FLORENCE ARNOLD-FORSTER'S
IRISH JOURNAL

Florence Arnold-Forster's Irish Journal

EDITED BY
T. W. MOODY
AND
RICHARD HAWKINS

WITH
MARGARET MOODY

CLARENDON PRESS · OXFORD
1988

Oxford University Press, Walton Street, Oxford OX2 6DP

Oxford New York Toronto
Delhi Bombay Calcutta Madras Karachi
Petaling Jaya Singapore Hong Kong Tokyo
Nairobi Dar es Salaam Cape Town
Melbourne Auckland
and associated companies in
Beirut Berlin Ibadan Nicosia

Oxford is a trade mark of Oxford University Press

Published in the United States
by Oxford University Press, New York

British Library Cataloguing in Publication Data
Arnold-Forster, Florence
Florence Arnold-Forster's Irish journal.
1. Ireland—Politics and government—
1837–1901
I. Title II. Moody, T. W. III. Hawkins,
Richard
941.5081'092'4   DA957.9
ISBN 0-19-822405-2

Library of Congress Cataloging in Publication Data
Arnold-Forster, Florence.
Florence Arnold-Forster's Irish journal.
Bibliography: p.
Includes index.
1. Forster, W. E. (William Edward), 1818–1886.
2. Arnold-Forster, Florence—Diaries. 3. Ireland—
Politics and government—1837–1901. 4. Ireland—
Social life and customs—19th century. 5. Statesmen—
Great Britain—Biography. I. Moody, T. W. (Theodore
William), 1907– . II. Hawkins, R. A. J. III. Title.
DA565.F7A66 1987   941.5081'092'4   87-7669
ISBN 0-19-822405-2

Printed in Great Britain
at the Alden Press, Oxford

PREFACE

WORK on the editing of Florence Arnold-Forster's 'Irish journal' was begun by T. W. Moody—with myself acting half as junior partner, half as research assistant—in the spring of 1972. At that time we hoped to complete it fairly quickly; a hope frustrated by the normal tendency of tasks to prove more laborious and complex in practice than in prospect, and by the pressure of other commitments that made sustained work on the project difficult, and for long periods impossible. Both of us were involved with *A new history of Ireland*; Dr Moody, among his innumerable concerns, was also completing and seeing through the press his great *Davitt and Irish revolution, 1846–82*, published by Oxford University Press early in 1982. *Davitt* is thus followed by the 'Journal', a narrative whose central figure, W. E. Forster, was in the forefront of the ranks opposed to Davitt. There is no anomaly here; for the personal integrity, the devotion to duty, and the human concern that appealed to Dr Moody in the character of Davitt were also the dominant characteristics of Forster. The different but no less strong appeal of the character of Florence Arnold-Forster herself cannot be better summed up than has been done in Dr Moody's introduction.

My own chief interest in the history of the land war—the policy and practice of enforcing law and preserving order—was much narrower in scope, and our differing concerns are reflected in the editing of the 'Journal'. Apart from the general work of annotation, in which we shared, my own contribution is virtually confined to comment (illustrated from the Gladstone, Ripon, and Spencer papers, from a handful of secondary sources, and from the records of the chief secretary's office) on the development of coercion policy and the working of the executive machinery. All the judgement, balance, and perspective in the editing came from Dr Moody. The experience of working with him on the 'Journal', as on the *New history*, has profoundly influenced my approach to historical writing and research. Since his death (11 February 1984), the final preparation of the typescript for the printer has been directed by Mrs Margaret Moody, whose critical judgement and eye for detail are fully worthy of her husband.

The 'Journal' would not have been published without the wholehearted cooperation and encouragement of Mrs Veronica Rowe, Florence's granddaughter, who made available the original typescript, other related documents, and much indispensable information. Among the others who have provided information, we are specially indebted to Dr A. B. Cooke and to the staff of the Surrey County Record Office. The extensive typing and retyping that has been necessary has been performed in exemplary fashion, as always, by Mrs Peggy Morgan of *A new history of Ireland*.

RICHARD HAWKINS

CONTENTS

ABBREVIATIONS

Abbreviations used by Florence are marked with an asterisk.

*C.S. Lodge	Chief Secretary's Lodge, Phoenix Park
*Cos	Cosmopolitan Club
cr.	created
D.M.P.	Dublin Metropolitan Police
D.N.B.	*Dictionary of national biography*
*F.	Frances Arnold-Forster
F.J.	*Freeman's Journal*
*govt	government
*H.S.C.	Hibernian School Chapel
I.H.S.	*Irish Historical Studies*
I.R.B.	Irish Republican Brotherhood
*L.C.	Lord Chancellor
*L.L.	Land League
Lyons, *Dillon*	F. S. L. Lyons, *John Dillon* (London, 1968)
Moody, *Davitt*	T. W. Moody, *Davitt and Irish revolution, 1846–82* (Oxford, 1981)
*Mr G.	W. E. Gladstone
*Mr P.	C. S. Parnell
*O. *Oakel	Oakeley Arnold-Forster
*P.M.G. *P.M. Gazette	*Pall Mall Gazette*
P.P.P. act	Protection of Person and Property Act, 1881
*R.H.M.S. *R.M.S.	Royal Hibernian Military School, Phoenix Park
R.I.C.	Royal Irish Constabulary
R.M.	Resident magistrate
Reid, *Forster*	T. Wemyss Reid, *Life of the Right Honourable William Edward Forster* (2 vols, London, 1888)
S.P.O., I.C.R.	State Paper Office, Dublin castle, Irish crime records, Returns of outrages, 1877–82
S.P.O., R.P.	State Paper Office, Dublin castle, Chief secretary's office, Registered papers
T.C.D.	Trinity College, Dublin
*V.R.L. *V.R. Lodge	Vice-regal Lodge

INTRODUCTION

THE years 1879–82 witnessed a conflict without parallel in Irish history—the 'land war'. It was a struggle between the tenant farmers and the landlords in which the established system of landlord–tenant relations was successfully challenged by the tenants acting together in a basically non-violent mass movement organised by a body set up for the purpose, the Land League. The land war dealt a deadly blow to the prestige of the landlords and to immemorial habits of deference on the part of the tenants. It broke the spirit of landlords as a class, undermined their will to continue as landlords, and predisposed them to seek a solution to the land problem by selling out their tenanted land to the occupiers on as favourable terms as they could secure.

The immediate outcome of the land war was a radical change in the land law. In his first administration Gladstone had grappled with the Irish land question and had carried a land bill in 1870 that for the first time interfered seriously with the rights of landed property in Ireland. The first Gladstone land act[1] had sought indirectly to curb the landlords' legal power of eviction by giving a tenant a right to compensation for his improvements and, unless the eviction was for non-payment of rent, compensation for disturbance. But the act offered far less to the tenants in practice than it did in principle, and its principle was repudiated by the Land League in favour of a demand for the 'abolition of landlordism' and the establishment of occupying ownership. Gladstone, as head of his second administration, responded with the land act of 1881,[2] which, though it did not concede the Land League's demand, went far beyond the act of 1870 by conceding what before 1879 had broadly constituted the tenants' reform programme: the 'three Fs'—fair rent, to be fixed by special courts, fixity of tenure so long as this 'judicial rent' was paid, and freedom for the tenant to sell his interest in his holding. The operation of the act progressively put an end to the old 'landlordism' and replaced it by a system of dual ownership of the soil by landlords and tenants, without compensation to the landlords for loss of their former rights of exclusive ownership. This, and the general and continuing reduction of rents by the land courts, made the landlords' position increasingly less desirable, and prepared the way for the eventual conversion of the tenants into owner-occupiers through state-aided land-purchase. This was substantially achieved by United Kingdom legislation, beginning with the Ashbourne act of 1885 and culminating in the Wyndham act of 1903. A social revolution was thus carried out by parliament in the quarter-century following the land war, which established the structure of landownership in twentieth-century Ireland

---

[1] Landlord and Tenant (Ireland) Act, 1870 (33 & 34 Vict., c. 46), 1 Aug. 1870.
[2] Land Law (Ireland) Act, 1881 (44 & 45 Vict., c. 52), 22 Aug. 1881.

and made possible the political revolution that secured self-government for twenty-six counties.

The occasion and the opportunity for the land war was an economic crisis, the combined result of three successive years—1877, 1878, and 1879—of bad seasons and crop failure, especially of the potato crop, aggravated by falling agricultural prices and general depression throughout the British Isles. It seemed in 1879 as if rural Ireland, especially the perennially impoverished regions of the west, was threatened with starvation and eviction on a scale comparable with that of the great famine. In reality there was no danger of starvation as in 1845–8, for conditions in Ireland had radically changed since then. The threatened calamity was averted by the timely efforts of voluntary relief organisations set up for the purpose and facilitated by government. The harvest of 1880 was generally bountiful, the danger of famine passed, and the great problem was the inability of innumerable tenant farmers on the verge of bankruptcy to pay their rents—and, still more, their accumulated arrears. The landlords, many of whom had reduced or remitted rents in 1879–80 and were themselves relatively impoverished, demanded their rents, and evicted or sought to evict defaulters in increasing numbers. The tenants reacted to this situation not as in the great famine with resignation or sporadic violence but by concerted resistance organised and directed by the Land League—the national body founded in Dublin on 21 October 1879 by Michael Davitt and other agrarian and political extremists, in combination with Charles Stewart Parnell and other 'activists' in the parliamentary home-rule party, for the immediate purpose of bringing about a reduction of rents and protecting tenants against eviction, and with the eventual object of achieving a settlement of the land question that would make the tenants owners of their farms.

The league, with Davitt as its inspiring genius and principal organiser, and with Parnell as its president, combined diverse social and political elements ranging from moderate land-reformers and moderate home-rulers on the right to agrarian revolutionaries and revolutionary nationalists (Fenians) on the left. The solid mass of the league's membership comprised tenant farmers great and small, agricultural labourers, the great bulk of the catholic clergy, shopkeepers, business men, and other interests in the country towns. Leadership came mainly from the militant group in the parliamentary party that centred around Parnell, and from opportunist Fenians who, without renouncing the Fenian aim of an Irish republic to be achieved by armed rebellion, were prepared to support parliamentary nationalists in a struggle for the land, the one vital immediate issue for the great majority of Irishmen. This new Fenian policy found its fullest expression in Davitt, the 'father of the Land League', in whom the Fenian passion for national independence was combined with a no less ardent devotion to social justice as he saw it. His closest colleagues at the centre of the league, Patrick Egan and Thomas Brennan, were also Fenians.

The Land League quickly devised an elaborate and sophisticated system of what was called 'moral force warfare'; and in the spirit of militant trade unionism conducting a general strike it brought tremendous pressure to bear on both the landlords and the government. Huge protest meetings, well organised and generally orderly though often menacing, were held regularly in most parts of the country, usually on a Sunday, and resolutions were passed demanding immediate reduction of rents, the 'abolition of landlordism', and home rule. A network of local branches coordinated local action in accordance with policy laid down by the central body and its executive in Dublin. The preliminary stage in evictions—the service of ejectment processes—and the execution of ejectment decrees granted by the courts were made the occasion of hostile demonstrations; legal defence was provided for tenants whose cases seemed to be sustainable in the courts; evicted families were sheltered and supported; an embargo was placed on farms from which tenants had been evicted; tenants able to pay their rents were called upon to show solidarity with those on the same estate unable to do so by withholding payment and accepting the consequences; persons involved in criminal prosecutions for Land League activities were defended, and the families of those sent to prison were cared for; above all, the terrible weapon of social ostracism, named the 'boycott' after its most conspicuous victim, was perfected as the ultimate sanction of the league against those who violated its code, whether evicting landlords or tenants who took farms from which others had been evicted. Money to finance these activities was forthcoming in abundance from the Irish in America, where Parnell and one of his most fiery lieutenants, John Dillon, conducted a memorable propaganda campaign early in 1880. An American auxiliary, the Irish National Land League of the United States, initiated by Parnell, was organised, and extended from New York to California, by Davitt, who spent six hectic months in America on this work (May–November 1880).

The land war, extended over the whole country outside Ulster, became the greatest mass-movement ever known in Ireland. For the first time the tenant farmers as a class stood up to the landlords, who as a class felt themselves the victims of an infamous campaign of organised intimidation, treachery, and violence. Class hatred blazed up in a way that seemed utterly to transform habitual restraints and personal relations, and the agitation was accompanied by a steep rise in the number of offences classified and regularly reported by the Royal Irish Constabulary as 'agrarian outrages'—threatening letters and other forms of intimidation, incendiarism, maiming and killing of animals, injury to property, assaults, shooting at persons and into dwellings, murders, and homicides. Agrarian outrages were exaggerated at the time: many of the offences enumerated were trivial, and the total of agrarian homicides for the four years 1879–82 was only 67, of which many had no direct connection with the agitation. But though there was no 'reign of terror' there was localised terrorism, which its victims—tenants as well as landlords—saw as the work of the Land League. Undoubtedly the system of intimidation inseparable from some of the league's procedures led to violence, but the leaguers themselves claimed that the basic violence sprang from the injustices of the land system, that without the restraining influence of the league there would have been vastly more violence, and that the league as such kept strictly within the law. It was true that the strength of the league lay precisely in the fact that it was technically a legal organisation, and for this reason the government had the greatest difficulty in coming to grips with it. Open insurrection could much more easily have been put down by the troops that were available in strength, and the commander-in-chief would have welcomed an open confrontation. But the Land League conducted a subtle, elusive, and sinister warfare that could only be countered by force at the particular points where breach of the law occurred.

When the crisis began, the conservative government in office under Beaconsfield failed to comprehend the situation and did little to cope with it. A general election in April 1880 brought the liberals back to power under Gladstone. In Ireland the election was fought on the land issue, and with the Land League solidly backing him Parnell won his first electoral triumph and was elected chairman of a reanimated home rule partly broadly committed to support of the Land League. His dual role as president of the Land League and chairman of the parliamentary party was at the heart of his behaviour in the land war. The association of revolutionary and constitutional elements within the Land League which made it so formidable to its enemies was a constant source of danger to Parnell himself: if either the left or the right wing were to have its head, the agrarian movement would probably split or be fatally weakened; and it was Parnell's constant task to preserve a balance between the two, while always keeping a vigilant eye on the farmers and the catholic clergy. Paradoxically, a landowner and a protestant himself, he was conservative in social outlook and his primary interests were political, not agrarian. But being a realist he threw himself into the land war because he knew that, at the time, this was what mattered most to most of his countrymen. He aimed at winning for the tenant farmers a maximum of practical benefit as quickly as possible, while at the same time committing them irrevocably to the cause of home rule. He was ready to use his authority to stop the land war and the disorder that accompanied it as soon as he was satisfied that substantial gains had been made for the farmers. But if that point were reached, his problem would be how to switch the national movement from the agrarian to the home-rule track without endangering his leadership. This goes far to explain why his public conduct seemed so devious and equivocal, especially after Gladstone's government had made a spectacular effort to remedy the land problem and undermine the Land League by the land act of 1881.

The Land League denounced the act as inadequate and deceptive, and Parnell, under the pressure of conflicting forces, encouraged this attitude and became more defiant of the government than ever. The government, armed by parliament with wide powers of arrest on suspicion and detention without trial under the protection of person and property act of 2 March 1881, set about putting down the agitation by force. During the next six months it imprisoned most of the Land League leaders, including Parnell, and suppressed the league itself (20 October). But the violence and disorder only grew worse, though at the same time the first decisions of the new land court (October), substantially reducing rents, began to demonstrate the far-reaching benefit the new land act could bring to the tenants. Parnell in Kilmainham jail was very much alert to political trends outside; and to Gladstone, from early in 1882, the coercion regime became increasingly repugnant. Indirect communications from Parnell to Gladstone disclosed a substantial community of interests between the two leaders. By the 'Kilmainham treaty', Parnell agreed to cooperate with the government in helping to restore order in Ireland on the understanding that the government would make provision for the problem of the tenants' accumulated arrears—as it effectively did by the arrears act of 18 August 1882.

When Parnell and the other interned leaders emerged from Kilmainham and other jails, the man who had been immediately responsible for the government of Ireland during the preceding two distracted years resigned in protest. William Edward Forster, born at Bradpole, Dorset, on 11 July 1818,[1] was the only child of remarkable parents. His father, William Forster, was famous alike as quaker minister, traveller, and leader in the anti-slavery movement. His mother, Anna Buxton, a beautiful and talented woman, who had become a quaker 'by convincement', was herself a minister and social reformer; and she moved in circles distinguished alike for piety, social position, and robust Christian action. Her brother was Thomas Fowell Buxton, Wilberforce's successor in the anti-slavery movement, and one of her cousins was Elizabeth Fry, the prison reformer. Both William and Anna Forster had a quaker 'concern' about Ireland. William spent nearly a year there in 1813–14, ministering to Friends' meetings in various parts of the country; Anna, accompanied by her cousin, Priscilla Gurney (sister of Elizabeth Fry), paid a 'religious visit' of three months to Irish Friends in 1818; and in 1846–7 William was again in Ireland, as the principal agent of English Friends in administering the funds they raised for relief of victims of the great famine.[2]

William Edward Forster enjoyed a happy childhood and youth, was given a good liberal education, and grew up to be a man after his parents' hearts—an affectionate son, a sincere but undogmatic Christian, high-minded, self-reliant, optimistic, public-spirited. He did not go to university—Oxford and Cambridge were not yet open to dissenters—but he combined intellectual

---

[1] There is a standard *Life of the Right Honourable William Edward Forster* by T. Weymss Reid (2 vols, London, 1888).

[2] *Memoirs of William Forster*, ed. Benjamin Seebohm (2 vols, London, 1865), i, 145–78, 197–200; ii, 210–40.

growth with a strenuous initiation into the textile industry, where his energy and his practical ability quickly brought success. In 1842 he set up a woollen manufacture in Bradford, in partnership with William Fison, son of a wool stapler of Thetford, Norfolk, with whom William Forster had become acquainted during one of his missionary journeys. This was his situation when in September 1846 he went for the first time to Ireland, to see for himself the ravages of the great famine in some of the worst affected areas of the south and west. He stayed a night at Derrynane as a guest of Daniel O'Connell, in whom he was quick to see 'the leader of a nation and king of the hearts of a people'.[1] He returned to Ireland in January 1847 to assist his father in famine relief-work, and his first important publication was a report to the English Society of Friends on his experience of Irish suffering that had made an ineffaceable impression on his mind.[2] In 1849 he visited Ireland a third time, to accompany Thomas Carlyle on part of his celebrated journey through the country with Charles Gavan Duffy, the Young Irelander.[3] Thus by the age of twenty-nine, Forster—described by Carlyle[4] as 'a most cheery, frank-hearted, courageous, clear-sighted young fellow'—knew something at first hand both of Ireland's social problems and her political condition.

In August 1850 a new phase of his life began with his marriage to Jane Martha Arnold, eldest daughter of Dr Thomas Arnold, the famous educational reformer and headmaster of Rugby School. She was a woman whose gracious and loving personality was matched by her qualities of mind and character. The poet Wordsworth, who was a friend and neighbour of the Arnolds in the Lake District, and knew her well,[5] is quoted as saying that 'in all that went to make up excellence in women, Jane Arnold was as fine an example as he had known'.[6] Another poet, Aubrey de Vere, of Curragh Chase, County Limerick, met her about 1845 while he was staying with his cousins, the Marshalls, of Coniston, a few miles from Fox How, the Arnold home in Westmoreland:[7]

I shall never forget what a bright and beaming creature she then was. I have often seen her since ..., though not so often as I should have wished ...; for she was one but to look upon whom was to strengthen one's belief in all that is good and true—one whom we associate with worlds that are all goodness and peace.[8]

[1] Reid, *Forster*, i, 178.

[2] See *Transactions of the central relief committee of the Society of Friends during the famine in Ireland in 1846 and 1847* (London, 1852), pp 153–60.

[3] See Charles Gavan Duffy, *Conversations with Carlyle* (London, 1890).

[4] Ibid., p. 24.

[5] A. P. Stanley, *The life and correspondence of Thomas Arnold, D.D.* (12th ed., 2 vols, London, 1881), i, 15, 210–13, 275; ii, 137; *The letters of William and Dorothy Wordsworth: the later years*, ed. Ernest de Selincourt (3 vols, Oxford, 1939), ii, 631, 633, 666; iv, 1089, 1127.

[6] Ellis Yarnall, *Wordsworth and the Coleridges* (New York and London, 1899), p. 244.

[7] *Recollections of Aubrey de Vere* (London, 1897), pp 126, 200, 218.

[8] Aubrey de Vere to Robert Vere O'Brien, 1 Nov. 1899, on the death of Jane Forster (Wilfred Ward, *Aubrey de Vere: a memoir* (London, 1904), pp 399–400; see also ibid., pp 64, 96, 158).

An American writer, Ellis Yarnall, who visited the Forsters about 1852, felt that 'intelligence, refinement, high and pure thought met in her together with all feminine charm'.[1] A third poet, her brother Matthew Arnold, had the highest respect for her judgment, and throughout his life discussed all important matters with her.[2] Her marriage at the age of twenty-nine to William Edward Forster made a rare combination. Yarnall, looking back over nearly fifty years, wrote:

Never was there a closer intellectual companionship than theirs, each, as it were, supplementing the other—his rugged strength, his quick mind, his wide knowledge of books, of men, and of affairs—her keen intelligence, her grace of manner, her sweet dignity, her tenderness of feeling.[3]

And their adopted son, Oakeley, wrote to his sister Florence, their adopted daughter, in 1888, on the appearance of Reid's *Life of Forster*:

Of course the great and inevitable gap in the book . . . is the absence of all reference to mother;[4] to her part in his life and to her influence over his thought. You and I were always agreed, I know, that it was the compound of the two natures, the mature wisdom of two different strains of thought about high things that gave unrivalled beauty and wisdom to their lives which we saw so much of and felt so often.[5]

The marriage that brought Forster such fulfilment also brought expulsion from the Society of Friends, which at that time disapproved of their members 'marrying out'. 'Your people turned me out of the Society for doing the best thing I ever did in my life', he said years afterwards to a deputation of quakers.[6] But there were no ill feelings on either side, and though he joined the Church of England, to which his wife belonged, he retained a warm attachment both to quakerism and quakers, while not sharing their pacifism.

In 1850 he and his partner moved their business from Bradford to Burley-in-Wharfedale, a village on the River Wharfe, about ten miles to the north in the west riding of Yorkshire. There they founded the Greenholme Mills for the manufacture of worsteds, an enterprise that eventually prospered and provided Forster with a steady and ample income. Near the mill buildings, on a delectable stretch of the River Wharfe, he built a house, Wharfeside, that was his permanent home from 1852. Living in intimate touch with his workpeople he was a model employer, and never lost the confidence and affection of the Burley community. From 1861, when he became M.P., he rented a house in

[1] Yarnall, op. cit., p. 244.
[2] See *Letters of Matthew Arnold, 1848–1888*, ed. George W. E. Russell (2nd ed., 3 vols, London, 1904); *Unpublished letters of Matthew Arnold*, ed. Arnold Whitridge (New Haven, 1923).
[3] Yarnall, op. cit., p. 244.
[4] She lived till 1899.
[5] Mary Arnold-Forster, *The right honourable Hugh Oakeley Arnold-Forster: a memoir* (London, 1919), p. 78.
[6] Reid, *Forster*, i, 266.

London for the parliamentary session; the third of these houses, 80 Eccleston Square, near Victoria station, which he chose for 1863, pleased him so well that he obtained a lease of it, and it continued to be the London residence of the Forsters for the rest of his life. Finally in 1873 he acquired a holiday retreat in the Lake District—Fox Ghyll, in the valley of the River Rothay, near Ambleside and the northern shore of Lake Windermere. It was in a region of great natural beauty, immortalised by Wordsworth, and with the added attraction that it was near Fox How, the home of Jane Forster's mother (who died in 1873) and of Jane's youngest sister, Frances. Fox How was to remain a Mecca to all the Arnold connection till Frances's death in 1923.[1]

As a young man Forster had hankered after a political career, but it was not till he was nearly forty that he felt financially in a position to contest a seat in parliament, which he did, unsuccessfully, in 1857 in the radical interest. In 1861 he was elected liberal M.P. for Bradford, a seat he retained for the rest of his life. He at once distinguished himself on the issue of the American civil war, strongly supporting the federal government and opposing all attempts to give British recognition to the south. He was called to office in 1865 as under-secretary for the colonies in the liberal administration of Earl Russell, and though in that office only eight months (from November 1865 to June 1866, when the government resigned), he acquired a deep and lasting interest in colonial questions which, in the closing years of his life, was to make him the leading exponent of imperial federation. He played a prominent part in the campaign that resulted in the second parliamentary reform act, carried by Disraeli's conservative administration, with the help of the liberals, in 1867. As vice-president of the council in Gladstone's first administration (1868–74), he was in charge of the education department, and was the author of the great elementary education act of 1870. He was also closely identified with the introduction of the secret ballot in 1872. In 1874, on Gladstone's resignation as head of the liberal party, he was strongly favoured for the succession but stood down in favour of Lord Hartington, who acted as leader till Gladstone returned to power in 1880. At that point Forster was assured of high rank in any liberal government and would have chosen to be colonial secretary. Instead he agreed at Gladstone's request to accept the lower-ranking but most critical office of chief secretary to the lord lieutenant of Ireland, or head of the Irish executive, with a seat in the cabinet. The man appointed at the same time as lord lieutenant, or titular head of the Irish government, Lord Cowper, was undistinguished as a politician, but was a well-intentioned and loyal colleague.

Forster's career as Irish chief secretary was to be a classic instance of the cruellest dilemma that can face a liberal in politics. He was a paragon of Victorian liberalism, a man of the highest moral courage and personal integrity, a humane and tender-hearted man, of marked simplicity of life. Behind a

[1] Reid, *Forster*, i, 332, 346, 362; A. P. Stanley, *Thomas Arnold*, i, 210–13, 293–4, ii, 42, 278; Mary Arnold-Forster, op. cit., pp 3–4.

gruffness of manner and indifference to his appearance[1] he had great charm and a wide range of intellectual and social interests. He was a firm believer in individual and political liberty and in social and international cooperation. Preeminently anxious to be fair-minded and just, he was infinitely patient, hard-working, and conscientious. He was greatly beloved by a large family circle, and a staunch friend. Yet, in an endeavour to pacify a distracted country, he felt it necessary to act in an increasingly despotic way in defence, as he believed, of those very social and political values with which his coercive regime was incompatible.

He came to Ireland with a very high sense of dedication to the poor and oppressed; yet very soon he was universally known as 'Buckshot Forster' a nickname that hurt him deeply and whose implication was undeserved; for though he defended the use of buckshot by the Royal Irish Constabulary against violent mobs as less deadly than ball cartridge, buckshot had in fact been adopted before he took office.[2] He endured constant vilification and abuse with stoical calm and even good humour. His life was repeatedly threatened (once by a letter-bomb),[3] but he showed himself entirely fearless, disliking the special precautions for his safety that the police sought to provide and doing his utmost to sidetrack them. Early in March 1882, when he was perhaps the most hated man in Ireland, he made a tour of distressed areas in Limerick, Clare, and Galway, and in some of the most disaffected districts he walked unarmed and without police escort among the local people and reasoned with them. At the workhouse in Tulla, County Clare, he visited a poor farmer who was dying of the injuries he had received in a midnight attack by armed men who had dragged him from his bed and shot him before his wife and five children as a punishment for paying his rent contrary to the Land League's 'no-rent manifesto'. On the way back to Dublin, Forster addressed a crowd from the window of his hotel at Tullamore, King's County, the centre of an 'outrage district', appealing to the reason and conscience of his hearers in defence of his policy, denouncing the moral cowardice that acquiesced in terrorism, and concluding, in answer to shouts of 'release the prisoners':

as soon as we can fairly say that outrages have ceased . . . and that men are not ruined, are not maimed, and are not murdered for doing their duty, or doing what they have a legal right to do, the suspects will be released.

Forster's presentiment that he would die in his bed and his indifference to personal danger proved to be justified. The secret assassination-club, the Invincibles, that butchered Thomas Henry Burke, the permanent under-secretary, and Lord Frederick Cavendish in the Phoenix Park on the day of the

---

[1] See, for example, Thomas MacKnight, *Ulster as it is* (2 vols, London, 1896), i, 383–6.

[2] *Hansard 3*, cclix, 1013–14 (8 Apr. 1881). Cf. Michael Davitt, *The fall of feudalism in Ireland* (London and New York, 1904), p. 265. And see below, p. 398.

[3] See below, pp 367, 378.

[4] Reid, *Forster*, ii, 390–403, and below, pp 387–96.

latter's arrival as Forster's successor (6 May 1882), had more than once lain in wait for Forster, but on each occasion had been foiled by some accidental circumstance. On the evening of his final departure from Ireland, 19 April, a group of Invincibles was waiting for him on the departure platform at Westland Row station where he was to have caught the 6.45 boat train for Kingstown. The intended victim unwittingly eluded his would-be assassins by yielding to the suggestion of his private secretary, Henry Jephson, that they should go to Kingstown together by an earlier train and dine there at the Royal St George Yacht Club before going on board the mail boat.[1]

The obloquy for a coercion policy that was the responsibility of the whole cabinet was heaped on Forster's head, not only by Irish land-leaguers but by English radicals (notably John Morley, in the *Pall Mall Gazette*), whereas credit for the land act, to which he actively contributed and on which he pinned his hopes, was entirely denied him by those who approved of it, while at the same time he was traduced for his connection with it both by the Land League and by Irish and English landlords who saw in it only an attack upon their property rights. Yet he persevered, shuttling between Dublin and London—he made the crossing between Holyhead and Kingstown more than thirty times in two years—to attend cabinet meetings and parliamentary debates, alternating the strain of directing the administration from Dublin castle with the torment of being baited both by Parnellites and by British radicals in the house of commons. He worked with prodigious and sustained energy, only once taking a holiday of more than a few days. Sadly aware that he could never do the good for Ireland he had fondly hoped to do, he never weakened in his conviction that Irish society could not be restored to health until the law of the land was made to prevail over the law of the Land League, and both landlords and tenants alike protected in the peaceful exercise of their legal rights. Again and again he contemplated resignation, and only remained at his post in response to Gladstone's urging. But when Gladstone, who had previously shared his low opinion of Parnell, changed his mind and decided that Parnell and the other imprisoned suspects, if released, could be relied on to help the government in restoring order, Forster's resignation followed as a matter of course (2 May 1882). It seemed that, as a politician, he was utterly discredited, and he never again held office. But within a few days of his resignation, the Phoenix Park murders (6 May) did much to rally British public opinion in his favour; and since his death (5 April 1886) his reputation has been substantially vindicated.

He is well commemorated in the words of a shrewd judge of men, whose career in the Irish civil service had not long begun when Forster was in Ireland:

Lord Cowper ... was well content to leave everything to his experienced chief secretary, whose steadfast honesty of purpose and burning desire to do what was righteous and just at all costs were almost superhuman. No other chief secretary that

[1] Reid, *Forster*, pp 428–9.

I have ever met possessed anything quite approaching Forster's divine obsession in this respect; but it was not a characteristic which could be helpful to him or likely to smooth the path for any Irish secretary. Opportunism and compromise had no abiding place in the tenor of his thoughts and actions.... Every man in the civil service loved Forster; he was tolerant, sympathetic, and as brave as a lion, and though harassed and vilified by the Irish press and people, he nevertheless bore no malice to anyone.[1]

It is here that Forster's adopted daughter Florence appropriately enters the story; for a journal that she kept during her adoptive father's chief secretaryship is a unique source of new light on his conduct and character. She was the second child of William Delafield Arnold (1829–59), a son of Dr Thomas Arnold and brother of Jane Forster. He had joined the Indian army, and in 1850 had married Frances Anne Hodgson, daughter of Major-General John Anthony Hodgson, surveyor general of India. William Arnold was director of public instruction in the Punjab when his wife died on 24 March 1858, leaving four young children, Edward Penrose, Florence Mary, Hugh Oakeley, and Frances Egerton, the eldest aged seven, the youngest two. It was arranged that they should go to their grandmother Arnold, and they travelled to England by the Cape route early in 1859. He himself followed by the Suez route, intending to meet them on their arrival, but he took ill on the journey and died at Gibraltar (9 April 1859). The place of the parents in the lives of their four children was immediately taken by W. E. Forster and his wife. Aunt Jane Forster met the orphans at Gravesend and brought them home to Wharfeside; and she and her husband, who were childless, took the momentous step of adopting them. It proved a dazzling success. The adoptive parents and their adopted children became permanently united in a relationship of mutual confidence and affection.[2] The children always regarded the Forsters, and always described them, as their father and mother; and when the youngest, Frances, was twenty-one, they all changed their surname to Arnold-Forster:

The idea of our doing so had been often thought of by father and mother, but with their usual generous lovingness they had resolved that all they have done for us should be so absolutely unreturned and one-sided that we should not be even asked to take their name.... We found that father and mother were as glad that it should be so as we were proud to add their honoured name to our own.[3]

Born in Bayswater, London, on 3 July 1854, Florence was twenty-five when Forster's chief secretaryship began. She was an altogether exceptional woman—charming, handsome, intelligent, witty, vivacious, well-read, well-informed, strong-willed, courageous, highly articulate. Though gay and light-hearted she was also serious-minded, and though no introvert was given to

---

[1] Sir Henry Robinson, *Memories: wise and otherwise* (London, 1923), pp 28, 34.
[2] *D.N.B.*, art. William Delafield Arnold; Mary Arnold-Forster, *Hugh Oakeley Arnold-Forster*, pp 6–11.
[3] Private journal of Florence Arnold-Forster, iv (1878–9), pp 193–4 (June 1879).

self-examination. Though well-favoured and well-connected she was not proud, or conceited, or condescending, but on the contrary was conscious of the many blessings she enjoyed (including unfailing good health) and never forgot to be thankful for them. Like the best of the great Victorians she 'cared' greatly for all that she did and she lived a full and happy life, never doubting that life was immensely worth living, and that responsibilities were more important than rights. Like all the Arnolds she was a writer: she published a book on the Hungarian patriot, Francis Deák (1880), she was a constant and distinguished correspondent, and besides her Irish journal she kept private journals during a large part of her long life. She was a shrewd and untiring observer of the political and social scene, and her comments on public events have a large and distinctive place in her journals. She was also a talented artist, and left many charming pen-and-ink sketches and water-colours. She had many friends, and thoroughly enjoyed the social round that brought her into touch with a wide variety of interesting and important people.

The large social circle in which the Forsters moved in London included a number of Irish landowning families who were liberal in politics and progressive and public-spirited in their social outlook: before she ever set foot in Ireland Florence learnt a good deal about Irish conditions from such friends as the O'Briens of Cahirmoyle, the de Veres of Curragh Chase, the Spring Rices (Lord and Lady Monteagle), of Mount Trenchard, and the Monsells (Lord and Lady Emly), of Tervoe, who formed an interrelated group of Limerick gentry. They in turn were connected by marriage with friends of the Forsters, the Marshalls of Headingly, near Leeds—Yorkshire textile magnates who had extensive estates in the Lake District, including houses on Lake Ullswater, Derwentwater, and Coniston.[1] Julia Marshall, who married Edward William O'Brien of Cahirmoyle (eldest son of William Smith O'Brien, the Young Ireland leader) early in 1880, was one of Florence's close personal friends.[2]

Florence visited Ireland for the first time in October 1878, with her father and mother, and they spent a week in County Limerick, staying with the Monsells at Tervoe and then with the Spring Rices at Mount Trenchard. She met innumerable relatives and friends of her hosts, among them Charlotte Grace O'Brien, poet, novelist, and social reformer, who, like her father, William Smith O'Brien, was untypical of her family and class in being a fervent nationalist—'a very clever and interesting woman, with a profound feeling of nationalism and the grievances of Ireland but not violently anti-English, and very glad to have the opportunity of meeting father'. After a trip in Clare to Kilkee, Lisdoonvarna, and the Cliffs of Moher, the Forsters went to Galway

[1] Mary Anne Marshall, eldest daughter of John Marshall, married Thomas Charles Spring Rice, 1st Baron Monteagle. Her brother, James Garth Marshall, married Mary Spring Rice, Monteagle's sister, and their daughter, Julia, married Edward William O'Brien. On the Marshalls see *The letters of William and Dorothy Wordsworth: the later years*; *Recollections of Aubrey de Vere*; Ward, *Aubrey de Vere*; Yarnall, *Wordsworth and the Coleridges*, pp 67, 70.

[2] Private journal, iv (1878–9), p. 100; v (1879–85), pp 18, 25.

and on to Connemara, visiting places Forster had visited with his father during the great famine, thirty years before. They stayed with Mitchell Henry, businessman and liberal M.P. from Manchester, who had acquired a large tract of Connemara and built himself a Victorian castle at Kylemore. They visited Leenane and Bundorragha, on the Killary, and wound up their tour at Westport. Florence enjoyed it all immensely, finding Ireland and the Irish very much to her taste.[1] The beauty of Connemara sank into her: from a hill above Letterfrack she saw

the frayed-out coast of Galway, the quiet sea running so deeply inland as to seem quite at home among the folds of the mountains, and rocky islands straying so far out to sea that they looked like ships in full sail, dimly seen in the mysterious evening sunlight.[2]

While she thus had some knowledge of Ireland before 1880, she was much better acquainted with the Continent, where she had travelled widely and often with her father since she was fourteen.[3] She had become especially interested in Hungary and its politics after a visit to Budapest in September 1876;[4] and this had led her to make a study of Francis Deák, the Hungarian architect of the *Ausgleich* or constitutional settlement of 1867 under which Austria and Hungary had entered on a new and happier relationship as partners in a 'dual monarchy'. He had died in January 1876, and only meagre accounts of his life had appeared in the English press. Florence began collecting information about him in French and German sources, and by November 1878 had made such good progress that she decided to write a book on Deák for the enlightenment of her countrymen. She accomplished this task, unknown to anyone except her brother Oakeley, in seven absorbing months at Wharfeside: 'when I have not been actually writing [the book] I have been thinking for it—in my walks, in the boat, out driving, at meals, on journeys, behind a newspaper, everywhere and at all times, even at most wrong times'.[5] In some trepidation she submitted her manuscript to a family friend, Mountstuart Grant Duff, M.P., a well-known authority on foreign affairs. His response was favourable, and in October Macmillan the publisher agreed to issue it at his own risk. The book appeared in April 1880, a few days before Forster accepted the Irish chief secretaryship.[6] Based wholly on printed material in French and German it had obvious limitations of which Florence, who insisted on concealing her authorship, was fully aware. But it was perceptive and well written, it carried an appreciative preface by Grant Duff, and it was generally welcomed by the critics as fulfilling the modest purpose announced in its author's introductory note—in the absence of an adequate biography of a great patriot, to bring his character and work before those English readers to whom he was little more than a name. Sales in England proved disappointing, but *Francis Deák* roused

[1] Private journal, iv (1878–79, pp 83–5, 91–106.
[2] Ibid., p. 104.   [3] Reid, *Life of Forster*, ii, 111.
[4] Private journal, iv (1878–9), p. 195.   [5] Ibid., p. 197.
[6] Ibid., pp 194–8, 221–2; v (1879–85), pp 1–2, 5–6, 66.

interest in Hungary. Count Andrássy, Deák's collaborator in the *Ausgleich* and chancellor of Austria–Hungary from 1871 to 1879, thought well of it and sent Florence a complimentary message about it through his friend, the Swedish minister in London.[1] Translated into Hungarian it was republished at Budapest in a standard series of cheap 'books for the people'.[2]

Florence's *Deák* was the work of a woman of lively mind and unflagging interest in public affairs at home, on the Continent, and throughout the world. The wide-ranging intellectual curiosity is fully reflected in her journals, and especially in her Irish journal, where her narrative of two crowded years as the chief secretary's daughter is interspersed with notes and comments on public events in Europe and beyond. Thus, for example, she follows with conflicting feelings the British military operations in Egypt and South Africa during 1880–82 that were scarcely less of an embarrassment to liberals than her father's regime in Ireland. At a time of extreme tension in Ireland she does not omit to assess (14 March 1881) the significance of the assassination of Tsar Alexander II. While all this is a tribute to the influence of her father and to the bracing intellectual atmosphere of her family, it is clear that she was a dedicated student of politics in her own right, without being a blue-stocking or a bore. Yet she was highly critical of her own performance as a writer. Though gratified at the reception of her book and 'unfeignedly glad to have been the means of bringing Deák before the notice of the English people', she reminded herself that

to some extent the political writing over which I have a tendency to waste my time is not really more valuable to the world at large than the successful efforts of a clever performing dog. It is very desirable that I should find some natural and useful channel for my political interest, and that I should not fritter away my time over writing which is of no worth to anybody.[3]

Still she could not help feeling that it was worth while to continue her habit of recording the chief events of the day.

The effort to arrange and set down in writing even the barest chronicle of events and opinions is good practice, and will, I think, be of help to me in case I should ever find myself gradually drawn into writing on some definite subject.[4]

But she felt that she had no natural aptitude for literary work.

My thoughts and imaginings do not come easily into intelligible and suitable language. My mind always seems to see an idea first in its general colour and effect, and not . . . in its form or outline; consequently I have great difficulty in expressing and defining my thoughts, even when they are clearly realised in my head.[5]

[1] Private journal, v (1879–85), pp 75–7 (May–June 1880).
[2] *Deák Ferencz*. . . . Translated into Hungarian by Agost Pulszky. Buda Pest: Franklin-Társulat, 1881. Florence's copy, dated 2 Feb. 1881, is among the Arnold-Forster papers in T.C.D. Library.
[3] Private journal, v (1879–85), 77–8 (May–June 1880).
[4] Ibid., p. 78.   [5] Ibid., p. 79.

If there is little trace of such difficulty in the apparently effortless style of her journals, it is a tribute to her self-discipline, her patience, and her determination to spare no pains.

And yet she was at times assailed by doubt whether she was really making proper use of her life. In May 1879 she wrote:

During the past month we have had about the usual amount of society, with going out and dinner parties at home. On the whole I like society of this kind though I have not lately come across anything specially interesting. What I thoroughly dislike is having to be sociable in the sense of entertaining odds and ends of people who drop in and spoil one's own occupations without giving much enjoyment, one would suppose, to anybody. The real interest of my life is still in trying to widen my knowledge of things and people and to improve my scanty power of feeling and seeing and judging rightly. I see clearly that the danger of this is in my neglect to do rightly. It is all very well to be interested, and, if one cares and professes to any knowledge about a subject however impractical, it is certainly better to try and have a right knowledge; but all the same I often see that the woman who teaches and helps, and enlightens two village children is really doing infinitely more for the fellow creatures in whom on a large and picturesque scale I profess to take such interest than I would do by vaguely reading and thinking and sympathizing for a lifetime. And yet this sort of thing is with me so entirely a part of my life that I cannot help trying to believe that it may be something more than a mere selfish indulgence, and long to bring it within those things which are 'done unto God'. I hope I am not altogether deceiving myself and living in a fool's paradise.[1]

Shortly before her twenty-fifth birthday she reflected:

Having lived through a quarter of a century of the world's history I have been little more than a spectator hitherto, though at times I have had as it were samples of the way in which men and women can really suffer and enjoy and hope and feel. Of bodily pain I know so little that when it comes it will be to me almost a new experience. Nor do I know the noblest of all experiences, which I might have learnt, if such things could be learnt, from mother and Francie—self-sacrificing, self-forgetting love of God. I am far enough from having taken as my motive for life the words which mother gave me in Advent 1877: 'The love of Christ constraineth us'. This is still my ideal of what one's motive [should be], but it seems almost a piece of hypocrisy even to write the words, so *very* far am I from living accordingly.[2]

On her twenty-fifth birthday (3 July 1879) she noted that it was probably a disappointment and surprise to some of her relatives that she was not married.

But happily father and mother have never given me the least reason to suppose that they would like to see me disposed of. As for myself I must confess that in some respects I should be glad of the 'enlargement and new fact' of marriage in the abstract, yet my feelings and interests and affections are so fully and constantly occupied that I am well content to remain as I am. I know what it is to feel sad and wistful and even what I, with my limited experience in that line, would call unhappy, and I also know what it is to feel absolutely excited with the pleasures of interest and sympathy and sometimes with the

[1] Ibid., iv (1878–9), pp 175–6. [2] Ibid., pp 176–7.

indescribable satisfaction of sharing in the life and progress of the world, which makes public events seem at times like matters of private interest. But as yet I do not know what it is to feel dull. No doubt this is in great measure owing to the discreditable fact that my intense vanity makes myself an object of such interest to me that at the worst my thoughts are never at a loss for a subject. This is my great sin and danger, my want of zeal, pure and unselfish, for the service of God. My mind is so thickly furnished with my earthly interests and cares that I become too much satisfied and lose sight of the true object of life, and the right relation of things; this is what makes me understand the need of the 4th collect after Trinity, which prays that 'we may so pass through things temporal that we finally lose not the things eternal'.[1]

She returns to the thought that romantic love has passed her by:

However full and interesting I may find my life at the present time, there is something deeply sad in the thought that I have past my youth for ever, that I have left behind the time of poetry and romance, that henceforth according to nature I can be only a sympathizing onlooker, and never an actor in those beautiful scenes which are the groundwork of half the best poetry that has ever been written. I foresee that the next few years will be rather sad and in some ways full of mortifications, but growing old is a thing which, whether or not it has its advantages, must at any rate be faced and accepted—it is to be hoped decorously and with a good grace. In some ways I think it will be pleasanter (inwardly) when I come to be generally regarded as an established elderly woman, with no need to condole with me or 'ménager' my feelings. . . . my great wish and endeavour is to be beforehand with my age rather than behindhand, especially, I mean, in such matters as behaviour, occupations and dress. I should dislike to cling obstinately to the ways of youth when I have lost the right to be there.

One thing of my recent youth I still retain and that is my distinct recollection of my own habits and inclinations of mind, my juvenile likes and dislikes; this makes me feel still quite on an understanding with children and young girls, and immeasurably older as I feel I am quite unable to patronize them, for in some respects I am still quite on their level, or it may be, far below them.[2]

Florence's twenty-sixth birthday (3 July 1880) was another occasion for spiritual stocktaking:

I am now really and decidedly becoming middle-aged, and should remember in all sincerity that whatever superficial observers may think—or at least say—I am no longer a 'young lady', and that to give myself the air of one is to make myself ridiculous. A woman approaching the age of 30 is not a 'girl' even in the conventional use of that term. I plainly detect the advance of age in my secret anxiety to avoid all reference to the question of dates and birthdays. My chief need now is to feel the responsibility of life and the duty of doing something, instead of merely interesting myself in an easy detached sort of way in the doings of others—above all to pray for a single mind and a pure heart, that I may love God and follow after goodness more than I love myself and follow after the various pleasures and interests of my daily life; that I may remember the Master whom I profess to serve, and that I may not by my head or my affections be led away from faith in our Lord Jesus, who is the light of the world, the source and

[1] Private journal, iv (1878–9), pp 203–5.   [2] Ibid., pp 205–7.

sanctification of all that is truly and eternally beautiful and good in the natural world and in our own selves—body, soul and spirit. 'For in him we live and move and have our being.'[1]

Some weeks later she had the painful experience of having to turn down an offer of marriage from Bertram Buxton, a second cousin of her adopted father's and a friend of her younger brother, Oakeley.

If respect and pity and a most sincere wish to help some one a thousand times more single-minded and noble than myself could have made me give a different answer I should have done so. But the giving would not have been equal on both sides. . . . Pity and sympathy are very near akin to love certainly, but they are not quite the same thing—would they grow into it or would they themselves die out, leaving only regret and wider experience? Shall I, when I am an elderly, perhaps solitary, woman feel that I have made a great mistake?[2]

It was all the more regrettable because she knew that Forster would have liked her to marry Bertram.[3] But three years later, when she was twenty-nine, what she had thought to be out of the question happened: she fell in love with an Irishman with whom she had become friendly during Forster's chief secretary-ship, Robert Vere O'Brien. He was a younger son of the Honourable Robert O'Brien, deceased, of Old Church, near Limerick, and of his wife Elinor, daughter of Sir Aubrey de Vere of Curragh Chase.

Robert ('Robin') O'Brien belonged to that cluster of Limerick–Clare landowning families with whom the Forsters had friendly connections: his sister was the wife of William T. Monsell, R.M., a relative of the first Baron Emly; one of his cousins was the fourteenth Baron Inchiquin, of Dromoland, County Clare; another was Edward William O'Brien of Cahirmoyle; one of his uncles was Sir Stephen Edward de Vere, of Curragh Chase, another was the poet Aubrey de Vere. He was clerk of the peace for County Clare, agent to Lord Inchiquin and other local landowners, and had a high reputation for good judgment, patience, business capacity and for humane and honourable dealing with tenants. He was a patriotic Irishman, in politics a liberal and a unionist. He and Florence had first met in October 1878, while she was staying at Tervoe and at Mount Trenchard; they met again in October 1880 during a visit she paid to the Edward O'Briens at Cahirmoyle, on several later occasions in Dublin, and in September 1881 at Chamonix where the Forsters were spending a short holiday. He proposed to her on 24 February 1883 and they were married in London on 10 July.

Florence and Robert were very deeply in love, and she found in marriage a fulfilment beyond all expectation.

Of all earthly and yet heaven-sent joys none ever has been or ever can be like this deep and satisfying and gracious revelation of what love is. It has seemed to light up and fill

[1] Ibid., v (1879–85), p. 87.
[2] Ibid., pp 106–7 (26 Aug. 1880).
[3] Ibid., p. 140 (Dec. 1880).

every corner of my being, and to have given me a sense of strength and protection and contentment which ought to make me stronger and more zealous to serve God and my fellow creatures. . . . It seems strange that the romance and passion of love should still have come to me when my youth was past and I had quite resigned myself to feel that this was 'an enlargement', an experience of life, which I was not destined to know. Full and happy and varied as my life has been in other ways, love and marriage have been a revelation to me, not only of what is but of what might be, of possibilities of sorrow as well as joy, of dejection as well as heights. They have illuminated poetry for me, and given me that sense of fellowship with the lovers and the beloved of all ages, with the husbands and wives from Hector to Andromache downwards, which I used sometimes to long for. . . . I am most humbly and truly grateful for the great blessing that has been given me and pray that I may be worthy of it.[1]

Her intimations of middle age at twenty-six proved quite unjustified. She had still in fact two-thirds of her life before her and was to spend fifty-three active and beneficent years in Ireland. On her own social level she had become one of the most distinguished Irishwomen of her day by the end of the century.[2] She revived a lace-making industry in Limerick, conducting a training-school for girls, introducing improved designs, and helping to popularise the lace among her large circle of friends in London. She inspired and maintained another domestic industry, the Clare Embroidery, at Ballyalla, near Ennis, County Clare, where she lived during most of her life in Ireland. A third enterprise in which she was prominently involved was a T.B. sanatorium, opened in April 1912 on the shore of Ballyalla lake. She died at Ballyalla on 8 July 1936, aged 82. Her husband, who was twelve years her senior, had died in 1913. They had four children, Aubrey, Hugh, Jane, and Florence, of whom Hugh and Jane married and had children. Two of these children, Elinor Vere (daughter of Hugh), who married Reginald Wiltshire, and Veronica Mary (daughter of Jane), who married David Rowe, inherited a large mass of family papers from their O'Brien grandparents. In 1970–71 the two cousins presented the bulk of the collection to the library of Trinity College, Dublin, where it forms MSS 4986–5117. It comprises letters and papers not only of Florence and Robert but also of their O'Brien, Arnold, Forster, and Arnold-Forster relatives. Florence's journals and other papers remain in the possession of Mrs Veronica Rowe, to whom we are deeply indebted not only for putting these manuscripts at our disposal but also for invaluable information and comment.

Florence began her long series of journals, written in plain bound notebooks when she was fourteen.[3] But by 1880 she had formed the practice of keeping on loose leaves a parallel series of records of current events. The private journal she described as 'Enlargements—new facts', the loose leaves as 'Contemporary

---

[1] Private journal, v (1879–85), pp 174–7.

[2] 'Distinguished Irishwomen, their professions, pleasures and pursuits' in *The Lady of the House*, Christmas 1895 (Dublin: Wilson, Hartnell & Co.).

[3] Her earliest journal, which she entitled 'The first journal, probably the last', records her first trip abroad and covers Aug.–Oct. 1868.

notes'. Many volumes of the former have survived, whereas only one bundle of the latter, covering the period 20 April–5 August 1882, together with a small sheaf covering 5–8 August and 2–3 October 1882,[1] are now extant. But a typescript copy of the complete 'Contemporary notes' for the period June 1880–5 August 1882, bearing the title 'My Irish journal', was made in the autumn of 1905, and this copy, well bound in six volumes and bearing the bookplate of 'Robert and Florence Vere O'Brien', has been preserved and is the source of the text printed below. An all too slight entry in Florence's diary for January 1906 records the making of the typescript:

During the autumn I have been having my Irish journal typewritten by Miss Davis (a costly business), and of late Robin has been reading aloud to me each fresh batch as it arrived—a very curious experience, combining strangely the past and present of my Irish life.[2]

This Irish journal, 'transcribed for my husband', Florence dedicated 'to the beloved memory of my father'.[3]

For the period June 1880–5 August 1882 the private journal can therefore be compared with the 'Irish journal': each contains both personal matter and comment on public affairs, but whereas the Irish journal gives constant attention to politics and is more than twenty times the length of the private journal,[4] the private journal contains personal details not in the Irish journal, its political content is comparatively slight, and from the end of 1880, when 'our public and private life became so intermixed',[5] it dwindles to a very thin thread of narrative. The private journal is a valuable supplement to the Irish journal but the latter, both as a personal and a political record, is well able to stand on its own feet.

The Irish journal opens with a short introduction on Forster's appointment as chief secretary, followed by a sequence of entries, the first dated 24 June 1880, each covering events of the several preceding days or sometimes weeks. These lead to a sequence of entries for almost every day from 6 December 1880 onwards, of an average length of over 300 words. The notes from which the journal in its present form was transcribed were sometimes written at the end of the day to which they refer, but usually at intervals of several days and occasionally after the lapse of a week or more. The journal consistently conveys a sense of immediate observation and experience. But the question arises whether the typescript copy might not represent a revised and 'improved' version of the original journal. There are five types of evidence to show that it

---

[1] 'Contemporary notes' for 20 Apr.–5 Aug. 1882 are in Mrs Rowe's possession; those for 5–8 Aug. and 2–3 Oct. are in T.C.D., MS 4986.
[2] Private journal, 1903–6.
[3] The MS of the title page containing these statements is preserved with the bundle of loose leaves referred to above.
[4] Irish journal = c. 210,000 words; private journal, June 1880–August 1882 = c. 10,000 words.
[5] Private journal, v (1879–85).

does not, but is on the contrary precisely what it claims to be, a true copy of Florence's 'Contemporary notes': (1) the section of the original journal that survives in manuscript, (2) extracts from the original journal printed by T. Weymss Reid, in 1888, in his *Life of William Edward Forster*,[1] (3) Florence's private journal for the years 1880–82, (4) a journal covering the same period kept by her younger sister Frances, and (5) the content of the Irish journal itself.

A collation of (1) and (2) with the corresponding parts of the typescript shows that the former are faithfully reproduced in the latter; and it is a reasonable inference, from the even, closely-knit texture of the Irish journal and the character of its author that what is true for these samples is true for the whole journal. This assumption is substantiated by the many internal links that connect the typescript journal with (3) and (4), which are unquestionably contemporary documents; for example, Florence often refers in her private journal to what she has written in her 'Contemporary notes', and Frances often refers to Florence's doings in very much the same terms as Florence herself uses. (5) Finally there is absolutely no trace in the typescript diary of any kind of hindsight. We may safely assume that any discrepancies there may have been between Florence's manuscript journal and the transcript are typing errors and not any revision of the original.

It might be supposed that the making of a typescript copy of the journal was intended to lead to publication, especially as, by 1905, any indiscretions the journal contained had become innocuous. But though Florence lived for another 31 years, it remained unpublished—perhaps because, within a few years, events occurred that changed the context of her personal life and the Irish political situation: the death of her husband in 1913, the home rule crisis of 1912–14, the Easter rising of 1916, the war of independence (1919–21), and the setting-up of the Irish Free State.

The authenticity of the diary as a record of events can be tested at innumerable points where it refers to facts that can be verified by independent evidence, both printed (for example, *Hansard*) and manuscript (for example, Forster correspondence in the Gladstone papers); it stands such testing extremely well, and the more so because as a rule everything in it is precisely dated. On the other hand there are frequent allusive references to individuals, especially relatives and close friends—and this may be an indication that Florence did not intend the journal for publication; all such persons have, so far as possible, been identified below.

Florence's style, even when her journal is in telegraphic English, is crystal-clear, fresh, and fluent. She has an artist's eye for natural beauty (as in her sensitive descriptions of scenes in the Phoenix Park, or in her picture of the

[1] Vol. ii, 316 (8 May 1881); 404 (8 Mar. 1882); 414–15 (5 Apr.); 449–50 (2 May); 459–60 (5 May). Variations between Reid's text and Florence's typescript are manifestly due to Reid's lack of scholarly precision. Variations between Florence's manuscript and her typescript for the period 30 April–5 August 1882 are insignificant: for example, figures in the MS are spelled out in the TS, abbreviations in the MS are expanded in the TS.

'peacock hills' of Wicklow, 27 September 1881) and in character-drawing she is deft, colourful, and perceptive. She can be critical, even severely so, but is never barbed or malicious. She is often sparkling but never cynical, sometimes ironical but never cruel, occasionally dejected but never despairing.

She has a delicate sense of humour and a pretty wit. She recounts a chance meeting in St James's Street, London, at a critical point in the parliamentary session of 1881, between her father and Sir Stafford Northcote, the amiable and not very effective leader of the conservative opposition. 'Well', said father, 'so you are going to oppose us tomorrow'. 'Yes' murmured Sir Stafford mildly, stroking on his black kid gloves and looking anything but warlike, 'we are going to draw the sword' (13 March 1881). She mentions a speech by Archbishop Croke 'advising the people to refrain from "the unmeaning and unmanly practice of hooting and stone-throwing" when the police and troops are present in such force at evictions and sales as to make the unmanly proceeding dangerous to the people' (10 June 1881). A propos of Tim Healy deploring the disorder he had witnessed in the French chamber of deputies, she remarks: 'it is pleasant to find that even Mr H. appreciates the beauty of order and decorum in the house, though he contributes so little to it himself' (16 June 1881). She quotes a Land League placard urging members to attend a meeting 'each man in his thousands' (21 January 1881), and the indignant assertion of a home-rule M.P.: 'so long as Ireland was silent, England was deaf to her cries' (21 January 1881). With less than her habitual charity she repeats a dinner-table *mot* of Judge Dowse's: 'Healy could not have been such a blackguard by nature—he must have taken great pains with himself' (15 November 1881). And she loves to record the amusing anecdote told her by others, as, for example, this one by Thomas Brady, an enthusiast for helping poor fishermen on the west coast. At a meeting he had called to discuss the terms of a loan, he took the opportunity of speaking plainly on the duty of paying just debts in spite of the Land League. Afterwards one of the men said to him privately: 'that was very right what you said, sir—I'm the biggest leaguer in the county, and I wish to God I could be put down and allowed to go about my business in peace' (18 October 1881).

The core of the journal is Forster's career as chief secretary seen by a daughter who was very much in his confidence and seen in the context of his inner family circle—his wife and the three unmarried children, who usually accompanied him on his many visits to Dublin during his two years in office. It illuminates not only Forster's political conduct during the crisis of 1880–82 but also the personalities and relationships of the Forsters, their splendid loyalty to one another, their grace and charm and good taste, their energy and courage, their interest in public affairs and their sense of public responsibility, their wide-ranging personal and social contacts, their intellectual and moral distinction. The diary is a rewarding source for the social round, both official and private, as well as of the inner life, of a well-to-do and well-connected Victorian family of the upper middle class, recording, as it does, their many guests, the constant hospitality (lunch parties, dinner parties, receptions, balls) they give and receive; their frequent churchgoing, their family prayers and bible-reading, their charitable work; their visits to picture galleries, exhibitions, the theatre, and concerts; their incessant journeys to and from their beloved Wharfeside, and between London and Dublin by the Irish Mail and the Holyhead steamer; their occasional weekend excursions from London to stay incognito at some small local hotel and to spend most of Sunday walking in the country (as at Arundel, 25–7 June 1881); the idyllic episode, at a time of great political tension in Ireland, of their weekend at Rostrevor, County Down, and their Sunday walk in the Mourne mountains (29–31 October 1881); their two trips abroad (to Chamonix, 27 August–12 September 1881, and to Normandy, 28 May–17 June 1882); their private conversation, and especially that between Florence and her father on their customary walks together from Eccleston Square to the Irish office when they were in London, and from the chief secretary's lodge to the Phoenix Park gates when in Dublin.

Though Florence writes of her father with unconcealed admiration and approval, her portrait of him is self-consistent and convincing: that of a strong personality in which great toughness of character and a stern sense of duty are combined with a buoyant and generous spirit, good temper, and a genius for happiness in personal relations. If he appears as in some sense a heroic figure, there is nothing awesome about him; and if as preeminently a righteous man, he is never self-righteous or solemn. In his natural element, English parliamentary politics, she sees him as a practical idealist, a leader and educator of public opinion. Of his election campaign at Bradford in April 1880 she writes in her private diary:

He has been hard at work, going round . . . to every ward in the town, and speaking with unfailing freshness, zest, and clear definite judgment on every imaginable topic, political and social, foreign and domestic, which intelligent self-governing Englishmen can take an interest in. There is so much that is unlovely and depressing in the advance of democracy, with its pretensions to decide complex questions of deep political and social import at the misleading dictates of class prejudice and one-sided passion, with its tendency to secure its ends by appeal to the half-knowledge and whole zeal of a numerical majority, that one looks with deep satisfaction at the example now being given by the working men of Bradford and of the manner in which a great constituency may take a wholesome and rational share in the government of the country.[1]

When he accepts the Irish chief secretaryship on 25 April 1880, 'it is felt', she writes, 'that the offer was below that (technically) to which he might have aspired', but

everyone is ready to acknowledge (and that not for the first time) that father is one of those English statesmen who have no hesitation in sacrificing their own claims if they believe they can do better public service thereby.[2]

[1] Private journal, v, 50–51.   [2] Ibid., p. 67.

He has no illusions about the burden he is shouldering as chief secretary:

To govern Ireland, as the new chief secretary will practically do, is a hard and thankless enough task at any time, and it seems doubly so now when the ruler will be called on to judge impartially, firmly, and kindly between the claims of poverty-stricken farmers and ill-used landlords, and to distinguish clearly between the respect due to sincere national patriotism and the relentless suppression of treasonable rant, needful in the interests of the United Kingdom.[1]

Florence's younger sister, Frances, comments in her journal:

For Ireland's sake I can be cordially glad he has made the sacrifice; for himself and for us all I wish it had been otherwise. For himself the burden and responsibility will be very great, and his very power of sympathy will cause him to suffer very keenly under all the real Irish grievances that will constantly be before him. However, happily, he is just now unusually well and vigorous.[2]

His public life had its consolations. In the midst of the anxiety and dis-appointment of his first parliamentary session as chief secretary, when his attempt to secure immediate temporary relief for Irish tenant-farmers by his compensation for disturbance bill was wrecked by the house of lords, he received, Florence records in her private journal,

a letter from an Irish priest acknowledging gratefully the good will of father and of his father before him towards Ireland—a letter which brought tears to father's eyes as he tried to read it aloud to us at breakfast.[3]

Timely words of encouragement, also from the prime minister,

who, throughout this whole session both in public and private backed up . . . the Irish secretary like a true friend and loyal colleague. The relations between father and Mr Gladstone have never been so intimately cordial as [at] this time; affection has been added to respect and admiration.[4]

And however great the demands of his public life, Forster was constantly involved in the life of his family, and they were with him in all his trials and difficulties. Even on his shortest visits to Dublin it was seldom that he was not accompanied by at least one of them (more than once by Florence alone); and whether Forsters were at 80 Eccleston Square or at the chief secretary's lodge or at Wharfeside, they brought warmth and friendliness, purposeful activity, and quiet enjoyment of life with them.

Next to her father the personality that emerges most impressively in Florence's pages is that of her mother—as gentle, sensitive, and tactful, as she is strong-minded, intelligent, and shrewd, with excellent judgment and a well-informed sense of duty, without illusions but never without hope, utterly

[1] Ibid., p. 67–8.
[2] Journal of Frances Arnold-Forster, iv (1879–83), pp 25–6.
[3] Private journal, v, 90 (July 1880).
[4] Ibid.

devoted to her husband and family, a tower of spiritual strength. When she conveys the news to Florence and Frances that Ireland is to be their fate, both daughters know that the prospect is very bitter to her personally.[1]

It is for mother I am most afraid. Not only will she share in all father's responsibility but she will have all the trouble, so utterly distastful to her, of setting up house anew in great state and entertaining people. . . . Mother however comforts herself with Havelock's[2] grand quieting principle that 'if it is right to do a thing at all' (and clearly in this case the going to Ireland is the right thing), 'then it is also right to take all the consequences'. Nevertheless there is nothing in the plan that she likes, and it is a veritable uprooting for her.[3]

Jane Forster certainly lived up to 'Havelock's principle'. Throughout the tensions and perils of her husband's two years as chief secretary her composure remains outwardly unshaken, though inwardly she longs for the day when his sentence will end. Not only her husband but she herself received anonymous letters (15 December 1880) threatening his life—'the vile cowardly cruelty of such a device was enough', Florence confesses, 'to make me for the time being hate Ireland and the Irish as cordially as so many of them hate us'.[4]

No one who saw her calm cheerful ways and heard her spirited courageous language when discussing public affairs would guess how acutely she felt every actual or possible difficulty and peril which father has to contend with. No wonder she looks worn and fragile; every now and then I have a glimpse into what she is feeling and enduring, but it is only rarely. As for the world in general they would not know that she had any anxieties on her mind.[5]

As hostess at the chief secretary's lodge she plays her part with grace and dignity (and an ample domestic staff), showing nothing of the distaste she feels for official entertaining. Her sympathetic ear is open to all kinds of people in trouble. Florence tells us of an Irish friend, Mrs Ball, 'a thorough radical' on land reform whose belief in the necessity of a revolution in the landlord–tenant relationship is 'sorely tried by personal intercourse with its victims', and who finds relief by 'pouring out her feelings volubly to mother, who she knows can sympathise with both principles and people' (19 May 1881). On the day after the murder of Lord Frederick Cavendish (6 May 1882) Mrs Forster calls at Devonshire House to convey sympathy to his widow. Lady Frederick asks to see her.

Mother found her perfectly natural [Frances writes], willing to speak freely of him, crying, and yet even at this time able to take comfort from the hope which mother expressed that this sorrow, by the very greatness of it, might cause a revulsion of feeling and so bring about a better state of things in Ireland—light out of darkness.[6]

---

[1] Private journal, v, 67.
[2] Major-general Sir Henry Havelock (1795–1857), the 'Christian hero' of the Indian mutiny.
[3] Journal of Frances Arnold-Forster, iv, 26 (May 1880).
[4] Private journal, v, 142 (Dec. 1880). [5] Ibid., pp 145–6 (4 Mar. 1881).
[6] Journal of Frances Arnold-Forster, iv, 132.

Lady Frederick is 'very sweet and affectionate' to Mrs Forster and in course of conversation remarks 'I suppose that among all your troubles you never feared *this*'—'not knowing', Florence notes, 'that mother never passed a day at the C[hief] S[ecretary's] Lodge last autumn without the fear of it before her mind' (7 May 1882). When Forster's spirited offer to return to Dublin and take the place of the murdered Lord Frederick is declined by the government, his wife counters his regret with unanswerable logic: his return to Dublin, she says,

... would certainly have been interpreted as a return to the 'old policy' and would more-over have caused exasperation in Ireland. With a view to the future prospects of the new policy, more than to the immediate stress of the present time, they are wise ... to decline accepting his services.

The only other member of the Forster family who occupies a comparable place with her mother in the diary is Florence's younger brother, Oakeley ('Oakel'), the eager, rising young politician, who interrupted a promising practice at the bar[1] to act as his father's unofficial private secretary and threw himself ardently into the struggle against the Land League.[2] Between Florence and Oakel there was not only intimate friendship but also close intellectual affinity. She believes him to be heading for a distinguished political career (as indeed he was), and follows with lively interest the writings and publication of the first two of his many articles on political questions—'A civilian's reply to Sir Garnet Wolseley' (*Nineteenth Century*, ix, no. 52 (June, 1881), pp 905–16), on the need for radical reform in the British army, and 'The Gladstone government in Ireland' (*North American Review*, cxxxiii, no. 301, (Dec. 1881), pp 560–77), an able defence of his father's policy.

Frances ('Francie'), her sister, and her brother Edward and his family, though frequently mentioned, are much more lightly sketched. Florence's private diary shows that she was warmly attached to both of them, but their interests were much less in politics than hers and Oakel's. Francie, the most other-worldly of the Arnold-Forsters, was deeply involved in Sunday-school work, and during most of her father's term as chief secretary was engaged in writing a missionary book,[3] of which Florence thought highly:

Though intended for children the book will be founded on such a basis of varied reading and information as will make it something far above the average in point of real value, and at the same time the liveliness and simplicity of the style will make it really delightful reading. As for the spirit of holiness which makes the whole book ... so singu-larly beautiful, I can only say it is what one might expect on anything written by Francie on a subject so near her heart.[4]

[1] See Mary Arnold-Forster, *Hugh Oakeley Arnold-Forster*, pp 28–30.
[2] He published on 1 Apr. 1882, under the pseudonym 'One who knows', a pamphlet *The truth about the Land League*, an indictment derived from statements of the league and its leaders.
[3] It was published in 1882 by Hatchard, of London, as *Heralds of the cross, or the fulfilling of the command: chapters in missionary work*.
[4] Private journal, v, 151–2 (Mar.–Apr. 1881).

Edward, who seems to have taken on the active management of the Green-holme Mills, lived at Burley-in-Wharfedale in a house called Cathedine (now The Court), where he and his wife Edith were raising a young family—nephews and nieces in whom Florence and Francie took great delight.

Of Florence's many Arnold relatives Uncle Matt (the poet Matthew Arnold) is the one who comes most vividly to life—personally amiable and endearing, but intellectually austere and sometimes exasperating as in his 'airy theorising' about Ireland (in which he had a historical as well as a contemporary interest).[1] Forster playfully warns him that if he comes to Ireland, the chief secretary will have to lock him up (6 April 1881)—though Uncle Matt and his wife, Aunt Fanny Lucy, stayed several times with the Forsters in the chief secretary's lodge. On the Forster side, after the death of Aunt Sarah at Tottenham (13 September 1880) the only relatives mentioned in the diary are the Buxtons, descendants of Sir Thomas Fowell Buxton, W. E. Forster's uncle. The widow of Charles Buxton, Sir Thomas's son, and Forster's first cousin, lived in the house in Surrey built by her husband, Fox Warren, which was within walking distance of Pain's Hill, Cobham, where 'the Uncle Matts' lived. The Arnold-Forster girls were frequent visitors there, as also at another house in the neighbourhood, Fox Holm, belonging to the Holland family. But relatives, friends and acquaintances galore keep cropping up in Florence's pages, staying with the Forsters for days on end or being visited by them, or joining them at breakfast, or lunch, or five o'clock tea, or dinner, or meeting them at other people's houses or in the street or at the house of commons, or exchanging letters with them. And all these, together with many others whom Florence meets on social occasions or whom, without ever meeting, she observed and comments on, make up an animated and infinitely varied tapestry in which men of letters, artists, prelates, landowners, industrialists, statesmen, politicians, judges, soldiers, administrators, and civil servants jostle one another.

As a source for political history in an age of crisis, the value of Florence's Irish diary depends on the accuracy of her knowledge, her grasp of the situations she describes, the soundness of her judgment, and the range of her sympathies. Her limitations can easily be identified. She viewed the Irish political scene from her father's standpoint, that of a liberal unionist, who firmly believed in the value both for Britain and Ireland of maintaining the union between them. She liked Ireland but disliked Irish nationalism. Yet she experienced something of the spell of the most persuasive advocate of Irish independence, Thomas Davis. In November 1880 Sir Charles Gavan Duffy sent her, as the author of *Francis Deák*, a copy of his new book, *Young Ireland*, with the request that she read it and see whether she did not find Davis as true a patriot as Deák. She did read it from beginning to end and recognised in Duffy's hero 'a man of rare nobleness of character':

[1] See *Edmund Burke, Letters, speeches and tracts on Irish affairs*, collected and arranged by Matthew Arnold (London, 1881); Matthew Arnold, *Irish essays and others* (London, 1882).

Like Deák single-minded in his devotion to what he believed to be the interests of his country, and having like him that complete freedom from personal vanity and self-consciousness, that large-minded kindliness which, joined to intellectual power and courage go far to make the sort of hero I incline to worship.[1]

Though convinced that Davis and his friends were mistaken, she sympathised with them as 'men working with eager brains and honest hearts in a cause they believed to be the regeneration of Ireland'.

I can well understand the excitement of that movement, and can feel for those whose hopes were so often disappointed and their calculations frustrated. Though Thomas Davis did not see his dream realized, though little permanent achievement seems the result of his untiring labour, yet, if he was really the man whom Sir Gavan Duffy describes, his life and character must in themselves be a heritage worth leaving to his fellow countrymen as a fine contribution to the traditions of Irish patriotism.

But among contemporary leaders of the Irish people she could see no such men as Davis. There were plenty of patriots who hated England more than Davis did, but few with such unselfish and enlightened love of their own country.[2]

It was Britain's heavy obligation to do justice to Ireland however unrewarding the task: 'we . . . must strive to do our best for Ireland and make up our minds to be hated and abused all the same' (27 December 1880). 'Doing justice' entailed, in 1880–82, effecting a revolution by act of parliament in the legal relations between landlord and tenant while at the same time stamping out the lawlessness and violence that accompanied the land agitation. She believed that the operation of the land act of 1881 would restore social peace and order in Ireland, but only if the ring-leaders of the agitation were thwarted in their attempt to usurp legitimate authority and make the crisis a stepping-stone to home rule itself. Like most of her countrymen she saw Parnell not as the brilliant leader of a struggling nation but as an unscrupulous and irresponsible schemer, appealing to the worst impulses of an ignorant and excitable people. Of his lieutenants, the only one she fervently wished to have 'with us, not against us' was Dillon, that 'honest and melancholy desperado' (25 February 1881), in whom, despite the criminal violence of his speeches, she perceived elements of true idealism. She saw the Land League only as a vast engine of intimidation and outrage, but was blind to its significance as an instrument of natural justice in the hands of a multitude of small farmers, effectively organised for the first time. Of Davitt, the league's founder, she was willing to believe that he was a sincere social revolutionary—'a peasant Mazzini'—, and here she differed from Oakel, who regarded Davitt as a murderer (8 February 1881); but she failed to perceive his nobility of character or his overflowing sympathy with human suffering.

[1] Private journal, v, 135–6.
[2] Ibid., pp 136–7; for an assessment of Davitt see T. W. Moody, *Davitt and Irish revolution, 1846–82* (Oxford, 1981), epilogue.

There is no doubt, I believe, that Mr Davitt was known to have circulated arms (not rifles, but revolvers, the weapons of assassination) and that he was privy to the attack upon Chester castle—a most clear attempt at murder. At the same time I cannot get rid of the impression that, with all his reckless revolutionary ideas of the laws both of the state and of civilisation, Davitt is not the sort of man who would be rightly punished or in any way reformed by subjecting him to the same prison discipline and degrading regulations as are suitable and necessary for an ordinary convict.

In all this she, like her father, was in much the same position as Gladstone himself until the Kilmainham negotiations of April 1882 caused him to change his mind. On the other hand she and her family were friendly with Murrough O'Brien and his wife, of Mount Mapas, Killiney, who were related to the Limerick O'Briens; and in Murrough they had within their own circle a strenuous defender of the Land League and admirer of Davitt. It was characteristic of Davitt himself that looking back on the land war, he formed a just estimate of Forster:

His intentions on accepting the chief secretaryship were of as sympathetic a kind towards Ireland as could influence an Englishman in that post. . . . But he found himself in a situation which, in a sense, compelled him to defend an impossible system of rule and of land tenure against . . . his personal sympathies.[1]

Florence's estimate of the Land League and its leaders, none of whom she knew personally, displays a lack of understanding and imaginative insight widely shared by intelligent and otherwise well-informed people of her class in Britain—and in Ireland. Yet she understood and was exceptionally well-informed about a large area of the political world: English politicians of both parties; Irish liberal M.P.s; a few Irish home-rulers—notably William Shaw, E. Dwyer Gray (editor of the *Freeman's Journal*), and, strangely enough, the ex-Fenian leader, John O'Connor Power; Irish landowners, especially such favourable examples as the Monteagles, Emlys, MacMurrough Kavanaghs, de Vescis, Longfords, and Powerscourts; civil servants, policemen, and soldiers. Many of these she knew at close quarters, from Gladstone himself—who appears not only as the charismatic leader of the liberals and a superbly able and inspiring parliamentarian but also as friendly and lovable, fascinating in conversation, of irresistible courtesy and charm—to Thomas Henry Burke, permanent head of Dublin Castle, the stern, dedicated pessimist, who spends, and eventually forfeits, his life in the service, as he conceives it, of his countrymen. She describes how Burke on one occasion, 'dilated with flashing eyes, and in his vigorous, trenchant manner, on the absurdity of trying to solve an insoluble problem—namely to carry on constitutional government in a country where the constitution is not based on popular support' (24 October 1881).[2] Within the circle of the Irish administration she was on familiar terms with

[1] Davitt, *Fall of feudalism*, p. 259.
[2] See also 4 Dec. 1881.

Henry Jephson and Horace West ('the occidental'), private secretary and assistant private secretary respectively to her father; Col. George E. Hillier, head of the Royal Irish Constabulary; Clifford Lloyd, most outstanding of Forster's special resident magistrates; and Sir Thomas Steele, commander-in-chief of the forces. What Florence has to say on the character and political conduct of all such men, based as it is on personal contact, on inside information, usually derived from her father, on regular attendance at the house of commons, and on systematic and critical reading of the press, British and Irish, is always worth hearing.

As a contribution to Irish history her journal is thus of special importance for the light it casts on the attitudes and experiences of landlords confronted by the Land League, on their relations with the Irish government, on the working of the Irish executive, the legal system, the police, and the army, on the use of police and soldiers to protect persons and property under the coercion act, on the operation of the land act, and, above all, on the policy and day-to-day action of Forster himself in endeavouring simultaneously to solve the land problem and to eradicate outrage and terrorism. His compassion and his humanity—as in his scrupulously considerate treatment of the political suspects whom he imprisoned without trial—are not less evident than his strength of will, his indomitable courage, and his good temper, constantly harassed as he was not only by land leaguers in Ireland and by Parnellites in the house of commons but also by tensions within the cabinet and the liberal party over the whole principle of his regime. Much of this Florence knew from her very acute and intelligent observation, and she is particularly interesting in her comment on the problem that the anti-coercion attitude of radicals within the liberal party, both inside and outside parliament, presented to Gladstone and Forster, and on Parnell's constant readiness to make political capital out of this situation. But whether she is drawing on her own observations or on public or private sources, Florence's relationship with the chief secretary gives her journal unique value as evidence.

Forster did not, of course, tell her everything of importance that was going on behind the scenes, but he obviously had the greatest confidence in her discretion, as in that of his wife, and told her a great deal that was known at the time only to the inner circle of government. Thus her journal brings out very clearly Forster's growing dissatisfaction with Cowper as lord lieutenant, regarding him as politically a cipher and seeking to have him replaced by someone who could share the burden of the Irish administration and so enable the chief secretary to give more attention to the demands of his office at Westminster (26, 29 May 1881). Forster's preference was for Earl Spencer, who had been lord lieutenant in Gladstone's ministry and was now president of the council with a seat in the cabinet; with Spencer as viceroy Forster thought he himself should be replaced as chief secretary by Shaw Lefevre (20 Nov. 1881).[1]

[1] See Reid, *Forster*, ii, 366–8.

If Gladstone could not spare Spencer, Forster thought of Goschen, raised to
the peerage, as the next best choice, Lord Carlingford being unlikely to accept
the office. He also toyed with the idea that he himself should exchange the chief
secretaryship for the lord lieutenancy, even if this meant that he would have to
be made a peer (23, 27 March 1882). Florence's journal makes it quite clear that
Cowper's decision to resign was entirely independent of the Kilmainham
negotiations. It has frequent references to the visits of Lord Frederick
Cavendish (as financial secretary to the treasury) and of Herbert Gladstone to
Dublin Castle, and both augments the latter's diary of his Irish mission[1] and
gives a convincing picture of him as an amiable, well-intentioned, and rather
ineffectual young man.

On the subject of the Kilmainham negotiations and the grounds of Forster's
resignation the diary provides a very telling statement of his case. Florence
misses nothing of the drama of his defence of himself in the house of
commons, followed by the Phoenix Park murders, his offer to return to
Dublin, and the great popular reaction in his favour. Though the diary ends
inconclusively, her final sketch of her father, 'in his enforced inaction and
isolation', is firmly drawn and appropriate. 'He seems as serene, as much
interested in everything (especially Irish affairs), as full of occupation, as
though he had never known any more exciting experience than presiding at
anti-cruelty meetings and attending emigration committees at the house'. But
she notices that

every now and then . . . a single sentence or tone of voice will show to those who know
him that his present position is not always as easy to bear as might be supposed from his
imperturbable cheerfulness and generous readiness to take up any useful work that is
still open to him.

At the height of the land war Florence reflects on Irish politics in a memorable passage (4 June 1881):

Perhaps this crisis, when nothing but evil seems uppermost, is but a phase in an onward
movement; . . . [perhaps] it is not so much to the deterioration, to the vices of the
present generation of Irishmen and women that these miseries are due, as to the
crooked corners of Ireland's past history.

The revolt against a bad system, the reaction after years of silent endurance and stolid
indifference on the part both of rich and poor—in short the revolution—has come in our
time, and come, as revolutions generally do, with very ugly accompaniments. . . .

However, I hope and believe that there may come a time, even in Ireland, when the
jar and distress and amazement caused by this painful readjustment of old relations
between man and man, and class and class, shall have passed away; when the mist of
falsehood conjured up by blind self-seeking leaders of the blind shall have been
dispersed, and Irishmen and Englishmen, gentry and farmers shall understand the new
foundation on which they stand, and dare to live together as friends and honest men,

[1] See A. B. Cooke and J. R. Vincent (ed.), 'Herbert Gladstone, Forster, and Ireland, 1881–2' in
Irish Historical Studies, xvii, no. 68 (Sept. 1971), pp 521–48; xviii, no. 69 (Mar. 1972), pp 74–89.

without fear of interference or incitement to violence on the part of either landlord or land leaguer.

It was in this spirit of sympathy, understanding, and hope that she herself was to spend the remaining two-thirds of her life in Ireland.

T. W. Moody

NOTE ON EDITORIAL TREATMENT

THE text is reproduced in full from Florence's typescript, collated at critical points with the portion of the MS of her journal that survives (see above, p. xxvii). Editorial additions to the text, such as expansions of abbreviated words, are shown within square brackets.

The spelling of the original is nearly always accurate, and the occasional lapses, almost certainly typing errors, are therefore silently corrected. The paragraph structure and the use of capitals are as in her typescript. But the punctuation is normalised (in accordance with *Irish Historical Studies rules*) and the titles of books and newspapers, which Florence usually gives within quotation marks, are uniformly cited in italics.

The dates marking the opening of diary sequences are not entirely consistent either in form or position in the typescript. These are here normalised on the pattern '24 June, Th.', in boldface, centred on the page. The date or dates on which the contents of each printed page were written is shown at the head of each page, at the inner margin, in the form '7 Dec. 80'. Florence's whereabouts, as stated or implied in her narrative, are shown centred at the head of each page.

The editorial annotation in footnotes relates to persons and events not treated in the introduction or the appendix.

MY IRISH JOURNAL

<OⵑⵑOⵑⵑOⵑⵑOⵑⵑOⵑⵑOⵑⵑOⵑⵑOⵑⵑO>

A Record—from the inside—
of the Chief Secretary's experiences
in
DUBLIN and LONDON
during the bad times
1880–1882

<OⵑⵑOⵑⵑOⵑⵑOⵑⵑOⵑⵑOⵑⵑOⵑⵑOⵑⵑO>

Dedicated to the beloved Memory of my
Father and transcribed for my
husband, Autumn 1905

Florence Verell Bren

MY IRISH JOURNAL

Contemporary Notes

June, July 1880

When Mr Forster was appointed Chief Secretary,[1] he entered on his Office with good wishes from all sides;[2] even, apparently, from the Irish Home Rulers, who were said to be gratified at the pledge given, in the appointment of so distinguished a statesman, of the Government's recognition of the claims of Ireland.

The Conservatives on their side were disposed to have confidence in Mr Forster's strength and fitness for the task of ruling Ireland, and there were many congratulations on this, the least objectionable of Mr Gladstone's new appointments.

At first matters went fairly smoothly in the House, even the Home Rulers seeming inclined to give the Government a chance. The Peace Preservation Act[3] was not renewed, a step which called forth some grave warnings, but which was on the whole accepted with equanimity on all sides. Moreover it was acknowledged that Mr Forster and Lord Spencer[4] had gone far to justify the action of the Government, when they pointed out—

(1) that the Executive Government in Ireland were still left with efficient means of dealing with disturbance;
(2) that the special powers now foregone were in practice of little special help;
(3) that the renewal of the Act afresh after the lapse of the necessary interval would have exasperated the Nationalist Party to a degree that would make the task of the Ministry in dealing with the more rational Home Rulers more hopeless, whilst it was not essential for the preservation of law and order.

---

[1] He was appointed on 30 Apr. On 3 May he paid his first official visit to Dublin, accompanied by Mrs Forster, Florence, and Edward. They all returned on 10 May (Private diary, v, 69–70).

[2] His predecessor, 'Jemmy' Lowther (see below, p. 41), in one of his last letters to the under-secretary, wrote: 'I am glad you have got Forster as he is head and shoulders over the head of Shaw Lefevre, who would have played the deuce and excited the mob with the notion that the days of the Commune were at hand. Forster is a plain-spoken man who you will find a good fellow to work with from what I know of him.' (Lowther to Burke, 30 Apr. 1880; N.L.I., MS 8501 (7).)

[3] The Peace Preservation (Ireland) Act, 1875 (38 Vict., c.14), last of a distinct family of repressive acts beginning in 1847; it served chiefly to continue, with amendments to 1 June 1880, some provisions of earlier acts designed to deal with agrarian crime. The question of its renewal is discussed in Richard Hawkins, 'Liberals, land, and coercion in the summer of 1880: the influence of the Carraroe ejectments' in *Galway Arch. Soc. Jn.*, xxxiv (1974–5), pp 40–57.

[4] See appendix.

Lastly, there seemed little reason why a Liberal Government should fear to take a step which it was pretty generally known would have to be taken by the Opposition had they remained in Office.

But however satisfactory the opening relations between the new Government and their opponents—Home Rule and Conservative—on the question of Ireland, the harmony has been short lived.

The Third Party, as the Irish Home Rulers who divide their favours between both sides of the House is now likely to be called, is showing its old affinity for 'obstruction' pure and simple; Mr Parnell,[1] the nominal leader (*vice* Mr Shaw) is outshone at present by Mr O'Donnell—the Irishman of all others whose line of action in the House seems to have least apparent relation to his presumed motive—namely, the furtherance of Irish interests and the relief of Irish suffering.

The only object hitherto achieved by this patriotic Irishman has been the spreading of his own notoriety by the highly successful method of first exciting the wrath and detestation of the House of Commons in the evening, and then writing a letter to the *Times* the following morning to explain why he had felt it his duty to do so.

Mr Parnell is believed to be reserving himself for a great demonstration of his principles on the Land Question.

24 June, Th.

As to Conservative opposition on Irish questions, the Government is about to experience it in full vigour on the introduction of Mr Forster's Irish Land Act. This is the great rock ahead at present; so strong indeed is the repugnance to this very drastic measure, not only amongst Conservatives, but amongst Liberal and even Radical Members, that it seems quite on the cards that the Government may fail to carry it through the Commons—a defeat which would probably involve Mr Forster's resignation.

Considering that in the Queen's Speech at the opening of the new Parliament it was expressly stated—to the disappointment, real or feigned, of the Irish Party—that the Government had no intention of bringing forward a Land Bill, but simply of proposing a measure for the relief of distress in Ireland, it may seem somewhat surprising that the Ministry should find themselves in the full crisis of Land Law reform.

How has this come about? The bare facts at any rate have been these. On June 4th late at night, Mr O'Connor Power brought forward a Bill on behalf of the Irish Party,[2] which, by comparison with the proposals of Land Reform

---

[1] See appendix.

[2] O'Connor Power (see appendix) introduced his Landlord and Tenant (Ireland) Act (1870) Amendment Bill on 28 May, when it was read for the first time without debate (*Hansard 3*, cclii, 740–41); the second reading was on 4 June.

usually set forth by Mr Parnell and his fellow agitators, was remarkably moderate; considering, however, that such proposals had included schemes for the complete extermination or buying out of Landlords 'en masse', this moderation by comparison was not necessarily very reassuring. As a matter of fact Mr O'Connor Power's Bill proposed to relieve the tenant by depriving the Landlord unconditionally of the right of eviction for non-payment of rent.[1]

On being confronted with this measure, it might to some have appeared a simple solution for the Government to refuse it all support, or rather to announce their opposition to it, on the ground, first, of the intrinsic defects of the proposed bill, and, secondly, of their own previously expressed determination to undertake no Land legislation this year. But to Mr Forster at least, as the Responsible Minister for Ireland, such a course, simple as it might appear, seemed inadmissible.

In the state of things against which Mr O'Connor Power's extravagant remedy was directed, there was a real grievance—a grievance, moreover, which was so intimately connected with the distress which the Government had pledged themselves to relieve that it was not easy to look upon the two as absolutely distinct questions to be dealt with at two separate times. Distress one session—Land question another.

To have professed total opposition to Mr Power's Bill would have been looked upon by the Irish and their representatives in Parliament as a disclaimer of all sympathy with that special form of distress (expatriation) which is at once most genuinely felt by the people, and is most easily taken advantage of by agitators whose wisdom is very far from genuine, whatever their feeling may be.

On the other hand for the Government to have accepted, or agreed to support, Mr O'Connor Power's Bill as it stood, would have been impossible.

There remained a third alternative, namely, to bring in a Government measure dealing in some degree, but in a different manner, with the state of things which had given occasion to the Irish proposal.

This course was the one advised by Mr Forster, who gained the consent of his colleagues (in some cases with great difficulty)[2] to introduce a measure having for its effect the suppression, for a limited time,[3] of the Landlord's right of eviction for non-payment of rent. By virtue of this proposed Act, a Landlord could be called upon to pay compensation, as in the case of 'disturbance', to a tenant whom he desired to evict for non-payment of rent, provided it could be shown to the satisfaction of the County Court Judge that the tenant was honestly unable to pay, not from his own fault, but from the pressure of distress caused by the famine.[4]

---

[1] The bill proposed to amend the land act of 1870 so as to give a tenant ejected for non-payment of rent the right to claim compensation for disturbance.

[2] The queen recorded in her diary for 19 Aug.: 'the duke [of Argyll] said that only four of the cabinet were in favour of the Irish disturbance bill' (*The letters of Queen Victoria*, ed. G. B. Buckle, series II, iii (London, 1928), p. 134).

[3] Till 31 Dec. 1882.   [4] The crop failures of 1877–9.

With the wish to emphasise the temporary and limited character of the measure and its connection with the special circumstances of distress, Mr Forster (on June 18th) presented it first to the House as a clause in the Relief Bill.[1]

But the Conservatives, horrified at this proposal to legalise fresh restrictions and burdens upon the Landlords as a mere supplementary clause in a Relief Bill, refused absolutely to consent to its presentation for discussion in this form, and Mr Forster was consequently compelled to bring forward the quondam 'clause' as a distinct measure in itself, having the title of the 'Compensation for Disturbance Bill (Ireland)'. If Mr Bradlaugh's case[2] is finished by that time, the new Bill is to be introduced to-morrow (25th) by Mr Forster, who will explain its true aim and character.

Never perhaps did a measure brought before the House by a Cabinet Minister depend more for its hope not only of success, but of bare toleration, on the power of its author to state and make good his case. Hitherto the opposition has been widely and freely expressed; not only do Conservatives talk of 'confiscation' 'communism' and 'injustice', but steady-going Liberals, and reasonable Irishmen speaking from experience of their country with its peculiar failings and dangers, are disposed to be alarmed at the encouragement which they conceive will be given to contempt of law and a feeling of misguided anti-landlord animosity.

The Chief Secretary has at least one like-minded and loyal supporter in the Lord Lieutenant. In a private letter to Mr Forster, Lord Cowper[3] has expressed his willingness to share responsibility for the Bill, and agrees with him as to the hatefulness of having to use the full legal and military tone[4] of the Executive in helping Landlords to clear their estates by evicting the peasants under the present circumstances of unavoidable distress and poverty. It is those who are specially responsible for the Government of Ireland who feel most keenly the importance of using the powers of the law only in those cases where the law does not in the eyes of the people run contrary to justice.

---

[1] The relief bill (Relief of Distress (Ireland) Act (1880) Amendment Bill) was introduced on 2 June. Forster's attempt to introduce the compensation provisions as an additional clause in the relief bill was made, and abandoned, on 17 June, not 18 June as Florence states (*Hansard 3*, ccliii, 201–2, 210–17). The compensation for disturbance bill as a separate measure was introduced and given its first reading on 18 June and received its second reading on 25 June.

[2] The election of the freethinker Bradlaugh (see appendix) for Northampton raised the question whether a member could take his seat without first taking the oath of allegiance. The course of the Bradlaugh controversy over the next six years is examined by Walter L. Arnstein in his *The Bradlaugh case: a study in late Victorian opinion and politics* (Oxford, 1965); the role of Irish M.P.s is discussed in his article 'Parnell and the Bradlaugh case' in *I.H.S.*, xiii, no. 51 (Mar. 1963), pp 212–35.

[3] See appendix.

[4] Should presumably read 'force'.

28 June, Mon.

On Friday afternoon the 25th, in a full House, with the Peers' Gallery thronged with anxious Landowners, Mr Forster explained and defended his proposed Bill. His endeavour was to show that the measure, however distasteful, was but an extension of the Land Act of 1870, and not the introduction of a new and revolutionary principle. That the proposal was not to prohibit eviction for non-payment of rent, but only to restrain eviction under certain special circumstances, and within a limited time and place; that the forbearance of Landlords cannot always be relied upon in periods of special and dangerous distress like the present, and that, whereas the law is now obliged to be put in force on behalf of unreasonable as well as reasonable evictions, it would under the provisions of the new Bill be employed in cases of the latter description only.

Mr Forster spoke with such conviction and feeling, and whilst showing his sympathy with the peasantry condemned so strongly the anti-rent agitators, by whom the people have been misled, that his speech made a very favourable impression on the House. On all hands it was acknowledged that the case for the much-abused Bill had been put as well as was possible, and that several mitigating features had been brought out which had been lost sight of in the first emotion of amazement and alarm. Moreover, the speech was not without its practical effect in the House.

2 July, Fri.

Amongst some of the English Liberals the Chief Secretary's speech produced a direct change of intention in the matter of voting (witness the private notes of Mr Playfair[1] and Mr J. K. Cross[2]). At the same time there can be no doubt that the objections to the Bill are as strongly felt as ever, and that an amount of opposition is to be expected which will make the probabilities of the Government carrying the measure, even in the Lower House, somewhat doubtful.

The Landlords are in a simple panic, and the *Times* is filled day after day with letters from Peers and Commoners, pointing out the evil consequences which the Bill, if carried, will entail, not only upon the Landlords, whom it will ruin, but upon the tenants, whom it will demoralize. From strong and calmly reasoned and, from some points of view, irrefutable arguments, down to frantic shrieks of denunciation, such as have greeted every reform touching the 'rights of property' since the world began, Mr Forster has to meet every form and kind of opposition. Nor [not] only the *St James Gazette* and *Standard*, but also the *Times* are dead against the Government on this question, and when the Bill was

[1] Dr Lyon Playfair (1818–98): professor of chemistry, University of Edinburgh, 1858–69; liberal M.P. for universities of Edinburgh and St Andrews, 1868–85; chairman and deputy speaker of house of commons, 1880–83; K.C.B., 1883; cr. baron, 1892.
[2] John Kynaston Cross (1832–87): Bolton cotton manufacturer and liberal M.P. for Bolton, 1874–85.

first produced even such Liberal papers as the *Spectator* and *Daily Chronicle* were guarded in their approval, and far from encouraging as to the Chief Secretary's prospects of success. His most thorough-going and intelligent supporter in the Press is the *Pall Mall Gazette* (now under Mr John Morley[1]). Amongst Irish Peers and Landowners he has *one* ally—Lord Bessborough.[2] As for the remainder, all alike, Liberals and Conservatives, are grieved and alarmed, even Lord Emly.

10 July, Sat.

The division on the second reading of the Irish Bill took place at 2 in the morning on July 5th, the result being a majority of 75 for the Government.[3] About 50 Liberals abstained and several (notably the Fitzwilliams, Lord Lymington, Lord Moreton[4] &c.) voted with the Opposition. The Irish resolutely refrained from speaking throughout the debate ('a silence more eloquent than words', according to Mr Gibson,[1] the late Attorney General, who made a long and vehement attack upon the Bill).

Amongst the speakers were Mr Gladstone, Mr Gibson, Lord Hartington,[1] Sir S. Northcote,[1] and Mr Forster, who warmed[5] up the debate in an effective little speech.

The majority was larger than had been anticipated, and the first impression was one of relief, and almost of triumph; but the clouds have speedily gathered again, and the present predicament of the Government Bill is in some respects more dangerous than before.

On July 8th an amendment was proposed by the Attorney General (Mr Law),[1] by which the whole character of the measure is declared to be altered, and the arguments used for and against it to have been rendered inapplicable. According to the new clause the Landlord cannot be called upon to pay compensation for disturbance on evicting a tenant if *he has given him the option of selling the interest in his holding*, and thereby leaving his farm not in a penniless condition, as may be the case at present, but furnished with a sum of money obtained *from the incoming tenant* instead *of from* the Landlord.[6]

[1] See appendix.

[2] Frederick George Brabazon (1815–95): succeeded his brother as 6th Earl Bessborough in Jan. 1880; owned about 35,000 acres in Ireland, almost all in Kilkenny and Carlow; chairman of the commission appointed in July 1880 to inquire into the working of the land act of 1870 (see below, p. 31).

[3] The division was 295 to 217.

[4] The brother and sons of the 6th Earl Fitzwilliam (owner of 91,423 acres, predominantly in Wicklow) sat as liberal M.P.s for Malton, Peterborough, and the West Riding of Yorkshire. Viscount Lymington, son of the fifth earl of Portsmouth (owner of 10,189 acres in Wexford) sat for Barnstaple. Lord Moreton sat for West Gloucestershire.

[5] Should presumably read 'wound'.

[6] The Fixity of Tenure (Ireland) Bill, introduced by a group of Ulster liberals on 21 May and dropped on 30 June, had included similar provisions. Government spokesmen held that Law's amendment did not change the bill, but merely made one of its original objects more explicit.

It is obvious that this proposal, which amounts simply to the introduction of Ulster Tenant Right, as a temporary measure of relief, into certain limited districts, cannot be denounced in the same terms of abuse which were lavished on the original Bill. But if rendered less odious in itself by the proposed amendment, the Compensation for Disturbance Bill is still a Government measure, and therefore no whit less objectionable in the eyes of all good Conservatives than it was before. Moreover, their 'zeal to destroy' has only become keener from the increased prospect of success afforded by the defection of the Parnell faction from the Government ranks. The leader of the 'Third Party' has given the 'mot d'ordre', and on the division upon going into Committee on Thursday night, Mr Parnell and thirty followers marked their disapproval of the new clause by walking out of the House in a body.

The majority for the Government was nevertheless 56.[1] Between Mr Parnell and the Chief Secretary there is now war to the knife, the latter having thus described their respective positions—that whereas the object of the Government was to protect the tenant in the possession of his property, the object of Mr Parnell (having in view his reputation in Ireland) was to enable the tenant to avoid paying rent.

It is acknowledged that the amendment as it stands at present will require some guarding if it is not to be made use of by the Landlords to compel a forced sale disadvantageous to the tenant, and there are some staunch Liberal supporters of the Government who regret this rather abrupt rectification of the Bill in a direction where some mitigation of the severely anti-landlord tendency was perhaps not uncalled for.

Meanwhile it remains to be seen whether the Liberals will be at all reconciled to the Bill by the proposed change. The resignation of Lord Lansdowne[2] (Under-Secretary for India) does not seem of good augury in this respect.

7 Aug., Sat.

The Compensation for Disturbance (Ireland) Bill passed the House of Commons on [26 July] by a majority smaller than was expected, 66.[3] On August 3rd, after a two nights' debate, the Bill was thrown out in the Lords by a majority of 231, only 51 voting for it. This result, though not surprising considering the strong opposition which had been evident from the moment the measure was brought forward, is much to be regretted by those who are responsible for the government of the West of Ireland. Unfortunately the only persons and the only principles which will be really strengthened by the

---

[1] The division was 255 to 199.

[2] Henry Charles Keith Petty-Fitzmaurice (1845–1927), 5th marquis of Lansdowne: owner of 120,616 acres in Kerry, Meath, and elsewhere in Ireland; under-secretary for war, 1872–4, in Gladstone's first administration; under-secretary for India, Apr. 1880, but resigned, as above, over the compensation for disturbance bill.

[3] The division was 304 to 237.

rejection of the Bill in the Lords are the anti-English political agitators, both in Ireland and in Parliament, whose theories will seem to have gained further justification by what has just happened.

There is not the consolation of thinking that if some opportunity of benefiting the poor tenants has been lost, the poor Landlords will at least be in a better position for securing their just dues. On the contrary, it is to be feared that the anti-rent agitation will have received a fresh impetus, and there will certainly be no lack of orators both in and out of Parliament to take advantage of this new opportunity of embarrassing the Government, and expatiating on the crying evils of 'Landlordism'.

On the other hand, there are some faint signs of a disposition, even amongst the more extreme of the Irish, to rally round a Ministry which has received such a severe rebuff in the sincere attempt to legislate for the benefit of the Irish people.

On August 5th the Government was called on by Mr Parnell and Mr O'Donnell to state what steps they meant to take in view of the rejection of the Disturbance Bill in the Lords, and whether they intended to call in the Military and Constabulary for the purpose of assisting at the eviction of poor tenants.

The reply of the Chief Secretary on behalf of the Government made a good impression on both sides of the House, from the firm and yet considerate language in which it was framed and the earnestness and feeling with which it was delivered. Whilst declaring plainly the intention of the Government 'to protect the officers of the law in the execution of the law', Mr Forster assured his questioners that the utmost consideration would be used towards the evicted tenants; he ended his brief reply with an appeal to all good citizens of whatever class, rank or condition, to aid the Government by their influence in endeavouring to restore friendly relations between classes in Ireland.

Meantime for the better security of individual life and property in the distressed districts of the West, a reinforcement of troops had been despatched to Ireland to be quartered in small bodies in those localities where outrages have been most frequent.

At present there is hope of a good harvest, which would do more than anything else to strengthen the hands of the Government, and take the bread out of the mouths of the agitators.

[10 Sept., Fri.]

The chief home event of interest, if not of importance, at the beginning of August was the illness of Mr Gladstone. Happily the feverish attack—brought on by over-work and exhaustion—was short, though severe. The demonstration of sympathy throughout the whole country, and indeed Europe and America, was very striking, and it gained in effect from not being confined to Mr Gladstone's political admirers. For days his house in Downing Street was besieged by enquirers of all ranks and parties, and every incident in his illness and convalescence has been eagerly treasured up and imparted to a sincerely sympathising and anxious public through the Press.

The cruise round the English and Scotch coasts which he is now making in a steamer provided by Mr Donald Currie[1] affords opportunity for repeated displays of affection and respect whenever the 'Grantully Castle' comes within sound of cheering, or within reach of enthusiastic addresses.

Meanwhile Mr Gladstone's colleagues are still toiling in this deserted City (Aug. 31). A week or two ago the work seemed harder and more thankless, the prospect of release more distant, than at any time in this long and toilsome session. Now, however, there seems to be light ahead, and if nothing unforeseen happens the Chief Secretary hopes to see and hear the last of Mr Biggar[2] and Lord Randolph Churchill[2] at the very beginning of next week.

The rejection of the Compensation Bill in the Lords, as was natural, did not contribute to make the Irish Party in the Commons more amenable than they had been, and there were ominous rumours of the revenge they mean to take later on, in the shape of acute obstruction.

The crisis as between the Parnellites and the Government was brought about by Mr Dillon, M.P. for Tipperary, who, in a speech at a Land League Meeting on August 15th,[3] used language which Mr Forster described in the House a day or two later[4] as 'wicked and cowardly'—the speaker having deliberately incited the people to illegal and punishable acts, whilst himself remaining so far within the letter of the law as to avoid the chance of conviction.

On Monday the 23rd,[5] the evening fixed for the discussion of the Irish Constabulary Vote, the obstructives gave battle all along the line, the text for discussion being a speech by Mr Dillon in answer to the Chief Secretary's vindication of his own offending speech. Mr Forster, having replied, reaffirming his original statement and dwelling more fully than he had done before on that part of Mr Dillon's speech which suggested the mutilation of cattle as an instrument in the Land League programme, the Irish Members got up one after another in formal array to assert their esteem and affection for Mr Dillon, and their abhorrence of the Chief Secretary and his insulting language (Sept. 10).

Finally the House divided, when only 21 Members were found voting for Mr Dillon's motion.[6]

The following evening and night were occupied by the Irish with a series of

---

[1] Donald Currie (1825–1909): founder of Castle (later Union Castle) Steamship Co., leading shipowner and active in South African affairs; liberal M.P. for Perthshire, 1880–85; K.C.M.G., 1881.

[2] See appendix.

[3] At Kildare, where he suggested the possibility of a general strike against rent. See appendix.

[4] 17 Aug.

[5] Forster had paid a second short visit to Dublin on 18–21 Aug. (Private diary, v, 97–8).

[6] His motion for the adjournment was defeated by 127 to 21 (*Hansard 3*, cclv, 1936 (23 Aug. 1880).

harangues on Home Rule, apropos of a motion of Mr Parnell's. This was evidently regarded by the Irish Members in the light of a demonstration necessary to satisfy their constituents, rather than as a political discussion. Some of the speeches were very able and moderate in language, notably those of Mr Parnell (to which Mr Forster made a courteous and conciliatory reply) and Mr O'Connor Power. The latter has apparently a genuine interest in Home Rule as a political experiment, which is more than can be said for many of the so-called Home Rulers, and land agitators.

After an interval of serious work at English measures on Wednesday, Thursday the 26th [August] was again given up to, or rather taken possession of, by the Irish. After a bitter attack on Mr Forster by Lord Randolph Churchill (the leader of the Fourth Party of Four)[1] and a reply by the Chief Secretary in which, amidst loud cheers from the House, he declined to enter into the personal charges made against him by Lord Randolph, the House was supposed to proceed to the final discussion of the Irish Estimates, including the Vote for the Constabulary. Instead of debating, however, in a rational manner, the Parnell party arranged a system of obstruction, which kept the House sitting till 1 o'clock in the middle of the following day. The English Members discreetly refrained from doing anything but support the Government with their presence and their votes, in the numerous divisions which were taken on the question of reporting progress; consequently the Irish and the Ministers bore the brunt of the debate—if that could be called a debate which consisted in a perpetual recapitulation of the wrongs of Ireland and the sins of England, winding up in each case with an attempt to extort some promise or pledge from the Government on the part of the Home Rule Members, and a perpetual repetition on the part of Ministers of their good will towards Ireland, their hopes for her improvement in the future, and their fixed resolve not to yield in a single point to the pressure put upon them by the Irish 'Party of action' at the present time.

Sir Stafford Northcote aided the Government as the Opposition had aided him on a similar occasion two years before, and at last about 12 o'clock an arrangement was come to, Mr Parnell pledging his followers, in so far as he dared, not to pursue the policy of obstruction on Monday night when the unfortunate Constabulary Vote was fixed to come on for final discussion and decision.

Mr Parnell is by birth and education a gentleman, and this cannot but tell to some extent, especially when he finds himself regarded by Ministers and ex-Ministers in the light of a responsible Parliamentary Leader, and treated as such. Moreover since Mr Dillon has acquired notoriety in the House as chief among English haters and would-be conspirators, Mr Parnell has clearly been anxious to establish his own chieftainship, on the ground of political ability and parliamentary tact.

[1] See appendix.

Whilst *he* is distinguished by Lord Hartington as the acknowledged leader of the Irish Party, the Member for Tipperary, with his popular name[1] and his dangerous faculty for 'out-Parnelling Parnell' in the matter of decrying land-lords and denouncing the English Government, sinks into his proper place as the violent young recruit who risks the prospects of the Party by his ill-judged zeal in the good cause.

There was some anxiety as to whether Mr Parnell would be able to answer for his followers, but for once matters turned out better than had been expected, and by half-past 10 on Monday night (30th [August]) every Irish Vote, including the Constabulary, had been got through peacefully.

At last the end of the Session seemed close at hand; the Burials Bill, the Hares and Rabbits Bill (most abused of all Government measures with the exception of the Irish Compensation Bill), the Employers' Liabilities Bill, fought their painful way through the Commons and the Lords (the Burials Bill having been begun in the Lords).

11 Sept., Sat. (Tenby)[2]

Just before the end, however, a violent little storm arose, which stirred up many angry passions. Ever since the rejection of the Irish Compensation Bill by the Lords, the Irish Members had been referring angrily from time to time to this indignity, and Mr T. P. O'Connor[3] had gone so far as to bring in a motion, and initiate a harmless little debate on the subject of the iniquity of the Upper House.

The Government, however, whatever they might have *thought* as to the Lords' demonstration against the Compensation Bill, had maintained a dignified silence on the matter. Their patience was more severely tried by the wanton aggravation of the difficulties of Irish administration caused by the rejection in the Upper House of two small and innocuous Bills, referring to the Ballot and the Registration of Voters.[4]

These were thrown out by the Lords[5] simply on the ground (suggested by Lord Redesdale,[6] Chairman of Committees) of the lateness of the Session, and

[1] He was the son of John Blake Dillon, one of the three most distinguished leaders of the Young Ireland movement of the forties (the other two being Thomas Davis and Charles Gavan Duffy).

[2] Forster and his wife, accompanied by Florence, went to Tenby, Pembrokeshire, on 8 Sept. for a few days' holiday. A telegram from Tottenham, where Aunt Sarah was dying, caused Jane Forster to return on 10 Sept., but Florence and her father remained at Tenby for the next two days (Private diary, v, 115–16).

[3] See appendix.

[4] Florence makes two bills out of one here, probably because Forster, speaking on 3 Sept. about the lords' rejection of the Registration of Voters (Ireland) Bill, compared it with their action on the ballot bill of 1871. In *Hansard 3*, cclvi, 1212, the date of the ballot bill is not mentioned, and it would therefore be easy for her to make such a slip.

[5] 1 Sept. 1880 (*Hansard 3*, cclvi, 962).

[6] John Thomas Freeman-Mitford (1805–86): 2nd Baron Redesdale; cr. earl, 1877; strong opponent of previous remedial measures for Ireland.

the inconvenience occasioned to their Lordships by having to discuss Bills at a season when they would naturally be out of town.

The large Conservative Majority in the Upper House, acting on Lord Redesdale's advice, exercised their privilege freely, and at once threw out the Irish measures on which Irish Members had set their hearts and which the Liberal government and majority in the Lower House were anxious to enact.[1]

The occasion was naturally made the most of by the ardent Radicals who love an opportunity of attacking the House of Lords, and who cheerfully contemplated the probability of a 'growing irritation between the two branches of the Legislature'.

But it was not only the Radicals unfortunately who felt deeply irritated and displeased at the conduct of the Upper House. On Sept 3rd, in reply to Mr Parnell, who had proposed to 'tack' the principal clause of the Registration Bill to the Appropriation Bill, and so compel the Lords to pass it, Mr Forster made a forcible speech which astonished both friends and foes by its vehemence of expression, and was considered to be nothing more nor less than a 'warning to the House of Lords'.

The Radicals were naturally enchanted; and many Liberals of the old school were not sorry that a protest should have been uttered against the tendency of the Conservative majority in the Upper House to gratify their feelings and embarrass the Liberal Government of the day by demonstration votes which brought no responsibility of power upon the voters.

At the same time everyone stood somewhat aghast at hearing a warning addressed to 'legislators by an accident of hereditary birth'[2] by a Cabinet Minister who had always been regarded, even by his opponents, as a Liberal who had in him no trace of the demagogue.[3] For this reason Mr Bright's[4] speech on the same occasion, though stronger in its denunciation than Mr Forster's, made less impression out of the House.

As to the latter, it made a sensation that no other single episode had done during the whole session.

In the House of Lords, Lord Granville[4] on the following day made an explanation, reading the correct and not the exaggerated report of the famous

[1] The lords rejected the registration bill on 1 Sept. by 42 to 30.

[2] Forster's 'warning', as given in *Hansard 3*, cclvi, 1212–13, virtually amounted to remarking that continued obstruction on the part of the lords' majority might lead many to consider whether a change in the constitution of the upper house might not be needed.

[3] 'If I had foreseen the rejection by the lords of the disturbance bill I hardly think I should have pressed it, but the fact was I thought they would hardly venture to eject so purely an administrative measure. . . . You will have been amused by the flareup caused by my innocent protest against the careless recklessness of your noble house. For the first time in my life I find myself dubbed a dangerous democrat; but little notice was taken of the point I mainly wanted to bring out—the necessity of making the lords feel their responsibilities. . . . If they felt that they might be called upon to try to govern the empire and especially Ireland they, that is the lords' majority, would be more shy of facing a hostile commons' majority.' (Forster to Ripon, 9 Sept. 1880, B.L., Add. MS 43537, ff 158–62.)

[4] See appendix.

passage, and explaining on behalf of Mr Forster that his Right Hon. friend had spoken for himself, and not as a Member of the Cabinet.

Abroad, the Continental papers used the speech as a text to be preached upon according to their respective views and desires, and the English Correspondent of the *Standard* regaled his readers with reports of the pious horror the expression of such revolutionary sentiments had aroused in France.

On the 4th Mr Gladstone reappeared in the House, in good health and spirits. Returning at once to his old duties, he signalised his return by a brilliant speech in defence of the Government policy in foreign affairs, contemptuously dismissing Mr Ashmead Bartlett[1] (who had suggested the despatch of a combined Fleet to the coast of Poland or the Caucasus), expostulating respectfully with Mr Cowen[2] who had libelled the Montenegrins, and reassuring Sir Wilfred Lawson,[3] who had feared lest the country might be taken into an isolated war out of pure activity of mind and philanthropic zeal on the part of its rulers.

On September 7th (Tuesday) the wished-for day at length arrived, and the House came to an end.[4]

4 Nov., Th.

The great question that has occupied the attention of Englishmen during the past three months has lain nearer home than Dulcigno. The excitement last autumn over the Davitt[2] and Killen prosecutions,[5] and the meetings which gave rise to them, were as nothing compared to the excitement of the present year.

The storm in Parliament over the Compensation for Disturbance Bill was but a prelude to the tempest which has been raging all over the United Kingdom this autumn concerning the state of Ireland. Not only [in] the English, but in the foreign press, the ills of this country and the remedies to be applied, are discussed from every point of view, and the whole aspect of the relations, past, present and future, between England and Ireland is a fertile

---

[1] Ellis Ashmead-Bartlett (1849–1902): born in Brooklyn, N.Y.; conservative M.P. for Eye (Suffolk), 1880–84, and Ecclesall (Sheffield), 1885–1902; a vigorous imperialist and party organiser, publishing *England*, the first conservative penny weekly, 1880–98.

[2] See appendix.

[3] Sir Wilfred Lawson (1829–1906): liberal M.P. for Carlisle, 1859–65, 1868–85, for Cockermouth, 1886–90, for Camborne, 1903–5, for Cockermouth, 1906; keen sportsman and leading temperance advocate; radical in politics, he supported Bradlaugh in the oath controversy (above, p. 6), opposed Forster's coercion bill (1881), and resisted the government's policy in Egypt (1882–3).

[4] Parliament was prorogued to 24 Nov.

[5] Michael Davitt, James Daly, editor of the *Connaught Telegraph* and a storm centre of the western land agitation, and James Bryce Killen, editor of the Belfast *Northern Star*, were arrested on 19 Nov. 1879 and charged with using seditious language at a land meeting at Gurteen, Co. Sligo, on 2 Nov. Examined before the Sligo magistrates (24–8 Nov.), they were returned for trial and released on bail, but proceedings against them were eventually abandoned. Their prosecution represented virtually the only action taken under the conservative government against the agitation.

theme for historical writers, pamphleteers, philosophical politicians, and republican agitators and adventurers.

Everyone who can find his way into print or on to a platform contributes his quota, either towards stirring up the excitement, or suggesting means by which to allay it—very often the latter produces exactly the effect desired by the former.

Nevertheless there are some encouraging symptoms of a real endeavour on the part of those most nearly affected by the present disturbed state of the country to aid the Government in the attempt to find a practical solution of their great problem, the Irish Land Question.

After the close of the Parliamentary Session at the beginning of September, there was a lull all over the Kingdom. The Irish tenantry were employed in getting in the abundant harvest, and the chiefs of the Land League abstained from holding meetings, or if they did speak they showed a disposition towards constitutional agitation, rather than towards the course of revolutionary menace adopted by Mr Dillon earlier in the summer.

It was during this short interlude, immediately before the rising of Parliament, that Mr Finigan,[1] as acting lieutenant for Mr Parnell, sought a private interview with the Chief Secretary, and obtained from him an intimation that, provided the approaching Land Meetings were of an orderly and legal character, the police should not be obtruded upon them in their military capacity. This arrangment was faithfully adhered to by the Government, and henceforth the Constabulary ceased to attend the meetings. The leaders of the Land League, with characteristic ingenuity of ill will towards a friendly English Government, did not fail to represent this concession—made in response to a humbly worded private appeal—as a triumph gained by the valiant Mr Parnell over a grudging and reluctant Ministry.[2]

Meantime if the speakers were in abeyance during the early part of September, the Land League papers were not, and the idea of resistance to the payment of debts was well kept before the people by the widely circulated motto of 'Hold the Harvest'.

---

[1] James Lysaght Finigan (b. 1844): lawyer, journalist, veteran of French Foreign Legion, and home rule M.P. for Ennis 1879–82.

[2] A circular issued on 21 Sept. by the inspector general of the Royal Irish Constabulary to the officers of the force directed that (i) if a meeting were held near a barrack, the men should stay inside, no armed men appearing unless absolutely necessary; (ii) in other cases, and where it was expected that a truncheon party would be enough to protect the reporters, the men should be near the meeting but preferably out of view; (iii) truncheon parties should be as small in number as was consistent with safety; (iv) the police should not provide protection for the professional reporters who were sent to the bigger meetings, if the reporters themselves thought it unnecessary (S.P.O., R.P. 1880/23468). Edward Gibson was later to allege that this circular was the product of collusion between the government and Parnell (*Hansard 3*, cclvii, 262; 7 Jan. 1881).

5 Nov., Fri.

The first sign of renewed activity on the part of the League and of impending hostilities between the agitators and the Government, may be said to date from September 23rd,[1] when Mr Forster received a memorandum from Mr Burke,[2] the Under-Secretary, enclosing information from a Magistrate near Cork, and strongly urging the summary prohibition of a meeting to be held in that neighbourhood at Charleville on the following Sunday, the supposed object of the meeting being intimidation of a particular Farmer who had incurred the displeasure of the Land League.

It was suggested that the whole proceeding might be stopped by virtue of an Act (quoted in the Memorandum) known as the [Whiteboy] Act.[3]

The case being a critical one, Mr Forster determined to shorten his short holiday, and go straight over to Dublin to consult in person with the legal authorities at the Castle.[4] The question, as he said, was of no less importance than this, 'Shall the Government declare war upon the League or not?'[5]

After due consideration it was decided that the instance in question did not furnish a good ground for the commencement of hostilities.

There was some sensation in Dublin for a few days, and rumours of intended prosecutions found their way in some mysterious manner into the Irish papers, but for the time nothing was done in the matter of either prosecution of individuals or suppression of meetings.

This passive attitude on the part of the Government coupled with the news (on Sept. 27th) of the murder of Lord Mountmorres, and the cold blooded

[1] Florence says in her private diary (v, 117–18) that Forster received this telegram on 22 Sept., the day on which he told her that he would have to leave for Dublin the next night instead of spending a few days with his wife at Fox How, as arranged.

[2] See appendix.

[3] Thomas Saunders, a Charleville J.P., wrote to the Castle on 18 Sept. forwarding copies of the placard announcing the meeting; he suggested that, as the meeting was calculated to intimidate, and uniforms would probably be worn, action could be taken under 1 & 2 Wm IV, c.44 (later designated the Tumultuous Risings (Ireland) Act, 1831, and also known as the 'Whiteboy Offences Act'). Saunders must have had in mind the earlier Whiteboy act of 1776 (15 & 16 Geo. III, c.21) for penalties on the wearing of uniforms. Burke agreed with Saunders (memo. to Forster, 21 Sept. 1880; S.P.O., R.P. 1880/23468). See below, p.35.

[4] Forster crossed to Dublin on 23 Sept., accompanied by Florence and Oakeley. Jane Forster and Frances joined them there on 27 Sept. (Journal of Frances Arnold-Forster, iv, 41). Forster was in London during 10–21 Nov., 25–8 Nov., and 13–16 Dec., but otherwise they all remained in Dublin till 29 Dec. (ibid., pp 41–8).

[5] In a letter of 22 Sept. to Burke, Forster stated the issue in more qualified terms: 'in our proclamation I hope we shall make it clear that we draw the line between meetings for legislative changes however extreme and expressions of opinion however violent, and meetings for the purpose of intimidating individuals. . . .' (N.L.I., MS 10219 (2)). There was not enough time to act in the Charleville case, but all subsequent meetings to denounce individuals were banned (memo. by Naish, 29 Dec. 1880; P.R.O., Cab. 37/4/95).

Forster did, however, follow this by making exhaustive inquiries of the law officers as to what action was possible against the league and its meetings, with particular reference to Parnell's speech at Ennis on 19 Sept. advising what was later known as 'boycotting'. The law officers, with great caution, eventually decided that prosecution of league leaders was possible; see below, p. 19.

speech of Mr Parnell delivered at New Ross, the scene of the recent murder of young Mr Boyd, produced a state of intense excitement, not only in Ireland but in England.[1]

As for the indignation of the Conservative and Landlord party against the miserable and criminal weakness of the Government, it found expression in every form of denunciation, lamentation and entreaty, whilst even amongst English Liberals who had been most consistently friendly to the Irish in their endeavour to reform the Land Laws, there was discernible a distinct revulsion against a party which was tending to exasperate English public opinion by its condonation, to say the least, of crime and outrage.

It was in vain that the *Freeman* maintained day after day that the Land League and its leaders were in no way responsible for the crimes committed on its behalf, and declared that the horror expressed was the outcome of panic and ignorance.

It was only too evident that in proportion as a Land League meeting was held, and the Land League organisation introduced into a district the number of crimes of more or less degree committed in that district at once increased.[2] The leaders of the Parnell Party, when posing before the British public, might plume themselves complacently on the legal and constitutional character of the agitation, and represent it as a Trades' Union, simply intended by means of passive resistance and refusal to take land from which tenants had been evicted, to bring down rents and improve the condition of the Irish peasantry.

But when addressing their countrymen, Mr Parnell and his coadjutors knew well how to give to the aims and nature of the Land League a very different aspect. The passion first appealed to, and invariably with success, so far as a ready response was concerned, was hatred of the English Government as personified by the Irish Landlords.

Reform of land tenure being an unpromising and perhaps somewhat dry subject for discussion at 'magnificent meetings', Mr Parnell consistently

[1] William Browne (1832–80), 5th Viscount Mountmorres, was killed near Clonbur on the evening of 26 Sept. by six revolver bullets; he had brought ejectment proceedings against some tenants, but it was believed that members of an agrarian secret society had killed him, suspecting him of giving information to government. Four men were arrested but discharged for lack of evidence (S.P.O., I.C.R., Returns of outrages, Sept. 1880). Allegations of callousness about his death on the part of the local people excited some controversy.

On the afternoon of 8 Aug., Charles Boyd, driving between New Ross (Co. Wexford) and Waterford City with his father, brother, and cousin, was fired at by a party of masked men with rifles and bayonets, and fatally wounded. Six men were arrested but discharged for lack of evidence; two others were sent to the assizes but discharged or acquitted (S.P.O., I.C.R., Returns of outrages, Aug. 1880). Speaking at New Ross on 26 Sept., Parnell remarked: 'I do wish to point out that the recourse to such methods of procedure is entirely unnecessary and absolutely prejudicial where there is a suitable organisation among the tenants' (*The Times*, 27 Sept. 1880).

[2] See *Return showing, for each month of . . . 1879 and 1880, the number of Land League meetings held and agrarian crimes reported to the inspector general of the Royal Irish Constabulary, in each county throughout Ireland*, H.C. 1881 (5), lxxvii, 793–804.

avoided making any suggestions towards practical legislation,[1] declaring plainly that this was not his business, and that it was only those who sought to sow discord among the National leaders who would press them to formulate plans for the settlement of the land question.

Under these circumstances it was natural to make the abolition of landlordism the main feature in the programme of an agitation which professed to be destructive in its aim, rather than constructive; if the people should interpret Mr Parnell's tirades against 'landlordism' as a hint to threaten, shoot or refuse the rents to their own particular landlord, it could hardly be denied that the connection of cause and effect between the 'constitutional agitation' of the Land League Leaders and the frequent wrongs and cruelties committed by their followers was not difficult to trace.

In point of fact the efforts of Mr Parnell and his Irish-American allies, working in the congenial atmosphere of Irish misery and discontent, have been going far to produce the 'social war' which was hinted at as a possible contingency during the coming Autumn by some of the Parnellites last session.

The only consolation is in the thought that, whereas Mr Parnell from the nature of his political ambition can never possibly be satisfied with any land reform introduced by an English government, this is not the case with the great bulk of the Irish people, even amongst the tenant farmers. Those well qualified to speak on the subject, from intimate knowledge of the Irish peasantry, do not despair of seeing a profound improvement in the state of this sorely disturbed country produced by the introduction of radical Land Law reform in the coming session.

Mr Parnell and a certain number of his friends are no doubt using the land grievance as a weapon of offence against England and any English Government present or to come, and so long as they can figure before the people as their sole champions in this vital question they will enjoy a popularity sufficient to gratify the most ambitious of demagogues.

But will the thousands who respond to the cry of 'down with landlords' and abolition of rents follow them with the same enthusiasm on the political enterprize to which this Land League agitation is but a stepping-stone? Will they do so at least, if in the meanwhile a strong and at the same time a friendly English government has by Parliamentary legislation taken from Mr Parnell his magic wand—the Irish land grievance?

In the middle of October the idea of State precautions[2] was again mooted, and for a few days rumours again made their way into the papers.

---

[1] In the margin, opposite the words 'towards practical legislation . . . and', the words 'Oct. & Nov.' appear in the original.

[2] 'Precautions' should read 'prosecutions'. The cabinet appears to have decided on 30 Sept. that the Irish government should prosecute the league leaders if there seemed to be a reasonable case. According to Bernard Holland (*Life of Spencer Compton, eighth duke of Devonshire* (London, 1911), i, 329), this course was a compromise, adopted because of the radicals' opposition to Forster's desire for the suspension of habeas corpus. Forster himself felt that the chief value of the prosecutions

The step had in fact been in preparation for some weeks past, and was in no way the result of the demonstration of landlords who came in a body (on October 13th) to interview the Lord Lieutenant and the Chief Secretary for Ireland at the Castle.

On the 16th October was published a letter from Mr Forster to Mr Richardson of Armagh, declining to be present at a banquet given by the Liberals of Ulster.[1] In this letter, which both from its tone and matter gave general satisfaction, the Chief Secretary, after alluding to the grave anxiety caused by the state of some parts of Ireland, and affirming the duty of the Government to preserve law and order, without depriving Her Majesty's Irish subjects, if it could possibly be helped, of the 'safeguards of personal liberty' went on to say—

As before, so now it may become[2] necessary to ask Parliament to enact special legislation; but I am confident that the Liberals of Ulster will agree with me that neither the present Government nor any Government ought to ask Parliament to resort to exceptional legislation for Ireland until the resources have been exhausted of those constitutional powers which suffice for the good government of Great Britain.

This was the first intimation that the suspension of the Habeas Corpus might eventually be considered necessary.

11-[16] Nov., Th.-Tu.

On the 18th October news of the attempted murder of Mr Hutchins, a landlord and land agent near Cork. Mr Hutchins escaped unhurt, but his Car driver was killed by a shot from behind a hedge. No evidence to lead to the discovery of the murderer was forthcoming.[3]

On the 22nd the statement as to the Government prosecution of the Land League Leaders[4] was openly confirmed and discussed—much parade of indignation and sorrow over the misguided Government on the part of the

would be to show that the government was doing all it could with existing powers (Reid, *Forster*, ii, 255–8). However, the law officers' conclusion on 10 Oct. in favour of prosecution was not so much the product of this compromise as the culmination of the inquiries Forster had instituted on 24 Sept. as to what could be done about the league and its meetings (above, p. 17). The lord chancellor, Lord Selborne, in a memo. of 2 Oct. had advised bringing charges of unlawful conspiracy, and possibly sedition, in far stronger terms than those of any of the Irish law officers (S.P.O., R.P. 1880/23687).

[1] See appendix. The banquet was given by the liberals of Armagh; Forster's reason for declining was that, in the present crisis, his membership of one party as distinct from another should not be stressed.

[2] In the margin, opposite 'went on to say .. may become', the words 'Nov. 10' appear in the original.

[3] Samuel Newburgh Hutchins of Charleville, who was on bad terms with his tenants, was fired at on 16 Oct. He usually drove his own car, and it is therefore likely that his driver, John Downey, was killed by mistake (S.P.O., I.C.R., Returns of outrages, Oct. 1880).

[4] The Irish government decided on 10 Oct. to prosecute Parnell and other Land League leaders for conspiracy to prevent the payment of rent; and on 2 Nov. the attorney general filed an information in the court of queen's bench accordingly (Moody, *Davitt*, pp 427–8).

Freeman's Journal. Reserve, inclining to approval, on the part of the *Times* and other English Conservative papers.

As might perhaps have been expected, the news of the prosecution was the signal for more vigorous manifestations from the Land League. Meetings were held all over the country, and the daily reports of outrages committed reached the Castle with depressing regularity.

Not from sensational stories of 'alleged outrages' in the newspapers, but from private and trustworthy information sent by sober-minded men not interested in promoting panic, the Government learnt day after day the state of the country. Terrorism extending, along with systematic refusal by the tenants to pay more than 'Griffith's Valuation'[1]—in this respect following the uniform advice given at every Land League Meeting.

The system of intimidation not only against Landlords but against Farmers, favoured by the Land League, was easily taken advantage of in the interests of private revenge: and though doubtless the League was not directly responsible for all the cases of 'malicious injury' perpetrated against life and property, yet the encouragement given by their leaders to deliberate defiance of the law naturally increased the normal tendency of the Irish people to regard a crime against their fellow men as justifiable provided it was an offence not against the 'unwritten law' of the Land League or of popular opinion, but merely against law and justice as understood by the British Government.

The meetings towards the end of October[2] and the beginning of November increased in violence, and the language of the agitators became, as might have been expected, more personally vindictive—Mr Parnell at Galway on Oct. 24th denouncing 'our hypocritical Secretary—Mr Buckshot Forster', [and] at the Banquet in the evening declaring openly that he should never have taken off his coat and gone to work at the Land League question, unless it had been as a step towards some ulterior object.[3]

He also took the opportunity of threatening England with American help to Ireland.

It has long been known that Mr Parnell's real interest was in a political rather than in a social revolution, but he has seldom declared so plainly that

---

[1] A comprehensive valuation, for purposes of local taxation (including the poor rate), carried out between 1852 and 1865 under the direction of Sir Richard Griffith, commissioner of valuation. Based on a scale of prices ruling in 1849–51, it was widely used as a yardstick of a reasonable rent, but it did not represent the true value of land after 1852, when prices were rising. When in 1877–9 the value of agricultural output slumped, it was commonly invoked as a measure of excessive rent. See W. E. Vaughan, 'Richard Griffith and the tenement valuation' in G. L. Herries Davies and R. C. Mollan (ed.), *Richard Griffith, 1784–1878* (Dublin, 1980), pp 103–22.

[2] In the margin, opposite the words 'The meetings ... October', 'Nov 11' appears in the original.

[3] 'I would not have taken off my coat and gone to this work if I had not known that we were laying the foundations in this movement for the regeneration of our legislative independence' (*F.J.*, 25 Oct. 1880). It was on this occasion that Matt Harris of Ballinasloe caused some sensation by remarking that if tenants were to shoot down landlords 'like partridges in September' he would not say a word against it.

he regarded the Irish Land grievance as a weapon to be used against the English, rather than as an object worth fighting for on behalf of the Irish peasantry themselves.

Meanwhile, in spite of the increasing excitement and bitterness on all sides, in spite of the prognostication of coming troubles and rising exasperation over the State Trials now impending, there is still some encouragement to believe that below the ferment a solid basis of agreement is slowly forming.

From various quarters the hands of the Liberal Government are being quietly strengthened for their great endeavour—never lost sight of in the midst of clamour and agitation—to legislate justly and generously for the Irish people.

Whatever may be the conduct of one violent man here and there, the Priests on the whole have lately been coming forward manfully, and attempting to stem the violence of criminal agitation, whilst at the same time professing open sympathy with the lawful objects of the land reformers.

From this point of view the Pastoral Charge of the Archbishop of Dublin (Dr McCabe),[1] the speech of Archdeacon McConnell on being invited to join a Land League Meeting, and the Resolutions passed by the Bishops and dioceses of Cork and Cloyne, have all tended to strengthen the cause of legitimate land reform and to discountenance the criminal acts committed under the auspices of the League.[2]

On the part of many of the landlords also, and their representatives in the press, there has been an ungrudging acknowledgement of the necessity for far-reaching alteration in the whole system of land tenure in Ireland, and a Committee has been formed including such men as Lord Monck, Lord Powerscourt, Mr O'Brien of Cahirmoyle, Judge Longfield, Dr McDonnell &c. for the express purpose of discussing and formulating practical suggestions of land reform.[3]

Amongst writers and speakers both in England and Ireland, there is apparent a spirit of fairness, a genuine anxiety to look at the question from all sides, and a desire to do justice even to the most exasperating of the agitators, so long as their proposals seem to be dictated by an honest wish not to defeat but to promote a satisfactory settlement of the Irish difficulty.

In the English press there is free and ample discussion of Irish grievances, and little complaint can justly be made of the tone adopted, whatever dissension there may be from the arguments used.

The *Pall Mall* (i.e. Mr Morley), the *Daily News*, and the *Spectator* are all

---

[1] See appendix.

[2] Ven. John O'Connell (not McConnell) was archdeacon of Ardfert. The diocesan assembly at Cork on 21 Oct. passed a series of resolutions advocating land reform on the lines of the 'three Fs', and condemning outrages.

[3] A list of 23 members of the 'Land tenure committee' appears in the *Irish Times*, 26 Nov. 1880, with a report of ten resolutions passed by the committee, including a proposal for the establishment of a 'court of tenures in Ireland'.

opposed to the idea of coercion—meaning thereby the suspension of the Habeas Corpus—and on first consideration even the State prosecutions were somewhat disapproved of.

On this point, however, the plain statement of the government indictment and the grounds for the prosecutions (supplied by Mr Forster himself) made a great impression. Without prejudging the issue, it was acknowledged, even by strong Radicals, that the charges against Mr Parnell and his twelve associates— of conspiracy for the promotion of intimidation and breach of the law—were sufficiently grave and sufficiently plausible to justify the Government in initiating such entirely constitutional and moderate proceedings as were contemplated in these State Trials.

Whether a conviction will be obtained against Mr Parnell &c. from a Dublin Jury is considered doubtful.

In any case the charges against the Land League method of 'constitutional agitation' will have been fully and effectively put before the public, and whatever the effect of the prosecution[s] they will at least not make a resort to coercion, if this should become needful, more difficult.

The danger of increasing the influence of the Land League chiefs by 'making martyrs' of them is of course obvious, but in Irish affairs at the present time every step taken must be only good in so far as it is the least of two evils.

In some respects there are signs of waning sympathy between the bona fide Radicals and the Parnellites—the latter becoming more and more identified with the American-Irish faction, and adopting more openly the line of class warfare, sedition and hostility to the British government (Nov. 16).

[18 Nov.,[1] Th.]

The principal incident at the beginning of this month was the 'Boycott affair'.[2]

Capt. Boycott, agent to Lord Erne, and living at Lough Neash [*recte* Mask] House, Ballinrobe, had for some weeks past been well known as a special object of Land League and popular hatred, and in a letter to *The Times* (during the 3rd week in October)[3] he had described with graphic simplicity the condition of isolation to which he and his family had been reduced by the absolute refusal of the people in the neighbourhood to work for him, sell to him, or serve him and his in any way whatsoever.

His own life was guarded by constant police protection; but any assistance to him was effectually prevented by a thoroughly organized system of intimidation amongst the peasantry and tradespeople of Ballinrobe.

A week or two later, a description in the *Daily News* by their 'Special

[1] See below, p. 28: 'To-morrow, 19th'.
[2] Charles Cunningham Boycott (1837–97). The fullest recent account of the 'Boycott affair' is Joyce Marlow, *Captain Boycott and the Irish* (London, 1972); see also Tom Corfe, *The Phoenix Park murders* (London, 1968), pp 88–103.
[3] *The Times*, 18 Oct. 1880.

Commissioner' of Captain and Mrs Boycott and their strange and dangerous isolation[1] excited public sympathy on their behalf still more strongly, and Lord Erne's plucky agent began to become quite a public character.

On Nov. 8th, Mr Forster and the chief authorities at Dublin Castle succeeded only just in time by prompt and vigorous intervention in preventing Captain Boycott from being made the pretext for downright civil war between Ulster and the West of Ireland.

It came to their knowledge in the course of the afternoon that an expedition of 100 armed men had been organized by some gentlemen in Ulster and their Tory friends in Dublin (notably Dr Robinson, editor of the high Tory and anti-Govt *Daily Express*), with the object of 'relieving' Captain Boycott, and reaping his crops for him.

It was obvious that the appearance of 100 armed Orangemen in Mayo, under the present circumstances and in the present excited state of feeling, would probably result in an encounter that might be the signal for an outbreak of mutual detestation between the Land League and their enemies all over Ireland.

The expedition had to be stopped. The Lord Lieutenant, the Chief Secretary and the Commander of the Forces[2] met at the Castle, and explained to Dr Robinson that, if the Ulster men went as an armed body into Mayo under pretence of reaping Captain Boycott's crops, they would do so in defiance of the Govt, who would declare such an expedition to come under the head of 'an illegal gathering'.

At the same time Mr Forster announced (not only to Dr Robinson of the *Daily Express*, but to representatives of the *Freeman* and *Irish Times* who had been sent for) that, though the Govt would not consent to the despatch of an independent force of armed men into Mayo, they would undertake to protect a convoy of bona fide labourers employed by Captain Boycott or his friends for the purpose of doing the necessary work on his property.[3]

Captain Boycott himself was not responsible for the projected 'invasion of Mayo', feeling entirely the danger of such a method of coming to his assistance. He asked for 50 labourers, and these he was to have, protected to the place, at it, and from it, by troops sent down for that special purpose by the Govt.

At 2 a.m. the Broadstone station was alive with troops, two squadrons of cavalry [of the] 19th Hussars, and one of infantry [of the] 84th,[4] who at these few hours notice were despatched to the wilds of Mayo for the purpose of

---

[1] Bernard H. Becker's despatches of 10 and 12 Nov. 1880 from Ballinrobe; later published in his *Disturbed Ireland* (London, 1881), pp 120–41. Becker (1833–1900) was special correspondent of the *Daily News* in Ireland.

[2] Sir Thomas Steele (see appendix).

[3] As Forster pointed out at the time, such a 'press conference' was an exceptional proceeding. Dublin Castle had no public relations system beyond the circulation of the *Dublin Gazette*.

[4] While the hussars and army service corps unit left from Broadstone, the 400 officers and men of the 84th entrained at the Curragh (*Irish Times*, 9 Nov. 1880).

protecting the expected contingent of Ulster labourers on their 15 miles march from Claremorris to Lough Neash [Mask] House.

The excitement all through Ireland was intense, and those responsible for the public peace passed some nervous hours until late on Tuesday night, when Sir Thomas Steele received news that the march had been quietly accomplished, and that the Ulster labourers, escorted by their strong bodyguard, and jeered at and cursed but not otherwise injured by the wrathful peasants of Mayo, were safely encamped on Captain Boycott's property.

The papers, English and Irish, have been full of long descriptions of the warlike encampment in the West, and 'Relief of Captain Boycott' has figured as a striking heading on the placards and papers.

On Nov. 9th Mr Forster went over to London for the Cabinets now being held in rapid succession. The demand for the suspension of the Habeas Corpus, though urgent in Ireland, is less unreservedly called for by the Conservative press in England, the *Standard* especially showing thorough appreciation of the objections, theoretical and practical, which might deter the Govt from summoning Parliament at once for such a purpose.

Mr Gladstone's speech at the Guildhall on the 9th[1] was generally acknowledged to be weighty and moderate, and quite free from any rash outburst that might have given undue cause for triumph to indiscreet friends or eager enemies.

His views on foreign affairs and the 'European concert' were pronounced by disappointed Conservatives to be a tardy imitation of Lord Beaconsfield's, and his most confirmed detractors in the Continental press could not deny that for once the fanatical Prime Minister had spoken of the Eastern problem with a prudence becoming a responsible European statesman.

On the vital subject of Ireland, Mr Gladstone's words won cordial approval from all parties. Whilst speaking with his habitual sympathy and respect for the Irish, and the unquestioned need for a change in their land laws, 'an enlargement of the Act of 1870', he employed his stately eloquence in enforcing the doctrine just laid down by Lord Selborne,[2] that 'law and liberty are the twin pillars of the State', and that neither public nor private liberty can be enjoyed in a state of society where 'the law as it stands' is not enforced.

There was no promise of an immediate suspension of the Habeas Corpus, which naturally disappointed some people, and there was no promise of a radical Land Bill, which disappointed others; but on the whole it was felt that, coming at such a time, from such a man, the speech was one well calculated to forward the cause of future peace and reform in Ireland.

All question of peace and reform seems far enough off at present in this unhappy country. From day to day there follows the same story of threatening, of outrage, and of widely spreading conspiracy to disregard all existing

[1] *The Times*, 10 Nov. 1880.
[2] See appendix.

contracts between landlord and tenant, and to render the relations between them more impossible.

There are not wanting men like Mr P. J. Smyth,[1] and others formerly trusted by the Irish people, to expose in plain language the impracticable and insincere character of the sort of proposals advocated by the Parnellites; but at the meetings in the West and South, it is men like Mr Dillon, with their fierce desire not to reform but to destroy the existing state of things in Ireland who get the ear of the people, and give the word of command.

For work such as this, hatred—class hatred and race hatred—is as potent as gunpowder, and with this moral gunpowder, Mr Dillon and his friends are amply supplied.

The newspapers of Nov. 13th contained the report of the murder of Mr Wheeler, at Oola in the Co. Limerick, a young man against whom there was no special rancour, and who was not one of the 80 persons at present under police protection.

Mr Wheeler's father was a land agent; the son was thought to have given offence by some private transaction in dispensing employment as labourers amongst a family of brothers, one of whom appears to have been discontented, and to have wreaked his vengeance by shooting Mr Wheeler from behind a hedge.[2]

At present however, no arrests have been made, and no evidence as to the murderer is forthcoming. The *Freeman* of course points out that specially brutal murder is no more connected with the Land League and its doctrines than are any of the crimes committed in great towns in England;[3] but nevertheless it is the deliberate opinion of many Liberal Irishmen familiar with the actual condition of society in the West of Ireland that such an outrage is the direct outcome of the present agitation, and that the suspension of the Habeas Corpus alone would have the effect of restoring some sense of security against personal outrage.

To know that the police have the power to arrest summarily the special ruffians on whom they have long had their eye would, it is thought, have a wholesome deterrent effect, not only upon these men themselves but upon others who now feel at liberty to indulge in any private brutality under the name of 'agrarian agitation'.

A circumstance that will not tend to make the path of the English Government easier is the recent subscription of three Catholic bishops, headed by the well-known Dr Croke, Archbishop of Cashel, to the Parnell Defence Fund, started by the *Freeman's Journal*.[4]

---

[1] See appendix.

[2] Henry Wheeler (aged 34) was shot in the head at about 2 p.m. on 12 Nov. while crossing a field with the brother of the suspected culprit. Both brothers were arrested but were discharged by the R.M. for lack of evidence. (S.P.O., I.C.R., Returns of outrages, Nov. 1880.)

[3] *F.J.*, 15 Nov. 1880.

[4] In addition to Croke, one catholic archbishop, John MacHale, of Tuam, and four catholic

Dr Croke is at present at Rome, using his influence with the Pope, and inserting articles in the *Aurora*, the papal Journal, which demonstrate the entirely 'constitutional and peaceable' nature of the Land League agitation, and represent the English Government as striving by the exercise of tyrannical power to crush the legitimate expression of discontent and misery for which they and the British Nation are solely responsible.[1]

It is said that Archbishop McCabe is shortly going to Rome, in which case it is to be hoped that Leo XIII will hear the other side to the story about the constitutional agitation, conducted by Mr Parnell, Mr Redpath,[2] Mr Brennan[3] etc.

Whilst the Cabinet is holding repeated councils, the newspapers are full of rumours, speculations and statements as to 'disunion in the Cabinet', some of the Ministers being represented as in favour of the immediate summoning of Parliament for the purpose of passing a Coercion Act, while others (Mr Bright and Mr Chamberlain)[4] are resolutely opposed to proposing the suspension of the Habeas Corpus, at least until the Govt can at the same time introduce a Land Bill.

Mr Bright's speech at Birmingham on the 16th, the day before the decisive Cabinet council, was taken to intimate his intention of resigning rather than sanction immediate coercion. He spoke with strong feeling on the claims of the Irish people to a complete rectification of the existing state of land tenure, but his strong words were not confined to a denunciation of bad laws and bad landlords; he referred to the proposals advocated by some would-be reformers as 'extravagant, impossible and unjust', and declared that such propositions were put forward by 'men who in their hearts hate England, much more than they love the tenant farmers'.[5]

His own suggestions were much the same as those he has made on former occasions—not compulsory expropriation, but greatly extended facilities for peasant proprietorship—in short, extension of the Bright Clauses.[6]

bishops—James MacCarthy (Cloyne), William Fitzgerald (Ross), George Butler (Limerick), and Patrick Duggan (Clonfert)—were among the subscribers to the defence fund.

[1] The *Freeman's Journal* carried extensive reports on the presence in Rome of Croke and his fellow bishops, under the heading 'Ireland and Rome'. On 17 and 18 Nov. articles reprinted from *Aurora*, and matching Florence's description, appeared under this heading.

[2] James Redpath (1833–91): Scottish-born American journalist; *New York Tribune* correspondent in Ireland since Feb. 1880; one of the most powerful propagandists of the Land League; author of *Talks about Ireland* (New York, 1881).

[3] Thomas Brennan (b. 1854): one of the originators of the land agitation, and one of the three original part-time secretaries of the Land League (the other two being Michael Davitt and A. J. Kettle); largely self-educated; employed as clerk in office of North City Milling Co. at Castlebar, 1872, and later in Dublin; full-time general secretary of the Land League, Mar. 1880; the most radical of the Land League chiefs after Davitt, and forming with him and Patrick Egan a triumvirate in the league executive; arrested under the P.P.P. act, 23 May 1881; released 16 June 1882; began a new and prosperous career in Omaha, Nebraska.   [4] See appendix.

[5] Bright's words 'force is not a remedy', delivered in this speech, were to become an anti-coercion slogan (*The Times*, 17 Nov.).

[6] The clauses of the land act of 1870 (33 & 34 Vict. c.46) intended to assist tenants to become

To-morrow, 19th, it will be known whether or not Parliament is to be summoned for an extraordinary Winter session, or whether proposals of either Coercion or reform are to be put off till an early Meeting in January. The Irish Conservative papers and the Irish gentry appear to be almost unanimous in the desire for Coercion; at any rate they are so in their denunciation of the 'palsied hands' of the Irish Executive and especially of the Chief Secretary.

20 Nov., Sat.

The conflict of statements and counter-statements as to the intentions of the Cabinet still continues. Rumours of dissensions—of dissensions made up—of the triumph of the 'Birmingham Ministers' over their 'Whig' and 'neutral' colleagues in the matter of immediate coercion—of the resignation of Lord Cowper, the resignation of the Chief Secretary—fill the newspapers.

Lord Randolph Churchill at Portsmouth and Lord Salisbury[1] at Hackney have made violent attacks upon the Govt with regard to Ireland, the former declaring that on Mr Forster's head is the blood shed in every agrarian murder since he came into office.[2]

The situation is further complicated by the intimation from Mr Gorst[1] that the Conservatives will oppose any attempt to introduce the 'clôture', in case Mr Gladstone should take this means of meeting obstruction on the possible proposal to suspend the Habeas Corpus.

On the 20th the Cabinet held a long sitting; on the 21st Mr Forster returned to Dublin; on the 22nd appeared the announcement that Parliament was prorogued to Dec. the 2nd.[3] This was interpreted by the public as meaning that a compromise had been come to in the Cabinet between those in favour of an immediate meeting of Parliament and those still anxious to postpone special legislation for Ireland.

On the 24th Mr Forster went back to London to be present at a Cabinet Council on the 25th, returning to Dublin on the 28th. The result of this last Cabinet has been that Parliament is summoned for January 6th 'for the despatch of business'.

During the next four weeks the Chief Secretary has a hard time before him, his three-fold task being, as he says, to govern Ireland, to frame a Land Bill, and to prepare a Coercion Bill. As regards the actual administration of the country from day to day, the difficulties are overwhelming.

The terrorism practised by the Land League is complete: no farmer can pay

owners. For the very limited operation of these clauses, see Palmer, *Irish Land League crisis*, pp 51–7.

[1] See appendix.
[2] Churchill's speech on 18 Nov., at the Portsmouth Workingmen's Conservative Club, is reported in *The Times*, 19 Nov. 1880.
[3] It was announced on the night of 20 Nov. in a special supplement to the *Dublin Gazette*.

his rent, buy, or sell [land]; no solicitor can take legal measures; no landlord can evict or even turn off a labourer without making himself liable to the vengeance of the Land League, or of those who take advantage of its system of terrorism; the cases of cruelty to animals are unhappily more frequent than ever.

As the propositions for the coming Land Bill take more definite shape, the symptoms of combined opposition on the part of the Conservatives become more unmistakeable. There is a drawing together between the moderate and the violent sections of the Tory party, Sir S. Northcote at Brecon, and Lord Salisbury, Mr Gibson and Lord R. Churchill at Woodstock, showing equally in their respective fashions their intentions to make the Irish Land Bill the great battle ground of parties during the coming session.

In Ireland the landlords are arranging a system of combination to meet the combination of the Land League, writing indignant letters to the *Express* and *Mail*, and to the Chief Secretary, and denouncing the 'Show Government' after the example set them by Lord Salisbury.

Behind the land agitation there are rumours of a well organized Fenian conspiracy, and every now and then startling paragraphs concerning 'revelations' and 'discoveries' find their way into the newspapers.

Meanwhile the Irish Govt is anything but asleep, and every precaution is taken to secure full and instant information from every part of the country. Fresh troops have been sent over, and the Constabulary are being constantly strengthened.

6 Dec., Mon.

The papers yesterday were occupied with two important speeches; Mr Parnell's at Waterford, and Chief Justice May's[1] in Dublin. Mr Parnell has taken this opportunity of affirming more plainly than before his intention to abide within the Constitution only so long as it suits his ultimate purpose—the establishment of a separate Irish nation—to do so.

The speech of the Chief Justice has caused a great sensation, and will be used as an effective weapon of offence by the Land League party, and by all those who wish to discredit the Law as administered in this country.

Apropos of a plea for the postponement of the trials in order to enable Mr Parnell and his friends to be present at the opening of Parliament on the 6th of January, the Chief Justice chose to deliver a strong and well-grounded denunciation of the Land League system of terrorism, and to draw a striking picture of the state of lawlessness which this system encourages in many parts of Ireland.

Unfortunately there can be no two opinions as to the impropriety of a Judge

[1] George Augustus Chichester May (1815–92): attorney general for Ireland, 1875; lord chief justice, 1877–87.

thus pronouncing condemnation beforehand on a case which he is about to hear tried.[1] Even the Conservative papers regret the vehemence of the Chief Justice's language on this occasion, and of course the *Freeman* and its clientèle triumph in exposing the unjudicial violence and prejudice of the man who is to be employed by the State in the prosecution of the Land League.

Every one we meet in Society here is gloomy enough about the state of the country, and feels uneasy about the bitter class hostility that is such a dangerous feature of the present agitation.

As for the landlords, they are going to mark their disapproval, we are told, of the present Govt by abstaining altogether from paying civilities to the Lord Lieutenant in the way of writing their names at the V. R. Lodge or attending any of the Castle festivities.

In fact, the season, we hear, is to be a dull one, which will be quite suitable. No one, I should think, will take this more philosophically than the Cowpers. They are both profoundly anxious to do their duty here, but they have absolutely no taste for state or society under ordinary circumstances, and at present Lord Cowper is so distressed and overwhelmed with the consciousness of the state of affairs in the West of Ireland that he is probably in less mood than ever for entertaining.

In Dublin they, the Cowpers, are, I imagine, respected and liked to a certain extent, but thought 'very quiet'. *Pat*, the Dublin comic paper, has just published a cartoon of Lord C. as 'The Invincible' carrying luggage labelled 'London and back'.[2]

As for ourselves, we are giving a succession of dinner parties, and are to give two balls. I suppose that however unpopular we may be, people—Dublin people at least—will come to them.

7 Dec., Tu.

We saw a variety of people: Mr Foster, the good, zealous clergyman of the Hibernian Military School where we go to Church, called in the morning. Mr Robert O'Brien[3] appeared at luncheon; Father was also at lunch and sketched his idea of a possible Coercion bill. We walked with him immediately

---

[1] The objectionable passage occurred when the chief justice stated that Parnell 'has endeavoured to carry out alterations in the law by violent speeches and violent means', adding 'I mean these are the accusations, these are the charges he has to meet' (*The Times*, 6 Dec. 1880).

[2] 'Invincible' should be 'invisible'. The cartoon (in *Pat's Christmas Box*, 1880) shows Cowper with a bag labelled 'State of Ireland', and a ticket marked 'London and back' in his hatband. The caption reads:

THE INVISIBLE
Invisibility, it is the thing for me
I'm the viceroy who can enjoy invisibility.

[3] The first appearance in the diary of Robert Vere O'Brien, of Old Church, near Limerick, whom Florence was to marry in 1883; see above, p. xxv.

afterwards to the Park gates with Mr O'Brien and Mr Illingworth,[1] who has just come over to call on his way through Dublin. Meantime we left mother entertaining the venerable old Judge O'Brien,[2] who looked a very Bird of Ages with his ample wig, and tall, rickety figure. However infirm he may be, he has the credit of having done his best to prevent the too vigorous Lord Chief Justice from absolutely committing himself in the matter of his recent address; it is said that it was old Judge O'Brien who, realising the very unjudicial and inappropriate nature of the diatribe being delivered by his learned brother from the Bench, gave the Lord Chief Justice a warning nudge, which had the effect of making him add the saving clause—'At least these are the charges of which you are accused'.

Miss Burke[3] came to five o'clock tea; she had lately been seeing something of Mr Blake (Terence McGrath)[4] and reports that he has grave fears as to what may happen in the West in consequence of the advice to use dynamite freely suggested to the people by Messrs Matthew Harris and Nally. Unless he is very much slandered this last is a man capable of any sort of revengeful ruffianism quite independent of Land League principles.

Mr and Mrs Kavanagh[5] dined and slept here. Father has a great respect for Mr Kavanagh's ability, and I believe he has done good service on the Land Commission, which, after receiving evidence in Dublin, has now closed its enquiry.[6] At dinner Mr Kavanagh spoke of the difference in his own experience between this and the Fenian time. Then there was no difficulty in getting information, he himself was able to do much in helping the police in their investigations; the people had no objection to 'split' on each other, and his personal influence amongst his tenantry went for a great deal. Now everything is changed; the silent combination is invulnerable; not a man will come forward to give evidence or information. Why do not the police do more in the way of

[1] Alfred Illingworth (1827–1907): Bradford cotton manufacturer and second liberal M.P. for Bradford, 1880–85.

[2] James O'Brien (1806–81): M.P. for Limerick city, 1852, 1854–8; second justice of court of queen's bench since 1858.

[3] Marianne Aline Alice Burke, sister of T. H. Burke; see appendix.

[4] Henry Arthur Blake, R.M. at Tuam, County Galway, had recently published (1880) a collection of portraits in words, *Pictures from Ireland*, under the name 'Terence McGrath'. For the second edition (ferociously reviewed in *F.J.*, 17 Nov.), he added a chapter on the distress of 1879–80. In Dec. 81 he was appointed a special R.M., one of the first three (below, p. 334).

[5] Arthur MacMurrough Kavanagh (1831–89): of Borris House, Co. Carlow; descended from MacMurrough kings of Leinster; born with only stumps for arms and legs, he learned to write, draw, paint, ride, shoot, fish, and sail better than most men, and lived a strenuous and adventurous life; archetypical paternalist landlord; J.P. for Counties Wexford, Kilkenny, and Carlow, high sheriff for Kilkenny (1855) and Carlow (1857); married, 1855, his cousin, Frances Mary, daughter of Rev. Joseph Forde Leathley, rector of Termonfeckin, and had children; conservative M.P. for Wexford County, 1866–8, and for Carlow County, 1868–80; member of Bessborough commission, 1880, and submitted a minority report advocating peasant proprietorship; vigorous defender of landlord position against the Land League; owner of 16,051 acres, valued at £7,905, in Co. Carlow; of 7,341 acres at £5,032 in Co. Kilkenny; and of 5,013 acres at £2,201 in Co. Wexford.

[6] The Bessborough commission, appointed in July 1880, reported in Jan. 1881. See appendix.

detection? it was asked, to which Mr Kavanagh answered that it is only surprising they find out as much as they do.

As for disguises, these are quite useless; the people recognise a stranger and hold their tongues; the police have a better chance of getting at information when they are in uniform, for as a rule they are popular, and when in a sociable mood the people occasionally let out rather more than they intend. But their difficulties are enormous.

'I should like to take you with me through the course of an enquiry', said Mr Kavanagh, 'what are you to do when the whole people is against you?'

With regard to expecting impossibilities from the police, Father agreed with Mr Kavanagh, though he acknowledged that it would be difficult to bring home to the minds of Englishmen that the absence of detection and prosecution of crime was not in some degree owing to inefficiency on their part; privately he informed Mr Kavanagh that he had lately been made uneasy by symptoms of an intention to try 'Boycotting' the police in outlying districts.

As it is, they are quite unable to engage cars, for whatever purpose they are wanted (on one occasion it was to convey a raving lunatic to the asylum), and under a constitutional government 'requisitioning' is impossible.[1]

Neither Mr [n]or Mrs Kavanagh spoke with the least tinge of vindictiveness or panic, but she especially was deeply desponding and sad. Her husband has been as good as a landlord can be, 'treating his tenants like his children', spending his money on the estate, living amongst the people; and it is disheartening to find that when the anti-landlord cry was raised throughout the country all this was forgotten—not only did his constituents return a stranger as their member[2] but they seemed to consider the defeat of their landlord to be as great a triumph and satisfaction as if he had been the worst rack-renting absentee in Ireland.

Like many others who have known the people for many years (Lady Ferguson[3] for example), Mrs Kavanagh declares that the present agitation, with its fatally attractive programme of repudiation of debts, is causing a visible deterioration in the character of the people. Every one asks the same desponding question 'How is it all to end: how can the harm that has been done already ever be got over?'

---

[1] A circular on the supply of provisions to 'boycotted' stations had been issued to the police on 30 Oct., and at the beginning of Dec. the treasury sanctioned the purchase of cars for police use, though it did not approve a permanent transport service for the R.I.C. until 1886 (S.P.O., R.P. 1881/21369). The army was given the power of requisitioning vehicles, under the lord lieutenant's warrant, by the army act of 1881 (44 & 45 Vict., c.58, pt III). This power proved very serviceable, but both army and police found it better to use their own vehicles when secrecy of movement was needed.

[2] Kavanagh and Henry Bruen (1828–1912), who had held Carlow County for the conservatives since 1857, were defeated at the 1880 general election by Edmund Dwyer Gray and Donald Horne McFarlane (b. 1830), both home-rulers.

[3] Mary Catherine, née Guinness, wife of Sir Samuel Ferguson (see below, p. 40).

8 Dec., Wed.

Father drove in to the Castle about twelve o'clock, much worried with letters— Mr G. in a high state of indignation over the Chief Justice's escapade. He returned soon after 7, dead beat.

'The worst day we have had; outrages on the increase.'

The chief facts in the papers to-day have been the Charge of Judge Fitz- gerald[1] to the Grand Jury at Cork, and the report of a scene over the prohibition of a pair of Meetings in Ulster, Land League and Orange.[2] The principal League orator has sent to the papers an indignant letter addressed to the Ch. Sec.

'O'Kelly[3] is furious', says Father, 'because the Govt have prevented his having his head broken by the Orange men who were prepared to attack the League Meeting'.

Mr Ball[4] and Captain Douglas Galton[5] dined with us, the latter fresh from London, and full of contemptuous disgust at the state of things here.

9 Dec., Th.

The papers announced (what we had heard on the previous night) the murder of a bailiff in Co. Tyrone—for once the murderer has been arrested; it remains to be seen whether he will be convicted.[6]

After two hours work with Francie over lists of names and invitations, I walked with Father to the V.R. Lodge. He told me that he had on the previous day written a very strong letter to Mr G. telling him plainly that he thought it was his duty to summon Parliament at once—for the sake of giving extra powers to cope with the state of things here; [letter] from the D[uke] of Argyll,[7] expressing his cordial sympathy with him in the peculiarly difficult position in which he is placed.

In the evening I went to bring Father from the Castle, and I heard that a

---

[1] See appendix. This charge stressed the sudden increase in serious crime, which he attributed to the Land League agitation.

[2] A league meeting at Brookeborough, County Fermanagh, on 6 Dec. and the Orange counter- demonstration, were banned on the grounds of danger to the peace.

[3] James J. O'Kelly (1845–1916): born in Dublin, the son of a blacksmith; a leading Fenian in London, 1861–*c.*1863; in French Foreign Legion, *c.*1863–7; again an active Fenian in London, 1867–70; served in French army during Franco-Prussian war; on staff of New York *Herald*, 1871– 80; joined Parnell's party, 1880; M.P. for Roscommon, 1880–85, for Roscommon North, 1885–92, 1895–1916.

[4] See appendix.

[5] Douglas Strutt Galton (1822–99): engineer, general secretary of British Association for the Advancement of Science since 1871.

[6] James Mulholland was shot while executing a civil bill decree on 8 Dec.; the murderer was sentenced to penal servitude for life (S.P.O., I.C.R., Returns of outrages, Dec. 1880).

[7] George Douglas Campbell (1823–1900), 8th duke of Argyll: lord privy seal, 1853–5; postmaster general, 1855–8; lord privy seal, 1859–66; secretary of state for India, 1868–74; lord privy seal, 1880– 81; resigned from govt over land bill, Apr. 1881, after a connection with Gladstone of 29 years.

cypher telegram had been received from Mr Gladstone from Hawarden which not a soul in the office could read.[1]

The unfortunate landlords continue to pour into the ear of the Chief Secretary their warnings, laments and remonstrances. Two ladies came to insist upon a personal interview, declaring that they had travelled 100 miles for that purpose. Each separate story has a dismal monotony in showing the state of terrorism in which all both rich and poor are living under the auspices of the Land League.

The Lord Lieutenant and Lady Cowper dined with us, all the official notables being invited to meet them—Archbishop, Commander of the Forces, Master of the Rolls, Attorney General, Lord Mayor, etc. I sat next the Lord Mayor (Mr Gray M.P.) a sallow, black-haired man, with a face capable of looking very forbidding, but wreathed in agreeable smiles when occasion required.

We had a good deal of harmless and suitable conversation on such safe topics as Irish ballads, statues etc., with only an occasional allusion on his part to subjects like Home Rule, and the state of the country, which I could hardly discuss with the Editor of the *Freeman* under present circumstances.

In the evening I had some pleasant talk with the Attorney General [Hugh Law], quite my favourite of all the Irish officials; also with Sir Thomas Steele. The Commander of the Forces strikes me as a vigorous, clear-headed man, preferring to deal with things from a purely military point of view, but quite capable at the same time of taking in the political bearing of the situation. He too wishes fervently that matters would come to a head, 'but no such luck; we should know by this time two months whether we were mice or men'. 'Oh, no, I am not afraid of the result—I should like to have a "go" at the Land League.'

Fortunately whatever the General's private views as to the best way of dealing with the Land question, he and Father work harmoniously together in the many matters they have to settle at the present time with regard to the moving and disposition of troops.

The arrival of the 1st Coldstream Guards in Dublin is the one and only act of the present Govt which has given satisfaction to elegant society here.

10 Dec., Fri.

A hard morning evidently with Father, but I did not walk with him and am ignorant of the special cause.

Lord and Lady Monck[2] left us. Bertram Buxton arrived. Spent the morning in riding with him, and writing ball invitations with Miss Burke and Francie;

[1] The exchange of telegrams between Gladstone and Forster resulted in the cabinet being summoned for 13 instead of 16 Dec. The incident is illustrative of the Castle's recurrent difficulties with communications, summed up by the conservative attorney general, Hugh Holmes, five years later when he told Churchill that there were two ciphers in use, 'one which everybody can read and one which nobody can read'. Cf. below, p. 131.

[2] See appendix.

went in to Dublin in the afternoon with Mr Ball and Bertram to see the new picture (a portrait by Palma Vecchio) recently bought for the National Gallery here.

The *Pall Mall Gazette*, irritated at the pressure for coercion which is being inevitably brought to bear upon the 'Birmingham Ministers' (and which has been considerably increased by the Judge's charges), has seized upon the Memorandum just issued by the Ch. Secretary to the Magistrates as the opening text for a series of attacks which are evidently going to be quite in the bitter personal vein of the Education controversy.[1]

'The Memorandum' (reminding the Magistrates of obsolete powers that may be exercised under various ancient and half forgotten Acts) is only a justification of the Radical resistance to extra-constitutional coercion. Why on earth were not these ordinary powers of the law employed earlier? If the Memorandum is of any practical use at all why was it not issued before? Miserable inefficiency of the Irish Executive—weakness of the Chief Secretary—Mr Forster may expect to be severely criticized for this as soon as the House meets, etc., etc.

Lord Emly, and Mr Mitchell from Athy,[2] introduced by Mr C. Parker,[3] and Mr O'Connor Morris,[4] dined with us. This last a most incessant and self-complacent talker; like every one else very anxious and despondent about the present crisis; in 1870 he wrote to the *Times* on the Land question: he is greatly disappointed at finding how mistaken he was in his belief then expressed that the Land Bill, though far from perfect, would at any rate have prevented such a state of things as the country is involved in now.

In the evening, [while] Mother was writing to the Duchess of Leinster[5] to explain that, as Father was going over to London for a Cabinet on Monday, we should be obliged to give up our visit to Carton, an excited note arrived from her Grace—'Sorry not to have the pleasure of seeing Mr and Mrs Forster, but owing to the disturbed state of the country, and the doubtfulness of getting rents, they were giving up their party, and felt obliged to reduce everything'.

[1] Forster's memorandum of 1 Dec., issued to all magistrates, simply drew attention to the powers given to magistrates under the Whiteboy act of 1776 and the amending act of 1831 (see above, p. 17) to summon persons suspected of moonlighting offences or intimidation, and to examine on oath persons believed to be able to give evidence (S.P.O., R.P. 1880/30945). A similar circular had been issued by Lord Naas in 1866. The Whiteboy acts were not particularly archaic or recondite, but there had been some uncertainty about the circumstances in which they might be applied, and the peace preservation act of 1870 had devoted a clause to clarifying the matter.

[2] James William Mitchell, J.P.

[3] Charles Stuart Parker (1829–1910): alpinist, champion of educational reform, biographer of Sir Robert Peel, and of Sir James Graham; liberal M.P. for Perth, 1878–92.

[4] William O'Connor Morris: author of *Letters on the land question of Ireland* (London, 1870); county court judge for Kerry, 1878; strongly opposed to land act of 1881.

[5] Caroline, wife of Charles William Fitzgerald (1819–87), 4th duke of Leinster, and premier duke of Ireland, and owner of 67,227 acres in Kildare and 1,044 acres in Meath. He was M.P. for Kildare County, 1847–52; colonel of Kildare militia; chancellor of the Queen's University in Ireland; and commissioner of national education.

This note is only an example of the feeling against the Chief Secretary and the Govt amongst the landlords. No doubt the poor Leinsters who have lately had some unpleasant dealings with reference to some form of lease on their estate obnoxious to the Land League are in a very natural state of perturbation; but there can also be little doubt that their Graces were glad to take this impressive if somewhat undignified manner of marking their displeasure with the Government.

11 Dec., Sat.

A dismal morning: gloomy in every direction. A very bad account of Lord Ripon; the papers one sheet of outrages, violence and law-breaking. Baron Dowse has followed Judge Barry and Judge Fitzgerald in giving a plain, unpolitical statement of facts as to the condition of society in the South and West of Ireland.[1]

If anything can bring home to the minds of Radical Ministers the urgent necessity for some remedy more immediately efficacious than a Land Bill, it will be these judicial charges; even the *Freeman* has hardly the face to maintain that the picture drawn by the Judges is coloured by fancied exaggeration.[2]

Francie and I, assisted by Miss Burke, spent the morning in writing invitations, haunted by the knowledge that things may happen before the 20th that would make ball-giving out of the question. The sight of Father's troubled care-worn face as he passed through the room once or twice, in search of Mother, or looking for a newspaper, made one feel keenly the curious double life we are leading here at present—Father occupied with reports of outrages in the study, and we with ball invitations in the drawing room.

In the afternoon walked round the Vice-Regal grounds with Francie and Bertram and the two dogs. Read 'Michael' to Kathleen Carpenter. Mrs Ball arrived, and Alice and Frederica Spring-Rice[3] to stay over Sunday.

At 6, I drove in to Dublin to bring Father back from the Castle. The evening was radiant with moonlight; clouds scudding past the moon, and the river rushing by at high tide with the light shining on the black waves. The poor Liffey and the ugly dirty quays looked quite glorified, and the pillars of the City Hall gleaming at the top of Parliament Street were stately and imposing.

Father seemed less exhausted that he sometimes is, but Mr Burke and Mr West[4] were in the carriage with us, so I had not much talk with him. He had

[1] Richard Dowse (1824–90): liberal M.P. for Londonderry city, 1868–72; solicitor general (1870–72) and attorney general (1872) for Ireland; baron of the exchequer, 1872–90. Charles Robert Barry (1824–97): former law officer; fourth justice of court of queen's bench since 1872; active in drafting the first land act of 1870; a catholic.

[2] Cf. Davitt, *Fall of feudalism in Ireland*, p. 264: 'This has been a notorious practice of these ermined partisans at all times of popular excitement. It was a glaring misuse of their judicial position in the service of the landlord class. . . . All these judges were mere promoted henchmen of the governing order . . . And so the chorus of the Castle-hacks was voiced at every assize. . . .'

[3] Sisters of Lord Monteagle.   [4] See appendix.

seen several more landlords, amongst them Lord Fitzwilliam, with whom, after a frank exchange of opinions on both sides apropos of a correspondence that had passed between them earlier in the autumn, he had parted on friendly terms.

We had several people to dinner—Dr and Mrs Neilson Hancock,[1] Father Healy, a clever and agreeable diner-out, with whom it appears Mr Gladstone had struck up a great acquaintance when he was over in Ireland,[2] Mr Vernon,[3] the well-known agent who by some good fortune or good management has succeeded in collecting all his rents this year, and is said to be unbearably self-sufficient and aggravating in consequence, Colonel James,[4] Mr Wallace,[5] etc.

I had a good deal of talk in the evening with Mr Evelyn Ashley[3] who had come to dine and sleep on his way back from his estate in Sligo. By dint of keeping his agent out of sight, presenting himself in person to the tenants and agreeing to accept Griffith's Valuation with a reduction on that, he had contrived to tide over matters very agreeably with his tenantry.

Unfortunately, he has only got the promise of the rents even such as they are; whether the money will be actually forthcoming after his departure, is still doubtful. Like many other people who have seen the agitation on the spot, Mr Ashley would like Mr Chamberlain and his friends to have the same advantage.

Amongst his tenantry there was no concealment of the fact that the combination against their landlord came from no sense of special grievance, but from the pressure of the Land League. They must be in line with the rest of Ireland, consequently a branch of the Land League has been set up with the local publican as Secretary; on this must naturally follow a refusal of rent, and probably outrages later on, if necessity should arise.

Like many other humane and Liberal men, Mr Ashley declares that the best thing for the country would be that matters should come to a head—a conflict in which the bloodshed would be small, but which would have the result of breaking the Parnell spell and re-asserting the power of the Queen's government. There is mischief brewing and until an outbreak has cleared the air not much good can be done.

12 Dec., Sun.

Day before a Cabinet, a hard one for Father, closeted in his study, writing, collecting materials to be laid before his colleagues, seeing Lord O'Hagan[3] and Mr Burke.

[1] William Neilson Hancock (1820–88): professor of political economy, Trinity College, Dublin, 1846–51; of jurisprudence and political economy, Queen's College, Belfast, 1849–53; editor of judicial and criminal statistics of Ireland, and writer of numerous reports to government on social and economic questions; keeper of records, Irish land commission; a champion of tenant right.
[2] 17 Oct.–12 Nov. 1877.　　　　　　　　　　　　　　　　　　　[3] See appendix.
[4] Lt-col. E. R. James, commanding Royal Engineers in the Dublin military district.
[5] Arthur Robert Wallace (1837–1912): first class clerk in the chief secretary's office.

He and Mr Ashley crossed together by the evening mail. The latter is a good friend both in public and private; he promised Mother to take care of Father on the journey, and he has written what I am told is an excellent letter to Mr Chamberlain, describing his recent impressions of this country.

At Miss Burke's, where I went with Mr Ball to 5 o'clock tea, I met Mr Christopher Redington[1]—another good Irish landlord, with the land question on the brain. His property is in Galway, and out of it he has to support his Mother and sisters; at present his tenants profess to be on perfectly friendly terms with him, but they either can or will pay no rent, and since the landlord cannot afford to be permanently without either his land or his money he will be forced in the Spring to begin evicting. What will become of the tenants' friendship then?

When this critical time comes, as it soon must in many hitherto peaceful parts of Ireland—when the landlords must take strong measures, if it is only to avert simple ruin from their families—then the fruit of the Land League teaching will be seen in its full bitterness.

13 Dec., Mon.

Mr and Mrs Ball left us. Mr Murrough O'Brien[1] came to lunch to meet Alice and Freddy. With all his quiet gentle manner, and courteous diffidence in argument, he is a most stern and thorough-going Radical at heart, with genuine sympathy for the Land League, and persistent incredulity as to Land League outrages. He is acquainted with Mr Michael Davitt, the man who is said to be the ablest and most sincere of all the League chiefs.

At the outset he (Davitt) abstained from the movement as not going far enough for him—a Socialist of the Continental type—now he is taking active part in the agitation, and is said to be more its mainspring than Mr Parnell himself; in his speeches he has never descended to the vulgar depths of some of his professional colleagues in the agitation, and has been more careful than most of them to discourage outrages upon man and beast.

In the afternoon Alice and I drove into Dublin, going to Mr Sim's, and to the Irish [*recte* Royal Hibernian] Academy.[2] I was amused at the old man in charge here, mildly remarking to Alice that he thought 'Miss Forster knew the collection almost as well as he did'; certainly in fulfilling my duties as 'cicerone' to our successive guests, I have been pretty often to the Academy, and also to my other favourite haunt the National Gallery.

The Spring Rices left us in the evening. As we were playing whist with Bertram [Buxton] after dinner, a note was brought Mother from Mr Jephson[1] at the Kildare St Club: it contained Father's telegram from London 'Parliament summoned for 6th with permission for suspension of Habeas Corpus'.[3]

---

[1] See appendix.   [2] At 34 Lr Abbey St.
[3] Forster had wished for an earlier summoning of parliament; the form which coercion was to take had still to be finally decided.

14 Dec., Tu.

A dismal wet day. Bertram left by the evening mail.

15 Dec., Wed.

Mr Broderick[1] arrived. Amongst the packet of answers to ball invitations which Francie and I were opening at tea time was a curious, ill-written note, purporting to come from one who wrote 'as a woman to a woman at the risk of her own life', to give warning that 'your husband will be shot before the end of the trials; the men are chosen to do it'.

Since then Mother received a second letter, this time professing to threaten and not to warn. Father has himself received numerous threatening letters (from both sides); but the cruel device of adding to a wife's natural anxieties for her husband at a time like this is a new invention of Irish malice. This will certainly be a curious autumn to look back upon.

16 Dec., Th.

The H[umphry] Wards, Lucy Ada and Mr Rutson[2] arrived in the morning. Went with Mother in the afternoon to a hot and crowded little ceremony of Prize giving at a Female Art Society. The Cowpers do all in their power to be gracious on these occasions but His Excellency has not a lively manner, and the hearing a Report read, however satisfactory its statements, can never be an incentive to brilliant oratory.

In the evening several of the party drove into Dublin to hear the speeches at the Roberts banquet.[3] Lord Waterford[4] in proposing the toast of 'Prosperity to Ireland' acquitted himself with discretion, and was not too funereal or too severe upon the Executive.

Lord Cowper, as Chairman, was well received, considering the circumstances, and of course avoided all allusion to dangerous subjects. Lord Monck's biographical sketch of General Roberts was informing but very dull and so comprehensive in its praise of the hero of the evening that it might have been applied equally well to Alexander the Great or Napoleon.

The General's own speech was perfect—vivacious, well expressed, and

---

[1] George Charles Brodrick (1831–1903): lawyer, journalist, and unsuccessful liberal candidate at general elections of 1868, 1874, and 1880; in 1881 he became warden of Merton College, Oxford, and published *English land and English landlords*; strongly opposed home rule and Irish land legislation.

[2] See appendix.

[3] In honour of Major General Sir Frederick Sleigh Roberts (1832–1914): of a Co. Waterford family; commander of British forces in Afghanistan, he had captured Kabul and relieved Kandahar (1879–80). In 1902 he became first Earl Roberts of Kandahar, Pretoria, and Waterford.

[4] John Henry de la Poer Beresford (1844–95), 5th marquis: liberal M.P. for Waterford County, 1865–6; owner of 66,684 acres, of which 39,883, valued at £27,707, were in Waterford.

charming in the ready tact with which he at once appropriated Lord Monck's eulogy, not to himself but to the soldiers and brother officers whom he claimed to represent.

17 Dec., Wed.

Father returned by the morning boat. Having carefully evaded or disposed of all our visitors, I contrived to secure a tête-à-tête walk with him to the Vice Regal Lodge. The carriage followed us and we drove to the Castle, picking up Mr Burke on the way.

The question of the day, the proposed prohibition of a Meeting[1] summoned by the Land League for the purpose of denouncing a particular man. Evidence forthcoming in placards issued by the promoters of the Meeting. Should it be stopped? The law officers hesitating—Mr Burke in a white heat of indignation against them, finding thorough support in this case, as he had expected, from the Chief Secretary.[2] The Meeting is to be stopped, and the Lord Lieutenant's proclamation will bear the signature 'W. E. Forster'.

In the afternoon rode in the Park with Mr Brodrick. Received from Mr John O'Hagan[3] *Lays of the Western Gael* by Sir Samuel Ferguson.[4] Dined at the V.R. Lodge. A large party and an 'at home' afterwards to meet Sir F. and Lady Roberts. The former took Mother in to dinner and made himself most agreeable. We, who are not yet 'blasé' as regards the small Dublin society, found the party amusing, and got through a great deal of miscellaneous chattering. I, with Col. Hozier, Colonel Boyle, old Sir John Lentaigne, Mr Heron, Sir Thomas Steele, Lord O'Hagan, Major Kennedy, Mr Doyle etc.[5] The C.S. Lodge was represented in great force, all our party having joined us in the evening.

18 Dec., Sat.

Aunt Fanny Lucy, Ted, and Oakel arrived. Morning spent over ball invitations and chatter. Walked round the Circular in the afternoon with Aunt F. L., Mary, the Lucies, Ted, Mr Rutson and Puck. Received ten volumes of Hayes's Irish

[1] At Cullahill, Queen's County.

[2] Burke's impatience is understandable, as the law officers had decided on 28 Sept. that meetings of this type should be banned; cf. above, p. 17.   [3] See appendix.

[4] Sir Samuel Ferguson (1810–86): born in Belfast and educated at Belfast Academical Institution and Trinity College, Dublin; poet and antiquary; deputy keeper of the public records in Ireland since 1867, and knighted in 1878 for his reorganisation of the department. The *Lays* were published in 1865.

[5] Lt-col. John W. Hozier, Royal Scots Greys. Lt-col. P. D. Boyle, assistant military secretary on the headquarters staff of the army in Ireland. Sir John Francis O'Neill Lentaigne (1803–86): eldest son of Benjamin Lentaigne, the émigré army surgeon who attended Wolfe Tone during his last days; inspector of reformatory and industrial schools, commissioner of national education, honorary member of general prisons board, and president of the Zoological Society of Ireland; knighted Apr. 1880. Denis Caulfield Heron (1825–81): third serjeant at law and formerly liberal M.P. for Tipperary, 1870–74. 'Mr Doyle' is perhaps Henry E. Doyle (see below, p. 46).

Ballads[1] from the Lord Mayor; the result of our conversation at dinner on the 9th. Dr and Mrs Kaye to dinner, and Mr Mahony, the famous improving landlord of Dromore Castle, Co. Kerry.[2]

19 Dec., Sun.

On meeting at breakfast found that Oakel had gone off by train with the troops to see the prohibited meeting in the Queen's County. To church at the [Royal] Hibernian [Military School]. Father at work all day with Mr Jephson and Mr Burke; Lord O'Hagan to tea; news that the Meeting at Culahill[3] had dispersed quietly. About 9 Oakley returned tired out and famished. Much impressed with the good temper of [*recte* 'and'] firm discretion of the Resident Magistrate,[4] and the patience of the troops.

20 Dec., Mon.

In the morning a lively gathering of juveniles in the smoking room, Mr West having permission also to remain at home and help in writing out the list of names for the papers.

Mary Monsell[5] arrived at lunch time to stay with us over the two balls. Walking and riding in the afternoon; gradual disturbance of the drawing room in preparation for the evening; preliminary dancing in the ball room after tea.

The ball was pleasant enough, and a pretty sight from the number of uniforms, and the highly successful decoration of the ball room and conservatory. There were about 200 people present, and everyone seemed to enjoy themselves.

Mr Liddell[6] and his band were in a good humour and played to the admiration of everyone; the floor was perfection; the military, the A.D.C.s and the youth of Dublin danced vigorously; the absence of the county people and the grandees, who, partly from the early time of year, and partly from disapproval of a Liberal Govt, did not favour us as they had Mr Lowther[7] last year, did not tell upon the spirits of those present; their Excellencies were amiable and did

---

[1] Edward Hayes, *The ballads of Ireland: collected and edited* (2 vols, London, Edinburgh, and Dublin, 1856). 'Ten' should probably read 'two'.

[2] William Squire Barker Kaye (1831–1901): LL.D.; formerly crown prosecutor of Armagh, counsel for the post office in the north-east circuit, and revising barrister for the city of Dublin; since 1878 assistant under-secretary and clerk of the Irish privy council. Richard John Mahony owned 29,163 acres in Kerry, valued at £3,071.

[3] The meeting had been 'adjourned' to Durrow, four miles away, in an attempt to circumvent the proclamation, but on Forster's instructions it was suppressed in spite of this.

[4] Thomas Hamilton, R.M. at Portarlington.

[5] Daughter of Lord Emly (see appendix).

[6] John Liddell, director of music by appointment to the lord lieutenant.

[7] James Lowther (1840–1904): chief secretary for Ireland, 1878–80, in Disraeli's ministry; in his imperviousness to Irish attack and his cheerful readiness to hit back, Lowther foreshadowed Arthur Balfour's style as chief secretary (1887–91). See above, p. 3.

their duty in every particular, Lord Cowper dancing the first quadrille with Mother, Lady Cowper with Oakel.

The only two who seemed at all out of harmony with the generally sociable spirit of the evening were my Puck, who was brought down—much to his annoyance—to see his friend Colonel Boyle, and the Lord Mayor—fingering his chair,[1] standing on his dignity and dissatisfied with his place in the supper arrangements; undoubtedly His Lordship was a little put out, for he talked with indiscreet candour to Mary later in the evening on subjects connected with the *Freeman* and its line with regard to outrages—finally avowing that 'he was not sure he should stop them if he could'.

Mother got through the labours of the evening wonderfully. Father roamed about, talking, looking benignant, and solacing himself with Whist in the little drawing room.

Oakel danced abundantly with the young ladies, and won the hearts of the dowagers by his polite attentions to them. In spite of my previous protestations and misgivings I danced too.

21 Dec., Tu.

Most of the party drove, or spent the day in Dublin. In the afternoon I walked round the Circular with the dogs, and finished 'Sohrab and Rustum'[2] to Kathleen Carpenter. Gaston Monsell[3] to dinner. The second ball in some ways an improvement on the first, there being more pretty people. Conducted Lord Cowper through the Lancers, and had much lively talk with him; in spite of our Parliamentary prospect I think he envies us returning to London.

Apropos of private theatricals, and the probable aptitude of the Irish for them if he were to get them up at the Castle during the season, His Excellency gently remarked 'I should think the Lord Mayor would act well', a delicate allusion to Mr Gray's supposed faculty for taking two sides, which rather amused me. However, Lord Cowper was quite of my opinion, that considered as a dinner party neighbour the Lord Mayor was quite one of the most agreeable and conversible of our official acquaintance.

Had much talk with Mr Edgar Vincent[4] (came over with the Guards, and lately with Lord E. Fitzmaurice[5] in Roumelia); he was very anxious to bet that the Cabinet will not exist as it is at present by that day (Dec. 21st) next year.

---

[1] ? chain.

[2] Matthew Arnold's long poem, first published in 1853.

[3] Thomas William Gaston Monsell (1858–1932): son of Lord Emly; later 2nd Baron Emly; held at this time the office of state steward in the viceregal household.

[4] Edgar Vincent (1857–1941): officer in Coldstream Guards, 1877–82; author of standard *Handbook of modern Greek*, 1879; financial adviser to Egyptian government, 1883–9; brother of Charles E. Howard Vincent (see p. 481).

[5] Edmond George Petty-Fitzmaurice (1846–1935): brother of Lord Lansdowne; liberal M.P. for Calne, 1868–85; commissioner at Constantinople under the treaty of Berlin, 1880–81.

The belle of the evening was a Miss Manley, a tall stately young lady, with splendid coils of yellow corn-coloured hair, and a yellow satin dress.

22 Dec., Wed.

Tory Dublin papers in virtuous indignation over the balls—'Mr Forster with the vicarious assistance of Mr Liddell'—like Nero fiddling while Rome was burning, etc., etc.

Lunched with Aunt Fanny Lucy at Mrs Bruce['s].[1] Called on Lady Ferguson to return books and say goodbye. Mary, Humphry, and Lucy Ada left us.

23 Dec., Th.

Rode with Oakel to Glasnevin; saw the Guards march through the back streets, playing 'The Campbells are coming' on the bagpipes. The people at doors and windows showed curiosity but no hostility; their pet aversion at present is the 19th Hussars engaged in the Boycott affair.

In the afternoon Lord and Lady de Vesci[2] called; a remarkably handsome couple. Aunt Fanny Lucy and Lucy left us, after the customary tea dinner in the smoking room.

24 Dec., Fri.

Morning occupied in helping Oakel cut out and classify extracts from the official reports of the Traversers' speeches.[3] A dreary painful business, so much coarseness and brutality mixed up with genuine emotions of patriotism and compassion for the poverty and wretchedness of fellow countrymen; much blatant commonplace rant from professional agitators, or local orators enjoying the glory of hearing their own voices from a platform; but at the same time some of the speakers evidently inspired by a national idea which they believed in with a sincerity that gave a certain pathetic dignity to their rather grotesque eloquence.

Interrupted in the middle of our cutting out and writing by an incursion of Vesey Fitzgeralds, father and son; happily Oakel and I were able to stave them off without their getting at either Father or Mother.

A bitterly cold afternoon. Mr Murrough O'Brien called; Mr Bryce[2] had been to see him, and has now gone to the West with introductions to Mr Davitt

---

[1] Mary Caroline, née Burgoyne, wife of Lt-col. Robert Bruce (1825–99), late of 23rd Fusiliers, deputy inspector-general of the R.I.C. 1877–82, inspector-general 1882–5.

[2] See appendix.

[3] Speeches made by Parnell and others accused of conspiracy in connection with their Land League activities.

and others; he will certainly hear all sides, for he was at our ball on Tuesday, and afterwards, I believe, at Lord Powerscourt's.[1]

25 Dec., Sat., Christmas Day

Francie, Mr West, Oakel and I went to the long musical service at Christ Church. Archbishop Trench[2] preached. A brilliant frosty day. After lunch Francie and I walked with Father to the V.R. Lodge. On the way he remarked, 'by this time next week, I shall very likely have ceased to be Irish Secretary'. I had hardly realized that his proposed Coercion Bill was so strong that it was likely to prove a stumbling block to some of his colleagues when once the main thing, the Suspension of the H[abeas] C[orpus], had been agreed to.

After Father had finished his interview with Lord Cowper the latter, accompanied by Osman, the Vice Regal collie, walked with us to the Zoological Gardens, where we wished Father to be introduced to the five lion cubs. Whilst we were in the lion-house, appeared Mr West to say that an orderly had brought papers and where should they be taken to? He also informed us that Oakel had been thrown by Phoenix, and though not seriously hurt was too much shaken to come out again.

On our walk back through the Park we were met by the orderly, sent by Mr West, with the papers, which the Chief Secretary received and read on the spot, to the interest of the passers by.

The park and the Dublin mountains looked beautiful under the clear frosty sunset, and I thought sadly of leaving this place for good and all.

On coming in, found poor Oakel decidedly stiff and bruised—no wonder, for Phoenix, after bolting into the wire fence by the front door, had pitched Oakel over his head on to the iron-hard gravel drive.

Miss Burke to 5 o'clock tea. Afterwards wrote at Father's dictation till dinner time. A small family party at dinner, Mr West dining out. We spoke much of Aunt Fan and the old Christmas Day gatherings at Fox How. After dinner wrote again for two hours, Father finishing the dictation of his Memorandum for the Cabinet on the Land Bill: an agreeable diversion in the midst of incessant schemes as to personal protection of landlords, movement of troops, and coercion.[3]

---

[1] See appendix.

[2] Richard Chenevix Trench (1807–86): archbishop of Dublin, 1864–84.

[3] This memorandum, together with a draft for the coercion bill, both dated 27 Dec., are in B.L., Add. MS 44625, ff 34–7. The land bill memorandum stressed the need to declare as soon as possible exactly how far the government was prepared to go. The draft coercion bill included, as well as the suspension of habeas corpus, restrictions on the possession of arms, and several other clauses from the peace preservation act of 1870, and clauses directed specifically against the agitation.

26 Dec., Sun.

To church for the last time at R.H.M.S. chapel. Francie, who has taken a class of little red-coated Hibernians at the Sunday school here for the past month or two, will be greatly missed.

After luncheon went into the study to copy out the Land Bill Memorandum with corrections. At work on this till tea time, Oakel meanwhile busy with his 'Sedition' (i.e. extracts from L[and] L[eague] speeches), and Mr Jephson and Mr West helping Father to arrange papers and despatch boxes in preparation for the general departure on Wednesday.

Sergeant Heron to 5 o'clock tea. More copying.

27 Dec., Mon.

A foggy moist day. Francie and I went to lunch and spend the afternoon with the Murrough O'Briens at Mount Mapas, Killiney. According to arrangement Mr O'Brien met us at Westland Row, and went down with us. A pleasant lunch with the O'Briens and their handsome intelligent little boy.

Francie spent the afternoon with Mrs Murrough, whilst I went with him a scrambling walk up Killiney Hill, and understood how beautiful the situation of Mount Mapas is, and how fine the views of the coast must be when they are not obscured by a rainy fog.

Theoretically Mr Murrough O'Brien is a Home Ruler, or rather is in favour of complete independence for Ireland, but he sees the impracticability of this at present, and meanwhile devotes himself in all sincerity to land reform, as an object in itself, not as a stepping-stone to Repeal.

Unlike some of the Land Leaguers with whom he sympathizes, he would gladly accept a strong Land Bill at the hands of an English Government, and give them all possible help and good wishes in their endeavour to legislate for the good of his country. He did not seem to believe as much as I did in the existence of a deep-rooted hatred of England amongst the Land League chiefs which would prevent their being ever really satisfied, or allowing the people to be satisfied with any measure of Land reform, however strong, coming through an English Parliament.

We in England must strive to do our best for Ireland, and make up our minds to be hated and abused all the same.

As I was driving through Dublin to the station on our way to Killiney, I looked at the faces of the men hanging about the streets (it was a Bank holiday), and realized with painful vividness the truth that, given a crowd of Irish in any town in Ireland, it would be easy, by a single inflammatory appeal from a professed patriot, to excite every man, woman and child present into a patriotic frenzy against England—against ourselves.

Antipathy to England and the English may be undeveloped, but it is latent in all Irishmen, unless perhaps in cases where this natural antipathy has been superseded by some special bond of sympathy and common interest, social or religious.

I have often had in my head during these days, the lines:

> I, with many a fear—for my dear country, many
> heart-felt sighs—
> Amongst men who do not love her, linger here.[1]

Mr and Miss Burke, Mr and Mrs Roberts, and Mr Edgar Vincent dined with us—the last of our pleasant Dublin dinner parties. Said good-bye to Mr Burke: he and Father have worked well together during these past difficult months, and Father's respect for Mr Burke's clear judgment, courage and impartiality has not been diminished by a close acquaintance.[2]

28 Dec., Tu.

Mr Becker the 'Own Correspondent' of the *Daily News* came to breakfast; his letters, and the Judges' charges, have in their different ways done more than anything else to impress Liberal public opinion with the dangerous and abnormal state of society in the West of Ireland.

A drizzling depressing day. Great precautions taken against an outbreak of popular excitement on this the first day of the trials. Fifty of the Guards at the Castle—the troops kept in barracks—Chief Justice May's house protected, expectation of broken windows for all the law officers connected with the Prosecution.

About 12 o'clock I walked with Father through the Park on his way to the Castle, everything quiet enough here, but anxious, wondering as to how matters might be going on in Dublin.

A gloomy morning—Mrs Henry Doyle[3] to 5 o'clock tea. Oakel back from the Four Courts. All had been quiet enough. The Chief Justice's announcement of his intention not to take part in the trials was received with respect; the scene Oakeley says was a painful one.

Judge May has behaved with dignity and consideration in thus withdrawing, and every one feels sorry for the judge who, by thus expressing on the Bench what many people thought and said off it, had brought himself into this embarrassing position.

The agitators and their friends in the Press have by this step of the Chief

---

[1] Wordsworth, 'Near Calais', 1802.

[2] 'Burke is the most efficient permanent official I ever came across, and my only fear about him is that he will literally work himself to death' (Forster to Gladstone, 20 Dec. 1880; B.L. Add. MS 44158, ff 80–81).

[3] Jane, wife of Henry Edward Doyle (1827–92), director of the National Gallery of Ireland, 1869–92, and brother of 'Dicky' Doyle, the caricaturist.

Justice's been deprived of an effective grievance, a fact at which some of them cannot conceal their regret.

Father and Mother dined in the evening at the V.R. Lodge. We have thoroughly liked, and got on with the Cowpers; they, poor people, cordially dislike their position both in its society and political point of view.

His loyalty to Father and to the Govt is just what might be expected from the best type of English country-gentleman statesman; and with all his shyness and ineffectiveness as a public man he has good judgment and ability, and will probably rise to the occasion when left at the Castle with more than the ordinary burden of work and responsibility upon his noble shoulders, if only he is strong enough.[1]

She has great force of character and a strong, if somewhat self-confident, desire to acquit herself conscientiously of the duties required of her. She has perfect simplicity of manner verging on brusqueness and though proud enough to all appearance is quite without fine-lady vanity or aristocratic exclusiveness.

Her evident desire to be on friendly terms with Dublin society, great and small, her genuine painstaking interest in all good works and institutions, and last but not least her strikingly handsome looks and dignity of carriage, are beginning to prejudice in her favour even those who were disposed to grumble at the extreme 'quietness' of their new Excellencies, besides having conscientious objections to their political principles.

29 Dec., Wed.

Drove with Father, Mr West and Oakel into Dublin after lunch. Oakel and I were set down at the Four Courts, and, thanks to Father's card, were soon provided with standing room inside.

The dramatic effect of the 'State Trials' was not striking. A small room, hot and crowded. Mr Law with his back to us making his speech, which went on for three days—Traversers in a semi-circle opposite (Mr Parnell I did not recognise at first from his having shaved off his light-brown beard)—Mr Dillon reading the *Pall Mall*—above, the two Judges[2] in scarlet—on the right the Jury— a throng of lawyers going in and out—a number of people standing about in the fine central hall of the Four Courts waiting to find room—perfect indifference apparently on all sides.

A message from Judge Barry to offer us seats, but this would have placed us behind the Traversers (regarding whom we were principally curious), and besides we had not much time, so we gratefully declined the Judge's polite offer and came away.

[1] Cf. below, pp 86, 157. In Sept. Spencer remarked to Gladstone that Cowper 'may want a little pressure, as he is more indolent than most men of his ability' (Spencer to Gladstone, 18 Sept. 1880; B.L., Add. MS 44308, ff 42–7).

[2] John David Fitzgerald and Charles Robert Barry.

On our way home, called on the Miss Glyns,[1] and then took an outside car through the Park to Miss Burke's and said good-bye to her. She is a strong Conservative so far as the Govt of Ireland is concerned—holding the theory of a benevolent despotism as the right thing for her countrymen. She said good-bye pleasantly enough and amiably wished us well through the coming parliamentary conflict but, like many other indignant and distressed gentlefolk whose relations are amongst the good landlords and agents in the West of Ireland, she will evidently see the Liberal Government called to account with keen satisfaction.

Before coming in went to say good-bye to Miss Higgins at the back lodge and to the Carpenters.

I shall look back with pleasure to my evening prowls through the garden during this autumn and winter—the quiet stretch of the Fifteen Acres—the distant lights of Dublin—the soft foliage of the ilexes by the iron gate—the fragrant twin cypresses in the kitchen garden—my Puck scouring happily about in the darkness—the bright rifts in the clouds, or the shining of the evening star which seemed like a promise of light and hope in these gloomy times; these are my impressions of our Dublin garden—I shall certainly be sorry to turn my back on Ireland for good.

We left by the evening boat from Kingstown—a large party including Rob and Puck. Yarrow remained behind at the C.S. Lodge, and Chattanooga had gone to London the day before with some of the servants.

A rough passage—Father and I came straight on to London, Mother, Oakel and Francie sleeping at Holyhead. At Holyhead parted with Puck, my constant companion during the past autumn.

Travelled in the sleeping car with Mrs White, née Considine, of Limerick; she had just been hearing from Miss Ellard herself the account of the attempt to shoot her—the mark of the bullet left on the carriage—Miss E. could hardly speak of the affair without breaking down.[2] The whole story has been ridiculed in the *Freeman* as a 'manufactured outrage' which never took place at all.[3]

30 Dec., Th.

Father and I breakfasted together, read the papers, and had much interesting talk. About 12 he went off to the Cabinet. Between 7 and 8 Mother and Francie arrived from Holyhead. Soon after Father returned to dinner. 'It's all right', I heard him call out to Mother as he came up the staircase. This crisis being

---

[1] Daughters of Major-gen. J. R. Glyn, general officer commanding the Dublin military district.

[2] Louisa Martha Ellard, who managed her father's property and had refused the local Land League's demand for 'Griffith's valuation', was fired at as she drove home from Oola station (Co. Limerick) on the evening of 23 Dec. Two shots hit her vehicle; she returned fire from her revolver (S.P.O., I.C.R., Returns of outrages, Dec. 1880).

[3] *Irish Times*, 28, 29 Dec.; *F.J.*, 29 Dec.

over, other difficulties are now before him. As things stand at present, a united Cabinet meets the House with definite proposals—(1) for Coercion, i.e. Protection of life and property in Ireland, (2) for Land Reform; the first measure to be entrusted to Father, the second to Mr Gladstone.

As regards Coercion a marked change of tone is perceptible (in the C[abinet]) since the Cabinet in November, the Radical and neutral members feeling distinctly that the weight of English public opinion is shifting in favour of repressive measures.

6 Jan., Th.

Parliament opened. Queen's speech. Debate on the Address. The Traversers present in person, there being no legal objection. Mr Parnell's Amendment on the address.[1]

I went down to the house in the evening—the first and familiar sight that met my eyes on looking down from the Gallery being Mr T. P. O'Connor declaiming against the Government. The cue of the Parnellites with regard to the Coercion Bill—'manufactured outrages', and 'conspiracy of the British Press'.

7 Jan., Fri.

Mr Parnell's speech on the Amendment moderate, absolutely different from his language in Ireland—evidently aimed at coaxing English Radicals.[2] Father's speech later in the evening made a good impression; without forestalling his coming statement on bringing in the Coercion Bill, he gave a few instances of recent agrarian outrage which were of much effect. Mr Gibson's speech much less a personal attack on the Chief Secretary than we had expected; in fact the landlord and feminine [? Fenian] virulence of Dublin to which we had become so well accustomed seems rather missing in the present debate.

8 Jan., Sat.

Met Lord Monteagle[3] and Mr Edward O'Brien[3] at the Spring Rices. There is much disappointment amongst Irish and English Liberals (even landlords) at the guarded nature of the allusion to the promised Land Bill in the Queen's Speech; it is declared that a strong Coercion Bill and a weak Land Bill will be a disastrous combination; 'the three Fs'[4] had been practically accepted as the

---

[1] Parnell gave notice of his amendment on 6 Jan., and introduced it next day.
[2] Parnell's amendment occupied the subsequent nights of debate on the address until 14 Jan.
[3] See appendix.
[4] Fair rent, to be fixed by special courts; fixity of tenure so long as this 'judicial rent' was paid; and freedom for the tenant to sell his interest in his holding.

basis of Reform by landlords as well as tenants;[1] to miss this opportunity would be a mistake, and would increase the power of the agitators.

In the evening to Lady Spencer's, people very cordial about Father's speech, Lord Emly nervously anxious to prevent Liberal magnates in Ireland 'boycotting the Lord Lieutenant at the Drawing Rooms'—had been speaking to Lady Spencer about it—'must speak to the Duke of St Albans'.[2] Mr Blennerhasset[3] was asked if it was true that there was going to be a split in the Home Rule party—did not deny it.

10 Jan., Mon.

Debate on Mr Parnell's Amendment continued. An eloquent speech from Mr David Plunkett,[4] quoting Shakespeare on Jack Cade against Mr Parnell.

11 Jan., Tu.

Mother and Francie to Tottenham. Walked with Father to the office. Humphry Ward and the O'Brien children to tea. Father home to dinner with Mr Stansfeld—much talk about the Agricultural Commission;[5] Lord Carlingford in practice though not in theory ready for the three Fs. Mr Stansfeld explained his device for meeting the objections to Free Sale.

Went down after dinner to the House, taking Mrs Percival. The first part dull—Irish members and Mr Chaplin;[6] at the end however a fine speech from Lord Hartington—a powerful indictment of the Land League 'which though discredited was certainly not injured' by the outrages which undoubtedly influenced local opinion in its favour by sheer intimidation, a speech well-worded and forcibly delivered; the House rang with cheers after he had sat down. Father delighted—every one acknowledging the speech as one of Lord Hartington's greatest efforts. Home at 1.30.

[1] 'Excepting extreme landlords, becoming fewer every day, and extreme agitators, I believe everyone in Ireland interested in the question wishes for and expects the 3 Fs' (Forster to Gladstone, 3[?] Jan. 1881; B.L., Add. MS 44158, ff 115–16; similarly his letter of 10 Jan., ff 121–2).

[2] William Amelius Aubrey de Vere Beauclerk (1840–98): 10th duke of St Alban's since 1849; hereditary grand falconer of England.

[3] Rowland Ponsonby Blennerhassett (b. 1850): M.P. for Kerry, 1872–85, and owner of 6,234 acres in the county; his cousin, Sir Rowland (b. 1839), had won the second Kerry seat at the 1880 election.

[4] David Robert Plunkett (b. 1838): former law adviser and solicitor general for Ireland under conservative governments; professor of constitutional and criminal law at King's Inn, Dublin; conservative M.P. for Dublin University, 1870–95.

[5] Appointed on 14 Aug. 1879 under the chairmanship of the earl of Richmond to inquire into the agricultural crisis in the United Kingdom generally; its preliminary report (dated 14 Jan. 1881) was almost entirely concerned with Ireland. Thirteen commissioners favoured emigration as a solution to the agrarian problem; the remaining six, headed by Lord Carlingford, produced a minority report favouring the three Fs (*Preliminary report from her majesty's commissioners on agriculture*, C2778, H.C. 1881, xv, 1–24) James Stansfeld (1820–98), liberal M.P. for Halifax 1859–95, and friend of Mazzini and Garibaldi, was one of the minority. For Carlingford, see appendix.

[6] Henry Chaplin (1840–1923): conservative M.P. for Mid-Lincolnshire, 1868–1906, for Wimbledon, 1907–16; noted huntsman and connoisseur of the turf; cr. Viscount Chaplin, 1916.

12 Jan., Wed.

London in deep snow and ice: walked with Father to the office,[1] and on with him to the House; spent an hour or two in the Gallery watching the Irish engaged in pure obstruction, preventing the debate on the Address being continued on pretence of not having known that it was to be proceeded with that day; obstruction further veiled under appearance of jealousy for the rights of private members—Mr Anderson and Mr Palmer[2] having voluntarily withdrawn their Bills at the request of the Govt.

After a plain avowal of intent to obstruct by Mr McCoan,[3] Mr Parnell prudently induced his followers to desist and allow a division,[4] after which (about 4 o'clock) the debate on the Address was continued till 6. Mr Cropper[5] and the Cumins to dinner.

13 Jan., Th.

Went to see 'Twelfth Night' acted at Mrs Simpson's. Father home to dinner with Mr Hibbert.[6]

14 Jan., Fri.

A long visit in the afternoon from Mr Grant Duff[5] and Mr Cropper, both driven from the House by Mr Synan[7] who was continuing the debate on the Address.

English and Scotch feeling against the Irish representatives is becoming strong—Mr Parnell's tender advances have not gained many; at the same time there is still an anxious desire for a thorough-going Land Bill; the zeal of English Liberals in this direction has been in no way diminished by the exasperation with obstruction.

The deputation of Liberal Irish Members to Mr Gladstone on the question of land reform last Tuesday has been warmly applauded: the separation of Mr Shaw and 18[8] Irish members from Mr Parnell hailed with great satisfaction.

[1] The Irish Office, 18 Great Queen Street, London, S.W.
[2] George Anderson (1819–96), liberal M.P. for Glasgow since 1868. Charles Mark Palmer (1822–1907): liberal M.P. for Durham North 1874–85, for Jarrow-on-Tyne 1885–1907; first mayor of Jarrow, 1875; shipowner and ironmaster.
[3] James Carlile McCoan (1829–1904): author of *Egypt as it is* (1877) and *Turkey in Asia* (1879); home rule M.P. for Wicklow County, 1880–85.
[4] 230 to 33.
[5] See appendix.
[6] John Tomlinson Hibbert (1824–1908): liberal M.P. for Oldham, 1862–74, 1877–86; parliamentary secretary to local government board.
[7] Edward John Synan (1820–87): liberal M.P. for County Limerick, 1859–74; home rule M.P. for the county, 1874–85.
[8] 18 may well be a typing error for 10. The *F.J.* of 18 Jan. lists the names of 12 seceders, including Shaw.

Mr Holms[1] to dinner; much fraternizing between him and Oakel over army reform.

First division taken on Mr Parnell's amendment to the Address, a smaller number (8) of English radicals voting with the Irish than might have been expected.[2]

15 Jan., Sat.

News of an attempt to blow up Salford barracks with dynamite; precautions against similar Fenian outrages in the great towns are being taken, the volunteer armouries being specially watched.[3]

In a clever speech on Friday, Mr Gray—our friend the late Lord Mayor of Dublin—ended with a significant warning to the Govt that coercion would be followed by real (i.e. not 'manufactured outrages' this time) in Ireland and England.

Walked with Father to the office; the question of a 'clôture' or some way of meeting obstruction is coming within the range of practical politics.

Bitterly cold. Cabinet dinner for Father at Mr Gladstone's. Mother at Lady Granville's. I joined her there afterwards with Father: small and dull.

16 Jan., Sun.

Father at work on a speech in answer to Mr Justin McCarthy,[4] who has moved the second amendment to the Address.

A call in the evening from Mr Ball, who suggests that the Govt should themselves adjourn the debate on the Address by way of cutting short these obstructive amendments. Father agrees, but does not find general support.

Mr Jephson to supper and work.

The prospective difficulties in the House, so far as regards the passing the Coercion Bill quickly, seem increased by the present diminution in the number, though not in the ferocity, of outrages. (Last week 31 head of cattle were driven over the cliff into the sea on the island of Arran; as usual no evidence forthcoming.) This diminution is traceable to a combination of causes—increased vigour of the magistrate in small cases, stronger denunciation than hitherto of 'unnecessary' outrages by such leaders as Davitt, last, but not least, the impending suspension of the Habeas Corpus Act. The experience was the same before the passing of the Westmeath Act.[5]

[1] John Holms (1830–91): liberal M.P. for Hackney since 1868; junior lord of the treasury.

[2] The division was 435 to 57.

[3] A boy was fatally injured in the Salford explosion on 14 Jan.; on 17 Jan. part of Glencorse barracks near Edinburgh was destroyed by fire, probably accidental (*The Times*, 17–18 Jan. 1881).

[4] See appendix.

[5] Protection of Life and Property in certain Parts of Ireland Act, 1871 (34 & 35 Vic., c.25); the first act to suspend habeas corpus in conditions of purely agrarian disturbance.

Meantime the plea for a Coercion Bill on the ground of urgency is being stultified by the continued postponement made inevitable by this prolonged debate on the Address. There are three Motions still to come, Mr McCarthy's, Mr Dawson's,[1] and Sir W. Lawson's.

17 Jan., Mon.

Father hard at work preparing his speech. Report in the morning papers of Mr Davitt's speech at Kilbrin—a furious and powerful invective against England who is threatened with 'the wolf hound of Irish vengeance bounding across the Atlantic'.[2]

Oakel to tea, just come from hearing Mr Gladstone's vehement and brilliant reply to Mr McCarthy. His amendment to the Address (praying that Her Majesty would prohibit the employment of Military, naval and constabulary forces in the enforcement of evictions) characterized by Mr Gladstone as an 'insult to the Throne', asking the Queen to suspend the action of her own executive Govt in the execution of the law; the Parnellites furious and aghast at Mr Gladstone's unexpected energy on this subject—complaining that he had misrepresented Mr McCarthy etc.; the effect of Mr Gladstone's plain speaking on the Radicals is much dreaded by the Parnellites, who have been carefully playing to the Government supporters below the gangway—not altogether without success.

18 Jan., Tu.

After a howling wind all night, we woke to a terrific snowstorm—snow whirling and drifting in the icy wind, and penetrating everywhere.

Father and Mr West to lunch. An afternoon in the house, the blinding snow and wind keeping all at home who were not positively obliged to be out of doors. Mother and Francie much inconvenienced on their journey back from Tottenham; already the drifted snow had made a barrier along our pavement, and they were obliged to leave the cab in the middle of the street, and pick their way through a cutting in the snow to the front door.

I gave up the children's afternoon dance, but Oakel persevered in going (by underground) to a ball somewhere in Holland Park, and found only five couples present.

Mr McCarthy having asked leave to withdraw his Motion, which was

---

[1] See appendix.

[2] 'Wolf-hound' should read 'wolf-dog'. Davitt's speech was delivered at Kilbrin near Kanturk, Co. Cork, following the banning of a meeting in the area. The 'wolf-dog', he stressed, was being held in check by the league, and would break out only if Ireland's legitimate aspirations were constantly thwarted. He added: 'repel every incentive to outrage and every inducement to give your enemies the opportunity of wiping out this movement in the blood of Irishmen'. (*F.J.*, 17 Jan.1881.)

refused, was defeated by a large majority—no English members voting in the minority of 37.[1]

19 Jan., Wed.

Papers filled with accounts of the disasters and miseries on land and sea caused by the storm—shipwrecks, trains snowed up, boiler explosions, floods in the river &c. Minor miseries, London streets impassable, snow still falling, cabs almost ceased plying—in less frequented districts a thoroughfare not opened through the snow and no wheeled thing able to pass.[2]

Lady Monteagle unable to come to lunch, but met me at the Ladies' Gallery by underground. I drove, our neighbourhood being already passable and the snow beaten into tracks.

An afternoon of Irish talk over Mr Dawson's amendment to the Address concerning Borough franchise in Ireland. The Mover spoke for 2 hours; Father followed, explaining the well-known willingness of Govt to forward such a Bill if there should be time during the Session, but their inability to bring it forward under present circumstances; the deputation that came to the Chief Secretary on the subject in Dublin a few weeks previously having expressly declared that land reform should have priority, Irish members could not now press forward with a Borough Franchise Bill on the ground of urgency.

Then followed the Parnellites, like puppets dancing to order—the same arguments, the same complaints, the same threats used by each in succession. No English Members spoke except Mr Walter James,[3] who provoked the only genuine and spontaneous speech of conviction from the other side, to wit from Mr Dillon. Finally the Amendment was talked out, without coming to a division.

A quiet evening at home, Father dining with the Speaker.

20 Jan., Th.

Papers full of the storm, and of ominous news as to the probable Greek and Turkish war. The Powers are trying to evade the responsibility of holding Turkey absolutely to the arrangement proposed by them at the Berlin Conference—France especially anxious to back out. Greece vehemently refusing to accept any frontier that does not include Janina—Turkey protesting her fervent desire for peace, but firmly refusing to cede this particular thing. Meantime both States arming, the Powers excitedly warning and lecturing each other and the two Mischief makers; something must be done to prevent war—how is the European concert to manage it?

[1] The division was 201 to 37.
[2] For reports of conditions all over Britain, see e.g. *The Times*, 19 Jan. 1881.
[3] Walter Henry James (1846–1923), liberal M.P. for Gateshead, 1874–93.

Walked with Father to the office—in the afternoon to the Hospital.

Oakel to dinner, just come from the House. Mr Dawson's Amendment disposed of at 6, Mr Parnell expressing regret that owing to his absence the division had not been taken yesterday.[1]

A quiet night with Sir Wilfrid Lawson and Basutoland.

21 Jan., Fri.

The House occupied with an interlude of discussion on the Transvaal. Mr Rylands'[2] Motion supported by himself and Mr Cartwright,[3] but not voted for by them in consequence of Mr Grant Duff's and Mr Gladstone's statements, which they considered satisfactory.

Mr Jephson and Ted to dinner.

One or two incidents connected with the agitation are rather amusing, i.e. the adjuration on a placard to members of a local Land League to come to a certain meeting 'each man in his thousands'—also Mr Synan's indignant assertion that 'so long as Ireland was silent, England was deaf to her cries'.

22 Jan., Sat.

Walked with Father to the office and brought away the rebel papers—the Fenian side to the Land League Movement seems coming into prominence.

A petition concerning the coming Land Bill signed by 20,000 Ulster farmers has been presented to Father by Mr Richardson. In spite of growing irritation at obstruction there is a persistent desire on the part of Liberal members and constituencies and the Liberal press to have a thorough Land Bill acceptable to such Irishmen as Mr Shaw and the Ulster members; the zeal for land reform is as unflagging and sincere as though Irish representatives had given no cause whatever for popular indignation in England, and the obvious ill-will and sedition preached by some Irish land reformers are not allowed to divert English Liberals from their intention to ensure sound land legislation for Ireland; calm discussion of the Three Fs, and historical disquisitions on the past wrongs and present grievances of Ireland continue to fill the magazines and newspapers.

At the same time provincial opinion as well as in London is accepting the necessity of coercion and is showing none of the signs foretold by the *Pall Mall Gazette* of a split in the party consequent on the introduction of a Coercion Bill.

In the evening Monteagle etc. to dinner: Father very tired, with the prospect of his speech impending. His bill is to be brought in on Monday.

---

[1] The division was 274 to 36.

[2] Peter Rylands (1820–87): liberal M.P. for Warrington, 1868–74; for Burnley, 1876–87.

[3] William Cornwallis Cartwright (1826–1915), liberal M.P. for Oxfordshire, 1868–85.

23 Jan., Sun.

London under snow. Father hard at work all day forging statistics and facts into shape for his speech. At last—12 p.m.—brushing his hand over his hair with a look of relief he announces to Oakel and me, who linger downstairs in the library, that he has done all he can, and has now nothing left but to try and make a good ending; this was to be done the next morning.

24 Jan., Mon.

Father and Mr West at lunch, after a final morning's work over the speech: Father in cheerful spirits not expecting to make a failure.

At 4.30 Mother and I in Mr Brand's Gallery;[1] Mrs Gladstone, Lady Spencer, Lady Ashburton, Duchess of Manchester also present. Francie in the Ladies' Gallery.

Questions till half past 5 when the Chief Secretary rose in a crowded and silent House for an hour and 40 minutes.[2] I have seldom seen a speech in the House make more evident impression on friends and foes. The appalling narration of plain facts—new to many of the listeners—the character of the speaker, the crisis marked by the very nature of these proposals coming from a Liberal Govt, the vigorous language and spirited action of a man who is known never to work himself into vehemence for the sake of mere oratorical effect—all this thrilled and astonished the audience, who only broke silence to cheer, or on the side of the Parnellites to remonstrate.

No one could help feeling that the Liberal Minister was not belying his Liberal principles by denouncing a lawful constitutional agitation, but was simply expressing in heartfelt, plain-spoken language the indignation of all honest men, English and Irish, Liberals and Conservatives, against those members of an Association or League, who, under cover of promoting a 'constitutional agitation', pursued their ends by a system of intimidation and crime.

When the Chief Secretary described by their right names the sort of men who carry out, by dint of outrage and terrorism, the 'unwritten law' of the Land League—and then, drawing himself up to his full height, and pointing his outstretched finger at the Parnellites, declared that the Member for Cork [Parnell], when this Bill were passed, 'would be unable to enforce his threats against landlords and honest farmers', 'because his policemen would be gone', the House cheered with enthusiasm; and when he sat down after expressing in words, which every one knew to be sincere, the pain and disappointment it was

[1] The gallery for visitors to the house, to which access was controlled by the speaker, H. B. W. Brand (see appendix).
[2] *Hansard 3*, cclvii, 1208–35; T. P. O'Connor comments favourably on the speech in his *Gladstone's house of commons* (London, 1885), p. 12.

to him to be compelled, after 20 years of public life to undertake the duty of bringing in this measure, it was obvious that he carried with him both the sympathies and the convictions of his audience.

Immediately after his speech Father came up to see us in the Gallery, Dr Lyons[1] being in possession of a thin House with an Amendment asking for remedies before coercive legislation.

On all hands Mother heard and received approving remarks and congratulations, amongst others from Lord Spencer and Lord Hartington, who came up also to the Gallery. Mr James Cropper was one of the first to congratulate Mother, and testify to the effect the speech had made on members sitting round him. Dr Lyons's dull oratory having soon emptied the House, we returned home to dinner at ¼ past 8. One more of these ever recurring crises in our present lives being over, there are plenty more to come.

After dinner Mother and I went back to Mrs Brand's Gallery, coming in to the middle of a clever anti-coercion speech by Mr Bradlaugh; a succession of Irish members followed, and we were at last put to flight by the uprisal of Mr O'Donnell about half past 12. We just missed unfortunately a speech from the gloomy sensitive Mr Dillon, which I should like to have heard; it must have been a most striking testimony to the impression made by the Ch. Secretary's speech[2] on a man who, with all his fierce fanatical hatred of England, is yet essentially an honest man, with whose principles and aims it would be possible to have some sympathy. He is the one man amongst Mr Parnell's followers who I fervently wish could be with us and not against us, as he is and always must be.

25 Jan., Tu.

Debate on Dr Lyons's Amendment continued. Mr. Biggar suspended, having been called to order three times.[3] The Irish retaliated by moving repeatedly the adjournment of the House.

The Govt having resolved that the division on Dr Lyons's Amendment should be taken at the close of the Tuesday's debate, arrangements were made for an all-night sitting, and after a plain exposition at 12 o'clock p.m. of the Ministerial intentions, the debate, carried on almost exclusively by the Parnellites, and varied by divisions on successive motions for adjournment, went on through the small hours of the night.

[1] Robert Spencer Dyer Lyons (1826–86): L.R.C.S.I.; liberal M.P. for Dublin City, 1880–85.
[2] Dillon had called it 'one of the most powerful he had ever heard [Forster] deliver in that house' (*Hansard 3*, cclvii, 1248).
[3] On Forster's motion for suspension; the division was 160 to 30.

26 Jan., Wed.

Father, having come home for a short interval at 6 a.m., was summoned back to the House at 8. At half past 10 Mother and I went down to the Ladies' Gallery, and as usual found Mr T. P. O'Connor in possession of the House, somewhat hoarse and haggard, and evidently wishing that he and his party were well out of the struggle over the 'lamentable incident', as Mr Biggar was always delicately styled.

In the course of the morning Mr Parnell reappeared, having just come from his 'ovation' at Dublin on the termination of the State Trials. The interest in these having quite subsided of late, the news that the jury had disagreed (two, one of them a Quaker, refusing to join in an acquittal) produced no more sensation in this country than did the eloquent speech of Mr [A. M.] Sullivan, which is said to have dissolved the Dublin audience in tears.

The debate lasted the whole morning with small incident except an encounter between the Chief Secretary and Mr Cowen.

Mr Gladstone, amidst warm approval from his own side, declined to accept an 'undertaking' made as usual by Mr Parnell to the effect that, if an adjournment were agreed to now by the Govt, the Parnellites would consent to the division on the Lyons amendment being taken without fail on Thursday; Mr Gladstone pointed out that this would happen any way since Wednesday, from a Parliamentary point of view had already disappeared and stated plainly that no bargain would be made and that the Parnellites might therefore continue moving the adjournment or vote straight off on the Amendment, just as they pleased.

Finally the last division on the adjournment was taken at 2 o'clock and the House dispersed for the day.[1]

Father, instead of being tired out with his 21 hours sitting, dined out and went afterwards with Mother to Lady Granville's. Oakel and I to a small party at the Childers's—Lord Spencer, whom we met here, told me how much interested he had been in the passage of arms between Father and Mr Cowen in the House that morning—had felt inclined to join in the cheers. The beginning of the thaw.

27 Jan., Th.

Walked with Father to the office, and brought back *Freeman*, *Irish Times* etc., to see accounts of Monday. Everywhere the effect of Father's speech upon the House is acknowledged; the cue of the Parnellites is to call it an 'inflammatory speech—an ingenious arrangement of misleading statistics—a slander of the Irish people', the object being more especially to represent the Chief Secretary

---

[1] This refers to the division on Gladstone's resolution that the protection bill should take precedence of other business; the house adopted it by 251 to 33.

as having called all members of the League as such 'village tyrants' and 'dissolute ruffians'.[1]

In the afternoon calls, and to the Hospital. Father home to dinner bringing Mr Pease.[2] It is said that Mr Parnell and Mr O'Connor Power both disapproved of the proceedings on Tuesday night—the latter on his return from the country and finding what had been going on, telling his friends plainly that they had 'been making fools of themselves' with their adjournments and obstruction over Mr Biggar's suspension.

28 Jan., Fri.

We had the pleasure of reading Mr Bright's speech. A fine utterance, which ought to do good both in Ireland and in the House; at any rate his outspoken support of the Government's Irish policy will abolish the theory that Mr Bright himself is an unwilling accomplice in the present legislation.

Meanwhile the Coercion Bill has not yet been brought in, and the country is groaning more and more with the Irish tactics. Every day the papers declare that 'something must be done'.

The Govt has been collecting information concerning the working of the 'clôture' in foreign Assemblies. Mr Thorold Rogers[3] and Lord E. Fitzmaurice have been exhuming and publishing ancient precedents for the suppression of obstructive Members, and the best friends of the Parnellites (even the *P.M. Gazette*) are warning them that Parliamentary patience is becoming exhausted.

Mother and I spent the day at Tottenham, returning in time to receive Aunt Fan, who has come to stay with us.

Father home to dinner with Mr Stansfeld. Rumour of bad news from the Transvaal.

In the evening with the Chester Square party to a dance at the Buxtons'. Oakel was to have gone with us, but instead went back with Father to the House to hear Mr Gladstone, who was expected to speak in the course of the evening. About 12 o'clock he joined me at Grosvenor Crescent. Had heard Mr Gladstone—a fine speech, but was afraid he (Mr G.) had put his foot in it. No explanation of this disagreeable intimation was possible till we were in the cab going home together at half past 2.

It appeared that, in illustration of a vehement and eloquent denunciation of the Land League system of agitation, Mr G. had read an extract from a speech

[1] 'Mr Forster, under the influence of excitement, has developed a savage vindictiveness against Ireland and Irishmen . . .' (*F.J.*, 27 Jan. 1881).

[2] Joseph Whitwell Pease (1828–1903): liberal M.P. for South Durham, 1865–85; prominent in trade, banking, and railways in north of England; brought in bill to abolish capital punishment, June 1881; first quaker to accept a baronetcy, 1881.

[3] James Edwin Thorold Rogers (1823–90): Tooke professor of statistics and economic science, King's College, London, 1859–90; liberal M.P. for Southwark, 1880–85, for Bermondsey, 1885–6; author of *History of agriculture and prices* (6 vols, Oxford, 1866–87).

purporting to have been made by Mr Parnell. The extract (one amongst a series of such passages) was handed to Mr Gladstone whilst he was speaking by Father; it was a piece of advice to tenants never to take a farm from which another had been evicted. Mr Parnell rose and violently denied that the passage quoted was from any speech of his, 'he had always said "unjustly" evicted'.

The House resenting Mr P's interruption of Mr Gladstone, who declared that the Hon. Member's memory must be fallible, for he was reading from an official report, refused to listen to any explanation and Mr Gladstone finished his speech.

As soon as it was over Father crossed straight over to Oakel who was sitting under the Gallery with horrible misgivings, lest a mistake should have been made through any blunder of his in the 'sedition' extracts. Happily the fault was not his: but it was unfortunately the case that the extract in question was not from a speech of Mr Parnell's but of some local orator (a Mr McDonnell). The fact was that an unrevised proof of the 'sedition' extracts had been allowed to go down amongst Father's papers from the office, in which the printers had omitted putting all the names of the speakers beside the passages extracted; hence the mistake. Mr Courtney,[1] in looking through the proof, lighted on the passage quoted, showed it to Father, who handed it up to Mr Gladstone.

The incident was unfortunate, but Mr Parnell was not so much misrepresented as he would have liked to make out, seeing that on other occasions he had not only sanctioned but actually used in Ireland the very expression which he so vehemently disavowed when quoted against him in the House.

29 Jan., Sat.

Walked and hansomed with Father to the office. Various annoyances: first, having unconsciously misled Mr Gladstone and prevented his accepting Mr P's explanation on the spot; secondly, by a printer's mistake the Coercion Bill has been issued prematurely, the First Reading having not yet been accomplished.

Lunched at 15 Chester Square—Coleridges, Havelock Allens, Dicksons, etc. dined with us.[2] At Mrs John Stanley's[3] afterwards Father met and had some talk with Mr O'Connor Power. Irish Members of the Parnell school are often to be

[1] Leonard Henry Courtney (1832–1918): liberal M.P. for Liskeard since 1875, and under-secretary for home office; leader-writer for *The Times*, 1865–81; professor of political economy at University College, London, 1872–5.

[2] John Duke Coleridge (1821–94): liberal M.P. for Exeter, 1865–73; solicitor general, 1868; attorney general 1871; chief justice of common pleas, 1873, and first Baron Coleridge, 1874; lord chief justice, 1880–94. Sir Henry Marshman Havelock-Allan (1830–97), V.C.: son of Sir Henry Havelock, the hero of the Indian mutiny; liberal M.P. for Sunderland since 1874. Thomas Alexander Dickson (1833–1909), liberal M.P. for Dungannon, 1874–80; for Tyrone, 1881–5; leader of Ulster liberals.

[3] See appendix.

met at Mrs Stanley's, her practice being, it is said, to invite her high Tory friends to dinner and the Home Rulers in the evening 'to see how they like it'.

30 Jan., Sun.

Father much occupied in revising in the statistics of outrages, which Mr Labouchere[1] and the Parnellites are trying to discredit and pull to pieces.

Johnny Temple and Mr Jephson to lunch; to church at St Michael's and tea at No. 15.

31 Jan., Mon.

Walked with Father to the office—some pleasant miscellaneous talk, but evidently something on his mind; only discovered just as we parted that he had that morning to come to a decision about arresting Mr Davitt.[2]

Mr Gladstone, I heard, had taken the explanation about the mistake on Friday in good part, and was much relieved at Father's at once assuming the whole responsibility and undertaking to write himself to Mr Parnell.

Rob and I came back together in a hansom.

In the afternoon Mother and Aunt Fan to the House where another all-night sitting and possibly a row expected.

Francie and I to tea at Roland Gardens. Met Mr Lucius O'Brien,[3] the clergyman of Adare. Like many others he was full of the mistake made by the Catholic clergy in yielding entirely to the Land League and countenancing intimidation and dishonesty. Even the cultivated, enlightened Father Flanagan,[4] when summoned to join the branch of the Land League at Adare, had compromised between his parishioners and his conscience by giving £1 to the band and withholding his name from the subscription list.

Mother and Aunt Fan returned from the House to dinner.

Mr Parnell had not yet spoken, though the letter to him 'from a Cabinet Minister' had been mysteriously alluded to by Mr A. M. Sullivan. Mr Parnell was expected to speak about 10, Father to follow him. After dinner I went back to the House with Mother and Aunt Fan. A bitter speech from Mr Parnell, but nothing about the letter—preparations made for an all night sitting—Father requested by the Whips to go home for an interval at 12 o'clock, Mother returning with him. Aunt Fan and I stayed till 3. Irish members arguing against

[1] Henry du Pré Labouchere (1831–1912), nephew of first Baron Taunton: in diplomatic service, 1854–65; liberal M.P. for Windsor, 1865; Middlesex, 1867–8; Northampton, 1880–1906; founded the magazine *Truth*, 1876; the radical equivalent of Lord Randolph Churchill, and in close contact with the Irish party.

[2] See Moody, *Davitt*, p. 463.

[3] Lucius H. O'Brien (1842–1913): Church of Ireland prebendary of Limerick and incumbent of Adare; son of William Smith O'Brien.

[4] John S. Flanagan, parish priest of Adare.

'indecent haste' in discussing the Bill. Mr T. P. O'Connor furious with Lord Hartington for his dry refusal to adjourn the debate; the Indian Secretary compared to Sancho Panza, and a comparison drawn between his manners and those of the absent Premier, much to the advantage of the latter.

1 Feb. 81, Tu.

Father after a sleepless night went back to the House at 8 a.m. and spent the day there. Aunt Fan and Mother to the Ladies' Gallery in the afternoon, and home to dinner at 8. Mr Parnell had not yet spoken, but was expected to do [so] about 10 when he would be followed by the Ch. Secretary.

After dinner I went down to the House with Oakel and found a seat in Mrs Brand's Gallery. Interminable repetitions from the Parnellites—Messrs Sullivan, A. O'Connor, Healy,[1] but Mr Parnell not forthcoming. At 12 Father came up for me and we started in a cab to come home together. Before getting out of Palace Yard were stopped by Mr Cotes[2] begging Father to return, for as far as he could make out Sir R. Cross[3] was in the act of proposing the 'clôture'.

I had to go home alone but was soon followed by Father—nothing had come of Sir R. Cross and the debate was still going on. Orders from Father to be called at 7, supposing the House were not up by then.

2 Feb., Wed.

Whilst at breakfast about 9.30. Father re-appeared. We ran out to meet him. 'Well, is the House up?' 'Yes, and a great deal is up besides.' It was the Speaker's Coup d'état.

During the long miserable night of obstruction and exasperation the Deputy Speaker (Mr Playfair) had been urged both from the Ministerial and Opposition benches to exercise his authority and suspend freely according to the new standing orders; his persistent toleration of the obstructionists at one moment so irritated the Opposition that Sir S. Northcote and several other Conservative members left the House in a body. Still the Parnellites were insolently and ostentatiously obstructive; still Mr Playfair took no strong measures to suppress them, still the so-called debate went on through the small hours of the night.

Shortly before 9, however, it seemed as though something were impending; the House filled, both Ministers and Opposition mustered in force; Mr Biggar, the obstructive on duty at the time still continued repeating the familiar argu-

---

[1] See appendix.

[2] Charles Cecil Cotes (1846–98): liberal M.P. for Shrewsbury, 1874–85; junior lord of the treasury.

[3] Sir Richard Assheton Cross (1823–1914): conservative M.P. for Preston, 1857–62; for Lancs. South-West, 1868–85; home secretary, 1874–80, 1885–6; notable for industrial legislation; cr. Viscount Cross, 1886.

ments of the last 40 hours; on the entrance of the Speaker, Mr Biggar, according to custom, resumed his seat, supposing that as usual the interruption was only momentary, but the Speaker remained standing, and then delivered the brief address which has suddenly made him the 'most popular man in Great Britain.

On his own responsibility he declined to call upon any more members to speak and announced that he should at once put the motion to be divided upon without further debate. The Parnellites, taken by surprise, took part in the division, and in the space of a few minutes the House found itself freed from the entangling net of organized obstruction in which it had been writhing hopelessly for the past days and weeks.

The Cabinet of course had been in the secret of the intended coup, but not even the other members of the Government; for once not a hint had leaked out as to how or when the long talked of measures against [obstruction] were to be taken.

As soon as the result of the division had been announced amidst the deeply felt cheers of the House, Mr Gladstone rose to announce that on the following day he should bring forward Resolutions for the better regulation of business in the House. The Parnellites, after standing up in their places and shouting 'privilege', left in a body.[1]

Father walked up the House and brought in the Coercion Bill, and after this exciting morning's work the House adjourned till 12 o'clock, and the Ch. Secretary came home to breakfast.

Amongst minor interests of this morning was the arrival of the Hungarian translation of my *Deák* by 'Forster Arnold Florence'.[2]

Drove with Father to the office at 11 and walked back. At 12 Mother and Aunt Fan went down to the House, the former returning to lunch; nothing particular had occurred, the debate on the Coercion Bill proceeding calmly.

A quiet afternoon at home; Father and Mother dined at the Harcourts',[3] going on afterwards to the Gladstones', and Father to the Speaker's levée.

3 Feb., Th.

Papers full of the House of Commons. General approval of the Speaker's action, but disposition to criticize Mr G.'s Resolutions as conferring too absolute power upon him (the Speaker). Various amendments and restrictions suggested.

In the afternoon to the Hospital.

Wrote a long letter to Charlotte O'Brien;[3] whilst writing this upstairs just before dinner, was called downstairs by Oakel—'bad news that would interest

---

[1] The division was 164 to 19.
[2] See above, p. xxii.
[3] See appendix.

me'. Mr Dillon suspended. There had been a great scene in the House, but no details in the evening papers. Oakel and I agreed in being sorry that it should have been Mr Dillon, thus placed in greater enmity towards us.

Uncle Matt and Aunt Fanny Lucy[1] to dinner, Father expected but did not come till so late that we had given him up. There had indeed been startling events in the House. A question from Mr Dillon[2] as to the reported arrest of Mr Davitt had set it all going.

'Was it true that Mr Davitt had been arrested?'[3] 'Yes, Sir', from Sir William Harcourt—a burst of cheering from the House. 'What conditions of his ticket-of-leave had he broken?' The Home Secretary declined to answer. The Speaker then called on Mr Gladstone to proceed with the speech in which he had begun to introduce his new Resolutions. Mr Dillon rising, the Speaker at the same time standing up, Mr Dillon refused to sit down, persisted [in] standing in grim silence, his arms folded, thereby disregarding the authority of the Chair.

The speaker thereupon named Mr Dillon, the motion that he be suspended from the service of the House being put by Mr Gladstone and the House dividing.[4]

On returning to his place after the division Mr Gladstone proceeded with his speech, but was at once interrupted by Mr Parnell who moved 'that the Prime Minister be no longer heard'.

The Speaker, ruling that by this motion Mr Parnell was guilty of wilfully obstructing the business of the House, named Mr Parnell, who, on the consequent division being taken, left the House amidst the cheers of his followers. The example set by their leader was followed by one after another of the Parnellite members, who adopted the further device of remaining in their places when the division on the motion for their several suspension was taken. For this proceeding, their names were taken down, and after being separately named by the Speaker the question of their expulsion 'en masse' was put to the vote.

When the result of the division was declared,[5] each suspended Member in turn made a little speech, denouncing the illegality of the measures taken and refusing to leave the House unless compelled by superior force.

The effect of this was to bring on the scene not only the Sergeant at Arms[6] but six aged attendants, to which display of overmastering force[7] each Member

---

[1] See appendix.

[2] Parnell, according to *Hansard 3*, cclviii, 68.

[3] Davitt's ticket of leave was revoked on 2 Feb., and he was arrested on O'Connell Bridge, Dublin, the next day about 2 p.m. (Moody, *Davitt*, pp 463–4).

[4] The division was 395 to 33.

[5] The division was 410 to 6.

[6] Captain Ralph Allen Gossett (1809?–85): son of Sir William Gossett, sergeant at arms, 1835–48; asst sergeant at arms, 1836; deputy sergeant at arms, 1854; sergeant at arms, 1875–85.

[7] 'The armed escort of the House's menials' (*F.J.*, 4 Feb. 1881).

successively yielded, after having received a touch on the arm and delivered his farewell denunciation.

After the expulsion of the principal body of the Obstructives a few remained who had not been present at the earlier stage; such were Mr O'Donnell and Mr O'Kelly, who having in turn moved 'that the Prime Minister be no longer heard', were successively named, suspended, protested, and finally 'yielding to superior force' were escorted out of the House by the Sergeant-at-Arms and his venerable assistants. The wild excitement and fury of the early part of the evening went off before the end of the two hours occupied by these strange proceedings, and the removal of the last stragglers—especially the blatant and unpopular Mr O'Donnell—finished amidst laughter rather than excitement.

The right tone must have been given to the temper of the House by Mr Gladstone's brilliant and eloquent speech, after it was all over, in which he expressed the indignation of the country against the degradation with which our Imperial Parliament had been threatened by the conduct that had reached its climax and found its punishment that night.

Distressing and trying as the scene he had just gone through must have been to Mr Gladstone both mentally and physically, there was no trace of anything but just and vigorous severity in the speech in which he brought forward his Resolutions proposing so momentous a transformation in the time-honoured customs and rules of the House of Commons.

The noble and pathetic words in which he referred at the end of his speech to the approaching close of his own public life must have moved his hearers as only such eloquent words coming from such a man as Mr Gladstone can do.

Merely as a piece of oratory unconnected with the historical crisis which called it forth, this speech will deserve to be quoted as one of the finest specimens of parliamentary eloquence which ever 'entranced'—to use Sir Stafford Northcote's expression—an English House of Commons.

The rest of the evening was spent in calm debate over the proposed Resolutions, and several important amendments suggested by the Opposition were accepted, and in a single night the House found its rules revolutionized.

The organized attempt to baffle and impede the English Parliament by using the letter of ancient observances with complete disregard of their spirit has been met by the creation of New Rules calculated to meet the new state of things.

The Obstructives in their professed regard for the forms of the House have remonstrated loudly against a course of action for which, they declare, there is no precedent—forgetting that there has also been no precedent for the conduct which made the arbitrary action of the Speaker a moral necessity.

Nevertheless the regret at our being forced thus to revolutionize our old forms and customs is very general, and there is great anxiety to do nothing which might at some future time be used against the just rights of a minority.

Of course there are already many critics to point out defects and mistakes in the method adopted of dealing with obstruction, and it is said that the absence of the Parnellite members from the debate on Mr G.'s Resolutions on Thursday night (though due as Lord Hartington observed to their own misconduct) 'will have an ugly look' in the papers. However, since the Obstructives had been warned day after day of the risk they were running, and finally forced their own expulsion upon the House, presumably for their own ends, it seems hard to blame the Govt and the great majority of the House for taking what advantage they could of the blunder committed by the Parnellites.

It is clear that the country at large, whilst as anxious as ever for fair play and justice to the Irish members, is fully prepared to support the Govt and the Speaker in their late despotic action. Thursday evening was certainly one to be remembered, and I hope not repeated.

There was a feeling of passionate excitement in the air, and one did not know what news of violence and outrage might not follow the strange scene in the House. Father evidently felt it keenly and his anxieties were not lightened by the knowledge that Michael Davitt was that night to be conveyed from Dublin to London with strong precautions against a rescue at every station, and all along the line.[1]

Even the Lobby and passages of the House were filled with police and it was thought advisable to prevent a crowd from collecting in the immediate neighbourhood of Westminster Hall.

One felt as if the events of the past few hours had raised the political temperature to boiling point, and that it was just possible there might be an explosion if the steam was not let off in some peaceful way.

4 Feb., Fri.

Walked with Oakel to Westminster Hall, and on to the Strand to see the Griffin[2]—then to his chambers at the Temple. He had been down in the Lobby for a long time the previous night, and seen a good many of the Parnellites hanging about with their press friends—some appearing angry and vehement, but others regarding the whole affair very complacently. Mr Dillon himself has gone over to Dublin; Mr Parnell, after assisting his friends in the preparation of a Manifesto to the Irish Race,[3] to Paris.

At Oakel's chambers I was introduced to Mr Guiry, an Irish barrister; he showed us a green satin tie he had received anonymously that morning with a gold harp and 'Land League' stamped upon it. If such decorations are being

[1] He was taken to London under strong guard via Holyhead on the evening of 3 Feb., arriving early the following day. The train in which he travelled was preceded by a pilot engine as a security measure (Moody, *Davitt*, p. 464).

[2] The bronze griffin by Charles Bell Birch (1832–93), surmounting the controversial Temple Bar memorial, costing over £12,000, which had been unveiled on 8 Nov. 1880.

[3] Probably the message to the American press, reprinted in Davitt, *Fall of feudalism*, p. 304.

sent gratis to many unsympathising Irishmen in London, the League finances must needs be in good case.

Mr Cropper to 5 o'clock tea; heard from him that Father had just made his speech on the 2nd Reading. The Parnellites, with the exception of Mr Parnell and Mr Dillon, had all returned to their places and were taking part in a quiet and decorous debate—no calls to order, no excitement, no wilful obstruction. It seemed curious to feel so glad at hearing of a long speech from Mr Biggar, but there is no doubt that the situation would have seemed even more strained than it is if the Parnellites had refused to reappear in the House.

The *Freeman* passionately 'exhorts, adjures, implores' its readers to 'keep calm', but so far the escapade of the Obstructives and even the arrest of Mr Davitt do not seem likely to cause special excitement or make Mr Gray's vehement adjurations necessary.[1] He meanwhile has entirely given himself over to Mr Parnell, declaring in one of his speeches (not in the House) 'that he is ashamed of the name of Liberal'—greatly to the delight and approval of the *Nation*, *Flag of Ireland* etc.

5 Feb., Sat.

Received a long letter from Charlotte O'Brien, very angry with us, and full of evil prophecies.

Drove with Father to the office—he silent and absorbed, but not from any specially bad news of that morning.

Lena Crofton and Dr Perry to lunch. In the afternoon to Twickenham to spend Sunday at the Grant Duffs'. Found there, Dr Farquharson, Dr Webster, Mr Errington (M.P. for Longford), and a Mr and Mrs Pearson.

The Death of Carlyle announced in the evening papers.[2]

6 Feb., Sun.

A brilliant day but bitterly cold.

To church in the morning at the old parish church of Twickenham.

Read the Irish (Rebel) papers, which are furious against Mr Bright.

After lunch walked with Father, Mr Grant Duff, the Pearsons, Dr Farquharson, Lord Dalhousie, Mr Errington, and a collie called Flora, in Richmond Park.

Mr Errington[3] is a Roman Catholic Home Ruler (?), M.P. for Longford, a lively, much travelled man about town, having, I should think, little sympathy

[1] 'We speak the language of studied moderation. ... The reign of terror has arrived. No one knows where the next blow will be struck.' (*F.J.*, 4 Feb. 1881).

[2] He died in London on 4 Feb.

[3] See appendix. For Errington's role in communications between the papacy and the British government, see C. J. Woods, 'Ireland and Anglo-papal relations, 1880–85' in *I.H.S.*, xviii, no. 69 (Mar. 1972), pp 29–60.

with Home Rule or any other agitation, and detesting the Land League and its representatives in Parliament. He gave me an interesting account of his interview with the Pope, and his endeavours to explain that there was another side to the Irish question than that expounded to His Holiness by Archbishop Croke.

The conversation being begun by the Pope in French and turning on the weather, Mr Errington began to fear that the interview would pass without the opening he wished for being given him; so, taking the bull by the horns, he ventured to change both the subject and the language, and explained (in Italian) what a pass matters in Ireland had really come to. The Pope seemed a little annoyed at having his ideas on the subject of Ireland, recently supplied to him by Archbishop Croke, disarranged, but he was not ungracious, and sent Mr Errington upstairs then and there to state his case more fully to Cardinal Jacobini.[1] The papal utterances in *Osservatore* and *Aurora* since this interview have certainly been less obviously inspired by an Irish Land Leaguer.

7 Feb., Mon.

Reports in the papers describe the state of things in Ireland as much quieter—the Land League losing its power; in a few cases—notably Captain Stackpoole's[2]—rents have been paid without reference to Griffith's Valuation. Is the calm a dangerous sign? There are plenty of prophets to foretell that the self-extinction of the Land League will mean the creation of secret societies and Ribbonism.

No doubt the critical time will come when the Coercion Bill shall have become law, and the landlords begin collecting their March rents (as for stress of poverty many of them must do); but it may be hoped that, now that some beginning of payment—and therefore defiance of League Law—has already begun, the outbreak of revolt and outrage will be confined at least to isolated cases, and not become general throughout the country.

The parliamentary fiasco of the Parnellites on Thursday may have made the people (or at any rate the press) very indignant, but its effect in showing the hollowness of Mr Parnell's bombastic language concerning the English Parliament will be very wholesome. The belief in his power to dictate to the Govt and the House, and to paralyze their action by the double method of well-planned obstruction in Parliament and intimidation in Ireland, will be rudely shaken by recent events. In proportion as the belief of the mass of the peasantry in his power to gratify their wildest dreams is diminished, will the possibility of pacifying the country by a strong and just Land Bill increase.

---

[1] Luigi Jacobini (1832–87): nominated cardinal-priest, 1879; secretary of state to the papacy.

[2] Richard Stackpoole of Edenvale, Ballyalla: owner of 1,381 acres in Clare, valued at £2,641; for his relations with his tenants, see Becker, *Disturbed Ireland*, pp 153–9, 165, 181.

Received a letter from Pesth and translation of the preface to my *Deák* from Mr Pulzsky. It is a pleasure to hear that the book has already done a good work, as its appearance has decided the Committee of the Franklin Publishing Company to undertake the edition of Deák's collected speeches.

8 Feb., Tu.

Accounts from Ireland (in the papers at least) still fairly satisfactory.

Mother and Francie to Tottenham. I walked with Father to the office—much pleasant talk; on going out he stopped to speak to the policeman who is now stationed here.

In various public places precautions are being taken, chiefly against dynamite outrages. The use of dynamite has been freely recommended by the *Irish World*, and though respectable members of the League scout the idea of outrages forming part of their programme there is no doubt that the *Irish World* is now recognised as the organ of the Land League, and admirers and readers of such a paper cannot be supposed incapable of occasionally attempting to practise the crimes there inculcated.

Having secured the *Freeman*, *Irish Times* and *Express* at the office, and found Oakel there, I walked with him to the Temple.

We do not agree on the subject of Mr Davitt. I am inclined to believe he is what one of the papers called him 'a peasant Mazzini', and though glad he is shut up at a time like this, am also glad that he should be spared personal degradation as a convict. Oakel considers him nothing less than a murderer, and says with much truth that the trumpeter is quite as guilty as the man whom he stirs up to violence. There is no doubt, I believe, that Mr Davitt was known to have circulated arms (not rifles, but revolvers, the weapons of assassination) and that he was privy to the attack upon Chester Castle—a most clear attempt at murder. At the same time I cannot get rid of the impression that with all his reckless revolutionary ideas of the laws both of the State and of civilization, Davitt is not the sort of man who would be rightly punished or in any way reformed by subjecting him to the same prison discipline and degrading regulations as are suitable and necessary for an ordinary convict.

It may be necessary in the interests of society on some future occasion to hang or transport Mr Davitt, and this he probably is prepared for; but in the meantime, whilst absolutely disagreeing with his views and restraining him from enforcing them, I hope our authorities will treat him with the consideration and respect due to a man who is self-denying, courageous, and sincerely conscientious—according to the lurid light by which he guides his actions.[1]

---

[1] Davitt was in fact treated with special consideration, on the instructions of Harcourt, the home secretary, during his second term of imprisonment, in Portland (Feb. 1881–May 1882) (Moody, *Davitt*, ch. XII).

Father and Mr Maskeleyne[1] to dinner. In the evening Aunt Fan and I to the House. A quiet debate on the Second Reading; the division was expected but the Parnellites moved the adjournment, mainly as usual on the ground of 'indecent haste', and also of Mr Parnell's absence owing to the weather.

After a division (420 to 40)[2] another Motion for the adjournment. The Speaker refraining from using his new powers, and the House being conscious of its ability now to free itself when it should think necessary, Mr Gladstone consented to the demand, and the House rose between 1 and 2 o'clock. Father came up to fetch us and we returned in an undignified manner—three in a hansom.

Mr Parnell is said to have gone to Frankfort, but his movements are mysterious, and unknown even to his confederates.

9 Feb., Wed.

The proposed Convention of the Parnellites is postponed. Mr Dillon has been speaking at Dublin[3] on the arrest of Davitt, and advising as to what the people are to do in the event of Land League leaders being arrested, or landlords proving insolent *in re* Mr Davitt—'organize a strike against rent, and protest by all means in their power—how, not specified—they will find out ways for themselves; meantime the time has not yet come for resistance by physical force'.

Mr Dillon's theory is that Mr Davitt has been arrested by the English Govt in order to provoke the Irish to acts of violence and facilitate the passing of the Coercion Act; consequently the best way to spite the Govt will be for the people to remain calm, and abstain from outrages. This is a most fortunate line of argument.

I went into Lillington Street in the afternoon and called on the Wyvills; saw on the placards 'Repulse of the Boers. British loss of 150 men.' The news is worse than this would have led one to suppose.

Sir G. Colley[4] on his way to the relief of Pretoria with a force of 800 men— anxious about his communications with Newcastle—had engaged the Boers with half his force on the road between Laing's Nek and Newcastle. The Boer riflemen planted skilfully behind cover on the surrounding heights had done terrible execution upon our small force, the guns being unable to come into play against them, and the gunners shot down in quick succession as they came forward to serve them.

Our small force narrowly escaped annihilation or surrender, and the Boers

---

[1] Mervyn Herbert Nevil Story-Maskelyne (1823–1911): F.R.S.; professor of mineralogy at Oxford; liberal M.P. for Cricklade, 1880–86; his daughter Mary married Oakeley in 1885.

[2] The division was 422 to 44.

[3] At the weekly meeting of the central Land League on 8 Feb. (*F.J.*, 9 Feb.).

[4] Major-general Sir George Pomeroy Colley (1835–81): of Co. Dublin family; first served in South Africa, 1854, later in China and Ashanti; accomplished watercolourist; military secretary to viceroy of India, 1876–9; K.C.S.I., 1879; commander in Natal since Apr. 1880.

are said to have been equally surprised and disappointed on finding at day-break that the remnant of the English had recrossed the Ingogo river and regained their camp.

The telegraphic account from the *Standard* correspondent at Newcastle has been most graphic—the anxiety and excitement amongst the inhabitants—the reinforcements not yet able to come to their relief, and the victorious Boers expected every moment to appear in sight.

This war is most depressing—all parties regret it equally, and yet there is a pretty general agreement that the Boers cannot be allowed to set up their very questionable Republic again simply on the strength of their having over-mastered the inadequate number of British residents and soldiers left in the Transvaal after the annexation.

By the original opponents of annexation, and by those who now wish to be out of the Transvaal on any terms, it is asserted that President Burger[s][1] and his colleagues in the Pretoria Govt did not truly represent the wishes of their countrymen when they consented to a voluntary annexation to the British Empire; that the English governor at Pretoria—Sir W. O. Lanyon[2]—justified the antipathy of the Boers to British rule by his unwise and arbitrary conduct; and finally, that the Boers are in the position of a free people struggling to regain their independence, and should therefore excite the sympathy and admiration, not the hostility of a Nation which has always professed more than any other to appreciate the blessings of political freedom.

This line is eagerly taken up by the Boers themselves, who have issued various 'Proclamations and Manifestos' to this effect; and also by sympathizers on the Continent—notably the Dutch, who have circulated a largely signed petition of the Boers amongst English M.P.s.

How far the demand of the Boers can be complied with effectually is a question that can hardly be discussed until our military disasters have been retrieved. Meanwhile the position of Sir G. Colley is critical, and news of the arrival of the reinforcements is anxiously looked for.

The Protection Bill to-day passed the 2nd Reading, the debate, which the Parnellites had insisted so earnestly on adjourning the night before, having run itself out sooner than was expected; the division thus came on earlier than was expected, and several Members arrived too late to vote.[3]

Oakel and I dined at Lady Monteagle's—met the Frederick Myers,[4] she very handsome in red velvet with a diamond crescent in her dark hair; also Mr

---

[1] Thomas François Burgers (1834–81): president of the Transvaal from July 1872 to the British annexation in Apr. 1877, which he did not actively oppose.

[2] Sir William Owen Lanyon (1842–87): administrator of the Transvaal since 1879; K.C.M.G., 1880; eldest son of Sir Charles Lanyon (1813–89), civil engineer and architect of roads, railways, and public buildings (including Queen's College, Belfast) in the north of Ireland.

[3] The debate ended at about 4 p.m.; the division was 359 to 56.

[4] Frederic William Henry Myers (1843–1901): poet, inspector of schools, and investigator of psychic phenomena.

Errington just come from the House. The question is still being vainly asked 'Where is Mr Parnell?'—the story that Mr Egan the Treasurer of the Land League has absconded with the funds, and that Mr Parnell is scouring Europe in pursuit, is, it is to be feared, too good to be true.[1]

10 Feb., Th.

In the afternoon to the Hospital, and to call on Agnes Ward.[2] Father in Committee and unable to come home to dine.

11 Feb., Fri.

Spent the morning with Lucy. In the evening to a dance at the Childers' with Mother, Aunt F[anny] L[ucy], Lucy and Oakel. Various arrivals from the House during the evening report Father 'left fighting' in Committee, and making some progress with the Amendments, of which there are more than 100.

Lady Holland[3] had come on from a party at Mrs John Stanley's, where she had been sitting at dinner next Mr Justin McCarthy, who was pathetic as usual over the social deprivations which obedience to his political principles had brought upon him.

Rumour of intention to blow up Windsor.

12 Feb., Sat.

Farewell visit to Aunt Fan from Ted and the Chester Squares. Uncle Matt and Nelly had also been at Mrs Stanley's party, where Uncle Matt's combined short-sightedness and amiability had caused him to make a very remarkable assertion. Seeing Nelly talking to Miss Justin McCarthy (whom she had been introduced to last year), he also went up to shake hands with her under the impression that the young lady was a Miss Bartle Frere[4]—'I hope you feel with my father?' enquired Miss McCarthy with her usual enthusiasm. 'Oh certainly I do', said Uncle Matt, 'but so does everybody'. An agreeable announcement which must have surprised even Miss McCarthy herself.

Departure of Aunt Fan and Francie for Woodhouse and Cathedine.

News in the papers that the Duke of Leinster's tenants have voluntarily paid their rents irrespective of Griffith's Valuation.

[1] Egan moved to Paris on 3 Feb. and there continued to function as treasurer of the Land League till Oct. 1882.

[2] Agnes Ward, sister of Humphry Ward, who married Mary Augusta Arnold, daughter of Thomas Arnold and granddaughter of Dr Thomas Arnold (see appendix).

[3] Margaret Jean, eldest daughter of Sir Charles Trevelyan, and second wife of Sir Henry Thurstan Holland (see appendix).

[4] Sir Henry Bartle Edward Frere (1815–84): governor of Cape Colony and first high commissioner of South Africa, had been censured during the Zulu war for exceeding instructions, and recalled to England in July 1880 for his conduct of the Transvaal question.

In one or two other places—notably on Captain Stackpoole's estate—the tenants have done the same, thereby encouraging the hope that when the dreaded time of March comes the revolt against rent paying will not be general all through the country. There are some signs that the all-pervading power of the Land League is waning, or rather that the power to enforce its decrees irrespective of justice or reason is diminishing.

The newly started Property Defence Association[1] is vigorously carrying out combined proceedings against well-to-do defaulters in the matter of rent. A tenant on Lord Digby's estate at Geashill[2]—a notorious example of the successful defiance of legal obligations during the autumn—having been served with a notice of bankruptcy, has after some demur paid his debts quietly; and in some cases of those who have finally refused to pay, the P.D. Association has undertaken the sale of their goods, themselves creating a demand and succeeding in realizing enough money to furnish the required rent.

Mr Parnell not back yet; much gossip in the House on the subject.

Father back from the Cabinet, and his game of whist in good spirits; dined with Mother at the Miss Hollands'; Oakel and I after a tête-à-tête tea joined them there and went on to a large party at Spencer House, where Father had much lively talk with the Prince of Wales.

13 Feb., Sun.

Father went with us to church at St James the Less. Afterwards to Lord Granville's to meet Sir W. Harcourt and consult about the answer to be given the next day to the charge of 'tampering with letters' at the Post Office.

In the afternoon walked with Father and Mother to Grosvenor Crescent. Met Mr Trevelyan,[3] just come from seeing the Anti-Coercion meeting in the Park, about half the people wearing Radical Clubs and old Tichborne banners etc.[4]

To tea at No. 15—met Mr S. Coleridge, Mr Rollo Russell and Bernard Holland[5]—every one had been to the Demonstration in the Park, which

[1] Founded in Dec. 1880, under the chairmanship of James George Henry Stopford (1823–1914), 5th earl of Courtown, the association was designed to provide landlords with a defence and counter-attack against the Land League.

[2] In King's County (now Offaly), where Lord Digby owned 29,722 acres valued at £12,745.

[3] See appendix.

[4] Between 50,000 and 100,000 people were estimated to have attended this meeting in Hyde Park, London, radical and labour associations being strongly represented. A similar meeting had been held the previous night in Sunderland (*The Times*, 14 Feb. 1881). The 'Tichborne banners' were relics of the widespread popular sympathy for Arthur Orton (1834–98), who returned from Australia in 1866 claiming to be the lost heir of the wealthy Tichborne family. After protracted and enormously expensive litigation, Orton was sentenced in 1874 to fifteen years' hard labour for perjury.

[5] Stephen William Buchanan Coleridge (1854–1936), second son of John Duke Coleridge (see above, p. 60). Francis Albert Rollo Russell (1849–1914), third son of the first Earl Russell; writer

appears to have been good humoured and orderly, but not impressive from a political point of view.

On returning home found Sydney Buxton calling at No. 80—he had been at the meeting, planted near the waggonette from which Mr Redmond[1] and Mr T. P. O'Connor[1] had been speaking back to back in order to address different portions of the crowd; there was no hooting and no special display of feeling of any kind.

The attempt of one of the orators to add dramatic effect to his address by burning a copy of the Bill unsuccessful owing to the wind. 'What shall I do with it?' the speaker had exclaimed waving the paper. 'Burn it!', said a voice from the crowd; matches were produced, but the Bill would not light even when protected by the orator's hat against the wind, and finally it had to be torn up.

14 Feb., Mon.

All day with Mother at Tottenham.

15 Feb., Tu.

Father much worried and anxious: Committee work is very trying and exhausting.

In the evening with Mother and Oakel to Lady Holland's. People full of Sir F. Roberts's speech on Monday at the Guildhall[2] denouncing our present Army system and the evils of short service; general feeling of respect for Gen. Roberts's opinion, but surprise that he should have taken a neutral opportunity when he was the guest of the evening to abuse a system for which the Commander in Chief and the War Minister (both present) were responsible. Oakel is delighted, having long been convinced of the defects and dangers of short service as at present worked in our Army. There is no doubt that Sir F. Roberts's speech whether well-timed or not has produced a great impression.

16 Feb., Wed.

Father much oppressed. A dense yellow fog—breakfast by candle light.

Mr Parnell heard of at last in Paris having interviews with Rochefort[3] and Victor Hugo[4]—explaining to them that his object was to obtain from England,

and meteorologist. Bernard Henry Holland (1856–1926): called to the bar, 1882; later private secretary to Lord Hartington and author of *Life of Spencer Compton Cavendish, marquis of Hartington and eighth duke of Devonshire* (London, 1911).

[1] See appendix.
[2] At the Guildhall, Roberts had been presented with the freedom of the City of London and a sword of honour; his speech was made at a Mansion House banquet in the evening, and argued strongly that Britain's small volunteer army could not be run on the continental system.
[3] Victor Henri, marquis de Rochefort-Lucay (1831–1913): French radical journalist, author and politician; founder and editor of *L'intransigeant*.
[4] The great French poet and novelist (1802–85).

of course by 'legal and constitutional means', the system prevailing in Austria–Hungary.

Nelly Boyle[1] to lunch. Ordered our things for the Drawing Room. Shaw Lefevres,[1] Smalleys, Edward O'Briens, Algernon West, Col. Colthurst, and Mr W. Livingstone to dinner.[2]

Father back from the House very tired and disheartened—'one of the worst days he has had'—the Parnellites behaving very badly, refusing to give him the opportunity to explain the intended treatment of prisoners under the Coercion Act. They persisted in keeping up an endless debate over an amendment concerning the flooring and boarding of prison cells to which the Govt could not agree, and on which it was impossible for the Ch. Secretary (owing to the New Rules) to make a second explanation or do more than repeat, what he had stated before, that at a later stage, if they would allow him to arrive at it, he would gladly describe in detail the arrangements made for the humane treatment of prisoners under the Act.

After our own party, Mother and I went on to Lady Harcourt's and Mrs Brand's. Everyone full of sympathy for the Ch. Secretary, and compassion for him in the way he is being treated, even Radicals like Mr T. B. Potter and Mr Arthur Arnold[3] making anxious enquiries of Mother concerning his health, Mr Potter declaring that the behaviour of the Parnellite Irish had the effect of shaking his democratic principles.

A good deal of criticism on the Speaker's new Rules—suggestions that new Amendments should not be allowed to be perpetually brought forward, but must be put on the paper at the beginning of the Committee.

17 Feb., Th.

All day with Mother at Tottenham. Father in Committee and not able to return home to dinner. Mr Parnell took his seat again in the House this evening. He has issued a Manifesto from Paris stating his line of policy, 'constitutional struggle'—'appeal to the Democracy in England against the landlord class and "shopocracy" represented in the present Parliament'—'vehement adjuration to the tenant farmers of Ireland not to "discredit the cause" by giving way', etc. etc.[4]

[1] See appendix.

[2] George Washburn Smalley (1833–1916): European correspondent for *New York Tribune*, 1870–95; edited Bright's speeches, 1868. Algernon Edward West (1832–1921): private secretary and close friend to Gladstone; commissioner of inland revenue since 1872; chairman of inland revenue board, 1881; father of Forster's assistant private secretary, Horace West. Col. Colthurst is perhaps Lt-col. David La Touche Colthurst (b. 1828), home rule M.P. for Cork County, 1879–85.

[3] Thomas Bayley Potter (1817–98): liberal M.P. for Rochdale, 1865–95; ardent champion of free trade and abolition of slavery; founder of Cobden Club. Arthur Arnold (1833–1902): liberal M.P. for Salford, 1880–85; author of *Free Land* (1880), *Social politics* (1881).

[4] Parnell's manifesto, in the form of a letter dated 13 Feb. to the Land League, replying to a request that he should visit the U.S.A., is in *F.J.* and *The Times*, 17 Feb.

It will be curious to see how far Mr Parnell's latest move— the attempt to establish a centre of Irish agitation amongst French Radicals and Communists—will advantage his position with the Irish farmers. Victor Hugo with whom he dined in Paris has had the Land League or Parnellite view of the Irish question fully placed before him by Mr Parnell and Mr O'Kelly, and has promised to write an ode in their favour to be entitled 'L'Oppresseur et l'Oprimée'.

On the one hand it is said that his new friends will cause scandal amongst Irish Catholics (a feeling to which Mr H. Bellingham[1] has just given expression in a letter to the *Times*);[2] on the other hand, the O'Donoghue[3] has replied to this that religious differences count for nothing in the present movement; it has further been stated that the 'popular party' in Dublin highly approve of the overtures lately made for French sympathy by the Land League Chief in Paris.

Mr Parnell's character and intentions are still the subject of much speculation: is he a determined revolutionary, or a sensitive and pliable fanatic? Has he perfectly made up his own mind what to do, and if he has, will he have courage—moral and physical—to face all the possible contingencies of his policy?

Why does he shirk the House, and leave his followers to struggle on with the system of organized parliamentary obstruction of which he is the author? One thing at any rate is certain: his personal hatred of the Chief Secretary is as keen as ever; he descended to depths of coarse abuse and allusion on Friday night of which one would not have thought an educated gentleman to be capable.

Received a long letter this evening from Mr Edward O'Brien saying that things were not so hopeless as might appear, and that Mr Forster would not be permanently hated in Ireland.

18 Feb., Fri.

An excellent letter in the papers this morning from Mr Shaw to the Bishop of Cloyne, speaking in terms as vigorous as their own of the Parnellites' obstructives and agitators, the result of whose policy is infinitely to diminish the chance of steady and lasting parliamentary reform for Ireland.[4]

Walked with Father to the office. I told him what Mr O'Brien had said; he was interested and thought there was some truth in it, but all the same there was no doubt his connection with the Coercion Bill would make him 'tabooed'

---

[1] Alan Henry Bellingham (1846–1921): private chamberlain to Pope Leo XIII; home rule M.P. for Louth Co., 1880–85.

[2] *The Times*, 17 Feb. 1881; the brief letter appeared under the heading 'Irish members and French communists'. Archbishop McCabe, in his Lenten instruction to the Dublin clergy a few days later, called the search for 'impious infidels' as allies 'a calamity more terrible and humiliating than any that has yet befallen' Ireland (*The Times*, 23 Feb.).

[3] Daniel O'Donoghue (1833–89), liberal M.P. for Tralee, 1865–85, changing his party label to 'home rule' in 1880.

[4] *The Times*, 18 Feb. The catholic bishop of Cloyne was John MacCarthy (1815–94).

in Ireland; he thinks that after they have done the Land Bill he shall give up at the beginning of next year.

On the whole a pleasant walk and much conversation concerning last night's debate and miscellaneous affairs.

Mr Jackson to lunch.

In the afternoon with Mother to Lady Collier's[1] 5 o'clock tea in the studio. The pictures by Mr John Collier and his handsome young wife (née Miss Huxley)[2] are very striking.

I drove with Father to the Office and left him at Downing Street for an early Cabinet.

Lunched with Amy Mulholland.

22 Feb., Tu.

A day of yellow fog. Francie in bed with cold. Drove with Mother in the afternoon. In the evening with O. to an evening party at Lady Holland's; heard that Father was getting on well with the Bill. Lady Young[3] asked if it was true that we all of us hated being in Dublin, and had said that we should never go back there; she hoped not for she had made bets that 6 months hence Mr Forster would be the most popular man in Ireland.

I had some amusing talk with M. Mori, the Japanese Minister. He had been in the House the night of the suspension of the obstructives. I suggested that he might congratulate himself on not having Parliamentary Govt in Japan; he seemed on the contrary quite to anticipate the prospect, but observed that, when they set up a Parliament, it would be copied from all the best models.

23 Feb., Wed.

Mr Parnell has written to the Sec. of the Clara Land League, retracting publicly the advice he gave the tenants to plough up their landlords' ground before leaving.[4] He states that he has since discovered that such an act would be illegal and though the law prohibiting it is 'iniquitous', he will not be responsible for advising the people to do anything contrary to the law.

Mother all day at Tottenham. She and Father were to have dined at M. House, but Father received counter orders to dine and sleep at Windsor.

---

[1] Isabella, wife of Sir Robert Porrett Collier (1817–86), a member of the judicial committee of the privy council, and himself a painter of note.

[2] John Collier (1850–1934), son of the preceding, had been exhibiting at the Royal Academy since he was 25; he married Marian, daughter of T. H. Huxley, in 1879.

[3] Alice Eacy (née Kennedy), of Dublin, wife of Sir George Young (see below, p. 88) since 1871; 'beautiful, witty, and most lovable woman' (*D.N.B.*).

[4] The advice was given at a mass meeting at Clara (King's County) on 20 Feb.; the object was to prevent the land from being turned over to grazing.

24 Feb., Th.

Mr Dillon in speaking at a Meeting of the Land League in Dublin[1] announced
that he had received orders from Mr P. to postpone the Meeting fixed for the
following Sunday, on the ground that the Coercion Bill would not be law by
that time, and that it would be well to have the Land Bill also to comment upon.
Mr Parnell's conduct is said to be very trying to his Parliamentary friends who
are kept in total ignorance of his whereabouts and his intentions. Mr Dillon is
at present doing the practical business of the League; in Dublin in his last
speech he protested eagerly against the statement now current that the tenants
are beginning to pay their rents, and declared that the report was due to a
conspiracy on the part of the English newspapers. He concurred that in some
cases large farmers with a great deal to lose had paid their rents rather than be
evicted, but he denied that their example was being widely followed throughout the country.[2]

Lunched with Julia and afterwards walked with her and Rob to Mrs
Smalley's. Heard from Mr E. O'Brien that Sir W. Gregory[3] lately returned
from Galway is creating quite a panic at the Athenaeum by his gloomy accounts
of the state of feeling in Ireland, and still gloomier prophecies as to the eventual
outcome of the embittered relations between classes and races.

He declares we are fast approaching separation, that the hatred of the Irish
against England and the English Govt is intense, and that at the next election
Parnell's following will be largely increased. Sir William is not influenced by
depression at not getting his rents, for they have been paid; in fact this is the
case in many places. Mr O'Brien hears the same from a bailiff in Limerick.

The afternoon placards announced 'accident to Mr Gladstone'. In getting
out of his carriage the previous night he had slipped and fallen with his head
against the step. The wound bled a good deal and thereby prevented inflamma-
tion, but the shock and the fear of cold will oblige Mr Gladstone to keep his
room for some days. There is the deepest anxiety and sympathy felt on all sides,
and the absence of the Prime Minister from the House at this time is greatly
regretted. He was to have made a statement as to the intended course of
business on Friday night, but this has been postponed.

25 Feb., Fri.

The debate of the previous night was signalized by a damaging exposure by Sir
W. Harcourt of the close connection and sympathy between the Irish Land
League and the atrocious doctrines of the Irish-American[s][4] represented by
such speakers as Devoy and Redpath, and such papers as the *Irish World*.

[1] On 23 Feb. 1881.
[2] *F.J.* and *The Times*, 24 Feb. 1881.
[3] See appendix.
[4] Harcourt had first raised this topic on 22 Feb. (*Hansard 3*, cclviii, 1553–5).

Mr A. M. Sullivan made a clever speech disavowing all responsibility for such a maniac as Devoy,[1] and ignoring the Home Secretary's other charges of complicity between the Americanized ruffians of this stamp and the professed 'constitutional agitators' in Ireland.

The Govt makes no secret of their belief in an organized Fenian conspiracy, but it is only rarely that Mr Healy and his associates in the House are publicly confronted with their disreputable acquaintance—whom they hasten as publicly to disavow.

Mother and I to the Drawing Room. Small but very pleasant and sociable.

In the evening to the House to hear the end of the Coercion Bill, fixed for this night. When we got down Sir J. McKenna[2] was speaking and was soon followed by Mr Cowen, who after some laudatory remarks on Mr Forster's general character compared him to Robespierre, and declared that the liberties of the people could no more be safely entrusted to his keeping than to those of the French Republican.

Mr Cowen has great natural eloquence, and very strong convictions, which he expresses in carefully prepared language, and with balanced phrases. He is a favourite in the House where his tendency to run counter to his own party, and his vigorous North country dialect, have gained him a reputation for honesty and originality.

He has formed an alliance with the Parnellites in the matter of the Coercion Bill, and delights his Irish friends by the oratorical fervour of his attacks upon the present Ministry, and especially the Ch. Secretary.

Mr Cowen's paper the *Newcastle Chron[icle]* is almost the only Liberal organ which has opposed the Govt in every part of their policy, coercion and the clôture. It does not appear that in this case Mr Cowen represents the general opinion of the working men whose champion and mouthpiece he has so often been hitherto.

The unanimity of the Provincial press in support of the Govt has been remarkable.

Nevertheless the prolongation of coercive legislation is a trying ordeal for the loyalty of Mr Gladstone's Radical supporters.

After a short speech from Mr T. D. Sullivan, Father rose to make his last speech on the Protection alias the Coercion Bill. He spoke with great vigour and replied most effectively to Mr Cowen's attacks and insinuations. He took the opportunity of declaring and dwelling emphatically in plain language, specially intended for the benefit of Irish readers, on the failure of Mr Parnell and his colleagues to keep their promise of making coercion an impossibility.

[1] John Devoy (1842–1928): joined I.R.B., 1861; organiser of Fenianism in British army in Ireland, 1865–6; imprisoned, Feb. 1866; amnestied, Jan. 1871, spending rest of his life in New York journalism; 'the most clear-headed, realistic, implacable, and incorruptible of the Fenian leaders' (Moody, *Davitt*, p. 136); cooperated with Davitt in 'new departure', 1878.

[2] Sir Joseph Neale McKenna (1819–1906): liberal conservative M.P. for Youghal, 1865–8; home rule M.P. for Youghal, 1874–85.

He has long felt and said in private that nothing did so much to keep up the violence of the agitation in Ireland as the belief of the peasantry in Mr Parnell's power to baffle the English Parliament, and he was glad to speak his mind on this subject in public. As to Mr Parnell himself, he referred to his continued absence from the House in a significant sentence which raised a loud cheer. At the same time, whilst pointing out the futility of Mr Dillon's boast of making Coercion impossible, he spoke of the Member for Tipperary with the respect which is generally felt for this honest and melancholy desperado.

The Ch. Sec. was followed by Mr T. P. O'Connor, a jovial eloquent young man who is hail fellow well met with all parties in the lobby, and in the House— can render valuable assistance to his friends by turning on a copious stream of oratory, pathetic, indignant or derisive, on any subject at a moment's notice. This evening he was mainly derisive, the chief object of his wrath being the Liberal Ministers—to wit, Mr Mundella[1] and Mr Chamberlain who had especially disappointed the hopes of their Irish constituents by their acquiescence in the Coercion Bill.

After a special denunciation of Mr Bright, Mr Ch[amberlain] was referred to as the one Minister who 'if he had not the courage of his convictions, had at least the silence of his shame',[2] a doubtful compliment which Mr C. can hardly have appreciated.

Mother and I left before the Division, not particularly wishing to hear our yell of triumph.

By some ingenuity of obstruction the Parnellites contrived to have 4 divisions before the Bill finally passed, their minority decreasing each time.[3] This curious procedure was no doubt intended to please constituents at home, to whom it would be represented in the desirable light.

Father followed Mother and me home in about an hour, and on finally separating for the night we had the pleasure of thinking that the special troubles and disagreeables of this particular epoch are over. It is not probable that Father will ever have to fight another Coercion Bill through the House.

It may be hoped that the next service he is able to render Ireland will be one that is less unpleasant in the execution.

Father goes to Dublin on Sunday; uncertain whether I go or not.

---

[1] Anthony John Mundella (1825–97): hosiery manufacturer; radical M.P. for Sheffield, 1868–85, and for Brightside division of Sheffield, 1885–97; cooperated with Forster in passing education act, 1870, and factories act, 1874; privy councillor 1880; as vice-president of council committee for education, introduced compulsory education bill, 1881.

[2] *Hansard 3*, cclviii, 1830, reads 'at any rate' instead of 'at least'.

[3] The four divisions were successively 321:51; 303:46; 282:32; and 281:36. Arthur O'Connor had attempted to move a further amendment, and F. H. O'Donnell had been stopped from speaking.

26 Feb., Sat.

Walked and hansomed with Father to the office; heard that he is going to stay at the C.S. Lodge whilst in Dublin and means to take me.

Went with Oakel in the afternoon to tea with Amy Mulholland. Father to dine with Lord Spencer in the evening, Mother and I to see the 'Cup'[1] at the Lyceum, and afterwards to a party at Spencer House.

Met Mr Errington; though forced to vote against the Coercion Bill, he rejoices in any check to the L. League which he detests most cordially; he could not stand my saying I had not wished to hear our cheer over the last division. I have heard since that he got behind a neighbour in order to be able to cheer heartily himself. According to him Mr Gray and the *Freeman* are tending to an abandonment of extreme Parnellism.

The Arms Bill is not to be postponed after all. There had been rumours to this effect and the Tories were getting very angry. Sir W. Harcourt brings it in on Tuesday. Mr Havand [Howard] has beaten Mr L[owther] by 30.[2]

27 Feb., Sun.

To church at St James the Less. Father at Sir W. Harcourt's with Mr Cullinan.[3] Mr Jephson preparing the Arms Bill.[4]

In the afternoon to St Peter's and then to 15 Chester Sq. Visit from Uncle Matt. Dinner at 7, and then with Father and Oakel to Euston. A quick journey and fine passage.

28 Feb., Mon.

On arriving at Kingsto[w]n, we were taken aback by seeing in the papers the terrible news of the defeat and death of General Colley.

For days we have been expecting decisive news, but the best was hoped, there being every reason to suppose that the reinforcements brought by Sir E. Wood[5] would enable Sir G. Colley to regain successfully the strong position of Laing's Nek where 7000 Boers were said to be entrenched.

[1] Play by Tennyson.

[2] George James Howard (1843–1911): nephew and heir of 8th earl of Carlisle; became 9th earl, 1889; liberal M.P. for Cumberland East, 1879–80; reelected on 26 Feb., beating James Lowther by 3071 votes to 3041 and making the constituency all-liberal.

[3] Probably William F. Cullinan, draftsman of bills at the Irish office in London.

[4] The arms bill received the royal assent on 21 Mar. 1881 as the Peace Preservation (Ireland) Act, 1881 (44 & 45 Vict., c. 5). It was originally to last to 1 June 1886, but was subsequently prolonged to 31 Dec. 1906. The act was applied by proclamation in specified areas, providing for regulating the possession, of use of, and trade in arms and ammunition, for search and arrest in cases where improper possession or use was suspected, and for punishment by 3 months' imprisonment or a fine of £20.

[5] Major-general Sir Henry Evelyn Wood (1838–1919): V.C., served in India, Crimea, Ashanti; called to the bar, 1874; served in Zulu war, 1879; commander of Belfast military district, 1879–80; K.C.B., 1879; second-in-command to Colley.

So far from a success we have met with a most disastrous defeat. Whilst Sir E. Wood was at Pietermaritzberg, Sir G. Colley with a force of 600 men left his camp early on Sunday morning [27 February] and succeeded by dint of a severe climbing march in establishing himself in a strong position on one of the high rocky plateau in the Majuba Mountains.

Here he was attacked by the Boers but for several hours the cover afforded by the rocks round the edge of the plateau was so complete that only three casualties occurred.

By this time however, the Boers had received large reinforcements, and poured a tremendous fire into the defending force, and finally stormed the British stronghold, driving out our troops and compelling them to retire towards the camp under a hail of bullets.

Of 600 men only about 100 returned to the camp from which their comrades had been eye witnesses, first of their success and then of their overwhelming defeat.

The fighting on both sides seems to have been desperate. Sir G. Colley himself and two other officers were killed, the rest all wounded or made prisoners. The regiments which have suffered so grievously are the 58th, 60th, 93rd [*recte* 92nd] Highlanders and a detachment of the Naval Brigade.

Besides the misery of this defeat from a military point of view, it is fearful to think of the evil consequences it will produce indirectly, not only in Africa but nearer home.

On all sides there is a tacit agreement that terms of peace cannot be thought of at present—every nerve is being strained to send out the necessary reinforcements wanted, and Sir F. Roberts is to succeed poor Sir G. Colley in the chief command.

We found Dublin in snow and the drive through the Phoenix Park was a long business, but the place looked as beautiful as ever. The house was warm considering its uninhabited state, and Yarrow neat [?] was delighted to see us.

After an interview with Mr Burke Father went into D[ublin] taking O. with him. I wrote and spent much of the afternoon in the garden. We all three dined at the Burkes'. A sociable evening, Father and Mr Burke, I believe, had some talk over the Land Bill.

1 Mar., Tu.

Papers full of the details of the battle; the behaviour of the troops on both sides seems to have been good; the Boers fighting splendidly and are said to be courteous in their treatment of our wounded and prisoners—not bragging, and attributing their success 'to the righteousness of their cause'.

Mr Cameron[1] the brilliant correspondent of the *Standard* was taken prisoner whilst with our troops but is I believe at liberty again.

A very bad outrage in the County Mayo. Mr Heam [Hearne], an old man much respected and liked but a Clerk of Petty Sessions and a land agent, has been fired at in broad daylight by two young men armed with revolvers. Mr Heam is not expected to recover.[2]

Father drove into Dublin with Lord O'Hagan.

I lunched and spent the afternoon with Miss Burke. I hear from her that the season is a very gay one, in fact things seem different enough to the time when the Ch. Sec. was severely taken to task for giving two balls.

The Cowpers are entertaining well, she especially is winning golden opinions. He remains hopelessly shy, and insists on clinging fondly to his old acquaintances at balls and parties, instead of launching out into new ones.

Father dined in Dublin; Oakel and I here, and afterwards went to a performance at the Richmond Barracks, a burlesque with Mrs B., Mrs C. W., and Miss S. performing. A very amusing entertainment. I was glad to meet a good many of our friends.

2 Mar., Wed.

Report of another outrage—the house of Mr Scott, a Head Constable, fired into by a party of men, one bullet grazing close by the head of a child in its cot.[3]

Sir W. Harcourt in bringing in the Arms Bill appears to have made a clever and aggressive speech which greatly irritated the Parnellites; and having once undertaken to expose the inconvenient and undoubted connection between some of the Land League members and the Fenian Irish in America, Sir W. works the idea with great effect, and to the extreme annoyance of would-be moderate men like Mr [A. M.] Sullivan and Mr J[ustin] McCarthy.[4] The Home Sec.'s remarks, too, at the expense of the absent Mr Parnell, the bold leader who ran away, 'but bade the rest keep fighting' are bitterly resented as

[1] John Alexander Cameron (d. 1885): joined the *Standard* as correspondent in Afghanistan; his work there and in South Africa was outstanding in quality and speed of reporting.

[2] John Hearne, agent for the F. H. de Montmorency estate, on which a tenant had not been reinstated as caretaker after eviction, was fired at near Ballinrobe about 3 p.m. on 28 Feb. and received six revolver bullet wounds. He recovered later. Two men were arrested and discharged for want of evidence but were later arrested under the protection act (S.P.O., I.C.R., Returns of outrages, Feb. 1881).

[3] The house near Ballina of George Scott, farmer and barony constable (not 'head constable', an R.I.C. rank) was fired at at *c.* 12.15 a.m. on 28 Feb. One pistol bullet penetrated the house, but was travelling upwards and caused no injury. A similar outrage occurred nearby soon after; the motive in both cases seems to have been to intimidate the victims into surrendering evicted farms. Six persons were given heavy sentences in 1884 for conspiracy to murder in this and other cases (S.P.O., I.C.R., Returns of outrages, Mar. 1881).

[4] *Hansard 3*, cclviii, 1963–2020. Harcourt's speech (1963–76), as reported, made in fact very little reference to American Fenianism, and was almost entirely concerned with shooting incidents and league incitements to resistance.

cowardly taunts against an absent man which Sir W. would not have dared to utter to his face, etc. etc. At the same time it is said that Mr P.'s prolonged absence does not please his friends and that they are telegraphing to him to return.

I went to church at the Hibernian [Military School] and afterwards walked with Father and O. to the park gates. In the afternoon drove into Dublin, called on Lady F[erguson] and had tea with the Monsells at their house in the Castle yard.[1]

Dublin society is very amiably disposed towards the Ch. Sec. just at present; as a fellow lady's maid expressed it to Williams 'Mr F's bill had made them feel so comfortable, and they thought his speeches in the House so clever'. As Father says, these sentiments will not last long. The Land Bill will soon restore us to our normal unpopularity out here with the landlord society and their satellites.

Father and O. dined in Dublin, and Yarrow and I spent a quiet evening together in the smoking room.

A telegram from L.C. to say the C[oercion] Bill received Royal assent.[2]

Father and O. home about 11 o'clock.

The actual work looking into evidence and preparing warrants begins I believe to-morrow.[3] Father is made uneasy by these fresh outrages, though Mr

---

[1] Gaston Monsell, as state steward, had lodgings in the viceregal apartments in Upper Castle Yard.

[2] Protection of Person and Property Act, 1881, 44 and 45 Vict. c.4.

[3] Forster in a letter to Gladstone dated 2 Mar. 1881 (B.L. Add. MS 44158, ff 138–9) says: 'I cannot cut through my work here before Monday—We have proscribed nine counties but our arrests will be under fifty. We are subjecting every case to most anxious and careful examination, and I have struck out many cases. . . .' The nine counties, for which the proclamations were published on 4 Mar., were Clare, Cork (West Riding), Galway, Kerry, Leitrim, Limerick, Mayo, Roscommon, and Sligo. Westmeath was proclaimed on 7 Mar.; the next proclamations were not for more than a month.

The Protection of Person and Property Act, 1881, which was to last to 30 Sept. 1882, empowered the lord lieutenant to issue warrants for the arrest and detention without trial of anyone 'reasonably suspected' of having since 30 Sept. 1880 been guilty of high treason, treason-felony, or treasonable practices, or (in a proscribed district) of violence, intimidation, incitement, or 'tending to interfere with or disturb the maintenance of law and order'. Those detained were to be treated as persons awaiting trial, according to regulations to be prescribed by the lord lieutenant; outdoor relief was to be made available to their families, and each case was to be reconsidered every three months.

The procedure for considering cases for arrest under the act is described by Forster in a letter to the queen on 7 Mar. 1881 (*Letters of Queen Victoria*, ed. G. E. Buckle, series II, iii, 199–200): 'Lord Cowper and Mr Forster, with the help of the chief officials here, have carefully examined into every case in which arrest has been recommended by the local police, and have cross-examined the sub-inspector of the constabulary and the resident magistrate of the district. The result is that warrants will be today issued for 40 persons. It is a most painful and anxious duty putting men in prison without the possibility of trial, and Mr Forster has deeply felt the responsibility; but he also feels that the men now arrested are all of them men against whom there is the most reasonable suspicion that they themselves have committed actual outrages, or worse still have incited others to commit them. The implication of the local land agitators in these outrages, and also the existence of secret societies has been brought out but too clearly; and nothing can be more plain that, without this act, many districts would have been subject to the tyranny of the worst men in their neighbourhood. Many of these men, however, have already fled, and Mr Forster has still much

Burke affirms that they were to be fully expected, and signalized the passing of the last Coercion Act.

Father however fears they may be the work of Secret Societies; the League he says will *see them with pleasure*, as proving the truth of the statement that the withdrawal of their influence would mean the commission of outrages.

Notwithstanding these acts of violence there are some signs of a turn in the tide which has been setting so strongly for the League Agitators all through the autumn and winter. There have been several resignations from the League; the character of the resolutions passed at a 'magnificent meeting' at Borris[o]kane on Tuesday were far milder than customary; several more cases of rent paying have occurred, always with large voluntary abatements by the landlord; the 'boycotting' of Mr S[aunders] of Charleville has come to an end, the labourers having asked to be taken back to work, and he consequently declining the services of the Emergency Men who were to have come to him.[1]

These may be chance straws, but it is possible they may show the set of the current. At the same time there can be no doubt that the Land League chiefs are doing all in their power to prevent the chance of a reaction in favour of parliamentary reform and honest dealing.

Moreover the lawlessness in the West and South has by no means ceased, and there is reason to believe in the mixture of a considerable Fenian element with the agitation, which the prospect of a Land Bill is not likely to influence. The search for arms is a favourite pretext for midnight raids, and a robbery of dynamite at Cork has been successfully accomplished.

3 Mar., Th.

A letter from Mother from Fox How.

The Parnellites do not act in harmony whilst absent from each other; the papers this morning contain a disavowal of 'a person called John Devoy' by Mr [Justin] Mc[Carthy] and a vehement protest by Mr Dillon against the vile conduct of the Home Sec. in reflecting on the character of an honourable gentleman like Mr John Devoy in his absence.[2]

Mr Dillon has announced his intention of coming over to London to defend his absent friend—the same gentleman to whose remarkable utterances Mr A. Sullivan referred as the 'raw head and bloody bones of Devoy'.[3]

The papers of this morning also contain a letter from Mr J. G. MacCarthy an

confidence in the good effect of the act; and having had the opportunity of seeing and testing the conduct of many of the officers of the constabulary, Mr Forster thinks he ought to tell your majesty that he had formed a very favourable impression of their loyalty, courage, and ability. . . .'

[1] *The Times*, 3 Mar. 1881; cf. above, p. 17.
[2] MacCarthy was speaking in the house of commons on the second reading of the arms bill, and Dillon at the weekly meeting of the Land League in Dublin on 2 Mar. (*F.J.*, 3 Mar. 1881, *The Times*, 3 Mar. 1881).
[3] *Hansard 3*, cclviii, 1706 (24 Feb. 1881).

ex-Home Ruler,[1] on the two policies—Mr Butt's and Mr Parnell's, very much to the disadvantage of the latter.

In the course of the morning Father and O. went into Dublin. I copied Father's Memorandum on the Land Bill for the Cabinet which he will not be present at. I hope we are now nearer the actual point than when I copied out his last Mem. on the same subject; that was on the 26th of Dec. and we had the C[oercion] Bill before us.

A call from Mr Foster of the H.M.S.,[2] otherwise a perfectly quiet day tête-à-tête with Yarrow, a howling wind and rain making it impossible to stir out.

Received a note from Father with invitation from the Lady C[owper] for to-night. Father adds 'Oakel is most useful in our inquisition'.[3]

Spent the afternoon writing, and reading Miss E's *Helen*.[4] Dined at the Cowper's, joining Father at the office. A pleasant evening, those being present being chiefly people staying in the house, Dalrymples[5] (she a blonde beauty), Mrs Elliot, two Miss Drummonds, also the Caulfields,[6] and Mr Jephson. In the evening had a tête-à-tête with his Ex[cellency] who seemed in very good spirits in his quiet way. He appears to be taking kindly to the Castle festivities, and I am told went through his duties of the drawing room with great éclat, but I much fear that in the deliberations with the Ch. Sec. and the authorities he shows no initiative power, and is little more than a figure-head. He is certainly, I should say, a man of strong convictions and principles, but he seems so absolutely without power of expression as to make him simply ineffective as a politician.[7]

4 Mar., Fri.

Mr Dillon has made a speech in the House in answer to Sir W. Harcourt's remarks about Devoy, so violent that even the *Freeman* 'deeply deplores' and 'emphatically condemns' his language.[8] He said amongst other things 'that were he an Irish Farmer and turned out of his holding he would decidedly shoot as many of the landlords as he could and then abide the consequences'.

Later on he remarked that there could be no civil war in Ireland for the people had no arms—'he wished they had'.

[1] John George MacCarthy (1829–92): home rule M.P. for Mallow, 1874–80; author of legal pamphlets and works on Irish politics.

[2] Rev. Robert Foster, Church of Ireland chaplain to the Royal Hibernian Military School.

[3] 'Inquisition' here means the investigation of cases for arrests under the P.P.P. act.

[4] The last novel, published in 1834, of Maria Edgeworth (1767–1849).

[5] North de Coigny-Dalrymple-Hamilton (1853–1906), son of the tenth earl of Stair, was adjutant of the Scots Guards.

[6] Colonel James Alfred Caulfeild was comptroller of the viceregal household; in 1892 he became 7th Viscount Charlemont.

[7] Cf. below, p. 157.

[8] *F.J.*, 4 Mar. 1881: 'we do not believe that Mr Dillon himself meant all that his words are capable of conveying.'

For this he was called to order by the Speaker for 'advocating civil war'.

It was hardly surprising that Sir W. Harcourt should take advantage of this speech to announce that now the House had heard the doctrine of the L.L. expounded by the man with authority to expound it, and that the doctrine was one of treason and assassination.

Mr D[illon] rose to explain that he had been misrepresented, but it is difficult to see how he expected his words to be understood if he chose to use such language as he had just employed. Even such men as Mr Gray and Mr Mc Coan disavowed and condemned his speech, and he found his champion in Mr Healy, who contrived in the course of his offensive remarks to get himself suspended.

In the division on this question only 15 voted in the minority including Mr H[ealy] himself.[1]

Later in the evening the debate was adjourned[2] and Mr Childers made his long expected and deferred speech on the proposed reform in our Army system.

A damp rainy morning. I drove to the Castle with Father and O. and after leaving them, and doing a commission for F. in Grafton Street, returned to the C.S. Lodge.

In the afternoon went with Miss Glyn to a Bazaar for the Eye and Ear Hospital.

Father did not return with O. but slept at the Kildare St Club, in order to begin work early the next morning. The work of enquiring into cases for arrest has been going on all day, Lord C[owper] present but taking little part—partly on account of his deafness.

The more the organization and 'personnel' of the L. League is examined, the more (according to Oakel) does the connection with Fenian and Ribbon Societies become apparent. In most cases the prominent Land League man is, or has been, prominent in other ways.[3]

5 Mar., Sat.

Miss Dixon to breakfast, Father having caused me to invite her, and then forgotten that she was coming.

Oakel went to the Castle after breakfast, the authorities now reckoning upon him to take down notes of the Constabulary statements.

At 12 went with Miss Dixon into Dublin; called with her on some Miss

---

[1] The division on Healy's suspension was 233 to 15.

[2] By 277 votes to 28.

[3] For preliminary reports by police and resident magistrates on persons who they considered should be arrested, see S.P.O., R.P. 1879/14767; 1880/34686; P.P.P. act proceedings, carton 2 (recommendations for arrest).

Darleys to see a picture of them in their young days by Mr Burton.[1] Looked in at the Irish Academy and called at the Castle for a newspaper. Drove out in a cab and lunched with Miss Burke.

On coming back had visits from Mrs Thompson, Miss Glyn and Monsells. In the evening dined at the Castle, a large party including Judges, Guardsmen, A.D.C.s and the people staying in the house.

Father dined with Mr Doyle, and the Royal Hibernian Academy.

6 Mar., Sun.

Went to church at the H.M.S. After lunching with Father walked with him and Sergeant H[eron] whom we met at the Park Gates. A lovely afternoon— reminded Father of our walk to the V.R. Lodge on Xmas Day, when our fate was hanging on the Coercion Bill. This time I suggested our return made doubtful by the Land Bill.

Yes, the Land Bill is a beast, said Father.

On coming in, I had a long visit from Sir G. Young[2] who has come over to hurry the printers with the 2nd Volume of the [Bessborough] Commission[3] evidence. He was of opinion that, in spite of Mr Dillon's fervent protestation, the power of the League to prevent payment is broken throughout the country. A marked change was made by the expulsion of the 37 members. The tenant farmers (according to Sir G.) had never seriously believed that Mr Parnell could get them their farms as a gift, or abolish rent, but they had great confidence in his power to paralyze and defy successfully the British Parliament in their behalf.

This impression was corrected by the summary treatment of the Obstructives, and the effect has been seen in the revived tendency to pay their debts on the part of Mr P's clients in Ireland.

The danger now, says Sir G., is 'not of the Agitators extorting too much from the Govt in the way of Land reform, but of the Conservative opposition rallying so strongly in consequence of the apparent pacification, as to prevent the Govt from carrying an effectual Land Bill through Parliament'.

Oakel and I dined with the Burkes, Father at the K[ildare] St Club.

---

[1] Frederic William Burton (1816–1900): born in Clare; Royal Hibernian Academician, 1839; director of National Portrait Gallery, London, 1874–94.

[2] Sir George Young (1837–1930): fellow of Trinity College, Cambridge, 1862; unsuccessful liberal candidate for Plymouth, 1874, 1880, 1881; member of various government commissions, and as secretary of Bessborough commission (above, pp 8, 31) wrote its report; invited by Lord Frederick Cavendish, on his appointment as chief secretary, to join him as private secretary, May 1882; charity commissioner under endowed schools act, 1882–1903; chief charity commissioner for England and Wales, 1903–6 (see above, p. 77).

[3] See above, p. 50.

7 Mar., Mon.

Another bad murder, this time of a respectable farmer in West Meath, Farrelly, shot from behind a hedge in broad daylight; it is supposed from being in possession of a farm from which a man (no longer in the country) had been evicted 7 years ago. Strenuous effort on the part of the *Freeman* to dispel the idea of an agrarian outrage in any way connected with the League.[1]

I lunched at the Castle and afterwards went with Miss Burke to a Fine Art exhibition opened by the Cowpers. Lady Cowper has become Vice-President of an Art Needle Work Society in Dublin which under the vigorous practical management of herself and Miss B[urke] promises to be a great success.

Rumoured death of Sir H. Wood.

Joined Father and Oakel at Westland Row, and returned by the evening mail to London, after a record fine passage.

Before leaving Dublin, the warrants had begun to go out. The principal people amongst those arrested are Mr Walsh, and Mr Boyle [Boyton], (familiar to us through the 'seditious' extracts).[2]

It was rumoured that Mr Brennan and other Land Leaguers were crossing in the same steamer as ourselves, so we had to be cautious in our conversation on deck.

In the sleeping car I made friends with Mrs S[ingleton], wife of a wounded officer.[3]

8 Mar., Tu.

Arrived in Eccleston Square at 7.30 after a very quick passage. Father and I had a pleasant breakfast together. He had been put into good spirits by hearing from Mr G. that the Land Bill had been re-drafted in the direction he wished. Mr G. also wrote having read the memorandum, but not expressing his intentions with regard to it.

There has been grave reason to fear that the Bill would not be as strong as is undoubtedly needful. It will be grievous if such Irish Liberals as Mr Shaw, Mr

[1] Patrick Farrelly was fatally wounded near Multyfarnham at about 8 p.m. on 4 Mar. and died the next day; in 1873 he had taken possession of an evicted farm (S.P.O., I.C.R., Returns of outrages, Mar. 1881; *F.J.*, 7 Mar.).

[2] Joseph B. Walsh, Castlebar publican, and Michael P. Boyton, Land League organiser, of Kildare, were both arrested on 8 Mar. for speeches made within the previous two months. Walsh was released on 22 Oct. and Boyton on 30 Nov. 1881. Both claimed U.S. citizenship (see below, p. 91, n. 1).

Of the first arrests under the P.P.P. act, one was made on 7 Mar., 5 on 8 Mar., 13 on 9 Mar. and 5 on 10 Mar.; only 9 were made during the rest of the month.

[3] Major Loftus Corbet Singleton of the Gordon Highlanders, who died on 1 May of wounds received at Majuba. His wife Emmeline Theodora was the daughter of Thomas de Moleyns (1807–1900), county court judge and chairman of quarter sessions for Kilkenny. See below, pp 90, 92, 98, 100.

Litton[1] and others, not to speak of the great body of rational English Liberals, were to be disappointed in their confidence in the Govt, especially after the strain that has been put upon their loyalty in the Protection and Arms Bill[s].

About 12 Father went off to a Cabinet. I spent the morning in arranging flowers brought from Dublin; had a visit from Mlle Stumfels, and Mrs Singleton and her brother, Major de Moleyns.[2] Mrs S. is very anxious to have a telegram sent to her husband through the W[ar] O[ffice] and would be grateful for our help *au près de* Mr Childers. I promised to do what we could, and sent Mrs S's message with a note to the Irish Office.

Lunched at No. 15, brought back Lucy to tea; had a short visit from Aunt Mala, and went to meet Mother at Euston at 5.45.

Oakel to dinner. Father not back; the Arms Bill in Committee, and though Sir W. H[arcourt] has charge of it Father could not be away from the division.

There is much discontent and uneasiness about the attitude of the Govt in the Transvaal affair. The news is confirmed that an armistice for 8 days has been concluded between Sir E. Wood and the Boers represented by General Joubert.[3] Mr Gladstone is besieged with questions to which he gives what are called 'evasive' answers, no one being certainly able to gather from his reply to Mr Ritchie[4] whether it was the Boers or the English who had first sued for an armistice.

On all sides there is deep regret at the present war and a sincere wish to avoid further unnecessary bloodshed; but there is also a strong feeling (not confined to Conservatives or so-called 'Jingoes') that the Govt will not soon be forgiven if they place England in the position of hurrying on an armistice and consenting to hitherto inadmissible conditions of peace simply because English troops have been three times defeated by the Boers, and because Radical opinion is seizing this favourable opportunity of repeating its protest against the original annexation of the Transvaal.

The annexation of the Transvaal was not an act of wanton injustice to gratify a lust of conquest and false Imperialism on the part of this country, but a measure thought advisable by just and humane statesmen both in the late and present Govt in the interest of the Boers themselves, of the Natives in the Republic, and of the general peace and safety of the South African colonies.

If the Conservative and Liberal Govts were both misled, the Boers have in great measure to thank themselves, and their now disavowed President Burgess [Burgers] for it. The misunderstanding as to the real views of the Boers on the subject is very much to be regretted on all accounts, and the conviction that a misunderstanding (*not* an act of injustice) has occurred is a reason for doing all

[1] See appendix.

[2] Townsend Aremberg de Moleyns (1838–1926), of the Royal Artillery.

[3] Petrus Jacobus (Piet) Joubert (1831–1900): member of the Transvaal 'triumvirate' separatist government; commandant-general in charge of Boer forces at Laing's Nek, Ingogo and Majuba, and chief Boer negotiator in the peace settlement.

[4] Charles Thomson Ritchie (1838–1906): conservative M.P. for Tower Hamlets, 1874–95.

we can to rectify the mistakes committed by British officials, and setting our relations with the Boers and Natives on a right footing for the future; but it is not a reason for making a defeat of our troops the apparent turning point of a new policy.

How is our Empire to be maintained if the precedent be once established that a successful though temporary overmastering of British troops is acknowledged to be ground sufficient for revoking measures adopted a short time before with the full knowledge and sanction of the Imperial Govt?

The Radical papers allow that a peace concluded immediately upon a third repulse, may seem a 'humiliation' for the country, but maintain that the affair altogether has been made too much of, and that now the only just and politic course is to get out of the Transvaal scrape as speedily as possible without further effusion of blood.

The French press is full of commendation of the 'moral courage' of the British Govt in their treatment of the Boer question, but in all our foreign policy during the past few years we have had such ample experience of the variations of foreign opinion that one is not accustomed to attach much value either to their praise or blame.

9 Mar., Wed.

An early call from Lord and Lady O'H[agan].

The chief staple in the papers, 'Further arrests under the Coercion Act'. Mr Michael Boyton declares himself to be an American citizen, and promises to give trouble on this account.[1]

The prisoners are all being brought up to Dublin and lodged in Kilmainham Gaol, where according to their own account 'they have nothing to complain of'; in fact some impatience is being expressed at the elaborate precautions taken by the Govt to secure not only comfort but luxuries for these men, who, if a tithe of the things charged against them are true, deserve very different treatment.[2]

[1] The question of imprisonment in the United Kingdom of persons claiming U.S. citizenship, and its influence on Anglo-American relations, is discussed by Owen Dudley Edwards, 'American diplomats and Irish coercion, 1880–1883' in *Journal of American Studies*, i, no. 2 (Oct. 1967), pp 213–32. See also P.R.O. Cab. 37/8/37 (23 May 1882) and (for British protests about inflammatory Irish-American speeches and writings) Cab. 37/10/34–6 (May 1883); and see below, p. 185.

[2] Under the P.P.P. act 'suspects' were to be treated as persons awaiting trial, but the regulations for their treatment might be altered at the discretion of the lord lieutenant, and this was done to their advantage. A list of eighteen regulations for the treatment of suspects (signed by Forster and dated 5 Mar. 1881) is given in *Third report of the general prisons board, Ireland, 1880–81*, pp 4–8, H.C. 1881, li, 672–6. Considerable work was undertaken to prepare cell accommodation for suspects—cells being 'floored, heated, lighted, supplied with bells, &c'—although at this time Irish prisons generally were being reorganised and improved; as 'the most important class' of prisoner they enjoyed the attention of the 'most experienced and reliable officers', upon whom the strain seems to have been heavy, and provision for extra prison staff had to be made (*Fourth report of the general prisons board, Ireland, 1881–2*, p. 6, H.C. 1882, xxxiii, 666).

In the evening dined at Abbey Lodge; I had much lively talk with Lady Ten-terden[1]—not on Irish subjects for a wonder.

After dinner I went with Father and Mother to Clarence House, and Lady Stanley's.[2] At the latter place Mother met Mr Errington, who was as despond-ent as many others at this time: 'if there was an improvement, he thought it was merely on the surface. As an Irish landlord, he had never felt more anxious than at the present moment'.

Mrs S[ingleton] is to have her telegram sent from the W.O.

10 Mar., Thu.

The papers full of the terrible earthquake in Italy, whereby some hundred people have been killed at the village of Casamicciola in the island of Ischia.

The armistice appears not to be a success in one respect, for the Boers, taking advantage of an unfortunate 'concession' made by Sir E. Wood, are ill-treating the well-disposed Boers and British subjects not included within the English lines, burning their farms and forcing them into the Boer camp.

Francie returned from Killerton, where she has been spending a very pleasant and quiet 10 days with the Aclands.[3]

Went to the Hospital. Oakel to dinner, but Father still attending on the Arms Bill.

11 Mar., Fri.

Walked with Father to the office—a bright morning, but the view from the Bird Cage Walk is not so beautiful as from the straight Road through the Phoenix Park. We spoke of Sir G. Colley's account of Laing's Nek.

Drove with Mother in the afternoon and called amongst others on Lady Alice Havelock Allan. We found her in great perplexity, Sir Henry being forced by the new Army scheme to choose between the alternative of leaving Parlia-ment or the army. If he does the former, a rabid and very able Home Ruler will succeed him at Sunderland; moreover his knowledge on military matters will be greatly missed by the Liberal leaders at this time of Army reform.[4]

Lady Alice told us that Sir E. [*recte* U.] K. S.[5] is in great despair about his

---

[1] Emma Mary Rowcliffe, née Bailey (d. 1928), second wife of Charles Stuart Aubrey Abbott (1834–82), 3rd Baron Tenterden.

[2] Probably 15 Grosvenor Gardens, home of Fabia, wife of Henry Edward George Stanley (1827–1903), 3rd Baron Stanley.

[3] Sir Thomas Dyke Acland (1809–98): liberal M.P. for North Devon, 1865–85 (see below, p. 430).

[4] Sir Henry Havelock-Allan, V.C. (1830–97), chose the army and on 11 Apr. the radical mayor of Sunderland, Samuel Storey (1840–1935), was elected to the vacant seat.

[5] Sir Ughtred James Kay-Shuttleworth (1844–1939): 2nd baronet; liberal M.P. for Hastings, 1869–80.

prospects at the Coventry election. The late M.P. (Sir H. Jackson)[1] got in by a small majority, and the Conservative candidate[2] has much local influence. The Parnellites have sent down Finigan and O'Connor to agitate amongst the Irish electors against the return of a 'Govt nominee'. It will be curious to see the result of this piece of Irish policy on the election.

Oakel dined with us. Father at the House.

Read Ellen [*recte* Charlotte] O'B[rien]'s very able article in the *19th Century* — 'Eighty years'.[3]

12 Mar., Sat.

Father in good spirits at having seen the last of the Coercion Bills[4] in the House of Commons. Sir W. Gregory called in the afternoon. His opinion as to our prospects in Ireland are, as we had heard, anything but cheering.

'We shall be worse before we are better.' Whereas there are now 30 Obstructives in the House, at the next election with better organization 60 or 70 will be returned. Even during the O'Connell agitation the hatred of England and things English was simply nothing to what it is now. The spread of education had enabled the people to read, but what they do read is 'poison'. From year's end to year's end they never see anything but such literature as the *Irish World* and the *Flag of Ireland*[5] etc.

The priests if they do discountenance outrages and violence do so on the ground that the commission of outrage will give the enemies of the people, i.e. the English Govt, an advantage over them, and are therefore undesirable.

Sir W's pessimist views are not the outcome of his own private sufferings at the hands of the Land League agitators, for he himself has been so unusually fortunate as to get his rents and maintain (apparently) a friendly understanding with his tenants.

He told us a curious story of the Land League procedure when seen at close quarters, and not idealised as it is in the descriptions of Mr Dillon and Miss [Charlotte] O'Brien.

A widow on his estate, renting a farm of fifteen acres, got so hopelessly into arrears with her rent that he was obliged to turn her out; but this was done entirely with the concurrence of the woman to whom he gave a house and three acres of her former holding, allowing her also to keep the purchase money from the sale of the remaining twelve acres. He also forgave her the arrears of rent, and from time to time gave her at her request a sovereign to 'keep her going'.

[1] Sir Henry Mather Jackson (1831–81): liberal M.P. for Coventry, 1867–8, 1874–81; appointed judge of high court, 2 Mar. 1881; and died on 8 Mar.

[2] Henry William Eaton (b. 1816–91): London merchant and Fellow of Royal Geographical, Horticultural, and Botanical Societies; conservative M.P. for Coventry, 1865–80.

[3] *Nineteenth Century*, ix, no. 49 (Mar. 1881), pp 397–414.

[4] The protection of person and property bill and the arms bill.

[5] One of three weeklies oriented to Fenianism, owned and edited by Richard Pigott.

When the local L.L. was started, the widow thought an opening had come for her to get back her former property. She accordingly stated her case to the local authorities and denounced Sir W. Gregory in due form as a bad landlord, heartless exterminator, etc. Unfortunately for the enterprising [tenant] the present occupier of her original holding is also a member of the local L.L., and a more powerful one than the widow. She was told that she had no case—had not a leg to stand upon, and was in short ignominiously sent about her business. Shortly after, the son of the widow came to Sir W. Gregory to show him privately a document his mother had received. This was a threatening letter of a most ferocious description, signed 'Rory', and decorated with the usual coffin, and intimating that if Mrs —— did not give up her land to her 'honest neighbours' she would infallibly be shot. The woman had been so frightened by this threat that for a fortnight she had never left her house; but on Sir W. assuring her son that he did not think there was much to fear from the letter, she ventured out and came to ask Sir W. for protection. 'Well, don't you think you are the worst old woman that ever lived to go denouncing me to the Land League and then coming to ask me to protect [you]', said the good-natured landlord, at which the widow cried and excused herself and said she was a foolish woman, as to which statement Sir W. does not appear to have contradicted her.

The threatening letter has not in this case been followed by any outrage, but the 'honest neighbour has been warned that he had better see that nothing does happen, as he being the person most likely to profit would be the first on whom suspicion would fall.'

Sir W. Gregory being very anxious to see Father and impress upon him his desponding views was invited to come to lunch the next day.

Spent the afternoon out driving with Mother, the afternoon so pleasant that we had the carriage open. Mr Cropper to five o'clock tea; he had been greatly delighted with Father's final speech the other night on winding up the Coercion Bill, being glad that the last words should have been spoken in a friendly and conciliatory spirit towards Ireland.

Father and Mother dined at No. 15, and I went in afterwards in order to go on with them to the Spencers. At No. 15 were Sir G. Wolseley,[1] Mr Browning, Mrs Proctor, Mrs J. Stanley, and Mr G. W. Russell.[2] I had some talk with Mr Browning concerning Mr Hunt the American artist, whose story Mr Browning had told with great interest at Uncle Matt's house the year before.

There is an exhibition of Mr Hunt's pictures now open in Grafton Street. Mr Browning has been to see them, but told me he was disappointed especially in the matter of colouring.

[1] See appendix.

[2] Robert Browning (1812–89), the poet. George William Erskine Russell (1853–1919): grandson of the duke of Bedford; liberal M.P. for Aylesbury, 1880–85; editor of *Letters of Matthew Arnold, 1848–1888* (1895, 2nd ed., 1904): author of *Collections and recollections* (1898), *Lady Victoria Buxton* (1919), and many other works.

At Spencer House we found all the party in great tribulation over the result of the Coventry election which had just become known. Sir U. S. defeated by a majority of over 400.[1] The withdrawal of the Irish vote would account for a great deal but not for such a beating as this. The long faces of such steady Parliamentarians as Sir C. Forster and others were almost comical. In these days, hoever, we are, at the Irish Office, accustomed to far more serious calamities than election defeats, [so] that I personally could hardly feel sufficiently depressed, and it was evident that Father, feeling relief from the nervous pressure of the C[oercion] Bills, was something of the same mind.

13 Mar., Sun.

To St James the Less in the morning, but Father occupied with Mr J[ephson], and unable to come. Sir W[illiam] G[regory] and Mr H. Goresell to lunch, the latter in London for a few days before returning to take charge of the Legation at Rio. His experience of the Irish population as they are in S. America far from unfavourable; several of the most wealthy and respected men in the Eng. community are Irish; one Irishman of Mr G's acquaintance who had made a large fortune on the River Plate determined to return to Ireland, and seek to establish himself in his native county (Limerick). Not long afterwards Mr G[oresell] to his surprise met him in the streets of Buenos Ayres, and enquired the cause of his return. The Irishman explained that he found that if he had bought a property and set up for himself in the County Limerick he 'should have been shot just like any other landlord', so he thought it more prudent to return with his fortune to S. America.

In the afternoon I went with Father to call on Lady Reay.[2] We met Mr Chamberlain, and there was some talk over Sir Stafford's [Stafford Northcote's] forthcoming letter to his constituents.[3] Mr C. could tell Father the chief points: 'urgency' demanded by Mr G. for Supply to be refused by the Opposition on various grounds—respect for the Constitutional privileges—discussion and redress of grievances before Supply—urgency not necessary in this case, there being no reason to know that the Parnellites meant obstruction; the Govt no right to claim it, for by their own mismanagement they had lost opportunities, as for instance on Friday night, when Sir J. Lubbock[4] was allowed to bring in his Ancient Monuments Bill.

'Well, what will happen', said Father. 'I know what I should like to happen', was the answer.

'Oh, but you can't always have what you want.'

'No', said Mr C., 'I never do get anything I want in this world'.

[1] Eaton polled 4011 votes to Shuttleworth's 3568.
[2] Fanny Georgiana Jane, who in 1877 married Donald James Mackay (1839–1921), 11th Baron Reay.
[3] The letter (dated 12 Mar.) is in *The Times*, 14 Mar. 1881.
[4] See appendix.

I do not know what this melancholy reflection can have been a propos of—perhaps reminiscences of the Coercion Bill.

There was some talk about the Parnellite members, the usual conclusion arrived at concerning Messrs Healy and Finigan, the *bêtes noires* of everybody; Mr McCarthy, Mr Ch. does not like, but like most people has a respect for Messrs O'C. Power, and Sexton.

I was amused and rather surprised at the unaffected candour with which Mr C. ejaculated 'What an extraordinary sentiment' when I had ventured to say something about liking the Irish. I suppose his ideas of the Irish are confined to his Parliamentary experience of that people, which in itself is certainly enough to disgust the most sympathetic Saxon and anti-coercive Saxon.

After leaving Lady R's, we walked towards Pall Mall; in St James' Street we met Sir Stafford who turned and walked a few steps back with us. 'Well', said Father, 'so you are going to oppose us to-morrow'.

'Yes', murmured Sir Stafford, mildly, stroking on his black kid gloves, and looking anything but warlike, 'we are going to draw the sword', and then followed a little explanation of motives as given in the Manifesto next day.

In Pall Mall we fell in with Lord K[imberley],[1] who also turned to walk a short distance with us. Some talk over the yesterday's Cabinet, and very voluble expression of opinion on the part of the Colonial Sec. 'Our Chief's' inconvenient habit of elaborate and unintelligible answers—'No answer yet received from Sir E[velyn] W[ood] to telegram sent him yesterday—Joubert getting nervous, etc., etc.'

If it were allowable to use such an expression of a Cabinet Minister I should say Lord K. was a chatterbox.

At the Reform Club I left Father and drove to No. 15, where as usual a levée was being held.

Call from Mr F. Buxton. About six Father came in asking if we had heard the news? The Czar shot at and badly wounded. He had first heard a rumour at the Athenaeum from the Bishop of Peterborough, and on going to Lady Granville's heard that the Duke of Edinburgh[2] had received a telegram to this effect: '*Gravement blessé*'. At 10 in the evening while we were at prayers a Cabinet box arrived—a telegram from Lord Dufferin[3] sent in the afternoon: 'Terrible news, a bomb thrown at the Czar's carriage on his way back from a review—the back of the carriage shattered, but the Czar stepped out uninjured. A second bomb

[1] John Wodehouse (1826–1909), Baron Wodehouse, 1846: 1st earl of Kimberley, 1866; lord lieutenant of Ireland, 1864–6; lord privy seal, 1868–70; secretary for the colonies, 1870–74, 1880–82.
[2] Alfred Ernest Albert (1844–1900): second son of Queen Victoria; son-in-law of Alexander II, by his marriage in 1874 to the grand duchess Marie Alexandrovna (1853–1920).
[3] Frederick Temple Hamilton-Temple-Blackwood (1826–1902), 1st earl (later marquis) of Dufferin and Ava: lord lieutenant since 1864 of County Down, where he owned 13,085 acres; ambassador to Russia, Feb. 1879–June 1881; author of *Letters from high latitudes* (1856), *Irish emigration and the tenure of land in Ireland* (1867).

thrown which exploded between his legs, one leg blown off. Evidently a mortal injury.'

14 Mar., Mon.

The Czar died two hours after he received his terrible wounds on Sunday afternoon. His death has been a most appalling and pathetic tragedy; and there was a thrill of awe and compassion throughout Europe when the details of this last and fatal attempt at the life of the persecuted Emperor was made known.

The Czar was killed by the second shell whilst enquiring about the victims of the first explosion. He had been urged to get back into his carriage and drive on, but he refused to do this.

He appears to have hardly been conscious before his death, almost the only words he spoke being the name of his son the Czarewitch.[1] There is very great sympathy with the new Czar, now taking on his shoulders the heavy burden which for so many years has weighed down, and at last crushed, the Emperor Alexander.

It seems as though the two powers which ought to co-operate in the work of reform and progress in Russia are doomed blindly to oppose each other—each side furnishes its victims—sacrifices the one to an evil system which has for its object the preservation of law and order, the other to an evil system which has for its main and worthy object the preservation of individual liberty and the spread of freedom. The Nihilist buried for life in a fortress or banished to Siberia, the Emperor murdered by his subjects in the streets of his capital, and both the innocent victims of a terrible disastrous misunderstanding.

There is much in common between the rulers and people, but so long as they remain each entrenched behind their separate systems which are and ever will be antagonistic, they must continue to be hateful and hating one another—not as men and Russians, but as Nihilists on the one side, and Imperial officials on the other.

All other news in the papers this morning seems uninteresting by comparison with the telegrams from St Petersburg. Even Ireland and the Transvaal seem of secondary importance, and one can talk and think of few public events besides the tragedy of Sunday afternoon.

There is great sympathy for the Duchess of Edinburgh who left London on Sunday night with her husband and [her] brother, the Grand Duke Alexis. She must have known the worst before she left. The Czarewitch is reported to have said to some of the officers of the guard, 'I should be sorry for my son to ascend

[1] Alexander Alexandrovich (1845–94): as Alexander III, reversed his father's liberalising trend in favour of 'orthodoxy, autocracy, and *narodnost* [faith in the Russian people]' (Sir Donald Mackenzie Wallace and M. T. Florinsky on Alexander III in *Encyclopaedia Britannica* (Chicago and London, 1970), i, 571).

the throne under these circumstances'. His son is a boy of 11 years old.[1] There are many speculations as to the future policy of the new Emperor and the effect of his accession upon European relations. During his father's lifetime he was always considered to be vehemently anti-German, and the Empress (Princess Dagmar of Denmark)[2] is said to throw her influence in the same scale.

M. E. de Brunner[3] always maintains that the great war of the future is between Germany and Russia—it may be that it is of no remote future.

In the course of the morning we had a call from Mr Hogarth, a Yankeefied Bradford man, just returned from N. Zealand and Australia, with a present of seeds and plants for his M.P. (whose 'good lady' had once helped in some benevolent institution started by him during the distress of 1879). He had come home with gloomy views as to the prospects of N. Zealand, which he declared was absolutely bankrupt, and with all his affections set upon New South Wales. He is trying to establish a little business out there, but is terribly hampered by the heavy duties of the Col. Govt.

'It passed his comprehension', he remarked, rubbing his forehead with a look of puzzled reflection, 'why so long as we professed to form one Empire the Colonies should be allowed to tax English goods so ruinously'.

It is curious and pleasant to find how Father's acquaintance with people of all ranks and callings brings us into close contact either by speech or letter with all the different parts of the world.

One day we are hearing of experiences in S. America, another in Australia, another in Africa. We have many outlooks into the world, beyond the confines of ordinary London society.

I walked with Father to the office.

In the afternoon in Lillington St. Father not home to dinner. The Urgency question raised in the Commons. Mr G.'s proposal defeated according to arrangement.[4] The desired effect however was produced, for the Parnellites, presumably to spite the Govt, took the highly satisfactory course of foregoing obstruction. Mr Gladstone['s proposal] was proved to have been unnecessary by the exemplary conduct of the Obstructives.

Supply was proceeded with happily and real progress was made with business. Never I should think was a Minister more thankful to be proved in the wrong than Mr G. on this occasion.

I heard from Mrs S[ingleton] that the W.O. have telegraphed as desired to her husband, and have sent her a good account of him.

[1] Nicholas Alexandrovich (1868–1918): later, as Nicholas II, last emperor of Russia.
[2] 1847–1928; daughter of Christian IX of Denmark, 'the father-in-law of Europe'; sister of Alexandra (1844–1925), princess of Wales.
[3] Maurice William Ernest de Bunsen (1852–1932): highly respected professional diplomat.
[4] It was passed by a majority of only 296 to 212, instead of three to one as required by the new rules.

15 Mar., Tu.

Walked with Father to the office. I told him of the account in the *Telegraph* of their Correspondent's interview with Joubert.

He agreed with me that peace looked less probable the last day or two.

Drove with Mother in the afternoon. Mrs Price and Mrs C. came to tea. As usual everyone full of the Czar's murder. Mrs P. said that the Cr. Prince of Germany[1] had told Mrs Max Müller[2] that it never for a moment entered his mind to imagine that he should die in his bed. Not at any particular time or season, but some day, he quite expected to die by violence, like the Russian Czar.

Father came home to dinner—a most unusual occurrence. Just at present we are enjoying a real breathing time, and the constant oppression and stress of work and anxiety seem to be somewhat relaxed.

The curious good conduct of the Parnellites in Parliament still continues. Even the debate on the Irish Estimates was moderate both in length and temper, and at one period in the evening the extraordinary phenomenon might be seen of Col. Tottenham expressing his agreement with Mr P., and Mr P. in his turn declaring himself much obliged to the right hon. gentleman the Ch. Secretary for some promise or [? of] inquiry he had given.

From Ireland the reports of outrages have decreased in number, but it is said that the temper of the people is still very angry and disaffected. There is some impatience again finding expression as to the delay of the Govt in producing the Land Bill. Mr G. has intimated that it is considered undesirable to allow a long period for criticism between the presentation of the Bill and the commencement of actual debate upon it, and that consequently the Govt may not bring it forward before Easter.

Meanwhile Mr P. who has been postponing his flaming indictment—before an Irish audience—of the Govt and their Coercion policy until he had the Land Bill to criticize as well, is forced to go on postponing, and has not in short visited Ireland since his Clara speech.

16 Mar., Wed.

Father dined in the evening with Mr Chamberlain, and Mother and I went to see 'Masks and Faces',[3] joining Father afterwards at Lady Rosebery's. Whilst having a cup before going upstairs we found ourselves alone in the room with Mr Gladstone. He was pale but wonderfully animated and genial, and his dark

[1] Friederich Wilhelm Nikolaus Karl (1831–88): son of the Emperor Wilhelm I; married Victoria Adelaide Mary Louisa (1840–1901), daughter of Queen Victoria, in 1858.

[2] Georgiana Adelaide, née Grenfell, wife of Friedrich Max-Müller (1823–1900), fellow of All Souls, and professor of comparative philology at Oxford.

[3] A play (1852) by Charles Reade and Tom Taylor on an episode in the life of Peg Woffington, the Irish actress.

eyes looked bright and eager as he discoursed pleasantly, chiefly about plays and actors, and conjuring us with fervour to go and see Charles Warner,[1] whom M. Coquelin[2] of the Comédie Française had pronounced to be the finest actor we had.

Amongst others whom we met upstairs were Capt. Lyttleton (who informed me that they had been telegraphing till they were black in the face at the W.O. about Capt. Singleton), Mr Baillie Hamilton, Lord Dalhousie, etc. The latter, like every one else, was struck with Father's flourishing appearance; he promised to go down next day to the House to see the Ch. Sec. confronting the Parnellites with a branch of shamrock in his coat.

17 Mar., Th.

This being St Patrick's Day I decorated Father with Shamrock, of which Carpenter had sent me a plentiful supply the night before from the C.S. Lodge.

In the afternoon as Mother and I were in a shop in Sloane Street, we heard the hoarse shouting which betokens sensational news. Men were parading the street with placards announcing 'Attempt to blow up the Mansion House— wonderful escape of the Lord Mayor'. On going to Mrs Stansfeld's[3] we heard the details from someone who had seen a paper.

A box of coarse gunpowder, 40 lb, has been found at night on a window ledge of the Mansion House. A piece of burning paper which first attracted attention was found attached to the box: and if a policeman had not come up and put out the flame, the explosion would have taken place in a few minutes. The street was one little frequented and at night there were not likely to have been any passers-by, but considerable damage must have been done to the house opposite. Some fragments of Irish and American papers were found in the box, but these gave no clue.

The Lord Mayor (McArthur, an Ulster Irishman)[4] was said to have given offence to the Irish by his support of the Govt in the Coercion Bills, and though the *Freeman* exclaims with horror at the notion it is considered probable that the attempt is the fruit of the teaching so long inculcated by such papers as the *Irish World*.

No doubt such events and crimes as those at St Petersburg are contagious.

In the evening Father spoke at the St Patrick Benevolent Dinner, and was very well received; he declared himself to be far from hopeless about Ireland,

[1] Charles John Lickfold (1846–1909), currently producing and acting in the title rôle of *Michael Strogoff* at the Adelphi theatre.

[2] Either Benôit Constant Coquelin 'aîné' (1841–1909) or Ernest Alexandre Honoré Coquelin 'cadet' (1848–1909), both prominent actors and writers on the theatre.

[3] Caroline, née Ashurst, wife since 1844 of James Stansfeld (see above, p. 50); they lived at Stoke Lodge, Hyde Park Gate.

[4] William McArthur (1809–87): woollen draper of Derry; liberal M.P. for Lambeth since 1868; sheriff of London, 1867; alderman since 1872; lord mayor, 1880; co-founder of London chamber of commerce.

and ended up his speech by declaring that it would be a great mistake if Irishmen forgot their nationality, and still greater mistake if England or Scotland asked them to do so.[1] Just before going to the dinner Father received a letter from an unknown Irishman at Kilkenny, so friendly and discriminating that it was a further encouragement, if one were needed, to make a sympathetic Englishman like the Ch. Sec. speak kindly of our Irish fellow subjects.

Oakel, Lucy, Julia O'B[rien] and I went to the St Patrick's Concert at the Albert Hall. Owing I suppose to the critical state of things about Ireland, the selection of songs was of the very mildest description—a succession of Kathleen Mavourneens and Aileens varied with gentle moralizings and farewells to Erin—a slight infusion of songs out of the *Spirit of the Nation*[2] would certainly have added to the interest of the performance, though on other grounds it was just as well to have nothing the least agitating.

18 Mar., Fri.

Walked with Father to the office. We talked of Archbishop Croke's violent and indecorous attack on Archbishop McCabe, in his letter to Mr [A. M.] Sullivan. Mr S. having indignantly protested against Archbishop McCabe's disapproval of the women's agitation in Ireland,[3] the Archbishop of Cashel has written to thank Mr S. and seizes the opportunity of an angry sneer at his brother Archbishop.[4] Father is inclined to think that the letter was not intended for publication, Roman Catholic prelates being accustomed to fight out their differences, if they have any, in private. However this may be, there can be little doubt that the outburst of Dr Croke's will do him no harm with the majority of the people in Ireland, whether it may discredit him with his ecclesiastical superiors or not.

In the afternoon Mother and I went to see the Millais Exhibition and the Swiss Collection in Bond Street. Father home to dinner—quite like old times. In the evening Oakel and I went to an evening party with music at Mrs Simpson's.

[1] Forster's speech to the ninety-eighth anniversary feast of the St Patrick's Benevolent Society, which supported 430 children in its schools, stressed the good qualities of the Irish people (*The Times*, 18 Mar. 1881).

[2] A collection of 'political songs and national ballads by the writers of *The Nation*'; first published in 1843, and by 1881 in its 50th edition.

[3] The Ladies' Land League, founded in Feb. 1881 under the leadership of Anna Parnell, Charles's sister, as an auxiliary of the Land League.

[4] 'His Grace will not be allowed in future, I apprehend, to ventilate unquestioned the peculiar political theories which he is known to hold in opposition to the cherished convictions of the . . . overwhelming majority of the Irish priests and people.' (*F.J.*, 18 Mar. 1881; *The Times*, 18 Mar.).

19 Mar., Sat.

Negociations with the Boers still going on. The armistice prolonged till Monday. President Brand[1] of the Free State is acting as mediator. Lord Kimberley in replying to a deputation who came to represent the danger of complete submission to Boer demands in the Transvaal, whilst fully acknowledging the force of some of the arguments brought forward, pointed out that the great point to be remembered was the being sure of developing the possibility of future friendly relations with the Dutch population in S. Africa.

Nothing certain is at present known about the prospects of a peaceful settlement. It is believed that the Boers' terms as at first proposed were declared inadmissible by the Cabinet to whom they were referred by Sir E. Wood. Joubert is said to be inclined towards peace, but there is a strong war feeling amongst the Boers, who are anxious to fight to the end for the restoration of their independence—*pur et simple*.

The feeling in England that the Govt were sacrificing everything in the desire to obtain peace and close the Transvaal question at any cost is diminishing; the bitter remembrance of the last defeat is wearing out, and the conviction that Sir E. W[ood] and the reinforcements now on their way under Gen. Roberts would be able to overwhelm the Boers' resistance, if necessary, is making the public more inclined to consider the possibility of a peaceful settlement and to indulge their natural sympathy for a brave enemy and a people fighting for their independence.

On Saturday evening Lord and Lady Monck, the Townsends, Lord Kensington, Bryces, Mitchell Henry,[2] etc., dined with us. Mr Townsend quite in his element in speculation and surmises anent the murder of the Czar. Apropos of the attempt to blow up the Mansion House, he declared that many more crimes of the same nature might be expected—'he only hopes they will not take the form of assassination; he has great fear of assassination of Mr Gladstone'.

We had a convincing proof how much news about ourselves we miss by not seeing the real authorities—the society papers. At dinner Mr T.[3] mysteriously remarked to Mother: 'I suppose I must not ask—but—is it true?' Finding Mother apparently quite ignorant as to any rumour true or false, he explained—'That you will be Lady Wharfedale before the end of the session?' Before leaving he spoke to Father on the same subject and told him of the rumour that he was to become Lord Wharfedale and President of the Council.

Who invents these curious statements, and for what purpose, is a mystery.

[1] Johannes Henricus (Jan Hendrik) Brand (1823–88): president of the Orange Free State, 1863–88; neutral during the Transvaal war.

[2] Mitchell Henry (1826–1910): F.R.C.S.I., 1854; surgeon at Middlesex Hospital; went into family business in Manchester and Huddersfield, 1862; early supporter of Isaac Butt's home rule movement; home rule M.P. for Galway County, 1871–85; bought an estate of 14,000 acres in Connemara on which he built a neo-Gothic castle on Kylemore Lake, providing extensive employment for the locality.

[3] Meredith White Townshend (1831–1911): owner and joint editor of the *Spectator*, 1860–98.

20 Mar., Sun.

To church at St James the Less in the morning. In the afternoon a call from Capt. Douglas Galton; Oakel and I went to see Mrs Murray and Miss Mulholland. To evening church at St Michael's. At supper Father read to us his Memorandum for the Cabinet on the Transvaal. Oakel a good deal oppressed with anxiety concerning an article he has just written in hopes of finding an entrance in the *19th Century*.

It is a civilian's reply to Sir G. Wolseley's article in favour of 'Short Service'. O. is deeply interested in all that concerns the army and its organization, and the Report of Lord Aire's Commission on the defects of the existing Short service system only confirms the views he has been impressing upon us for a long time past.

I thought his article (founded on the facts of the Report) interesting and clear, but of course there are 10 chances to 1 against its ever appearing in the *Nineteenth Century*.[1]

21 Mar., Mon.

Papers full of the grand and solemn ceremonial of the lying in state of the Emperor Alexander II. Since the crime on Sunday, the most appalling details have come to light showing the desperate and thoroughly organized character of the Nihilist murder association. If the Czar had not been killed by the first bombs, other young men (volunteers for the purpose) were prepared with the same missiles at a further point of the road. Owing to the discovery of a plan, a mine has been discovered under one of the streets of the city charged with explosives enough to have destroyed the whole surrounding district. The open triumphing of the Nihilist party over the murder of the Czar, expressed in America at a public meeting, and in other countries, even in England, in Socialist newspapers, has been almost as revolting as the crime itself.

The bright spring weather has changed to an East wind and snow storms.

Went in the afternoon to the Hospital, and afterwards to tea with Amy Mulholland.

In the evening Father dined at Grillion's; Mother and I went with Ted to see the *Colonel*[2] at the Prince of W[ales Theatre]. This skit on the modern high-art Mama is amusing and well acted, but too long drawn out. The acting of Mr Coghlan as the American Colonel is inimitable—I have not seen anyone like him since Mr Jefferson.[3]

[1] Wolseley's article 'Long and short service' appeared in the *Nineteenth Century*, ix, no. 49 (Mar. 1881), pp 558–72; Oakeley's 'A civilian's reply to Sir Garnet Wolseley' in no. 52 (June 1881), pp 905–16.

[2] A three-act comedy, which opened on 2 Feb. 1881; by Francis Cowley Burnand (1836–1917), editor of *Punch*, 1880–1906, and one of the foremost Victorian humorists.

[3] Charles Francis Coghlan (1844?–99); Joseph Jefferson (1829–1905), Philadelphia actor who had appeared all over the English-speaking world.

22 Mar., Tu.

There seems reason to hope that the Boers will finally accept our terms: the armistice has again been extended.

An event of interest in the House last night was the announcement by Mr G. that he intends to bring in the Land Bill on April 7th, the day before the House rises for the Easter vacation.

From abroad the news is far from reassuring: in spite of the most strenuous diplomatic efforts the[re are] prospects of a war between Turkey & Greece. Experience has generally shown that when warlike preparations have been made to the extent which Greece and still more Turkey have made, war may be staved off but not averted—neither power can afford peace.

Alice S[pring Rice] and Miss Fitz G[erald], a niece of the Knight of Kerry, came to lunch. According to Miss F. there has not been an estrangement between them and their tenantry as far as friendly relations are concerned, in spite of Mr C. Russell's visitation[1] and the ill offices of the priest in their district, who shares in a strong degree the common hatred of England and all who are in any way connected by position or office with the English Govt.

In the afternoon Mother went down to Weybridge. Francie and I with Aunt F[anny] L[ucy] and L[ucy] to Miss Holland's. Father came home to dinner, bringing Mr Chevison with him. They brought news of the conclusion of peace in the Transvaal, the Boers having accepted our terms. The suzerainty of the Queen acknowledged—complete self-government—appointment of a Royal Commission (Sir H. Robinson, Sir H. de Villiers, Sir E. Wood) charged to insure the protection of Natives under the Boer autonomy—a British Resident at Pretoria—the Boers to disperse and go home—British troops not to advance into the Transvaal, but to remain there and in Natal until a final settlement has been made.

It remains to be seen how this arrangement will be taken by the country.

In the evening Father returned to the powerful discussion of foot and mouth disease to the House, and we went to an 'at home' at Mrs Buxton's.

23 Mar., Wed.

As might be expected, opinions on the Transvaal settlement vary greatly, the one side highly delighted, the other discontented, and full of prophecies of the evil to come from this temporary submission on the part of the British Govt.

Judging from the telegraphs from correspondents in Africa, the public there is bitterly aggrieved and considers not only that the prestige of England is fatally damaged, but that English residents in Natal and the Transvaal will find life insufferable. There is much anxiety expressed as to the fate of the loyal

[1] See Charles Russell, *New views on Ireland . . .* (London, 1880). Reprinted from the London *Daily Telegraph*, for which Russell was special correspondent; and see appendix.

Boers, whose interests, it is thought by the Opposition, are not sufficiently considered by being relegated to the subsequent decisions of the R. Commission.

On the whole, however, there is a feeling of relief at the war being over, but the circumstances under which it began and ended are equally disagreeable.

Mr Dillon's speech attacking Judge Fitzgerald for his strong remarks on the behaviour of Irish juries has apparently been a little too much even for some of his L.L. colleagues. At a meeting in Dublin yesterday, attended by Mr Lander [Louden],[1] Mr Sexton etc., attempts were made even by Mr M. Harris to explain and excuse away the violence of Mr Dillon's language.[2] According to Mr Bryce (who is very strongly in sympathy with the most advanced of the Home Rulers), the Parnellite party is splitting up, and Mr T. P. O'Connor (not himself a pattern of moderation) is said to have denounced Mr D. as a firebrand.

Certainly for some reason or other the vice seems to have gone out of the Parnellite phalanx, and they have condescended to observe the ordinary courtesies of debate; on the amendment on Friday night to reduce the Supplementary War Estimates, only 6 voted in the minority.[3]

Walked with Father to the office, joining company on the way with Mr Thorold Rogers, who carried under his arm a great folio, printed and edited by him from a MS at the Bodleian. Father dipped into this as we walked along the Bird Cage Walk, and the talk fell upon the tranquil subjects of ancient books and matters quite foreign to the Irish and Transvaal questions.

Went in the afternoon to Bond St and to tea with Nelly Boyle. In the evening we dined at the Peases's and went afterwards to Lady Tenterden's.

I had forgotten the fact of Court mourning and to my dismay and abasement found myself about the only person present not in black or white. Much talk about Sir W[illiam] H[arcourt]'s pistol which he received this morning in a box.

24 Mar., Th.

Walked with Father to the office—a bright morning. Lunched with the Kensingtons in Grosvenor Sq. Nelly and Mary B[oyle] to tea; their father has just returned from Ireland, unable to get his rents but in fairly good spirits I am told—I shall like to know why.

Father and Mother dined at the F. Cavendishs' where I joined them, going

[1] J. J. Louden of Westport, Co. Mayo: barrister; chairman of Mayo Tenants' Defence Association, Oct. 1878; associated with Davitt since April 1879.

[2] Dillon's speech was made on 20 Mar. at Woodford, Co. Galway (*F.J.*, 21 Mar. 1881; *The Times*, 22 Mar.); the reaction of his colleagues is reported in *F.J.*, 23 Mar.

[3] The amendment was in fact introduced on Monday, 21 Mar., and accepted by 109 to 6.

on afterwards with Mother to Lady R's [? Reay's]. We left Father at the House where the Candahar debate was going on.

Mr G. had made a moderate and good speech 'for a bad cause' and Lord Lawrence likewise.

Mr H[erbert] Gladstone[1] and Lord Baring made their maiden speeches on this occasion.

25 Mar., Fri.

Papers full of the Candahar debate.[2] Sir C. Dilke's[3] answer to Mr G. appears to have put the case of the Govt in the best possible light. He announced the fact that the new Czar has signalized his accession by recalling Gen. Scobel [Skobeleff] from his onward campaign in Central Asia. As might be expected, the anti-Russian papers do not attach much importance to this as a factor in our Indian frontier policy.

The various items of news from S. Africa are decidedly saddening reading this morning. The correspondents' letters now arriving describing the last fatal battle of Majuba Hill do not conceal the fact that our troops did most certainly take to flight, before they had attempted to confront the enemy at close quarters; the officers, however, appear to have maintained our honour so far as they were able; each one of them from Sir G. Colley downwards behaving with perfect coolness and courage.

To bring the war to a close as soon as possible was no doubt admirable on general grounds of policy and humanity, but it is impossible not to sympathize with the bitter feelings of our troops as they watched the Boers marching away from Laing's Nek wearing portions of the 'kit' of the British soldiers whom they had defeated.

The telegrams also from the correspondents in Natal and at the Headquarters are very depressing; both parties seem equally discontented with the terms of peace; the Boers are sulky and indignant at not having got all they wanted, whilst our people feel deeply humiliated and cannot forget that the war has closed with a disgraceful defeat which we have not been allowed to retrieve.

Sir F. Roberts and the bulk of the reinforcements are to return at once

---

[1] See appendix.

[2] In *Hansard 3*, cclix, 1831–1916, 1938–2036.

[3] Sir Charles Wentworth Dilke (1843–1911): liberal M.P. for Chelsea, 1868–86; succeeded his father as 2nd baronet and to proprietorship of the *Athenaeum* and of *Notes and Queries*, 1869; close ally of Chamberlain in radical section of liberal party; under-secretary for foreign affairs, 1880–82; declined Irish chief secretaryship, Apr. 1882, on ground that it did not carry seat in cabinet; president of local government board, 1882–5; favoured home rule, and voted for Gladstone's bill of 1886; his political career cut short as result of divorce suit (Cranford v. Cranford and Dilke), 1885–6; returned to public life as M.P. for Forest of Dean, 1892–1911; vigorous and capable reformer, art collector, and publicist; author of *Greater Britain* (1868) and other important works on contemporary affairs.

without landing, but some small additional force will be left in the Colony—according to all appearance this is by no means an unnecessary precaution.

Walked with Father to the office. In the evening I dined at the Sellars'. Sat between Mr Grant Duff and Mr Wodehouse[1] of the Colonial Office. He had been reading the papers in the morning with the same feelings I had; in fact, he made no secret of his despondency and disgust at the present state of things.

His father was for many years Gove[r]nor of Natal, and he himself has the strongest interest in our Colonial Empire, and especially in our treatment of the Native races for whom by conquering them we have become responsible. He does not believe at all in the efficacy of the precautions taken in the recent settlement to secure the independence and good treatment of the Transvaal natives.

A Resident! what can he do in a country as big as France, to prevent the Boers as they extend from dispossessing and enslaving the natives on their borders.

Territory to be divided off from the Transvaal proper, according to a future settlement by the Royal Commission! If they actually do insist upon this, British troops can enforce the protests of the Resident, if the Boers transgress the regulations concerning native treatment. The Boers are perfectly sure that come what may the British Govt won't do anything to risk another war in the Transvaal.

As to the Boers themselves Mr W[odehouse] had but a poor opinion of them, believing amongst other things that the 'sentimental craving for national independence' had been a good deal developed for British consumption at home. What they do crave for no doubt is personal independence of all authority especially in any matter affecting their dealings with the natives. When I spoke of their courtesy in the field towards our British soldiers, Mr W. drily remarked: 'Wait till you see Colonel Anstruther's Report of the affair on the Ingogo'. Mr O'Brien to breakfast, more cheerful.

26 Mar., Sat.

Maud Goschen[2] and Lucy and Nelly to lunch. An afternoon at home. Father and Mother dined at the Buxtons', we at No. 15.

27 Mar., Sun.

In the morning to Church at St Michael's. In the afternoon walked with Father to the Club. To tea at No. 15; a visit from the Monteagles.

Mr Aubrey De Vere's[3] continued protests against the doctrines and morals

---

[1] Edmond Robert Wodehouse (1835–1914): son of Sir Philip Edmond Wodehouse, governor of the Cape Colony, 1862–70; private secretary to Lord Kimberley, 1870–74; liberal M.P. for Bath from 1880.

[2] Lucy Maud Goschen (1858–1909), eldest daughter of George Joachim Goschen (see appendix). [3] See appendix.

of the L. League have embittered the priests against him—a painful state of things for a devoted Catholic and an Irishman. It is said that there is a strong feeling against Rome amongst the bulk of the Irish priesthood, who go entirely with Archbishop Croke as opposed to Archbishop McCabe, whose view of the situation is supposed to be the one adopted by the Pope.

It is a curious fact that in Clare several L. Leaguers have been defeated as Guardians.[1]

Mr Parnell spoke on Saturday at a Meeting to inaugurate an English branch of the L. League.[2] A moderate speech, seasoned with the inevitable abuse of the Ch. Sec. and prophecies that he and the land system which he tried so hard to prop up would come down with a run together.

28 Mar., Mon.

Uncle Matt to lunch. At Mrs S[tanley's] he had been introduced to Mr T. P. O'Connor—'Letters are neutral'. Father at a Cabinet in the morning. In the afternoon Mother and I went to see young Mr Browning's[3] picture for the Academy and Gro[svenor Gallery] exhibited in an empty house at Queen's Gate, with his Father acting showman.

Father returned to dinner in good spirits. The Land Bill tending in his direction.

29 Mar., Tu.

Walked with Oakel to Westminster, returning in a hansom, and afterwards with Father to the office. Mrs R. and May to lunch. Spent the afternoon with Mrs G. at Weybridge in the S. K. Woods. Brilliant and fine but very cold at sunset. Father returned home to dinner, and we went in the evening to private theatricals at the Colliers'. The second piece, 'Modernes Precieuses Ridicules', was amusing, the subject of it being something the same as in 'The Colonel'; if it had not been really cleverly written one would get tired of these everlasting sarcasms upon false aestheticism as symbolized by peacock feathers and sunflowers.

30 Mar., Wed.

In the morning called on O. at his lodgings and walked with him and Rob to the Temple, returning also on foot.

[1] Member of boards of poor law guardians, the elections for which had just been held all over Ireland.
[2] The inaugural meeting of the Land League of Great Britain, attended by several Irish M.P.s, was held on Friday and Saturday in the Westminster Palace Hotel (*F.J.*, 26, 28 Mar.); see Moody, *Davitt*, p. 481.
[3] Robert Wiedemann Barrett Browning (1849–1912), son of the poet; known as 'Pen'.

In the *Standard* of this morning a full and deeply interesting account by their Corr. (Mr Cameron) of the defeat on the Majuba Hill. The Officers to a man appeared to have behaved well, and the 92nd H[ighlander]s like veterans of the Peninsula, but they were not supported by the young troops with whom Sir G. Colley had made up his contingent of 360 men.

In the evening Father, Mother and F[rancie] dined at the Lawrences'. I went with O. in the evening to a pleasant party at the Lubbocks'.

Lord Beaconsfield is seriously ill, but the accounts of him this evening rather better.

31 Mar., Th.

F. and I went with Mother in the afternoon to tea at Lady Mowbray's and Mrs Mundella's. Everyone enquiring latest news of Lord Beaconsfield.

Mr and Mrs Rathbone,[1] Mrs Buxton and Sydney, Sir H. Verney,[2] Mr Vadal and Mr Richardson to dinner. Father received a small parcel addressed 'Not dynamite, but a sample of bread supplied to prisoners at Kilmainham'.

1 Apr., Fri.

There is some discontent amongst the Liberal papers at the Govt prosecution of the *Freiheit*, the wretched little Socialist print which published a revolting article on the Czar's murder, Sir W. Harcourt having explained in the House that the prosecution is not undertaken by the Govt in deference to pressure from abroad, but simply with a view to punish the open publication of incitements to murder whether of an Emperor or of a peasant.

In the morning Francie went to have her first sitting to Mr Tayler[3] for her picture in water colour. By Mother's wish we are both going to have our heads done by him. I lunched with Nora Lucy, and went afterwards to examine the old English china at the S[outh] K[ensington] Museum with a view to getting such fresh light on our own collection.

Lady Kensington and Mrs Ball to tea.

Lord Cairns's[4] speech in the H. of Lords on Thursday in denunciation of our Transvaal policy has made a deep impression: even the *Pall Mall* is visibly impressed, and has to get what comfort it can out of the situation by abusing Lord Kimberley.

[1] William Rathbone (1819–1902): liberal M.P. for Liverpool, 1868–80; for Carnarvonshire, 1880–85; for North Carnarvonshire, 1885–95.

[2] Sir Harry Verney (1801–94): liberal M.P. for Buckingham, 1832–41; for Bedford, 1847–52; for Buckingham, 1857–74, 1880–85.

[3] See appendix.

[4] Hugh MacCalmont Cairns (1819–85): conservative M.P. for Belfast, 1852–66; solicitor general for England, 1858–9; attorney general, 1866; 1st Baron Cairns, 1866; lord chancellor of England, 1868, 1874–80; cr. 1st Earl Cairns, 1878.

The dissatisfaction with the conditions of affairs produced by the recent peace both at home and abroad seems only to increase with time. From South Africa the accounts as to the prospect of peaceful relations between Dutch and English in the future are most discouraging. The English Colonists who have settled and bought land in the Transvaal, under the belief they would continue to be British subjects, are leaving the country with bitter complaints against the Govt which has betrayed them to the Boers by a humiliating peace. Meetings of protest have been held at Newcastle, and Mr G's effigy has been burnt in the streets. The Boers on their side refuse to be committed to good behaviour by Joubert and are making their position unbearable to loyal Boers and Englishmen in the Transvaal.

The Commission will either prove a delusion and a snare to those who hoped that it would assist claims left in abeyance by the peace negotiations; or it will insist upon concessions which the Boers seem in no mood to grant, and the demand for which will provoke a new war, this time with more fiercely embittered feelings on both sides.

Uncle Matt and Uncle Walter to dinner.

2 Apr., Sat.

Gloomy accounts of state of things in S. Africa. 7th Hussars and 58th are to remain in Natal.

Walked with Father to the office. A Sunday [sunny] morning but a continuance of this bitterly cold east wind and driving dust.

The prospects of a holiday for Father at Easter fast diminishing. He remarked to-day that he was not at all easy about the condition of things in Ireland, either as regards disturbance or distress. Also he has come to the conclusion that he cannot with an easy mind leave everything to Lord C[owper] in times like these—'he is a reflex of Burke'.

Lucy to Lunch, she and Francie in the afternoon to the Sat. Popular Concert, I with Mother to Mrs Hamilton's and the Spring Rices'. At 6.30 I dined with the Balls and went with them afterwards and a M. and Mme. Cumuret to the S[outh] K[ensington] Museum to investigate further into the china. The Museum was full of people, and looked very bright and attractive; I felt quite as if I were in some foreign town, there was something so strange in strolling about amongst my fellow creatures in a public place in the evening in one's bonnet. The cartoons looked finer than I have ever seen them.

Father and Mother dined at Mrs J. Stanley's.

3 Apr., Sun.

The *Observer* contained the report of a conflict in Co. Sligo on the estate of Mr Ffrench between the people and the police engaged in protecting a process.

The police being attacked were at last ordered to fire; three of the people were killed and others wounded. One of the police was mortally injured.[1]

Father and Mother to church at the Savoy, we to St James's with Oakel who is at present living in the house.

Mr Jephson to lunch—always a sign of stress of work and anxiety at the Irish Office. In the afternoon, Father, Rob and I walked to Curzon St to enquire for Lord B[eaconsfield] a throng of people in the hall writing their names and reading the bulletins.

A crowd outside watching the arrival of enquirers. The account a little more favourable, but far from reassuring.

Home from the Athenaeum in a hansom, calling at No. 15. Sir F. Buxton[2] to tea. Mother much delighted with Watts's[3] portrait of Uncle Matt, which she and Aunt F[anny] L[ucy] had been to see this afternoon in the studio.

At 6 Father returned with papers, evidently of bad import. It was a letter from Mr Naish[2] to Mr Johnson[2] giving a most glaring account of the state of things: the dogged resolution not to pay rent, and determination to resist by active or passive resistance every operation of the law; the insolent and menacing behaviour of juries even towards the lawyers conducting a case. In Kerry the immediate effect of the Coercion Bill dying out, all fear of further arrests passed away, the conclusion being that more arrests were necessary.

I have seldom seen Father more profoundly depressed by any budget of public news. It seemed as though we had gone back to the dark mornings that we passed through during the autumn in Dublin.

I went in the evening to St John's. Read the *Irishman*; less violent than usual. A remarkable article in the *Irishman* on 'Land policy'.

4 Apr., Mon.

Details in the papers of the 'fatal affray' in Co. Sligo. Mr Dillon, on reading to the meeting he was addressing the telegram describing what had happened, declared that 'the blood of the men killed and the curses of their children would be on the heads of G[ladstone] and F[orster] who had refused to step in

---

[1] At about 10.30 a.m., on 2 Apr., Constable Robert Armstrong with three sub-constables was escorting a process-server to Clogher, a village in south Sligo, about five miles from Ballaghadereen. They were met by a hostile crowd and stones; Armstrong tried to make an arrest and was beaten to the ground, whereupon the other police fired into the crowd and killed two men. A verdict of murder was later found against the police by a coroner's jury; see p. 166 below. Armstrong died of his injuries on 6 Apr.; three men were committed for trial for his murder but the case was not proceeded with (S.P.O., I.C.R., Returns of outrages, May 1881; 1882).

[2] See appendix.

[3] George Frederic Watts (1817–1904): earnest and prolific painter and sculptor; R.A., 1868; now reaching the height of his popularity. The *Annual Register* describes his portrait of Arnold (now in the National Portrait Gallery, London) as 'somewhat coarse and markedly Semitic in aspect ... nevertheless a striking likeness' (*Ann. Reg. 1881*, p. [454]).

to prevent evictions before the Land Bill'. 'That's rather too bad' was the poor Ch. Sec's comment as he read aloud the passage.[1]

England is not the only country that has its troubles in distant parts of its Empire. France is in high excitement over the destruction of a band of French soldiers by a marauding raid from some Tunisian tribe on the borders of Algeria. There has for some time been considerable friction and jealousy between France and Italy with regard to the question of influence and ultimate supremacy over the Bey of Tunis. The present outrage seemed to give the French a good pretext for asserting themselves actively. Reinforcements are being promptly despatched to the Tunisian frontier. Meantime Italy takes alarm, and the Bey of Tunis seems likely to find himself in a somewhat dangerous predicament between his two European neighbours, each desirous to conciliate his feelings and respect his independence, but still more anxious to 'score off' each other at his expense if necessary.

Monday morning walked with Lucy to Miss Wood's, in the afternoon to read to Francie during her sitting to Mr Tayler, and afterwards to the Hospital.

Budget night. A note from Father saying he must go to D[ublin] at once.

Mother and I dined at Lady Erskine May's,[2] where we were joined by Father from the House. A pleasant informal party. Mrs Gladstone and the W. H. Gladstones[3] came in from the House and Mrs Brand's gallery, also Sir J. Lubbock and Mr Leveson Gower.

After we had sat down to dinner the great man himself appeared, very bright and lively, and seeming in no way exhausted by his 2 hours speech. I was sitting between him and Mr W. H. Gladstone, and had the pleasure of hearing much pleasant talk between him and Father who was sitting next to Lady May. Every now and then he turned to me, and there was something very attractive in his bright benignant dark eyes, and courteous manner.

The talk was anything but political, turning a good deal on the characters of the Kings of England. Which was the worst, propounded Mr Gladstone to Father, explaining that he measured a man's badness by his selfishness. On this account he gave Chas 1st, Hen. 8th and G. IV as the three worst. Charles 1st had very many good points, only he was possessed with the unfortunate notion 'that it is the privilege of a king to lie'. He told Father that as Irish Sec. he ought to have a friendly feeling for James 1st, since it was in his reign that the first attempt was made to deal rightly with the Irish question; it was under him that for the first time the Irish became not enemies but subjects.

From the dining room Mr Gladstone went back to the House, but in half an

---

[1] Cf. below, p. 127. Dillon was speaking at a meeting at Clough, near Castlecomer, Co. Kilkenny, on 3 Apr.

[2] Louisa Johanna, née Loughton, wife of Sir Thomas Erskine May (1815–86), clerk of the house of commons 1871–86, and author of *A treatise on the law, privileges, proceedings, and usages of parliament* (1844; many later editions), as well as a constitutional history of England.

[3] William Henry Gladstone (1840–91): eldest son of the premier; liberal M.P. for Chester, 1865–8; for Whitby, 1868–80; for East Worcestershire, 1880–85.

hour reappeared in the drawing room, welcomed by vociferous clapping from Mrs G., saying: 'there has been a great flare-up about the Transvaal, and they are saying it's all our fault'.

However I suppose the flare-up had died out, for Mr G. had not gone back to the House when Mother and I left to go on to Lady Thurlow's.

Here we saw Uncle Matt, Monteagles, Alma Tademas, Poynters[1] etc. but did not stop very long. The cold still intense.

5 Apr., Tu.

Mr G's Budget is considered unsensational, that is, somewhat disappointing. The surplus all gone in defraying War expenses.

Mother in the afternoon to Sydenham.

Father back to dinner.

6 Apr., Wed.

The cold bright weather continuing. A visit in the morning from Uncle Matt. From all we hear his article in the new *Nineteenth* [*Century*]—which I have not yet seen—is somewhat startling.[2] Mother shirks reading it, fearing that its airy theorizing may be taken hold of by the enemy and so tend to increase the Ch. Sec's political difficulties. Father laughingly tells Uncle M. that he had better not come to Ireland, for from all he hears, he should have to arrest him on the strength of his article.

Uncle Matt told me that Mr Lowell,[3] on the other hand, said to him 'It is only poets and artists amongst men, and young countries amongst nations like mine, that can see straight, and from what they tell me of your article, it must be just common sense'. If only the poets and artists could be got to administer in politics, as well as prescribe, they would find that 'seeing straight' is only half the battle.

Dorothy Blomfield to lunch. May and Humphry [Ward] with their children, also Mrs and Miss Mulholland to tea. Dined in the evening at the Mundellas'. I sat at dinner between Mr Stopford Brooke[4] and Lord Hartington. With the former I had much talk. I found him interesting and agreeable but somewhat affected; probably it was natural to him to be so.

[1] Laurence Alma-Tadema (1836–1912): the Dutch-born painter (chiefly of classical subjects), now at the height of his career. Edward John Poynter (1836–1919): principal of the National Art Training School and writer on art.

[2] Arnold's two-part article, 'The incompatibles' [England and Ireland], appeared in the *Nineteenth Century*, ix, no. 50 (Apr. 1881), pp 709–26, and no. 52 (June 1881), pp 1026–43.

[3] James Russell Lowell (1819–91): perhaps the foremost American man of letters at this time; humorist, and U.S. ambassador to London, 1880–85. See appendix.

[4] Stopford Augustus Brooke (1832–1916): born in Letterkenny, Co. Donegal; ordained, 1857; seceded from Church of England, 1880; famous preacher and author of many religious and literary works.

I was rather amused at the mild but decided disapproval he expressed of the moon and its effects, which he thought unnatural. A moonlight and love, he considered too like the Opera, and by the repeated sight of the moonlight reflection on the sea he had been positively bored from its sameness and monotony.

Like every other pair of talkers at this particular season we spoke of course of Carlyle's *Reminiscences*;[1] he did not, like me, feel angry with Mr Froude for having published unsorted and unsifted these *Reminiscences*, which with all their interest and vividness have so much that is ill-natured and petty mixed up with them. On the whole, Mr Brooke thought the picture they presented of Carlyle himself and of his manner of thought an interesting and not unfair one. He was especially struck with the way in which the artist in Carlyle, as distinguished from the philosopher, novelist, and historian, comes out in these miscellaneous writings. 'It is curious', said Mr B.,

how with all his talk about the veracities and his professed contempt for art, Carlyle was essentially and before all things, an artist, seizing and transfiguring a character, or an event by the force of his own vivid imagination till you realized the object as he saw it, and wished you to see it, with perfect clearness, but perhaps never once saw it in the plain light of historical fact.

After dinner I had some talk with Mrs Poynter, a pretty, close-fitting little lady, who made herself very pleasant and has asked me to come and see her.

Before leaving I consulted Mr Mundella about an embossed white tea service, a specimen of which I had brought to show him. He was much interested, but could not positively tell me what it is; he inclined to think, Bow.

From the Mundellas' Father returned home to meet Mr Chenney.[2]

The appearance of a long 2-column in the *Standard* in the morning, apparently giving on authority the terms of the Land Bill, and evidently based on some actual though defective information, has caused a great sensation, and highly incensed the other papers.[3]

O. having come in the carriage he went with us to Mrs Playfair's, and afterwards on with me to Mrs J. Stanley's. At Mrs P's he had a long colloquy with Mr E[rrington] who it appears was begging for some of O.'s 'eloquent extracts' from the *I.W.* [*Irish World*] to take with him to Rome and shew to the Pope.

At Mrs Stanley's we found the party almost melted away. Uncle Matt and Nelly still there however, also the Bancrofts, Mrs Smalley, and the Hawthornes. From Mr H. I heard that all the Parnellites had been present earlier in the evening, including Mr P. himself. Mr H. further had a story of Mr Parnell,

---

[1] Published in two volumes by Longmans earlier in the year for his literary executor, James Anthony Froude (1818–94).

[2] Possibly Thomas Chenery (1826–84), editor of *The Times*, 1877–84.

[3] The *Standard* article was reprinted in the 2nd edition of the *F.J.* of 6 Apr. 1881.

having walked off on finding himself standing close by 'Forster'. It was no use my assuring Mr M. that 'Forster' had not been there that evening. He stuck to his story, though as I found afterwards there was very little foundation for it, Mr P. not having been present either.

7 Apr., Th.

The day for the introduction of the Land Bill. Walked with O. to V[ictoria] Station, and on to Chester Sq.; heard that, when Mrs Stanley was 'denied' to Father on Sunday afternoon, she had been closeted with Mr P., [and] her intelligent maid, taking matters into her own hands, had under the circumstances refused to admit the Ch. Sec.

Soon after my coming in, a note arrived from Mrs Brand saying that Princess M. and Mrs Lister had just sent round to say that they were coming to the Gallery, therefore Mother could only have one place. I was sorely disappointed, and poured our my feeling very emphatically to Father as he walked down to the office. I had much wished not to miss this link in the chain of events connected with Irish history, and felt that I was turning into a rabid Republican at this instance of Royal privilege used against myself.

Freddy Spring Rice and Miss Fitzgerald, and Aunt Mala to lunch. In the afternoon Mother went to the House, I to tea with Mrs Smalley, where I met the Alma Tademas and Mrs A. Dilke;[1] had the melancholy satisfaction of hearing that Miss Gladstone had been treated as I had, there having been a rush of Grand Duchesses on Mrs Brand's Gallery.

Called at Grosvenor Crescent on my way home. About half past 8 Mother and Aunt M. returned from the House. Mr G. had spoken for less time than was expected—under 3 hours—a densely crowded House, all sides listening with such eager attention and interest that there was little cheering and few signs of remonstrance either from Tories or Parnellites.

The peroration was beautiful, and quite in Mr G's best manner, and of course there were loud cheers when he sat down. He had been followed by Mr Shaw (on the whole approving), Sir S. Northcote, Mr P (very guarded and enquiring rather than critical), and others.

After dinner Mother and I went down to the House but found the Land debate over, and Mr Pell haranguing to a thin House on floods and drainage, so returned immediately.

8 Apr., Fri.

On the whole the first impression of the Land Bill as set forth in Mr G's masterly and moderate speech seems to be distinctly favourable. At any rate

[1] Margaret, wife of Ashton Wentworth Dilke (1850–83), brother of Sir Charles Dilke, and liberal M.P. for Newcastle-upon-Tyne, 1880–83.

there is a frank acknowledgment that the Measure is thoroughgoing and states-manlike in its conception of the situation and in its elaborate and painstaking attempt to meet it by careful, just and far-reaching remedies.

The very elaboration and diversity of the scheme, however, accounts perhaps for the absence of violently hostile criticism at the outset.

The Conservatives and Parnellites may well be trusted to supply their criticism later, but just at first there seems a general agreement to try and fully realize the working and purport of the Bill before attacking it.

The same papers that contain the report of Mr G's great speech announce the resignation of the D[uke] of Argyll in consequences of a disagreement with his colleagues on some points of the Land Bill. Remembering how very nearly the Duke left the Cabinet last year on the Compensation for Disturbance Bill, this step is not in any way a matter of surprise, though it may be of regret.

An early call from Mr Seebohm[1] and a slight discussion between him and Father over the new Bill. Before leaving the dining room, in answer to some remark of Mr Seebohm about the extreme intricacy and difficulties of the Measure, Father observed that some of these came from the fact that Mr G. had had so many difficulties to get over in his own mind. At the same time it cannot be said that these complications seemed to present any difficulties to Mr G., judging from the mastery [he showed] of all the elaborate details involved.

Our plans for the Easter recess still unfixed. Father and Mother certainly going to Dublin, the rest of the family doubtful, perhaps to Wharfedale. This morning decided that I am also to go to Dublin, Francie to Woodhouse.

At lunch decided that Francie should also go to Dublin. In the afternoon I went with Mother and Lucy to the Exhibition of Ancient Needlework at S. Kensington; afterwards to see Aunt Mala. Father home to dinner.

Mr T. P. O'Connor had taken a last opportunity before the House separated for Easter to insult the Ch. Sec. A short reply by the latter to Mr O'C. and by Mr G. to Mr Justin McCarthy.

The 2nd Reading of the Land Bill to be taken on Monday fortnight, the 24th.[2]

9 Apr., Sat.

The whole party including Oakel and Rob left Euston at 7.10 for Dublin. Contrary to our expectations we had a brilliantly fine passage, and spent a good part of the time very sociably on deck. Amongst our acquaintances on board

---

[1] Frederic Seebohm (1839–1912): banker and historian; author of *The English village community* (1883) and other books on English social history; a leading quaker.

[2] Monday fortnight was 25 not 24 Apr.

were the O'Hagan[s], Mr Law, Mr Melder,[1] Mr Shaw, Mr Blake (M.P. for Waterford)[2] etc. At 4 o'clock, Lucy, O. and I presided over a 5 o'clock tea in the stern, at which we entertained a select company very pleasantly. Mr Shaw is on the whole well pleased with the Bill; Mr Blake also.

We reached Dublin in good time, leaving Father at the Castle and to dine at the Club.

It is certainly pleasant to come to Ireland fresh from a Land Bill, rather than from a Coercion Bill.

10 Apr., Sun.

To church at the Hibernian R.M.S. Father walking home with H[is] E[xcellency] across the 15 Acres.

In the afternoon Father, O. and I paid a long visit to the Zoo; filled with people; the Park parched up, and grey from the long continued east wind, but signs of a change of weather visible.

A call from Miss Burke, and a quiet family dinner in the study, Father having contrived to extricate himself from an engagement to dine with the O.H. [? the O'Hagans].

11 Apr., Mon.

Papers this morning full of speeches by Mr Parnell and others on the Land Bill. The tone is not unsatisfactory or unpromising for future discussion, so Father agreed as we walked to the Park gates. The cue evidently given by Mr P. to his coadjutors is: criticize first half of the Bill (dealing with relations between landlord and tenant and practically establishing the Three Fs), as unsatisfactory and inadequate; distrust the efficacy and fairness of the Courts of Arbitration; and denounce the 17 traitors i.e. non-Parnellite members who separated from the Obstructives in the House; and oppose the 2nd part of the Measure (dealing with facilities for purchase by loans to the tenants, and disposition of waste lands), as practically the adoption of a scheme recommended by a self-constituted Commission of which Messrs P. and Davitt were members.[3]

Lord Carlingford is to succeed the D[uke] of A[rgyll] as Lord Privy Seal—a Liberal, a Land Reformer, and an Irishman.

The latest news from the Cape is not reassuring; the Boers appear to be

---

[1] Charles Henry Meldon (1841–92): lawyer and senator of Dublin University; home rule M.P. for Kildare, 1874–85, and home rule whip, 1874–9.

[2] John Aloysius Blake (1826–87): mayor of Waterford, 1855–7; inspector of Irish fisheries, 1869–78; liberal M.P. for Waterford City, 1857–69; home rule M.P. for Waterford County, 1880–85.

[3] Parnell had spoken at a dinner at Cork on Sunday evening; Irish M.P.s addressed several other meetings elsewhere to similar effect on the same day (*F.J.*, 11 Apr. 1881). The 'self-constituted commission' evidently refers to the land conference of 19 Apr. 1880; see Moody, *Davitt*, pp 374–6.

behaving very ill to the British and loyal residents; in spite of the felicitations of the Cape Parliament on the conclusion of peace and the laudation of President Brand, there is said to be every prospect of a renewal of the war at no remote period.

Father and Oakel spent the day at the Castle, Mother, F., and I a quiet, bookreading, letter-writing afternoon at home.

The rain has come to the delight of everyone, and the brilliant harsh weather of the past few weeks is exchanged for cloudy grey skies and misty horizon.

I went to have tea with Miss Burke, and hear from her about the progress of the Art Needlework Exhibition which is to be held in St P[atrick's] Hall at the beginning of May. She told me that the Mr Knox whom I met at her house in November, and who so relished his opportunity of abusing the Irish Govt for my benefit, is now getting his rents, but most of the landlords round him are still in great distress. She also told me that Archbishop Croke was said to have been in D[ublin] yesterday dining with Archbishop McCabe.

The latter it appears was greatly distressed at the passage of arms between himself and the Archbishop of Cashel—went about looking miserable, and saying 'when will the Govt give us the Land Bill and get us out of this hot water'.

In the evening Mother, O. and F. dined at the V.R. Lodge. Father having caught a slight chill stayed at home and went early to bed.

12 Apr., Tu.

Mr Dillon has been speaking against the Bill—as might have been expected.[1] He is to attend a great L. League Conference in a day or two, to consider the attitude of the Parnellite party towards the Bill in Parliament and in the country, at which there seemed likely to be a strong divergence of opinion between himself and Mr Parnell. Mr Dillon carefully avoids the responsibility of actually advising in so many words to reject the Govt measure, but he gives them plainly to understand that he thinks they will be wise to do so. At bottom all his objections to the Bill seem founded on distrust of the Courts.

Father all day at the Castle, Mother driving into Dublin with him. A quiet afternoon. At 4.15. Mother, Francie, and I drove in the open carriage to Woodlands to call on Lady O'Hagan.[2] Father back in good time; he seems to have recovered from his chill. At dinner we had some talk over Col. Cotton's trouble at the R.H.M.S. etc.[3]

---

[1] Speaking at a meeting near Nenagh, Co. Tipperary, on 11 Apr., Dillon prophesied that the bill would, if passed, result in the eviction of all tenants with heavy arrears, a rise of rent on all low-rented estates, an increase in absenteeism and 'a terrific flood of litigation' (*F.J.*, 12 Apr. 1881).

[2] See appendix.

[3] Col. L. S. Cotton was commandant of the Royal Hibernian Military School.

Some further arrests have been made—notably Mr Matt Harris and Mr Gordon, a ruffian unless the language does him great injustice.[1]

Father hears that at the private L. League Conference to-day Mr P. was strongly attacked for his favourable reception of the Bill.

A peaceful, and seemingly cheerful, evening, but plenty of anxieties of mind for Father. Standing with his back to the fire in the drawing room after dinner he asks Mother:—'Don't you think that after the Land Bill is passed, I might write to G. and tell him I have had enough of this?' 'The Irish will never forgive me' he adds reflectively, 'they are not a forgiving people'. Poor Mother only sighs, and says that it sounds very tempting.

13 Apr., Wed.

Bad reports in the papers of successful defiance of the law. A process server in Co. Cork forced to tear up his writs though defended by ten constables; the whole band surrounded and rendered helpless by a crowd of shouting angry men to the number of 200. In another case eviction peaceably carried out, the priest dissuading from violence, the constabulary engaged themselves subscribing £5 for the relief of some of the evicted tenants.

At the League meeting yesterday[2] Mr Dillon appears to have been the only speaker in favour of total rejection of the Bill. The *Freeman* still continues to support it with apparent sincerity: as the *Freeman* follows but never leads public opinion in Ireland the value and permanence of its support is never a factor to be taken into much account on its own merits.[3]

Lord Beaconsfield's condition is very critical, but all hope of his recovery is not yet given up.

The Liberals have lost a seat at St Ives, Mr Pendarves having been very decidedly beaten by Mr Ross, successor to Sir C. Read.[4]

Father all day at the C[astle]. In the afternoon O. Rob and I went down to K[ingstown] and spent an hour and a half on the *Belleisle*; we were kindly

[1] Matthew Harris of Ballinasloe, Co. Galway, and Patrick J. Gordon of Claremorris, Co. Mayo. Warrants were issued on this day for the arrest of both men for incitement to violence, but Gordon was not arrested until next day and Harris not until 16 Apr. In July Gordon was sentenced at assizes to twelve months for incitement to murder; Harris remained in prison as a 'suspect' until 3 Feb. 1882, when he was released.

[2] *F.J.*, 13 Apr. 1881. At this meeting Dillon seconded Parnell's motion for a convention of the league to consider the land bill; rather than advising total rejection, he appears to have stressed the serious obstacles which the bill, if passed, would place in the way of continued agitation (F. S. L. Lyons, *John Dillon: a biography* (London, 1968), p. 49).

[3] 'The *Freeman* seems to be taking a fair and moderate line, which I suppose means that the R.C. Bishops accept it' (Spencer to Gladstone, 14 Apr. 1881; B.L., Add. MS 44308, ff 125–6).

[4] Sir Charles Reed (1819–81) had been liberal M.P. for Hackney, 1868–74, and was elected for St Ives in 1880. In the by-election after his death, Charles Campbell Ross (b. 1849), a Penzance alderman and banker, received 462 votes against the 360 for William Cole Pendarves (1841–1929), former high sheriff of Cornwall.

received by Commander Hay,[1] and two lieutenants who insisted on our making a most thorough inspection of the ship. I was taken into every corner from the 'ram to the conning tower' and finished up by firing a cap on one of the 26 ton guns. The last time I did this was on the Austria H[ungarian] gunboat *Maro* off Belgrade.

We did not reach the C.S. Lodge till 8 o'clock, but Father was still later, having been solacing himself after his labours with a game of whist at the K[ildare] St Club; as usual he had had a hard and anxious day's work—had seen the usual variety of people—an ex-Bradford man wanting a place—a sub-inspector from the West—Lord Cork's agent—Sir E. G., this last not in the best of spirits, reporting ill-feeling between the soldiers and the people and much depressed (as every soldier is) at the recent finale in the Transvaal.

Between the Ch. Sec. and him the personal relations are fortunately still very friendly.

In talking quietly over things after dinner Father's mind again recurs to the idea of yesterday—'Before the end of the year I may be out of it all'. Mother and I both silent—she wishing it so much, I dis-wishing it so much, Oakel suggesting that in some ways it would be a pity as he knows so much about things; to which Father agrees—a new man would certainly be at a disadvantage compared with him after his experience. 'It is impossible for a man not to be humbugged by them for the first six months.'

There is no doubt that the present aspect of the country is disheartening—the first good effects of the Coercion Bill are wearing out, the good effects of the Land Bill have not begun to be seen, in so far as the disorderly conduct of the people is concerned. On the other hand one cannot but feel that the present bad fit was sure to come sooner or later, as soon as the evictions began; this had been entirely foreseen months ago; and the present crop of disturbances and collisions is but the fruit of the seed sown by the L.L. meetings in the autumn and winter.

14 Apr., Th.

Before going into Dublin Father came into the drawing room to astonish us by reading some charming complimentary verses which he has composed in honour of the pretty Mrs Dalrymple, who stopped a runaway horse in Dublin the other day and saved a child's life.

We had a curious illustration of the varied duties and responsibilities of an Irish Secretary in a case which Father brought in to consult Mother about. An order had come up to the Castle for the Ch. Sec.'s signature for the discharge of two children from a Govt Industrial Home, the father of the children being a well-to-do man who had now sent for them to join him in Africa. Since the

[1] Probably Commander James B. Haye. The *Belleisle*, 4720 tons, was an armour-plated corvette of the first reserve, stationed at Kingstown.

discharge had been applied for, it was discovered that the father was a professed atheist, and the question now came before the Ch. Sec. as to whether the Institution should still under these circumstances allow the children to be given back to their parent.

In the afternoon I went into Dublin with Williams to see the Dublin Royal Academy—Royal Hibernian. Home with Oakel. Miss Burke to tea.

15 Apr., Good Friday

To church at the H.M.S. church. Walked with Father in the park.

Reports in the papers of an Ulster meeting on the Land Bill, at which Mr C. Russell, Mr Shaw, Mr Litton, and Mr Givan[1] spoke. Mr Shaw as sensible and vigorous and fair-minded as usual; his speeches are a pleasure to read. I wish a man like him was not such a 'lusus naturae' in Irish politics.

Mr Burke and Mr Vincent to 5 o'clock tea, the latter as much interested as ever in Eastern politics, and getting quite tired of Dublin. The question of peace or war between Turkey and Greece still hangs in the balance, a 'diplomatic note' more or less inclining the scale now one way now another.

16 Apr., Sat.

A cold dreary morning with a dense sea fog over everything.

We were sincerely grieved and shocked to see in the papers the sudden death of our old Danube friend, Sergeant Heron.[2] He was a man whom we all liked, and to Father his personal friendship and bright cheery ways were a real refreshment amongst the crowd of strangers and official aquaintance with whom he has been so constantly surrounded during his hard times at the Castle.

At 12 o'clock Father, Mother and I went by train to Bray, and from there drove to Lord P[owerscourt's] to lunch. Unfortunately Lady P. was not well and did not appear, and the fog was so thick we could see nothing of the view or even the grounds; but under the circumstances we got on well enough and Lord P. was a most amiable host. I was surprised to hear his moderation and even approval of the new Land Bill. He most eagerly agreed with Father that the great danger would be lest the English should take fright and imagine they were all going to be tarred with the same brush; he had been exhorting Lord Leicester when last at Holkham[3] not to take this alarm, and explaining to him the different position in which the Irish landlords stood from the English.

[1] John Givan (1837–95): home rule M.P. for Monaghan, 1880–83. The occasion was a general meeting of the tenant-right associations of Ulster in the Music Hall, Belfast, on 14 Apr. (*F.J.*, 15 Apr. 1881).
[2] Denis Caulfield Heron collapsed while fishing in the early morning of 14 Apr., and died at 3.30 p.m. (*F.J.*, 16 Apr. 1881; see above, p. 40).
[3] Thomas William Coke (1822–1909): 2nd earl of Leicester; Holkham Hall, near Wells, Norfolk, was the family seat.

Judging from some details of his own dealing with tenants, I should imagine the Bill will do little more for Lord P. than legalize practices in force with him already.

Besides ourselves at lunch were Col. and Mrs Wingfield, Lord and Lady W. Seymour, and Judge Ormsby.[1]

We returned to D[ublin] about 5, Father going straight to the Castle, where he was occupied with further arrests. In the evening he and Mother dined at the V.R. Lodge.

17 Apr., Easter Sunday

To church at the Hibernian at 2. Father had a visit by appointment with [O'Connor] Power. His object was to obtain the release of a Mayo man[2] in whom Mr P[ower] (M.P. for Mayo) appears to have a parliamentary, but not otherwise very keen, interest. He had never heard the extracts from Mr Daly's paper for which he was accused of inciting to crime, but acknowledged that they were wild words, but declared himself positive Mr D. did not write them. In any case he is editor of the paper. Mr O'C. P. and the Ch. Sec. appear from Oakel's account to have conducted their interview with the greatest courtesy and good-understanding on both sides, and Mr O'C. P. was probably neither surprised nor heartbroken at his request not being granted.

Mr Burke and Miss Burke to tea. In the evening Father, Oakel and I dined at the O. H[agans'] meeting Mr Chevey, Mr Hayward, the Keenans[3] and J[ohn] O'H[agan]s.

18 Apr., Mon.

Went into Dublin with Father and O. Helped Miss B[urke] at the Castle in unpacking some of the cases of old Needlework for the Exhibition. Lunched with her at the C.S. Lodge.

We all left Kingstown by the evening boat and slept at Chester. A rough passage, the North east wind having returned in all its bitterness. Yarrow very low at our departure.

Heard of the death of Lord Beaconsfield.

---

[1] Henry Ormsby (1812–87): former secretary general and attorney general for Ireland; judge of landed estates court 1875–8; judge of chancery division of high court of justice in Ireland since 1878.

[2] James Daly: editor of the *Connaught Telegraph*, Castlebar; chaired the first meeting of the agitation at Irishtown, Co. Mayo on 19 Apr. 1879; arrested on 14 Apr. 1881, under P.P.P. act, for incitement to violence and imprisoned at Galway; see above, p. 15 and below, p. 135.

[3] Sir Patrick Joseph Keenan (1824–94): resident commissioner of national education since 1871; K.C.M.G., July 1881.

19 Apr., Tu.

Father, Oakel, and F. left Chester at 10 for London via Hawarden. Mother and I coming to Wharfeside. Bitterly cold weather with driving snow. Puck enchanted to see me.

20 Apr., Wed.

A quiet day at Wharfeside: visits from Dr Murry, Mr Clarke, Mr Fison,[1] and Mr Black.[2]

The dear children[3] down to spend the day with us. Del[afield] a very manly sweet little boy, Vernon as fascinating as ever and full of cleverness; the baby [Iris Mary] tall, sturdy and blue-eyed, much character in her rosy face, and a strong likeness to Edward.

Everything gone through according to precedent, including the performance of the machinery mouse and the stereoscopic photos.

21 Apr., Th.

Papers full of Lord B[eaconsfield]. Mr Gibson's attack on the Bill. A long interesting letter from Father describing their morning at Hawarden, which had been very pleasant. They had stayed to lunch, and been shown over the Castle by Mr G. and the whole family, and come on to London about 4 o'clock.

Mother and I left dear Wharfeside at 2, and coming up to London by the Midland, arriving soon after 8.

Father home to dinner in good spirits; he had had a thorough quiet talk with Mr G. over the Bill and its prospects. There seems a feeling that it will not be absolutely thrown out by the Lords—the great cry now rising on the Tory side is for compensation of the landlords.

22 Apr., Fri.

The opposition to the Bill from the L. League side is gathering force. Mr P. at a 'convention' to consider the Report on the Bill made by the L.L. Committee, has been speaking in no friendly terms, and there are many Leaguers who will try to follow Mr Dillon's lead and reject the Govt Measure root and branch. There are plenty of hard times coming in Parliament during the next month or two, but at any rate it will be pleasanter for Father fighting over an Irish Land Bill, than an Irish Coercion.

[1] Frederick William Fison (1847–1927): only son of William Fison of Greenholme, Burley-in-Wharfedale (see above, pp xiv, xv).

[2] Charles Ingham Black (1821/2–96): born and educated in Ireland; vicar of Burley-in-Wharfedale since 1855.

[3] Of her brother Edward.

23 Apr., Sat.

Papers full of letters on the Land Bill, chiefly stating the landlord objections.

From abroad there comes still warlike rumours from the Mediterranean; the French are pushing their expedition against the Kroumins with great vigour; there is some anxiety lest the result should be dangerous for the European residents, whom the Bey of Tunis may be unable to protect in the event of a fanatical outburst caused by a French invasion.

It is said that papers are forthcoming showing the justification given at one time by Lord S[alisbury] for annexation by France of Tunis.[1] However this may be, there is no doubt that the French have got their blood up about the affair, and are inclined to be very irritable at any suspicious remonstrance on the part of England or Italy.

The latter meanwhile is in a state of great perturbation as to the probable fate of her influence in Tunis if France goes much further with her present action. At the same time Italy is by no means prepared to drift into war on the subject. The Caroti [Cairoli] Ministry, after being forced to resign on the ground of not being sufficiently warlike and patriotic as regards the Tunis question, has returned to office, on the advice it is said of S. Selea, who declared himself unable to form a Cabinet.

In Russia (St Petersburg) the state of terror and apprehension continues and it would seem with only too good reason. The prisoners, including the woman, have been hanged, and the Nihilists have announced a terrible retribution for the executions; not only on the Czar but on his wife and children.

It is said that the P. of Wales returned from his recent visit to St Petersburg, deeply depressed with all that he had experienced there. As for the poor Czar, he told the Prince in parting that he never expected to see him again.

A quiet day. Ted to lunch. Father home to dinner in the evening.

24 Apr., Sun.

Father at work all the morning preparing his speech for the 2nd Reading debate on the Land Bill. A visit in the afternoon from Lord Monteagle and the F[owell] Buxtons. Much talk between Father and Lord M. over the Bill and Ireland generally. Lord M. reports that the landlords, though of course not liking it, are not prepared to oppose absolutely; this is more likely to be done by the English landlords who have property in England as well as Ireland. As for the others, they were like Ld Longford,[2] with whom Lord M. had been over to Dublin, comparatively resigned: 'they knew it was coming'.

In the west and south the phase of complete rent refusing seems passing

---

[1] Cf. below, p. 149.

[2] William Lygon Pakenham (1819–87): 4th earl of Longford; owned 15,014 acres in Westmeath and 4,555 in Longford.

over, but there has been a sudden revival of the practice in the north of Leinster, where agents are now in dismay at meeting with flat refusals of well-to-do farmers to pay any rent at all—perhaps hoping that some clause in the Bill will 'wipe out arrears' if they have been left long enough to accumulate.

The Irish papers of Saturday contain full reports of the Land League Convention, which lasted two days.[1] Mr P. was in the chair and the debate appears to have been conducted with much spirit and decorum. The point in question was embodied in a Resolution conferring power on the parliamentary rep[resentative]s of the League to use their discretion in supporting, criticizing, or rejecting the Land Bill during its passage through the House.

The more fiery spirits in the Convention, led by Mr Dillon, were in favour of enjoining their representatives to reject the Govt proposal without further parley as being inadequate and dishonest.

The majority including Mr P. M. O'Kelly, Mr Louden, and Mr Sexton were for leaving freedom of action to members, and acknowledging that the present Bill would do something if not much, to improve the position of tenant farmers. Mr Sexton's speech was excellent, quite justifying the good opinion that has been formed of him over here.

A favourite point of attack in the Bill, and one that lends itself to much fervent oratory, is the emigration proposition. This is described as a deeply laid insult and injury to the Irish people, whom a cruel Govt are trying to drive from their native land. It is especially enjoined on the League party in the House to strive for the rejection of these emigration clauses as a condition of any further toleration of the Bill.

25 Apr., Mon.

The mild weather has returned again; this time it may be hoped not to be succeeded by a fresh series of snow storms.

Walked with Father to the office. His speech concocted in his mind. In the afternoon we went to the House, Francie and I having places in Capt Gossett's Gallery.

It was expected that Mr Gladstone would speak of Lord B[eaconsfield] but our hopes were disappointed. Mr G. was not present at the opening, and the only notice taken of Lord B's death was an intimation by Lord R. Grosvenor[2] that the Premier will a fortnight hence propose the erection of a national monument in the Abbey.

After the questions, the debate on the 2nd Reading of the Land Bill began

[1] At the Rotunda, on 21–2 Apr., attended by over 1000 delegates; see Moody, *Davitt*, pp 483–4.
[2] Lord Richard Aquila Grosvenor (1837–1912): second surviving son of the 2nd marquis of Westminster; vice-chamberlain of the royal household; liberal M.P. for Flintshire, 1861–86; chief government whip, 1880–85.

with an able and ungenerous speech from Mr Gibson, who criticized, apparently with great effect, many of the details of the Measure, demonstrating with great force the injustice of some of the provisions regarding 'a fair rent' to the landlords, who were being distinctly mulcted of a large portion of their incomes without any shadow of compensation being offered them. At the same time Mr Gibson did not announce his intention of voting against the Bill on the 2nd Reading.

After the discharge of their great gun, the debate threatened to collapse in a most extraordinary way. Mr Richardson (of Armagh) made a rather ineffective speech from the Liberal side, but after him no Ministerialist was found to take up the cudgels; Mr Warton and Mr Chaplin scolded and complained that Mr Gibson's crucial questions had not been, and ought to be at once, answered from the Treasury Bench.

The Treasury Bench meanwhile was almost empty, the Ch. Sec., Mr G. and the Law officers being (as it turned out afterwards) in private consultation.

A division on the 2nd reading at this unwonted hour of the evening (7) appeared imminent. Thereupon Mr Warton and Mr Gorst moved the adjournment. Mr Gladstone and the other Ministers returning, a very pretty quarrel took place as to who was to blame for this curious state of things. Mr G., Sir S[tafford Northcote], Mr Forster, Sir W[illiam] H[arcourt] and Sir R. Cross all joining in with much zest. After a short tempest, and two motions for adjournment, both of which were withdrawn, the House calmed down and the debate on the 2nd reading proceeded.

At 10 Mother and I went back to the House, I this time to the Ladies' Gallery; coming in for the middle of a speech by Lord Ly[mington] which was much approved for its good sense and practical knowledge by the authorities on our side. He was followed by the Ch. Sec. who spoke for about an hour and a quarter in reply to Mr Gibson, very conciliatory in tone and conventional in manner, and reassuring in some of its statements to those who were in fear lest Mr Gibson's interpretation of certain clauses in the Bill should indeed be the Ministerial one.

After this the debate was adjourned till Thursday, the House till 9 on the following day, to give time for members to attend Lord B[eaconsfield]'s funeral at Hughenden.

26 Apr., Tu.

A bad murder near Clifden, a caretaker[1] being shot by a party of men who visited his house at night. Several other instances of lawlessness. A verdict of 'wilful murder' returned.

---

[1] John Lydon, herd: his son Martin, shot at the same time, died on 21 May (S.P.O., I.C.R., Return of outrages, Apr. 1881).

Uncle Matt to lunch. Father home to dinner. Stanley Fleming to dinner, and taken down to the House afterwards by Father, so coming in for the Bradlaugh scene, this affair having come up again in the same way as last year.[1]

27 Apr., Wed.

Papers full of Lord B's funeral.

Mr Dillon, in a speech at a meeting of the Land League Executive in Dublin, has announced that a final effort will be made next week to induce Parliament to suspend all evictions and sales of farms for a year; that if this is not done the people will resist evictions by force, and that the public opinion in Ireland will support him in saying that, should blood be shed, the guilt will be on the heads of Mr Gladstone and Mr Forster.[2]

The afternoon occupied by the House over the Bradlaugh affair.

Edith arrived from the I. of Wight. A dinner party at home including the F. Hollands,[3] Seban, Mr Hughes, Lady F[rederick] C[avendish], etc.

28 Apr., Th.

To Bond St in the morning. In the afternoon to the Hospital. Dined in the evening at Sir H. Verney, to meet Mr Lowell, Father snatching an interval from the House to come with us. Heard from him that Lord Elcho[4] had been speaking against the Bill, vivacious but not seriously damaging, also Mr C. Russell.

Notice of an amendment given by Lord J[ohn Manners][5] to the effect that the state of things in Ireland did not require legislation on land tenure but promotion of industry, in short 'protection'. This is the nearest approach to a direct negative of the Bill on the 2nd Reading which the Conservatives have as yet brought forward.

---

[1] See above, p. 6.

[2] *F.J.*, 27 Apr. 1881. This speech, and the similar sentiments he expressed at Grangemockler, Co. Tipperary (*F.J.*, 29 Apr.; Lyons, *Dillon*, p. 50), formed the grounds for his arrest for 'inciting persons to forcibly oppose and resist the execution of process of the law for giving possession of lands, and to riot and assault'. Dillon's actual assertion was that if a man were shot by the police in resisting eviction, a verdict of wilful murder would be brought against Gladstone and Forster instead of the police. This does not seem to have happened, but Dillon's warning influenced Forster's policy towards mass resistance to process-serving; see below, p. 160, n. 5.

[3] See appendix.

[4] Francis Charteris Douglas (1818–1914): son of 9th earl of Wemyss; conservative M.P. for East Gloucestershire, 1841–6; for Haddingtonshire, 1847–83; lord of treasury, 1852–5; succeeded his father, 1883.

[5] John James Robert Manners (1818–1906): 2nd son of 5th duke of Rutland; the model for Disraeli's 'Lord Henry Sidney' in *Coningsby* (1844); enthusiast for social reform under aristocratic leadership; conservative M.P. for Newark, 1841–7; Colchester, 1850–57; N. Leics., 1857–85; postmaster general, 1874–80.

29 Apr., Fri.

Father much pleased with the speech made last night by Mr Law—quite a success, and a very satisfactory answer to Mr Gibson.

The Catholic Archbishops and Bishops have held a conference on the Bill, and passed resolutions recommending strong, very far-going amendments in Committee, all in the interests of the tenants.

In the morning with Edith, Aunt F[anny] L[ucy], Lucy, and N[elly] to the private view at the R. Academy—very pleasant, meeting many acquaintance, but the rooms not over-crowded. Uncle M's picture disappointing at first sight, Watts' peculiar style being done great injustice to by the brilliant surroundings on the Academy walls.[1]

On the other hand Mr Collier's picture of Hudson looks finer than even when we saw it in the studio—it has been bought by the Academy for £1500.

In the afternoon with Edith to Abbey Lodge, where I was introduced to Mme and Mlle Cataigé of Bucharest, and to the daughters of the Greek Minister.[2]

Greece is in a high state of excitement at present, the people being furious at the compromise with Turkey; there are even fears lest the King's position may be endangered, so great is the unpopularity of all in authority who are considered responsible for the recent arrangement.

Father home to dinner, bringing with him Sir W. Gregory, and Sir F. Herschell[3]—the former most amusing and agreeable—full of anecdotes of Lord B[eaconsfield] whom he had known intimately as a personal friend from the 'Young England' days down to last month, when he met Lord B. at one of the last houses he dined at.

In spite of his personal friendship Sir W[illiam] however is not—on public grounds—well pleased at the proposal of a national monument, an honour only paid to 5 out of 20 of our last Prime Ministers. It is evident there will be some opposition when the question comes before the House.

The House occupied this evening with Mr Pease's Motion on the Opium question.

30 Apr., Sat.

An anxious morning for Father—clearly something impending. Mr Jephson summoned and sent off with a message to Mr Law: evidently Mr Dillon is to be arrested. I had known this was becoming more likely of late, but have seen so little of Father during the past week that I have only gathered vaguely the state of affairs.[4] This morning again my hopes of a talk with him were disappointed,

[1] See above, p. 111.

[2] M. A. A. Contostavles.

[3] Farrer Herschell (1837–99): Q.C., 1872; recorder of Carlisle, 1873–80; liberal M.P. for Durham City, 1874–86; solicitor general for England, 1880–85; lord chancellor, 1886, 1892–5; Baron Herschell, 1886.

[4] According to Dilke (Gwynn and Tuckwell, *Dilke*, i, 370), the decision to arrest Dillon was

for just as I was ready to start with him for the office, Lord Monteagle appeared 'with suggestions' concerning the Bill, and went down with him instead of me.

Edward arrived from a flying visit to Havre. An afternoon at home. Mr Cyrus Field[1] to tea, just fresh from a journey round the world.

Father home at 6.30. to dress for the Academy dinner; on going up to his dressing room for a few moments I heard there had been a hitch caused apparently by not having prepared the warrant in time for the arrest to be made that day.

Mother having taken Father in the carriage to Burlington House, returned to 7 o'clock dinner, after which she and F. and I went to see Mme Modjeska and Mr Forbes Robertson[2] in *Romeo and Juliet* at the Court Theatre. Very good, both looking the part well, and Mme M. a thoroughly 'interesting' actress, with real force, and capable of playing passion without the effect of tearing it to pieces. Her voice and manner have not the winning charm and variety of Sara Bernhardt,[3] and there seems a slight monotony of tone and gesture in the lighter scenes, but when wrought up with grief or fear she was very fine and convincing.

1 May, Sun.

A gloomy day for Father. Report of fresh outrages in the *Observer*; the cruel barbarities practised by bands of armed men upon helpless and unoffending individuals, men, women and children, are sickening.

A spirit of random cruelty and lawlessness seems at work, and in one or two instances there is no apparent motive for the crimes committed—especially in the case of Lyden, an old man who was brutally murdered near Clifden.[4] Mr Dillon with his courageous plain-speaking has very much to answer for.

To church at St James the Less, but Father not able to come. The Academy dinner had not been very lively, and Uncle Matt's speech was unfortunately not well heard.

made at a cabinet meeting at which the opponents of arrest consisted of Bright, Chamberlain, Childers, Carlingford, Northbrook, and Dodson; Spencer and Granville were both absent but, if anything, were against arrest. Harcourt was neutral. The advocates of arrest consisted of Kimberley, Hartington, Selborne, Forster, and Gladstone, who declared that there were six on each side and gave a casting vote as chairman for arrest.

[1] Cyrus West Field (1819–92): entrepreneur; promoted first Atlantic telegraph, 1857–8; helped to restore Anglo-American relations after 1865 through his personal contacts with Gladstone, Bright, and others.

[2] Helena Modjeska Chlapowska (1844–1909): born in Cracow, Poland; settled in U.S.A. since 1876; specialised in Shakespearian roles. Johnston Forbes-Robertson (1853–1937): a well-established actor who, however, considered himself primarily a painter; knighted, 1913.

[3] Henriette Rosine Bernard (1844–1923): former chief actress of the Comédie Française; played at the Gaiety Theatre, London, 1879; resigned from the Comédie next year to begin a series of world tours.

[4] Above, p. 126. The police report on the Lydon case ascribed the motive to an attempt to enforce a boycott of the Lydons' employer (S.P.O., I.C.R., Returns of outrages, Apr.–May 1881).

Mr and Mrs Cyrus Field to lunch. By way of a variety on Irish business Father called off from lunch to a circulating Cabinet box, and obliged to write off then and there a Minute on the French Commercial Treaty.

In the afternoon he called on the D. of Manchester[1] who lamented to him over the poor opinion entertained of England at Berlin in consequence of the Transvaal peace. A short time ago our kind friends in Germany shook their heads disapprovingly at us in consequence of the Transvaal war, so it seems almost hopeless to win their admiration or esteem.

Visits here in the afternoon from Lord Spencer, and from the Dean of Durham with his bride-elect, Miss Katherine Gladstone.[2] I did not see them as I was out with Oakel calling on Mr and Mrs P. and Mrs Ball.

In the evening looked through the Rebel papers, not so violent as usual—some rational criticisms and comments on 'Mr Forster and the Land Bill', apropos of his reply to Mr Gibson on Monday.

2 May, Mon.

'Dublin proclaimed', 'Expected arrest of Mr Dillon'—the columns of Irish news as unpleasant as it used to be in the autumn. In Dublin a boy (Farrell) has been shot (probably killed) in consequence of his having informed the police of some rifles concealed in a house he was painting. There seems general agreement that this is a Fenian outrage, and that there may be more to follow. In this case however the police have a clue to some of those concerned.

The news from the Transvaal very unsatisfactory; the Boers becoming constantly more aggressive and insolent towards loyal Boers and English inhabitants, the prospects of any compliance with the demands of the Commission decreasing as the warlike 'Africander' party in the Transvaal get the upper hand over Joubert and those leaders who are professedly anxious to keep terms and maintain peace with the British Govt.

The Natives are said to be discontented at the prospect of a return to Boer supremacy, and the anti-Boer European inhabitants threaten to revenge themselves by inciting this discontent against their now jubilant enemies.

It looks as though Sir F. Roberts might have to take another voyage before long unless all idea of maintaining English laws and rule in S. Africa is to be abandoned. The only satisfactory statement from this quarter of the world is the announcement that thanks to the mediation of Sir H[ercules] Robinson, the Cape Govt have at last made peace with the Basutos.

In the morning Aunt F[an] arrived on her way from O. to C. I drove with Father to the office. We talked of Oakel, and the tempting suggestion made by

---

[1] Probably William Drogo Montagu (1823–90), the duke of Manchester, who owned 12,298 acres, worth £17,164, in Co. Armagh.

[2] William Charles Lake (1817–97): dean of Durham since 1869; married Katherine Gladstone, niece of the premier, in June 1881.

Humphry that he should stand for Oxford. From the office we drove on to Sir E. May, Father having meanwhile received a telegram reporting Mr D[illon]'s movements as far as known.

Father home to dinner in the evening. A disagreeable meal—Mr P. C. very deaf, all the efforts of Mother and the family, including E[dward] and E[dith] directed to keeping up the semblance of a lively conversation, Father being absorbed in silent anxiety and annoyance.

In the middle of dinner, a cipher telegram brought in, a struggle to make it out by the aid of the accompanying dictionary, the result evidently unsatisfactory, Father's gloom and worry increase. Just before we leave the dining room he mutters under his breath 'they've made a complete mess of it'. In fact the arrest which ought to have been got over on Saturday had missed fire again.

About half past 11 Oakel appeared after making a speech on the L. Bill at his Debating Society—informed us that Mr Dillon had been arrested at Portarlington and taken to Kilmainham. It had to be done, and it is a good thing it is over.[1]

3 May, Tu.

A fuller report of Mr D[illon]'s last speech given in *The Times* would in itself be ample justification for not leaving him at large while smaller men are arrested for 'inciting to break the law'. A more deliberately cruel hounding on to the persecution and ruin of innocent men than his exhortation to his Tipperary audience as to their treatment of process servers and all others engaged on the unpopular side I never heard or read.

It is clear that the 'irreconcilables' amongst the Parnellites are determined to make hay while the sun shines, and excite the passions of the people to such a pitch in the present that no possible Measure of Land reform in the future can pacify them. Mr Dillon plainly avowed his fear the other day that the passing of the Land Bill would mean the break up of the Land League, and he is consistently doing all in his power to prevent the people from accepting or profiting by any reform coming from Parliament instead of through the Land League.

There have lately been rumours of a split between the Members for Cork and Tipperary and their respective followers on the question of dealing with the Land Bill, but of course Mr P. will now be compelled to become Mr Dillon's champion in the House if only for the sake of appearances in Ireland. He did attempt to bring forward the affair last night.[2]

[1] Cf. Forster to Gladstone, 16 May 1881: 'There was one mistake but only one mistake about Dillon's arrest—not holding an early Council on the Saturday—but Burke *is* a very good man though sadly overworked'. Burke's instructions to the inspector general on 1 May enjoined the greatest discretion in making the arrest, and concluded: 'It is the wish of the Government that Mr Dillon, if arrested, should be treated with every possible consideration', including transport by first-class rail instead of the customary second-class (S.P.O., R.P. 1882/15406).

[2] Parnell had asked the chief secretary during question time what object the government had in suspending the constitution in Dublin (*Hansard 3*, cclx, 1554).

A busy day for Father. Mr Jephson and Mr Law here an hour after breakfast—later on Judge Ball, Lord C.,[1] and Lord Emly, the latter to discuss University business.

At 12.30. Father obliged to go down to the office to prepare for question time, when he fully expected 'a row', and advised Mother and me to come down to the House.

Lord C. and Lord E[mly] to lunch.

On one or two estates hitherto at peace, the well-to-do tenants have lately refused point blank to pay any rent at all—on one of these (Lord C's brother) the rents had been lowered to an almost extreme point during the famine, and never been raised since.

Mother and I spent an hour and a half at Mr Tayler's (my first sitting) and afterwards went down to the House; on going up to the Gallery heard from Wilson that question time had passed over quietly and that the House was now occupied over some peaceful Motion of Mr Blennerhasset.

Father home to dinner, also a Dr Smith,[2] Moderator of the Presbyterian Church in Ulster. A pleasant man, with much kindly feeling towards the Ch. Sec., and by no means hopeless as to the future.

A private meeting in the House in the evening between Father and Presbyterian Ministers come up to watch the L[and] B[ill] (including our friend D[r] Smith and Dr Boyd Kinnear, M.P. for Donegal).[3]

Before the end of the evening Mr P. endeavoured to bring on a scene over Mr Dillon's arrest, but his method of doing so was ruled out of order by the Speaker, and nothing exciting happened.

After dinner Mother, O. and F. went to one of Mrs G[ladstone]'s Tuesday parties. Mr Knowles,[4] of the *19th Century*, told Mother than an Irish Member had spoken to him of Mr D's arrest as no matter of surprise to any one: 'it was evident that the only reason the Govt had left him at large so long was that he might divide the party'.

As a matter of fact the only surprise to people generally in this arrest is that it was not made sooner. Even the *P.M.G.* seems to think that having a Coercion Act at all it was not unnatural for the Govt to make use of it in a case where the deliberate incitement to law breaking was more flagrant than usual. At the same time the *P.M.[G.]* does not lose the opportunity of pointing out with mournful self-satisfaction the fresh justification of its own opposition to the Coercion

---

[1] Very probably Major-general Eyre Challoner Henry Massey (1830–97): 4th Baron Clarina, 1872; served in Crimea and in Indian mutiny; J.P. and deputy lieutenant of Co. Limerick, where he owned 2,012 acres.

[2] Jackson Smyth, D.D. of Armagh, moderator of the general assembly of the presbyterian church in Ireland, 1880–81.

[3] John Kinnear (1824–94), D.D. presbyterian minister for Letterkenny since 1850; liberal M.P. for Donegal, 1880–85. For John Boyd Kinnear, author, see p. 255, below.

[4] James Thomas Knowles (1831–1908): architect, editor of the *Contemporary Review*, 1870–77; founder and editor of the *Nineteenth Century*, 1877–1908; founded Metaphysical Society, 1869; close friend of Gladstone and Tennyson.

Bill in their logical [?   ] for imprisoning a Member of Parliament whose criticism on the Land Bill would have been valuable. 'Lettres de cachet', it observes, 'are fundamentally opposed to all our system of constitutional parliamentary govt'.

This may be true, but is it not also true that legislators who incite to lawbreaking are quite as fundamentally opposed to it. Mr Dillon practically took this course long before the Govt took to coercing, and it is hardly fair to dwell on the evils of coercion without alluding to the prior events which made such unconstitutional legislation necessary.

4 May, Wed.

A lamentable disaster in the Navy. H.M.S. *Doterel* blown up, 135 lives lost.[1]

Mr Jackson arrived. A large party to dinner including the Brands and Northbrooks, G[ran]t Duffs, Seton Ross, Sir T. Acland, Lady Reay, Mr Brown, M.P., etc. Mr B. told me that several of the Parnellites had been dying to get up a scene over Mr D[illon] the night before, and were much disappointed at the course things had taken. Father making himself most agreeable to his neighbours at dinner, and full of lively talk in the evening but very tired, and quite refusing to go on to Lady Airlie's.

Oakel and I to Mrs Tennant's, the remains of a party—John Collier, F. Myen [Myers], Mr Courtney etc.; with the latter I had some talk about Mr D. Like many others he expressed respect for Mr D's honesty and good motives, but thought he was crazy—it is very unfortunate when in political and social agitations heads and hearts go so very little together, as seems the case now in Ireland.

5 May, Th.

With Mr Jackson to the Academy in the morning, in the afternoon to the Hospital.

Dined with O. at the Croppers'. Mr C[ropper] back late from the House, having been kept by a division over the Vote of thanks to Sir F. R[oberts]. Mr Healy's opposition, with a minority in the div. of 20 to 300.[2]

6 May, Fri.

Mr Dillon has effectually divided the party. Mr Parnell and 17 of his allies have resolved to mark their sense of the Govt's base conduct in arresting their friend and colleague, by refusing to vote for the 2nd Reading of the Land Bill.

---

[1] On 26 Apr., the six-gun sloop *Doterel*, 1,137 tons, blew up in the Magellan Straits; only eleven men survived. In spite of Fenian claims to have caused the explosion, it appears to have been accidental.   [2] The division was 304 to 20.

12 Parnellites on the other hand, of whom the spokesman is Mr A. M. Sullivan, decline to follow their leader in this course, and declare they will still give the Govt a chance of getting their Bill into Committee, where as they all agree it will require radical alteration and amendment.

There seems a general impression that Mr P. has made a decided blunder in this matter. Even Archbishop Croke has written a letter to the *Freeman* full of admiration of Mr D[illon]'s patriotism, heroism, chivalry etc., but regretting Mr P's decision thus to go against the resolution of the recent Convention in Dublin.

The *Freeman* likewise regrets the split, and the *P.M.G.* reflects that Mr P. is evidently not so well qualified to direct parliamentary strategy as he is to conduct an agitation outside Parliament.

There have been several fresh outrages in the West—two attempts to destroy the life of a process server and his family by dynamite, an outcome doubtless of the advice given by Mr Harris and others in the autumn.

Also attempts which caused an explosion, but no serious damage in either case, to blow up the barracks at Chester and Wolverhampton.

The credit of such performances as the Mansion House affair and other similar attempts has been openly claimed by writers, in the Irish-American papers, of the 'Skirmishing Fund', so there is no great injustice in the popular ascription of these outrages to 'the Fenians'.

Friday morning spent with Francie at Mr Tayler's. Aunt M[ala] to lunch. In the afternoon with Mr J[ackson] to the Travenners, and afterwards with O. to tea at the John Colliers'.

To Mrs Collier's great disappointment, her picture 'A coming Tragedian' has not been accepted by the R. Academy. She intends by Mr Tadema's advice to send it to Liverpool, and if not sold there to the Salon at Paris next year.

Father not home to dinner. In the evening Mother and I went down to the House, thinking the Dillon affair might come on. We found the House discussing Mr Callan's[1] Motion regarding the bad condition of Irish agricultural Labourers. Mr Newdegate, Mr Senior, etc. Father had spoken earlier, 'a conciliatory speech', so much so that Mr C[allan] had agreed to amend his motion at the Ch. Sec.'s suggestion, in which form it was accepted by the Govt. Unfortunately Mr B[right] in a plain-spoken speech, concerning the real source of Irish labourers' misery—'want of enterprise and security for capital' causing a generally low standard of living and wages throughout the country— had irritated the Irish members, who kept up an angry series of remonstrances for a long time after the question might have been otherwise peacefully disposed of.

Between 11 and 12 Mr A[shmead-]Bartlett brought on his long-postponed motion of censure upon the foreign policy of the Govt. To my regret we came

[1] Philip Callan (1837–1902): liberal M.P. for Dundalk, 1868–74; home rule M.P. for Dundalk, 1874–80; for Co. Louth, 1880–85.

away in the middle before hearing Sir C. Dilke, who had little difficulty in making a satisfactory reply.

Father not home till 4 being kept for a division on the everlasting Bradlaugh affair.

The Land Bill debate is not making much progress, and there is some grumbling in consequence, though the most sincere detractors of the Govt cannot make out that the blame for this is all due to themselves.

7 May, Sat.

The brilliant May weather continues and London looks as bright and clean as Paris.

Drove with Mother in the afternoon to call on the Fletchers and Hansons, and to the private view of Mr Herbert's[1] pictures, including his great new picture for the H. of Lords—as gay in colouring as a Kidderminster carpet— and the subject out of the Apocrypha—'The Judgment of Daniel' in the case of S[usanna] and the Elders.

A large party to dinner, Mount Temples, Selbornes, Childers, C. Russell, Croppers, Mr Stanley, etc.

A few minutes talk with Father in his dressing room—had had a hard day's work, complicated with questions about releasing one of the Kil[mainham] prisoners, J[ames] Daly, the newspaper editor, whose wife is ill, and who has written a humble letter of apology for his past offences.[2]

I dined upstairs but had a pleasant evening afterwards. Lord M[ount] T[emple] informed me, on the question coming up after dinner, that they had been talking about the Land Bill, a fact which did not surprise me, as no two people are ever in the house without beginning to do so. He added that the general opinion amongst them had been that the Lords would probably not reject the Bill, but would send it back to the Commons with so many amendments as to make it awkward for the Govt to know how to take it.

8 May, Sun.

To church at St James the Less, but Father not able to come. His speech at Bradford on Wednesday to be thought over, and a letter to H.M. to be written. The Queen was informed that it was true that there had been several serious cases of outrage lately, but that during the past few days they had decreased; though still much cause for grave anxiety, matters however not so bad as before the passing of the Protection Act.

[1] John Rogers Herbert (1810–90): R.A. since 1846.
[2] O'Connor Power on 4 May sent Forster an abject letter from Daly, begging to be released as his detention might be fatal to his pregnant wife; he was released on 8 May (S.P.O., R.P. 1881/ 19558). See above, p. 122.

The prospects of the Bill not unfavourable in the Commons, since Mr P's abstention would make small difference to the majority; his opposition would rather incline some others in favour of the Bill, and most of the Conservative Irish would vote for it. The danger would be in the Lords.

To church in the afternoon at St Michael's. The Howsons,[1] C. Cropper, Frederick Verney,[2] Mr Rutson, and Sir F[owell Buxton?] to tea. Father read aloud to us Mr Robinson's[3] Report about the reception of the Seed Potato gift to the people at Belmullet (Co. Mayo). This has been an altogether delightful incident, and it was a pleasure to hear the Ch. Sec. reading anything so different from an Outrage Report.

'I wonder whether they would call me "Buckshot Forster" if I went down there' pondered Father. They certainly would, if a Land League orator had an hour's start of him and arrived on the scene in time to prepare the minds of the people with the doctrines of the *Nation*, *Irish Times*[4] etc.

A quiet evening; Father up in the drawing room to read the Psalms and Lessons.

After supper looked through the Rebel papers. The *Flag of Ireland* and *Irishman* opposed to Mr P's proposed retaliation upon the Govt by abstaining from voting for the 2nd Reading. Full of admiration for Mr D[illon] as the most sincere and courageous of all the Land Leaguers—but 'Dillon is not Ireland'; to reject the Bill would be doing an injury to Ireland.

In the *Nation* and *Weekly News* an allusion to the recent split amongst the Parnellites and no opinion expressed as to its wisdom, but extra allowance of rancour against the Govt and especially the Chief Sec.

One article headed 'Conciliation a la Forster' enumerating various unsatisfactory and unsympathetic answers to questions given by the Ch. Sec. in the House—the moral drawn being that this made it the more necessary for good Parnellites to keep on questioning.

9 May, Mon.

On the whole less black accounts from Ireland this morning. Several fresh arrests have had to be made—notably one in Dublin of a man reasonably suspected of having something to do with the late shooting case.[5] This arrest is

[1] John Saul Howson (1816–85): dean of Chester since 1867; and his wife Mary, daughter of John Wakefield Cropper of Dingle Bank, Liverpool.

[2] Frederick William Verney (1846–1913): third son of Sir Harry Verney (above, p. 109); relinquished deacon's orders, 1873; called to bar, 1875.

[3] Henry Augustus Robinson (1857–1927): inspector of the local government board; author of *Memories wise and otherwise* (1923) and *Further memories of Irish life* (1924).

[4] This must be an error, as the *Irish Times* was the most favourable of all Irish newspapers to the government; cf. below, p. 175.

[5] John Leavy, whipcord manufacturer of Richmond Hill, near Kilmainham; a warrant was issued on 6 May for shooting at and wounding with intent to murder, and he was arrested on

said to have caused a considerable sensation in Fenian circles, where the possession of such accurate information on the part of the police has given much surprise.

Lord S[alisbury] has been formally accepted as the leader of the Con[servative] party. A choice of evil omen for the Land Bill in the Lords.

Walked with Father to the office, a bright morning and St James's Park in brilliant looks. In the afternoon to Mr Tayler for my 2nd sitting: tea at the Hughes'.

Father home to dinner, full of admiration at Mr G's speech on proposing the Monument to Lord Beaconsfield. It had been simply perfect, and not a word said that was not true: in the Division of Mr L[abouchere]'s Amendment 50 to 300 and something.[1] Father much pleased at Mr G's candid appreciation of T. Cooper, for whom he and some others have been trying to get a pension. This it appears cannot be done, but privately Mr G informed Father that he thought that £300 might be given to T[homas] Cooper who is now 76. Mr G. told Father that he had been very much interested in the autobiography which Father had sent him. He gave proof of this by an allusion to Thomas Cooper in his speech, which Father thinks will give great pleasure.[2]

10 May, Tu.

General agreement in the papers as to the excellence of Mr G's speech, the *Standard* agreeing with Sir S. Northcote that it was nobly expressed, and still more nobly conceived. To have accomplished this difficult task so successfully must be a great relief to Mr G., who had been oppressed at the prospect before him.

Mother received this morning from Mr Penrose an interesting little book— The Memoirs of our great grandfather, Mr Penrose of Medborough [Fledborough].[3] In these troubled worrying times it is very pleasant for Father and Mother to be taken back as they are by this book and the old Tottenham letters to the quiet good lives of their grandfathers and grandmothers; to return for a short time to familiar intercourse with the Josiah Forsters[4] and John Penroses,

7 May. On 8 Aug. he was discharged, having signed an undertaking (S.P.O., I.C.R., Protection of Persons and Property Act, 1881, lists of arrests).

[1] Labouchere, supported by Arthur O'Connor, moved that the chairman leave the chair, with a view to producing a division unfavourable to Gladstone's proposal. The motion was defeated by 380 to 54.

[2] Thomas Cooper (1805–92): chartist, had been imprisoned 1843–5 for sedition and conspiracy. Disraeli had helped him to publish his political epic poem 'The purgatory of suicides'. Cooper had returned to Christianity, and his *Plain pulpit talk* (second series) had been published in 1880.

[3] John Penrose (1754–1829): sometime rector of Fledborough (Notts.); his daughter Mary married Dr Thomas Arnold. Elizabeth Penrose (1780–1837), who as 'Mrs Markham' wrote history textbooks for children, was his daughter-in-law. Francis Cranmer Penrose (1817–1903), mathematician, architect, and antiquary, who sent Mrs Forster the memoir, was his grandson.

[4] Josiah Forster (1782–1870): quaker educationalist; committee member of Anti-slavery Society, and writer; uncle of W. E. Forster.

whose peaceful, leisurely surroundings were so unlike those of their poor descendants.

The principal news from abroad just at present concern the French operations in Tunis. The expedition against the Kroumins is evidently regarded by the French in the light of an 'experiment' as to the fitness of their Army for more serious work in the future, the unfortunate Tunis being a convenient subject. So far France has had every reason to congratulate herself. The military operations have been conducted with great promptitude and success; the people, as represented at least by the Parisian press, are in good spirits at their return to public life and activity, and the influence of France over Tunis is completely assured by the recent military display whether annexation is formally declared or not.

England lectures and shakes her head over conduct which certainly does not seem consistent with very scrupulous international morality, but none of the Great Powers show signs of any intention to withstand France or to support the Sultan in the feeble claim he is raising on behalf of Ottman Suzerainty over the Regency.

It seems to show how completely the natural antipathies of this country to one or other of the European Powers has been transferred from France to Russia, when one observes the comparative indifference with which the extension of French influence over the Mediterranean is regarded. At the same time one can never be sure that more ill-feeling and jealousy is not being engendered by the present action of France than would be supposed from the continued friendliness and apparent confidence of our Govt. From their point of view it is not surprising to hear that Bismarck is said to watch these wise but somewhat questionable French demonstrations in Tunis with complacent satisfaction.

In Vienna at present there is great national rejoicing over the marriage of Princess S[tephanie] of Belgium with the Archduke R[udolph]. The future Empress is a grand-daughter of the old Palatine Joseph and bids fair to become a good Hungarian. She appears to be charming all Vienna by her pretty ways, and patriotic remarks; in a State like the A[ustro]-H[ungarian] Monarchy, this personal popularity of the Royal family is a matter of public importance, and if the young Archduchess and her husband help by their conduct to keep up the traditions of serious attachment to the Hapsburg dynasty amongst the various nationalities they will be doing good service not only to their own Empire, but to the peace of Europe.

In Bulgaria there is an excitement over a very different cause. The Prince Alex. has issued an Ultimatum announcing his fixed intention to resign the Crown if he is not allowed by the National Assembly which he is about to convene to govern Bulgaria according to his own views of what is best for the good of the country. The Constitution presented by Russia would appear to be broken down; at any rate the Ministers have proved themselves objectionable to the Prince, who it is said is influenced by Austrian machinations.

Uncle Tom to tea and dinner. Father not home to dinner, but appeared to our surprise at about half past nine.

Mr P's Motion for the adjournment of the House apropos of Mr D[illon]'s arrest had actually been allowed to pass, and the H[ouse] had adjourned at this extraordinary hour.

It had been an ill-conditioned evening, Mr P. having attacked the Govt on this Motion for adjournment instead of by a direct censure which could be met and voted upon. Mr G. refused to entertain the discussion, and neither he nor the Ch. Sec. would reply. 'He was no doubt right', said Father, 'but it was very disagreeable to sit and hear oneself abused without being allowed to answer'. Several Irish and Radicals joined in, and Mr Jesse Collings[1] took occasion to make a speech so wide of the mark that he was rebuked by Mr Gibson, who then to the surprise of Ministers made a violent attack on the Irish Executive, charging them with not having done what they might to stop the agitation by using the ordinary powers of the law.

Father highly indignant at this attack to which neither he nor Mr G., having already spoken, were able to reply. He said as much to Mr W. H. Smith and Sir M. Beach[2] on coming across them privately before leaving the House. They said 'it was all from Mr Gibson's hot Irish blood'.

Father anxious to work at his Bradford speech, but was dissuaded and went to bed instead.

11 May, Wed.

Father and Mother left for Bradford at 11 o'clock, intending to dine with E[dward] at the Vic[toria] Hotel at six, the Meeting being at half past seven. Father preoccupied and anxious, Mother not so. Considerable chance of a disturbed meeting in spite of the fact that the Irish in Bradford, having taken a prudent course, had announced through the papers their intention to protest against the Ch. Sec. by abstention from his meeting.

Considering the proportion the Irish in Bradford bear to the rest of the Ch. Sec.'s constituents, their absence was not likely to make a large void in the audience at St George's Hall.

The afternoon spent by F. and me at Mr Tayler's. In the evening Oakel and

---

[1] Jesse Collings (1831–1920): son of a small builder; mayor of Birmingham, 1878; retired from business, 1879; liberal M.P. for Ipswich, 1880–86, and for Bordesley, Birmingham, 1886–1918; active for educational reform and the welfare of agricultural labourers; close friend and ally of Chamberlain.

[2] William Henry Smith (1825–91): creator and owner of lucrative network of railway bookstalls; conservative M.P. for Westminster, 1868–91; first lord of the admiralty, 1877–80; chief secretary for Ireland, Dec. 1885–Jan. 1886; first lord of the treasury, 1886–91; *Punch*'s 'Old Morality'. Sir Michael Hicks-Beach (1837–1916): conservative M.P. for East Gloucestershire, 1864–85; for West Bristol, 1885–1906; under-secretary for home department, 1868; chief secretary for Ireland, 1874–8, 1886–7; colonial secretary, 1878–80; chancellor of the exchequer, 1885–6, 1895–1902; cr. Viscount St Aldwyn, 1906; earl, 1915.

I to parties at the Powells' and Childers'. On telling Mr P[owell] that my Father had gone down to address his constituents, he was much astonished, having been told that under present circumstances he did not venture to go down to B[radford].

'On whose authority had he been told this?'

'The Chief Constable's, who had himself informed Mr F. that he would probably be shot at if he did go down.'

This was news to me, but I believe that as a matter of fact the Bradford police authorities have been in a great state of alarm on the subject.

A pleasant party at the Childers': met Lord Dufferin, the Trevelyans, the Roumanian Minister and daughter, the Greek Minister and daughter, the Japanese, etc., etc. Oakel had some talk with Mr Knowles, who told him that he thought his article (on Short Service) a very good reply to Sir G[arnet] W[olseley], and that he meant to have [it] put in type, though he could not promise that it should appear next month. This is more than we had ventured to expect.

12 May, Th.

A rather sleepless night with 'Meeting' on the brain, aggravated by Mr Powell's remarks; the papers brought up to my room, very satisfactory and re-assuring. The Meeting had gone off very well, the Irish Ch. Sec. receiving an ovation when he made his appearance, the audience standing up waving their hats, and cheering for a long time.

The speech itself was worthy of the occasion, and, in spite of occasional attempts at interruption and insult from a scattered minority of Irishmen, the audience remained thoroughly attentive, and cordial to the end.

To anyone who had lived with the Irish Sec. during the year of hard labour which he described since he took office, and read the few words in which, before this friendly Yorkshire audience, he referred to his own position and the experiences it had involved, it was difficult to keep from tears.

At the end of the Meeting the Resolution expressing approval of the Govt Land Bill was carried all but unanimously—twelve hands held up against.

After the Meeting Father and Mother went by train to Wharfeside, and were met at the Station by a large crowd of village friends, Mr Black escorting Mother to the carriage.

Before leaving Bradford they had an affectionate meeting with Father's old friend and supporter, Mr Byles.[1]

Francie and I, after reading the papers, spent the morning in Sloane Street.

[1] William Byles, founder of the *Bradford Observer*, which later passed to his son William Pollard Byles (1839–1917).

Nelly Boyle to lunch. In the afternoon to the Hospital, and to tea at Grosvenor Crescent.

Dined with the C[ropper]s at James's, and went with them afterwards to see 'Patience' at the Opera Comique. Mr C., just back from the House, had been hearing Mr Shaw make an excellent speech on the Land Bill—strongly in support—but with amendments.

On coming home at 11.30 found Mother returned from Wharfeside, Father having been left at the House.

Before leaving Bradford he had made a speech to the Ch. of Commerce on the proposed Fr[ench] Commercial Treaty. There is much excitement in B[radford] and elsewhere on this subject, the French Govt raising great indignation by threatening to raise the Duty on our Woollen goods. This at least is what I understand. At any rate one thing is clear, and that is that the possibility of some return to Protection by this country is being now talked of in quarters where formerly such notions would have been scouted as hardly worth arguing against. Long continued depression is severely trying the Free Trade principles of our manufacturers.

In this respect Bradford is peculiarly liable to temptation, for trade there is more completely at a standstill than anywhere else.

13 May, Fri.

Bad accounts from Ireland: fresh cruelties committed upon helpless process servers; a riot at New Pallas apropos of a Dillon Meeting—where but for the efforts of the officers of the R.M. there must have been a downright battle between the mob and the soldiers.

Walked with Father to the office—talked of the Bradford Meeting—it had been a touch and go affair with the immense audience but he had succeeded in keeping it in hand to the end. Mr Illingworth had been less successful, his voice failing him.

The precautions taken by the Ch. Constable had been a decided reality—more so than Father at all liked: in fact, when he found 12 of the Wakefield police quartered in Burley, he sent a message to the C.C. intimating that another time he would rather be shot.

I believe however, though I did not know it till today (Monday), that a warning had really been received by the police which it was impossible for them quite to disregard.

Friday afternoon spent with Francie at Mr Tayler's, the first picture of her not being satisfactory, or doing at all justice to her eyes, Mr Tayler has of his own accord begun another.

Father home to dinner, a pleasant leisurely time. Father much delighted at finding a full report of his Bradford speech with a not unreasonable leader in the *Freeman*—a paper, as he says, that is really read by the violent people in

Ireland. It is a great satisfaction to think that an ungarbled version of his speech is to be allowed to reach them.[1]

As for comment in other papers, both English and Irish, they have been universally friendly and appreciative, and anxious to do justice to the Ch. Sec. personally.

14 May, Sat.

In the afternoon with Mother and Cousin C. to Bridgewater House; rather a disappointment as we were not admitted to see the Raphael and other pictures in the dining room. However the Teniers, Gerard Dows and other Dutchmen in the Picture Gallery are well worth seeing again.

Father dined with Mr Escott[2] of the *Standard*, meeting there a curious medley, Lord Carnarvon, Mr Traill ([of] the *St J[ames's] G[azette]*), Mr Mudford, ed. of the *Standard*, Dr Quain, etc. etc.

I dined with Mrs Buxton and went with her and Mrs Stanley to the St James's Theatre to see the Kendals[3] in the 'Money Spinner'. An inferior piece but the acting exquisite, and Mrs K. more charming than ever.

Received from the Rev. R. Kennedy, at the instance of Miss O'B., the Resolution passed at a Labourers' Meeting in the Co. Limerick.

15 May, Sun.

Father and Mother to church at St Margaret's, I with Cousin C. to St Peter's, Vere St, to hear Mr Page Roberts. Father not home to lunch, being occupied with papers at the office (probably outrages).

Spent the evening with him in the library; arrears of private letters to be got through: Thomas Cooper, the O'Connor Don, Mr Pears of Constantinople,[4] etc. We looked at the rebel papers, the *Irishman* for a wonder containing a civil article on his speech—civil not apropos of the Land Bill of which they are rather by way of being [? critical]—but to him personally. We agreed that this paper should be framed and glazed as a curiosity. The *Nation* as usual very bitter.

[1] *F.J.*, 12 May 1881.

[2] Thomas May Sweet Escott (d. 1924): professor in classical literature, King's College, London, 1866–73; leader-writer for the *Standard* since 1866.

[3] William Hunter Grimston (1843–1917) and Margaret 'Madge' Shafto, née Robertson (1848–1935), his wife since 1869. Grimston had been since 1879 lessee and manager of the St James's; he and his wife, according to Boase, espoused an 'ostentatious cult of respectability'.

[4] Charles Owen O'Conor (1838–1906): liberal M.P. for Co. Roscommon, 1860–80; member of Bessborough commission, 1880; senator of Royal University of Ireland; member of Irish privy council. Edwin Pears (1835–1919): barrister and historical writer; practised at the consular bar, Constantinople, 1873–1914.

16 May, Mon.

The papers full of the French Treaty with the Bey of Tunis, who yielding to superior force, in the shape of a French army stationed round his palace, has yielded everything required of him, and allowed the Regency to become a province of France.

High indignation in Italy. Cairoli has this time insisted on resigning, and Signor Selea has undertaken to form a Cabinet. As the French occupation of Tunis is a 'fait accompli' and neither Italy nor any of her allies are prepared for the moment to resent it, there is no apparent object to be gained by this change of Ministry at Rome.

English irritation against the French Republic appears to be on the increase; the Tunis affair, coming on the top of the Commercial Treaty, is creating annoyance and jealousy in different quarters at once. This is unfortunate for the Foreign policy of our Govt, the keystone of whose policy of alliances was a good understanding with France.

Lord Salisbury will probably not fail before long to point out the contrast between the Conservative success in establishing an alliance with the German-speaking Empire, and the Liberal attempt to carry out a satisfactory foreign policy with such unsatisfactory allies as France and Russia.

On the other hand it may fairly be retorted that it was the example and encouragement given by Lord S. in the annexation of Cyprus which induced France to act in the present high-handed manner towards another dependency of the Turkish Empire.

Accounts of the lawlessness in the West of Ireland still very discouraging. A general complaint that the effect of the Coercion Bill is wearing out, and defiance of the law, or indeed of the simplest rules of Morality, as universal as before.

Difficulties of administration not lessened by the exaggerated reports in the papers of every disturbance that takes place; the circumstantial account of the New Pallas riot turns out, according to the R.M. present, to have been greatly exaggerated.[1] About 50 people engaged in hooting—only at the last moment, when the soldiers were re-entering the station, were stones thrown, and nobody was hurt.

Uncle M[att] and Lucy to lunch—in the afternoon to the Hospital. Father late home to dinner, also Dean Neville[2] and Mr Errington and Oakel. They had all been detained at the House listening to Mr Gladstone's speech on the Land Bill, which was only just over.

[1] Forster wrote to Gladstone to this effect on this day (B.L., Add. MS 44158, ff 154–7); but he added: 'I think the late arrests are doing some good:—but we *are* in this position that if & when the landlords collect their rent, it will be at the point of the bayonet. . . . What we want is to stop the unreasonable eviction, while showing that we will make the fraudulent man pay.'

[2] Monsignor Henry F. Neville (1822–89): professor of theology at Maynooth, 1852–69; dean and vicar-general of Cork since 1875; rector of the Catholic University, Dublin, since 1879.

Mr G. had been expected to speak later in the evening, and Mr Johnson had moved the adjournment and so would naturally have opened the debate, but the ordinary course had to be altered, for Mr G. was not well, and his doctor had said that if he spoke at all it must be got over at once and that he must then come home to bed. Father had been informed of the state of the case by Lord R. Grosvenor and was therefore 'miserable' from 5 to 7, during which time two successive Motions for adjournment (one by Mr Healy apropos of himself: the other by Mr M. Guest on Tunis) prevented Mr G. from speaking and kept him chafing in suspense on the Treasury Bench, with his speech undelivered. A good one, Father was certain, from Mr G's avowed anxiety 'to get it off'.

A good one it was indeed, all the four who had just come from hearing it agreed. He had seemed ill and feeble when he began, leaning on a stick, and asking indulgence for the irregularity he was committing on the ground of his indisposition; but he soon revived, under the magic of his own voice. A few interruptions, or fancied interruptions from the other side, roused him into all his usual vivacity—'The honourable Member shakes his head—why does he shake his head?'—and then would follow a vigorous exposure of the honourable member's error or absurdity.

The first part of the speech, said Dean Neville, was reasoning, the last pure eloquence. He had never shown a more wonderful grasp of his whole subject. 'What is left for the Solicitors?' said Mr G. 'There really seems nothing more to be said, though unfortunately this would not prevent people saying it'.

However it is expected, says Father, that the division on the 2nd Reading will be taken on Tuesday. Sir Stafford seems to wish it, and when the party whips on both sides are agreed in desiring a division it is pretty sure to come off, even if it involves sitting up far into the night.

As for Father's own experience this evening, it had been of the usual kind. A question from a Parnellite (Mr Healy) as to the conduct of the police in tearing down some violent placards?

Explanation from the Ch. Sec. stating that they were justified. Further question from Mr D. [F. H. O'Donnell]. Were they torn down because they contained a reference to the Ch. Sec. as 'Buckshot Forster'?

Pause. The Ch. Sec. on this explained that it was the duty of Ministers to reply to questions but not to insults, and that he should decline to answer the inquiry of the Member for Dungarvan.

Mr Errington was probably only expressing the feeling of a great many others in the House when he told Father how delighted he had been at his at last taking this line with Mr D. and his allies—'You have been patient with them too long'.

Aunt Fan, Mother and Cousin C. to the Ladies Gallery in the evening, but nothing interesting going on.

A letter from C.M. asking to see Mr D[illon?] in Kilmainham.

17 May, Tu.

Went down with Aunt Fan to see Ted at East Grinstead, returning about 6 o'clock.

Read the full report of Mr G's speech; understood what Father had meant by saying last night that, fine as it was, it was somewhat imprudent. Mr G. in the fervour of his parliamentary appeal to the Conservative opposition, explaining the really moderate character of the proposed measure etc., left out of his consideration and remembrance for the moment the effect of this on the Home Rule opposition, a thing which the Irish Sec., daily responsible for the administration of Ireland and painfully familiar with Irish opinion, cannot for the space of a single sentence afford to do.

Father home to dinner in the evening, returning afterwards to the House only to find it counted out.

18 May, Wed.

The state of affairs in the Transvaal continues very critical. The Boers have not yet given up the guns taken (under false pretences) at Potchefstroom; until this has been done the Commission refuses to proceed further in their deliberations. The natives are said to be very hostile to the Boers, and quite ready at slight instigation to resist a return to Boer supremacy. Considering the bitter hatred of the loyalist British inhabitants in the Transvaal against the now triumphant Boers, this instigation is not unlikely to be forthcoming.

The present excited feeling may calm down before the expiration of the 6 months during which British rule in the Transvaal is to continue, but if it does not the prospect of a Boer and Native war, with Europeans joining in on either side, seems only too likely.

In the present state of things very much will depend on the personal weight and influence of the Commissioners. In Sir H. Robinson's ability at any rate there seems general confidence, and Sir E. Wood also appears to be the right man in the right place.

Continued excitement in Italy over the French 'coup' in Tunis. General disappointment amongst the admirers of the F[rench] Republic in this country over this return to Napoleonic practices. The Republic taking to military glory and telling downright diplomatic falsehoods! Who would have thought it!

Aunt Fan and Cousin C. left us in the afternoon. Oakel all day at Woolwich with Mr Childers, seeing gunnery experiments.

A dinner party in the evening, Erskine Mays, Blennerhassets, T. B. Potter, Sir R. Collier, Hardcastles, Lord Lymington, Mr Ashley—this last as pleasant as when he last dined with us in Dublin. I enquired after his tenants. The particular ruffian of the district—the local inn-keeper—had withdrawn to Liverpool on the passing of the C[oercion] Bill, but had unfortunately been encouraged by his wife's relations to return to his native town, and was now engaged in promoting various small annoyances and depredations on the landlord's property. As to the rents due in Dec., they really had been paid and not merely promised; the doubtful point now was would the spring rents be forthcoming? Mr A[shley] is going over at Whitsuntide so he will have the opportunity of renewing personal intercourse with his tenants, who do not seem to have any special aversion to him—a matter of great thankfulness and surprise in these Land League days.

Like many others he is getting tired of this interminable 2nd Reading debate—not at all from a surfeit of the whole question of Irish land reform, but from impatience to make real progress.

Speculation between him and Father and Mr H[ardcastle] as to the division—what will the English tenant farmers do?

Apropos of divisions I alluded to the ill-fated Compensation Bill of last year, an unfashionable subject and one to be mentioned cautiously before those of Whig leanings—rather to my surprise Mr A[shley] murmured in a tone of conviction 'Ah, if that Bill had been passed we shouldn't have needed a Coercion Act'![1]

In the evening Mother and I went to the State Concert—Father to bed. He knew that if he appeared Irish landlords would come up asking and cross-questioning 'about the state of the country'. He has so much of this in the House that an escape on Wednesdays and Saturdays is to be prized.

We met various people, amongst them Mr Dodson[2]—who mild though he be in general felt compelled to observe to Mother of the Parnellites—that he considered them not men: 'they are fiends'.

19 May, Th.

Apropos of a paragraph in one of the papers to the effect that, if the Govt made some promise to prevent evictions for 'famine arrears', the Parnellites would re-consider their threat of abstention from the 2nd Reading, Father told us that Lord Selborne had come voluntarily to have two hours talk with him as to possibilities in this direction. Very good of the Lord Chancellor, father thought—'and of course anything that he would accept in this matter, meant its acceptance by the Cabinet'; he did not like the idea at all, but quite came to see the difficulties of Father's administration of the present situation.[3]

Mr Plunkett has been speaking against the Govt at Bristol.

[1] Cf. Forster to Ripon, 17–21 July 1881: 'It is no use crying over spilt milk, but I still believe that the passage of my compensation of [*sic*] disturbance bill last year would have stayed the strike against rent' (B.L., Add. MS 43537, ff 180–86).

[2] John George Dodson (1825–97): liberal M.P. for E. Sussex, 1857–74; Chester, 1874–80; Scarborough, 1880–84; president of local government board.

[3] Selborne's later account of his views on the land act and the land commission is given in *Memorials*, II, ii, 20–27.

Spent the morning at Mr Tayler's, my fourth sitting. Mrs Ball to lunch, full of excited wailings over the state of her country—cowardice, ingratitude—Americanization—demoralization; she is really unhappy, and certainly reads and hears enough from her landlord friend and relations to make her so. She is a thorough Radical in her principles, and in her wishes as to Land reform, but the despair and bitter indignation she witnesses at close quarters amongst her friends who are being ruined and exiled individually in the course of this readjustment of relations between landlord and tenant are enough to distress and perplex the most determined Radical; she evidently finds her philosophy as to the necessity of this social 'revolution' sorely tried by personal intercourse with its victims.

What with feeling pity for them as ruined landlords, and contempt for the landlord 'principles' and complainings, which they din into her ears, it is no wonder if she becomes agitated and excited, and talks in a somewhat incoherent and contradictory manner and glad of the relief of pouring out her feelings volubly to Mother, who she knows can sympathize with both principles and people.

Certainly the despair and discouragement of educated Irishmen at the present condition of their country is one of the most saddening features of this crisis. If cultivated patriotic Irishmen throw up the game, and say that the character of the people is changed and that no more good can be expected of them either for themselves or for England—how is an English Govt to keep up its faith in the power of just laws and patient sympathy to improve not only the condition of Ireland itself but of its relations to our own country?

'It is lucky for the Balls', says Mr Lecky,[1] that 'they like himself are so cosmopolitan, and do not need to have much to do with Ireland'. Mrs Ball herself declares from what she has seen and heard that such a feeling of hatred has been created between the two classes that there will be nothing left for the landlords but to leave the country; good and bad landlords are treated alike—there is as little gratitude or kindly feeling shown to the one as to the other.

This, Mother suggested, may pass away, the apparent ill-feeling towards old friends coming not from ingratitude but temporary fear. Mrs Ball agreed, declaring that the Irish were like the French, brave enough in physical courage, but quite without civil courage—or rather moral courage making them dare to stand against a strong external opinion whether represented by the Govt, as in France, or by local public opinion, as in Ireland. As regards Italy too Mrs Ball was unhappy and angry.

Spent the afternoon with Mother leaving cards, calling etc.

At $\frac{1}{4}$ to 8 Father home to dine and go with Mother to the Selbornes'. I ran to have a word with him as he walked heavily up to his dressing room. 'Well, how have things been going with you?'

[1] William Edward Hartpole Lecky (1838–1903): historian; the first two volumes of his monumental *History of England in the eighteenth century* had appeared in 1878.

'Oh pretty well', rather drearily, 'two men shot at—a landlord and a farmer—not killed—one in Kerry, the other in Co. Cork'.[1] Only last night he announced to us with satisfaction that there had been only 6 returns of outrages that day, and of these 4 were threatening letters.

The debate on the 2nd reading closes, it is *hoped*, tonight.

20 May, Fri.

An excellent division—two to one against Lord Elcho's Amendment, which was rejected by a majority of 176—352 to 176.[2]

Mother and Francie, having gone on from the Admiralty to the House, were present at the division. After this the 2nd Reading was carried without opposition. 150 was the largest majority that had been expected, and this overwhelming majority is very satisfactory to the Govt.

The absence of Mr Parnell and his chosen few made little perceptible difference. Now comes the real tug of war in Committee; both Parnellites and Conservatives make their future attitude towards the Bill depend on its being radically amended in the direction they wish, whereas the Govt, whilst prepared to accept minor improvements and suggestions, are pledged to maintain the character of the Measure as defined in Mr G's speech on the 1st Reading.

With what majority the Bill will be sent up to the Lords is a matter of great uncertainty; the division on Thursday can hardly be taken as a guide, considering all that may happen in Committee.

A speech of Lord S[alisbury]'s at a Merchant Taylors' dinner, reported in this morning's papers, decidedly unpromising as regards the probable reception of the Land Bill in the H. of Lords, at any rate by the responsible leader of the Conservative party.

The House of Lords, the best abused body in the Kingdom—what is their duty? To respect the will of the country as expressed by a majority in the H. of Commons. All very well, but, suppose the majority only expresses a passing whim favoured by the Govt for party motives—what other reason can there be for a Measure of confiscation brought forward to meet some cry of 'land hunger' in Ireland? Land hunger—amongst the Irish people—why if it comes to gratifying all such tastes as these, why not do something for those who suffer from 'silver plate hunger' which doubtless is felt by some people. He himself, he was not ashamed to aver, was at this time suffering from 'place hunger' etc. etc.

---

[1] George Swanton, J.P. and landlord near Skibbereen, was driving home at about 9.30 p.m. on 18 May when a shot was fired and several stones thrown at him, without injuring him. His supposed part in bringing about a protection act arrest had made him unpopular. No case of firing at a farmer in Kerry is recorded in the returns of outrages (S.P.O., I.C.R., Return of outrages, May 1881).

[2] On 2 May Elcho had moved, during the debate on the second reading of the land bill, 'that this house, while willing to consider any just measure . . . is of opinion that the leading provisions of the . . . bill are in the main economically unsound, unjust, and impolitic'. After long and repeatedly adjourned debate, the motion was defeated on 19 May (*Hansard 3*, cclxi, 928).

No doubt this sort of language was intended rather for after-dinner pleasantry than as a serious specimen of Conservative criticism on the Bill, but coming from the newly chosen leader of the party it does not look well.

On another matter Lord S. does not appear before the public in a favourable light. The same paper that publishes the report of his lively oration at the Merchant Taylors' contains extracts from the foreign office correspondence of 1879 concerning France and Tunis. From a long statement of M. Wadding-ton's[1] to the French Ambassador in London (the general accuracy of which is acknowledged in a subsequent letter of Lord S's) it appears that the English Representative at Berlin gave carte blanche to France to do as she liked in all her future dealings with Tunis, assuring him that no measures towards the Regency, however stringent, would have any effect on the friendly relations between England and France.

In short Lord S. appears to have contemplated if not suggested, so immediate an assertion of French claims over Tunis that M. Waddington thought it well to explain that for the present at least, France—though gratified at the cordiality of England in the matter—was not prepared to make such a decided move (in short to follow the example set by us in the adoption of Cyprus).

The publication of this Tunis correspondence has created some sensation, and is very embarrassing to those Conservatives who had been inveighing against the present Govt for their tame acquiescence in the outrage upon inter-national morality being committed by the French Republic upon the Sultan's unoffending vassal.

Of course the *P.M.G.* is triumphant and self-satisfied, and points the moral against Lord S. and the 'showy foreign policy' of the late Govt with much gusto.

Walked with Father to the office, talked of plans for Whitsuntide. He has had thoughts of going over to Dublin this week, but will probably not go now before Whitsuntide.

Another idea has been for Father and all of us to migrate to the Phoenix Park for good before the end of the session—'and let them holla after him and abuse him from over here as much as they liked'.

On reaching the office Father told me to come in and hear how many outrages were reported this morning—he expected a heavy tale—but to his surprise only 4—'more reports would come in later' said Mr Jephson, who is not given to optimism.

Oakel to lunch, being engaged to a Meeting of the Liberal Counties Union, of which he is on the Executive Com[mittee] in the afternoon.

Drove with Mother in the afternoon. A farewell call before his marriage from the Dean of Durham at $\frac{1}{2}$ past 6.

A dinner party in the evening, Sir J. and Miss Lubbock, Prices, Lady S.,

---

[1] William Henry Waddington (1826–94): son of an English manufacturer naturalised in France; French minister of foreign affairs since 1880.

Trevelyans, Col. Johnson Webster. At $\frac{1}{4}$ to 8 Father not home from the House, only arriving after half the people had come. I not dining in, had an interview with him in his dressing room. 'There has been a grand "row" over the arrest of Father Sheehy'. General chorus of abuse from the Parnellites, Lord R[andolph] C[hurchill] joining in—'their only English ally', as Mr G. observed.[1]

To a demand for reasons of the arrest Father could only say that he would not enter into these on a Motion of the Adj[ournment].[2]

To Father's great satisfaction Mr G. has given Tuesday afternoon for a regular discussion of the Ch. Sec.'s conduct in the administration of the Coercion Act. 'It was getting quite time to say something', Father remarks, and having no scruples as to the arrests, no one of which has been made without his full knowledge and consent, he is thankful for this opportunity of justifying the action of the Irish Executive.

The prospect of having his tongue loosed and being allowed to speak out instead of being forced to hear himself abused and misrepresented in silence— as was again the case last week over Mr D.[3]—produced an evident effect on his spirits, and he went down to dinner brisk and cheerful. He and the other Members went back to the House in the evening, the Irish Sec. being again on duty—this time with a Saturday Public House Closing (Ireland) Bill, patronised by Mr Meldon.

21 May, Sat.

Defeat of Mr T[hompson] at Preston, in spite of Irish support.[4]

Anxious news from Ireland. Disturbances in the West, chiefly in the Eastern corner of Co. Limerick. Father and Mother drove into the City together in the morning. O. to lunch. The proofs of his article 'A civilian's answer to Sir

---

[1] *Hansard 3*, cclxi, 963–1004. The arrest of Fr Eugene Sheehy on 20 May—the first catholic priest to be arrested during the land war—was naturally exploited by the Irish party to the full, and Forster was from the first somewhat defensive on the matter. Fr Sheehy was president of the Kilmallock (Co. Limerick) branch of the Land League; nearly all the committee were arrested on the same day (20 May) and the Kilfinane committee were arrested four days later. These first *en bloc* arrests of local committees were generally ignored in parliament. Clifford Lloyd, R.M., had taken over this critical district on 12 May, and on 19 May had gone to Dublin to argue before Cowper, Burke, Naish, and Anderson that law and order depended on paralysing the local Leagues, 'the hostile power in occupation' (*Ireland under the Land League*, pp 59–103). The reasons for the arrests were variously given as sedition, unlawful assembly, intimidation, and issuing threatening notices; all these refer to recent actions by the committees.

Following Gladstone's witty and attacking speech, the Irish delivered a typical 'cab-rank' attack, sixteen or seventeen short speeches being made. Parnell (*Hansard 3*, cclxi, 992–5) was the first to mention Lloyd; subsequent speakers dutifully, if ignorantly, developed this theme. Cowen (ibid., cclxi, 1000–1001) gave the Irish some support.

[2] Forster is recorded in *Hansard 3*, cclxi, 967, as saying that he could not give the exact reasons for the arrest without having the wording of the warrants before him.

[3] Probably F. H. O'Donnell; see above, p. 144.

[4] In the by-election for Preston on 20 May William Farmer Ecroyd received 6004 votes against the 4340 for Henry Yates Thompson (1838–1928), proprietor of the *Pall Mall Gazette*.

G. Wolseley'. Went with him in the afternoon to pay calls, and afterwards in
the Square with Rob and Roy. Weather lovely.

Father and Mother in the evening to the Deanery, meeting there a large
party of ecclesiastical dignitaries. Much talk at prsent about the Revised
Edition of the New Testament which has just been published. In the evening to
Lady Spencer's, where we stayed but a short time, Father being dog-tired.

22 May, Sun.

Bad news as usual in the *Observer*—continued rioting in Limerick, the mob,
having taken possession of a castle on the estate of Col. Hare, have so far defied
the military and police and made all attempts to serve processes fruitless.[1]

Another disagreeable item from Dublin was, the publication in the *Freeman*
of the Private Instructions issued by the Constabulary Inspector to the police,
urging them to be more zealous and efficient in detecting the perpetrators of
outrages—men who were frequently known to the whole countryside, and yet
against whom the police seemed unable to furnish evidence, or establish
'reasonable ground for suspicion'.[2]

The publication of this document will like most other things add to the Ch.
Sec.'s difficulties. Of course it was necessary, and he is prepared, as he wrote to
Mr Burke, to defend it in the House, but there will be no end to the attacks it
will give rise to—charges of inciting the police to manufacture evidence etc.

Father unable to go to church. Mr Jephson at lunch—talk over this unlucky
publication—how did they get it—probably through a clerk at Thom's, the
printing office.

After a mouthful of lunch, a Turkish bath, and a call on the D.[3] of Manchester, Father returned home to send off a letter to Mr Burke by the Sunday
Messenger. Being in the library I have the opportunity of hearing this, a generous assurance of his intention to make himself entirely responsible for the
Circular in the House, and a request that Mr Burke will engage any extra

[1] From the report of the sub-inspector at New Pallas, this incident seems to have been less
serious than the *Observer* suggests, although entered on an outrage form as a case of agrarian riot
and assault on police and military (S.P.O., R.P. 1881/19115). A force of 100 constabulary and 200
military, under two resident magistrates, accompanied the sub-sheriff to serve writs of *fieri facias*
on the Hare estate on the morning of 21 May. On reaching Thomas Anderson's farm, the force was
stoned not only by a crowd in the farmyard but by men in the upper galleries of a ruined castle next
to the house. A few were struck, but the crowd on the ground were dispersed; the men in the castle
'were not driven therefrom, there being no means of doing so without probable loss of life, except
by starving them out' (sub-inspector's report). The whole incident lasted half an hour. Several
suspected rioters were later arrested under the P.P.P. act.

[2] For the text of the circular of 7 May, see *F.J.*, 21 May 1881. Nationalist views of 'that most
extraordinary, that most unparalleled secret circular' (McCarthy), 'worthy of the worst days of a
Mouravieff in Poland' (O'Donnell), assumed Forster's authorship, but this is denied by Forster
himself. N. D. Palmer (*The Irish Land League crisis* (New Haven, 1940), pp 279–80) uncritically
accepts Forster's authorship and condemns him for attempting to shift the responsibility for the
state of Ireland on to the police. The circular was issued to only 18 county inspectors.

[3] Probably the duke of Manchester; see above, p. 130.

assistance in the office that he needs—'I will make myself personally responsible for the salaries', supposing the Treasury should make difficulties, which
however there is no fear of their doing.[1]

It has been determined to arrest Mr Brennan.[2]

A stream of people at 5 o'clock, Colonel Dease[3] from Dublin, Sir F. Buxton
and his brother, Laws, Cecil Boyle,[4] Lord Monteagle, Mr Ball—much talk
about Ireland, also of the landlord distress in England, caused not by un-
willingness, but inability, of farmers to pay rent or take farms. One instance
after another quoted from personal knowledge of landlords having thousands
of acres thrown on their hands—the richer taking the farms into their own
management and working them through a bailiff, others simply shutting up
their places and leaving the estate.

Col. Dease in discussing the Land Bill from the moderate landlord point of
view, agreed with Father as to the desire of Irish landlords that it should pass—
with some amendments; in fact, according to a story now being told, the unnatural Liberalism of Irish landlords on this question is disgusting to good
Conservatives in this country—'as long as they get their rents and are not shot,
they don't care what happens'—one of the great Tory chiefs is reported to have
said with indignation.

Lord Monteagle has not yet got into difficulties with his tenants; but Mr
O'Brien is expecting to have violent dealings with some of his, and consequently he and Julia have given up the idea of going back to Cahirmoyle as
they had intended.

Up to about a month ago rents were coming in freely, in spite of the L.
League—but now there is a general spirit of refusal, probably in the hope of
making something out of waiting for the Land Bill.

Lord M[onteagle] left with us a letter from Sir S. de Vere[5] giving his opinion
as to the advisability of abolishing the Jury system in Ireland. On the whole he
thinks not, at present. We must have patience a little longer; there is to his
thinking a lull in the storm; the outrages—though infamous—when they do
occur, are not on the organized system that they were; the Land League party is
breaking up; with the introduction of the Land Bill, and a vigorous administration of the present coercive powers, he has still hope that an improvement may
take place without necessity for a further infringement of constitutional Govt in
Ireland.[6]

---

[1] Extra clerks were engaged and paid by the treasury.

[2] The warrant, for incitement to riot and assault for the purpose of obstructing the execution of
process (in his speech at a meeting at Ballyroan, 15 May), was issued on 23 May and executed the
same day; he was held in turn at Naas, Kilmainham, and Kilkenny, and released on 2 June 1882.

[3] Gerald Richard Dease (1831–1903): honorary colonel, 4th battalion, Royal Irish Fusiliers:
chamberlain to the lord lieutenant (see below, p. 289).

[4] Cecil William Boyle (1853–1900): great-grandson of 7th earl of Cork and husband of Nelly, a
second cousin of Florence's.

[5] See appendix.

[6] On the following day the house of lords approved a motion by Lord Salisbury for the

As to the lull in the storm, Father to some extent agrees; certainly there was a remarkable falling off in the returns of outrage last week—a proportion of 50 to 90.

No doubt the arrest of Father Sheehy will make a temporary revival of excitement and perhaps outrage, but on the other hand it may be hoped that this proof that a priest is not to be allowed by virtue of his position to incite the people to violence and outrage, any more than a layman, will have a wholesome effect.[1]

There is no denying however that it is a bold step, and one result will certainly be to increase the bitter hatred against the Ch. Sec.

Just of late he has received threatening letters, but under the present circumstances he had told Oakel to enquire whether our special policeman is still on duty here; if he was ever wanted it is likely to be at this time. 'They will be very angry at what is being done, and will fasten it specially on me.'

Of course this was only said to Oakel and me when alone with him in the library on Sunday evening. These are not the sort of anxieties which weigh much on his mind.

Mother and F. to the Abbey to hear the Bishop of Exeter.[2]

23 May, Mon.

No special news from Ireland that we had not seen in the *Observer*. Letter from Lord Cowper, 'not very happy about the state of the country, and expressing his agreement with Father in the line they were taking, and congratulating him on having an opportunity of defending and explaining their conduct in the House'—'was sure he would make out a good case'. As to the publication of the 'Instructions' he had never seen a man so overwhelmed as Burke when he came to tell him of it.

'Poor Mr Burke is', Mother says, 'the man most to be felt for next to Father in the present crisis'. He is almost killed with work and anxiety. Father at work all the morning preparing his speech for tomorrow.

appointment of a select committe to inquire into the working of the Irish jury laws in criminal cases. The committee was nominated on 30 May; met for the first time on 31 May; held sixteen sessions and examined 43 witnesses including six R.M.s and Robert Vere O'Brien; and reported on 12 Aug. in favour of change of venue and an extension of the summary jurisdiction of magistrates for riot, aggravated assault, forcible repossession, assaults on peace officers, threatening letters, and other forms of intimidation (*Report from the select committee of the house of lords on Irish jury laws; together with the proceedings of the committee, minutes of evidence, and appendix*, H.L. 1881 (430), xi).

[1] As early as 22 Feb. the sub-inspector at Kilfinane, the county inspector of Limerick, and the R.M. then in charge of the district had unanimously recommended Fr Sheehy's arrest (S.P.O., P.P.P. act proceedings, carton 1). Forster was later to quote with effect a speech made by Sheehy on 3 March, urging that priests should put themselves in a position where the government would have to incur the odium of arresting them (*Hansard 3*, cclxi, 1247–8 (24 May 1881)).

[2] Frederick Temple (1821–1902): headmaster of Rugby, 1858–69; bishop of Exeter, 1869–85; bishop of London, 1885–96; archbishop of Canterbury, 1896–1902.

Father at work till 1 preparing his speech for Tuesday. Walked with him to the office. In the afternoon with Fr[ancie] to Mr Tayler's. Father home to dinner and Major Neild, just appointed temporary R.M. in Ireland.[1]

Heard from Mother the last thing at night that Father would probably like me to go over to Dublin with him the next day.

24 May, Tu.

In the morning to Mr Tayler, my last sitting. At 4 with Mother to Mr Brand's Gallery. We came in for the latter portion of Mr O'D[onnell]'s lengthy harangue in support of the Motion of censure upon the Ch. Sec.[2] Mr Litton followed with a courageous defence of the Govt and an outspoken assertion that the Land League had the approval of only a section of Irishmen, however they might choose to pour [? portray] the Parnellites in the House.

Father rose to speak at 20 to 5, and, after regretting that the other side had no real arguments to follow Mr O'D's personalities, he dealt in order with the various counts of the indictment against him, the proclamation of Dublin, the arrests of Mr D[illon] and Father Sheehy, and the now famous Circular to the Constabulary. As to the arrests and the necessity and grounds for them, he proved his case mainly by the extracts from speeches delivered by both the 'suspects', showing how they were direct incitements to violence, and how invariably outrage upon individuals and defiance of the law followed on their delivery.

As to the Circular, he certainly kept his promise to Mr B[urke] and took the whole responsibility for it upon himself, defending its main drift, and only allowing that there were one or two passages which, if he had read it over more thoroughly, he would have had otherwise.[3] Towards the end of his speech he dwelt very impressively on the responsibility that would rest on those who should deliberately incite the people to defiance of the execution of the law. After all, the soldiers who are sent to protect process servers and others in carrying out

[1] Four temporary R.M.s had been appointed in 1880, and a total of fifteen were appointed in 1881. Major Thomas Kent Neild (1839–87): commissioned in 1st battalion 6th Royal Warwickshire Regt, 1858; served in India; brought to Forster's notice by his efficiency as adjutant of Volunteers at Bradford; app. R.M. for Dartry district, Co. Monaghan, 30 May.

[2] Justin McCarthy had brought in early that morning a motion censuring the Irish government on the grounds that the arrest of Dillon, Fr Sheehy 'and many other men of high character and good conduct', the 'state of siege' imposed on Dublin, and the protection by crown forces of 'the wholesale execution of wanton and cruel evictions', constituted an abuse of the powers entrusted to them, and were calculated to promote disaffection. He suggested that Castle officials were trying to provoke an insurrection, and ended by urging the cabinet to 'throw their Jonah overboard' (*Hansard 3*, cclxi, 1174–81). On the resumption of the debate that afternoon (ibid., 1214–62), O'Donnell opened with a two-hour speech suggesting, among other things, that Sheehy's arrest was a result of the circular of 7 May. The rest of his speech is of equal value.

[3] Forster's main point, which ran directly contrary to the nationalist interpretation, was that the circular was intended to urge the police not to propose more arrests, but to provide more substantial evidence, without which the government could not issue warrants.

their duty are flesh and blood, and they will not stand for ever to be insulted and stoned by an angry mob, who rely on the disinclination of the authorities to order the troops to fire.

'There are people that in the wish to see the Govt embarrassed and discredited would be glad to witness a fatal conflict between the troops and the people, but I hope still we shall disappoint them', said the Ch. Sec. He further explained that the Govt, whilst fully recognising the need for 'remedial legislation in Ireland, was firmly resolved not to permit a combination for the purposes of robbery—even of landlords'.

That the policy of enforcing the law and preventing resistance, by an overwhelming force if necessary, would be continued, and that no man, whether clergyman or Member of Parliament would be allowed with impunity to incite people to violence and lawlessness.

I have often seen the Parnellites exhibit their feelings in the House with an insolent disregard of all Parliamentary decency, but I never saw them behave quite as they did during this speech. They were evidently much exasperated, and showed the loss of their temper in a most distressing manner. Mr Finigan, who really looked as though he would have a fit, Mr T. P. O'Connor and Mr Healy could with difficulty sit quiet on their seats, and relieved their minds by shouting out comments, questions, and insulting epithets at the Ch. Sec., who, keeping his temper and carrying the House entirely with him, as able to retort several times with great effect and much to the enlivenment of his speech.

The rest of the debate was occupied by speeches from Mr Plunkett, Mr G. and Mr Parnell. The Parnellites refused to divide on the Motion of censure, probably, as Mr G. told them with great warmth, because they did not dare. The debate was adjourned at 7 to some problematical time when the Govt shall be induced to give facilities for its resumption.[1]

After a hurried dinner at 7, Father and I left by the Night Mail for Dublin. Father's principal object in coming over now, I believe, is to consider at the Castle the advisability of issuing a proclamation pronouncing that, in future cases of resistance to the law and attacks on the police and soldiers, the latter are to be ordered to fire.

The unfortunate scrape about the Police Circular had naturally made the Ch. Sec. anxious to see in person that no document of this important nature for which he is responsible comes from the Castle without his knowledge and approval of every word of it.

[1] The speeches following Forster's were all brief; O'Sullivan and Callan moved the adjournment. On 27 May (*Hansard 3*, cclxi, 1459–60) it was agreed to resume the debate on 30 May, but this did not in fact happen. Parnell complained (cclxi, 1750), and Hartington agreed to allocate time on 3 June; see below, p. 168.

25 May, Wed.

A perfectly calm passage. As we were going from this to the Vice Regal Lodge and did not want to arrive there early in the morning, we breakfasted and spent an hour or two at Kingstown, going up to Dublin at 11.25. Father remained at the Castle, and was soon deep in an interview with Mr Burke.

Williams and I, after doing some shopping in Grafton Street, drove to the V.R. in time for lunch. The Cowpers quite alone—the Dalrymples staying at the P[rivate] Sec.'s Lodge.

Visited Yarrow in the afternon at our own place, and was received very pleasantly by him, also C[hattenooga], the Carpenters, Mrs Adams, Kelly, etc.

Dined alone with Father and Mr Jephson, at 8, the Cowpers having dined earlier in order to go to the Opera to which they were engaged. Had some pleasant talk with Father in his room before going to bed. Mr Burke had been glad to see him, which I can easily believe. We talked about the Circular—'the most awkward affair he had ever had in his life—the only thing to be done was to be perfectly honest'. In spite of these immediate difficulties he is more hopeful about the state of the country.

An interesting letter received from Mr E. O'Brien confirms the opinion of Sir S. de Vere that, bad as the isolated outrages are, there is not the same utter lawlessness and organized violence that there was in the autumn.

26 May, Th.

The worst item in the papers this morning a mischievous speech by Dr Croke in vindication of Father Sheehy. The mainspring of the Archbishop of Cashel's action is said to be hatred of England—a statement fully borne out by this enthusiastic harangue.[1]

In the morning wrote letters for Father and walked with him through the park, which is looking quite lovely, though I have not yet had a glimpse of my favourite view of the Dublin mountains.

After lunch read Mr Blake's 'Sunrise', and walked over to Miss Burke's where I was very kindly received and stayed to tea. Mr Burke has not yet broken down in health though he is much worn, and has of late been specially distressed by this affair of the Circular. As for Col. Hillier[2] he does not like even to speak to him on the subject. According to Miss B., the traitor was in Thom's printing office, whence it is supposed private papers have before now found their way into the *Freeman*.

Dined at 7 and went afterwards with Lady C[owper], Lord W[illiam][3] and

[1] Croke's speech was delivered in response to an address from the parishioners of Loughmore and Castleiny (Co. Tipperary), who included Fr Sheehy's father and brother; the *F.J.* version of it (26 May 81) is not conspicuously anti-English.

[2] See appendix.

[3] William George Spencer Scott Compton (1851–1913), second son of the fourth marquis of Northampton; private secretary to Lord Cowper.

the Dalrymples to St Patrick's, to hear an Oratorio Service for Ascension Day, the Lobgesang[1] and parts of 'Israel in Egypt'.[2]

The Cowpers are very kind and well meaning, but one thing is melancholy plain—the Lord Lieutenant is a cypher. All the sound political judgment and good sense, which we thought latent beneath a quiet rather shy manner, remains so entirely latent that it is practically non-existent; on such a matter as the discussion of this important Proclamation Lord Cowper contributes no opinion whatever, either for or against, and though he assists at the deliberations at the Castle on the subject, it is solely with his bodily presence. As to the legal authorities meanwhile, their opinion seems to be divided—the Master of the Rolls[3] on the whole in favour of issuing some such document, the Attorney General[4] against.

A short interview with Father before bedtime—the outrages have not yet gone up again. As to the culprit in the Circular affair, Miss Burke was wrong— they know who he is but he is not in Thom's office.

27 May, Fri.

The London Correspondent of the Irish papers full of speculation and rumours as to the cause of the Ch. Sec.'s sudden visit to Dublin. 'Why did he go?' 'At any rate something important will be come of it'—'the suppression of the League', 'a Proclamation in the Gazette', etc.

Meanwhile the House appears to have made some progress with the Land Bill which last night got into Committee. Mr G. has declined to give any definite answer as to Govt intentions on the matter of suspending evictions for arrears of rent until the return of the Ch. Sec. In the expectation that he will be in his place in the House on Monday, a large store of questions is being prepared for him by the Parnellites.

The *Freeman* on the other hand states that he will remain in Dublin over Whitsuntide. I have not the least idea which of these suppositions will turn out to be correct.

Spent the morning writing; in the afternoon went to the C.S. Lodge, and walked round the V.R. Grounds with Lady C[owper] and Lord William. The laburnums overhanging the water are in their full glory.

Before coming in to dress F[ather] read me his letter to Mr G.[5]

Mr and Mrs D. to dinner. The whole party to the Mansion H. ball in the evening, with the exception of Father and me.

After we had gone upstairs I helped him in the way of blotting and turning

[1] 'Song of praise'; spelt 'lobgesary' in the TS.
[2] Oratorio by Handel.
[3] Sir Edward Sullivan.
[4] Hugh Law.
[5] Forster to Gladstone, 27 May 81 (B.L., Add. MS 44158, ff 161–4); quoted in Reid, *Forster*, ii, 320–21.

over whilst he signed 306 search warrants for use under the Arms Act. It took just an hour.[1]

28 May, Sat.

Father walked with me to see Yarrow at the C.S. Lodge, and then on with him to the park gates—much preoccupied at first and silent. Before parting however we had some lively talk. He told me of his interview the day before with a friend of Mr Dillon's sent to represent some grievance of the latter's about the conduct of the Kilmainham doctor. A long letter from Mr D. to Mr Powell setting forth his grievance and denouncing the Ch. Sec. referred to the latter by the prison authorities for decision whether it might be sent or not. Of course the letter was forwarded, only with the proviso that a copy containing the specific charges against him should be given also to Mr Dillon's enemy, the Infirmary doctor.[2]

Meantime everything is to be done for Mr D's comfort and convenience that can be done without transgressing the prison rules.

Amongst other things, he has demanded the *Pall Mall Gazette*, which is to be supplied to him.

In the afternoon went with Lady C[owper,] Mrs D[alrymple] and Lord W[illiam] to Herr Elsner's concert at the Ancient Concert Rooms. At half past 7 walked to meet Father. Whether we return before Whitsuntide or not still uncertain.

The plan of issuing a general Proclamation definitely given up. A middle course has been decided upon; in those districts where evictions and organized resistance are known to be impending a Proclamation with all the authority of the Castle will be published, warning the people that if they assemble to obstruct the execution of the law they will do so at their peril.[3]

Mr and Miss Burke, Colonel Hozier and a Capt. Welby[4] of the Scots Greys to dinner.

[1] For the development of procedure in the issue and execution of warrants under the arms act, see C.S.O., R.P. 1881/19669. The warrants signed by Forster would have been prepared by sub-inspectors of constabulary, on their own judgement on whether reasonable grounds existed for searching the premises specified, and sent up to the Castle for signature without further inquiry.

[2] There is nothing on this matter in the file relating to Dillon's arrest and detention, C.S.O., R.P. 1882/15046. The doctor is probably William Corfe, physician and surgeon of the Royal Hospital, Kilmainham, and medical officer of Kilmainham gaol.

[3] See below, p. 163. A number of circulars had already been issued to the constabulary on matters arising out of resistance to the execution of processes; notably those of 22 April (on the importance of having a sufficient force on hand), of 3 May (on the arrest and prosecution of ring-leaders at riots), and of 21 May (setting out the legal penalties for assault on constables); see C.S.O., R.P. 1881/22731. On 28 May Samuel Lee Anderson showed Burke and Forster his proposals for the immediate arrest of rioters. These were approved but, probably because of the adoption of other measures, there is no record of corresponding instructions being issued to R.M.s or police until August 1886 (C.S.O., R.P. 1886/15933). For Anderson, see below, p. 270.

[4] Alfred Cholmeley Earle Welby (1849–1937), conservative M.P. for Taunton, 1895–1906.

Father read to me with great amusement Mr [Mc]Coan and Mr O'C. Power's answer to Mr Egan in the *Freeman*.[1]

29 May, Sun.

All idea of returning to London before Whitsuntide given up. To church at Christ Church in the morning with Lady C. and Lord W. After luncheon copied letters for Father to Mr Bright and Mr C[hamberlain] explaining a scheme of Mr Shaw's for dealing with arrears of rent in cases of tenants under £8 or £10—and a letter from Father to Mr G. of which he had told me the main purport the day before.[2]

'The Irish Executive cannot safely go on as it is at present. Burke and Naish both first-rate men, but cannot and indeed ought not take responsibility on themselves. Three courses open—either [1] the Ch. Sec. must give up Parliament and remain in Dublin, which would have a bad look, or (2) Cowper must be replaced by Spencer, an arrangement which could not be made without giving pain, and would moreover seem like a confession of failure, or (3) the Lord Chancellor must be replaced by Sullivan (Master of the Rolls)—this change on various grounds might be the most easily accomplished. Will Mr G. talk it over with Lord H[artington] and Spencer and get their opinion so that the change might be made during Mr F's present stay here.'

As to Mr Shaw's scheme, afraid it will hardly do—most of the evictions are in cases of over £10 rental. If anything is done, better an Amendment to be moved by Mr F. immediately after Whitsuntide. Meantime another effort must be made to enforce the law—nine out of ten of the cases in which resistance is made are simply combinations for robbery.

After finishing the letters Father went for a walk with Mr Burke—I to tea with Miss B. and afterwards to the C.S. Lodge, to tell Mrs Adams that we should come over the next day to stay for a week or ten days.

Heard from Father just before dinner that there had been another bad

---

[1] Egan's letter of 22 May to Brennan, describing O'Connor Power as a welsher for voting with the government on the land bill, and McCoan as a carpet-bagger, was published in *F.J.* on 26 May 1881; Egan used much harder words about the government. Power and McCoan made effective replies, stressing the anomaly of the Land League treasurer's retiring to Paris.

[2] The letter here referred to (B.L., Add. MS 44158, ff 167–71) contains the following: 'Cowper does not attempt to steer the ship.... Questions then which ought to be decided without delay and on the spot, are referred to London for my decision guided by the law officers. Here again the difficulty is increased; were I here I should almost always feel I could act on the opinion of the law adviser,... but in London I must be guided by Law and Johnson, & they, away from the facts, can hardly avoid taking a *dangerously safe* side. With all this O'Hagan our chancellor is useless. He does nothing & if he did anything he would probably be worse than useless.... O'Hagan is rich, tired of work & in poor health, & above all he is shy of responsibility.'

'I suppose it is impossible to get Spencer to replace Cowper...' Forster had remarked to Gladstone on 16 May 81 (B.L., Add. MS 44158, ff 154–7).

[3] Forster and Florence stayed with the Cowpers at the Viceregal Lodge from the 25th (above, p. 156) to the 30th (below, p. 161).

murder in Galway—a respectable man, formerly a gardener, had taken a farm on the property of Lord Dunsandle,[1] from which another man had been evicted. On Sunday morning he was shot whilst going to Mass with his two young children, and died without recovering consciousness.[2]

30 May, Mon.

A very black Monday. Bad reports from the South and West of lawlessness and outrage. Details of the murder of Dempsey—also of the rioting and hideous brutality at Mitchelstown, where nothing but the behaviour of the R.M. can have prevented fatal bloodshed.[3]

A story of cruelty perpetrated by men and women to a bailiff near Bantry too loathsome to believe without further confirmation.

Mr Dillon in his comfortable retirement at Kilmainham will have the satisfaction of seeing that his advice to his savage countrymen is being carried out to the letter. It is hard to believe that a prosperous future for the poor Irish tenantry is to be built on such a foundation of cruelty and dishonesty as is being laid by the present agitators, with the blessing and assistance of prelates like Dr Croke and Dr Nulty,[4] and the complacent toleration of *Pall Mall Gazette* Radicals, who say apropos of agrarian outrage, 'there are some things it is wise for a Govt to shut its eyes to'—vide *P.M.G.* of May 12 1881.

Walked with Father to the park gates—very much oppressed—'You have got the Proclamation on your mind?'

'I have got a great deal on my mind—things are as bad as they can be.' Presently after striding along in silence, he suggests to Mr Jephson: 'I should think it will be a relief to the R. Magistrates to have my proclamation to act upon; if there is a verdict it will be returned against me not them.[5] In the

[1] Denis St George Daly (1810–93): 2nd Baron Dunsandle, owned 33,543 acres in Co. Galway and 3,514 in Tipperary, valued at a total of £17,393.

[2] Peter Dempsey, shot at about 11.30 a.m. on 29 May. The other details are as Florence records. The former tenant and his nephew were arrested and discharged for lack of evidence; six arrests were later made under the P.P.P. act (S.P.O., I.C.R., Returns of outrages, May 81).

[3] Severe and prolonged rioting at Mitchelstown (Cork, East Riding) on 27 May accompanied the attempt by the sheriff to execute seven ejectments on the Kingston estate, supported by a force of 70 constabulary, 70 men of the 25th infantry regiment, and a troop of dragoons, commanded by Richard J. Eaton, R.M. Eaton reported: 'I found it necessary to use very vigorous action in dealing with the stone-throwing mobs & several of their members no doubt got very roughly handled, but not more than they deserved . . .'. He had several times to read the riot act and order bayonet charges by the police, and eventually dispersed the crowd only by ordering six soldiers to load and prepare to fire. The local Land League tried to restrain the people, but feeling continued to be bad for some time and several P.P.P. act arrests were made. See C.S.O., R.P. 1881/19125; *Cork Daily Herald*, 28 May 81.

[4] Thomas Nulty (1818–98): ordained 1846; served mostly in Meath, of which he became coadjutor bishop in 1864; bishop 1864–98; held radical views on the land question; one of the small number of catholic bishops who were well known to approve of the Land League.

[5] Forster's stress on this point probably derives from Dillon's speech at Grangemockler on 28 Apr., asserting that bloodshed at evictions would be charged as wilful murder against Gladstone

present excited state of the people, and the certainty of there being more evictions, some collision is imminent, the next time probably not without fatal results, for after the warning to be given in the Govt proclamation the troops employed are bound to fire.'

No one who does not personally know the Irish Secretary and his feelings towards the Irish peasantry can quite realize all the trials involved in such a position as he holds at present. But whatever he feels or endures no one can say of him that he shirks responsibility.

From the Park gates Father and Mr Jephson went on to the office on a car. I with Miss Burke in the train and afterwards in her carriage to do various errands of hers at the School of Art Needlework. Miss Burke very despairing about the country—'the French Revolution impending'.

In the afternoon I went with Their Ex[cellencie]s and Lord William to a Cricket Match at Trinity College—four horses and 2 outriders—the afternoon brilliant and the ground with its ring of spectators a very pretty one. I sat next Sir T. Steele who had just come from a Council, where he had thought Father seemed rather tired. As for himself he declared he was never better in his life— whatever happens he does not fret. He and father still get on very well together, which, considering there are so many military arrangements to be made now-a-days at the Ch. Sec.'s office, is very fortunate.

The Ardilauns, Ladies St L. (2), Col. Boyle, Mr Winn, Mr Stopford, etc. to dinner.[1] Lady A. Father reported 'very insolent in manner', Lord A. also making himself disagreeable, and implying that he was obliged to close his works on account of getting no rents—which is hardly the fact.

At the end of the evening Father and I migrated to our own Lodge, not impressed with the liveliness of existence in Vice Regal circles.

31 May, Tu.

Mr Kettle of the Land League has been arrested and taken to Naas, where there was a scene of some excitement amongst the crowd on his way to the prison.[2]

and Forster (*F.J.*, 29 Apr.); he had quoted that passage in the house of commons on 24 May (*Hansard 3*, cclxi, 1234–5).

[1] Arthur Edward Guinness (1840–1915): second baronet, created 1st Baron Ardilaun 1880; conservative M.P. for city of Dublin, 1868–9, 1874–80; owned 25,341 acres, predominantly in Galway. Henrietta Eliza St Laurence, who married Ardilaun's brother in Sept. 1881, and her sister Geraldine Digby, were half-sisters of 4th earl of Howth.

[2] The arrest of Andrew J. Kettle, a pioneer of the land agitation and a joint secretary of the Land League, is described in C.S.O., R.P. 1881/42487, by Superintendent John Mallon of G Division of the D.M.P., who escorted Kettle to Naas, where they had to drive from the station to the gaol without a police escort. Kettle began shouting 'No rent'; Mallon's car broke a shaft, and 'McCormack and I were obliged to wade through the crowd with Kettle.... We got some rough handling, but are not seriously hurt, and Kettle came in for his share of kicks and cuffs.... Mr J. J. Clancy who accompanied Kettle did his very best to pacify the people and got badly beaten for his pains. The crowd consisted chiefly of women and men of the lowest class. ... They continued to howl like

The House last night was taken up for two or three hours over the quarrel between Mr P. on the one side and Mr McCoan and Mr O'C. Power on the other, the affair having been brought on by a Motion of Mr M[itchell] Henry's declaring Mr Egan's violent denunciation of Messrs Mc[C.] and O'C. P. to be a breach of privilege.

There have been several signs lately that the extreme wing of the L.L. party were disgusting more reasonable Members, and Mr Egan's letter and Mr P's apology for him will not tend to conciliate would-be independent Home Rulers.

No doubt, however, Mr P. may rightly reckon on extreme violence being popular at the present time in the majority of Irish constituencies. On the other hand too persistent opposition to the Land Bill, and too complete a severance from the moderate Home Rulers on this subject will be probably rather dangerous except in the case of professional Land Leaguers.

A letter from Mother to say that she arrives tomorrow morning and perhaps Francie also. A long day alone with Yarrow in this beautiful garden—writing, and reading *East Lynne*.[1]

Father and Mr Jephson home at 11.30 after dining with the 'Strollers',[2] where Father had enjoyed himself and had made a speech on behalf of the 'Visitors'.

1 June, Wed.

Mother arrived to breakfast, after a fine passage. She brought with her the June *19th* with O's article in the place of honour.

Another brilliant day—outwardly. The papers as usual anything but cheerful reading. A bad riot at Clonmel on the occasion of a sale of 20 farms, Mr Goddard[3] and the Emergency Men being present. As on previous occasions the resistance evidently well organized beforehand, the priests first inciting the disturbance at the sale, and afterwards—when the police and soldiers were obliged to charge and danger seemed imminent—endeavouring to stop it. In spite of the attack made on them by the mob with stones, bricks and bottles, the troops and police were not ordered to fire, and the only life lost will probably be that of a soldier, who was badly injured and is not expected to recover.[4]

furies outside the gaol for over half an hour.' The incident led to a tightening-up of procedure for escorting prisoners; see C.S.O., R.P. 1881/20672. Details of Kettle's detention until his release in Dec. (for which his landlord wrote to thank Burke) are in R.P. 1881/45908.

[1] The immensely successful novel (first published 1861) by Ellen Wood, 'Mrs Henry Wood' (1814–87).

[2] A society founded in 1865 for promoting amateur dramatic and musical activity, limited to seventy members.

[3] Norris Goddard, Dublin solicitor and legal director of the Property Defence Association. The 'emergency men' were labourers and other auxiliaries supplied by the Orange Emergency Committee, a landlord association of Orange sympathies.

[4] Norman Dunbar Palmer's account of the Clonmel collision (*The Irish Land League crisis* (New Haven, 1940), p. 276), recording numerous fatalities, is taken from the *Evening Mail*; other

Before going into Dublin, Father brought into the drawing room to show us a copy of the Proclamation to be posted in the district of New Pallas, where there will be evictions and probable resistance on Friday. The Document, headed Cowper and signed W. E. Forster, warns the people that if they assemble to obstruct the execution of the law they will do so at their peril.

Fortunately this critical case in which the Executive have to undertake this disagreeable duty, is one that will bear examining; there is no pretence that the people about to be evicted are unable to pay their rent or that the rent demanded is an unjust one. But non-payment of all rent, and resistance to the law having been earnestly preached by the extreme Members of the Land League, such consequences as these at New Pallas were inevitable.

Dr Croke has just been making another speech in which he tries to modify the effect of his last exhortation, by insisting that an 'unjust rent' is all that he would have the people object to; but of course His Grace has not been occupied for days past exciting the passions of his flock against everything connected with the law and Govt for nothing, and he will hardly be surprised if the people insist on serving the good cause by refusing to pay rent, and resisting the enforcement of the law in all cases indiscriminately.[1]

Mother walked with Father to the park gates. At half past 5 I called for him in the carriage at the Castle; after waiting half an hour brought him away with me, very silent and annoyed, evidently something had gone wrong—presently the cause of the vexation appeared—'it was a wonder he had any temper left at all'—after all arrangements had been made by the Govt for the support of the officer of the law in the execution of his duty at the coming evictions—the land-lord communicated with—the troops under orders—the officer himself, the sub-sheriff of Limerick, shirked the task and declined to act. What was to be done? No wonder that all Dublin Castle from the Ch. Sec. downwards were indignant and annoyed.[2]

However, Father seemed to feel that the sub-sheriff's behaviour would not be allowed finally to overthrow his arrangements, and by the time we reached home he had somewhat recovered his spirits.

We found Mr Vincent with Mother: had tea on the lawn, and after Mr V's

---

newspapers (e.g. *Derry Journal*, 3 June) give quite different accounts. The police reports show that no one was killed; two hussars had bad falls from their horses, and a soldier and a policeman were badly injured by missiles (C.S.O., R.P. 1881/19414). A report by the officer commanding the troops present was read by Childers in the house of commons on 10 June (*Hansard 3*, cclxii, 240–41).

[1] Croke's speech, made on Tuesday at the culmination of his 'more than Roman triumph through his great archdiocese' is reported in *F.J.*, 1 June 1881.

[2] Negligent or irregular conduct by sheriffs, process-servers, and similar officers was a frequent annoyance to the executive; cf. the behaviour of the sub-sheriff of Cavan a week later (C.S.O., R.P. 1881/20735). The power of sheriffs and magistrates to requisition police and military protection, virtually at discretion, also caused much confusion and waste of manpower. Steps were accordingly taken to place the arrangements for protecting the execution of sales, writs, and other legal processes completely in the hands of the police; see below, p. 170.

departure Father and I played a short game of tennis, during which time he had a brief respite from his anxieties, being quite absorbed in the game.

On going indoors everything closed round him again.

While we were dressing for dinner a telegram was brought on from the office saying that failing the sub-sheriff the Sheriff of Limerick, Mr Considine,[1] would do the work himself. This information gave Father great satisfaction.

After dinner, his head evidently full of the coming prospect, he read us his instructions to the R.M.,[2] explaining to Mother what must be expected—the troops will fire into the mob—many will be killed—the responsibility for the troops' action will be clearly brought home to the Ch. Sec. whose instructions can be produced—and a verdict will be returned against him by the Jury.[3]

After dinner came more telegrams and messages from the Castle—also London papers and letters. Mr G's answer[4]—I have not read this, but from what Father tells me, it appears not impossible that Mr G. may approve of the 1st suggestion—the Ch. Sec. to give up Parliament this Session and remain here. Father seems to think that the Lord Lieutenant would not resent this—would be glad rather to figure merely as the social head of the Irish Govt and consent to have all the real work of the Executive taken out of his hands, ostensibly as well as practically.

Mother on the contrary is of opinion that Lord Cowper under these circumstances would feel himself bound to resign. I can hardly believe at any rate that Her Excellency would willingly stay for the sole and only object of entertaining Dublin society.

Another unpleasant result of such an arrangement would be that the Ch. Sec. would become identified exclusively with the present administration of Ireland, and not at all with the remedial legislation of the Land Bill.

Considering all things this would seem very hard and very unjust. However nothing is settled, and whatever happens, Father and Mr G. between them may be trusted to do what is best for the good of Ireland, if not for our personal satisfaction.

The London papers full of reports of the immediate return of the Ch. Sec. to attend the next Cabinet, bringing with him proposals for the complete suppression of the Land League.

---

[1] Heffernan James Fritz Considine (1846–1912): owned 950 acres in Limerick and 1124 in Tipperary; became R.M. in 1882 and deputy inspector-general of R.I.C. in 1900.

[2] Major C. F. Rolleston.

[3] The instructions, as later reported by Forster to the house of commons (*Hansard 3*, cclxii, 356–7), emphasise that the sheriff's business must be executed, and in the event of resistance crowds are to be dispersed and the ringleaders arrested; however, the R.M. is to give due warning to the people, and should not order firing unless no alternative remains (C.S.O., R.P. 1881/18280).

[4] To Forster's letter of 29 May 1881; see above, p. 159.

2 June, Th.

A bad morning—further rioting at Clonmel. Another reported attempt at murder near Loughrea—a land agent badly wounded. Report of a terrible collision between police and people in Clare—five people killed; as yet there is no official information of this.[1]

An early visit to Father from Mr Burke, with whom he has gone off to the Castle. Mother was to have walked with him, but he came in to the drawing room to say he must go at once with Mr Burke. 'It is no use to attempt to think of other things'

A quiet day in the garden. A visit in the afternoon from Col.[2] and Miss B[urke], and from pretty Mrs D[alrymple]. The latter full of excitement about the sudden departure of the Guards this evening. 'Where are they going to?' people ask her but she can't tell them. All that is known is that 300 of the Coldstreams, and 100 of the Scots Guards are to go off as a flying column somewhere; the officers seem much pleased, and say this is really serious work, they will have bottles thrown at them etc. etc.

Mrs D. in her capacity I suppose of 'adjutant's wife' left us with the intention of riding to the station to see 'her boys' off, i.e. the 100 Scots Guards.

She did not the least know where they were to go from, or at what time, but trusted to finding out from some of her brother officers.

Father home about 7 in time to have a game of tennis. The report of the land agent fired at is untrue. In the riot at Bodyke in Clare, one man was killed, not 6.

During dinner a telegram received from O. proposing to come over.

3 June, Fri.

Papers full of the 'fatal affray' in Clare. The only wonder is that more people were not killed, for on two separate occasions during the day the police were fired on by the people concealed behind hedges.

Went in during the morning to borrow books from Miss Burke. In the afternoon Mother and I drove to the Hawthorne dell, and afterwards into Dublin,

[1] The riot occurred at the village of Bodyke when a crowd estimated by the police at about 600 assembled to obstruct the service of writs on the notorious O'Callaghan estate, just before noon on 1 June. The force present consisted of 80 police, with six mounted police, under the sub-inspector, county inspector, and William O'Hara, R.M., but the crowd readily used not only stones but pitchforks and the contents of a beehive, and during the arrest of a rioter another was fatally injured. In addition, rifle fire was later opened on the force at a range of some 600 yards, and both the C.I. and R.M. were fired on as they were returning home. In all cases fire was returned, but apparently without injury on either side. Twenty-one arrests were made, and several under the P.P.P. act were made later.

The inquest on the dead rioter produced a verdict of wilful murder by a policeman 'at present unknown'; a sub-constable was later accused, but not prosecuted. See C.S.O., R.P. 1881/19900, 24293.

[2] Theobald Hubert Burke (1833–1909): brother of Thomas Henry and Marianne Burke; lt-col. (retired) of 18th regiment of foot; succeeded as 13th baronet of Glinsk, 1884.

bringing Father away from the Castle about 6 o'clock. In better spirits than the last time I went for him—'he thought his blows were beginning to tell'.

Up to the latest report, the New Pallas expedition was being got through quietly. Before leaving Dublin called at the K[ildare] St Club to hear the latest telegrams from the House. A row going on apparently among the Parnellites—speeches from Mr G. and Mr P.

A lovely evening, interrupted in the middle of lawn tennis by the arrival of a telegram—an appeal from Sir W. Harcourt—Ministers evidently being worried for information about the state of things here. Answer sent off, and tennis finished.[1] Mr Naish, Law Adviser, to dinner—'a big-brained man' says Father; it is to be wished there were more like him here. Much talk at dinner concerning the recent verdict of murder against the policeman engaged in the Galway affray in which Sergeant Armstrong was killed.[2] What is the best way of dealing with this flagrantly unjust verdict of the Coroner's jury? Shall Mr Law as Attorney General and Crown Prosecutor enter a *Nolle prosequi*, or shall the bill simply be left to be thrown out by the Grand jury when it comes before them?

In the one case, the Govt would take on themselves the responsibility of publicly reversing the Coroner's verdict, in the other they would leave it to be done by a body of men, who would certainly be accused by the people of class prejudice in so acting.

As to the depositions made before the Coroner's jury, Mr N[aish] who had read them through declared that in any other country the witnesses would infallibly have been prosecuted for perjury, so glaring and obvious were the lies told upon oath.

About 10 o'clock a telegram arrived announcing the proceedings for the day at New Pallas were over quietly.

4 June, Sat.

To my great delight Oakel appeared in my room about half past 7 o'clock, having come by the North Wall. It is a very great pleasure having him. I went down at 1 o'clock with Williams to Killiney to see the Murrough O'Briens; this time I could see the view which had been hidden from Francie and me in the winter by a thick fog. After lunch we set out for a walk, Mrs Murrough going part of the way with us afterwards I went with Mr O'Brien to see some new cottages built by a Mr Bramley[3] for the benefit of Artizans—the rent 6s. a week being too high for labourers.

We also went into the little reading room just started by Mr O'B[rien] and

[1] See *Hansard 3*, cclxii, 21–3 (3 June 1881).

[2] 'Galway' should read 'Sligo'; see above, pp. 110–11. 'Sergeant' is a curious anachronism: Armstrong's rank was constable, a designation which was changed to sergeant on 1 Oct. 1883; before that date the rank of sergeant did not exist in the R.I.C.

[3] W. Jennings Bramley, of Strathmore, Killiney.

this Mr Bramley—a plain room for smoking and talking supplied with English illustrated papers, and the three Dublin dailies, *Ex[press]*, *Freeman*, and *Irish Times*.

If this sort of thing had been done more by the resident gentry throughout the country and in the great towns, would there have been the bitter class hostility, the dangerous ignorance and violence which every one is now complaining of so sorrowfully?

It may be quite true as Sir W. Gregory says, that at the present time no literature but such wretched, one-sided stuff as appears in the so-called National prints, would have the least chance of being read by the peasantry, even if it were pressed upon them gratis; but is not this partly because for generations past no effort was ever made to influence and interest the minds of the people by those who should have been their natural leaders, the landlords, who lived amongst them, and received their money?

In spite of our political differences, I like Mr Murrough O'Brien as much as ever, and to a great extent sympathize with his ideas and way of looking at things. He may be an enthusiast, but he is not a fanatic, and whatever change he would make would be from an honest love of Ireland not from hatred of England.

We had some talk about Mr Dillon, who is, I believe, a personal acquaintance of Mr O'Brien. He disapproves greatly (as might be expected) of his imprisonment, and maintains that in all his violent speeches, Mr Dillon had never meant his words to be understood as an incitement to break the law, or resort to actual violence.

I could not help saying that however little the English were supposed to understand the Irish character, Mr Dillon must understand them still less, if he had really thought that his Tipperary audience would take all his strong expressions about dealing blow for blow at the landlords, and pursuing process servers to their ruin, simply as literary metaphors, which they were never meant to act upon.[1]

If Mr O'Brien takes the *Freeman* line, and thinks the alarm about the state of the country much exaggerated, his wife, a sister-in-law to Mr Mahony of Dromore, is quite alive to the other side of the question; indeed she told me she was even more despondent than in the autumn, and spoke, as people often do of the French Revolution.

The running after new leaders—the forsaking and forgetting of old ties—the sordid ingratitude, the weak cowardice, the open disregard of moral obligations in the matter of justice or even the barest honesty, the indifference on the part of women as well as men to any amount of suffering and cruelty when inflicted on the unpopular party—all this may well make an Irish lady despair, and feel as if on her and in her time the end of the earth had come, so far as her country was concerned.

[1] Cf. Lyons, *Dillon*, p. 41.

And yet there is some hope in the thought that perhaps this crisis, when nothing but evil seems uppermost, is but a phase in an onward movement, that it is not so much to the deterioration, to the vices of the present generation of Irishmen and women that these miseries are due, as to the crooked corners of Ireland's past history.

The revolt against a bad system, the reaction after years of silent endurance and stolid indifference on the part both of rich and poor—in short the revolution has come in our time, and come as revolutions generally do with very ugly accompaniment—the worst and most puzzling circumstance is that those who have suffered least, and have least interest and excuse for revolt seem to be those who make the loudest outcry—do the most harm—profit the most largely by the present dislocation and distress, and impose most easily with their lies and false doctrines upon the ignorance and misery of the really suffering people.

However I hope and believe that there may come a time, even in Ireland, when the jar and distress and amazement caused by this painful re-adjustment of old relations between man and man, and class and class, shall have passed away: when the mist of falsehood conjured up by blind self-seeking leaders of the blind shall have dispersed, and Irishmen and Englishmen, gentry and farmers, shall understand the new foundation on which they stand, and dare to live together as friends and honest men, without fear of interference or incitement to violence on the part of either landlord or land leaguer.

I left Killiney at 5, Mr and Mrs Murrough coming with me to the station. I found Lord de Vesci having tea with Mother. He is one of the sort of Irishmen whom Ireland will always be the better for having. Like many other good landlords he has had much cause for disappointment and annoyance in the conduct of his tenants, though this has not had the effect of embittering him against his countrymen.

So far as he knew, the New Pallas affair was going off quietly; the Guards were expected back that evening.

Father and Oakel home from the Castle about 8 o'clock. No fresh event. Mr Jephson back at night after dining in Dublin and seeing Magistrates—more depressed and gloomy than ever about the state of the country.

Mr Parnell's last speech, reported in today's papers, is more openly treasonable than usual. His 'threat' disguised under the veil of prophecy of what would happen if the Govt did not cease to carry out the law, the recovery of rent, was replied to by Lord Hartington, who declined on behalf of the Govt to surrender the powers of the Executive in Ireland into the hands of the Land League—or even of the Archbishop of Cashel.[1]

---

[1] *Hansard 3*, cclxii, 91–102; Holland, *Devonshire*, i, 341. Parnell, apparently seriously, advocated the adoption of Croke's proposal that crown forces should be withdrawn from Tipperary, and the clergy entrusted with the preservation of the peace.

5 June, Sun.

To church at the Hibernian—Father coming with us. Mr Aubrey de Vere to lunch. A call from the Monteagles and their little boy, immediately afterwards on their way to Mount Trenchard for a short visit—'before they have asked their tenants for anything, and are still on good friendly terms with them'.

Spent the afternoon walking about the grounds with Mr de Vere. Mother with Father in the study, afterwards going for a walk with him, Mr B. and Mr de Vere.

A pleasant family dinner in the evening. In a note from Lord de V[esci] he told Mother that 'the G[uard]s had come back from New Pallas much impressed with the villainous faces of the men, the beauty of the women, and the wonderful influence of the priests'.

6 June, Mon.

No special murder or riot in the paper this morning. Our movements as to going, or staying on here quite uncertain. Parliament meets on Thursday, but the Land Bill not to come on till Monday.

Father is much impressed with the importance of his presence here at this critical time. But how about the Cabinet on Friday? Will he go to this and then come back here again, or shall we all wait and go home together on Sunday—or shall we stop on here indefinitely, and tell Francie to join us? We do not know ourselves, and certainly no one else can tell us—not even the London correspondents of the Irish papers, who profess to report almost daily on the Ch. Sec.'s movements and intentions.

A wild stormy day, with showers of hail and rain, and bright gleams over the mountains in the intervals. Mother and I spent a long quiet day at home, writing, reading, and trying to get out of doors between the downpours.

In the evening we all four dined at Woodlands.[1] Met there Archbishop McCabe and his secretary, the Chief Baron and Mrs Palles,[2] John O'Hagans, Lord and Lady Alex. Lennox, and Mr Naish. Father was very glad to meet the Archbishop and had a great deal of talk with him—finding him not by any means brilliant but sensible, and seeming thoroughly to understand all the bearing of matters connected with his own office.

In appearance His Grace is not striking, even with the assistance of his purple robes, and long gold chain. Both he and his secretary the Rev. Mr Frickers[3] were pleasant and ready to talk—both very quiet and as it were small, retiring in their manner.

With the former I had only a short tête-à-tête, towards the end of the

[1] Residence of Lord O'Hagan, at Castleknock.
[2] Christopher Palles (1831–1920): solicitor general for Ireland, 1872; attorney general, 1872–4; lord chief baron of exchequer, 1874–1916.
[3] M. A. Fricker, P.P., administrator of St Mary's parish, Marlborough Street, Dublin.

evening on the subject of potatoes. With the latter, who sat next me at dinner, I had a good deal of talk concerning the inhabitants of [?] who happened curiously enough to be the parishioners of Mr Frickers, and well known to him.

One is glad to think that these miserable districts are not so utterly squalid and Godforsaken as they appear when one merely passes through them.

Father I think liked his evening—was glad to meet both the Archbishop and Mr O'Hagan, of whose ability he has a high opinion.

7 June, Tu.

Another Circular in the papers this morning signed by Col. Hillier; it fills the *Freeman* with dismay, but does not seem to have this effect on people in general. The purport of it is to direct the Sheriffs to give full information beforehand to the Executive as to the places where evictions requiring the aid of the constabulary and troops are to be carried out, in order that the Govt may make arrangements accordingly.

This clear proof of an intention on the part of the Govt to support the landlords in the enforcement of their just rights[1] causes great satisfaction to some, and disappointment to others who had believed or professed to believe that their next move was to be abdication of their functions in this respect, and compliance with Mr P's advice 'to leave the landlords and their tenants to fight it out'.

A violent and vulgar speech of Mr H[ealy] reported in this morning's papers, full of coarse abuse of the Ch. Sec. but prudently free from any such language of incitement and sedition as can be used safely in the House.

A cold stormy day with heavy downpour of rain and hail. Drove into Dublin in the afternoon—Mr and Mrs Murrough O'Brien who had called going part of the way with us.

Apropos of Lord M. having come up to Dublin to examine witnesses with regard to the Shannon Commission,[2] Mr O'B. casually mentioned that he was afraid his visit would prove abortive, as one of the witnesses had been arrested and the other would not appear.

There are fresh arrests every day varying in the excitement they produce.

We called for Oakel at the Castle to take him on with us to see the Athletic Sports (or College Races) at Trinity for which we had tickets. He told us that 'rather a bad thing had happened'.[3] A cypher telegram from Co. Cork reported

[1] Forster more accurately described its purpose to a colleague as 'letting the sub-sheriffs and landlords know that they must tell us what protection they want, and when and where, thereby preventing them from being masters of the situation' (Reid, *Forster*, ii, 323).

[2] Lord Monteagle was one of the eight commissioners appointed in Oct. 1880 to examine the inland waterways connecting Belfast, Coleraine, and Limerick. The commission held its seventh meeting on 8 June, and its fourteenth and final meeting on 7 Dec. and reported on 8 Feb. 1882 (H.C. 1882, xxi, 101–22).

[3] The disturbances in the area Skibbereen-Ballydehob-Schull form the chief ground for N. D. Palmer's assertion that 'guerrilla warfare had broken out in many parts of Ireland' (*The Irish Land*

that the police barracks at Ballydehob had been attacked—the police forced
to retreat, the telegraph wire cut—a reinforcement of Marines was to be sent
from Bantry—12 miles off—Details were not known, but it seemed as if the
excitement was connected with the arrest of a man named Mahoney, who had
been arrested, rescued, and retaken again in that district, a day or two
before.[1]

Everything seemed to point to the likelihood of a serious riot and difficulty—
the newly discovered device of cutting telegraphic wires causing much inconvenience.

On returning to the Castle after the Sports, where we did not stay very long
owing to the pouring rain which came on, we found Father too busy to leave
and had to drive back without him.

We dined at the Burkes', a very cheerful party; no one but themselves and a
friend Miss Gough.

Heard from Father of his interview with Lord Lismore[2] concerning a
suggestion about arrears of rent.

Mr Burke did not believe that the Cork affair would turn out to be much
more than a riot.

After we got back to the C.S. Lodge, a telegram arrived saying that there had
been no firing and that the mob was dispersing.

League crisis (New Haven, 1940), p. 276); as in other cases at this time, rumour thrived on lack of
information. A concise account of the episode was given by Forster in the house of commons on
13 June (*Hansard 3*, cclxii, 347–50). The district, like many others, had for a long time been well
under the police strength it should have had (C.S.O., R.P. 1881/19298). Reinforcements (plus 44
marines backed by the gunboats *Orwell* and *Britomart*, and some 300 soldiers from Cork), together
with the issue of a proclamation, rapidly quietened the district, but a renewal of attacks on barracks
continued to be feared for some time, and the military 'flying column' was not withdrawn until the
end of July. Sub-inspector J. E. French, detective director of the R.I.C., sent special reports to
headquarters from the district, and assisted in selecting rioters for arrest. On 12 June Captain
Plunkett, R.M., took command of the pacification, and probably laid the foundation, by his
handling of it, for his selection as one of the first special R.M.s in Dec. (see below, p. 334). On
17 June twelve rioters were brought before him at Schull petty sessions; their solicitor and the local
clergy offered in effect to guarantee peace if the defendants were released on their own recognizances. According to French, 'Captain Plunkett in a very lucid and impressive manner explained
that the government were quite able to assert the authority of the law and to preserve the peace of
the country without the intervention of any third party ... and that peace and order would be
established here, and maintained at any hazard, even tho' it should become necessary to take away
human life in doing so' (C.S.O., R.P. 1881/20498).

[1] Henry O'Mahoney (another 'returned American') was arrested in Ballydehob at 6.45 a.m. on
4 June, rescued by a crowd, rearrested and rescued again, after which the sub-inspector and his
nine men were forced to withdraw. The 'suspect' then drove to Limerick and gave himself up; on
9 June he wrote facetiously to T. M. Healy that in future the chief secretary should save the cost of
police escorts and send each suspect a copy of his warrant and his travel expenses to gaol; he
contemplated claiming £4 1s. 6d. for his own expenses. (S.P.O., I.C.R., P.P.P. act, list of arrests;
R.P. 1881/21205.)

[2] George Ponsonby O'Callaghan (1815–98): 2nd Viscount Lismore; lieutenant and custos
rotulorum of Tipperary, in which he owned 34,945 acres, with a further 6067 acres in Cork and 1194
in Limerick.

8 June, Wed.

The papers full of the rioting in the Co. Cork, roads torn up, telegraph wires cut, the police and even the soldiers attacked with stones—houses of unpopular inhabitants wrecked. It appears that the origin of the disturbance was the groundless rumour of the arrest of a priest—Father Murphy. Having become once thoroughly excited the people, men, women and children, took advantage of their opportunity, and are committing all the violence they can with impunity. There was no firing on the mob, but the presence of troops in the district for some little time to come is thought necessary.

Miss Dixon to breakfast. Miss Glyn and Miss Burke to play tennis in the afternoon.

Oakel returned to England by the North Wall in the evening. Mr and Mrs Litton to dinner, the former as usual personally agreeable, and politically amenable; he is responsible I believe for about 80 amendments on the Land Bill, but his interference in the debate will certainly not be in a hostile spirit, or with the purpose of obstruction.

For one thing, he is not in the least afraid of his constituents or of the Land League, and therefore is able to discuss the Land Bill, to suggest or withdraw amendments according to his own judgment, without reference to the dictates of Mr Parnell or the threats of Mr Egan.

The last thing before going to bed Father received a telegram saying that things were quiet at Skibbereen.

9 June, Th.

The sale at Mullingar, where troops had been sent down and the Proclamation posted, has gone off without the slightest disturbance. In one or two other cases, sales and evictions have been got through quietly. On the other hand an expedition near Glin on the Shannon to effect a seizure of cattle for rent has proved a failure, everything having been removed before the arrival of the sub-sheriff and troops.

There has also been another cruel and cowardly attack by a mob of people on a process server, who has been so badly injured that his life is despaired of.

A fine morning, but very cold. The fifteen Acres covered with troops exercising under Gen. Glyn.

Mother walked with Father to the Park gates, and after lunch called on Lady C[owper] who returned from Abbeyleix on Tuesday. The latter very gloomy about the state of the country—no hope from the Land Bill—neither landlords nor tenants seem to like it.

The Cowpers have even less chance than we have of being sanguine about the prospects of the country, seeing that they never hear of anything except through the landlords.

At 6 I drove into Dublin to fetch Father, who after leaving the Castle, spent a happy half hour at the K[ildare] St Club over whist whilst I drove about and waited for him.

Things look rather better. There are signs that the exasperation and resistance policy is becoming discredited, and that the vigorous measures of the Govt are beginning to tell.

As Mr Litton and many others have said, the Irish peasants are like children trying how far they can go.[1] The New Pallas expedition, with the Proclamation, amongst other things have made them and their leaders see that they cannot safely go a step further in the direction of violent resistance to the law and they are prepared to stop short accordingly.

The publication of this Proclamation has clearly had a good effect. The impression that the police and troops would never fire under any circumstances, and that they would be condemned by the Govt if they did, seems to have been wide-spread both amongst the people and the constabulary—at least such is Oakel's opinion after hearing the talk of numerous police constables and Magistrates, who have been up at the Castle during the last few days from different parts of the country.[2]

Father and Mother dined at the Dalrymples'. Mr Jephson in Dublin, so I had an evening to myself. Read some cantos of Dante and afterwards the papers including the 'rebels'. The *Flag of Ireland* reads Mr H[ealy] a severe lecture for his vulgar speech at Swords the other day, and speaks with unusual civility of the Ch. Sec. who 'means well to Ireland' according to his lights. *The Nation* and *Weekly News*, whilst reprobating and bewailing and marvelling at the conduct of Mr Forster and the Govt in the usual orthodox fashion, shows a wise appreciation of the meaning of the recent Proclamation and Circulars, by strenuously warning the people to desist from further violence by which means they will defeat the 'sly and vicious object of the latest constabulary Circular'.

An excellent speech[3] by Mr C[hamberlain]—'The Liberals detest coercion, but they detest the disorder more'.

10 June, Fri.

A speech from Archbishop Croke at Tipperary, advising the people to ['refrain'] from resistance, and from the 'unmeaning and unmanly practice of hooting and stone-throwing' when the police and troops are present in such force at evictions and sales, as to make the unmanly proceeding dangerous to

[1] Edward O'Brien had used this simile in a letter of 4 Nov. 1880 to Forster (B.L., Add. MS 44157, ff 195–204).

[2] It is doubtful what can have given this impression, except perhaps the insistence in the circulars of 22 Apr., 2 May, and 21 May on the less drastic methods of dealing with crowds.

[3] At Birmingham on 7 June; quoted in J. L. Garvin, *Life of Joseph Chamberlain* (London, 1932), i, 336–7.

the people.[1] Dr Croke also advises a combination of 'judicious flexibility and firmness' in the treatment of the Land Bill by the extreme party in Parliament, and hints plainly to the 'immortal Parnell' that he and his party must be very cautious in opposing or obstructing the Bill, even if all the desired amendments are not incorporated in it.

Oakel sends me today the *Daily Chronicle* containing a letter from himself on evictions, and the mistaken presumption that they are, in most instances, cases of hard dealing on the part of the landlords, and points out that in each of the four cases brought forward by the League as specimens of 'unjust evictions' their statements proved on enquiry to be absolutely false or without foundation.

The *Chronicle* not only inserts this letter (signed 'H') in a prominent place, but has a leader upon it which is very satisfactory.

It is much to be wished that English public opinion should understand that the Govt in supporting the landlords in the exercise of their legal rights is not necessarily supporting them in injustice, as seems to be the assumption with some people.

The House has met again, and actually got straight into supply without intermediate obstruction. Telegrams on the state of Ireland were read from the Ch. Sec. by Sir W. Harcourt, and an extract from a letter explaining the origin of the Schull riots, and the exaggeration of the state of things there in most of the newspaper accounts. It was announced by Mr G. that the Ch. Sec. will be in his place in the House on Monday.

I wish I thought we should be there too, but I fear Mr G. and others seem to contemplate the possibility of the Irish Sec. remaining in Dublin—in which case we should stay here and he would return with Francie in a few days.

Father received a long letter this morning (whch also appears in the *Freeman*) from Miss Anna Parnell remonstrating against the appearance of some Constabulary officers on the platform at her Meeting on Saturday, and reminding him of the 'constitutional fear which many women have of firearms'—the letter written on emblazoned 'Ladies Land League' paper is signed 'respectfully Anna Parnell'—the usual formula 'yours respectfully' would have been held I suppose to have compromised her with the Govt.

A persistently wet morning, and still so threatening in the afternoon that Mother would not go to Lady O'Hagan's garden party.

We dined at the V.R. Lodge. Heard from Father of the attempt to blow up the Liverpool Town Hall. Two men caught in the act. Fortunately an English jury can be trusted to do justice, and, as seems to be the case, if there is

[1] 'No bad news today. Archbishop Croke's speech yesterday is I cannot but think a good result of our late proclamations—but there is much naïvete in his advice to the mob not to attack the police when they are in large numbers and supported by troops' (Forster to Gladstone, 10 June 1881; B.L., Add. MS 44158, ff 181–2).

sufficient evidence on which to convict these men, they will not be acquitted with flying colours—the usual course of proceeding with a jury in this country.[1]

The party at dinner consisted of ourselves, the D.s, Sir A. Liddell, Capt. Carpenter of the *Bellisle*, and Col. Gibbs of the Scots Guards. Not very amusing.

11 June, Sat.

No special outrage in the papers this morning. The rioting at Cork has been serious, but more connected with drink and the Cork races than the Land question.

The two men pursued and arrested at Liverpool turn out to be Irish Americans. This fact, coupled with the circumstance that the men had about them badges and papers bearing Fenian inscriptions, leads the *Freeman* to suggest that the whole affair is a 'plant' got up by the English for the purpose of further discrediting this unhappy country. It does not do more at present than mysteriously hint at the very plausible suspicion, but intimates that 'we shall watch this trial with curiosity—it will probably result in revelations'—this is quite possible.

As regards the Land Bill, there are signs in the *Freeman* and others, who may be trusted to 'jump with the cat' that even the extreme party will not venture to obstruct progress openly.

Walked in the morning to the Park gates. In the afternoon Mother and I to a Musical afternoon at Mrs Palles—wife of the Chief Baron.

Mr Naish to dinner. Father was deeply annoyed by an article in this evening's *Times*, written in a tone of angry despair at the state of lawlessness in Ireland, and entirely ignoring the efforts being made (not unsuccessfully) by the Govt to deal with it, and giving the impression that everything hitherto done by a weak and frightened Executive had quite failed to check the violence of the mob, and the influence of the Land League.

Such an article, appearing in the *Times*, would do real harm Father thought—moreover the task of governing Ireland at a time like this, is made almost hopeless if on one side every step that the authorities take is abused and misrepresented, and on the other their efforts to restore and keep order are absolutely ignored and unsupported.

The one paper which during the present crisis is giving the Executive intelligent support and appreciation is the *Irish Times*.

[1] James McGrath (alias Robert William Barton) and James McKevitt had attacked Liverpool police station on 16 May with a gunpowder device, causing minor damage. On 10 June they were caught by police at the town hall while planting a dynamite bomb which exploded ineffectually. McGrath was sentenced to life imprisonment and McKevitt to 12 years. See K. R. M. Short, *The dynamite war: Irish-American bombers in Victorian Britain* (Dublin and London, 1979), pp 63–7; and below, p. 216.

12 June, Sun.

To church at the Hibernian. Afterwards, Father and Mother walked over to the V.R. Lodge to say good bye to the Cowpers, it having been finally decided that we should all leave together on Sunday night.

At luncheon Father charged Mr Jephson to be sure to remind Mr Burke about having the 'sewer' attended to at once—'never mind about waiting for the Corporation, if they like they can prosecute the Govt afterwards, provided the thing is done first'. I supposed of course that the 'suspects' at Kilmainham were dissatisfied with the drainage there and are insisting on the Ch. Sec. having it set right. It appeared however, that the 'sewer' is a small river now used for this purpose which runs under the Castle, and that when—as at the present time—there is a talk of blowing up the Castle precautions are taken by putting a grating at the mouth, to prevent persons from creeping up it.

Spent the afternoon in seeing about the flowers, and calling on Miss Burke, who with her friend Miss Gough also came to see us. Mr B. who was to have come to Father between 3 and 4 did not arrive. At 5 o'clock he had not appeared and we began to suppose that something had happened—the Mill-street Meeting gone wrong.

However to our great relief when Father at last came in to join us in the dining room at half past 5, after his interview with Mr B. he brought us no bad news. On the contrary all had gone off well at Millstreet—gone off in the literal sense, for the Meeting, having obtained leave from the R.M. in command to march into the country a short distance and back, had availed itself of this opportunity to demonstrate in silence.

As it is the inflammatory stuff which is poured into peoples ears at these Meetings by professional agitators that leads to outrages and excites a district, and not the Meetings and brass bands themselves, it may be hoped that this arrangement of a silent meeting was satisfactory to all parties.

We returned to London in the evening by the evening Mail—I having been nearly three weeks, and Mother a fortnight in Ireland.

We had a perfectly smooth passage, and remained on deck for two hours; amongst our fellow passengers were Lord and Lady Alex. Lennox (she Lady O'H's sister and very nice), Lord W. Compton, Mr Hatchell, Capt. Carew, and Mr Healy.

13 June, Mon.

Arrived in such good time that Francie was not quite prepared for us. She came back from the Dingle on Saturday. A hard day's work before Father—a Cabinet in the afternoon, and a string of questions (14) to be answered in the House.

I spent the morning over the flowers we had brought from Dublin. In the afternoon drove with Mother to Mr Tayler, calls etc.

At 4.30 to Mr Brand's Gallery. Questions had begun, so we did not hear the cheers with which the Ch. Sec. was received when he made his first answer. However we heard most of them, I had the pleasure of seeing how well he got through his ordeal, how entirely the ill-meant questions and insinuations of the Parnellites (notably Healy and T. P. O'Connor) were made to recoil upon themselves, and how respectfully and approvingly the House generally listened to his straightforward statement of what the Irish Govt had done with regard to disturbances in the past and meant to do in the future.

Apropos of an impudent question of O'Connor's which he gratified the House by not answering, Father had the opportunity of reading his recent Instructions to the R.M. of Limerick in the matter of firing, which he was glad to avail himself of. In answer also to Lord R. Churchill he was able to read to the House a detailed account of what had actually taken place in the riots at Skibbereen, as to which there had been much excitement and some exaggeration in this country.

After the questions were over Father came up to see us, and shared our tea in the recesses of Mrs Brand's Gallery.

Mother and I left about 7 o'clock, the House being in full swing over the Land Bill—a quiet rational discussion, even Mr Leamy[1] debating calmly like an ordinary civilized member, and Mr P. actually compelling Mr Biggar to withdraw an amendment on the ground that in substance it had been already decided upon by the House, and that to press it now might seem like obstruction.

Father home to dinner bringing Mr Cropper with him.

14 June, Tu.

The *Times*, *Standard*, and *Daily News*, all friendly towards the Ch. Sec. this morning, the clear and full information given by him yesterday afternoon with regard to the state of Ireland has given general satisfaction.

The Land Bill really made some progress yesterday—several amendments were got through, and many others will be withdrawn after discussion amongst their respective movers. Mr G. is said to be putting his foot down firmly and showing his intention to press the Bill through very much as it stands.

Drove with Father via Conduit St to the office. A visit in the afternoon from Uncle M[atthew] and Aunt F[an] just come from Miss Farrar's wedding at which both Sir S[tafford Northcote] and Mr G. had been assisting.[2] Mother and Francie out driving in the afternoon, I to Lillington Street.

Father home to dinner in cheerful spirits. Some talk about future plans. Is

[1] Edmund Leamy (1848–1904): home rule M.P. for Waterford city, 1880–85; for Cork N.E., 1885–7; for Sligo S., 1888–92; for Kildare N., 1900–04.
[2] On this day Hilda Cardew Farrar (d. 1908), daughter of Frederic William Farrar (1831–1903), dean of Canterbury, married John Stafford Northcote (1850–1920), third son of Sir Stafford.

Father or any one else at the Irish office to have any holiday this summer?
Whatever happens Mr Burke must get away. The Cowpers' movements need
not affect ours, there would be no reason against their being away at the same
time as Father, since matters might be left in the hands of the Lord Justice. The
Master of the Rolls[1] can at least be as much relied upon as Lord Cowper to
keep things straight in the absence of the Ch. Sec.

Again this evening Father reverted to the idea of his resignation—'It is
seriously to be thought of whether after the Land Bill is passed I should not get
out of it all. The Cabinet would make arrangements for me—I can never do
now what I might have done in Ireland—the Coercion Bill, and Buckshot, will
be always hung round my neck—there are some things that the people will
never get over—the arresting a priest.'

I wonder whether this is really so. Some Irishmen who might be supposed to
know, tell one that the violent language now the fashion amongst the people in
speaking of the Ch. Sec. does not represent their real permanent feeling about
him, and that after being the best abused he might not improbably become the
most popular Englishman in Ireland.

Of course this is nonsense, but at the same time I do believe that a great deal
of the outcry and professed hatred against him is artificial, and that if after this
agitation had died away, the Ch. Sec. were left alone for a year with the Irish
people they would come to understand and appreciate him as they are quite
forbidden to do under the present circumstances.

It will seem cruelly hard if Father with his inextinguishable liking and good-
will towards our Irish fellow-subjects should be known by them only as the
author of the Coercion Bill of 1881. However, even if the Irish are never
allowed to do him justice, justice will be done him.

After dinner Father (who had only one question put him to-day) went back to
the House, which was engaged on Sir W. Lawson's Local Option Resolution.
Mother and I to Mrs Gladstone's where I enjoyed meeting a good many of our
acquaintance after my three weeks in Ireland.

Everyone was in cheerful mood about the prospects of the Land Bill and the
improvement of the tone in the House. Many nice enquiries after Father, and
guarded congratulations on the state of things in Ireland being a little better
than when we went over to Dublin.

Father's vigorous action at the Castle has certainly not been for nothing.
Amongst those we met were Mr Knowles—very friendly and complimentary
about Oakel's article—Mr Childers, who declared that Oakel was a confirmed
Tory in his views on the Army—of course the Duke [of Cambridge[2]] and all the
officers were delighted.

[1] Sir Edward Sullivan.
[2] George William Frederick Charles (1819–1904): cousin of the queen; 2nd duke of Cambridge
since 1850; commander-in-chief of the British army since 1856.

He spoke pleasantly however of Oakel himself, and acknowledged that whatever his arguments might be, he had made no blunders in his facts.

Mr Sellar who thinks that if the present amiable conduct in the House is maintained the Bill may be through Committee on the 20th of July—Mr Errington full of admiration as usual at Father's wonderful patience towards his aggravating fellow countrymen—Mr Vincent on his way from Dublin to join General Hamley and the Greek Frontier Commission—not at all sorry to leave Ireland, and thoroughly displeased with the Irish character so far as he had seen it at New Pallas and elsewhere. I pointed out to him that if the two men who tried to blow up the Town Hall were Irishmen, so were the policemen who pursued and captured them, but this did not seem to make any change in his opinion—Mr Hayward—Mr Rutson, the Yates Thompsons, Mr Doyle, etc. etc.

Before coming away I went with Mrs G. into the Cabinet room, and tried to seek inspiration in the darkness of this august chamber, every corner of which must be impregnated with State secrets.

15 June, Wed.

The papers very quiet. The most important fact so far as Irish affairs are concerned being Mr G's statement with regard to Major Nolan's[1] bill, which was brought forward late at night.

The object of this is to suspend evictions for 6 months[2] in those cases where a half year's arrears of rent is paid. There had been some talk of such a proposal, but Father himself was rather startled at finding in this morning's papers (for apparently he had not been in the House at the time) how kindly and almost approvingly Mr G. had spoken of Major Nolan's bill, which he imagined was blocked for some time to come by Mr Warton.

As for Mother she declares that there seems a fatality about Irish affairs—just as Father's vigorous assertions of the law in Ireland was at last convincing tenants that dishonesty was not the best policy, and that when rents were beginning to come in steadily and without disturbance, appear Major Nolan and his Bill, in such a way as to force the Govt to choose between opposing and accepting it, and in the latter case, holding out encouragement to the tenants to renew the wavering resistance to the enforcement of the landlords' legal and in most cases just claims.

Aunt Mala and Mrs Hayes to lunch. In the afternoon to Mr Tayler for my very last sitting.

Father and Mother to dinner at the C. Russells', I with Mother afterwards to

[1] John Philip Nolan (1838–1912): artillery officer, with a distinguished record of active service; home rule M.P. for County Galway, 1874–85; for Galway N., 1900–06.

[2] Properly, until 1 Oct., so as to allow time for the passing of the land bill; the bill in fact became law on 22 Aug.

Lady Salisbury's. A great crush and very hot. Hardly any of our colleagues present.

16 June, Th.

The prestige of the Land League can hardly have been improved by one or two circumstances that have happened lately—notably a curious law-suit to which full publicity has been given between a Land League farmer, O'Shea, and an agent, Mr Barry. The farmer prosecuted Mr Barry for libel on account of some statements published by the latter as to Mr O'Shea's conduct towards both his landlord and his fellow-tenants. Mr O'Shea did not profit much either in pocket or reputation by his move—a verdict (by a special jury transported from Limerick to Dublin) was given against him and instead of receiving damages, he has had to pay £5 costs.

The Proclamations have had their effect in stopping the sort of violence which came to a head in the Mitchelstown riots, and of late evictions and sales have been conducted without disturbance in different parts of the country.

The facts pointed out in Oakel's letter with regard to the supposed hardship in the eviction cases brought forward by the League, have been noticed in several quarters. The *Pall Mall Gazette* in a leading article has acknowledged that the four specimen cases of unjust eviction did certainly break down and the London correspondent of the *Freeman* complains angrily that by these mistakes on the part of the League authorities in Ireland, a dangerous opening is given to the enemies of the truth here.

Walked with Father to the office. Col. Pearson and Mr Fitzgerald to lunch. In the afternoon to the Hospital, and afterwards with Oakel to call on Mme Catargi and Mrs Childers.

Every one of all sorts is full of enquiries and commiseration for Mr Forster. The Sister at the Hospital, Mr Tayler, Mme Catargi, Mrs Glyn—with anyone to whom I speak it is the same story. As for the way in which people talk of Ireland and our experiences in Dublin during the past three weeks, one would think that we had been living in a barbarous country infested with brigands and assassins, and on the verge of civil war—I can quite believe that if we had gathered all our impressions of the state of things from the London papers instead of from the facts in Ireland we should have been.

After every fresh piece of legislation such as the Land Act, or the Church act, their natural disposition has been to rest and be thankful, and consider the new Law in each case as final, as removing the necessity for further exertions on the part of Irish representatives. This would not answer with English constituences and it has not answered with Irish constituences, who were always pressing for some new reform, and demanding improvements on what has been already effected.

The great want in Ireland at present, says Dr Lyons, is an independent newspaper—the people hear only one side, and can hear only one side, for the other side is never put before them. As to paying, it would not pay at first, but the money spent in supporting such an enterprize would certainly not be thrown away.

I believe Father also thinks that a great deal might be done to improve things in Ireland by a wise expenditure of money, he had been saying as such to Lord F. Cavendish and Sir R. Lingen[1] this very afternoon when he went to speak to the Treasury about a certain railway. 'If I had £200,000 Secret service money I could do a good deal' Father said to us in the evening.[2]

On the whole Dr Lyons was decidedly pleasant, and I thought sensible though perhaps a trifle inclined to be lengthy.

He amused me by a story of Mr Healy with whom he had fallen into conversation in a railway carriage—'Mr Healy informed me that he had lately been in Paris and assisted at a debate in the Assembly—he had been much scandalized at the disorder and confusion, and drew comparisons between the French and English Parliaments, greatly to the advantage of the former [should be 'latter']'. 'The President of the Assembly', he remarked, 'seemed quite powerless to keep order, now with us the Speaker has a great deal of influence'.

It is pleasant to find that even Mr H. appreciates the beauty of order and decorum in the House, though he contributes so little to it himself.

19 June, Sun.

The *Observer* of this morning contained the report of further ravings of Mr O'Donovan Rossa,[3] and the statement that Lord G[ranville] had called the attention of the U.S. Govt to the publications in which they appear.[4] He has again claimed credit for the destruction of the *Doterel*, and proclaims it to be the further duty of patriotic Irishmen to compass the assassination of the 'hypocrite' Gladstone and 'Buckshot Forster'.

To church at St James the Less. In the afternoon with Oakel to call on Mrs Dugdale, Mrs Simpson and the Bishops. Mrs Dugdale charming as usual, and seemingly much interested in the Irish affairs, and appealing seriously to me whether after all when I was in Ireland, I did not feel that I was in a foreign country. I said no, and engaged that if she would come and stay with us in the Phoenix Park, she should not feel so herself, by the time she went away.

---

[1] Ralph Robert Wheeler Lingen (1819–1905), permanent secretary to the treasury, 1869–85.

[2] The amount of secret service money spent by the chief secretary's office in the financial years 1880–81 and 1881–2 (approximating to Forster's tenure of office) was £5,449 8s. 2d. and £3,414 17s. 7d.; see Eunan O'Halpin, 'The secret service vote and Ireland, 1868–1922' in *I.H.S.*, xxiii, no. 92 (Nov. 1983), p. 353.

[3] Jeremiah O'Donovan Rossa (1831–1915).

[4] Rossa, speaking at Fall River, Massachusetts on Saturday, called Forster 'an assassin of my race . . . a poltroon and a liar', and offered to meet him in France 'eye to eye and sword to sword' (*F.J.*, 20 June). For Granville's representations to the U.S. government see P.R.O., Cab. 37/10/36.

A visit from Mr Ball at 6 o'clock. A peaceable evening at home. After supper assisted Father's memory through the last fortnight of his Journal; Oakel at the same time copying a letter or Mem. to Sir W. Harcourt on the advisability of stopping or trying to stop the *Irish World* coming into Ireland.[1] Read the 'rebel' papers. The *Nation* and *Weekly News* as usual far the most bitter and personally abusive of the Ch. Sec.; their attitude towards O'Donovan Rossa very curious: thinking it necessary to disavow sympathy with his style of politics, assassination, dynamite etc., but anxious to take advantage of it, and impressing upon the Govt that such threats as O'Rossa's are only the natural outcome of the present Irish policy. The *Flag of Ireland* continues warmly to support the Land Bill, and follows its fortunes through Committee with as much friendly interest as the *Daily News*.

An 'eloquent' speech by Mr Redpath, announcing his intention to come to Ireland and not be arrested.

20 June, Mon.

Received an interesting letter from Mr Balgszky [Pulszky] acknowledging the copy of the Land Bill, which at his request I had sent him. The elections in Hungary are now going on, and with result he thinks as much the same as three years ago—M. Tisza[2] keeping his majority, the Liberal opposition being content for the present with trying to consolidate and discipline their party in order to vindicate the influence of parliament and administrative reform.

Drove with Father to the office and afterwards went into Lillington St.

Drove with Mother in the afternoon; Mrs Potter to tea, also Mrs Rutson and Bernard Holland. Mr R. had been hearing lately from Mr Fortescue,[3] Lord F's brother's agent, his experiences in going back to their Waterford property—a melancholy change in the manner of the people, in consequence of an edict from the L. League that no mark of respect was to be paid to the landlord's family—the priest being a violent Leaguer, this is carried out by all except a few women who persist in courtseying to Lady C[amilla]. Even some of the men are rather shamefaced over their compulsory rudeness, and the F.s notice that as they drive to church on their outside car, they will cross over the road in order to avoid the question of taking their hats off altogether.

As regards the Bill, Mr F. unlike his brother is in favour of its passing. He is

[1] Since the repeal in 1875 of sect. 30 of the Peace Preservation (Ireland) Act, 1870 (33 & 34 Vict., c.9), there had been no power to seize newspapers containing treasonable material, whether produced in Ireland or abroad. A close check, however, was kept upon the circulation of the *Irish World* in Ireland (C.S.O., R.P. 1879/22696; 1880/5141, 7312, 14733); and in one P.P.P. act case Naish recommended arrest on the ground that the 'suspect' distributed the *Irish World*, constituting a treasonable practice (1881/20919).

[2] Kálmán Tisza, leader of the Hungarian liberal party and minister-president of Hungary, 1875–90.

[3] Dudley Francis Fortescue (1820–1909), 3rd son of 2nd Earl Fortescue; married Camilla, daughter of earl of Portsmouth, 1852.

a thoroughly good agent to a kind landlord, and just, and for a long time past, the practices of free sale etc., now to be legalized in the Bill have been practically in force on the Fortescue estate—all that the landlord will lose is the 'power to be unjust if he chose'.

Father not home to dinner. Mr McCall dined here.

21 June, Tu.

Report in the papers of a great anti-English Meeting at Marrachurch [? Massachusetts] at which O'Donovan Rossa spoke, and also a certain Judge Brennan, presumably a bona fide American citizen, not an Irish-American, and therefore with less apparent reason for his violent and offensive language towards this country.

There are some disagreeable signs in extracts from American papers as to the way in which the U.S. Govt may be expected to receive Lord G[ranville]'s representations. The Radical papers here are by no means pleased at this step having been taken, and some of the Conservatives, gratified for any opportunity of 'sniffing' at the Govt join with the *Daily News* and *Pall Mall* in their regrets and disapproval.

The situation seen from the outside is rather disagreeable, but no doubt the Foreign Secretary knew what he was about when he made his public representation to the Washington Govt and had good reasons for doing so.

The riots at Marseilles continue, several people have been killed, and the excitement between French and Italians runs very high.

The morning occupied in arranging flowers. Visits from Mr Tuke[1] and Lord Monteagle. The latter has just returned from the Co. Limerick—rather saddened at the change in the bearing and manners of the people since he was there in the winter; the Land League edict against courtesy to the landlord had produced its effect in his neighbourhood also. Still his tenants are not personally hostile to him, and I believe he does not despair of being paid his rents; but his general conclusion is that 'the levelling process' has begun in serious earnest, and that the relations between classes in Ireland will never— for good or bad—be what they were again.

Charles and Janie Penrose to lunch. A short call from Mr Bonamy Price[2] afterwards. Mrs Yates Thompson to tea. Mr Rutson, Lord Emly, and Gaston Monsell dined here.

I dine at Mr Cropper's, meeting John Weston, Miss Sellar, and Sydney Holland. Mr Cropper is becoming quite as implacable against the Parnellite Members in the House as Oakel himself; in fact wherever one goes in English

[1] See appendix.
[2] Bonamy Price (1807–88): economist; professor of political economy at Oxford since 1868; member of Richmond commission on agriculture; praised by Gladstone for his ability to apply economic principles to Irish circumstances 'exactly as if he had been proposing to legislate for the inhabitants of Saturn or Jupiter'.

society one hears the same strong aversion expressed—not always I think with quite sufficient discrimination.

22 June, Wed.

Mary and H. Ward to lunch. In the afternoon to a garden party at the Dulwich Gallery. Met amongst others Mr Haweis who was anxious to communicate to me grievances of some persons arrested under the C[oercion] Act. A lady friend of his had received complaints of the bad effect of the whitewashed walls on their eyes. The 'suspects' do not seem to have much difficulty in bringing their complaints before the authorities, judging by the details of prison management with which the Ch. Sec. is often called upon to deal. I could not promise to tell him of Mr H's poor friend, which I expect was what was intended.

In the evening Father and Mother dined at the Croppers', Oakel and I at Sir J. Lubbock's—meeting the Derbys, Lady Wade, Lord Lymington, the Brands, Mr Plunkett, Sir F. Leighton[1] etc.

I went down to dinner with Sir F. who made himself very pleasant, as is his wont. We had much talk with reminiscences of Abestone [Atherstone] where we had last met at the same dinner table—then a few words, as is natural and indeed inevitable nowadays, on Ireland and Irish representatives; then a long dissertation on the appropriate topic of the Royal Academy School—where the female students are embarrassing by their numbers, and in some ways aggravating—as they rarely take to art as a profession in the end and keep out boys who would do so. On the subject of women as painters Sir F. was certainly not complimentary; up to a certain point they had ambition—and then stop short—there is no growth, no development.

'Look at my poor friend Miss Thompson's picture in the Academy this year ("Rorke's Drift"). She has made no progress. The fact is women have not the creative power—quick perceptions, quick understandings. There has never been a great female composer or painter.'

Apropos of Mrs Collier's picture, he said it had not been rejected but simply not hung on account of want of space. 'The picture was clever, but it need not have been so large. When you say a thing so big, it should be better worth saying—everything in this picture might have been told on a much smaller scale—the justification for great size is either the character of the beauty represented which may require large proportions to do it full justice, as with the Venus of Milo, or the extreme and varied interest of the subject, which cannot be fully expressed within small limits.

Neither of these things can be said of Mrs Collier's picture; the idea was

[1] Frederic Leighton (1830–96): R.A., 1869; knighted 1878; president of the Royal Academy since 1878.

perfectly simple; the girl looking at herself in the glass, was not of a high order of beauty—on the contrary, she was commonplace, and rather ugly'.

In spite of Sir F. Leighton's severe criticism on women artists in general and Mrs C's picture in particular, I have great hopes that her development at least has by no means stopped short yet; to have reached the point she has before 25, promises well, and in her case she has the advantage of being able from an early age to give up her whole time and thoughts to her painting, as so few women artists have hitherto been able to do.

After dinner I had some pleasant talk with the Speaker, and told him of Mr Healy's appreciation of his authority in the House.

Of course we talked a little of the Land Bill and its prospects; the Speaker is pretty sanguine of its getting through Committee before the end of July, but thinks there will be a long stoppage over Report, when various postponed questions and amendments will be brought forward again—not [by] Mr Heneage, if he is wise; he would not again get such a division as he did the other night.[1]

In the evening Father and Mother called for me, and we went on to Lady Harcourt's—a small party to meet Prince L.—a large proportion of beauties and diplomats, amongst the latter our dear friend Mr L[owell] looking less amiable than usual. Communications between him, Lord G[ranville] and Father.

'Well' Mother said as we were going on to Devonshire House, 'you got some business done with Mr Lowell.'

'Very little' was the answer, 'he is very cross about the arrests.' Evidently things are not quite pleasant in that quarter.

A great crowd at Devonshire House—the 'party' present in great force. While waiting for the carriage we met Sir G. Wolseley.

'Well, have you seen what my impudent boy has been writing about you?' Father asked.

'Yes he had, and had even been thinking of writing to the author though he did not know him—he was pleased with the article and thought it well written though he did not agree with it.' 'Tell him so from me' said Sir G. who went on to enquire with some surprise how 'the impudent boy' came to know and care so much about military matters—was he going into the army, he hoped not!

Altogether nothing could have been more charming and gracious than Sir G. Wolseley on this occasion. It made me quite understand how it is that whilst he has by his speeches and writings made such bitter enemies, thanks to his manners and conversation he has a circle of such admirers.

[1] Edward Heneage (1840–1922): liberal M.P. for Lincoln, 1866–8; elected for Grimsby, 1880; on 16 June his proposed exclusion of 'English-run' estates from the land bill was defeated by 225 to 200. But see below, pp 218, 223.

23 June, Th.

The Land Bill is moving on slowly, but of late there are beginning to be murmurs against Mr Gladstone from the Irish Members, who say that his concessions are too exclusively to the Conservatives.

It is even rumoured that an amendment conceded by Mr G. to the wish of the Conservatives concerning the instructions to be given to the Land Courts in the matter of fixing rent, has so alarmed the Ulster tenants, that their Members will have to coalesce with the Parnellites in opposition to the Govt on this point.

Went in the morning with Mother to see the Spanish Loan Collection at S. Kensington. Lunched at the Balls'—calls in the afternoon on Mrs Pease, and Mrs Cartwright.

Mother and F. to see patent fire extinction on the Thames Embankment, I to the Hospital, and afterwards to meet O. and F. at Lady Monteagle's. Met there Mr Bute, Mrs de Vere, Miss Elliot, Lady Gore Brown, etc., as usual many enquiries and much condolence about Father.

Miss E[lliot] remarked that she had seen him in a hansom the other day, and that his hair and beard had become much whiter. This is true but it is the first time I have heard it noticed by a stranger.

Land Bill in the evening. Father not home to dinner.

24 June, Fri.

Heard from Father that they had had a tiresome evening at the House last night, and made little progress; he suspects there was some deliberate obstruction on the part of the Parnellites—it is probable they have received orders to this effect from America. As nearly every farthing of the L. League money now comes from there, it is obvious that the Irish leader must do something to please their active patrons there, as well as to satisfy the Catholics and Archbishop Croke party in Ireland.

The funds of the League are now estimated at £100,000, and the great mystery still is what is to be done with the money, now and in the future.

There are several bad cases of outrage reported from Ireland this morning—cruelties perpetrated on individual farmers and process servers, and near Loughran a deliberate and nearly successful attempt to murder a landlord and his son, by shooting from behind a hedge.[1]

The effect of the Proclamation in preventing riot at sales is still apparent.

Walked with Father to the office. We spoke of O'D[onovan Rossa] and the American Govt, also of the articles now being reproduced in large type in the

---

[1] At 11.30 a.m. on 20 June J. H. Lambert and his son John, who acted as his agent, were fired at three times but escaped by rapid driving. A tenant who owed Lambert £50 for rent was suspected, but no arrests were made (S.P.O., I.C.R., Returns of outrages, June 1881).

D[*aily*] T[*elegraph*] from the *New York Herald*—advising England to adopt a Federal Parliament, with Colonial and Irish Representatives on a similar footing.

This is what it will come to in time, (said Father), we shall not keep the Colonies for ever with the present relations; when we admit the Federal principle in their case, and have to alter our present constitution accordingly, then the arguments I have always used against the Home Rule scheme proposed by such men as Butt will cease to apply. I have often wondered the Irish don't make more of this.

Drove with Mother in the afternoon—a perfect June afternoon. F. and I went to have tea with A[my] Mulholland and the Lubbocks. A visit late in the afternoon from Mr Cropper. He too spoke with disgust and annoyance of the bad evening they had had in the House the night before; it was said that the Parnellites had friends in the Strangers' Gallery and felt it their duty to get up an Irish scene in the House for their amusement.

Mr C[ropper] very indignant at this idea. 'This is what Parliament has come to, English members made a sport for Irish spectators'.

Mother tried to interest Mr C[ropper] in the true side of Miss O'Brien's Emigrant grievance, but even her eloquence upon Mr C[ropper] seemed for once to produce little effect, so persuaded was he that Miss O'B[rien] was merely an untrustworthy Irish advocate of a case which had been proved by demonstration to have nothing behind it. He took her papers out of courtesy to Mother, and promised to look them over, but like many other people he has been deeply predisposed against poor Charlotte and her clients by her unlucky mistakes when she first appeared before the public with *P.M.G.* and afterwards in her curious self-contradictory letters read by Mr Chamberlain in the House.

A dinner party in the evening—Mr and Lady C. Bellingham (he a Catholic Home Ruler, a pervert from a staunch Orange family in the North—a young lively man looking, as O. said, like a jockey—she, a Noel and niece of Lady V. Buxton) the Mundellas, Miss Benson, Lord Carlingford, the Humphry Wards, Mr Cullinan, Mr Errington, and Mrs Fry.

In the evening Father summoned to a conference with Mr G. over the Labourers' Clause in the Land Bill, so Mother and I forced to go to the Court Ball without him; Sir F. Herschell whom we met here told me that a friend of his travelling lately in Ireland had been informed in the course of conversation by an enthusiastic patriot that when the news of Dillon's arrest was received in London, Mr and Mrs Forster waltzed round the room for joy.

25 June, Sat.

Having no engagements for this evening it was decided that we should go down to Arundel for the Sunday, in order that Father might have a day in the country. The Saturday Cabinet was fortunately early in the afternoon, so Father could meet us at Victoria at 3.55.

A grey afternoon following a wet morning—gradually clearing towards 6 o'clock when we reached Arundel. By Oakel's advice we had taken rooms at the small Bridge Hotel just over the river, where we were most hospitably entertained, and found the sitting room filled with beautiful roses. After a cup of tea, we all walked forth, dear Robbie of course of the party. Wandered up the steep streets of Arundel, and peered curiously like veritable tourists through the great gateway of the Castle, where we were forbidden to enter, Saturday not being a show day, and no blandishments or entreaties availing with the gate-keeper.

We looked into the Duke's[1] magnificent modern Cathedral where confessions were going on, and our presence was not desirable, and at last found our way into the Park, at the entrance of which we were compelled to leave poor Rob behind under penalty of his being 'destroyed' by the Duke's orders.

However the evening was soft and pleasant, and the park with its steep grassy slopes and masses of tall trees was very beautiful and very quiet.

After dinner we sat in the balcony looking over the small tidal river passing under the bridge below, to the dark pile of the battlemented castle, and the delicate spires of the Gothic Cathedral, rising in all their grandeur over the modest town of Arundel, and the flat meadows of the Arun valley.

Every cloud had vanished from the sky, only thin wreaths of vapour lay stretched over the quiet valley, and straight in front poised over the dark towers of the Castle hung the comet in all its splendour.[2]

26 June, Sun.

A perfect June day. To church after a leisurely prowl through the streets of Arundel at the old Parish Church. Father was very anxious to see the tombs of the Earls of Arundel in the chancel, which has been walled off from the body of the Protestant church by the Catholic Duke. However here again he was disappointed—the Estate steward was the only man who could give the order and he was away.

After lunch Father did two hours work—wrote a long Minute on the important question of arrears of rent. Between 4 and 5 we went for a walk along the towing path beside the river. After about a mile Mother and F. turned back and we made our way further up the flat fields and country lanes, and by the reedy margin of the river, where Father and Oakel helped to gather yellow irises for my splendid handful of wild flowers.

It was a glorious afternoon with a bright sun and cool breeze, and we much enjoyed ourselves; no one talked of Ireland or the Parnellites.

About 6 o'clock we came to the little old Church of Burpham with its fine Norman arches, and then being within a stone's throw of the Drewitts' house,

[1] Henry Fitzalan Howard (1847–1917): 15th duke of Norfolk since 1860.

[2] The brilliant comet 1881b, first sighted in Australia a month earlier, became visible in Britain on 23 June.

Oakel persuaded us without much difficulty to call with him on the chance of finding any of his friends at home. We were very kindly received by the whole family, Mr and Mrs Drewitt, three daughters and Dr Drewitt; they gave us tea and roses, and made Father happy with large tomes of county Histories, in which he could increase his knowledge of the genealogy, intermarriages and various titles of all the noble proprietors of Arundel Castle from W[illiam] the Conq[ueror] downwards.

Dr Drewitt walked nearly the whole way back with us by a path leading past the other side of the valley, and helped to carry my flowers and flags and rushes, which by this time had accumulated to more than my two hands alone could manage.

We reached the hotel about half past 7, finding Mother and Francie gone to evening Church. Dinner at 8.15 and a little more Irish work for Father afterwards.

This has been the first time since September that the Ch. Sec. has spent a single day or night out of walking distance of the I[rish] office either in London or Dublin, with the exception of the Bradford meeting.

27 June, Mon.

Left the Bridge Inn and the amiable Tilly family at 10.45, besides my other flowers we took with us a large basket of roses presented to Mother by the landlady.

Arrived in London at 1 o'clock. Father read aloud his Minute on arrears. No special Irish news in the papers. Received kind note from Mr Pears about Father and Ireland.

I lunched with Nelly Boyle. Father not home to dinner in the evening, in consequence of L[and] Bill in Committee.

28 June, Tu.

Heard from Father that they had made little progress with the Bill, a whole hour had been taken up simply with abuse of him by the Parnellite gang, led off by Mr T. P. O'Connor.[1] This gentleman's language was so strong that it seems surprising the Speaker should have allowed some of his expressions to pass. It is sometimes said that the Speaker's apparent indulgence towards misconduct comes from a deliberate intention to let the Parnellite Members bring matters in the House to such a pass that a radical reform may be inevitable.

Father has received a friendly letter of Resolution in support of his policy from the Leicester Liberal Association.

[1] In the course of a debate on the proclamation of the city of Waterford under the P.P.P. act, O'Connor called Forster a 'Brummagem Castlereagh'. The *Hansard* report (27 June; *Hansard 3*, cclxii, 1366–75) shows Power, Leamy, and O'Donnell as opening the debate.

Spent the morning in shopping and arranging flowers from Arundel and Dublin.

Francie left in the afternoon for Cobham and Fox Holme. Called on Mary, cheery Mr and Mrs Green in Kensington Square. Freddy and Amy S. to tea.

A dinner party in the evening, F. Cavendishes, Wilfred Lawson, Jacob Bright,[1] Pyms, Mr Pierce (U. S.) Philips. Father obliged to leave his dinner in the middle, having promised Mr Errington to go down and keep a house for some Irish bill of his. The House being counted out in spite of his efforts, Father reappeared before dessert with a good conscience. Mr G. has carried his Motion to take the L[and] B[ill] every day.

In the evening we went to Mrs W. H. Smith's, and Mrs Gladstone's.

29 June, Wed.

An account in the *Standard* of an interview with Gen. Grant[2] on the subject of Fenian plots against this country; according to this, Gen. Grant's language friendly and sensible, though of course as he says 'he does not speak for the Govt'.

Walked with Father to the office, told him that even Mr B. [Jacob Bright], who at the beginning of the Session was full of sympathy for the extreme party, had said to me the night before 'that they really were behaving very badly, it was difficult not to lose all patience with them'. 'Yes' said Father, 'I think he has almost more patience with them than I have'—which is [not] true of most people.

We dined in the evening at Sir G. Campbell's[3] at their fine new house in Southwell Gardens—a large party but few people we knew. I went in to dinner with Mr Frank Dicksee, A.R.A., the young artist who gained his Diploma with the beautiful picture called 'Harmony' two or three years ago.[4] We had a great deal of talk about painting—pictures, artists and sitters.

Went on afterwards to the State concert, where we met many people and stayed late. Christine Nilsson sang: a pleasure to hear even for unmusical people.[5]

---

[1] Jacob Bright (1821–99): brother of John; liberal M.P. for Manchester, 1867–74, 1876–85.

[2] Ulysses Simpson Grant (1822–85): American soldier; appointed commander-in-chief of Union armies, 1864; secretary for war, 1867; president of the United States, 1868–76.

[3] Sir George Campbell (1824–92): lieutenant governor of Bengal, 1871–4; liberal M.P. for Kirkcaldy, 1875–92.

[4] Francis Bernard Dicksee (1853–1928), who exhibited 'Harmony' in 1877.

[5] Christine Nilsson (1843–1931): born in Sweden; then in the front rank of opera singers. At this concert, at Buckingham Palace, she sang the 'Baccarolle' from Offenbach's 'Tales of Hoffman', 'Connais-tu le pays' by A. Thomas, and the Scena from 'Mireille' by Gounod (*The Times*, 30 June 1881).

30 June, Th.

In the afternoon Mother and I called on Mrs Kosute and on Madame and Mme [Mlle] Catargi. Met here M. Marinovics the Servian envoy in London who was delighted to hear of my having been at Belgrade and knowing his dear friend and colleague M. Cristics—now at Vienna. M. Marinovics spoke with great respect and almost enthusiasm of 'Déak', which in a Slav and a Servian pleased me greatly.

1 July, Fri.

Walked with Father to the office. Lady Monteagle, Katie Greenhill, Arnold and Mr Reade, formerly our Consul at Rustchuk now at Corfu. It was interesting to hear his opinion on the present State trials in Constantinople. The conviction of Midhat Pasha and other great officials of being accessary to the murder of Abdul Aziz has created a great sensation in Europe; confessions and revelations having been made all round, and the trial of the accused persons has been apparently conducted with European impartiality and decorum, the final result being sentence of death upon Midhat. Mr R[eade]'s account of the affair is that this sentence, and not a wish to bring the murderers of the late Sultan to justice, is the end and object of the whole trial, which is nothing more than a gigantic imposition from beginning to end. Abdul Hamid is afraid of Midhat who has always insisted that no effectual reforms can be made without limiting the autocratic power of the Sultan. The revival of the assassination theory concerning Abdul Aziz is solely for the purpose of incriminating Midhat, the Sultan's brother-in-law being accused at the same time in order to give an appearance of impartial justice to the proceeding.

As for M[idhat] himself, Mr Reade is a firm believer in his political ability and honesty, this last virtue seemed to impress him particularly.

'Why' he said enthusiastically, 'Midhat is an honest man—he is in debt!'

Father and Mother dined at the G. Trevelyans. O. and I in the evening first with Mother to Lord Northampton's, and afterwards drove to a dance at the G. Smiths'.[1] At Northampton House we were surprised to see Their Excellencies, come over for a few days holiday on private business at Panshanger. The party at Northampton House profoundly 'silent' and aristocratic; at the Smiths' literary and aesthetic: in the matter of looks, both dress and faces, the 'barbarians' certainly had the advantage.

The contrast in coming suddenly from one party to the other was very curious.

[1] Probably George Smith (1824–1901) the publisher, and his wife. Head of the firm of Smith, Elder & Co. since 1846, he published works by Ruskin, Charlotte Brontë, Thackeray, Matthew Arnold, Robert Browning, and other leading writers; founder of the *Cornhill Magazine* (1859), the *Pall Mall Gazette* (1865), and the *Dictionary of national biography* (1882).

2 July, Sat.

The papers full of the murder of Mr Gold on the Brighton railway, and the escape of the murderer Lefroy.

In the afternoon went with Mother to the Anti-Cruelty prize-giving by Lady Spencer at St James's Hall.

Left Waterloo by the 4 o'clock train for Fox Warren, Father and Mother leaving at the same time for Midhurst to spend the Sunday tête-à-tête at the Angel Inn.

A family party at Fox Warren including Gen. and Mrs Crofton. Francie at Fox Holme. Oakel gone down to spend Sunday with the Robinsons.

3 July, Sun.

My birthday—27. A burning hot day—to church in the morning at Byfleet. At luncheon we were startled by the news calmly announced by Sydney [Buxton] out of the *Observer* of the attempted murder of President Garfield.[1] He had been twice shot in the waiting room of the railway station at Washington on Saturday morning. According to the latest report in the *Observer* the President was 'sinking fast'.

Walked over to Pains Hill Cottage in the afternoon. Uncle Matt and Mr John Morley returning with us to tea at Fox Warren. Mr Lowell was also to have come down to Uncle Matt for the Sunday, but on Saturday afternoon the rumour of the attempted assassination of the President caused him to give up coming.

4 July, Mon.

Francie and I returned to London in the afternoon: Father and Mother had much enjoyed their Sunday at Midhurst. Aunt F[anny] Lucy and Nelly to dinner. Father also came back from the House and drank my health. In the evening with Aunt Fan, Nelly, and Oakel to a ball at Mrs Benson's in Lowndes Sq.

5 July, Tu.

Woke to a day of excessive heat—blazing sun and sultry air without a breath of freshness in it. Cousin Martha Buckland, Sydney Buxton, and Johnny Temple to lunch.

Drove with Mother and Cousin Martha in the afternoon—heat tropical.

[1] James Abram Garfield (1831–81): Ohio soldier and politician; elected president of the United States, 1880; shot by Charles Guiteau on 2 July; died on 19 September.

Mlle Frölich, Uncle John, Mrs Poynter and Lucy Ada to tea, the latter to spend the night. Father home to dinner with Mr Laing.

A violent thunderstorm in the night.

6 July, Wed.

President Garfield rather better—a slight chance of his recovery. From the first he has behaved heroically, and increased the strong sympathy which would naturally be felt for any man under the circumstances.

Mrs Buxton to lunch. In the afternoon to Lillington St. A dinner party in the evening—Sir G. and Miss Bowen,[1] Gen. Armstrong (a pleasing and interesting American, head of an Agricultural College for the training of young Indians and Negroes—and at present over here as Secretary of State to the Kalakua—King of the Sandwich Islands),[2] the Arthur Arnolds, Leathems, Mr Aubrey de Vere, Mr and Lady C[amilla] Fortescue, and Mannie Brook.

In the evening Father and Mother went to the Royal Academy, and Oakel and I to private theatricals at Mrs Bishop's. Here we found ourselves in quite a different set; met Col. Burke, Mrs Ball, the Simpsons, Mr Ranken[3] (Editor of *The Tablet*) and last but not least 'Pauline', Mrs Craven's sister.[4] I was introduced to her by Miss Bishop, and felt no shock of disappointment, for in the small elderly lady with her delicate aquiline features, and kind gracious manner, it was not difficult to imagine the charming Pauline to whom Alexandrine and Eugenie were so devoted, and who in her turn immortalized her sisters in her wonderful book.

I said something about knowing Mr Grant Duff, upon which she spoke kindly of my book, and said that it had told her something quite new; she had wondered if it was I who was the writer, but had thought I looked too young! 'Looks' I told her 'are sometimes very deceitful.'

7 July, Th.

Uncle Matt to lunch. In the afternoon to the Hospital, and to the Dean's Flower Show party at Westminster. Father home to dinner. Mother with Mrs Giveen to the House in the evening.

---

[1] George Ferguson Bowen (1821–99): K.C.M.G., 1856; governor of Mauritius since 1879.

[2] David Kalakua (1836–91): elected king by the Hawaiian assembly in 1874 after a successful revolt against the previous king.

[3] George Elliot Ranken (1828–89): converted to catholicism, 1849; privy chamberlain to Pius IX, 1871; edited the *Tablet*, 1871–8; now consulting editor.

[4] Pauline Marie Armande Aglaé (1808–91): married Augustus Craven, 1834; her *Récit d'une soeur* (1866) was translated two years later as *A sister's story*.

8 July, Fri.

A Deputation (so-called) of Labourers, brought by the L. League to see Father at the Irish office this morning,[1] and private labourers imported by Mr Fitzpatrick to see this house.

Drove with Mother in the morning and did the flowers. At 2 o'clock with Oakel to Lords', the 2nd day of the E[ton] and Harrow. Before I had been there half an hour found myself undergoing a lecture on the Land Bill, this time from J. K. Cross who walked across the ground with us, in order to explain to me his views on the clause under discussion the previous night when he had not been able to make a speech.

On reaching home found Edward who has come up for the Volunteer review on Saturday.

Sarah Bruce, Mrs Playfair, Mary Cropper, and Col. Burke at tea. Apropos of Father's 'arrears' proposal, Col. B[urke] mentioned that, whilst sitting in the Park, he had involuntarily overheard Lord Powerscourt's opinion of it, expressed to a gentleman he was with—'Very clever scheme of Forster's, offers us half a loaf instead of a whole one—when we shouldn't get the whole—for my part I shall take it'.[2]

On the whole the proposal seems to be regarded by the papers as ingenious, and an expedient worth trying to lessen the probability of evictions for arrears—there is no strong outcry from any side, and as the compromise between landlord and tenant must in every case be voluntary on both sides, the landlords, however little they may wish to seem content with half a loaf instead of a whole, will have no ground for complaining of confiscation or injustice on the part of the Govt as in the case of the Disturbance Bill.

A dinner party in the evening—Penrose-Fitzgeralds,[3] Sir T. Acland and Miss Acland, Mr Johnson, Sampson Lloyds, George Young, Mr Herbert Gladstone, etc. Mr Fitzgerald and I made great friends, a handsome, keen-eyed man, high spirited and intensely pugnacious—a fervent Irishman, letting it plainly be seen that he thought us and our Govt Saxons and aliens—but with absolute detestation of the modern Irish patriot as represented either by Nationalist or Land Leaguer—a vehement Tory, but with friendly personal feelings towards the Ch. Sec., who he believed had always tried to 'go straight' in spite of difficulties—i.e. his Liberal and Radical colleagues.

[1] At 1 p.m. on Friday, a deputation of five representatives selected by a recent meeting of labourers at Kanturk, headed by Fr Richard O'Kennedy, catholic curate of Kilmeady, Co. Limerick, asked Forster to promote state aid to labourers in the form of cottages and land. Over thirty M.P.s, of varying allegiances, appear to have attended (*F.J.*, 9 July 1881).

[2] Forster had prepared to empower the land commission to advance 50 per cent of the arrears due for 1878 and 1879, in the case of tenants who had settled with their landlords for the 1880 rents (6 July, *Hansard 3*, cclxiii, 160–65), the clause embodying this was agreed to on 21 July (ibid., 1538–9).

[3] Robert Uniacke Penrose Fitzgerald (1839–1919): owner of 5307 acres in Cork; director of Property Defence Association and Cork Defence Union; married Jane Codrington, 1867.

A well-meaning, right-acting, genial landlord of the old type, turned sour by the Land League, who had contrived to set his tenants and neighbours in relations of sullen discontent or open enmity against him, and obliged him to lead a life of constant warfare and self-defence, if he would not follow the example of other landlords and turn his back on his Irish home for good and all.

I expect Mr Fitzgerald has not made matters in the Co. Cork smoother by his bold defiance of the Land League, his aristocratic sentiments, and his over-bearing, impulsive manners; no doubt it would be better if he could take the calmly philosophic and historical view of the present situation in Ireland that comes natural to writers in the *P.M. Gazette*; at the same time he has been, I believe, a genuinely good landlord according to his ideas—making personal sacrifices many a time to help his tenants during times of famine, living amongst them on friendly sociable terms, an Irishman amongst Irishmen, as far from tyrannizing or rack-renting as any sensible landlord in England or Scotland.

And it is on such a man, and others like him who happen to be Irish and not English or Scotch landlords, that all the sins of a bad system and bad landlords of other generations, and other parts of the country are now being visited; whilst philosophical land reformers in England look on with calm indifference, considering that the grievances and disappointments of individual landlords are beneath attention in the great process of agrarian reformation in Ireland.

Of course individuals must suffer in times like these, and it is well for critics to be able to look at the question broadly, but from those who are actually suffering in the process of transition from one state of society to another, it is hard to expect a perfectly impartial insight into the historical origin and bearing of the present agitation conducted by men who in many cases are to say the least, quite as far from being disinterested and purely unselfish as the landlords themselves.

As I was not dining this evening I went in as usual to have a few words with Father in his dressing room. He told me that he had got well through his Arrears speech, on the whole it seemed likely to be favourably received, and he was in good spirits.

'Oh, by the bye, my dear' he said, 'I have been amusing people down at the House by telling them of a unique compliment you have had this morning'—this turned out to be a threatening letter from a man in Dublin, who informed him 'that he had meant to have shot him on a former occasion, if it had not been for the lovely (*sic*) girl who was walking with him, and whom he did not wish to deprive of a Father'—'but now' the letter went on—'to H[ell] with such weak fancies, etc.'

I asked Father how far he thinks such productions are purely coarse jokes, written in a sort of bravado and love of composition; he thinks they are mainly this, but that they are written with the cognizance and approval of leaders who are glad to produce effect if they can by all possible means.

In the evening Mother, Oakel and I went on to a party at the Rathbones'. I had the pleasure of receiving a message from a Hungarian gentleman, a friend of the Rathbones, telling me that my book had been reviewed in most of the Hungarian papers and on the whole approved of. I suppose this is since the appearance of Mr Pulzsky's translation.

9 July, Sat.

Mr Cropper to lunch: in the afternoon with Father and Mother to the Arthur Peels'[1] at Sandy in Bedfordshire. Father arriving at the station only just in time for the train, having been kept hard at work at the office up to the last minute. On the whole in good spirits; the outrages lately have considerably gone down—on Saturday only three were reported.

A small party at the Peels'—no one staying in the house except ourselves, and an elderly Mr Stephenson, M.P. for somewhere in the North—a steady, sensible man greatly interested I believe in the Licensing Bill, but otherwise very dull. A Colonel and Mrs Stuart[2] to dinner. The former talked to me a great deal about the agricultural depression, and the impossibility for English land-lords to let or otherwise profit by their land; however he thinks the present extreme distress is not permanent, and explained that a period of just the same sort had been gone through in the first quarter of the century.

Father was much interested in finding that old Col. Stuart was a descendant both of Judge Jeffreys and William Penn, whose families appear to have inter-married.

10 July, Sun.

A quiet Sunday: to church at Sandy in the morning with Mrs Peel and her children—whose delightful young black poodle (named Afric) insisted on following them into church, and had to be forcibly expelled.

Father remained at home to work at the Clause for the benefit of the Labourers which it is proposed to insert in the Bill. In the afternoon Mr Peel, Mr S[tevenson], Father and I, accompanied by Afric, went for a two hours and a half walk—over high ground, partly cultivated, partly bracken, commanding views over the flat Bedfordshire country and the low line of the Chiltern Hills, returning through Mr Peel's beautiful woods, which are like a bit of Surrey imported into Bedfordshire.

The weather was fine and not too hot, and the Peels are thoroughly nice

[1] Arthur Wellesley Peel (1829–1912): liberal M.P. for Warwick, 1865–85; under-secretary for home department, 1880; speaker, 1884–95; married Adelaide Dugdale (d. 1890), daughter of W. S. Dugdale of Merevale Hall, 1862.

[2] William Stuart (1825–93): honorary colonel of the 3rd battalion, Bedfordshire Regiment; M.P. for Bedford, 1854–7, 1859–68.

people, with pleasant well-conducted children, the eldest 'coming out' next year, the youngest a boy of 7.

The great hero of the place is the purchaser and late owner, Sir William Peel. The garden is adorned with cannon brought by his sailors from Sebastopol, and in the church there is a fine statue of him by Tweed.

11 July, Mon.

Father's birthday. In spite of present difficulties and hard work, it must be allowed that to Father personally this birthday seems to have been a brighter one than the 11th of July last year, when he was in the thick of the Disturbance Bill, and all the worry and oppressive annoyance that this involved.

No special news in the papers, except of the brilliant success of the Volunteer review. Everything went off well, and the railway companies conveyed the 50,000 to Windsor without the smallest hitch or delay.

We got back to London at 11 o'clock, Edward meeting us at the station in order to have a word with Father as he was obliged to return to Burley that afternoon.

Aunt Sarah to lunch. In the afternoon to see the Russian pictures in Pall Mall, and to the Panorama of Waterloo at Westminster.

Father returned home to dinner, having explained to Mr G. that it was his birthday, and that we should be expecting him. He seemed in cheerful spirits—informed us that for two hours the Parnellites had been enjoying a violent personal attack on the Irish Secretary, apropos of some questions about arrests, or as to the reasons for which he had refused to give the full details they required.

Mr G. had said a few words in vindication of his colleague (whom it is the aim of the Parnellite gang to dissociate from the Premier) with the grace and fitness of language which is natural to him.

'He said to me sotto voce' said Father, when one of them was talking something about a Message of Peace to Ireland, 'you're the best message of peace I have sent them'.[1]

Considering that the Parnellite theory is that whilst Mr Gladstone is the benevolent statesman to whom some indulgence is due even from Irishmen, Mr Forster is the despotic tyrant, the evil genius of the Liberal Cabinet in its dealings with Ireland, they would have been greatly surprised and aggravated if they could have overheard this remark.

In the evening with Oakel to Mrs Fletcher Moulton's, and afterwards to a small dance at Mrs Benson's—I was glad to hear from a Mr Tennant whom I met there that he had been making acquaintance with Francis Deák through my book.

[1] The 'message of peace', the first step towards which should be Forster's dismissal, was suggested by T. P. O'Connor (*Hansard 3*, cclxiii, 520).

12 July, Tu.

The Bill is not getting on quite so well. Drove with Mother in the afternoon; called on Mrs T. and were initiated into the mysteries of the Ladies Dress Reform Assocation, of which Lady Harburton is President, and Mrs T. a zealous member. Already however there has been a schism amongst the Reformers, the more moderate members refusing to follow Lady H[arburton] in the propagation of 'bloomers' as the ideal feminine garment.

Father home to dinner. Symptoms of obstruction under cover of opposition to the Emigration clause.

13 July, Wed.

Hansomed with Father to the office, the heat being too great for walking. Perry, Johnny Temple and his fiancée, Miss Carrington, to lunch.

In the afternoon to a garden party at Lambeth. Irish question as usual to the fore—this time in the person of Lord Monteagle who pressed into my hand a letter from an R.M. in the Co. Cork, respecting the grievances (very genuine ones) of the Constabulary in the disturbed districts. I was also charged with other messages for the Ch. Sec. concerning the Irish harvest labourers in the North of England who are behaving very well, and beginning to pay their rents again.

Father dined at S. Kensington with Lord Spencer to meet H.R.H. We all went to a brilliant party there in the evening, Oakel and I going first to Sir J. Lubbock's. Lord and Lady S[pencer] considered to have made a great success with their S.K. party. Everybody there, from the Prince of Wales and the King of the Sandwich Islands down to the humblest Radical members in the Party. Everyone in good humour—the coolness and space is most delight-ful, an unusual feature in a great London 'at home'—the art treasures, the china and glass—the cool tiled floors, the fine ladies' diamonds, sparkling and shining under the electric light—cosy corners fitted up with carpets, sofas, and banks of flowers—the Hungarian and Royal Artillery Bands playing in different parts of the building, but in such a large space not overpowering with their loudness as is generally the case—altogether a very pleasant gathering.

14 July, Th.

The heat fiercer than ever.[1] Aunt Sarah and Nelly to lunch. Mother and I in the afternoon to a garden party at Marlborough House; heard rumours from various members present of the probability of an all night sitting, the Parnellites shewing signs of intention to oppose the Emigration Clauses by the familiar

[1] On 15 July, temperatures of 98 °F in the shade and 123 °F in the sun were recorded in the Strand.

method of obstruction; the Govt being warned of this intention, and resolved not to allow the Parnellite minority to defy the House in its wish to see the Bill make real progress, were quite prepared to resist Mr Parnell's tactics by all available means.

Father not home to dinner. In the evening to Lady Trevelyan's where I had a long talk with my old friend Mr Kinglake—of course about Ireland. Like many other people he spoke with much good feeling and respect of the Ch. Secretary.

15 July, Fri.

There was not an all night sitting after all. Father had come home at 4 o'clock, in good spirits Mother reported, for they had quite overcome the obstruction and carried their Clause.[1]

The sitting however appeared to have been unusually lively and the conduct of the Parnellites so ill-judged as to bring down very severe denunciations on their heads first from Mr Bright, and later in the evening from Mr Gladstone himself, in a speech of such extraordinary force and burning well-merited rebuke, that it produced instantaneous effect upon the House, even upon the Parnellites themselves, who very shortly gave up the game of obstruction, ceased reporting progress, moving sham amendments, etc., and allowed a division to be taken on the original clause, in which their numerical weakness, even among Irish members, was as usual strikingly apparent.

At the same time owing to some members having left the House, they were able to claim that amongst the Irish 3 more had voted against the clause than for it.

The real truth about this violent opposition to the Clauses providing for the State assistance and State regulation of Emigration, seems to be that they afford a convenient opportunity for some of the Parnellites to gratify their sincere desire to obstruct and discredit the Land Bill, and to all they are a useful text on which to harangue by the hour on English cruelty in the past and present.

By simply understanding the permission to emigrate with comfort and decency, as compulsion to emigrate under pressure from a despotic Govt, a patriotic Irishman, follower of Mr Parnell, can work himself up into a frenzy of noble indignation which is none the less agreeable to himself and gratifying to his constituents from the fact of its being occasioned by a purely imaginary grievance.

In the afternoon Mother, Francie and I to the Crystal Palace to meet the Hodgsons, and see the Panorama of the Siege of Paris. This, by Philopoteau, is the finest panorama I have seen—a real work of art.[2]

[1] The division was 126 to 23.

[2] The panorama, covering 22,000 square feet and depicting an incident of the siege in Jan. 1871, is described in *The Times*, 2 June 1881.

Oakel and I dined at the Parkers' in Gt Queen St. Met the Roundells, Dr Farquharson, Mr Broderick, etc. Like every one else who heard it Dr F. had been thrilled by Mr G's speech—he said also that judging by the faces, the disappointment of the Parnellites at their favourite Radical Mr Jesse Collings turning against them was very severe. They had called vociferously for him to speak instead of Sir R. Cross, and when he did speak it was to deplore their conduct instead [of] to back them up as they had fondly expected. In fact judging from the tone of the *P.M.G.*, and other Radical provincial papers, the Parnellites made a serious blunder on Thursday night, and have done much to estrange their warmest English sympathizers.

A personal insult and ingratitude to Mr G. creates more indignation than any amount of mere obstruction, and Mr Healy and Mr T. P. O'Connor are not wise in their generation when they extend their coarse sneers and insinuations from the Ch. Sec. to the Prime Minister.

16 July, Sat.

Tried to guess the names of the 3 [Land] Commissioners, but with all manner of hints from Father only succeeded in guessing one, Mr O'Hagan. Had O. been told the other two?

Katie Temple to lunch. Mother and I in the afternoon to Mr Spencer Bell. Father Thamen in the morning from Fox Ghyll, and in the afternoon a box full of mosses, and ferns and flowers from the Co. Limerick by Charlotte O'Brien. Father dined at the Colonial dinner, at the Mansion House.[1] We at home, going in the evening to Mrs Childers.

17 July, Sun.

A very pleasant leader in the *Observer* this morning about the Ch. Sec. beginning:

When the events of the present day pass into history Mr F. will probably meet with a far more just estimate of his services than is accorded to him at this moment. Nothing indeed can well be more unfair than the attacks of which the Sec. of State for Ireland is made the object. . . . The experiment now being tried by Mr G's Govt may be destined to failure, but it could hardly have been tried with better chances of success than under the management of the present Sec. of State for Ireland.

The leader on Ireland and Mr Forster in last Tuesday's *Times* was a curious contrast to the article in it whilst we were in the thick of difficulties at Whitsuntide, and which so tried and discouraged Father by its petulant injustice and misapprehension of the real state of affairs.[2]

[1] A banquet given by the lord mayor of London to persons connected with the British colonies; guests included the prince of Wales, the king of the Sandwich Islands, and Lord Kimberley (*The Times*, 18 July 1881).   [2] Above, p. 175.

At the same time it must be allowed that if the Irish Sec. is now finding more appreciation and support in some quarters, this coercive policy of the Govt, with its natural and inevitable results in the way of numerous and apparently arbitrary arrests, is beginning to be chafed against in others. The *Daily News* is becoming the organ of complaint, and letters from agitated English travellers relating the stories of petty tyranny on the part of police authorities are made the text for renewed remonstrances and laments over the present coercive policy of the Govt.

Considering that the necessity for a Coercion Bill was reluctantly admitted as being least of two evils, even by the *D[aily] News* itself, it seems unreasonable to complain of the Govt using the powers conferred on them according to their own discretion, and to ground a serious attack of [*recte* on] the policy of Coercion on the strength of two or three instances of misused authority on the part of subordinate officials.

However in spite of the concentrated hatred of the Ch. Sec. which the Coercion Act has no doubt created, the encouraging facts remain, that a good Land Bill is slowly advancing through the House, that outrages have diminished and that no open conflict has as yet taken place between police and people, notwithstanding some earnest wishes for this consummation on both sides.[1]

As to the decrease in the number of outrages, this of course is attributed by the *P.M.G.*, not to any action on the part of a misguided Govt, which would not take the advice of the *P.M.G.*, but simply to the fact that the people are otherwise occupied for the moment with agricultural pursuits.

A visit to Father after breakfast from Mr Escott. As I supposed, he had come to try and find out the Comm[issioners], and had gone away in ignorance. 'I shall always be glad to see you on the understanding that I don't tell you information, but only explain'.

To church on Sunday morning at St James the Less. In the afternoon Father called on Lady Bective[2] and had an amusing talk with her over her benevolent scheme for improving the prospects of British farmers and manufacturers by persuading fashionable ladies to wear exclusively home-made goods instead of French.

Mother was entreated to become one of the patronesses of this well-meant Association, but has entirely declined to promote Father's Bradford business in this way.

We had visits from Mrs and Miss Baden Powell, whose acquaintance Mother has sturdily resisted for a long time, but who are not to be kept out, Mrs B. Powell[3] having the interests of her sons always in view and evidently

---

[1] Cf. Forster to Ripon, 17–21 July 1881 (B.L., Add. MS 43537, ff 180–86), quoted in Reid, *Forster*, ii, 329–30.

[2] Alice Maria, daughter of the 4th marquis of Downshire, and wife of Thomas Taylour (1844–93), earl of Bective, M.P. for Westmorland 1871–85.

[3] Henrietta Grace (née Smyth), who in 1846 became the second wife of Baden Powell

meaning them to get what benefit she can secure from acquaintance with Mr and Mrs Forster.

We had also Dr Farquharson and Mme and Mlle Catargi, the Roumanian ladies who to their regret are about to be transferred from London to Paris. The handsome daughter who speaks very good English has made many friends here, and Mme Catargi too likes her present surroundings. I enquired about M. Marinovics, the Servian Envoy, and was told that he was 'très comme il faut'—that there were two Servians who were 'comme il faut'—one was this M. M[arinovics], and the other of course turned out to be the inevitable M. Cristics.

Mother and Francie went to the Abbey in the evening to hear the B[ishop] of Manchester,[1] and returned very late—they had been greatly shocked and startled at hearing the Dean of Westminster[2] prayed for in church, the Bishop of Manchester closing his sermon with a few beautiful words that were in effect a funeral elegy.

For a day or two past we had known that the Dean was unwell, but on sending to enquire on Sunday no alarming account was given, and Mother was therefore greatly overcome and taken by surprise at hearing on Sunday evening of his dangerous and almost hopeless condition. Erysipelas had set in, and Sir W. Jenner declared that it would be a miracle if he recovered.[3]

18 July, Mon.

The report of the Dean of Westminster slightly more favourable.

The heat still upon us in all its fierceness. Walked with Father to the office, and was told to come in and hear the last outrage statistics. Things still keep rather the better, the figures for this month being 109 against 197 for last month.[4]

On enquiring for the Dean in the afternoon Mother heard that he was a shade better.

Father home to dinner. The names of the Comm[issioners] announced in the House.[5]

(1796–1860), professor of geometry at Oxford, and bore him six children, including the future defender of Mafeking.

[1] James Fraser (1818–85), bishop of Manchester since 1870.

[2] Arthur Penrhyn Stanley (1815–81): former pupil and biographer of Thomas Arnold; appointed professor of ecclesiastical history at Oxford, 1856; as dean (since 1864), attempted to attract all religious opinions to the Abbey.

[3] William Jenner (1815–98): F.R.S., 1864; baronet, 1868; K.C.B., 1872; president of Royal College of Physicians.

[4] These figures correspond roughly with the total of recorded agrarian offences for each month, with the figures for threatening letters and other forms of intimidation deducted.

[5] Edward Falconer Litton, John O'Hagan, and John Edward Vernon (see appendix).

Some talk between Father and O. about the threatening letter prosecutions.[1]
O. to see the Solicitor to the Treasury tomorrow.

Latest report of the Dean very hopeless.

19 July, Tu.

The death of the Dean of Westminster. This is a great sorrow to Mother and indeed to all Grandpapa's sons and daughters by whom 'Arthur Stanley' was almost looked upon as a brother.

His loss is very deeply felt by men of all ranks and persuasions throughout the nation; he was loved as well as honoured and on all sides it is agreed that his special place in the Church can never be filled by another.

The Newspaper tributes to him are unusually interesting, and seem written with a genuine sympathy and appreciation quite different from the usual perfunctory style of obituary notice.

Hardly anyone writes about the Dean of Westminster without alluding to his friend and master Dr Arnold of Rugby . . . [*sic*].

The papers to-day all contain criticisms on the Commission. The names were received with a howl by the Parnellites, but as they had probably come provided with howls to be used against any three names announced by the Govt this demonstration was not specially significant.

With the public at large the chief feeling seems disappointment of the 'obscurity of the new Tribunal of which so much has been said', and from whom so much is demanded.

The *Times* however is on the whole gracious, acknowledging the extreme difficulty of selection, and the general disappointment is negative rather than active. According to Mother's expression the Commission is one 'that will have to justify itself by its intrinsic excellence, since it starts with none of those advantages of prestige and dignity which would in themselves have given it influence with the public'.

The heat today greater than ever. Amy Mulholland, Conny Lubbock, and the Bruces to tea. Father home to dinner; heard of O's interview with Mr Stevenson of the Treasury. The man Hickey was brought up at Bow Street today. Mr West gave evidence of the letters in question having been received by the Ch. Sec. at the Irish office, and the man was remanded for a week—bail being refused.

Of course Father has received cartloads of threatening letters, and Hickey's was only one more, but as in this case there could be little doubt of who and what the writer was, it was thought desirable to prosecute him.

The Land Bill is making real progress.

[1] Patrick Trafford Hickie (or Hickey), aged 18, born in Drumcondra (Dublin), had written to Forster threatening him with death if the suspects were not released. Hickie pleaded that the letter (obviously inspired by Rossa's earlier 'challenge') had been meant as a joke. See below, pp 209, 217–18.

20 July, Wed.

Reports in the papers of the charge of threatening the Irish Secretary.

The great heat has passed away, and we woke this morning to a rational temperature.

Uncle John and Miss Manley to lunch. In the afternoon with Mother to Mrs Birchall's. A dinner party in the evening; as usual a varied assortment—the Aberdares,[1] Hughes, Miss Elliot, Mr Shaw, M.P., Mr Clifford Lloyd[2] (the vigorous and much abused R.M. of Kilmallock), Mr Villiers Stuart,[3] Mr Maskelyne, Sir J. Rose,[4] and Mr Chenery.

Mr Clifford Lloyd certainly looks a man quite equal to putting down in any form, he is keenly alive to the disagreeable [? necessities] which his present experience involves; he is obliged to go out always with a revolver and police escort, and submit to floods of abuse and curses from his neighbours on the smallest provocation; but at the same time, he does not seem at all bitter against the people, and in exercising his authority evidently tries to keep a clear distinction between political agitation, and downright lawlessness and disorder.[5]

Mr Shaw as usual made himself very pleasant, and I think enjoyed his evening; it is sad to consider how much he will have lowered himself in the estimation of some of his compatriots if it comes to their knowledge—as through the gossip of a 'London Correspondent' it very likely will—that he has sat at the same table with the Ch. Sec. and Mr Clifford Lloyd.

In the evening we went on to Mrs Brand's, the Hungarian band played on the Terrace, and the coolness was delightful; the tide was up and there were lights of different colours in every direction, some stationary as the stars—the lamps along the embankment, some moving past on carriages passing over Westminster Bridge and steamers gliding up the river.

Every one spoke of the Dean, not as a mere formality but with real feeling and regret.

As usual too there were many friendly words to the Ch. Secretary, especially apropos of the threatening letter episode in the morning papers.

[1] Henry Austin Bruce (1815–95): liberal M.P. for Merthyr Tydvil, 1852–68; for Renfrewshire, 1869–73; home secretary, 1868–73; cr. Baron Aberdare, 1873.

[2] See appendix.

[3] Henry Windsor Villiers Stuart (1827–95): liberal and home rule M.P. for Waterford County, 1873–4, 1880–85.

[4] John Rose (1820–88): born in Aberdeen; emigrated to Canada, 1836; first minister of finance for Canada, 1867; created baronet for his part in the treaty of Washington, 1870; K.C.M.G., 1872; G.C.M.G., 1878.

[5] Lloyd describes his precautions against attack in *Ireland under the Land League*, pp 91–3, and quotes some fairly coarse abuse against him in a report of 8 Dec. 1881 (C.S.O., R.P. 1881/43733). In theory, he could certainly perceive the distinction between agitation and crime, but in practice his duties obliged him to look for connections; and in Dec. 1882 he could write 'Crime and agitation in this country are synonymous. Mr Trevelyan says "agitate by all means, but if crime is committed we will punish it". If the people again get the upper hand of us, all the police in the world will not stop crime of the most hideous nature. An outburst of agitation means an outburst of crime.' (Lloyd to Spencer, 7 Dec. 1882; Spencer papers, Althorp, Lloyd correspondence.)

With regard to Ireland generally there seems a more hopeful spirit, and everyone is cheerful about the Bill which of late has made such progress as to justify Mr G's sanguine expectations.

We did not go on to Lady Granville's, Father declaring that he had a bad day before him tomorrow with the discussion of his Labourers' Clause, and would rather come home to bed.

21 July, Th.

Report in the papers this morning of a speech of Mr Goschen to his constituents at Ripon, giving an account of his diplomatic experiences, and bearing emphatic testimony to the genuine effectiveness of the much derided European Concert in settling the Greek frontier question without war. 'A victory in which no one was defeated'—a settlement made in good faith by sincere agreement amongst the Great powers, in which the amour propre of neither Greece nor Turkey was sacrificed to the exigencies of Europe.

In what he said with regard to home politics and to Ireland, in his fine tribute to Mr Gladstone, in his definition of weak-kneed Liberals—not those who hold by their old principles when the current of public opinion is rushing past them, but those who go over to the extreme party, principles and all, as soon as the onward movement becomes strong enough to make standing against it difficult—in every part and every sentence of his speech, Mr Goschen spoke like a true statesman and a loyal colleague, and a cultivated orator who knows how to make a political speech that is a pleasure to read from a merely literary point of view.[1]

Johnny Temple to lunch. In the afternoon to the Diploma Gallery at Burlington House, and to the Hospital.

At 7 o'clock rode with Mr Cropper on Mary's horse, and afterwards dined with them at James Street. Uncle Matt dined here. Both he and Father have been asked to be pall bearers at the Dean's funeral on Monday.

22 July, Fri.

Father got through both his Labourers' and his Arrears Clauses last night to his great satisfaction.

Applications are now beginning to pour in for posts under the Commission. I received one this morning through Miss Palmer on behalf of Mr K. Bruce—Father received three by letter, and before we had finished breakfast Mr Price came in person to enquire as to the possible chances of a third. Mr Price is delighted with the appointment of Mr Vernon; this is certainly the choice which meets with most general approval, but the whole Commission seems to [be] becoming accepted with greater equanimity.

It is said that in the Lords an amendment will be proposed to increase the number from 3 to 5.

[1] *The Times*, 21 July 1881.

Miss Whately and Mr White of Bucharest[1] to lunch, the latter as friendly as ever. Uncle Walter to dinner. I dined in the evening at the Monteagles to meet Sir C. Gavan Duffy.[2] I sat at dinner between him and Mr Aubrey de Vere, two curious contrasts of Irish character and Irish experience—both alike cultivated men, and sincere in their patriotism and in their devotion to an ideal for Ireland, but with having little enough sympathy or perhaps even comprehension of each other's hopes and fears, aspirations or regrets.

I had much pleasant talk with both my neighbours on various subjects—Carlyle—Irving—Déak—Thomas Davis—England and Ireland, etc. I was glad to hear Sir C. Duffy acknowledge most emphatically the marked absence of exasperation amongst the English people against the Irish, even in spite of the provocation given by Fenian outrages—blowings up, obstruction, and such like. He declared that it was perfectly amazing to him, and that up to this time there had never been such a thing known as this continued desire for kindness and justice towards Ireland in the face of continued irritation.

It is to be wished, as Oakley says, that Sir C. Duffy, and men with his influence, if they think these things would say them sometimes to their own countryman, instead of harping exclusively on the misdeeds of Englishmen in the past, and their Ministers in the present.

In the evening I had some talk with Lord Emly—as usual not inclined to be sanguine—he had been told by men well qualified to speak by intimate knowledge of the country (e.g. Mr Goddard the Emergency man) that there would be more trouble than ever in Ireland during the coming autumn and winter—the disturbances coming rather from Fenianism and Ribbonism than Land League agitation. He allowed that (according to what we were told last Autumn by Mr Kavanagh and others)[3] this would in some way be less dangerous and easier to deal with than the Land League agitation.

23 July, Sat.

The Land Bill got through Committee last night. Walked with Father to the office. In the afternoon with Mother to call on Miss Temple and to a garden party at Mr Mitchell Henry's. Here we met several of the loyal Irish connec-

---

[1] Probably Mary Louisa Whately (1824–89): resident in Cairo since 1861, organising schools for Moslem children; writer on Egyptian life; daughter of Richard Whately (1787–1863), archbishop of Dublin 1831–63. William Arthur White (1824–91): C.B., 1878; ambassador to Bucharest since 1879, the first catholic ambassador since the reformation.

[2] Sir Charles Gavan Duffy (1816–1903): founder, with Thomas Davis and John Blake Dillon, of the *Nation*, 1842, organ of Young Ireland school of nationalism; imprisoned, 1848–9; initiated Irish Tenant League (1850) and independent Irish party in parliament (1852); independent M.P. for New Ross, 1852–5; emigrated to Australia, where he had a highly successful career, becoming prime minister of Victoria (1871–2) and speaker of the house of assembly (1874–80); knighted, 1873; K.C.M.G. 1877; he spent the rest of his life in Europe, mainly in the south of France; published *Young Ireland: a fragment of Irish history, 1840–1850* (London, 1880) and other important historical works.

[3] Cf. above, pp 31–2.

tion—Mr Villers Stuart and his wife, the Monteagles, Sir W. Gregory, Col. Colthurst, Mr Johnson, the Littons, etc.

Dined at home. Aunt Fan arrived at 8.30 having come up from Fox How to be present at the Dean of W[estminster]'s funeral on Monday.

24 July, Sun.

The President[1] not so well, grave cause for anxiety about him.

To church in the morning at St James the Less. Mr Jephson and Uncle Walter to lunch. Walked and drove with Father in the afternoon, taking Rob with us.

A Land League meeting being held this day in the Phoenix Park, a telegram to be received in the evening to say how it had passed off.

We have begun considering where we shall go to abroad this summer—everyone being agreed that the 'Irish Sec.' must on everybody's account take a short holiday—I was therefore much taken aback to hear Father doubt this afternoon whether he should be able to go after all—'the first fortnight after the L[and] Bill passes will be a critical time, and he may have to be in Ireland'.

We discussed a little whether this Session had been as bad as last—he thought that (what with the ill-meant questions and opposition of the Parnellites) it had been as bad, but that it had perhaps not seemed so simply because he was more accustomed to it.

As usual in the course of our walk we came across an Irish landlord who at once buttonholed the Ch. Sec. This time it was Mr Fitzwilliam Dick of the Co. Wicklow.[2] The customary observation 'What a dreadful state of things we have been having in Ireland'. He however had no cause to complain, for he had got all his rents, even from the secretary and treasurer of the local L. League, who had paid him with apologies to their fellow Leaguers for doing so. 'But, mind you, your Land Bill will do no good'—was Mr F. Dick's parting remark—however as this goodnatured landlord is an ex-Tory M.P. his opinion on this subject is naturally conclusive.

Mr V. Fitzgerald, Mr and Mrs Horace Pym, and Mr Baden Powell to tea.

Father and Mother, Aunt Fan and Francie to the Abbey in the evening to hear the Bishop of Peterboro' on the Dean. I to St John's.

Read the rebel papers. The *Irishman* has an article disapproving of Hickey's threatening letter. This paper has now been bought by the L.L. and will appear daily.[3]

[1] Garfield; see above, p. 192.

[2] William Wentworth Fitzwilliam Hume (1805–92): assumed the name 'Dick' by royal licence, 1864; high sheriff of Wicklow, 1844; conservative M.P. for Wicklow, 1852–80; owned 4,770 acres, valued at £2,534.

[3] The contract of sale of Pigott's weeklies—the *Irishman*, the *Shamrock*, and the *Flag of Ireland*—to Parnell's recently formed Irish National Newspaper and Publishing Co. Ltd. was signed on 2 Aug. The *Flag* was replaced by *United Ireland* (also a weekly edited by William O'Brien (see appendix), which first appeared on 13 Aug. (Moody, *Davitt*, p. 485).

A telegram received late at night stating that all had gone off quietly in the Phoenix Park.

25 July, Mon.

Great sensation in the papers concerning discovery of infernal machines at Liverpool, sent over in barrels of cement. Full details in all the papers except the *Times* which disbelieves the whole story.

The *Standard* has lately been taking pains to make known, by copious extracts, the full villany of O'Donovan Rossa's teaching and incitement to murder in his American paper the *United Irishman*, consequently this illustration of the doctrines of the 'assassination press' comes with the greater effect.

Father's letters this morning included three typical specimens—1, a severely worded appeal to his conscience from an Irishwoman living in London, requesting him peremptorily to release those innocent persons the 'suspects'—2, a friendly letter from a Newcastle man, assuring the Ch. Sec. of the loyalty, support and appreciation of the majority of his townsmen—3, a threatening letter adorned with the usual coffin and cross-bones, from an Irishman purporting to be a sub-constable in Ulster.

On my noticing to Father Judge Fitzgibbon's favourable statement about crime in Galway,[1] he told me that it was undoubtedly the case, that the counties in which the agitation had begun longest back were beginning to show signs of quieting down: at present Cork and Kerry are the worst.

A telegram in the *Standard* stating that Captain Elliot's murderers in the Transvaal had been acquitted by a jury composed of 8 Boers and 1 Englishman. 'Well' said Father, apropos of the debate on the Transvaal affair tonight, 'I'd rather have had my job than that—in fact I should have resigned'.

Walked with Father and Oakel to Mr Lowell to enquire for the President, but no fresh news had been received.

Uncle Matt and Aunt F[anny] L[ucy] to lunch. In the afternoon we all went to the Dean's funeral. Father and Uncle Matt were pall bearers, the others being Mr Spottiswood, D[uke] of Westminster, Mr W. H. Smith, Mr Sorey (Presbyterian), Dr Stoughton (Nonconformist), Mr Jowett, Canon Westcott.

Aunt Fan was in Edward the Confessor's Chapel, Mother and Francie and Aunt Fanny Lucy in the Record Room, and I in the Choir with Lady Holland. The crowd was immense, both in and outside the walls of the Abbey.

The procession of mourners that followed the coffin up the Nave into the Choir was a very impressive sight—every rank of life, every school of thought, every domain of intellectual knowledge was represented, and one felt that in paying this act of sincere and affectionate homage to the memory of the Dean of Westminster, all—princes, statesmen, poets, men of science, historians,

[1] *F.J.*, 25 July 1881. Gerald Fitzgibbon (1837–1909): solicitor general, 1877–8; lord justice of appeal, 1878–1909; an active freemason and prominent in Church of Ireland affairs.

leaders of thought and leaders of action—were consciously doing honour to the spirit of goodness, of true charity and of purity, which had been embodied in Dean Stanley, both in his character as a Christian gentleman and a Minister of the Church of God in this land.

To know and love such a man was in some degree to know and love goodness, and in this extent at least, all the various mourners however widely separated in other ways, were for the time united. . . . [*sic*].

Father home to dinner. Heard from Oakel that Father is not likely to be summoned in the Hickey case, as the defence will probably not call any witnesses.

A policeman has been shot dead near Loughrea.[1]

The story about the discovery of infernal machines and dynamite is quite true, they were discovered 3 weeks ago but the police authorities had not wished the affair to get out and so prevent them continuing their investigations in private.

In being questioned in the House Sir W. Harcourt last night[2] made a full statement of the facts, and dwelt strongly on the connection between these murderous attempts and their instigators in the Fenian newspapers, papers which some persons in this country (presumably the *P.M.G.*) insist should be treated merely with contempt and ridicule.

The division last night on the Transvaal purely party, each side showing their full strength.[3]

26 July, Tu.

Miss Temple and Agnes to breakfast. In the afternoon to Lillington St and afterwards with Aunt Fan and Francie to tea at Lambeth. Father and Mother dined with Sir A. Hobhouse. Francie with the Croppers, O. and I at home with Aunt Fan. O. and I afterwards to a dance at Lady Aberdare's.

I was interested in hearing from Lady Cross that it was by the Dean's special wish that Father had been chosen as one of the pall bearers.

27 July, Wed.

Considerable dismay at the narrow Govt majority last night on Lord E. Fitzmaurice's Amendment—to exempt farmers of over £100 rent from the benefits of the Bill.

[1] Constable James Linton, who had been active in working the P.P.P. act and the licensing laws, was shot in Loughrea town at 10 p.m. on 24 July, and bled to death in half an hour. A man and his wife were arrested, but were acquitted at Galway spring assizes.

[2] In fact on Monday 25 July (*Hansard 3*, cclxiii, 1750–54).

[3] Sir Michael Hicks-Beach's resolution criticising government policy on South Africa was defeated by 314 to 205, Parnell and several other home-rulers voting with the government.

The Amendment was only defeated by 4 [? a.m.], a majority of 36.[1] Mr Goschen and one or two other Moderate Liberals voted with the Opposition, and many others abstaining; it is feared that this result may have a bad effect in the Lords.

Of late there has been less apprehension of total opposition to the Bill in the Upper House (Lord Salisbury himself announced the other day that they did not mean to divide on the 2nd Reading) but this Whig demonstration in the Commons will it is feared encourage the Lords in a bad tendency towards mutilation and limitation of the Measure.

The papers full of excitement over the infernal machines.

The U.S. Govt seem quite as alive as we could wish to the necessity for action on their part in the way of tracing out and punishing the promoters of such devices, whether American-Irish or not. Mr O'Donovan Rossa, probably apprehending this, is for once anxious to disclaim credit for the affair, and does not venture to boast his responsibility for the Liverpool cargo.

Some of the Parnellite Members it is said are anxious publicly to disavow all connection with the Irish dynamite politicians and to express their horror at such proceedings; but as was to be expected Mr Parnell objects to their doing any such thing, on the ground that 'it has nothing to do with us'.

It is quite possible or indeed probable that this particular cargo of explosives has nothing to do with the Parnellite Members, but considering however that the use of dynamite as an agent of warfare against England is constantly recommended by the *Irish World*, and that it is through the medium of the *Irish World* that Mr Parnell and his fellow Land League members receive the bulk of their subscriptions, they can hardly be said to have 'nothing to do' with the recent event at Liverpool in the same sense in which this may be affirmed of their non-Land-League compatriots, who are in no way under obligation to the *Irish World* and its contributions.

The truth is that though Mr P. the respectable member of the British Parliament 'views with horror' all attempts to influence the English Govt by threats of outrage and assassination, Mr Parnell the Land League agitator cannot afford publicly to disavow or condemn the principles of the Irish-American press on which he is dependent for his money.

Uncle Matt to lunch. Francie to assist at the St James the Less school treat at Hampton Court.

The Bishop of Exeter with Mrs Temple and their little boy to tea. A dinner party in the evening—Mr and Mrs Locke King, Lady and Miss Campbell, Sir Patrick and Lady O'Brien, the Barrans, the Roundells, Mr John Conybeare,[2] and Mr White.

I asked Mr White 'what do they say about the Irish question abroad—do they

---

[1] The amendment was rejected by 241 to 205.

[2] John William Edward Conybeare (1843–1931): married Frances Anne, daughter of James Cropper, 1870; vicar of Barrington (Cambs.) since 1871; published *La morte d'Arthur*, 1869.

really believe that we ill-treat them?' 'Yes', was the laconic answer; as for the King of Roumania, he thinks the Land Bill is not half radical enough, and does not go to the root of the matter—but the fact is they do not understand the question—Mr White explains, 'one is constantly being asked to advise some book of good authority on the subject'.

I suggested that Cavour's Letters of 1854 showed a thorough grasp of the situation, a complete understanding of the relations between England and Ireland—to this he entirely agreed, and observed that they 'ought to be so published'.

The evening on the whole a pleasant one. 'Your scratch parties, my dear' as Father observed to Mother when the guests had departed 'are often a great success'. No more evening parties, so Father able to go early to bed—'I am less low about things in Ireland than I have been for the last few days' Father said to me—'but they are a forlorn people to have to do with'.

28 July, Th.

In the afternoon with Mother, Francie and Oakel to an afternoon dance at Mrs Grant Duff's, their last party at York House before their self-banishment to Madras. A pleasant party with a judicious mixture of talking, dancing and walking about the garden.

Had a good deal of talk with Mr Blennerhassett, who seemed much impressed with the need for Irish members to speak out to their constituents during the coming autumn—if only they have the courage and opportunity to do this.

He declared from his personal experience of the tenant farmer that they do not share the bitter personal hostility to the Ch. Sec. expressed by the Land League papers and agitators—and they believe that he and Mr G. mean well by Ireland, but say 'they had bad advice about the Coercion Bill'.

Like many others he disapproves very strongly of Lord E. F[itzmaurice]'s Amendment on the ground that such exclusion would make enemies of 12,000 farmers, and plant the seeds of a fresh agitation for no practical advantage to the landlord. If there were no Irish-Americans to be supported by agitation in Ireland he believes the country would quiet down rapidly after the passing of the Land Bill—but as things are it is imossible to be sanguine of much improvement for some time to come.

There is some reason to expect that Mr P. may cease to be the leading spirit, simply because he will in all probability be called upon before long to lead an openly Fenian movement, and being (according to Mr B[lennerhassett]) a thorough coward he will decline the honour and be shelved in favour of a more daring leader.

Father not home to dinner.

29 July, Fri.

Walked with Father to the office. He returned to dinner in the evening —after dinner Mother and I went down with him to the House, to see the Land Bill pass the 3rd Reading in the Commons. We were almost alone in Mrs Brand's Gallery, only Helen Gladstone, the Miss Dodsons and one other lady.

Our side of the House crowded, the Conservative benches nearly empty, the bulk of the party and the responsible leaders declining to go to a division on the 3rd Reading, returning only to vote on Lord R. Churchill's very sweeping and condemnatory amendment (for which he has been severely rebuked by his own party) or on Lord Elcho's now before the House.

Everyone eager for the division, which but for the conduct of Mr Warton and other such Conservatives would have been taken before 7 o'clock—every fresh speaker received with an outburst of impatient groans.

Mr Healy disclaiming for himself and the 'Irish people' the least feeling of gratitude towards the Prime Minister or those who sat with him, provoked some remonstrance from Mr McCoan, and Mr Blake, but was entirely backed up by Mr R. Power[1] who contrived to raise a personal question over some apocryphal remark of Mr Gladstone's to Lord R. Grosvenor, repeated to Mr Litton—who had repeated the offensive message to Mr Callan who had reported the same to Mr Power.

After an angry little scene the division was allowed to be taken at half past 10. Mr P., Mr Healy, Mr A. O'Connor[2] and one or two others not voting—the numbers 14 to 240.[3]

As the Members returned to the House crowding in from the Lobby and filling up the doorway, Mr Gladstone made his way amongst them and marched up to the Treasury bench carrying his red box in his hand, followed by a loud long cheer, which was repeated again when he left the House, and walked out behind the Speaker's chair.

The Irish Land Bill has now left the stormy waters of the H. of Commons and passed into the dangerous smoothness of the Lords.

By eleven o'clock the interest and excitement of the evening had quite died out, and English Members and Ministers went happily away leaving Irish affairs behind them for some little time to come—all except the Ch. Secretary, who was left on the Treasury Bench with an Irish Member exhorting him from the opposite benches.

---

[1] Richard Power (1851–91): home rule M.P. for Waterford City, 1874–91.
[2] Arthur O'Connor (1844–1923): home rule M.P. for Queen's County, 1880–85, for Donegal E., 1885–1900.
[3] Should be 220.

30 July, Sat.

Papers full of the reflections on the Land Bill, and Mr G., complimentary and otherwise—with regard to Mr G. however, it must be said that the splendid power, the marked skill, and genial untiring patience with which he has personally conducted his great and complicated Measure through its difficult career, are acknowledged on all sides.

It is curious to contrast the respect paid to Mr Gladstone (whether from friendly or unfriendly sources) with the half contemptuous, half angry admiration, which was the common tone in speaking of him at the time of his great electioneering demonstration in Mid-Lothian.

It certainly is a pleasure to see our greatest English statesman in a position to use his magnificent powers, as a responsible statesman, and not as an electioneering orator.

It may be said that if he had not been the one, he would not now be the other.

Whatever Mr Healy may say, it is probable that Mr G. will receive some gratitude and kindly feeling even from Ireland for the work he has done this Session. His name will always be connected with the Land Bill of 1881, as Mr Forster's will with the Coercion Bill, to which some bitter allusions were made on Friday night; and the public will never know the laborious and minute care which for months back the Ch. Sec. has spent upon the elaboration of Irish land reform, or the influence he has had upon the final character of the Bill.

At times a sense of the perverseness and rather hopelessness of things in regard to Ireland is depressing. When Father came down to breakfast on the morning after the passing of the L[and] Bill through the Commons, and I seized his hand and congratulated him, he said, rather sadly—'I don't know that there is much reason for congratulation.'

I think it was a passing feeling that as long as there are Irishmen like Mr Healy and Mr Power whose sole occupation and pleasure it is to plant and water seeds of hate and discord, it is little use for Englishmen to send messages of peace.

Father went down in the afternoon to Osborne. I with Uncle to Cobham for the Sunday. Found Lucy going on well, but still quite unable to put her foot to the ground—a pretty little figure on a reclining chair in the drawing room window with 'Max' the handsome brown dachsund—successor to 'Geist'—constantly in attendance.

Mr Lowell, Admiral and Lady L. Egerton,[1] and Mr Sumner the curate to dinner.

---

[1] Vice-admiral the honourable Francis Egerton (1824–95) son of 1st earl of Ellesmere; naval A.D.C. to the queen; liberal M.P. for East Derbyshire, 1868–85; married Lady Louisa Cavendish, only sister of Lord Hartington, 1865.

31 July, Sun.

A wet stormy morning—to church at Cobham in the morning—in the afternoon for a short walk with Nelly and the dogs. Mr L[owell] and Uncle Matt going up to visit the Egertons and their Roman camp.

Lord and Lady Enfield,[1] Mr E. Lushington, and Sydney Buxton to dinner. Lord Enfield, whom I had never seen before, much surprised me by enquiring at the beginning of dinner if I was a relation to the person who translated a book about Deák. I was very much pleased to find that Lord E. had read the book, and had been very much interested in the character of Deák whom he admired as fervently as I could wish. I have promised to get him from Pesth a photograph of Deák, which he wishes to hang up opposite 'that of Cavour'. 'If only the Irish had a man like Deák amongst them!' he said, to which I entirely agreed.

1 Aug., Mon.

Mother's birthday. I came up to London with Mr Lowell who made himself a perfectly charming companion. I bought two newspapers at Walton, but having satisfied himself that the President was going on well, Mr Lowell showed such a disposition to talk instead of read, that my twopence was agreeably wasted, and I had the pleasure of being entertained by word of mouth all the way up to London, and indeed to our own door, for my kind escort insisted on depositing me actually 'at home'.

Heard that Father had had a pleasant but not exciting time at Osborne, and was already gone off to the office. There was a bad attempt to murder in the Co. Cork (or Kerry) on Sunday—an old man of 80, Mr Swainton, who is not expected to live.[2]

Oakel and I spent the afternoon at Clapham helping Miss R. Potter entertain her Whitechapel people.

Father dined at Grillion's. Louis arrived to stay for a day or two.

2 Aug., Tu.

Mr Parnell was suspended last night. This is the 2nd time of asking. The ostensible cause of his excitement was the refusal of the Govt to allow him to discuss the Coercion Bill on Supply, instead of moving a Vote of Censure at a later period as suggested by Mr Gladstone.

[1] George Henry Charles Byng (1830–98): eldest son of 2nd earl of Strafford; styled Viscount Enfield, 1860–86; liberal M.P. for Tavistock, 1852–7; for Middlesex, 1857–74; parliamentary under secretary of state for India, 1880; married Alice Egerton, daughter of 1st earl of Ellesmere, 1854.

[2] At about 5.30 p.m. on 30 July, Robert Swanton, gentleman farmer, was badly wounded around the left eye by a charge of small shot, as he drove home from Skibbereen. He was thought to have been responsible for the arrest of local league members. No one seems to have been arrested for this offence (S.P.O., I.C.R., Returns of outrages, July 1881).

There is however every reason to believe that the excitement was carefully calculated and the whole scene arranged with a view to Mr P's character for enthusiastic and uncontrollable devotion to his imprisoned compatriots.[1] It is said that Mr Dillon and his friends have been much displeased with their Parliamentary leader for his not having taken an earlier opportunity to protest against the Coercion Act.

The party of action naturally requires some activity on the part of their leader, and if Mr Egan and Co. cannot expect Mr Parnell to go the length of encouraging the use of infernal machines against England, they may at least require him every now and then to make a 'scene' in the British House of Commons, by way of a passing protest and keeping up the spirits of his followers.

Full reports in the papers this morning of the adjourned Land Bill debate in the Lords. A formidable array of criticisms and denunciations, and evident signs of intentions to 'improve' and moderate the Measure very thoroughly.

In the morning with Mother, Oakel and Francie to Johnny Temple's wedding, and the breakfast afterwards at Mrs Carrington's. Aunt F[anny] L[ucy] to tea. Father home to dinner with Mr Vernon (one of the Land Commissioners) and Mr O. Cullinan. He had been in the Lords hearing the D. of Argyll call his late colleagues 'jelly-fish'.

Mr Vernon deeply impressed with the difficulty and odium of the task the Commissioners have undertaken—'they will be the best abused and best hated men in Europe—if he had taken his wife's advice he would certainly never have undertaken it—however he had felt that it would be at least one stroke for Ireland, one more attempt to see if some good could not be done.'

Father back to the House immediately after dinner and not home till 3 a.m. The Parnellites have resolved to obstruct on all the Estimates, English and Scotch as well as Irish, on the ground that they concern Irishmen living in England and Scotland.

3 Aug., Wed.

Mr Parnell has been speaking at a Land League Meeting in Dublin—very gently. A Convention to be summoned for Sept. 15th to consider the further action of the League. Meanwhile Mr P. advises tenants not to rush into Court, but to wait and see how test cases brought forward by the League are decided by the Commissioners. He does not believe that the effect of the Bill will be to lower rents. A violent letter read from Mr Egan protesting against a favourable reception of the L[and] Bill.

The Lords have also been criticizing the Bill from their point of view, Monday's debate being continued on Tuesday.

The papers full of details of the manufacture and discovery of elaborately

[1] Parnell said as much in the house (*Hansard 3*, cclxiv, 390).

constructed infernal machines in America. More extracts in the *Standard* from the O'Donovan Rossa press, signing the assassination of Mr Gladstone, and describing some Meetings of rhetorical ruffians in which 'sentence of death' had been passed upon the Premier, and impressively recorded in red ink.

McGrath and [Mc]Kevitt, the men concerned in the Liverpool explosion, have been sentenced to penal servitude, one for life, the other for 15 years.[1]

Walked with Father to the office—'I am to be baited all day' he told me—the Irish Estimates including the salary of the Ch. Sec. and Lord L[ieutenant] come on today and afford a valuable opportunity for invective.

On my way back from the office met Mr Cropper, hurrying down like many other Members to be in time for the expected Bradlaugh scene—Mr Bradlaugh to assert his right of entrance, and make his way by physical force into the House.

Nelly Boyle to lunch. At 4 with Mother, Francie and Louis to St Martin le Grand's to see over the Telegraph and General Post Office. Mother having orders from Mr Fawcett,[2] we were very kindly treated, and shown everything most thoroughly, being occupied for two hours with a short interval for tea in Mr Fawcett's room. He himself was not present but his secretary did the honours, and every successive head man in the different departments explained everything with great civility.

The press telegraph department was in a great bustle sending off the latest news about Mr Bradlaugh. He did attempt this afternoon to force his way into the House, and had to be forcibly turned out by policemen after a struggle in which his coat was torn, and his moral position in no way improved.

No further news of Father this evening as he dines with the clothworkers, and did not return home to dress.

Oakley all day at Southend helping Mrs Barret[3] with 400 Whitechapel children.

Father home about 12—a family gathering in Mother's room to hear his adventures of the evening. Moderately amusing. Mr Trevelyan's speech for the Navy a great success 'really beautiful composition'. Father's correspondence this evening included as usual a threatening letter, and a request for an appointment under the Comm[ission]. His communications from Ireland at present are usually of this nature.

[1] See above, p. 175.

[2] Henry Fawcett (1833–84): blind since 1858; professor of political economy at Cambridge, 1863–84; liberal M.P. for Brighton, 1865–74; Hackney, 1874–84; radical reformer, known as 'member for India'; 'Fawcett's act', 1873, abolished all remaining religious tests in Trinity College, Dublin; postmaster general, 1880–84; introduced parcel post; a leading member of the Commons Preservation Society.

[3] Henrietta Octavia Weston, née Rowland (1851–1936): wife of Samuel Augustus Barnett (1844–1913), rector of St Jude's, Whitechapel, both being involved in all forms of social work; Henrietta was appointed D.B.E., 1924.

4 Aug., Th.

Papers full of Mr Bradlaugh's 'scene in the House'—'another account' etc. etc. Everything connected with this affair is disgraceful and degrading, and the amount of false sentiment, false principles, and false heroism exhibited on all sides in connection with it is disgusting.

Mr Bradlaugh kicks and struggles with the officials—Mr Labouchere poses as the friend of the political martyr and the champion of the British electors generally—Northampton in particular—whilst the *P.M.G.* lectures everybody, points out the mistakes that have been committed by everyone all round, and indicates the line that must now be taken by the Govt under pain of making fresh mistakes and again incurring the disapprobation of the *Pall Mall Gazette*.

The announcement made today of the appointment of Mr Leonard Courtney to be Under Sec. for the Colonies. This will probably give satisfaction to the Boers and the extreme Radicals, whose views about the Colonies are represented by Mr Goldwin Smith. Lord Rosebery is to succeed Mr C[ourtney] at the Home Office.

From the Transvaal the news comes that the Convention between the High Commissioner and the Boers has been finally completed. The Native chiefs to whom the terms of the Treaty were made known, are said to be grievously displeased at the re-establishment of Boer supremacy, and amongst all Colonists and military men in South Africa, there is much discontent and irritation.

There can be no doubt that the work the Govt has had to get through in S. Africa since the beginning of the session has been singularly disagreeable however necessary.

With regard to Indian policy, Conservatives have been very triumphant over the so-called humiliation of England through the defeat of Abdul Rahman. This Ameer who was supposed to represent British interests in Afghanistan has been completely defeated by Ayoub Khan—supposed to represent Russian interests. Candahar from which we withdrew our troops at the beginning of the year has now been taken by Ayoub Khan.

By the consistent supporters of the Liberal policy however it is maintained that recent events prove nothing against the wisdom of our withdrawal from Afghanistan, all that is shown is that we 'bought the wrong man'. Now that Ayoub has proved himself the better man, all we have to do is to buy him—making him understand that he will not be interfered with by us, and leave it to his native Afghan love of independence to insure his refusing to become the tool of Russia.

Walked with Father to the office—the hot weather has come back, more to Father's satisfaction than mine. In the afternoon to the Hospital. At 7 Oakel arrived from the Old Bailey and gave us an account of Hickey's trial before

Judge Lindley.[1] The Crown prosecutor Mr Poland[2] did not magnify the offence, but treated the sending of it rather as a nuisance. Mr A. M. Sullivan for the defence ridiculed the whole affair, suggesting also that the prisoner was partially insane, and came of a family in which there was insanity. Mr West was briefly examined, asked whether Mr Forster received many such letters etc. A statement was made by Mr Poland to the effect that Mr Forster had. The judge in summing up remonstrated against the affair being treated as a practical joke, and the jury after a short absence gave a verdict of Guilty but recommended mercy. Sentence was deferred.

Father home to dinner—discussion of the Hickey affair, and hopes on Father's part of a light sentence.

5 Aug., Fri.

Report of the Lords in Committee on the Land Bill. Mr Heneage's Amendment restored, Lord E. Fitzmaurice's not approved of even by Lord Lansdowne.

A burning hot day. Mother walked with Father to the office. Drove with Aunt Fanny Lucy and Mother and Francie in the afternoon.

We were amazed and rather horrified to find in this evening's *P.M.G.* that Judge Lindley had sentenced Patrick Hickey to 15 months hard labour. One cannot help wishing that those 15 months could be distributed amongst 15 other threatening-letter writers instead of being all accumulated on Patrick Hickey.

We all dined in the evening at the Horace Pyms'. Heard from Father on the way that he had been seeing Father Nugent who had made a very good impression on him—as to the stories told by the Parnellites in the Emigration debate about the failure and misery of Irish emigrants to Canada they were complete falsehoods.

Heard also that a 'capital despatch had been received from the American Govt quite as good as we could expect'.

A pleasant evening at the Pyms', only ourselves and Mr James Payne the novelist.[3] A real holiday for Father—no Irish or political talk of any sort or kind—plenty to see and discuss amongst Mr Pym's collection of books and pictures, Father being specially interested in Sir Joshua Reynolds' portrait of Sheridan, and in an unfamiliar edition of Pepys' *Diary*.

[1] Nathaniel Lindley (1828–1921): judge of court of common pleas, 1875; lord justice of appeal, 1881; writer on law.

[2] Henry Bodkin Poland (1829–1928): barrister, 1851; bencher, Inner Temple, 1879; recorder of Dover since 1874; counsel to treasury and home office.

[3] James Payn (1830–98): editor of *Chambers' Journal*, 1859–74; reader to Smith, Elder & Co.; his forty-second and forty-third publications, *From exile* and *A grape from a thorn*, both three-volume novels, appeared in 1881.

On our way home we left him at the House of Lords to hear the continuation of the debate in Committee.

Heard that he had spoken to Mr G. about his allusion to the proposed reform of the H. next Session—explaining that he had only spoken for himself not as pledging the Govt. However Mr G. was quite content, and prepared to endorse what he had said. Apropos of Mr G. it was also mentioned that Herbert Gladstone will probably come to us in the autumn for a short time, in order to go with Father to the Irish office, and prepare himself to act as his unofficial lieutenant in the House on Irish matters. At least this I believe is the idea.

6 Aug., Sat.

Papers full of M. Gambetta's speech at Tours at the opening of the Election campaign in France. His language towards the President eminently respectful—towards the Senate also respectful but with an inclination to be threatening—in consequence it would seem of the rejection of *Scrutin de Liste* by the Upper House. M. Gambetta[1] has become more convinced than he was a month or two ago (when speaking at Cahors) of the possible need for reform in the election and constitution of the Senate. Without positively committing himself, he is beginning to question in his mind whether the existence of 'life Senators' is not an anomaly in a Democratic Republic; where every movement, every manifestation of the administrative machine should correspond accurately with each impulse of the great heart of the nation—with each fresh wave of popular feeling as it rises, gathers force, comes to its full height—and then as generally happens collapses.

Ought not an ideal Second Chamber, like Burke's ideal representative, look indeed not to the opinion of the people—but to such opinion as they must have 5 years hence?

Would not this independence of merely temporary opinion become more difficult in proportion as the members of the Senate owed their political position to the favour of a popular constituency who should decide on their qualification not once for all on the broad question of public merit, but on their conformity to the popular opinion on every sucessive measure as it arose.

I rode at 6 with Mr Cropper. Oakel and I dined at James St afterwards. Mr Cropper was much pleased with some statistics made by Mr Playfair shewing that Members have spent 7 days in the Lobby divisions since the beginning of the Session, which up to the present time has been longer than any session except 1832, and will soon be much longer than that.

Father and Mother dined at the Mansion House, going afterwards to meet the Medical Congress at Lady Granville's.

[1] Léon Gambetta (1838–82): as French minister of interior and minister for war organised resistance to Germany after fall of Napoleon III, and opposed cession of territory to Germany; at present president of the chamber of deputies.

7 Aug., Sun.

Francie's birthday.

The dinner last night seems to have been very pleasant; the Ministers were very well received, notably Mr G., Lord H[artington], Mr Bright, and Father. The chief fact of the speeches was the undertaking given by the Prime Minister and Lord H. to readjust the machinery of the House of Commons—'to take steps to save the Parliamentary machine from further humiliation'.

Mr G. made a beautiful reference to our Colonial Empire, disclaiming for the Liberal party the charge that they were indifferent to the privileges and the duties it involved upon this country—'there is no man worthy the name of a statesman, no man known to me in the sphere of political life who is not sensible that the business of cherishing those Colonies is one which has been so distinctly entrusted by Providence to the care of the people of this country, that we should almost as soon think of renouncing our name as Englishmen as of renouncing the great duties, which pressing beyond these, are imposed upon us in regard to the more distant, but not less dear portions of this great British Empire'.[1]

With regard to Ireland Mr G. and Mr Bright both spoke with grave hopefulness, but with no too sanguine expectation of immediate improvement.

Father had only to return thanks for the Lady Mayoress in a few graceful sentences—'it was a very pretty little speech' Mother said—referring to the help that women gave to their husbands, and especially what this was to men in public life.

Francie celebrated her birthday by going with Mother to hear Mr F. Holland at Quebec Chapel, I to St James the Less.

Father paid a call by appointment on Cardinal Manning,[2] whom he found as usual very amiable and friendly.

In the afternoon he called on Lord Granville, Mother and I walking through the Park with him. A visit at 6 o'clock from Sir T. Acland, much delighted to have a thorough talk over details of the Land Bill with the Ch. Sec. He had been lately meeting Mr Christopher Redington, who I am sorry to hear is very despondent about the prospects of the bill doing much to pacify the country.

Speaking from his experience in Galway, Mr R[edington] thought that the feeling between landlord and tenant had gone too deep for any legislation to restore the old relations.

It must be owned that if we do have a bad autumn again in Ireland, and if for the time the Land Bill seems to do little good in satisfying the people, our trouble this time will not have the added bitterness of disappointment. There

---

[1] In *The Times* report (7 Aug. 1881), these words, with slight variations, were given as coming from Bright.

[2] Henry Edward Manning (1808–92): ecclesiastical statesman; as anglican clergyman, was prominent in Oxford movement; converted to Roman Catholicism, 1851; archbishop of Westminster, 1865; cardinal, 1875; friend and controversial opponent of Gladstone.

will be no longer even a pretence on the part of the Parnellite representatives of a desire to help a Govt that meant well by the Irish people. The warfare will at least be an open one, and the evident intention of Mr Parnell and his adherents to prevent the people from accepting the Bill in the spirit it is given, will save much useless trouble and misunderstanding.

After all the consolation remains that Mr Parnell, Mr Healy and the *Weekly News* do not represent quite all Irishmen or Irish papers.

8 Aug., Mon.

Father received this morning an intimation from a Mr Baine that a scheme is on foot for publishing a letter from English Liberals to the Irish people, explaining the true aim and nature of the Land Bill.

According to the experience of a Protestant Clergyman writing from the West of Ireland, the people are kept in absolute ignorance and misunderstanding of Mr G's bill, which they are taught to believe will do them no good.

Father is much inclined to approve of Mr Baine's scheme, and Oakel is greatly interested and anxious to further it through the agency of his Home Counties Liberal Union of which he is an active member.

The papers of this morning announce the release of Mr Dillon. The ground of this is the state of Mr Dillon's health. He refused to be examined by the official doctor, but on the report of his own doctor that his life was likely to be endangered by long imprisonment, an order was instantly made out for his release.[1] The rumour that this was the prelude to a general release of all the 'suspects', contradicted in this evening's *Pall Mall*—Oakel having been sent by Father to Mr Stead[2] to explain the state of the case.

Mr Stead and Mr Cropper dined with us, Father also returning home to dinner.

The Lords have read the Bill a 3rd time.

Mr Cropper full of interest and admiration concerning Mr Mundella's speech in introducing the Education estimates. It appears he has made several changes, the most interesting of which is the permission to University men who have taken a degree to become National school masters, with no other qualification than a year's work as under-master in which they shall have satisfied the inspector of their efficiency.

Father apparently in cheerful spirits this evening—more leisurely than usual having received an intimation whilst at dinner from Lord R. Grosvenor to say that if he had no objection the Irish estimates would not be taken that evening.

Some talk about Mr Dillon. What will he do? Come back and receive an

---

[1] Florence's account is not quite accurate; see Lyons, *Dillon*, pp 52–3; S.P.O., R.P. 1882/15406; Forster ordered Dillon's release on 6 Aug.; he was released next day.

[2] William Thomas Stead (1849–1912): editor of liberal *Northern Echo*, 1871–80; assistant editor of *P.M.G.*, 1880, later editor; inaugurator of the 'new journalism'.

'ovation' from his compatriots in the House. Will he deny that it is on account of his health he is let out, and maintain that he is quite well. He himself will hardly do this, but the other Parnellites will be quite capable of maintaining that the Ch. Sec. and the Govt have been frightened into releasing him. 'Each man who has sent a threatening letter will think that it was just his letter which did it.'

'I got the most ferocious threatening letter this morning that I have had yet' said Father.

'Ah, then the writer of that will certainly think he has got Dillon released' said Mr Cropper.

'Yes, only it came after he had been let out.'

'A curious thing happened to me today' Father informed us, 'I had to go into Gladstone's room to speak to him about something, and found him lying on a sofa actually doing nothing.'

Before going back to the House, Father had some talk with Mr Stead about the Lords' Amendments. Mr S[tead] anxious to know the line to be taken. 'Fight them all round' was the 'mot d'ordre', which the *P.M.G.* will no doubt do cheerfully and ably.

Judging by extracts from the Provincial papers of all shades—English, Scotch and Irish—there is every disposition to back the Govt thoroughly in resisting the alteration made by Lord Salisbury.

9 Aug., Tu.

Great prominence given in most of the papers to some proposed Fenian Convention to be held in Chicago—quarrels over the Money of the Skirmishing Fund—resolves of 'active war' against England—designs for destruction of British ships—differences of opinion over O'Donovan Rossa etc. etc.

Francie read Mr Mundella's speech aloud to Mother. Lord Monteagle called and walked with Father to the office, thereby usurping my favourite privilege. Drove with Mother and Francie in the afternoon. Mr Rutson to tea. At 6.30 went down with Mother to the House. Father coming up to see us in Mrs Brand's Gallery—rather tired and depressed—no hope of his coming back to dinner.

The House in full swing of quiet reasonable debate over the Land Bill as amended by the Lords—Mr Healy and Mr Parnell accepting legal explanation from Mr Law and Sir F. Herschell as though obstruction and malice were far from their thoughts.

Returned home at 7.30.

10 Aug., Wed.

Drove with Father to the office—very silent. Mr Parnell's Motion of Censure on the Coercion Bill is impending, and the uncertainty as to when and in what precise form this bitter attack will be made is very trying. Also the Irish

Estimates will soon be coming on, a disagreeable prospect, considering the fixed intention of the Parnellites to obstruct and harass to the best of their ability on this occasion.

In the afternoon to the Hospital. In the evening dined with Oakel at the Bensons' in Kensington Square. Mr Tuke and Mr Jephson dined at No. 80. Father to bed very tired.

11 Aug., Th.

The great subject of interest at present is the Lords and the Land Bill. The Commons still proceeding with consideration of the Lords' Amendments. The D[uke] of Argyll's (practically Mr Heneage's) exempting English-managed estates from the operation of the Bill, has been accepted (with limitations) but this is about the only concession. The Govt have their party well united at their backs, and the Liberal opinion throughout the country is strongly in favour of Mr Gladstone's bill being carried in the shape he thinks most desirable. Even Mr Goschen and Mr Brand voting with the Govt.

The Liberal papers of all shades join in delivering addresses more or less threatening, persuasive, contemptuous or argumentative to the House of Lords, and the general opinion seems to be that the resistance in the Upper House will be a sham fight.

Everyone seems agreed that the part of wisdom would be for the Lords to make the best of a bad bargain and accept the Bill when it comes back to them without further attempt to mutilate it; at the same time one cannot help feeling that—'human nature being what it is'—even amongst Peers—the bullying lecturing tone of some Liberal writers is rather calculated to drive the Lords into bad courses than to induce them to act with prudent and patriotic moderation.

It is to be hoped that not many Conservative lords read the *P.M.G.*, the *Freeman* and the Liberal papers, for if so a collision between the two Houses would be almost inevitable.

Called in the afternoon on Mme Catargi to say goodbye, as they are going to Paris and will be replaced here by Prince Jon Chikai.

Tea with Nelly Boyle at the Miss Hollands'. Fr. to Dr A. Clark.[1] To the G.F.S. Room in the evening. Father not home to dinner.

12 Aug., Fri.

The House last night, after an interlude of obstruction and offensive language from Lord R. Churchill and Mr Healy, finished the consideration of the Land Bill at 4 o'clock and sent it back to the Lords, 3 or 4 of whom were sitting up to receive it.

---

[1] Probably Andrew Clark (1826–93), who at this time had the largest practice of any London doctor.

Mr Dillon has not yet appeared in the House; it is said that he intends when he does come, to express his disapproval of his colleagues' action (or inaction) with regard to the Coercion Bill policy, and that they do not look forward to his return with unmixed satisfaction. Meanwhile Mr Dillon is to address a meeting of his constituents at Tipperary where he will naturally be welcomed with genuine enthusiasm.

Francie and I drove with Father to Jermyn St leaving him there enjoying temporary happiness in a Turkish bath.

Nelly and Charley Benson to lunch.

I came down in the afternoon to Merevale to stay over Sunday with the Dugdales. Left Euston with Williams at 3, reached Atherstone at 5.40. A very fine park, and large handsome house, standing on high ground surrounded with trees (remnants of the forest of Arden)—at the foot of the grounds the remains of the old Monastery, and two large fish ponds which reflect the evening sun—wide views in every direction, but set in a foreground of ancient trees, and the middle distance filled up with woods and cornfields.

A quiet evening—no one here but myself and Miss Macauley.

13 Aug., Sat.

Bitterly cold with howling wind and rain, and low grey clouds over all the wide horizon. Spent the morning in-doors—wrote to Sir Gavan Duffy (to thank him for sending me a picture of Thomas Davis) and to Mr Pulzsky to thank him for sending me a photograph of Deák for Lord Enfield.

At 12.30 the *Times* and *Daily News* arrived—'gloomy prospect'—'sinister outlook', leading articles full of grave respect and disapproval over the conduct of the Lords who, acting on the advice of Lord S[alisbury] have put back all their Amendments, and so defied the House of Commons. What will happen next?—supposing the Govt resigned, it is impossible for Lord S., says the *Times* to undertake to form a Ministry under the present circumstances—and if he appealed to the country he would not fare any better.

If, as the *Daily News* intimates, there is to be an autumn Session to give the bill a second chance of being passed in its entirety by both Houses, the interval will be a very trying one for those responsible for the Govt of Ireland.

Meanwhile a Conference between the two Houses will be held, and much is hoped (judging at least by the *Times*) from the prudent counsels of Lord Cairns with his own party.

For the present, Lord S. and the rank and file of the English Lords have it all their own way.

The Bill goes back to the Commons on Monday.

I went for a drive with Mr Dugdale in the afternoon; there is much variety and much charm about this country—pleasant bye-roads looking through woods, over bits of common with tangles of gorse and heather and bracken, between thick hedgerows and broad bands of turf, past isolated red cottages almost smothered in their own little gardens; on all sides the varied rural landscape stretching away into the distance, but distinguished from the ordinary rural landscape by the sight here and there of a tall colliery chimney, and the consciousness of Birmingham on the horizon. I wished much that the grey clouds would have lifted, but though it did not actually rain, I never for one moment saw the beautiful view under the magic of a gleam of sunshine. On the contrary the wind was so bitterly cold that I was thankful for my ulster, and longed for a muff.

Assisted at a school feast in the afternoon.

14 Aug., Sun.

Received a note from Mother this morning in which she says—

You may imagine that the proceedings of the Lords are greatly agitating our minds. Father brought back Mr Shaw to dinner last night (Friday) and things had looked bad when they left the House—at 10 Father went back by appointment to meet Mr Gladstone and consult with him, returned about half past 1 with the news that the Lords had done their bad work. I can still hardly believe that they will not recoil from the responsibility and throw over Lord S. as their evil genius. The Cabinet meet at 12 to-day (Saturday). J. P. Smyth is coming to dine here. Oakel was in luck last night for Father got him into the House of Lords to hear the close of the debate; he said Lord C[arlingford] spoke well and with dignity, but Lord Salisbury was tempestuously cheered at the last in his 'No Surrender'. It is a serious prospect for all and most of all for our beloved Chief Secretary, but I think he is the more cheery already for the conflict with difficulty.

Spent a quiet Sunday: walked with Mr Dugdale to church at Atherstone in the morning—2 miles off. Atherstone is a quiet looking red town of 3800 inhabitants, devoted to the manufacture of felt hats, and also of helmets for the French army which are supposed to be of French manufacture.

The church is a fine one, with a small and beautiful octagonal tower. After service we called on a Rev. Mr and Mrs Compton; he is Vicar of All Saints, Margaret St but has a country home in Atherstone. Apropos of the excitement over the Lords with the Land Bill, Mrs Compton expressed a fervent hope that the Lords would be staunch—a sentiment which rather took me aback, having forgotten what a sound Tory atmosphere I was now in. After lunch went to the view of over two or three neighbouring counties from the top of this house—Bosworth, Burton-in-Trent, Lichfield Cathedral, the chimneys of Birmingham, the faintly seen hills of Shropshire, were all pointed out to me by Mr Dugdale.

At 3 to afternoon church at the little Pilgrim Chapel at the foot of the park—containing some rare old stained glass windows, and the beautiful marble effigies of an ancient Lord Ferrers and his wife, also a mutilated recumbent statue of the first Lord Ferrers, crusader and founder of Merevale Abbey.

On our way home I was taken to 'inspect' an old family nurse named Mrs Coxe, who in her youth had seen Lord Nelson and Lady Hamilton walking down the streets of Coventry.

Tea in the nursery—a talk with Mrs Dugdale in her room—dinner at 8.

Tomorrow I return to London to the excitement of an acute constitutional crisis. What will Lord Salisbury do? and what will happen in Ireland?

15 Aug., Mon.

Leader in the *Times* speaking with becoming gravity of the situation, but deprecating any hasty assumption that no way can be found out of the difficulty but by resignation, dissolution or an autumn session.

Letter from Lord Pembroke[1] stating the facts of the case, and pointing out exactly the difference between the original Bill and the Lords' Amendments.

The *Standard* as before refuses to believe in any serious collision between the two Houses, and remarks that the Liberal Clubs throughout the country will be found to have been exciting themselves very needlessly.

Up to the present time the excitement has apparently been chiefly expressed by Clubs and newspapers, even in Ireland no general agitation has as yet begun amongst the people.

I left Merevale about 2 o'clock, and after missing the train at Rugby reached home a little before 6. Found everyone out. Mother and Francie having gone as I expected to the House. Saw in the papers that Father had been having an interview with Mr G. that morning, and also that he as well as Lord G[ranville], Mr Gladstone, and Lord Salisbury had been out of town on Sunday; this however was, I heard afterwards, untrue as regards Mr Forster, who had been much too busy to leave London.

According to the newspaper extracts and reports in the *Pall Mall G.* the weight of public opinion against the conduct of the Lords is overwhelming in England, Scotland and Ireland. Even such an Irish Tory paper as the *Express* regrets Lord Salisbury's action, and looks forward with alarm to the probable effect upon the country if the passing of the Land Bill should be longer delayed.

Mother and Francie back from the House a little before 8. Mr Gladstone had simply proposed the consideration of the Lords' Amendments seriatim, and had declined to accept the suggestion of Mr Parnell that he should make a statement of the Govt's intentions with regard to their future conduct. The attitude of the House self-restrained and dignified—proceeding quietly with the discussion of the Amendments as desired by Mr G., but venting their excited feelings in vehement cheers at every expression of fixed disagreement with an amendment on the part of the Govt. Mr Parnell and his followers of course resisting every concession however trifling with dismal protestations in each case that the Bill was now rendered practically worthless.

[1] George Robert Charles Herbert (1850–95): thirteenth earl; under-secretary of state for war.

Oakel had been spending the afternoon at a Meeting of the Liberal Federation at the Westminster Hotel in support of Mr G., Delegations being present from Birmingham and other places.

He is greatly impressed with the extraordinary power that Mr Gladstone has to influence the most advanced members of the Liberal party. 'If he was to go in for yielding the country would yield.'

'He could make us do anything' said one of them; and the general feeling evidently is that in spite of the strong excitement against the Lords, if Mr G. was to give the cue for conciliation and concession it would be at once responded to.

I was much interested in hearing that Oakel has undertaken to write an article on the Irish policy of the Govt for the *North American Review*. Father was asked to write one himself, but he pointed out that, however common in America, in England a Minister could not defend his policy in a Magazine; he told the *N. American* emissary however, that he knew of some one who could do it—he thought well—and mentioned Oakel. After telegraphing to the Editor the suggestion was accepted and Oakel is already hard at work on this important paper.

Father not home to dinner. The letters he receives are not always threatening ones—Mother showed me this evening a letter from a Nonconformist Liberal to Mr Gladstone, with a friendly message of sympathy and approval which the writer begged might be conveyed to the Chief Secretary. The other day Father received a letter of the same kind from the Quakers begging that it might be sent on to Mr Gladstone.[1]

16 Aug., Tu.

Very bad account of the President.

General impression that the Crisis (as the daily papers love to print it in large type) will end quietly. An intimation in fact in the *Standard*, [as] though there could be no doubt of the matter that Lord Salisbury will this evening advise the Peers to accept the Bill in the form in which it will now return to them from the House of Commons. Practically Mr Gladstone with all his conciliation and courteous manner last night has made so little modification as to satisfy even Mr C. Russell, but nevertheless, as the *Standard* points out, there will be room for the leading articles on both sides to claim a victory for their respective chiefs—the true fact being that the Commons will have conceded a little, and the Lords a good deal.

After breakfast wrote to Oakel's dictation for his Article; walked with Father to the office. I told him about my visit to Merevale. On the way stopped for him

[1] The letter (12 Aug.) recorded gratitude for the government's 'earnest and sincere desire to act on Christian principles' (B.L., Add. MS 44158, ff 211–12).

to buy a new stylographic pen for Miss Dixon. Met Mr Evans, a Midland Counties Whig, who congratulated F. on the probable passing of the Bill.

'You are all going away' said the Ch. Sec. 'and leaving me to fight it out with the Irish'.

'Yes, I am afraid you will have a bad time over the estimates' was the encouraging answer.

The worst of these numerous departures is that there will not be enough Members left to vote Urgency and so stop the obstruction which is being planned by the Parnellites. 300 Members will not certainly be found in London.

Mother and Francie drove in the afternoon thereby missing Mary Buxton who paid a long visit. At 6 o'clock Humphry Ward appeared straight from the House of Lords, with the news that the Land Bill is at last fairly passed. The closing scene had been most peaceful: Lord S. spoke with chastened dignity and moderation, expressing his lasting disappointment of [*sic*] the Bill, and pointing out that the Lords having allowed it to pass in the present condition the Govt would be entirely responsible for its results. He could not answer for Lord Lansdowne, or for the Duke of Argyll, whom he regretted not to see in his place (the D. was married on Saturday to Mrs ?[1] and is on his honeymoon), but as regards his own party he should not advise them to reject the Bill as sent back to them from the other House.

Lord Lansdowne followed, and Lord Carlingford ended the debate with a few amiable expressions. Lord G[ranville] did not speak, but testified his good feeling and friendliness by sitting on the front Opposition bench in affectionate conjunction with Lord Salisbury and Lord Cairns.

This account may be inaccurate as it is not founded on the newspapers, but simply on Humphry's report which is all that we have yet heard.[2]

With the exception of the extreme Parnellites (who showed their exasperation by their more than usually offensive conduct in the House at the close of last night's debate) everyone is deeply thankful that the dreaded 'crisis' had been averted, and that the Land Bill had at last become law.

Father home to dinner, tired but not feeling quite so low as he had done lately—for the last few days his chief feeling had been uneasiness.

The immediate prospect is not cheering, the Irish estimates have now been fixed for to-morrow, and will probably be debated over till Saturday. Father says 'he expects they (the Parnellites) will be worse than they were last year even, but at any rate he is more hardened to it'.

The Whitebait dinner in Greenwich[3] comes off to-morrow, and it is to be

[1] On 13 Aug. the duke married Amelia Maria Anson (née Claughton), daughter of the bishop of St Albans and widow of the second son of the earl of Lichfield.

[2] According to *Hansard 3*, cclxv, 13, Granville did make a brief speech stressing the government's difficulties.

[3] An annual banquet for members of the cabinet, held at this time at The Ship Hotel, Greenwich.

made the occasion of a great demonstration to Mr Gladstone by his former constituents.

17 Aug., Wed.

A bad account again of President Garfield, it is hardly thought possible that he can live.

News from Ireland not very satisfactory—several cases of attacks on the police, etc. The worst county still is Cork—Limerick rather better.

Spent the morning in writing for Oakel: his Article I think promises well. Mother went down immediately after lunch to the House to hear the opening of the attack on the Ch. Secretary apropos of Mr Parnell's long-talked-of Motion of Censure. She returned about 3 having left Mr P. in the midst of a tame oration, the main ground of his argument being the unexceptionable character of the 'suspects' as vouched for by their wives and families. Mr Parnell having undertaken to criticise the operation of the Coercion Act in Mayo, his followers were intending evidently to do the same for other counties.

Later in the afternoon Mother again went down to the House returning in time for tea, as also did Oakel who had been 'choked off' as he expressed it by the prospect of an unending harangue from Dr Commins.[1] The House very empty, not half a dozen Members on the Conservative benches and only 16 on the Liberal. Father reported to be well, and suffering the great onslaught of the Parnellites with perfect equanimity. Had told Oakel that at present the difficulty was to know what to answer, the charges against him having been so vague and feeble.

Mr Cropper and May Benson to tea.

Uncle Matt to dinner: had been much amused by a statement in a Scotch paper to the effect that he was going to give up inspecting, take entirely to literature and politics, and probably come into Parliament as Member for an Irish constituency.

18 Aug., Th.

Account of the President slightly more hopeful. Concerning foreign news, the papers are mainly occupied with M. Gambetta's rebuff at his Belleville meeting, where such a disturbance was raised, that he was obliged in great anger to withdraw without making his speech. In spite of his speech at Tours the other day advocating revision of the Senate, M. Gambetta has not succeeded in commending himself to the ultra Radicals of Belleville where his opponents MM. Revillon and Lacroix are making an unexpectedly successful canvass; besides not going far enough to satisfy the political views of a portion of the

[1] Commins did not in fact speak for long (*Hansard 3*, cclxv, 195–7), but Oakeley was well-advised to miss the speech, which was both pedestrian and superficial.

constituency; his acquaintance with General Callifet of Commune celebrity is being used as a powerful cry against him.

At the same time according to Sir C. Dilke, a personal friend of Gambetta's, this rebuff from the ultra Radicals of Belleville will only have the effect of ensuring his election if he so wished in every county constituency throughout France, so strong is the feeling in Paris against the Moderate Republicans of the provinces.

The Whitebait dinner yesterday had been decidedly pleasant. Next to Mr Gladstone the Irish Secretary was the best cheered of all the Ministers by the crowd of Liberals who came to make a demonstration and present an emblazoned morocco chair to Mr Gladstone. Lord Roseberry (the new Under Sec. for the Home Office) presided at the dinner, and made a most excellent and amusing chairman. Everyone seems to have entered into the spirit of the evening, Mr G. announcing that he was sorry not to be able (I do not know for what reason) to do as he had intended and explain to the company the principles of the Land Bill.

Mr Herbert Gladstone was also present in his new capacity of unpaid Junior Lord of the Treasury.

The papers of this morning contain the report of a satisfactory address of Archbishop Croke's at Charleville, recommending the people to accept the Land Bill, it had been given in a gracious, wise and statesmanlike spirit, and should be received with gratitude by the Irish people.[1]

It is all the more satisfactory that the Archbishop of Cashel should take this line, since it becomes daily more apparent that the Land League will do their utmost to discredit the Bill, and induce the people to continue the Land League system of defiance and intimidation.

Spent the morning in writing for Oakel. Uncle Matt at lunch, also Father, having been at home all the morning preparing his speech. Mother walked to the office with him. Francie and I at 5 o'clock this afternoon to Mrs Brand's Gallery. After a gentlemanly speech from Mr Molloy,[2] the Chief Secretary rose at 5.30 to make his defence of the whole conduct of the Irish Executive in the administration of the Coercion Act. When he began the House was very empty—there being only 2 members (one of them asleep) on the Conservative benches, but it soon filled up, and what with the large numbers present in the Stranger's Gallery and a respectable array of Peers over the Clock, there was enough to make a considerable audience.

The Ch. Sec. began with taking up and replying one by one to the various charges made against the Executive in the speeches of the day before—above all that the [Coercion] Act had been used differently from what he had led the

---

[1] Croke's speech was made on 17 Aug. (*F.J.*, 18 Aug. 1881).

[2] Bernard Charles Molloy (1842–1916): served with distinction in the French army, 1870–71; private chamberlain at the Vatican; home rule M.P. for King's County, 1880–85; for King's County (Birr), 1885–1900.

House to expect it would be in his speech on the original introduction of the Bill—that the powers conferred by it had been used for the suppression of legal and constitutional agitation, and not solely for the arrest of persons reasonably suspected of committing or instigating to outrages, or of treasonable practices. 'This I deny' said Mr Forster emphatically.

Going then through the other charges—that arrests had been made of 'respectable persons', that the motives for arrest had been, in some cases, spite on the part of police—and the local authorities, that the suspects had not been tried before a jury, etc. etc.—he took great pains to show by reference to particular instances, and by explanation of the method of arriving at a decision in the case of suspected persons by himself and the Lord Lieutenant, that the powers of the Coercion Act had been employed in the spirit and for the purposes which the House of Commons intended when they entrusted the Govt with the responsibility of administering it.

As regards the arrests made on the strength of speeches delivered by prominent members of the League, he read a few extracts from recent speeches by Messrs Boyton and Brennan which helped considerably to point his argument, and which evidently created a disagreeable sensation amongst the Parnellites.

All through the speech, they, notably Mr Healy, expressed their feelings by shouting rude interruptions from their seats, conduct that at last obliged the Speaker to interfere. But in spite of the ill-manners and irrepressible acrimony of Mr Healy and Mr Parnell, the atmosphere even in the Parnell quarter of the House was very different from what it had been on the January afternoon when the Ch. Sec. introduced the Coercion Bill.

His own tone throughout was uniformly courteous and conciliatory, and once or twice even his enemies opposite could not refrain from joining in the laugh when some insolent sally of Mr Healy's was adroitly and good-humouredly turned against himself. As a matter of fact Mr Forster both felt and said that the Irish Members were only fulfilling a right and a duty in pressing (however unpleasantly) for an exposition of the Govt's conduct in the matter of the Coercion Act, and in justice not only to them but to the English Liberals who from the beginning had felt such a natural repugnance to endorsing the exceptional legislation demanded by the Govt, he was not only willing but anxious to enter into a full and extended explanation of his motives and actions since the passing of the Coercion Bill.

At the same time he was obliged to explain the reasons why the Govt could not consent to an immediate release of all the persons arrested under the Act. Much was hoped from the Land Bill, but the Land Bill if it was to benefit the Irish people must have a fair trial. Would the chief members of the Land League be willing to promote this—were they likely to cease from agitation, and from seeking to enforce their views by the familiar method of intimidation? It was to be feared, judging from certain speeches (extracts read from Mr Healy, Mr

L[ouden] etc.) that this silence from bad words, giving fair play to the Land Act, was hardly to be expected. With the removal of legal grievances, and with the excuse if not the justification for agitation, the duty of the Govt did not come to an end, it was still their duty to preserve order and to enforce the observance of the law, and so long as the condition of things in Ireland was such as to enable persons to incite to lawlessness with impunity from conviction under the ordinary law, so long the Govt must refuse to resign the exceptional powers conferred on them.

No one would be more rejoiced than the Govt if they were able to let all the suspects go free to-morrow, but until it seemed clear that their influence on the country would not be for harm, this could not safely be done.

After the Chief Secretary had finished his speech, which lasted for an hour and ¾, he was followed by Mr Gibson who expressed his entire approval of the course the Govt were taking, his full appreciation of the difficulties of their position, and his intention, however much he had opposed the Land Bill during its passage, to do all in his power now to insure its doing what good it could for Ireland.

Mr Gibson's friendly little speech was followed by a gentle appeal for the eventual release of some of the coercionists by a young English Member, Mr Reid,[1] and then Mr Redmond addressed some angry remarks to a thin House, in the course of which F. and I came away—with Father who had come up to the Gallery in very good spirits, and expecting to find Mother there.

Home at 8.15 to find Mother and Oakel at dinner, also Mr Litton who had been invited unawares. Mother and Francie back to the House in the evening in order to hear Mr G. who was expected to speak.

19 Aug., Fri.

Oakel's birthday.

Mr Gladstone had indeed spoken last night, and to some purpose. He rose to reply to the old O'Gorman Mahon, and the gracious courtesy, the generous sympathy of tone and language with which he answered the veteran Irishman's somewhat eccentric speech in favour of a total amnesty might have made Mr Healy and his fellows feel that there is a more effective way of producing an impression on an English Minister than the only one they are acquainted with, which consists in a mixture of bullying and insulting and complaining.

In the course of his speech Mr Gladstone made a friendly tribute to the Ch. Sec. declaring that the power placed by Parliament in the hands of the Irish Govt had been used with as much firmness, discrimination and clemency as any executive govt could have brought to so painful and odious a task.

As regards the release of the 'suspects' he was obliged entirely to corroborate

[1] Robert Threshie Reid (1846–1923): liberal M.P. for Hereford, 1880–85; later lord chancellor and 1st Earl Loreburn.

what had been said by his right Hon. friend; under the present condition of things it was not possible. He believed that a very large majority of the Irish Members are completely united with the rest of the H. of Commons in the desire that full and free working [*sic*] shall be given for the working of the beneficial provisions of the Land Bill. But the declaration of a minority—a very small minority—had not tended to inspire the Govt with that confidence which they could have wished to feel, and their course was clear.

We must under no circumstances compromise the peace of the country. We must use the powers which we have so long as they are necessary. We must not contract that use, but we shall rejoice to place it in abeyance when we find them superfluous. When they are insufficient it is equally our duty to enlarge them. But I myself desire to record my full adhesion to the declaration of my right hon. friend whose own antecedents and disposition, I think, drawn from the recollection of other days, must be known to be such as will never allow him to be at any rate the conscious instrument of unnecessary aggression on public liberty. It lies not in our hands—it lies in the hands of others, to place us in a position to bring about the consummation that seems to be so warmly desired.[1]

It is very satisfactory to think how entirely the efforts to dissociate the Prime Minister and the Chief Secretary, and make one appear as the benefactor, the other the tyrant of Ireland, have failed. During the whole course of this long, painful, wearisome session nothing is pleasanter to look back [upon], and to remember, than the generous support in public, the kindly sympathy in private which Mr Gladstone has given to his much abused Irish Secretary.[2]

The debate last night ended with a division of 30 to 83—no single English Member voting with the Minority.

Papers full of commendation: general approval of the firm moderation of the P.M. and Ch. Sec. The *Freeman* as usual in its anxious care for the credit and success of the Govt 'has read Mr F's speech with feelings akin to despair'.

Spent the morning writing for Oakel. In the afternoon drove with Mother, going in to the National Gallery to see the new Leonardo da Vinci.[3] Father not home to dinner, being in the thick of his Irish Estimates, in which the first vote had been taken the night before. At 10 o'clock Mother and I went down to the House, which we found calmly occupied on the question of reducing the Salaries of Crown Solicitors. Mr P. speaking, followed by T. P. O'Connor, Mr Healy, etc., each provided with an immense folio or blue book of some kind. Amiable and somewhat too lengthy replies and explanations from the Irish Attorney General.

[1] Quoted from *Hansard 3*, cclxv, 298, Florence's text differing as follows: 3rd sentence—'We must contract that use, we must rejoice . . . find it is safe'; 4th sentence—'When it is unsafe . . . to enlarge it'; 5th sentence—'whose own disposition . . . of unnecessary aggression'; 6th sentence—'which seems so warmly desired'.

[2] Cf. Forster to Gladstone, 21 Aug. 1881, thanking him for his support (B.L., Add. MS 44158, ff 205–6).

[3] The 'Madonna of the rocks', from the collection of the earl of Hamilton.

Father came up to visit us in Mrs Brand's Gallery, seemingly in cheerful spirits. The vote over his own salary had been got through—first a vulgar attack upon him by Mr Biggar, followed by Mr Parnell in one of his smooth-spoken moods—deprecating personal abuse of the Ch. Sec., lamenting the anomaly of his official existence, dwelling on the advantages of extended self-govt to Ireland, and hoping that if the Land Bill did really result in lowering unjust rents it might prove beneficial and be accepted by the people as such.

To this extraordinary and moderate speech Father replied in the same strain, speaking of it as interesting and suggestive, whilst at the same time declining to enter into questions of general policy on the present occasion. With regard to himself he had at any rate tried to do what was best—only time could show. Of Mr Biggar's denunciation he took no notice whatever, of which that gentleman complained later on whilst yielding to the suggestion that he should withdraw his amendment (for the reduction of the Ch. Sec.'s salary). Two English Members spoke in vindication of the Ch. Sec.

Mother and I remained till about 12. Father home at 3; the all-night sitting for which arrangements had been made was not thought necessary, as some reasonable progress was made with the Votes.

20 Aug., Sat.

Father down to the House at 3, a Saturday sitting which may last far into night. A Motion apropos of Mr Davitt is coming on, and the Constabulary Estimates are still to come so Father and Sir W. Harcourt have plenty still before them.

Our prospects however of getting away seem becoming a little clearer. If all goes well, Father hopes to go over to Dublin on Monday, returning in time for us to go abroad! on Thursday or Friday.

The idea of leaving London and the Irish Members entirely behind us for a fortnight with the sea, not merely the Irish channel, between them and the Ch. Secretary, seems almost too good to be true, and I shall not believe in the possibility of our going abroad till I see us on the pier at Calais.

Mother and Francie looked in at the House between 5 and 6, and came back with the report that they had only got into supply, the Davitt affair having taken up the whole afternoon.[1]

Father not home to dinner—at 11 the light on the Clock Tower still burning—at 12 the pleasant sound of the latch key fumbling at the lock of the hall door, and presently Father's voice announcing in very cheery tones 'Well, we've done the job—my parliamentary work for the session is over'. O. and I who were at work over the *N.A.* [*North American Review*] article followed him into Mother's room to hear the latest news. The Constabulary estimates had been got over much more quietly than had been expected, Mr O'Donnell proposing that they should protest by taking a division on the whole vote and

[1] See Moody, *Davitt*, pp 485–8.

not on the several items. Finally after some comparatively intelligent discussion of the Irish Education Estimates and other miscellaneous matters the House rose at 11.35.

21 Aug., Sun.

Father came down in the morning looking more cheerful than for some weeks past—fresh troubles will soon accumulate, but for the moment the weight of the Parliamentary nightmare being taken off his shoulders may well make him feel light and free.

We in the morning to St James the Less, Father to call by appointment on Cardinal Manning. Mr Law and Mr Jephson to lunch: plans for the holidays discussed. Uncle Walter to 5 o'clock tea. In the evening helped Father write up his journal—read the rebel papers. They are a good deal occupied at present with a wholesome scheme for regenerating Ireland (and it is hoped annoying England) by the promotion of Irish manufactures; letters and suggestions on the subject pour in, and it is much to be hoped—though perhaps hardly expected—that some real impulse to Irish trade and manufactures may be the result. As regards the Land Bill, the writers in these papers are uniformly ungracious—nervously anxious to prevent the farmers from deriving any advantage from a measure with which they are not connected. Agitation is of course to be carried on with unabated vehemence during the autumn, that is as far as the young men connected with the Nationalist press are able to promote it.

A thoroughly vicious speech from Mr Dillon in this morning's papers urging the people at Tipperary 'never to forget or forgive'.[1]

22 Aug., Mon.

Father and Oakel left by the mail for Dublin, intending to sleep the first night at the C.S. Lodge, and the two following at Lord Monck's. Mother went down at 12 o'clock to Wharfeside for two nights (taking Challoner with her) and Francie and I to Fox Warren.

Drove with Nelly over St George's Hill, and called on Lady Herschell.[2] Dined at Fox Holme, now in possession of the Bayleys.

23 Aug., Tu.

A quiet day: spent the wet afternoon in reading aloud amongst us—Miss Riddle, May and Sybil—the 'Blythedale Romance'.

[1] This should appear under 22 Aug.; Dillon's speech at Thurles (Tipperary) on 21 Aug. was reported on the following day (*F.J.*, 22 Aug. 1881).

[2] Agnes Adela, née Kindersley, wife of Sir Farrer Herschell (above, p. 128).

24 Aug., Wed.

Francie and I came up to London at 4 o'clock. Mother arriving at 6 from Wharfeside with a very good account of the dear Cathedine people. I found awaiting me a note from Sir Charles [Gavan] Duffy enclosing the promised autograph of Thomas Davis. He also sent me the *Freeman* of Monday, containing in full his long and admirable letter (to Canon Doyle) on the Land Bill. It is a comfort that at least one Irishman should have been found to explain to his countrymen in plain popular language the true scope and effect of the new Bill, and to point out to them the downright benefits which the much vilified, much insulted British Legislature has bestowed upon those Irish farmers who have the sense and the enterprise to take advantage of their new position.

What an extraordinary difference it would make in English and Irish politics if the popular cause in Ireland were represented by men like Sir G. Duffy. Very likely the ultimate disagreement might remain as marked as ever, but how entirely the tone and temper in all the relations between the two peoples would be transformed.

25 Aug., Th.

The President it must be feared is slowly sinking; even the doctors are ceasing to appear sanguine.

We have had little news of Father since he left except through the papers which say that he is hard at work all day at the Castle having interviews with the Land Commissioners, enquiring into 'suspects' cases,[1] etc.

A hopelessly wet stormy day, the prospects for the unfortunate farmers are becoming daily more hopeless.

Uncle Walter to dinner.

26 Aug., Fri.

Father and Oakel arrived this morning after a fearful passage: on the whole in good spirits, Father having found things not worse than he had expected, and feeling able to leave tomorrow morning for his short, much-needed holiday.

An amusing report from Oakel of the continuous rush of applicants for the post of Asst Commissioners. There are 12 appts—8 to be still filled up, and at a modest estimate 500 applicants—each one with quite convincing proofs of his eminent fitness for the post. A released suspect took advantage of an interview with the Ch. Sec. to press the claims of his brother, and one of the applicants (according to Oakel) has recently left Kilmainham himself.

---

[1] These would not be new arrests, of which only ten took place in Aug., but reconsiderations, after the statutory three-month interval, of persons arrested in May.

Some Irishmen happily are not so magnificently rancorous and unforgiving as Mr Dillon would have them be.

Francie left us at 11.30 for Wharfeside. She is going for Edward and Edith's sake to be at Wharfeside whilst we are abroad.

As for our starting it is again uncertain—since 10 o'clock this morning Father has discovered that the Parnellites have put a long row of questions for this afternoon, and unless Mr Johnson can undertake to answer them our departure is again postponed.

Father home at 11.30 (having dined at the Club) with the tidings that all had been arranged and we could start next morning. Lord R[ichard Grosvenor] assured him that he could not possibly get a House on Saturday large enough for the I[rish] Members to ask questions in—that is to say a quorum sufficient to be prorogued, but was not sufficient to constitute a House for other purposes, and therefore the Parnellites would have to ask their questions at some other time.

27 Aug., Sat.

We left England. London to Paris. Hotel Meurice.

28 Aug., Sun.

Paris. Elec. Ex. President Garfield a shade better.

29 Aug., Mon.

Paris to Geneva. Hotel Beau Rivage.

30 Aug., Tu.

Geneva to Chamonix. Hotel d'Angleterre. Birthday of William Allen.[1]

31 Aug., Wed.

Father and Mother to the Montanvert; home in pouring rain.

1 Sept., Th.

Miss Dixon appeared—walked to the Boisson [Les Bossons] glacier in the rain.

Speech of Mr Dillon's announcing his intention to retire from public life for

[1] William Howard, b. 30 Aug. 1881 (typescript has 'William Allen'), third son of Edward Arnold-Forster.

a time, and expressing fear that the Land Bill would strike a blow at the League.[1]

Mr Cullinan and Mr Fitzgerald[2] to tea and whist.

2 Sept., Fri.

Rain. Walked with Miss Dixon, and the German (Dr Mayer) etc. to the Boisson glacier.

3 Sept., Sat.

Letter in the *Freeman* from Dr Croke, enclosing friendly explanation of the Land Bill signed 'the Farmer's friend'. Drove in the afternoon to the Argentière glacier. Mr [Robert V.] O'Brien and Mr Redington to tea and whist. Farewell visit from the German and his daughter. The former presented with a copy of the Land Bill by Father.

4 Sept., Sun.

Church in the morning: in the afternoon Father and Oakel to the Montanvert for the night. Mother and I prevented going by the rain.

5 Sept., Mon.

A fine morning, with glorious views of Mont Blanc. Chamonix empty—everyone gone [on] an excursion. After lunch Mother and I to the Montanvert on Mules, taking letters and papers with us.

Letter from Mr Naish to Father—bad outrage in Kerry. Much excitement over the progress of the Tyrone election. Liberal prospects everywhere gloomy. Mr Lowther has beaten the Liberal (Col. Tomline) in North Lincoln-shire[3]—expected that the Conservative and Land League candidate between them will make Mr Dickson's return for Tyrone impossible. Mr P. and Mr Healy using all their eloquence against him.

A large party of us at the Montanvert. Mr Davidson,[4] Mr and Mrs Grant, Mr Fitzgerald, the 2 Mr Cullinans,[5] Mr O'Brien, Mr Redington, and four of

[1] Speech in Dublin on 29 Aug., at a banquet celebrating his release (*F.J.*, 30 Aug. 1881; Lyons, *Dillon*, pp 54–5).

[2] Gerald Fitzgerald (1849–1925): 3rd son of John David Fitzgerald (see appendix).

[3] The seat had been vacated by the death on 14 Aug. of the liberal Robert Laycock (1798–1881). At the by-election on 2 Sept., Lowther beat Tomline by 4200 votes to 3729. George Tomline (1812–89), now honorary colonel of the North Lincs. militia, had been liberal M.P. for Sudbury, 1840–41; Shrewsbury, 1841–7, 1852–68; Great Grimsby, 1868–74.

[4] Possibly William Edward Davidson (1853–1923): barrister, assistant to crown land officers; honorary secretary of Alpine Club, 1880–85.

[5] See appendix.

ourselves and Robbie. A pleasant evening of mountaineering talk, whist, with an undercurrent of Ireland and Land Bill.

6 Sept., Tu.

Walked down from the Montanvert after breakfast. Quiet afternoon at Chamonix. Oakel sent his article to the *N.A. Review*. Saw in the *Journal Officiel* that Sir G. Elliot, assisted by Mr P. and Mr Cowen, had beaten the Liberal Mr Laing for North Durham,[1] by a large majority. Another seat lost.

7 Sept., Wed.

A fine day. Oakel went for a long walk with Mr Darley the clergyman. Father, Mother and I with Rob in the afternoon to the Chablettes—the first chalet on the way up the Brévent.

8 Sept., Th.

Left C[hamonix] for St Gervais. Father and I starting at 10 to walk over the Col de Voza—drove the first four miles to Les Houches—a beautiful walk in fine weather to the top of the Col. At half past 2 began to descend, and were soon drenched with rain—reached St Gervais about 4, at the same moment as Mother and Oakel who had driven in the afternoon from Chamonix, bringing letters and papers. Irish papers full of accounts of an alarming riot at Limerick between the police and people—in which many people on both sides had been injured by buckshot and stones.[2]

9 Sept., Fri.

A beautiful place [? day] on which to see this very beautiful place. Walked about the village all the morning: Oakel and Rob went up the Mont Joly. Father, Mother and I down to the Baths of St Gervais. In the evening fraternized with a French family in our little hotel, and introduced them to Mrs Barclay and her daughter (the 'Pleiades') whom Oakel made acquaintance with at Chamonix.

[1] In a by-election caused by the death of the sitting member, John Joicey, Sir George Elliot (1814–93), conservative M.P. for this constituency, 1868–80, defeated James Laing by 5,548 votes to 4,896.
[2] On 4 Sept. Limerick station was unusually crowded, and a fracas between civilians and a few members of the Scots Greys developed into a riot in which the police charged with fixed swords and fired on the crowd. A dozen police and a similar number of civilians were injured (*Irish Times*, 5, 6 Sept. 1881).

10 Sept., Sat.

A telegram from Mr G. in the morning telling Father that he had sent a letter to him at Chamonix. We were to start for Anneçy via Bonneville at half past nine immediately the letters had arrived. Whilst waiting for the carriage Rob and I went to join Father at the little post office, where the civil postmaster was doing his best to struggle with English telegrams and addresses.

It was my good luck to receive from this worthy our *Pall Mall Gazette*, and announce to the Ch. Sec. our victory in Tyrone—Mr Dickson at the head of the poll, Col. Knox a good second—and Mr Harold Rylett nowhere. 3 figures to the others 4—a hundred and something to 3 thousand and odd.[1] This unexpected good news rejoiced us all inexpressibly—bad as the effect of Mr Parnell's triumph in Ulster would have been, we had been teaching ourselves to face it, and the most we had ventured to hope was that at least Col. Knox might succeed in beating Mr Rylett.

The morning was fine as we set out on our 28 miles drive to Anneçy, but if it had been pouring cats and dogs the news from Tyrone would have kept us cheerful.

Reached Bonneville between 2 and 3—changed carriages, lunched and drove on to Anneçy which we reached about 8 o'clock, intending to stay there over the Sunday and Monday.

11[–12] Sept., Sun.[–Mon.]

Father received his expected letter from Mr G. by the early morning post. The main drift—'Can anything be done in the way of letting out the suspects apropos of the Tyrone election'.[2]

The need for us to be back had been coming daily more apparent, and the wish to consult with Mr G. on this question decided Father to return as speedily as possible. Mother too was very anxious that, if it turned out that an immediate release of all the suspects was practicable, the Ch. Sec.'s absence should not be the cause to prevent it. Accordingly instead of remaining two days at Anneçy we left at 2 on Sunday afternoon, and travelled straight through to London, where we arrived on Monday Evening about 7 o'clock. The stoppages on this hurried journey had been at Aix les Bains where the Spencers came down to spend half an hour with us at the station,[3] and

[1] In the by-election for Tyrone County on 7 Sept., T. A. Dickson (liberal) was returned with 3,168 votes, Col. W. S. Knox (conservative) receiving 3,084 votes and Rev. Harold Rylett (home ruler) 907 votes.

[2] Forster's reply of 11 Sept. (B.L., Add. MS 44159, ff 5–7) is in Reid, *Forster*, ii, 336–7. He had already written on 9 Sept. stressing that release of suspects should be guided by the state of crime (ibid., ff 2–3).

[3] In a letter to Gladstone, written on 12 Sept. at Aix-les-Bains, Spencer generally supported Forster, with much reference to his own experience in 1869 of the release of Fenian suspects (B.L., Add. MS 44308, ff 151–6).

Paris where we stayed for three hours and breakfasted at the Hotel du Nord.

Oakel and Rob remained behind in Paris in order to try and see something of the French Manoeuvres.

13 Sept., Tu.

80 Eccleston Square.

Rather a black list of outrages from Ireland this morning—making the total amnesty idea seem less feasible. H[umphry] and M[ary] Ward to lunch, the former telling us that he is now going to write on Ireland in *The Times*.

Day spent in shopping, seeing about the packing, etc.

14 Sept., Wed.

Visited Mrs Carlile our pretty travelling companion. Dined with Uncle John and Aunt Susy at Garland's Hotel. Father with Mr Chenery.

15 Sept., Th.

Left London at 12 for Hawarden, Mr Gladstone having suggested that Father and Mother should spend a night there before going over to Dublin. We reached Chester about 5 and drove the 7 miles over to Hawarden Castle—a fine evening—mild and sunny, very different from the violent capricious weather we have been encountering in Switzerland for the past fortnight.

We found a large family party assembled in the drawing room over 6 o'clock tea and finishing letters for the post. All very friendly and cordial in their manner, the great man himself emerging from his study to receive us, being the very embodiment of serious courtesy.

After tea a stroll in the bright flower garden in front of the house, enclosed amongst the green slopes and fine trees of the park, and lying at the foot of the hill on which stands the ruins of old Hawarden Castle.

We naturally fell into pairs, Mother and the Warden of Keble[1]–Helen Gladstone and I–Mr Gladstone and the Irish Secretary–already deep in discussion of their Irish problem, as one could gather from overhearing various familiar words and names as they paced up and down in earnest confabulation.

Late in the evening the Bishop of Winchester, Mrs Harold Brown[2] and their daughter arrived from touring in Scotland: and the party at dinner consisted in

[1] Edward Stuart Talbot (1844–1934): first warden of Keble College, Oxford, since 1869; influential in establishing Lady Margaret Hall as a Church of England women's college, 1878; married Lavinia Lyttelton, 1870.

[2] Edward Harold Browne (1811–91): bishop of Ely, 1864; of Winchester since 1873; and his wife Elizabeth.

great part of the [Gladstone] family including the Warden of Keble and Mrs Talbot, Mr Alfred Lyttleton,[1] and Mrs Wickham.[2]

We had intended to leave early the next morning and cross to Dublin by the midday boat, but Mr Gladstone, partly from his natural instinct of hospitality, and partly from a wish for further consultation with his colleague, set himself so strongly against this project, and demonstrated so earnestly by reference to Bradshaw and other time tables that it would be easier and more agreeable for us to go by the night boat instead of the day, that Mother was obliged to yield with a good grace, and agree to spend the best part of next day at Hawarden instead of on the voyage to Dublin.

16 Sept., Fri.

A large and cheerful family party to breakfast including two of Mrs Wickham's little children to whom their distinguished grandfather showed the same courtesy as to his grown-up companions, stooping as he went by to pick up a ball dropped by the fat two-year-old baby, and breaking off in the midst of his conversation to kiss and wish good morning to an elder child whom he had apparently overlooked when she first appeared upon the scene.

There was a good deal of talk about press reporting—Mr G. and Mr Forster both having enough experience on the subject. Both agreed that the worst reporting was of speeches made in the house. If either of them made a speech on however insignificant an occasion in any other place, they were far more likely to have a full and adequate report furnished to the papers.

Mr G's solution of the question why Parliamentary reporting was so inferior was that the reporters themselves became so intensely bored with the amount of the speechifying they were compelled to listen to.

After breakfast Mr G. and Father vanished into the study. The question of the suspects kept to the fore by a telegram forwarded to Father from an Ulster deputation (including Mr Dickson and Mr Givan) asking for an interview on this subject with the Ch. Sec.; they had already been out to the C.S. Lodge in the hope of seeing him.

After luncheon a large troop started for a walk through the woods, being met half way by another contingent brought by Mrs G. in a waggonette. At one time we were a party of 9, including Mr G. and Father, the Bishop of Winchester and his wife and daughter, Helen Gladstone, Mr L[yttleton] and the Talbots, but gradually from various causes the numbers diminished, and the last half hour we were reduced to Mr G., the Bishop, Father, and myself, which I thought much more agreeable. There was pleasant non-political talk between

---

[1] Alfred Lyttleton (1857–1913): son of 4th Baron Lyttleton and brother of Lavinia Talbot; barrister, 1881; later liberal unionist M.P. and colonial secretary.

[2] Agnes, eldest daughter of the prime minister; in 1873 married Edward Charles Wickham (1834–1910), headmaster of Wellington school, 1873–93.

the three, concerning various persons and things—Mr G. enquiring of the B. as to the probable capabilities of Dr Westcott as a Bishop—had he the administrative faculty—in these days it was not enough to look for learning and acquirements in a bishop—these had become of secondary necessity—and it was perhaps a good thing that this was so.

Apropos of foreign bishops, and a reference by Father to Archbishop Haynald,[1] Mr G. was moved to pronounce a fierce little diatribe against the Hungarians, which I thought was a hard fate on me, as I had to stride along in respectful silence beside him.

A subject on which he spoke with eager interest was a book he had just been reading, and now recommended to Father—'and to all who took an interest in the French Revolution'—*Lettres d'une Bourgeoise* written during the Reign of Terror, and now edited by her grandson.

It was pleasant to hear him discourse on this, on 'Mr Burke' as he always respectfully called him, on Erasmus etc.—and I was sorry when we got back to the house and 5 o'clock tea.

A little before 6 we left Hawarden for Chester, Mr Gladstone escorting Mother to the carriage, and the kind goodnatured Mrs Gladstone at the last moment pressing into my hands at the carriage window a handful of geraniums, flowers and leaves which she had just torn out of the bed on the lawn. She had noticed that I was carrying away a few fronds of bracken gathered in the woods, and evidently thinking that I was treasuring it as a relic of Hawarden presented me with these flowers instead.

It is pretty to see the profoundly admiring affection with which all his family regard and wait upon Mr Gladstone, and they are evidently accustomed to see their visitors demonstrate their veneration in the same way.

We dined at the Railway Hotel at Chester, read the papers, and went on at 10 o'clock to Holyhead, crossing by the Mail—my favourite steamer the *Leinster* and a perfectly smooth passage.

17 Sept., Sat.

The Irish papers full of the Convention now being held in Dublin—Mr Parnell in the chair, 1700 delegates from the Land League branches throughout the country—and also from America—the Meetings held in the Rotunda decorated sumptuously with green hangings, and crownless harps.[2]

The accounts of President Garfield are very unfavourable—the good effects of the move to Long Branch seeming to have quite passed away.

The house and gardens here looked very familiar and very attractive, and in a

[1] Ludwig Haynald (1816–91): bishop of Kalocsa, Hungary, since 1867; botanist and promoter of education; leading opponent of the doctrine of papal infallibility.

[2] The convention sat for three days, beginning on 15 Sept.; the *Freeman* estimated that 1,200 delegates attended (*F.J.*, 16 Sept. 1881). See Moody, *Davitt*, pp 492–4.

short time we seemed to have spread our belongings about us, and quite settled down.

At 12 o'clock Father and Mr West (who had joined us on the steamer the night before) went into Dublin, Father having the Ulster deputation to receive, the L[ord] L[ieutenant] to see and a great deal of work before him.

Francie and Mr Jackson arrived by the Mail at 7 o'clock. Francie has been spending two days at the Deanery at Durham,and struck up a really cordial friendship with Mrs Lake.[1]

18 Sept., Sun.

To church in the morning at the Hibernian School, where by the way they were having several 'little difficulties' as Mr Forster would say, since we were last here.

Sir William Gregory to lunch. In spite of the bad state of things round him he is still personally on good terms with his tenants, and was apparently pretty cheerful. He amused us with the story of the latest Irish grievance—a man lamenting that 'sure they didn't know what they'd do for the pigs this year, as to the potatoes there was not so much as a black one amongst them!'

Sir William, like most of Father's friends and acquaintance at this time, had been charged to make interest for some protégés for an appointment under the Commission; however he was not very urgent or embarrassing in his appeals. His real errand to the Ch. Sec. was to obtain the release of some particular suspect, which I believe has been done.

In the course of the afternoon Mr West was allowed a half-holiday, and I wrote at Father's dictation a letter to the Ulster deputation in reply to their request for a general release of the suspects.[2] 'A very difficult letter to write' Father said—in fact it was the Govt statement of their policy on this important matter, and every word had to be carefully considered.

The letter begun by expressing full recognition of the claims of Ulstermen to be heard, and their opinion to be considered on this question—reminded them however why the Coercion Act had been passed—solely for the prevention of outrage,[3] not for punishment—showed that the diminution of outrage and terrorism had not so far been such as to justify the Govt in giving up the powers that had been entrusted to them for this purpose—explained, that whenever the state of a particular district would allow the Govt to release the prisoners from that district consistently with regard for the preservation of law and order, they

[1] Katherine Gladstone, wife of William Charles Lake, dean of Durham.

[2] The request came from the Ulster tenant right associations and was forwarded to the chief secretary by Dickson and Givan. As printed in the *Freeman*, it is dated 14 Sept., and Forster's reply 19 Sept. (*F.J.*, 20 Sept. 1881).

[3] Although, in the past, suspensions of the habeas corpus act had had this objective, the use of the P.P.P. act for prevention was in fact a new development in the autumn of 1881.

would gladly do it—but that liberation must depend on the consideration of each individual case, and could not be donated en masse.

Lastly the Ch. Sec. expressed his hope that before long the Govt might be able to protect person and property from outrages without making use of the exceptional powers which Parliament has entrusted to it for this purpose.

Julia O'Brien to 5 o'clock tea. She and Mr O'Brien have come over on a fly- ing visit to Dublin from Westmoreland to see about the possibility of Mr O'Brien being offered or accepting a Sub-Commissionership.

19 Sept., Mon.

Read after breakfast the Irish papers of this morning containing lengthy reports of the last days' proceedings of the Convention.

The important point with regard to this Convention has been the nature of its attitude towards the Land Act, and the consequent effect upon the peace of the country. Mr Parnell was placed in rather a delicate situation by his joint obligations towards the Fenian and Socialist party in America, and the tenant farmers in this country. The former had announced in so many words through the *Irish World* that the acceptance of the Land Act would discourage and even put a stop to Land League contributions from America—the latter were known to have a lurking desire to derive practical benefit from the Act in spite of the abuse heaped upon its authors by Mr Parnell and his associates.

To seem sufficiently hostile to the Act to satisfy the *Irish World*, and yet to avoid such absolute repudiation of it as would prevent bona fide tenant farmer protégés of the Land League from taking practical advantage of its benefits, was the task of the President of the Convention, and it must be said that this being the case he conducted the proceedings with great diplomacy.

The keynote of his own speech was 'abolition of rent'[, a] principle which had the merit of commanding the full sympathy and approval of all sections of the assembly, and of being equally satisfactory whether regarded in the light of a theory or practice.

It need not be said that the various topics suggested by the Resolutions were taken advantage [of] for a great display of highly coloured oratory, on all sorts of subjects.

Some of the speakers, especially on the congenial subject of 'alien rule', used genuine eloquence, and others in the discussion of the Labourers' question, showed a power of application and mastery of detail which would have done credit to a Committee of the House of Commons. But on the other hand the amount of mischievous rubbish and vulgar bombast mouthed out and relished apparently by speakers and audience, was most depressing.

If Grattan could have heard some of the speeches, which were said to have visibly recalled him, he would have shuddered both as an Irishman and an orator.

A notable element in the Convention was the large part played by the American cable; at frequent intervals, a telegram from some Irish American branch of the Land League was read out by the President: this trans-Atlantic element was also largely represented in the person of various Irish American patriots (notably Mr Redpath) whose fervour of anti-British, anti-Ulster, anti-landlord hatred, and almost injudiciously thorough Boycotting doctrines, it was difficult for the most ardent Irish Land Leaguer to rival.

On the whole as regards the Land Act the conclusion arrived at by the League Convention has been summed up by one of their organs—(*United Ireland*) under the heading 'Test the Act, don't use it'. Tenants have been enjoined not to take separate advantage of its provisions, and so run the risk of producing what Mr P. called 'sectional contentment'; but the League engages to select test cases on certain specified estates, in which they propose to defray at public cost the expense of bringing the Landlord into court, and endeavouring to obtain a substantial reduction of his rents.

By way of compromise however with the American section who are in favour of repudiating and ignoring the Bill altogether, Mr P. and Mr Sexton have promised that the American moneys sent through the *Irish World* shall not be used for this purpose.

With respect to the test cases—the policy of the League—as avowed in an unguarded moment by Mr Dawson—is to select Estates on which the rents are notoriously low, and then when the Court declines to reduce them, proclaim aloud the worthlessness of the Act, and the inability of the Court to do justice or satisfy the natural requirements of the Irish farmer.

The great hope of the Govt and the Ch. Sec. is that Ulster may prove the 'fulcrum' as some one has said for working the Act rightly. The farmers there will probably prefer using the benefits offered them at their own discretion and without the intervention of Mr P's executive, and it may be that the southern farmers will in time wish to follow their example.

20 Sept., Tu.

The telegram in the *Irish Times* of this morning told us that President Garfield died the previous night. Ever since Sunday the 2nd of July, when the *Observer* announced the attempted assassination of the President, the attention of Englishmen has been fixed with unfailing interest on the daily bulletins from Washington or Long Branch; the first shock of horror and indignation, such as would be felt at the news of any such public crime, was soon succeeded by a feeling of deep personal interest in the President himself, a feeling which as days went on and more came to be known of the sayings and doings of the wounded man, of the beautiful courage and patience with which he was bearing his hard sufferings—of the devotion of his wife, who never left his sick bed— indeed of every pathetic detail brought to light in the full glare of English and

American journalism—grew into a sentiment of intimate affection and anxious sympathy, which to thousands of men and women has made the news of his death come like a personal sorrow.

There has been something very striking in the way in which the dying President has drawn the two great English-speaking countries together.

In America and England the expression of the national feeling—on the one side of cordial heartfelt sympathy, on the other of grateful response and acceptance of our sympathy—has been spoken by a woman.

The Queen's messages to Mrs Garfield have not been mere conventional forms, but words of true feeling, which even at such a time as this must have given her pleasure and consolation.

The new President Mr Arthur[1] has not the best of reputations politically, and it is thought doubtful whether he will have the will and the courage to fight against the abuses of State jobbery as General Garfield would have done, but at the same time there is a disposition to make allowance for the difficulties of his position, and credit him with good intentions.

It is to be feared that England will not find in him such a trustworthy friend in Fenian matters as was his predecesor.

After a long morning's work at home, Father drove in to the Castle to begin his work there, an interview with Dr Gillooly, Bishop of Elphin[2]—one of the few bishops who at times has the courage to express publicly his condemnation of Land League morality. Father asked him to come and dine with us in the evening—he said, that he would like much to do so, but could not venture, as there would be such a fuss made about it.

Julia and Mr O'Brien to dine and sleep. Mr Joseph Pim to dinner. A sensible and honest man (of Quaker origin); Father had consulted him as to whether it would be desirable for him to subscribe to the Guarantee Fund for the proposed Exhibition next year of Irish manufactures in connection with the 'Irish industries' movement. He has heard since that his £250, so far from being thrown back in his face, gave great satisfaction which was expressed apparently by little Mr Dawson the Lord Mayor elect, and one of the hysterically violent— though harmless—Land League men on the Committee.

This Irish Industry Movement was intended by the Land League in which it was started to have been a weapon of offence for their own peculiar use. The idea of Boycotting English goods (as a speaker at the Convention suggested also that they should Boycott 'English ideas and English intellect') was very attractive, and patriotic Boards of Guardians had passed resolutions pledging themselves to use in the workhouses only Irish linen and Irish woollen goods.

The scheme however of peace and prosperity in Ireland, by encouraging home-made manufactures and trade, has been warmly taken up by all sides and

---

[1] Chester Alan Arthur (1830–86): son of a Co. Antrim clergyman; vice-president, 1880; accused of adherence to the old 'spoils' system, he proved to be a reforming president.

[2] Laurence Gillooly, bishop of Elphin (1858–95).

all classes, and long lists of contributors to the Guarantee Fund have appeared in the *Freeman* including the Lord Lieutenant and Mr Dawson.

This benevolent interest in a movement which was meant to have struck a blow at English prosperity quite as much as to have promoted Irish, has been very annoying to the Land League, and they have been trying to raise an outcry against 'patronage' in connection with the proposed exhibition.

However the tradespeople and manufacturers throughout Ireland are so keenly alive to the advantages of this last patriotic movement as a medium for advertising, if for nothing else, that they will probably be unwilling to abandon it, even if discredited by English approbation and support.

21 Sept., Wed.

Uncle Matt, Aunt F[anny] L[ucy] and Nelly arrived from Fox How. A very nice letter to Father from Mr Lowell.

22 Sept., Th.

Father and the two secretaries hard at work all the morning over applications for Sub-Commissionerships—there are 12 vacancies, and between 4 and 500 applications.

Mr Fox, author of a pamphlet on 'Distress in Mayo' dined with us, and had much useful talk with the Ch. Sec. about the state of things in the West.

I read the rebel papers. The new one *United Ireland* [1] is the cleverest of all of them. Very violent about the Ch. Sec.'s letter to the Ulster deputation: calling him every kind of opprobrious name, and indulging generally in language worthy of Billingsgate whenever having occasion to allude to him.

23 Sept., Fri.

Father again at work all the morning over the L[and] Comm[ission] appointments. A leader in the *Irish Times* on Mr Healy's *Handbook on the Land Act*, which is said to be very good and not biased by his ill-feeling towards the Measure.[2]

Mother, the Uncle Matts and Francie to Howth. I rode Paris in the park,

---

[1] See above, p. 207.

[2] 'It is not bad & will tempt tenants into court. The man's intellect has got for a time the better of his vice.' (Forster to Gladstone, 23 Sept. 1881; B.L., Add. MS 44159, ff 18–21.)

Puck going with me. Sir S[amuel] and Lady Ferguson, Dr and Mrs Moffat,[1] and Mr Naish to dinner. The latter told me that the new paper *United Ireland* is edited by a man named O'Brien, formerly on the staff of the *Freeman*—'a very clever fellow, but a born rebel, and always will be'.

24 Sept., Sat.

The three Land Commissioners to breakfast and to spend the morning with Father over the appointments.

Mr Webber and the Countess of Kingston,[2] of the Mitchelstown estate, came to see the Ch. Sec. and suggest that he should suppress the Land League which was making their part of the country unendurable.[3] They have been very badly treated by their tenants, and poor Lady Kingston, an elegant interesting woman, seemed deeply melancholy as well she might. They stayed to lunch, as also did Mr Law.

In the afternoon Uncle Matt and I went to Killiney and had a pretty view, full of passing lights and shadows from the Obelisk Hill.

We met the Murrough O'Briens, who took us to their house and gave us tea. Mr O'Brien has been appointed secretary to the land-selling department of the Commission, a work he will do 'con amore'.

The Dowdens, Keenans, Dean Neville, Burkes, Sir Hubert Miller, and Mr Jackson to dinner.[4]

25 Sept., Sun.

Oakel arrived from France by the mail boat this morning. He and Rob have been staying at Chartres, seeing what they could of the manoeuvres and making friends with every one they met.

Mr Jackson preached to the little Hibernian boys at the morning service. He left us in the evening to return to England. Mr Errington to dinner. After dinner helped Father make up his journal fallen into arrears since Chamonix. He told me of their intention to release Father Sheehy—Mr Clifford Lloyd being of opinion that this can be done with safety to the peace of the district.[5]

[1] Thomas William Moffett (d. 1908), president of Queen's College, Galway, and professor of history, English literature, and mental science.

[2] William Downes Webber (1834–1924): landowner and agriculturist, married Lady Kingston in 1873.

[3] In the early summer, the local league branch seems to have tried to secure a settlement and reduce disorder; see C.S.O., R.P. 1881/19125, and above, p. 160, n. 3.

[4] Edward Dowden (1843–1913): professor of English literature at Dublin University, 1867–1913. Charles John Hubert Miller (1858–1940), 8th baronet.

[5] Fr Sheehy and two other committee members of the Kilmallock Land League were released on 27 Sept., the last of the Kilmallock–Kilfinane suspects of 20–24 May to be released.

26 Sept., Mon.

Papers full of the 'ovation' to Mr P. A torchlight procession and presentation to him of an address from the Dublin Land League.[1] His speech and Mr Sexton's made from a balcony, fiery enough to suit a torchlight procession audience—denunciation of alien rule—compliment to the Irish people—threats against the English—'to be swept back across the channel, etc.'.

The crowds appear to have been terribly rough, and the Dublin 'corner boy' evidently took advantage of his opportunity—several people were robbed and others, mostly women and children, knocked down and injured.

Father had to receive a deputation of Publicans this afternoon—to protest against a recent Circular issued by the Castle Authorities enjoining Magistrates to revoke Licences when an innkeeper refused to entertain persons. The tone of the address presented was respectful and reasonable, and the publicans themselves said little; the speaking—of a very violent character—was all done by the M.P.s who accompanied the deputation, including Mr Gray and the O'Donoghue.

The Ch. Sec. declined to order the revocation of the Circular, but explained that in cases where the innkeepers were genuinely intimidated allowance should be made for the inability to carry out their legal obligations.

On Monday afternoon Mother went in to the Castle to have an interview with Mr G. Pim, about the Social Science votaries, to whom the Ch. Sec. will have to show hospitality on a large scale.

I with the Uncle Matts and Nelly to Trinity where we were shewn everything by Dr Ingram,[2] Mr French (sub-librarian), and Professor Dowden.

27 Sept., Tu.

The Uncle Matts, Nelly, Mother and Francie started at 10 for Bray, whence they were to take a drive up the Dargle, and Uncle Matt go on to Glendalough to dine and sleep at a Mr Booth's and have some fishing.

Leader in the Irish papers on Mr F's reply to the Licensed Vintners' deputation, according to the *Freeman* and *Express* a weak concession to the League—the *Irish Times* a reasonable and generous comprehension of the facts of the situation, and of the peculiar difficulties of intimidated innkeepers.

Walked with Father to the Park gate. On comparing notes after an interval of silence it appeared that we had both been reflecting on the curious fact that in spite of such language as was used about him on Sunday ('To hell with Buckshot')—the Chief Sec. has never been personally insulted in Dublin or the

[1] The *Freeman* reported participation by sixteen league branches and a total attendance of 100,000 (*F.J.*, 26 Sept. 1881).

[2] John Kells Ingram (1823–1907): librarian of Trinity College, 1879–87; regius professor of Greek, 1866–77; economist and poet; founded the journal *Hermathena*, 1874; president of Dublin Statistical Society, 1878–80; author of 'Who fears to speak of '98'.

park. On the contrary by unknown people he is now and then greeted with respect, just as happens in our walks to the office in London.

Oakel and I in the afternoon to Miss Burke's. The Dargle expedition had been a great success and the weather lovely. In fact these sweet 'peacock' hills are more endearing and lovely, even with their many changing colours and fleeting gleams of sunshine.

Received autograph from Mr Dowden.

Father very late back having been kept at the Castle till 7. The outrage report today worse than any day since last December.

28 Sept., Wed.

Announcement of the release of Father Sheehy. Tuesday's Report of Land League Meeting; Mr Sexton and Mr Parnell are straining every nerve to prevent the tenant farmers from 'ruining the cause' by going into court on their own account. Above all, rack-rented tenants are conjured to bear their sufferings patiently and not give the Court an opportunity of reducing their rents, as this might give an appearance of fictitious fairness to the decision of the Commissioners.

To ensure discipline amongst the people in this respect, minor Conventions of Land League members are to be held throughout the country which are to decide as to the fitness of cases to be brought before the Court.

Mr Parnell spoke at the Maryborough Convention on Monday, explaining the principle on which test cases were to be selected.

The Rules of Procedure of the new Land Court published in the papers this morning.

Drove into Dublin with Father and Aunt F[anny] L[ucy] and Nelly—to the Zoological [Gardens] with the two latter on the way back.

A dinner party in the evening. Judge and Mrs O'Hagan, Dr and Mrs Kaye, Sir Bernard and Lady Burke,[1] Col. Hillier and Sir J. Lentaigne. I sat next Dr Kaye, whom I like. He told me that Mr Adams, one of the editors of the *Freeman*, had just returned from the West of Ireland, he had volunteered to him the information that he believed the Land Act would be made eager use of by the tenants.

Apropos of the *Freeman* and its apparently lurking desire to see a fair trial given to the Act, notwithstanding Mr Parnell, I was told that its spasmodic but violent Parnellism is caused to a great extent by dread of successful competition on the part of their paper *United Ireland*.

This has already a very large circulation, and if the *Freeman* should flag in its

---

[1] Sir John Bernard Burke (1814–92): Ulster king of arms since 1853; knight attendant on the order of St Patrick, and keeper of state papers of Ireland since 1855; annually re-edited his father's *Peerage* from 1847 to 1892; C.B., 1868; married Barbara Frances, daughter of James McEvoy of Co. Meath.

extreme anti-Governmental doctrines there would be every probability of the *United Ireland* taking its place as the popular daily paper; at present it comes out weekly.

I was interested in hearing from Dr Kaye his reminiscences of Isaac Butt[1] for whom he had a great admiration and liking.

According to him there was something of real genius in Mr Butt—sound political ability, foresight, power to take a wide view of things—and not least, perfect truthfulness—this at least was Dr Kaye's testimony as a lawyer who had had frequent intercourse with Mr Butt on circuit and in the law courts, where he had the deserved reputation of being fair and truthful in his dealings.

I could not help thinking of my *Déak*—If only Mr Butt had had more of what Uncle Matt calls 'conduct' as well as ability, eloquence, and a genial generous nature, the present Chief Secretary might be having a very different experience from what he is going through now, and this generation might have seen what an honest, far-seeing Irish Statesman with the Irish people behind him, and an English statesman with the weight of a kindly-disposed English public opinion behind him, could have done towards giving justice to Ireland, and beginning an era of peace and goodwill between the two countries.

But Mr Butt is dead, and the men who profess now to lead public opinion in Ireland, and who certainly exasperate public opinion in England, are such patriots as Mr Parnell, Mr Healy, Mr T. P. O'Connor, and others, Irish and American.

29 Sept., Th.

Full report in the papers of Father Sheehy's triumphant reception at Kilmallock, and of his speech, or rather yell, on the occasion. Chiefly occupied with abuse of the Ch. Sec. 'his infamous character' etc.[2]

As Father remarked to the 5 bishops who came to him at the Castle to-day— 'Father Sheehy was quite safe as long as he kept to this topic'.

The object of the Bishops (including Archbishop Mc Cabe, and the good bishops of Elphin and Ossory)[3] was to bring some Catholic Education demands before the Ch. Sec. He had a long and interesting talk with them over this peaceful and once familiar subject; before parting he made allusion to the bad state of the country—'a mere passing irritation' said one of the Bishops, and on which Mr Forster, to show the form which passing irritation was taking,

---

[1] Isaac Butt (1813–79): barrister and statesman; professor of political economy, Dublin University, 1836–41; conservative M.P. for Harwich, 1852; liberal conservative for Youghal, 1852–65; defended Fenian prisoners, 1865–9; home rule M.P. for Limerick, 1871–9; founder of home rule party, 1870, and leader till his death, though his policy as leader was increasingly challenged by Parnell.

[2] This speech was made at Naas on his release; he did not reach Kilmallock until Thursday, when he spoke chiefly against Clifford Lloyd (*F.J.*, 29, 30 Sept. 1881).

[3] According to the *Freeman* (30 Sept. 1881), these three were the only bishops present.

rang the bell and sent for 5 telegrams which had just been received each detailing some serious outrage in different parts of the country. He also read them a passage from a speech made by a priest at Maryborough,[1] advocating and advising the people to 'Boycott' those who displeased them 'without mercy'.

The bishops shrugged their shoulders, and it was evident that they either could not or would not make any use of their powers to stay such language.

However at their recent conclave at Maynooth the Bishops have passed Resolutions speaking in warm praise of the Land Act, advising the people to make use of it, and protesting against outrages—good so far as it goes—says the Ch. Sec.—but he had hoped they would have taken the opportunity of pronouncing emphatically against 'boycotting'.

Archbishop Croke was absent from the Conclave or the language of the Resolutions might perhaps have been less satisfactory.

It is said that the priests themselves are becoming frightened at the pass things have come to; in spite of their compliance with the popular sentiment in all its worst manifestations their influence now goes for almost nothing, and if their flocks wish to commit outrages, as they very often do, the priests seem quite powerless to restrain them.

Spent a good part of the morning watching a sham fight on the Fifteen Acres in honour of General Glyn, who is going to be succeeded as Commander of the Dublin District by Lord Clarina.

Made out lists and invitations for dinner parties to the Social Science notables.

Mrs and Miss Bruce, and Dr and Mrs Graves[2] to lunch. Father back to dinner looking very tired, as well he may.

The old story of last autumn is now beginning again for the Ch. Sec.—a daily struggle with crime and violence, of word and action—accompanied by daily abuse and criticisms from opposite quarters—Father Sheehy and the *Freeman* in the morning, counter-balanced by the *Morning Post*, *Dublin Mail* and the *Standard* in the evening. A very black outlook.

30 Sept., Fri.

Lord F. Cavendish arrived by the morning boat. Walked to the Park gates with Father, Uncle Matt, and Mr Jephson.

It is delightful having Uncle Matt here, but one cannot help feeling sometimes a little tried by his airy indifference to the extreme difficulty and gravity of Father's position. He seems to think that he is quite absorbed in his work, and evidently considers that if he let things alone a little more, and ceased to

[1] Fr Edward Rowan, C.C., comparing the power of boycotting to 'a Nasmyth steam hammer of a thousand tons' (*F.J.*, 29 Sept. 1880).

[2] Probably Charles Graves (1812–99), protestant bishop of Limerick, Ardfert, and Aghadoe.

worry himself he might have a much easier time, and need be less constantly at the Castle.

When he does discuss the political situation, it is touched off with an easy critical style, and he is of course able to regard Mr Parnell, Mr Sexton and their fellows with the sympathy of an amiable literary observer, who can admire the vigour of their rhetoric, and philosophize on the charms of the Celtic temperament, without an after thought as to the effect of these brilliant orations on the next outrage returns.

The papers this morning contain accounts of the attempt yesterday to blow up the house of Capt. Lloyd and his Emergency men at New Pallas, with gunpowder. The walls were shattered and the roof partially destroyed, but happily no one was injured.

Mr Moffat a land agent has also had a narrow escape, he was fired at from behind a hedge, the car and his ulster riddled with shot but himself uninjured.[1]

Another speech reported from Father Sheehy, this time foaming at the mouth in personal abuse of Mr Clifford Lloyd, whom he described as being like Richard III in mind and body—this last being an allusion to some rheumatic stiffness in Mr Clifford Lloyd's neck which gives him rather a high-shouldered look.[2] In spite of Father Sheehy's violence and Mr Clifford Lloyd's unpopularity with the Land League the fact remains that he has the mastery of Kilmallock.

So at least says the Chief Secretary referring this evening to the report in the morning papers of Mr Lloyd's cool, temperate proceedings as a magistrate—dismissing some cases—committing others for trial, and showing himself apparently quite sufficient master of the situation to account for the ferocious vapourings of the Land League agitators, who object to any strong hand over the people except their own.

Friday afternoon—Uncle Matt spent in Dublin going over the Marlborough Street Schools with Sir P. Keenan, and visiting St Patrick's and Christ Church. He is full of admiration as we were of the beautiful statues of Archbishop Whateley and Captain Boyd—both by Farrell,[3] a sculptor who seems so much less famous than he deserves to be.

1 Oct., Sat.

The Uncle Matts and Nelly left by the morning boat to return to Cobham.

Lord Monck and Lord Monteagle arrived in the evening to stay over the Sunday. Lord Monteagle and his wife are now established for the winter at

[1] On 28 Sept., O. B. Maffett, who was using emergency men on his farm, was fired at as he drove into Drogheda. An arrest was made under the P.P.P. act (S.P.O., I.C.R., Returns of outrages, Sept. 1881).

[2] Lloyd reprinted Fr Sheehy's 'Richard III' speech in full in *Ireland under the Land League*, pp 178–94.

[3] Thomas Farrell (1827–1900): later knighted and president of the Royal Hibernian Academy.

Mount Trenchard, endeavouring by patience and self-denial to live through these hard times, and do the duties of an Irish landlord without an open breach between them and their tenants.

Up to this time Lord Monteagle's richly deserved popularity with his own people has stood him in good stead, but he has his enemies in the local Land League and they are carefully seeking for opportunities to annoy him. The last device has been to 'boycott' his school in the village of Shanagolden. The pretext for doing this is of the flimsiest, but the real reason is not far to seek; the priest of Shanagolden—like many other more or less active adherents of the Land League—is desirous to serve his own turn out of the present movement: his object in this case is to secure the Management of Lord M[onteagle]'s school and he hopes by inducing the people to withdraw their children, and threatening to set up a school of his own, to bring the landlord to terms in this matter.[1]

Every day the feeling that 'something must be done' is growing stronger, even amongst genuine Liberals, not susceptible to the praises of the *Daily Express* and *Post*, and not in any way prejudiced against the tenants.

The fact that the Land League organization is not merely a defensive Trades Union, as the *Pall Mall Gazette* loves to argue, is becoming more and more painfully evident. With the leaders of the League there is no pretence of the kind, and the fact that the organization is now used for the purposes of intimidation and terrorism, enforced by boycotting and outrage, is scarcely concealed: opinion at headquarters seems tending towards the conviction that such an organization, under however innocent a name, will in the end have to be treated as illegal and criminal, if the well-disposed and neutral tenantry throughout the country are to have the smallest chance of profiting by the Land Act, and daring to be honest without fear of injury to person or property.

In the universal gloom of the present situation, some of the papers have been drawing comfort from the recent Land League Circulars, inviting the local branches to assist in furnishing and sending up 'test cases' for the judgment of the court. It is said that this shows an intention to make use of the Act, and sanction the farmers doing so—but as Mr Parnell avows an intention to demand from the Court an impossible reduction of moderate rents, the bias of his action in this respect is not likely to be favourable towards a fair working of the Act.

2 Oct., Sun.

To church in the morning at the Hibernian. Mr Laing M.P. to lunch. Mr Laing has just returned from fishing in the West of Ireland, and like Mr Boyd Kinnear[2] and other tourists has been writing his impressions of the state of the

[1] See below, pp 349.
[2] John Boyd Kinnear (1828–1920): Scottish landowner, lawyer, writer, and agriculturalist; author of *Ireland in 1881* (London, 1881) and many other works.

country to the newspapers, in this case to the *Freeman*—as usual under these circumstances, he has discovered that the disturbance has been much exaggerated—as for rents—he is convinced from what he was told on the spot, that Griffith's Valuation is decidedly above what the standard of rent ought to be—a statement which a good deal surprised poor Lord Monteagle.

Father came in to lunch after a hard morning's work in the study over a letter to Mr Gladstone. Mr Laing's optimist views must have been a good deal disturbed by the conversation at lunch of those who like Lord Monck, Lord M[onteagle] and the Ch. Sec. had special reasons for knowing and if possible for hoping.

In plain, forcible words, Father described the difficulties and perils of the present situation, not drawing an alarmist picture, but simply stating facts as they are, and looking the possible consequences fairly in the face.

The afternoon taken up with minor anxieties over the proposed garden party to the Social Science Congress; finding that this would involve asking 1000 people, and having no secretary or assistant at leisure to help her arrange things at such notice, Mother has determined to give up the idea, and give a more limited evening party instead.

Before post time two copies of a long letter to Mr Gladstone[1] to be made, Mr West and Oakel doing one, Mother and I the other. 'A sad and saddening letter' as Mr G. called it in his reply.

'Tell Herbert' Father had written at the end of his letter (Mr H. Gladstone) 'that I shall be ready for him whenever it suits him to come—but I have some compunction in bringing him into this mess: if he really gets into it he will find life almost unbearable'.

Lord and Lady O'Hagan, Mr Burke and Col. Burke to tea. Mr Burke to say goodbye before starting on his holiday—he has not had one for 4 years—and Father has been very anxious for him to go, though this is rather an unfortunate time for him to be away.

Some pleasant talk in the evening after dinner between Father and Lord Monck over old House of Commons stories, and afterwards on the condition of the country, and the different circumstances of the tenantry and landlords of the West. Father's minute and thorough knowledge of these matters would rather astonish some of the professional agitators, whose stock in trade consists so often of generalities, more or less false.

3 Oct., Mon.

The first thing to be ascertained on the arrival of the post and newspapers this morning—what had Mr Parnell said in his speech at Cork yesterday? Mr Gladstone had been informed by the Ch. Sec.[2] that Mr P. might make it

---

[1] Forster to Gladstone, 2 Oct. 1881 (B.L., Add. MS 44159, ff 29–36; inaccurately reproduced in Reid, *Forster*, ii, 340–44), urging that the League must be paralysed by stretching the P.P.P. act in a general arrest of central and local leaders.

[2] In Forster's letter of 26 Sept. (Reid, *Forster*, ii. 339–40).

necessary to arrest him for sedition, but he did not think it likely. It has not proved to be necessary, Mr Parnell having talked mischief but not treason.[1]

As before he makes a great point of the duty of the farmers to bear any sacrifice and inconvenience in the matter of rents, rather than act independently of the Land League by going before the Land Court on their own account.

Lord Monck left us this morning. He is the most charming and cheering of visitors, but I am told that even he is in reality excited and perturbed at the present state of the country. As one of the Lords Justices he, like Father, has the opportunity of hearing in detail, and from day to day, the same monotonous report of lawlessness, intimidation and outrage sent up from all parts of the country.

A lovely afternoon. Walked with Mother and accompanied by Puck and Yarrow to call on Mrs Tremble—the Aunt of our little Irish kitchen maid, living in Black Horse Lane; on the way back we met Mr C. Russell, cheerful and anxious to assure us that things were not so bad as they seemed—a great deal was mere talk—as for Father Sheehy's speeches they had only done good, by opening people's eyes more plainly to the character of the men the Govt has to deal with. He had been travelling in Fermanagh, and Donegal and found things quiet enough there.

Dined at 6.30 and spent an hour reading the rebel papers by Father's request. Judging by these a poor prospect for the Act receiving a fair trial. Went afterwards to hear Lord O'Hagan's inaugural address to the Social Science [Congress] at the Exhibition Palace, Father joining us on the way from the Kildare St Club, where he had been dining. The Address was in itself something dry—a categorical review of Social legislation for the last 20 years—health acts, jury reforms, reformatories, asylums etc.—but at any rate it was an agreeable interlude from politics and agitation, and pleasant to see the Ch. Sec. sitting calmly on an Irish platform without opportunity being given to attack or abuse him.

The names of the 8 (or 12) Assistant Commissioners published this morning, to the great relief I should imagine of every one concerned—certainly to that of our poor young Mr West who has had to stand the brunt of a constant invasion of importunate or pathetic applicants, who came in shoals to the Castle in hopes of a personal interview with the Ch. Sec.

The *Freeman* has an article, on the whole favourable to the new appointments[2]—this paper would go more decisively in favour of the Land Act, if it dared, but with Miss Fanny Parnell writing poetry with the refrain 'Tear up the Parliament [*recte* parchment] Lie!' in the Rebel papers, it behoves every would-be Nationalist paper to be at least moderately violent.

[1] On 29 Sept. Forster had told Gladstone that Parnell's speeches were 'treasonable by construction' but did not merit arrest under the original concept of the P.P.P. act.

[2] Forster had secured this favourable response by a previous interview with Gray—'very risky, but in this case necessary'—as well as with the editor of the *Irish Times* (Forster to Gladstone, 4 Oct. 1881; B.L., Add. MS 44159, ff 43–6).

Mr Doyle and Mr Baden Powell to 5 o'clock tea: also Lord and Lady P[owerscourt] and Sir John and Lady Smale[1]—these 4 latter to dine and sleep.

A dinner party in the evening, Lord Monteagle, Mr Jephson, Sir G. Owens (High Sheriff of Dublin), Sir Robert Kane (of the R[oyal] I[rish] Academy, Dr Lyons, Miss Burke, and Mr A. Burke, Major Byng, Rev. Fleming Stevenson, Mr Hastings, M.P., and Mr Joseph Brown (these two latter Social Science notables).[2]

Heard from Father that there had been another murder—a man shot near Millstreet, Co. Cork—said to be for paying his rent.[3]

5 Oct., Wed.

Walked and took the train into Dublin with Williams to have my 'Irish Manufacture' ulster tried on. Father is giving me one to be made of Irish cloth—he suggests that if it turns out a sucess Mr Geary (the Tailor) shall advertise it as the 'Buckshot Ulster'.

Lady Powerscourt left us in the afternoon, Lord P. having gone earlier. She is a thoroughly nice woman, and we all took to her. She was rather despondent but not despairing, and spoke with much good sense and gentleness, that one felt glad that in times like these the future Lord Powerscourt had such a wise landlady for his mother.

A dinner party in the evening, Sir Thomas Jones, Mr and Mrs Brooks, M.P., Dr Croker King, Mr Goldwin Smith and Lord Monteagle.

In spite of his sour looks, and unpatriotic sentiments about the colonies, Mr Goldwin Smith pleased us by his friendly words to the Ch. Sec. as to his actions here. Whatever may be his un-English sympathies in other respects, he is at any rate not a Fenian or a Land Leaguer.[4]

In the evening Oakel and I went to a ball at the Mansion House as representatives of the Ch. Sec. and Mrs Forster: we were very hospitably received by the Lord Mayor,[5] the Lady Mayoress, and Mr and the Miss Moyers, and had rather an amusing evening. I danced in the same set of Lancers with the Lord Mayor elect, the funny little Home Ruler and Parnellite, Mr Dawson. I could hardly keep my countenance as we bowed and curtseyed at each other, and

[1] John Smale (1805–92): chief justice of Hong Kong since 1866; knighted 1874.

[2] Sir George Bolster Owens (1810–96): M.D., lord mayor of Dublin, 1876; knighted, 1876. Sir Robert John Kane (1809–90): president of Queen's College, Cork, 1845–73; knighted, 1846; president of R.I.A., 1877; vice-chancellor of Royal University of Ireland, 1880. Major G. S. Byng, assistant secretary and A.D.C. to the lord lieutenant.

[3] At about 11 p.m. on 3 Oct. Patrick Leary (22), a farmer's son, was shot by a gang of moonlighters who allegedly 'thought he was a detective'; he died the next day (S.P.O., I.C.R., Returns of outrages, Oct. 1881).

[4] In 1885 Goldwin Smith was to urge treating Ireland as a crown colony, since Irish political instincts and habits 'are those of the tribesman, not those of the citizen' (Goldwin Smith, 'The administration of Ireland' in *Contemporary Review*, July 1885, pp 1–9).

[5] George Moyers (1836–1916): architect and civil engineer; according to *Who Was Who, 1916–28*, he was the last lord mayor of Dublin to receive a viceroy at the Mansion House.

I thought of the last time I had seen him—wagging his little head fiercely at the Govt across the floor of the House of Commons.

6 Oct., Th.

Lord Monteagle left us. Walked with Father to the Park gates, he going on with Oakel to be photographed at Chancellor's—where Robbie was also photographed gratis.

Read in the papers Mr Parnell's speech at Dungarvan defining the duties of the Court—to reduce rents at a rate of 20/- to 2. If they do not do this in all the 'test cases' submitted to them, the tenants are to return to their former method of proceeding and 'bring the landlords to their senses by refusing to pay any rent at all'.

A lovely afternoon. Rode with Oakel, he on Paris, I on Mr West's pony which suits me very well. In the evening Father, Mother and the Smales dined at the O'Hagans'—Francie, Oakel, Mr West and I went to see Mr Irving and Miss Terry in the 'Merchant of Venice'.[1] The house[2] crammed from floor to ceiling, and the performance altogether delightful—'it seemed so human', as Mr West remarked, to be in a theatre again.

7 Oct., Fri.

The morning occupied mainly with sending off final invitations for the evening party to-night. Walked with Father to the tram-way. We talked of Mr Parnell's Dungarvan speech, of the Rebel papers, and of the mysterious assassination in Co. Cork. The young man killed was the son of a Land League secretary, and it is now said that he was shot by mistake.

To-morrow Mr Gladstone makes his great speech at Leeds, which is looked forward to with eager interest by every one. What will he have to say about Ireland, and how will he say it? It is possible there may be a Cabinet next week.

Captain Talbot[3] to 5 o'clock tea, having called in order to hear Mother's plea on behalf of a policeman (brother to the still-room maid here) who has been turned out of the force for drunkenness. Capt. Talbot explained that the offence was for the 8th time and could not be overlooked, which in fact Mother did not urge.

Capt. Talbot, the head of the Dublin police, is a man who gives one the impression of being thoroughly up to his work—he is said to be very able and

[1] Henry Irving (1838–1905): the most famous actor and theatre manager of his age, and the first to be knighted (1895); revived popular interest in Shakespeare. Ellen Terry (1848–1928): now established as an outstanding actress and working regularly with Irving since 1878.

[2] The Gaiety Theatre.

[3] George Talbot (1823–1914): formerly of 13th Light Infantry; chief commissioner of Dublin Metropolitan Police, 1877–82; dismissed after Phoenix Park murders; owner of 1,341 acres, valued at £953, in Co. Wexford.

cool-headed, and he certainly talked about his special subject in a way that gave that impression.

He says, what one often sees stated, that in all but agrarian crime Ireland shows better than England, and his Dublin statistics at the present time are not unsatisfactory in this respect. But according to him the really dangerous symptom now-a-days is 'the decline of religion'—the influence of the priests over their flocks having almost disappeared.

A dinner party in the evening, Mr B[onamy] Price, the Vernons, Dr and Mrs Cameron, M.P. (Social Science), Dr and Mrs Moffett (Social Science), and Mr Dudley Field, brother of Mr Cyrus Field.

Afterwards Mother had an evening party to which about 100 Social Science notables and Dublin acquaintance came. An amusing gathering, but rather difficult in some ways considering that many of our guests were unknown to us and to each other.

In the midst of much miscellaneous talk with people known and unknown I had a few serious words with Mr Naish, a man for whom I have a great respect and liking, as a strong trustworthy Irishman. He is very gloomy about the present state of things 'with a body of men living on the agitation, and having a large income to work with' and he is not hopeful of peace or a fair trial to the Land Act, and as to not despairing 'well, it is difficult not to'.

Our guests did not depart till past 12 o'clock, so it is to be hoped they had enjoyed themselves.

8 Oct., Sat.

Mr Gladstone's speeches at Leeds—the first in the Victoria Hall on Free Trade and Fair Trade—the second, and to us all-important, one on Ireland at the Banquet in the evening.

Father eagerly turned to the report of this in the *Irish Times* and after a hurried look seemed well satisfied. Mr Gladstone has indeed been plain spoken in his denunciation of Mr Parnell's policy, and his fine exposition of the duty of the Imperial Govt with regard to Ireland.

He did not denounce the Land League, because

dangerous as that association has brought itself to be, it has many members, and perhaps many local branches who have no view but the attainment of lawful and reasonable objects, and whose exertions and the credit of whose name and character others are endeavouring to pervert to purposes neither lawful nor reasonable,[1]

but he did speak in very plain terms of Mr Parnell 'a man of considerable ability' and of 'the small body of men who are not ashamed to preach in Ireland the doctrine of public plunder'.

After drawing a contrast, point by point, between the political aims and

[1] This and Florence's other extracts from the speech are not always literally accurate.

doctrines and conduct of O'Connell and Mr Parnell, Mr Gladstone described carefully the attitude of the Land League President towards the Land Act, and his avowed intention to make the Court obey his behests in the matter of rent. Saying with reference to this, amidst the cheers of his audience:

You know gentlemen as clearly as I do that the Parliament of this country is not going to overturn the principles of public right and public order [to please Mr Parnell[1]], and I think you also know, what I fully believe, that the people of this country in any such question relating to a portion of the Queen's territory, weak as it[2] may be if their cause is unjust, in a just cause are invincible.

From this Mr G. passed to the 'secondary evil of Ireland'—the great cowardice prevailing amongst the upper class and land owners, who should exert themselves in support and aid of the laws.[3]

And then came a passage which was of special interest to us as the Ch. Sec. read it aloud to us at breakfast. 'I am glad to see opposite to my eye[4] the name of Mr Forster' (loud and continuous cheers),

I am glad that my reference to that name has been the means of provoking this testimony of your admiration which has been equal to the occasion and to the recollection of the splendid services personally rendered to the People of Ireland from pure and disinterested philanthropy. He represents in Ireland that cause which I hope will triumph. I have not lost confidence in the people of Ireland. . . . We ought to rely on Ireland but they have advantages and temptations offered to them—such as never before were presented to a people, and the trial of their virtue is severe.

After referring to the great impending crisis during which it would be seen what course the Irish people elected to follow, Mr G. ended his speech by saying:

when we have that short further experience to which I have referred, if it should then appear that there is still to be fought the final conflict in Ireland between law on the one side and sheer lawlessness on the other, if the law purged from defect and from any taint of injustice is still to be refused and the first conditions of political society to remain unfulfilled, then I say without hesitation that the resources of civilization are not yet exhausted. (cheers)[5] I shall recognise in full when the facts are ripe, and their ripeness is approaching, the duty and the responsibility of the Govt, I call upon all orders and degrees of men in these two kingdoms—in these three kingdoms—to support the Govt in the discharge of that duty—and in acquitting itself of that responsibility: and I for one—in that state of facts, relying upon my fellow countrymen in these three nations associated together, have not a doubt of the result.

[1] These four words are added from the report of the speech in *Irish Times*, 8 Oct. 1881.
[2] 'they' in *Irish Times* report.
[3] The passivity of the law-abiding was extensively discussed in the correspondence between Forster and Gladstone throughout October, with regard to the possibilities of raising special constables or other forms of aid from society.   [4] 'a name opposite me' in *Irish Times* report.
[5] Forster had suggested the theme 'now that we have made the law just, we are called upon to put down lawlessness with a strong hand' (Reid, *Forster*, ii, 346–8); an echo of his views at the time of the compensation bill.

Report in the morning papers of the Land League Meeting in Dublin—Mr P. in the chair.

Much annoyance expressed by some of the speakers at the conduct of Mr Fitzwilliam Dick, 'the richest man in Ireland' who is the moving spirit of the new anti-Boycotting Association in the Co. Wicklow, and who insists on supporting with his money a Boycotted Bank (the Munster Bank) which the Land League intended to ruin by a simultaneous withdrawal of deposits.

Walked with Father to the Park gates. He repeated the speech he was to make at the Lord Mayor's banquet in the evening in reply to the toast of the House of Commons—'must be very careful always to speak of the Imperial, not the British Parliament'.

On coming in I performed my unpleasant duty of reading the rebel papers. *United Ireland* is going ahead in every respect, and I believe its circulation is already very large. It is certainly the ablest of the whole set, and evidently wishes to appeal to the more educated class of Irishmen for their respect, being more akin to the *Nation* in the days of its editorship by Thomas Davis, Gavan Duffy and others.

I always come away from my study of these papers with my fists metaphorically clenched and feeling a Saxon to the backbone; the amount of lying, the misrepresentation, the gratuitous insolence they contrive to compress into a small compass is sickening, and yet at the same time there is a fervour of nationalism, an enthusiasm of hatred, a spirit of genial camaraderie of Irishmen of which I can quite understand the attraction. If ever there is civil war between England and Ireland, the *United Ireland* may fairly claim credit for a large share of the responsibility.

In the afternoon Mother, Oakel and I drove to Artane, and were hospitably entertained, and shown over the wonders of the great Institution by Sir John Lentaigne, Father Hoop,[1] and Brother Flynn.

The Duke of Teck[2] called about half past 5 in hopes of seeing the Ch. Sec., and being prompted for his speech at the Mansion House in the evening. He has come over to Ireland, it is said, in connection with some scheme promoted by a Mr Orrell Lever for the purchase of waste lands. He was asked to stay here, but declined, arrangements having been made for him at the Shelbourne.

Mother, Francie and I dined alone, all the rest of the party being at the Mansion House.

A quiet evening over the London papers—full of Mr Gladstone's great demonstration at Leeds—on the whole general approval of his speech about Ireland—the Conservative papers however being astonished at his 'audacity' in

[1] Fr Thomas Hoope, corresponding manager of the Industrial School for Catholic Males at Artane Castle, Artane, Co. Dublin.

[2] Francis Paul Charles Louis Alexander (1837–1900): only son of Duke Alexander of Württemberg; cr. prince of Teck, 1863; duke, 1871; married Mary Adelaide Wilhelmina Elizabeth (1833–97), daughter of 1st duke of Cambridge, 1866; naturalised in England, cr. colonel in British army and served with Wolseley in Egypt, 1882.

venturing to describe and denounce so plainly a state of things in Ireland for which he himself is responsible.

There can be no doubt that the mass of the Liberal party are thoroughly prepared to support the Govt in any strong measures they may think necessary to take in dealing with Mr Parnell, and his agitators.

From different quarters there comes evidence that the impatience and indignation at the continuance of outrage and intimidation is daily increasing. The Radicals, who before the passing of the Land Act were most strongly opposed to Coercion, will feel less scruple in applying strong measures now to those who defy the laws. Now that the law as Mr Gladstone says 'has been purged from defect and from any taint of injustice'.

Father and Mr B. Price did not get back from Dublin till past midnight. The evening had been a decided success, and the Ch. Sec. well received and allowed to make his speech (in which he had so far ventured on politics as to ask for a fair trial for the Land Act) without interruption, and even with applause.

This has been a great relief, for with such an assembly as was collected at the Mansion House, there was every chance of the Ch. Sec. being refused a hearing, or at least treated with some unpleasantness.

A very good speech had been made by the Mayor of Cork, whom Father had invited to dine with us the next day to meet Prince Teck.

9 Oct., Sun.

To church in the morning at the Hibernian; Father not able to come. Mr Jephson and Mr Cullinan to lunch, the latter leaving for London in the evening to have documents printed for the Cabinet that is to meet on Wednesday. With all important papers it is now becoming necessary to be more than ever careful.

It is pretty well ascertained that the post office here is no safe medium of communication, a recent letter from the Ch. Sec. to Mr Law having evidently been detained somewhere; as for the printing office here, that, it is known, cannot be trusted.

Walked in the afternoon with Father and Mr Price—some talk about Mr G's speech—and the future. It will have to be followed by action if necessary.

'Just what I have been telling Gladstone' says Mr Forster, 'his speech has done everything that words alone can do, but that will not be enough'.

Between post time and dinner a long visit to Father from Lord O'Hagan.

Prince Teck, Sir Patrick Keenan, Sir Bernard Burke, the Mayor of Cork[1] and Mrs O'Sullivan to dinner. Prince Teck, good humoured and easy mannered, with a certain amount of fun in him, and considerable perception of the relation of things and persons out here.

He amused me by informing me that my Father had been quite enchanted with the Mayor of Cork's speech at the Banquet the night before, and that he

[1] D. V. O'Sullivan.

was quite sure he had only invited him (Prince Teck) to dinner as an after-thought, and by way of 'buttering' Mr O'Sullivan. I assured His Serene Highness that I would tell my Father how completely he had been seen through, though I did not think in this particular case the Prince was quite right.

In the evening I had some talk with the Mayor of Cork, a vivacious fluent little man, who of course was barley sugar itself towards us, and very pressing in his invitation that we should come to Cork—at any rate next spring, when he believed the present state of things would be at an end. Whether or no the Govt could rely upon Mr O'Sullivan's loyalty, in any emergency requiring a great display of moral courage, is I think very doubtful; but at any rate one thing is certain, and that is that he has no sympathy whatever for Mr Parnell.

Like many others who dare not say so, he resents the tyranny of the Boy-cotting League, and has so far jumped the ditch which separates the Parnellites from moderate men of all classes, that, if he gives way to them, it will be from fear, not from sympathy.

Unfortunately the terror of being 'denounced' in the Land League papers (a fate which Mr O'Sullivan is daily expecting) or being otherwise injured is so great that up to the present time moderate men are just as little use in stemming the tide of lawlessness as the most active sympathisers.

Mr O'Sullivan told Mother that quite recently a series of violent Resolutions were drawn up at Cork and sent round for signature—out of 19 who signed them 14, to Mr O'Sullivan's own knowledge, entirely disapproved of, and detested the sentiments of the Resolutions, yet dared not refuse. Mr O'S. was probably one of the 14.

The only hope is that as the number of victims from boycotting increases, the chance of a successful combination against its cruelty will increase also. If the Govt take strong and sudden measures against it now, it may come just at the right time to strengthen a movement of resistance of which faint symptoms are becoming visible throughout the country.

The difficulty with these efforts of the anti-Parnellites to help themselves, is that from being accustomed to look to the Govt for everything, when they do begin to take matters into their own hands they have a tendency to break the law. Apropos of this Father mentioned on Sunday morning that late on Saturday afternoon he had been informed that the 'loyal Protestants' in Co. Wicklow had proclaimed their intention to attack and disperse a Land League meeting to be held at Baltinglass on Sunday afternoon.

It was too late to stop the meeting, so all that could be done was to send down extra police, and hope there would be no collision.

During Sunday afternoon and evening Father received 5 telegrams from different parts of the country reporting the effect of the various meetings. All reported quiet. From Wexford, Parnell reported to be making a violent speech, but no disturbance.

It was arranged that Oakel should go down to Belfast early the next day to take a message from the Ch. Sec. to Sir Thomas Steele: again the post appeared to have played false, a certain letter from Sir Thomas known to have been sent off not having arrived.

10 Oct., Mon.

Oakel went off before breakfast to Belfast. Mr Price also left us. Report in the papers of Mr Parnell's speech at Wexford—chiefly occupied with violent abuse of 'William Ewart Gladstone' but nothing to invoke immediate arrest.

Also a mischievous speech from Archbishop Croke, depreciating the Land Act, and urging the people not to pay rent till they had satisfied all their natural desires and requirements in the way of lodging, food and clothing. 'As bad a speech as it could possibly be', said the Ch. Sec.

Reports of the speeches at the Mansion House on Saturday—Mr Forster said by the *Freeman* to have been enthusiastically cheered. This curious phenomenon has surprised us a good deal, in fact both Sir Bernard B[urke] and Sir P. Keenan told us that when they saw who and what sort of people were going to be present at the Banquet, they had been quite prepared for some sort of disagreeable scene.

Mr G's great meeting in the Cloth Hall at Leeds has gone off splendidly—25,000 people present. This time the speech was mainly a review of the foreign policy of the Govt.

We are so much absorbed in Ireland that I have said nothing of the events that have been occupying attention in other places—Egypt—where there has been a revolt of the military against the authority of the Khedive and the Anglo-French control, and, in the complications that followed, threatening of more serious international danger from possible difference of opinion between France and England with regard to their respective claims.

The *Spectator* came out the week before last with a most warlike article on the necessity for England maintaining a paramount influence in Egypt, even at the cost of a rupture with France, and of course there has been no lack of disposition in France and elsewhere to take up a similar tone with regard to England. It now seems however that harmony is likely to be restored, and that the Governments of the two countries are united in the intention to maintain a joint control over Egypt and the Egyptian Govt without interference from the Sultan, who has been shewing a strong desire to meddle in the character of the Khedive's suzerain.

Our difficulties with the Transvaal are by no means at an end. The Volksraad has refused to ratify the Convention agreed to by the Boer Triumvirate and Sir E. Wood at the close of the war. They demand important modifications in the terms, and intimate that they intend to be satisfied with nothing short of complete independence and entire control over the Native population.

Such Radicals as Mr Passmore Edwards (of the *Echo*)[1] and to a certain degree the *Pall Mall Gazette* seem disposed to grant the Boers anything they may require, but the country generally is more likely to support Mr Gladstone when he declared on Saturday that

what we attempted to do was equal justice, and in attempting to grant that justice to the Dutch population we never for a moment forgot what was due to other considerations, to the rights of the native tribes, and to the general peace of S. Africa. Those men are mistaken—if such there be—who judge that our liberal concessions were the effect of weakness or timidity, and who think because we granted much that it was only to encourage them to ask for more.

Monday afternoon Mother and I drove into Dublin, and went to see Mr A. Burke's picture of the Wexford coast at his studio in Stephen's Green—also to Chancellor's for Mother to protest against their publishing the photograph they have just taken of Father; it is so bad that to exhibit it in the shop windows would be to play into the hands of the Land League.

On coming back to tea we found Mr Tuke arrived from Mayo to dine and sleep before returning to England. His picture of the state of society in those desolate regions was very graphic, and he had every opportunity of seeing things for himself—driving 300 miles about the country on an outside car with Mr Henry Robinson, the popular poor-law inspector.

Certainly the picture was disheartening enough—the miserable tenant families turned out of their cabins on the roadside—the landlord who had turned them out (or, in the specially sad case, the landlady, Mrs Blake of Renvyle) nearly as miserable as themselves—with no money, hardly food enough to eat, and the concentrated hatred of the whole district directed against herself and her family—men known to have planned or committed murder going about their daily business, their employer not daring to turn them off much less denounce them for fear of being himself 'boycotted' or murdered—the unpopular land agent obliged to drive about the country fully armed, the driver of his car instinctively lowering his head and lashing on his horse when they came to a wooded ascent of the road, to avoid the bullets which might at any moment be fired over the hedge.[2]

The priests—all but two, Father Hewson and Father Ronayne—marked men, tolerating if not encouraging the general lawlessness, and teaching the people that the Land Act was the fruit of agitation and crime, and that to extract the full advantage it needed a continuance in the same easy and congenial procedure.

Mr Tuke is by no means an excitable man likely to be impressed with a panic-stricken view of things, nor is he in the very least prejudiced against the

---

[1] John Passmore Edwards (1823–1911): philanthropist, editor, and liberal M.P. for Salisbury (1880–85); proprietor of the *Echo*, first halfpenny newspaper, 1876–96.

[2] Mrs Blake's view of the situation at Renvyle is given in a series of letters to the Castle (S.P.O., R.P., 1881/44601), exemplifying the apprehensions of landowners.

people, but after this further close personal acquaintance with them, he is very much impressed with their incapacity for self-government, and with the misfortune of having to deal with Ireland on the principle of its being as well-fitted for constitutional government as England.

In fact, at the present time, even such a benevolent liberal-minded Quaker as Mr Tuke, fresh from his recent experience in many of the actual conditions of society, would be almost prepared to tolerate the introduction of Martial law, and the complete suppression of the Land League.[1] What would the *P.M.G.* say?

The O'Conor Don dined with us. It was evident at dinner that the day had been a bad one with Father. Presently it came out that there had been fresh outrages in Clare—also another disagreeable fact, the reversal by the Magistrates of Major Traill, R.M.'s[2] recent sentence on Father Conway,[3] the notorious priest of Clonbur. For an assault on a process server, Major Traill had sentenced Father Conway to 2 months' hard labour—knowing that the sentence would be reversed on appeal, but wishing to prevent the man getting off triumphantly with the payment of a fine.

The Magistrates, not having the courage of Major Traill, have annulled the sentence altogether—a complete triumph as Father says for the Land League. 'Things are worse now' he says 'than they have been yet'.

Oakel returned this evening from Belfast. Sir Thomas Steele also coming up to Dublin in order to see the Ch. Sec. before his going to the Cabinet.

11 Oct., Tu.

The sight of the headings in the *Irish Times* this morning was enough to depress the most sanguine. 'Fatal Riot at Ballyragget, Kilkenny. One man killed and several wounded'—'Incendiary Fires in Co. Kildare. Burning of Haggards'—'Daring Outrage in Co. Clare'—'Fearful outrage near Doneraile'—'Attack on a Process serving party at Westport'—etc. etc.

Another speech of Mr Parnell's at Wexford—which has been giving him an enthusiastic welcome.

A long visit to Father this morning from Sir Thomas Steele—all preparations have to be made for a certain possible contingency, i.e. the arrest of Mr Parnell, and his principal accomplices.

For once no rumour of this possibility has leaked out. Last year the *Freeman* and others were busy with reports of what was coming, sometime before the State Prosecutions were announced.

Apropos of the *Freeman* Mr Gray has run away and left no address. He is said

---

[1] Cf. Tuke, *Irish distress and its remedies . . .* (London and Dublin, 1880), p. 89, accepting the need for repression if remedies could not be applied.

[2] Robert Gayer Traill (1839–1908): formerly major in the 19th Foot, now R.M. at Ballinrobe, Co. Mayo; younger brother of Anthony Traill, later provost of Trinity College, Dublin.

[3] See below, p. 306.

to have declared to someone that his position was intolerable, as he richly deserves it should be. His fear is of being outrun and perhaps denounced by the more violent papers of the same party with whom he has never had in reality, I imagine, much sympathy, but in whose wake he has allowed his paper to follow. Now if the extreme party desert it, the *Freeman* will be left with little enough support, having quite forfeited the claim it once had to be considered a decent independent paper.

As an organ of the Land League it will soon be outdone by *United Ireland*, and as anything else it has no standing at all.

Drove with Father to the Castle, whence he crosses to-night to London. The decision of this Cabinet will be critical.

Calls this afternoon from Mrs Litton and Mrs Robinson (of the Local Govt Board) and Mother of Mr H. Robinson of Mayo. Mrs Litton has promised to get us seats for the opening of the Land Court on Thursday week the 20th.

Aunt Fan arrived by the evening boat, accompanied to our surprise by Mrs Vaughan, who was staying near Holyhead and had come over for one night to see us.

12 Oct., Wed.

Speeches reported this morning by Lord Salisbury, and Sir S. Northcote at Newcastle, and Mr Dillon at the Land League Meeting in Dublin. Lord S., as might be expected, a vigorous and epigrammatic attack on the Govt—especially with reference to Ireland—

for the present state of the country Mr G. was responsible—he having undertaken for electioneering purposes to govern Ireland on an absolutely new policy—that of concession to violence—on the principle of 'Squeeze and you shall obtain'. As to Mr Parnell and his doctrine of public plunder, plunder was the basis of Mr G's own policy—the practice of the Liberal party being to 'cleanse its conscience with regard to Ireland by robbing the landlords of their property in order to pacify the people', etc. etc.

Mr Dillon's speech consisted mainly of a vindication of himself from the charge of deserving Mr Gladstone's 'compliments'.[1] He explained once more his attitude of entire hostility to the Land Act, but protested his entire adhesion to his leader, Mr Parnell, and his intention not to oppose the policy of 'test cases' as decided upon at the Convention.

Before the close of the Meeting a speech was made by the English Democrat Mr Frederick. In allusion to this Mr Dillon observed that he had given up believing in much support from the English working men—a well-founded scepticism.

[1] In his Leeds speech, Gladstone had claimed Dillon as 'an opponent whom I am glad to honour' for not opposing the land act (Lyons, *Dillon*, p. 56).

A lovely morning. Mr West and I had a gallop in the Park immediately after breakfast; this place is certainly a paradise for horses.

A telegram from Father reporting that he had not been ill, and his cold better.

A call in the course of the morning from a Miss Isabel Trench to consult Mother as to a proposed 'Association for the relief of distressed Irish Ladies', some of whom from the sudden failure of all means of support by the withholding of rent have actually been forced to go into the workhouse.

Mother gave Miss Trench all the encouragment and advice in her power, and we have promised to do what we can towards making the association known amongst our friends in England.

A letter will be sent to the newspapers on the subject, and the Dublin correspondent of the *Times* has promised to mention it, and I quite expect that people in England will be very glad to help. Indeed there is every reason to encourage any attempt that may be made by private and voluntary endeavour to meet the distress caused in various ways by the present deliberate attack upon property.

There are signs that a spirit of combined resistance to the selfish and cruel tyranny of the Parnellites is beginning to arise in different parts of the country: a desire, as a correspondent of the *Evening Mail* puts it, 'to leave off railing at the Govt' and show Mr G. that after all there is some moral support to be found amongst law-abiding people in Ireland.

There never was more need of combination against evil than at this time; the most cruel outrages are daily committed against defenceless persons who are suspected of having paid their rent, or worked for a 'boycotted' man, and on one estate after another—now on Lord Rosse's, now on Judge Fitzgerald's[1]—the tenants have combined in refusing absolutely to pay any rent at all.

Certainly, honest and well intentioned Land Leaguers—if such there be—must feel that the cause of the Land League is being terribly discredited.

Mrs Vaughan left us by the evening mail to return to Llandaff. A quiet evening, and a family party, Mr West having gone to the theatre with Prince Teck.

It was arranged that Oakel should meet Father the next morning at Kingstown.

13 Oct., Th.

Father and Oakel did not arrive at the usual time from Westland Row, having gone round I was told by the Castle.

I wondered whether anything particular was happening. Before I left my

---

[1] Laurence Parsons (1840–1908): 4th Earl Rosse since 1867, owned 22,513 acres in King's County and 2,633 in Tipperary, worth £8,964 and £1,496 respectively. Judge Fitzgerald owned 2,717 acres, worth £1,324, almost equally divided between Clare and Limerick, as well as 9 acres in Dublin worth £124.

room Mother came to tell me that the warrant was out for the arrest of Mr Parnell. Father had arrived 'seeming well, and with the satisfaction of feeling that he had come back with full power to act as he thought best—the Cabinet was very strong about Mr Parnell'.[1]

At that moment he was closeted with Sir Thomas Steele, making the necessary arrangements about troops, etc. in case a display of force should be necessary.

We all sat round the table at breakfast this morning in a curious state of quiet excitement, Father looking wonderfully fresh and untired after his two journeys, and, as usual with him after a crisis has come and a resolution definitely taken, seeming cheerful, composed and vigorous.

Oakel's face wearing an expression of calm satisfaction—Mr Jephson's not less.

In the middle of breakfast a note was brought to the Ch. Sec.—'My dear Mr Forster, Anderson[2] has just written to you to say that Parnell has been arrested and is by this time in Kilmainham, yours very truly, John Naish'.

Very little comment on this welcome piece of intelligence—an ejaculation of relief from Mother that it had been accomplished without a hitch (she no doubt having vivid recollections of the bungle over Mr Dillon's arrest), and a subdued but emphatic hand clapping from Mr Jephson.

Their secret has been wonderfully well kept this time, though Mr West says the idea was beginning to get out in Dublin yesterday that 'something was up' as one of the A.D.C.s said to him. The newspaper accounts of the Cabinet discussion are even fuller than usual but there is no suggestion of the truth, it being even stated that the question of Ireland was relegated to a second Cabinet to be held in a day or two.

Father went into Dublin with Oakel and the two secretaries almost immediately after breakfast, leaving us to a quiet day here.

At this moment—3.25—the rain is falling in torrents, and half shuts out the view—always peaceful enough. As I sit here writing with Chatty[3] curled up on my lap and Yarrow lying beside me, we seem far enough removed from all danger and excitement, and yet I cannot help fancying that I heard just now the sound of a bugle—then of shots in the distance, the shouting of a mob—it is probably all fancy—and I hope that when they come out from Dublin this evening they will know nothing about it.

[1] According to Gladstone's report to the queen, the cabinet, after careful consultation with the Irish law officers and Lord Selborne, agreed to the following course of action: (i) the immediate arrest of Parnell and other central leaders, followed by provincial arrests; (ii) arrests for treasonable speeches; (iii) prohibition, at the discretion of the Irish government, of meetings endangering the public peace or tending to intimidation (*Letters of Queen Victoria*, iii, 242–3).

[2] Samuel Lee Anderson (1837–86): brother of Robert (see below, p. 449), crown solicitor for Kilkenny and Waterford; like his brother an expert on Fenian matters, he worked closely in the chief secretary's office with Sir Thomas Larcom and Thomas Henry Burke, successive undersecretaries.

[3] Chattenooga, the Forster cat.

The arrest of Mr Parnell will I hope give strength and nucleus to all the isolated efforts that are being made throughout the country on behalf of law and justice: it will come just at the right moment, and will give proof—if proof were needed—that the Govt have not resigned their powers into the hands of the Land League, and the arch-representative of treason and anarchy.

Mr Parnell's influence during the past few weeks has been used wholly and solely in encouraging the Irish people to break the law themselves, and to punish by the infliction of cruel and malicious injuries those who refuse to do so.

Whilst lesser men have been arrested and imprisoned he has been parading the country in triumph—defying the Govt, defying the Land Court, defying the power of law-abiding citizens to resist the terrible pressure that he can bring to bear through the organization of the Land League upon Irishmen who refuse to become Parnellites.

And yet though he has carried his policy of defiance and insult to this length, there will probably be no man in Ireland more surprised at his arrest than himself.

The sounds I heard yesterday were all imaginary, I am thankful to say. At 6 o'clock Father and Oakel returned from Dublin, and it was at once evident from their bearing and tone of voice that no catastrophe had taken place since they left us in the morning.

The Ch. Sec. had had a hard day's work, but seemed in no way disheartened. He had been well satisfied with the way in which the secret had been kept, and all those immediately concerned had done their business—especially Capt. Talbot, to whom he had spoken very warmly on the subject—not even Mr Hamilton[1] (now taking Mr B[urke]'s place at the office) knew what had been done till he arrived at the Castle yesterday morning. As Father explained to him this was from no want of confidence, but simply from the importance of no one but those actually concerned knowing what was going to be done.

The possibility of Mr P's arrest being decided upon had induced the Ch. Sec. to make preparations before leaving on Monday.

As soon as he reached London and saw that 'he was going to have his way' he telegraphed to Dublin to have the warrants made out, and on reaching Kingstown on Thursday morning all he had to do was to go straight to the Castle and sign his name to them.

Mr Parnell, he told us, had behaved like a gentleman—the police inspector, on going to Morrison's hotel about 8.30, was informed by the servants that Mr Parnell was not there, but he assured them that he knew to the contrary, by informing them that Mr P. was in No 21, and that if he was not shown to his room at once he should be obliged to have every room in the hotel searched by the police force which he had with him.

Mr Parnell seemed surprised but perfectly composed—asked leave to finish

---

[1] Thomas Hamilton, previously R.M. at Portarlington, who, on 18 July, had been appointed a first-class clerk in the chief secretary's office, with special responsibility for police and crime.

and post three letters, and himself suggested that he should leave the hotel by a back door in order to avoid a scene. This however the inspector assured him was not necessary, and as soon as Mr Parnell had dressed and breakfasted he drove off quietly in a cab with the inspector from the front—there being at that time in the morning no crowd or excitement of any kind.[1]

As to disturbance in the evening, Father did not think there was much cause for anxiety—placards announcing Meetings and processions were being issued, but all precautions had been taken—troops were quartered in every part of the city, and two small guns had even been placed in the Castle yard. The place where there was most fear of riot was Cork.

Another bad murder to-day—a man shot in the Co. Longford, it is believed for having given evidence in a Boycotting case.[2]

Mr Herbert Gladstone arrived from Hawarden by the evening boat. He had not heard till Father told him of the arrest of Mr Parnell; apparently there had been no talk of it on the boat or in [the] train, and no placards or other signs of excitement to enlighten him in Dublin.

The idea of Mr G. coming here is that he may learn by practical experience something of official work, especially of Irish work in order that as 'Junior Lord of the Treasury', he may be able to officially assist the Ch. Sec. in the House by answering questions, getting up special subjects, etc. There is considerable interest and speculation in the papers about his visit here—the *Irish Times* and *Freeman* stating in an imposing paragraph that he has come to represent the Treasury in the financial dealings of the Govt apropos of the new Land Commission.

He seems an amiable, intelligent young man, and we all feel kindly disposed to him from the way he has just been speaking about Mr Forster at Leeds, telling the people in speaking of his coming here that 'he could not be going to serve under a greater or worthier chief'.

Report in the *Evening Mail* of Mr Gladstone's speech at the Guildhall. In the middle of his speech Father's telegram was brought to him announcing Mr P's arrival at Kilmainham. When he announced the fact of Mr P's arrest, the audience rose to their feet, cheering and waving their hats, in appreciation of the fact that the Premier's strong words at Leeds were being followed by strong action.

These demonstrations of triumph over the imprisonment of a man who should be our fellow-countryman, and not our enemy, are rather painful—though it must be allowed that the expression of hostile feeling against a man who has for many years past lost no opportunity to insult and vilify the English people and the English Govt is not unnatural.

Father Sheehy and Mr Egan have left Ireland.

[1] See R. B. O'Brien, *Parnell*, i, 307–14; F. S. L. Lyons, *Parnell*, pp 167–9.

[2] At about 7–8 p.m. on 12 Oct., William Lawlor, a letter carrier, was knocked down by two men who emptied their revolvers into him. However, he did not die; three men were arrested and later discharged, and another was acquitted at the assizes (S.P.O., I.C.R., Returns of outrages, Oct. 1881).

14 Oct., Fri.

A terrific gale in the night, and great devastation amongst the trees. Carpenter does not remember having seen such havoc since the storm of 1839.[1]

In one respect we were grateful to the weather, for it effectually prevented any exhibition of feeling in the way of processions and out-of-door meetings last night.

Miss Dixon to breakfast: it was evident from Father's face as he looked through the Irish papers that something was deeply annoying. This turned out to be the report of an interview with Mr Parnell after his arrival at Kilmainham. How could this have been allowed? The carriage was ordered for half past 10 and word was sent off to Capt. Barlow and Mr C. Bourke[2] to meet the Ch. Sec. at the Castle at 11.

The language of the *Freeman* is just what might be expected: happily, both in its leader and in Mr Dillon's speech at the Land League Meeting, the people are conjured not to let their indignation make them transgress the law, and O'Connell's saying about the 'man who commits a crime' etc. is again quoted—rather late in the day unfortunately.

In the afternoon Mother, Miss Dixon and I drove into Dublin, calling first on Miss Burke whom we found deploring the wreck of her favourite trees. Seven elm trees in their garden have been blown down—in some cases torn clear up by the roots, carrying quite a large tract of field with it.

Mr Burke is expected back to-morrow, having been recalled by telegram from Paris. Lord Cowper returns either on Saturday or Monday. Miss Burke I need hardly say is delighted at the arrest of Mr Parnell. Apropos of this she told us that Mr Teeling—a relation of Lord O'Hagan's first wife,[3] and much connected by family association with the extreme party—met Mr John Dillon in the street yesterday. 'This is a strong thing your friends have been doing', he said—to which Mr Teeling answered 'well now, between you and me and the post, don't you think that it was not a bit too soon?' On which Mr Dillon only laughed, and then went his way to make a flaming speech at the Land League Meeting.

Before coming out of Dublin Mother went to call on the Ch. Sec. at the Castle. She found him overwhelmed with work, he had been busy all day seeing police inspectors and others from different parts of the country—getting detailed information as to the necessary people to arrest, and preparing a Proclamation on the subject of Boycotting.

Other leaders will soon follow Mr Parnell, Mr Sexton I believe is already by this time in Kilmainham, and Mr A. O'Connor will probably join him.[4]

[1] The gale, the worst recorded since 1855, affected Europe generally; wind speeds of 84 m.p.h. were recorded at Kingstown pier.

[2] Capt. J. Barlow, vice-chairman of the general prisons board, Ireland. Charles Fowler Bourke, C.B., son of 5th earl of Mayo, and chairman of that board.

[3] Mary, daughter of Bartholomew Teeling (1774–98), United Irishman.

[*See p. 274 for n. 4*]

There is rioting going on in Cork, but we know no details.

Nothing could look quieter or less excited than the streets of Dublin this afternoon—here and there a placard—'Latest Outrage—Arrest of C. S. Parnell—Indignation Meeting', etc. but these were few and far between, and there were no crowds, or other signs of the Citizens of Dublin feeling much impressed by the appeals made to them. No doubt the danger will be in the country districts, where Father fears a fresh epidemic of isolated crime and outrage.

Father dined in the evening, with Sir Thomas Steele at the Royal Hospital.

15 Oct., Sat.

Reports of the Meeting at the Rotunda to protest against Mr Parnell's arrest. Mr Dawson (Lord Mayor elect) in the chair. Speeches of indignation from Mr Dawson, Mr Dwyer Gray; Mr Biggar as usual confined himself chiefly to personal abuse; Mr Dillon strongly incited to the Non-payment of rent as an effective measure of retaliation.[1] The meeting appears to have been very crowded and enthusiastic, but the police kept the street outside clear, and there was no disturbance . . . [*sic*].

The Irish papers are full of reports of indignation Resolutions passed by various Land League branches all over the country, but there does not appear to have been any serious disturbance even in Cork where there was the most cause for anxiety.

As for the English papers, they are almost unanimous (the exception being Mr Cowen's paper) in approval of the strong measures taken by the Govt. Even the *P.M.G.* has been carried away for the moment with the current of opinion; it also publishes a very helpful and on the whole approving letter from Mr Goldwin Smith, on the action of the Govt with regard to the present crisis.

Some even of the Irish Liberal papers allow that matters had come to such a pass that the Govt had no choice between defying Mr Parnell, and allowing themselves and their policy to be defied by him—but the great majority— Liberal as well as Land League—declare the arrest to be, at best, a gigantic blunder—proving once more the inability of English statesmen to deal with Ireland. The expression of this opinion was of course a foregone conclusion.

Walked with Father to the Park gates.

A brilliant afternoon, drove with Mother and Aunt Fan to Abbotstown and Woodlands. Mr Hamilton of Abbotstown,[2] whom we had not yet seen, came to

[4] Sexton was arrested at 3.00 p.m. on 14 Oct.; a warrant for O'Connor had been issued but not executed, and he indeed visited Kilmainham on this day.

[1] Dillon did not propose 'no rent' as a policy advised by the league executive, but left it open to local branches to adopt it on their own initiative; see Lyons, *Dillon*, pp 57–9.

[2] Ion Trant Hamilton (1839–98), conservative M.P. for Dublin County, 1863–85, his father having represented it 1841–63; owned 3,647 acres in Co. Dublin and 2,245 in Queen's County.

the carriage door to introduce himself, and express his approval of Father's conduct—'he only hoped the Govt would not stop there'.

A call on coming in, from Mr Aubrey de Vere who varied the usual strain of Irish conversation by discoursing pleasantly of Wordsworth.

Of course however, there was also talk of the crisis and the arrests, of which Mr de Vere quite approved, as tending to free the people from the demoralising tyranny of the League.

Father very late home to dinner. A summons to me from Oakel to come to his room and hear what had been going on. Mr Dillon re-arrested—Mr William O'Brien, editor of *United Ireland* also arrested.

There had been symptoms of a disturbance over the arrest of Mr Dillon, and Captain Talbot had hurried up to the Castle with a request for troops to clear the streets if necessary—Father had gone to the Turkish Baths near Kildare St Club, whence Oakel had to bring him back to the Castle. The appearance of the Guards upon the scene soon produced the desired effect and there seemed no fear of further disturbance.

An evening over the newspapers—hearty support still from all sides in England—even Mr Ashton Dilke and Mr Burt having spoken in approval of the Govt.

At 12.30 we were startled by a ring at the front door. Col. Hillier came to ask for extra troops to support the Constabulary at Limerick, where disturbance was expected the next day. Father had to be roused from his bed, and go deeply into the question of military possibilities. 500, as asked for, could not be spared, but 200 of the Guards were to be sent off by special train that night.

From here Col. Hillier went off to 'knock up' Lord Clarina:[1] and a little later Father sent off an orderly to Sir T. Steele, his answer also arriving in the middle of the night, so that there was no peaceful division between the anxieties of Saturday and Sunday.

16 Oct., Sun.

By the time we came down to breakfast Father was already up, and had begun to receive telegrams. Rioting at Mallow—All quiet so far at Limerick—Rioting in Dublin last night.

A lovely autumn morning. Father, Aunt Fan, Oakel and I drove into Dublin in the open carriage intending to go to service at the Chapel Royal. As we were too early we went first to the Ch. Sec.'s Office, and here the Ch. Sec. found it necessary to remain, so we had to go to the lonely grandeur of our State pew in the Chapel Royal without him.

The sermon was preached by Archdeacon Bell of Cashel,[2] who at the end spoke a few grave helpful words about the present crisis, and of our own responsibility, which made me glad to have been there.

[1] Now G.O.C., Dublin military district; above, p. 253.
[2] Robert Bell (1808?–83): canon of St Patrick's, Dublin; archdeacon of Cashel since 1872.

From the Chapel we drove to the office to take up Father: Mr Law, Mr Jephson, and Mr Naish came up to speak to us, but they were not encouraging as to the possibility of the Ch. Sec.'s getting away. The Land Leaguers, after intimating their intention not to hold a park meeting, were meaning to do so, and the Govt were going to stop it; consequently due precautions had to be taken.

As Aunt Fan and I waited in the carriage we had the opportunity of seeing various members of the Irish Executive—Mr Burke (who has just returned), Mr Johnson, Lord Clarina, Capt. Talbot, etc., etc.—all the legal and military authorities seemed congregating round the Ch. Sec., and our chances of carrying him off more and more doubtful. This was unfortunate, as Prince Teck had invited himself to lunch, and we knew Mother would not wish to entertain him alone.

At last a little before 2, Father and Mr Law emerged and joined us, seeming in no way depressed—all was quiet at Limerick, Mallow, and Cork, and no one appeared much afraid of disturbance in Dublin over the prohibited meeting.

As we drove along the quays and through the Park we met swarms of people—at one time a regular crowd, all trooping towards the City. Various suggestions as to what it could all mean—preparation for the meeting?—but why did they all come from, as well as go towards the same place?—had they been holding an indignation meeting already in the Park? At last Father stopped the carriage and asked a policeman—then the mystery was explained— the crowd was simply coming away from the Sunday Wrestling Match which takes place every week on the Nine Acres.

Certainly the demeanour of the people was anything but threatening or disagreeable, and though Father was evidently the object of much curiosity there was not a word of incivility or insult.

On coming home we found Prince Teck already arrived: he had been making poor Mother uneasy by describing the crowds in the streets, and urging her to telegraph to the Ch. Sec. not to venture back from the Castle. He himself had just been recalled to England by a telegram from the Queen—and would be obliged to give up dining at Woodlands, and return by the evening boat.

After lunch Father took Prince Teck out for a short walk but was soon brought in by Major Browne[1] with a message from Sir Thomas Steele, and was then closeted for the best part of the afternoon in the study with Mr Law— chiefly I believe over the question Shall the Govt seize the Land League office in Dublin?—eventually decided in the negative.[2]

To afternoon service at the Hibernian with Mother and Aunt Fan. Lord and Lady O'Hagan to afternoon tea—they having driven down in a state of much anxiety to know what was happening in Dublin, and what was the meaning of

[1] Aide-de-camp to the commander of the forces.
[2] In accordance with the law officers' opinion of 30 Sept. that committees could not be dispersed or offices closed without risk of legal actions in reply (B.L., Add. MS 44627, ff 85–8).

Prince Teck's note announcing his immediate departure, and adding mysteriously—'Mr Forster will explain all'.

Between 5 and 6 Father was persuaded to lie down in the study and sleep—Mother meantime intercepting the telegrams which arrived for him, reporting the state of things at different places where meetings were to be held—all quiet so far.

Soon after 7, Father, Mr H. Gladstone, Oakel and I drove over to dine at Woodlands. Met the Ardilauns, Archbishop McCabe, Sir Patrick Keenan, John O'Hagans etc.

On our return a little before 12, Father found a telegram from Limerick—'stone throwing going on, and some shots fired on the police'—not a pleasant message to go to bed upon.

Still on the whole the day which everyone considered to be a very critical one has passed off without serious disturbance in any part of Ireland—and this is something to be very thankful for.

17 Oct., Mon.

The Irish papers full of detailed accounts of the 'violent conduct of the police in clearing the streets last night'—'Scandalous scenes' etc.

The police do appear to have carried out their instructions to clear the streets and prevent the mob taking possession of the thoroughfares with great vigour, and to have used their batons perhaps too indiscriminately [I think not—W.E.F.] but on the other hand it is clear that if they had not done so the rowdy element, the 'corner boys' and public house men, would have been in riotous possession of the streets as they were on the night of the Torch light procession.[1]

The police themselves suffered a good deal, and this is not surprising, as the *Freeman* itself mentions incidentally that a gang of roughs, collected round the Nelson Pillar, made a point of attacking every 'individual' policeman they could lay hands on.

However the sturdy Dublin police appear to have held their own, and there was no occasion to call in the aid of the Military who are nowadays kept strictly to barracks.

Walked with Father to the Park gates. For the first time I realized (Herbert Gladstone pointing out the fact)[2] how carefully the Chief Secretary is looked after; two mounted constabulary follow him down the road, one policeman walks behind on one side and a detective in plain clothes on the other.

I must own they manage it as little disagreeably as they can, which is

[1] Above, p. 250.
[2] Cf. Herbert Gladstone's diary entry for this date in A. B. Cooke and J. R. Vincent (ed.), 'Herbert Gladstone, Forster, and Ireland, 1881–2 (I)' in *I.H.S.*, xvii, no. 68 (Sept. 1971), pp 530–31. And also West, *Recollections 1832–86*, ii, 115.

fortunate, as poor Father dislikes being confronted with any of these pre-cautions. As for me I have been hitherto quite unaware of them, and was under the agreeable delusion that in our daily walks through the Park I was the Ch. Secretary's policeman.

On coming in read the Sedition papers.

Mrs Vernon and her daughter to lunch. A brilliant afternoon. Mother, Aunt Fan and Francie to the Zoological Garden—I for a ride in the park on Paris. My favourite view of Dublin and the Liffey from the Magazine Hill, more beautiful than ever.

Oakel and I in the evening to the [Gaiety] theatre to see 'Olivette',[1] Col. and Mrs Dease having offered us two seats in the V.R. Box. Any allusion to arrest or locking up taken up at once with cheering by the audience.

On coming out we were told there had been a row going on, but we saw nothing of it; heard from Mr Morris that the mob had been breaking the windows of the *Evening Mail* at the top of Parliament St.—when we passed, however, all was quiet there.

On coming in found Mr West also just returned from Dublin; a cypher telegram (expressing her uneasiness) had been received from the Queen, and Mr West had been obliged to ride off at 11 o'clock to the Castle to bring out the key.

He reported that a Constabulary orderly carrying letters from here to the Castle had been stoned by the mob in Parliament St, and nearly knocked off his horse. Considering that Mr West had ridden along the Quays and up to the Castle within a quarter of an hour of the poor constabulary man, it was fortunate that he had not come in for any rough treatment himself.

However, as he points out, he was not in uniform, which is the great provocation to insult.[2]

In the course of the day Father had received a deputation of the Lord Mayor and Members of the Corporation to protest against the conduct of the police, and request that it might not occur again. The deputation was the result of a lively meeting of Town Councillors, at which the Lord Mayor (Mr Moyers) had been obliged to preside, and at which Mr Dawson, Mr Gray and others had spoken.

Mr Gray (who has returned from the Continent in consequence of Mr Parnell's arrest) worked himself up into a state of frenzy, expressing his deliberate belief that the Govt had ordered the police to irritate the people in order to provoke disturbance, and give an excuse for firing upon them.

The reply of the Ch. Sec. to the remonstrance of the deputation was a plain statement of the necessities of the situation, and a defence of the police, who

[1] H. B. Farnie's *opéra comique*, produced by Charles Windham's and Richard D'Oyly Carte's Olivette Opera Company. This was its first night at the Gaiety; it had already had 300 perform-ances at the Strand theatre, London, and was still playing there.

[2] This is possibly the incident referred to in West, *Recollections 1832–86*, ii, 112–13.

had received orders to clear the streets and were quite justified in doing so. If the gentlemen on the deputation knew the facts as he did, they would acknowledge that the executive could not have done otherwise if it meant to protect the law-abiding citizens. As for consulting the Lord Mayor about the measures to be taken, the Executive Govt and not the Lord Mayor was responsible for the peace of the city, and to have evaded this responsibility by professing to consult with him would have been cowardly. As for not using similar measures in future, he could not undertake to give any such promise.

18 Oct., Tu.

Walked with Father to the Park gates, afterwards going with Oakel to the Constabulary Barracks to enquire on Father's behalf after the man who was hurt yesterday. He is in hospital, but will soon, it is hoped, be all right again. He behaved very pluckily, galloping straight through a shower of stones, one of which all but knocked him out of the saddle.

On the way back read the accounts of yesterday's meeting of the Corporation and the Deputation. Mr Gray has sent a letter to the papers to say (amongst other things) that after hearing the Ch. Sec.'s statement, he feels bound to retract the charge he made before the Corporation as to the Govt's intention to provoke a collision.

A call in the afternoon from Lady Ferguson, and Miss Guinness. The mob had streamed past their house in North Gt George St on Monday night, breaking some of their windows in sheer rowdiness—in fact, as Lord Monteagle put it in a letter I had from him, the rioting both in Dublin and Limerick had seemed to be more 'rowdyism than agrarian'.

Mr and Mrs Murrough O'Brien arrived about 7 to dine and sleep. A dinner party in the evening—Robinsons, Mrs and Miss Williams, Findlater[1] (he, like Mr Maurice Brooks, M.P.,[2] has fairly jumped the ditch and has nothing to hope from keeping on good terms with the Land Leaguers) Mr Brady (Inspector of Fisheries), Mr Anderson, Mr Cornwall, and Mr Gerald Fitzgerald (our Chamonix friend).

Everyone full of the rioting in Dublin; anxious enquiries 'was it quiet when you came through?' The Robinsons had seen knots of roughs parading the streets, and declared that their carriage had been hissed as they drove along the quays. Mr Cornwall—very gloomy about the bad state of feeling in the city.

The most cheering talk I have had for a long time about anything Irish was with Mr Thomas Brady[3]—a good humoured, vigorous looking man, with a rosy weather-beaten face, and twinkling blue eyes. His work at least, in helping the

[1] William Huffington Findlater (1824–1906): president of Incorporated Law Society of Ireland, 1878; liberal M.P. for County Monaghan, 1880–85.
[2] Maurice Brooks (b. 1823): home rule M.P. for Dublin city, 1874–85; lord mayor of Dublin, 1874.
[3] Thomas Francis Brady (1824–1904): inspector of Irish fisheries since 1860.

poor fishermen along the western coasts, has not been labour thrown away; instead of ruin caused by misfortune, or prosperity produced by dishonesty, his stories were of genuine good results obtained by giving timely assistance and helping the starving peasants to help themselves by honest work. Mr Brady's enthusiasm about his protégés was quite touching, and I believe that he is personally known and loved by every fisherman along the Irish coasts.

'Oh, Miss Forster' he exclaimed, when I asked him some questions about the Fisheries—'I am glad you are interested about it, it's a subject about which I am positively insane'.

Apropos of these small Western farmers of whom he has such an intimate knowledge, Mr Brady told Mother a curious incident. He had called an assembly of them together to settle some question as to the terms of a loan, and took the opportunity to speak to them very plainly about the duty of behaving like honest men and paying their just debts in spite of the Land League. When he had left one of the men followed him to say 'that was very right what you said Sir—I'm the biggest Leaguer in the country, and I wish to God I could be put down, and allowed to go about my business in peace'.

There have been various signs (even in the Land League papers) lately that the tyranny of the Local branches is becoming a nuisance in their respective neighbourhoods, and the inconvenience of promiscuous boycotting is evidently beginning to be resented.

19 Oct., Wed.

The Land League has taken a bold and decisive step. The papers this morning contain a Manifesto signed by the chiefs of the League—Messrs Davitt, Parnell, Sexton, Brennan, etc. calling on the tenant farmers of Ireland to punish the British Govt by refusing to pay any rent at all. The word of command is no longer 'A fair Rent', but 'No Rent'.

'It is as legal to refuse to pay rents, as it is to refuse to receive them' says the Manifesto, which except for this very plain statement, is written in general in a rhetorical and eloquent style.[1]

It was read at a Meeting of the League at which Father Cantwell (Administrator to Archbishop Croke at Thurles) took the Chair. How far the command will be obeyed is the general question—how far the tactics of passive Resistance will be attempted, and will be successful.

Even the *Freeman* seems a little staggered by the injunction for which of course it holds the Govt responsible.

An excellent and spirited address at Quarter Sessions on the Land Act by a Mr Waters at Dungarvan, and an equally excellent leader upon it in the *Irish Times*, which is just now behaving admirably.

There was a good deal of indiscriminate stone-throwing and window-

---

[1] *F.J.*, 19 Oct. 1881. The manifesto was written by William O'Brien.

breaking in Dublin last night; this could not have been caused by the irritating influence of the police, for they did not appear upon the scene till 10 or 11 o'clock, when they sallied out in force and quickly cleared the streets of the roughs who melted away before them.

To-day the papers have begun to repent of their violent denunciations of the police, and even the *Freeman* tries to speak them fair. There seems to be no doubt however that a good many innocent people did get knocked about in the previous rows, and the individual sufferings of some newspaper reporters and Town Councillors were quite enough to account for the indignation of the Press and the Corporation on Monday.

Walked with Father to the Vice Regal.

The Murrough O'Briens left us. He (Mr O'Brien) is as personally friendly and amiable towards us as ever, and will, I believe, do his duty in the Commission with perfect loyalty. But there can be no doubt that he thinks the 'suspects' martyrs, and nothing will ever make him believe that the Land League chiefs are not all as guiltless of encouraging intimidation and outrage as he is himself.

'If that fellow was not on the Commission' is Father's comment to me after speaking of his conversation with Mr O'B[rien] the night before, 'he would be in Kilmainham'.

Lord de Vesci & Lord Courtown to dinner. Both of them good landlords, desirous of helping the cause of law and justice, and supporting the anti-Land League, and Boycotted farmers in their districts.

Edward arrived from Ebworth by the North Wall boat—quite disappointed at finding Dublin so quiet. After the newspaper accounts of the state of things here, he was not at all prepared to find the streets quite peaceful, and no signs of rioting.

As for the newspapers, they must certainly be very alarming to our friends in England. Large print and sensational headings accompany the columns and columns of Irish news which fill the papers. As for rumours and startling paragraphs they abound—one day it is 'the attempted assassination of Mr Herbert Gladstone'—another it is a statement reproduced in all the papers 'that Mr Forster drove from the Phoenix Park to the Castle in his brougham attended by a mounted escort of cavalry'. 'This is the first time he has had to be so protected.'

On the whole, English public opinion seems still strongly in support of the Govt with the exception of course of the *P.M.G.* and the *Echo*, which have returned to their normal attitude.

On the Continent approval of the arrests appears very doubtful, and the American papers have become entirely hostile on the subject. Mr T. P. O'Connor has had a warm reception from his compatriots, and at Boston the Mayor presided at his Meeting, and Mr Wendell Philips[1] denounced British rule. No

---

[1] O'Connor was in America on the first of six missions there on behalf of party funds (see *Memoirs of an old parliamentarian*, i, 206–11). Wendell Phillips (1811–84): American abolitionist;

doubt so far as pure American sympathy with Mr Parnell goes, it has a good deal to do with the Irish vote, which has to be conciliated by American politicians.

A letter this evening from C[harlotte] O'Brien, bidding us goodbye in sorrow and anger.

20 Oct., Th.

An eventful day. On coming down to breakfast, Mother informed me that Archbishop Croke had come out against the No Rent Manifesto—Father had already got the morning papers in the study, and was possessed of this satisfactory piece of intelligence.

In a letter to the *Freeman* the Archbishop expresses his 'dismay' at the last step taken by the League—declaring at the same time his devotion to the principles of the League in so far as they are based on the demand for 'fair rents'.[1]

The appearance of this letter, says Father, is a justification of the Govt's resolution not to arrest Father Cantwell for the part he played yesterday. They had been strongly disposed to do it, but if they had they would certainly never have got this letter from the Archbishop.

On the other hand the League have sent their Manifesto to all the Branches, also a Placard 'No Rent' signed by Parnell and others.

At half past 11, Mother, Aunt Fan, Francie and I drove to Mr Litton's house in Merrion Square, going on thence with Mrs Litton and her two daughters to be present at the opening of the Land Court in Merrion St.

A sober Queen Anne house, in a quiet street, no crowd or appearance of public interest outside—inside a busy going to and fro of lawyers, secretaries, solicitors—a cheerful bustle of preparation and appearance of friendly interest in the coming proceedings.

We were taken through the Legal Secretary (Mr Fottrell's)[2] room into a small wooden pen in one corner of the handsome large room, in which the Land Court was to begin its existence. There were several other ladies—Lady O'Hagan, Mrs O'H[agan] etc.

Beside us at the end of the room was a raised platform, and canopy of red cloth, under which were set chairs for the three Commissioners—below sat the Clerk and secretaries—facing them the solicitors and barristers. A long row of reporters down one side, and the rest of the room filled with a constantly increasing crowd of men.

In a few minutes the three Commissioners quietly came in and took their

president of Anti-slavery Society, 1865–70; championed prohibition, female suffrage, penal reform; introduced colloquial style of oratory; his speeches were edited by James Redpath in 1863.

[1] *F.J.*, 20 Oct., p. 5. See below, p. 290.
[2] George Fottrell jun. (1849–1925): solicitor to the land commission.

places, and the Clerk declared the Court open—by a slip of the tongue he called it the 'Court of the Land League', an announcement received with an outburst of laughter, in which the three Commissioners joined heartily; then Judge O'Hagan drew out a roll of much-corrected MS and began to read a short opening address, mainly a businesslike explanation of the functions and procedure of the Court, but ending with a dignified and well-worded statement of the spirit in which the new Tribunal meant to enter on its labours.

After this short address the business began of making applications on behalf of tenants (mostly wishing to have a judicial rent fixed under the new Act).

Prominent amongst the Solicitors was Mr [Peter C.] McGough, acting for the Land League, who applied on behalf of such a large number of tenants that the Judge set aside a day to be reserved for the consideration of his cases only. Mr McGough however, like most of the solicitors, was so insufficiently posted up in the facts necessary for appearing before the Court that time had to be granted for him to collect the requisite details as to names, dates of eviction, etc.

Throughout all the proceedings the most perfect good humour prevailed, and at the same time there was no want of vigour and decision in Judge O'Hagan's laying down of the law; he seemed to have every detail of the Act at his fingers' ends, and no enquiry however perplexing it sounded seemed to find him in any way at a loss even for a moment. At 2 o'clock the Court rose, to sit again every day till the 29th.

I was very glad to have been present at what we all fervently hope is the opening not only of the New Land Court, but of a new and happier era of agrarian experience for Ireland.

There can seldom have been a Tribunal on whose decisions more will depend for the good or evil of an Empire—nor one whose power of doing good was more dependent upon external conditions over which the just intentions of the Judges have no control and no influence.

Certainly I have seen a great deal happen since the autumn of 1878 when my eyes were first opened to the magnitude of the Irish Land question.

How well I remember when we were being rowed across the Killaries my questioning Father as to the meaning and the possibility of 'fixity of tenure', an expression which had quite lately come within the range of my vocabulary.

A quiet afternoon at home—walked with Francie and the dogs to look at my favourite view from the Magazine Hill. The wreck amongst the poor thorn trees in the Park caused by the late gale is quite melancholy.

Miss Burke to afternoon tea; by no means disposed to be jubilant over Archbishop Croke's letter, she thinks that his influence for good will not be as great as his influence for harm, and whatever his present tendency to comparative moderation he will not be able to control his clergy. Her model ecclesiastic is Archbishop McCabe, who certainly does know how to keep his diocese in order, and makes short work of those priests who meddle with the Land

League. He has just suspended a certain Father Kenny for having sent an abusive letter and subscription to the *Freeman* (apropos of the arrests), and then refused when summoned by the Archbishop to bring him within 2 hours time a written apology to be published also in the *Freeman*.

The chief event of the day was still to be known. Father, as usual nowadays, came back so late from the Castle that we did not see him before going up to dress. On coming down to the drawing room before dinner, Mother handed me a paper headed with the Royal Arms—the supplement to the *Dublin Gazette*—proclaiming the Land League.

The answer of the Queen's Government to the 'No Rent' Manifesto issued by the Executive of the Land League Govt has not been long delayed.

The language of the Proclamation is firm and explicit, and the ground on which this most critical step is taken is set forth in terms which will commend themselves even to those who would be most disinclined to sanction such a measure.

The reasons given for declaring the Land League 'an unlawful and criminal association' are 'that its designs have been sought to be effected by an organized system of intimidation', and that it has now avowed its purpose to be 'to prevent the payment of all rent, and to effect the subversion of the law as administered in the Queen's name in Ireland'.

All persons are warned that the 'Association styling itself the "Irish National Land League"', or by whatsoever other name it may be called or known, is an 'unlawful and criminal association'; and that all meetings 'to carry out or promote its designs or purposes are alike unlawful and criminal, and will be prevented, and if necessary, dispersed by force'. 'And we do hereby make known' says the Proclamation

that all the powers and resources at our command will be employed to protect the Queen's subjects in Ireland in the free exercise of their lawful rights and the peaceful pursuit of their lawful callings and occupations; to enforce the fulfilment of all lawful obligations; and to save the process of the law and the execution of the Queen's writs from hindrance or obstruction.

The Proclamation was already posted up in Dublin and published in the evening papers.

'Well', said Father, at dinner, 'it is not often three such events happen in one day as Archbishop Croke's letter, the opening of the Land Court, and the Proclamation of the League.'

Mr West left for his holiday.

21 Oct., Fri.

Everything quiet as yet. The *Freeman* urging the people to keep calm in the face of this new attempt to exasperate them. The *Irish Times* gravely approving. Another Manifesto from the League Executive telling the people not to attempt holding Meetings. The Land League offices are closed: the Ladies [Land] League having been at work late at night, arranging, and carrying off and destroying books and documents.

It is not quite known where the headquarters of the Association will be transferred to. It has been said to Holyhead, Liverpool, or to Paris. The chief members of the League at present at large—but not in Ireland—are Mr Healy, Mr Egan, and Mr Arthur O'Connor.

Read the sedition papers, very violent of course and full of abuse of the police.

A quiet day—walked with Mother and Edward towards the Park gates, and afterwards called on the pretty Mrs Dalrymple. Mr Law home to dinner with Father. Father rather tired and preoccupied; amongst his duties during the day had been an interview with Mr Parnell's brother-in-law,[1] who explained that he did not at all agree with Mr P's political views, but came to ask to be allowed to see him in private as his 'legal adviser'. The difficulty was that under cover of consulting with his 'legal adviser' Mr Parnell had already been having private interviews with the Land League solicitor, and therefore his brother-in-law could hardly claim to see him under this head.

There are few of his present duties that are evidently so painful to the Ch. Sec. as having to decide in all these details of actual prison management. Since Mr Parnell's arrest he has been obliged even more than usual to watch over what went on inside Kilmainham for on one or two occasions Mr P. has endeavoured—very naturally, perhaps—to communicate with the public through the medium of Reporters, or (what is still more difficult to meet) the Land League doctor.[2]

To shut up Mr Parnell and then allow him to address the public from inside Kilmainham would of course be an absurdity, and the authorities with every wish to treat the 'political prisoners' with courtesy are obliged to keep a careful watch over the nature of their communications with their friends—be they doctors or legal advisers.

22 Oct., Sat.

A wild stormy day; much anxiety as to Edith and the four children, who were to arrive by the North Wall from Ebworth. A dinner party in the evening, Talbots, Master of the Rolls and Mrs Sullivan, Sir Thomas Steele, Col. and Mrs Taaffe Ferrall, Col. Lockwood, etc. I had a good deal of talk with Capt. Talbot about his beloved Dublin Police, of whom he is very proud; also with Col. Lockwood, who explained to me the nature of a 'picket' (we have a picket of ten Dragoons

[1] Alfred McDermott had married Sophia Katharine, one of Parnell's sisters, who died in 1877. He was Parnell's solicitor.

[2] Dr Joseph Edward Kenny (1845–1900): medical officer to North Dublin Union; arrested, 24 Oct. 1881.

quartered here now), and assured me that the Coldstreams would be glad to come over from the Richmond Barracks for our defence if required. Apropos of defence, Sir Thomas Steele was very anxious to impress upon both Mother and me the precaution he had taken for the protection of the Chief Sec.'s Lodge in case of a rush of the mob. 30 of the Guards at the Mountjoy Barracks, with a regular system of orderly communication, etc., etc., etc.

It appears that at the time of the arrests Sir T. Steele had seriously advised Father to send us all away—the danger feared being that the mob after holding a Meeting in the Park might turn to and wreck this house, as they did to some extent in Dublin during the late riots.

Edith and the four dear little children arrived about midnight—well and blooming, and not having been in the least discomposed by the storm.

23 Oct., Sun.

To the Hibernian Chapel in the morning, but without Father. Mr Edward O'Brien to lunch, passing through Dublin on his way to Limerick.

Approves, but with great regret, the strong measures the Govt have been taking. His cousin, Mr Robin O'Brien,[1] he says is becoming more sanguine about the possibility of things settling down—in three years time, according to him, the landlords will be selling their land at 28 years purchase. This is what Father expects himself.

Everywhere just at present there seems to be a sense of relief as though the worst was over and the clouds were breaking. At any rate, the feeling of help-lessness in face of an organization which under pretence of a lawful agitation was really being used for the persecution of the unpopular minority, has been removed by the Govt's recent measures, and quiet, law-abiding people have been made to feel that the Queen's Government is after all more powerful than the Government of Mr Parnell and his associates.

The great danger apprehended now by all competent persons is private out-rage; and it is prophesied that the next month will be a bad one over the collection of the November rents.

Helped Father make up his journal, and heard from him of the impending resignation of the L[ord] C[hancellor], at present a deadly secret.[2]

Walked with Father after lunch to the Dalrymples, and through the V.R. grounds.

We talked of Sir Thomas Steele and his precautions: Father was not too well pleased with him for having expatiated on his fears to us, and agreed that he did not think there was much cause for alarm in that direction; 'but I believe there are two people who want to murder me' he told me; 'two sets, the O'Donovan

---

[1] Robert Vere O'Brien, whom Florence married in 1883.

[2] O'Hagan had wanted to resign for reasons of health or private business, but hung back now to avoid giving the impression of disagreement with the government (B.L., Add. MS 44159, ff 66–8).

Rossa lot, and some of the friends of men who have been arrested'. 'I think Parnell would not be sorry to see me knocked on the head', Father remarked, reflectively, as we were walking back. 'I believe he hates me, and I am sure I don't wonder.'

I enquired about Mr Sexton, and heard that he was better; but Father is much inclined to send both him and Mr Dillon away, asking them to sign no conditions except to keep out of Ireland for the present.

Home in time for the post, Father being anxious to write to Mr Vernon about the small evicted tenants, whose position before the Court, according to an article in the *Freeman* of Saturday is unfairly prejudiced by the arrest of Mr Dorris, a Land League solicitor, who had been charged to bring forward their cases at the first sitting of the Court, and is now unable to do so.

A call from Mr Burke after tea—came not to see Father on business, but actually to pay a visit to Mrs Forster, a statement which he had to make in explicit terms before Mother could believe it. He told us that he had been talking to men at the club, who all agreed that in their respective districts a better and more wholesome state of things was beginning to prevail.

Lord Lansdowne (amongst others) has just gone home and been well received by his people—more no doubt from a sense of expediency than from any more amiable motive, but satisfactory all the same.

A quiet evening: Father early to bed with a slight chill—no telegrams.

Poor Carpenter has been attacked with apoplexy, and is very dangerously ill.

24 Oct., Mon.

The country seems to have been quiet yesterday—no Meetings were held which required to be dispersed by force.

A bad murder reported from Co. Clare; a farmer on the estate of Mr Stafford O'Brien, shot dead while sitting at table in his own house—uncertain whether from private revenge or because he had paid his rent.[1]

A vehement 'whip' in the *Freeman* in support of Mr Gray's Motion to confer the freedom of the City on Mr Parnell and Mr Dillon.

Walked with Father, Aunt Fan and Mother towards the Park gates. A quiet afternoon, wet and grey. Mr W. Cullinan and Mr Gerald Fitzgerald to 5 o'clock tea. Heard from the former that Dr Kenny, the Land League doctor, had been arrested: he was 'wanted' on Saturday and Sunday, but could not be found.

Aunt Fan left us to return to Fox How by the evening Mail—general regret of everybody.

Carpenter is a shade better.

[1] At about 7 p.m. on 22 Oct., Michael Moloney was killed by a charge of shot from a gun thrust through his bedroom window. The probable cause was a dispute with his brother over inheritance of a piece of land. (S.P.O., I.C.R., Returns of outrages, Oct. 1881).

Father, Mother, Mr H. Gladstone and I dined at the V.R. Lodge—a small party—Lord Clarina, a Mr and Lady Margaret Ormsby Gore, the Burkes, Capt. Legge, the Sullivans, and Major Byng.

Some speculation as to the result of the Corporation division the next day on the question of the freedom of the city.

There is no man of all the Land Leaguers for whom aristocratic Dublin has such a vehement detestation as for Mr Dwyer Gray; the Ch. Sec. could not do a more popular thing—in this circle—than arrest Mr Gray under the Coercion Act—on general grounds, if he did not bring himself under any special indictment.

It is said that Mr Gray has been going round the last day or two, warning the small tradesmen on the Corporation to 'be careful about their business', implying that if they did not vote for his proposal, he could have them 'boycotted'.

The present Lord Mayor (Mr Moyers) has declined to summon the Meeting, and given his reasons for doing so.

Apropos of this proposal to confer the 'Freedom of the City' on men arrested by the Govt on charges of intimidation and sedition, Mr Burke dilated with flashing eyes, and in his vigorous, trenchant manner, on the absurdity of trying to solve an insoluble problem—namely to carry on constitutional government in a country where the constitution is not based on popular support, where it lacks the necessary groundwork of success, and where its privileges and rights are only used by the people as a weapon to be turned against the authorities and the powers that be.

As an instance of the anomalies that may be produced by the extension of constitutional rights to Ireland, he referred to what had happened when the Act was first brought forward in Parliament for giving to Irish Corporations the right of conferring the Freedom of the City. A member present, remembering just in time what would be the probable result of the extension of English customs to Ireland, moved an Amendment to the effect that it should not be permissible for the Corporation to bestow the Freedom of the City on persons sentenced to penal servitude. The necessity for this proviso was at once recognised, and the amendment stands in the Act to this day.

25 Oct., Tu.

The papers on the whole not unsatisfactory this morning: in an interview with a correspondent of the *Daily Telegraph*, Archbishop Croke has confirmed the opinion expressed in his letter about the 'No Rent' Manifesto.

This famous document appears to have been mainly the work of Mr Patrick Egan acting on the advice and suggestions of Mr Ford of the *Irish World*.[1] In America the 'No Rent' programme met with general approval amongst the

---

[1] It was the work of William O'Brien; above, p. 280.

Irish Americans, and money is promised in abundance if the tenants will only hold out and defy their landlords.

A fine autumn day—Edward and I rode over to Celbridge Abbey to lunch with Col. and Mrs Dease. It seemed very curious in riding through the roads and villages in Ireland to see the familiar signature 'W. E. Forster' at the foot of a Proclamation posted in conspicuous places.

We were very kindly received by the Deases, and spent a pleasant half hour after lunch, walking in their grounds—beautiful grassy banks under flame-coloured beech trees bordering the Liffey—here a wide brimming stream, with a mill-race flowing into it with a rush of brown foaming water. In Celbridge itself, and again above Celbridge Abbey there are large disused flax mills—the masonry still intact and in good repair, water power in abundance—but everything deserted, and silent. A year or two ago we were told some Englishmen had thought of setting them at work, but the 'state of the country' had driven them away.

The Deases' house (which they rent from the Langdales of Yorkshire) is a curious place, with intricate little passages and unexpected flights of steps. Col. Dease's study is the room in which Swift found Vanessa when he came to bring back her letter to Stella.

Colonel Dease, who had just come back from a rent-collecting expedition, had been on the whole successful. On one property in West Meath the tenants would not pay—but on another near Drogheda they had all paid up, after a long resistance for the sake of appearances, for it was a case in which the farmers were well off, and had no difficulty whatever about their rents.

Edward and I had a pleasant ride home, returning not through Woodlands, but along the Strawberry Beds.[1]

On the road to Lucan we were escorted by a good natured and very sporting gentleman—evidently a small Squire of the neighbourhood—who insisted on riding with us in full conversation for about 2 miles, and finally suggested that we should come with him to his house and have a glass of wine—true Irish hospitality, we thought. He was very communicative about his own circumstances, and would clearly have liked to find out who we were. Judging from his remarks on the 'diabolical state of the country' he was evidently not a Land Leaguer.

About 7 o'clock Mr H. Gladstone returned from the Castle with the news that the Corporation had been 23 for and 23 against conferring the Freedom on Mr Parnell and Mr Dillon—the Lord Mayor being called on to give his casting vote, and giving it against the proposal, just succeeded in defeating it—a very good result.

A small party at dinner, both Mr H. Gladstone and Oakel dining with the Strollers[2] in Dublin.

[1] I.e. along the road north of the Liffey between Lucan and Chapelizod.
[2] An amateur dramatic and musical club, founded in 1865, its number limited to 70.

26 Oct., Wed.

The Convention with the Transvaal has been ratified.

Speeches reported in the papers this morning from Mr Chamberlain, Sir W. Harcourt, and Mr Plunkett. A wonderful agreement of tone as to the duty of the Govt to enforce the law in Ireland, and of all loyal subjects to support the Govt.

The *Freeman* comments only in a single short article on the result of yesterday's discussion and vote in the Corporation; the *Irish Times* on the contrary dilates with great satisfaction in three successive leaders on the result, and congratulates the Corporation on their spirit of independence.

Another murder has been committed in Co. Clare—this time it is said, of a Land Leaguer (McMahon, a local secretary), who had apparently irritated some of his neighbours by his threats against non Land Leaguers. However, this account, Father remarks, sounds improbable, and as yet the whole affair is a complete mystery.[1]

A letter from Archbishop Croke to the *Freeman*, denying the truthfulness of the language attributed to him by the *Daily Telegraph* reporter, and adding that he had been given to understand the interview was private.

Walked with Father to the Park gates. A call from Lady Cowper before luncheon. In the afternoon Mother, Edith and I drove into Dublin: we called at the Land Court but found it was already adjourned. The Commissioners are overwhelmed with work (1800 applications have been made up to the present), but the work, for the Dublin Court at least, is of a kind to be done privately and not in session.

One hears of several hopeful signs as to the prospects of the Land Court now occupying the prominent place in the tenants' minds rather than the Land League. Meanwhile the prohibition of all attempts to hold Land League meetings or committees is being vigorously enforced all through the country, and arrests are still being made.

It is greatly to be hoped that the cause of the tenants will not be injured by the total suppression of the League organization—the landlords are forming Landlords' Defence Associations to ensure that the landlords' claims shall be duly brought before the Court, and no doubt the farmers and clergy will be allowed to take similar bona fide measures for the representation and defence of the legal rights of the tenants under the Act.

Mr Cullinan to afternoon tea. Oakel home early from the Castle in order to see something of his little nephews.

He had been interviewed at the Castle by a reporter from the *Manchester Guardian*—vainly desirous to see the Ch. Sec., and anxious to find out from Oakel the reason why so many troops are still being sent over to Ireland.

[1] Thomas McMahon was found, shot dead, on the morning of 25 Oct.; the police concluded that he had been shot for refusing to participate in an outrage (S.P.O., I.C.R., Returns of outrages, Oct. 1881).

'There was a strong feeling arising about it in England—anxiety to know the reason, etc. etc.' Oakel of course gave him no information, so the curiosity of the M[*anchester*] *Guardian* remains as ungratified as mine on that subject.

There are from time to time rumours of an 'apprehended rising' in Limerick or elsewhere—usually dating from the 'Press Association' and one cannot help connecting some idea of this kind with the continuous influx of troops. And yet, those who ought to know say there is no cause for alarm, and certainly the Ch. Sec. does not seem uneasy. However, for that matter, no more he does about himself, and at the same time the head of the Detective Department here is said to have told the Press Association that there were two men in Dublin come over from America for the express purpose of murdering Mr Forster, that their names were known, and their movements watched by the police.

'Mr Forster is fully aware of his situation' says the paragraph at the end of the Irish letter in *The Times*, 'but shows complete indifference to the danger'.[1]

A small party at dinner, Mr H. Gladstone and Oakel dining with Mr Law; Edward at the theatre. Father brought back with him from the Kildare St. Club, Mr Cogan, an Irish Privy Councillor, and land owner. A respectable but rather dull elderly gentleman.

We heard that the Lord Mayor on opening a new Market in Henry St[2] this afternoon had been hooted and groaned at by the mob, so that his words in opening the building could scarcely be heard.

On the other hand nearly all the members of the Kildare St Club, Mr Cogan told us, intended calling on him 'en masse' at the Mansion House—a demonstration of approval for which little Major Byng was said to be chiefly responsible.

27 Oct., Th.

The calm may be deceitful, but for the present there is a distinct feeling of relaxation in the strain and excitement of the past few weeks—or even one may say months.

The change for the better is apparent in the newspapers, which have become much less painful and irritating reading for the last day or two. The *Freeman* has begun to turn its attention a great deal to the Land Court, and today has a peaceful article on the advantages of 'peasant proprietorship' to be established not through agitation for the 'abolition of landlords' but by reasonable agreement and ordinary methods of sale between landlord and tenant.

The Berwick[-on-Tweed] election has resulted in the victory of Mr Hubert Jerningham, a Liberal and a Catholic, by a majority of 517 (Jerningham 1[046], Trotter [529])[3]. A most well-timed success for the Government.

[1] 'was quite aware of the serious position in which he stood, but exhibited the utmost indifference to danger' (*The Times*, 26 Oct. 1881).

[2] Should read 'George's Street, South'.

[3] Hubert Edward Henry Jerningham (1842–1914): writer, diplomat, and later governor of Mauritius; Henry John Trotter (1836–88): B.L., conservative.

Father not feeling obliged to go into Dublin till 1 o'clock—Oakel and Mr H. Gladstone followed his example and spent an hour before lunch playing tennis at the V.R. racquet court with Mr Jephson and Edward.

Walked with Father and Francie to the Park gates at 1 o'clock, going on with him by the tram to the Castle. I went with him to his room and began to share his sandwiches, but was dispersed after a few minutes by the Lord Chancellor who called to see Father.

After doing a commission in Grafton St I returned home by tram, walking, and cab.

Owing to my stupidity in taking the wrong tram, I had to find my way down to the Quays, through Castle St, and Fishamble St, a part of Dublin in which I had never walked alone before. I was amused by the cautious enquiry of the cabman, whom I took off a stand on the quays, when I told him to take me to the Chief Secretary's Lodge—'Will I go up to the door Ma'am?' He evidently thought that a 'fare' taken off the road-side, could not aspire beyond the lodge or the back door.

Mother, Edward, and Edith spent the afternoon at Artane.

Mr Mawson,[1] the Bradford architect of the new Market in Henry St, dined with us. Oakel dined with the Littons.

A letter to Edward from Major Neild, the Resident Magistrate in Leitrim, with whom he is going to stay. He gave some details of the bad outrage just committed in his district—a poor boy of 15 shot at (and probably killed) for being the son of a bailiff.[2]

Major Neild, like others of experience in the country districts, fears that in the matter of outrages like this 'things will be worse before they are better'.

28 Oct., Fri.

Another bad outrage reported this morning, a man named Walsh in the Co. Cork, fired at and dangerously wounded by a party of armed men, visiting from house to house and warning the farmers not to pay the rents due the next day. Walsh declared his intention of paying in spite of intimidation, and has consequently been half murdered.[3]

The farmers in the neighbourhood now declare that in spite of their previous intentions, they dare not now pay their rents.

[1] Richard Mawson: architect, of the Bradford firm of W. & R. Mawson. He designed the south city market in George's Street.

[2] John Magoohan herded for his father's employer, who had become 'obnoxious' to the tenants. At about noon on 26 Oct. John was knocked down and shot twice by two men. The police arrested four men who were later discharged for lack of evidence (S.P.O., I.C.R., Returns of outrages, Oct. 1881).

[3] At about 2 a.m. on 27 Oct., Michael Walsh was visited and warned by a gang of moonlighters. After the warning, he closed his door and a shot was fired through it, wounding him *slightly*, according to the police return. A man was arrested but later discharged for lack of evidence (S.P.O., I.C.R., Returns of outrages, Oct. 1881).

On a good many estates whether from intimidation, or from obedience to the Land League, the tenants are refusing in a body to pay rent.

The 'suspects' in Naas Gaol, following the example of Kilmainham have, it is said, appealed to the tenantry not to pay anything till they are released. On the other hand, the Bishop of Cork and Cloyne (Dr Fitzgerald)[1] has published his thorough approval of Dr Croke's Letter against the 'No Rent' Manifesto, and the Bishop and Clergy of Kildare have done the same.

The English papers, and some of our private English friends, are full of felicitations on the improved state of things here, but Father himself, though seemingly cheerful and vigorous, feels that he has a great deal of trouble before him during the next month or two. It is a great comfort to know that he is thoroughly well served and supported by those who work with him in the Executive Govt here—not to speak of the cordial support and sympathy given him by his colleagues and fellow countrymen generally. I should think that, next to Mr Gladstone, there was not at this time in Great Britain a more popular member of the Cabinet than the Irish Secretary.

Report in this morning's papers of Mr Gladstone's speech to a Liberal deputation received by him at Knowsley. Mainly occupied with the question of Ireland, and in this following very closely on the line of his Leeds speech— Contrast between the O'Connell and Parnellite agitation—the latter having for its object first 'sheer rapine' and the dismemberment of the Empire—denial that the Land Act was due to the League[2]—hopeful signs of the Corporation's refusal to confer the Freedom of the City on Mr Parnell and Mr Sexton (a mistake for Mr Dillon)—satisfactory prospect of the Land Courts being really made use of by the people—sanguine belief that Parliament, the great Legislature of this country having fearlessly and wisely endeavoured to do full justice to the people of Ireland, will meet the due acknowledgment of that justice in the ready recourse of the people to the judicial means which they have provided for them between man and man, and in the future peace and improved order and prosperity of the country.

Walked with Father to the Park gates. A scheme in preparation for spending Sunday at Rostrevor, and taking a long walk in the Mourne Mountains. Whether I go or not uncertain; 'my claims to be considered along with those of others'.

We talked about the tenants' defence question in the matter of preparing their claim for the Land Court. The difficulty is, Father says, that these so-called 'tenants' defence associations' are very likely to turn into Land League branches again, with the old system of intimidation and boycotting; however a letter has been written on the subject to the local authorities and of course every fair opportunity will be given to the tenants—already the 'first sitting' of

---

[1] William Fitzgerald was in fact bishop of Ross.
[2] Cf. Gladstone's statement in the house of commons on 3 Mar. 1890: 'Without the Land League the land act of 1881 would never have been placed on the statute book' (*Hansard 3*, cccxli, 1686–7).

the Court in Dublin has been extended by nearly a fortnight, thereby removing Mr McGough's cause for complaint as to the tenants, who by the sudden suppression of the Land League were prevented from having their cases presented to the Court in time to reap the advantage of the 'first sitting'.

We also spoke of Dr Kenny. He has not only been arrested, but since then has been removed by the Local Govt Board from his appointment as Dispensary doctor.

His cause has been vehemently taken up by the *Freeman* which has opened a subscription for his benefit,[1] and prints day after day fierce letters of sympathy for Dr Kenny, and abhorrence of the 'mean' or 'tyrannical' or 'cowardly' or 'vindictive' action of the Local Govt Board, and the Chief Secretary.

The *Pall Mall* and *Echo* have also taken up the cry, the former declaring that, considering that Mr Forster and Mr Burke are both ex-officio members of the Board which has thus acted towards Dr Kenny, it is difficult for the most moderate Liberal 'not to smell Castle vindictiveness' in the affair.

'It was impossible for us to keep a man in the post of a Government official who was suspected of breaking the law' is all that Father says to me on the subject of Dr Kenny's ill-treatment.

Privately I have a strong suspicion that the Govt here know quite enough about Dr Kenny's political proclivities to justify their conduct towards him, even in the eyes of the *Pall Mall Gazette*; I do not of course know anything, but I suspect that the Fenian side of the Land League is occupying the attention of the Irish Govt more at present than the English public is at all aware.

In the afternoon Mother, Francie and I went to a Meeting of the Association for the Relief of Irish Ladies in distress, in the Palace, Stephen's Green.[2]

A dinner party in the evening, Judge and Mrs Ormsby, and one of their pretty daughters, Dr Grimshaw, Mr and Mrs Kane (he[3] is one of the Sub-Commissioners going down on Monday to begin work at Castle Blaney in the Co. Down),[4] Col. and Mrs Conolly,[5] Mr Jephson and Mr Guiry, the Irish barrister who shares Oakel's rooms in London. A very laborious evening.

---

[1] Kenny was arrested on 24 Oct.; on 27 Oct. the *Freeman* announced the opening of its testimonial fund.

[2] Cf. above, p. 269; at this meeting the executive committee of the association was formed. The list of donations recorded gifts of £100 from Lady Cowper, £50 from Mrs Forster, and £5. 5s. from Florence and Francie (*Irish Times*, 29 Oct. 1881). The Palace, 16 St Stephen's Green, was the official residence of the Church of Ireland archbishop of Dublin, then Richard Chenevix Trench.

[3] Robert Romney Kane (1842–1902): professor of jurisprudence of King's Inns, Dublin, 1873; son of Sir Robert John Kane (see above, p. 258).

[4] Castleblaney is in Co. Monaghan.

[5] John Augustus Conolly (1829–88): V.C., assistant commissioner of the Dublin Metropolitan Police.

29 Oct., Sat.

A letter from Mr Parnell to the Editor of the *Freeman* protesting against the formation of 'Tenants' Defence Associations', on the ground that

freedom of speech and the right of combination have been forbidden by the Govt; and the proposed associations would be tolerated by Mr Gladstone only so long as they appeared disposed to carry out his views and policy, and so far as they appeared likely to attempt to undo the work which the Irish Land League has done during the last 2 years.

No organization will be tolerated by our rulers for an instant unless it promises to be of a reactionary and Whiggish nature, willing to assist the Govt in their attempt to repress, mislead and demoralize the Irish tenant farmers.

In an Editorial note to this letter (printed in leaded type in the *Freeman*), it is explained that parts have been omitted in consequence of the Govt proclamation.

The fact that such a communication from Mr Parnell should have been allowed to appear from Kilmainham, is annoying, but as far as the matter of the letter goes Father is not sorry that it should have been published.

As for enforcing greater strictness in the supervision over the 'suspects', this is not so easy; they cannot be treated on the same footing as convicted prisoners, and what with constant association amongst themselves, and visits from their friends outside (though this has lately been restricted) it is very difficult to prevent a letter finding its way out.

However I believe there is some talk of removing Mr Parnell from Kilmainham to some other place where he would be under less temptation to carry on his functions as active leader of the extreme party by means of smuggled out documents and Manifestoes.

I heard in the course of the morning that I was to be allowed to go with Father to Rostrevor, consequently after reading the papers, and copying a letter for Father (to the Queen) I had to go and see about the packing. Dearest Mother was half inclined to come with us (it was she who discovered and suggested Rostrevor), but finally decided not to.

At half past 1 Rob and I called at the Castle; after waiting what I thought a dangerously long time, considering we had a train to catch, Father and Oakel at length appeared, and we drove off to the Amiens St station, where Mr Frederick Cullinan, who was coming with us, had already taken the tickets.

A fine afternoon, settling down into a clear, frosty evening, with a splendid golden sunset over the low hills to the west of Drogheda. Changed at Goragh Wood and reached Warren Point at the head of Carlingford Lough, about half past 5. A cold but pleasant drive with Father in an outside car to the Mourne Hotel two miles from Warren Point.

An excellent hotel, on a small terrace overlooking the Lough—nothing but the quiet road between the house and the star-lighted waters of Carlingford Bay, a narrow inlet of the sea with heath-covered mountains on either side, and woods and moss-grown stone walls running down to the water's edge as they do at Windermere.

Mr Cullinan had telegraphed for rooms, and an amiable landlady showed us at once to a cosy sitting-room with a good fire burning.

'Would we dine at the table d'hôte, which had only just begun?' At first we declined, but a second invitation made it so plain that a separate dinner later would be so inconvenient to the household, which was in excitement over an Amateur concert to be held that evening in Rostrevor, that Father decided in favour of our pleasing the landlady, and hurrying down to the coffee room to dinner within 10 minutes of our arrival.

A small room, about half a dozen ladies and gentlemen dining, apparently local people, or visitors from Newry—very steady and respectable, but not of a social turn of mind, even Oakel's conversational powers being almost defeated by the extreme demureness of the ladies opposite, with whom he made valiant efforts to engage in conversation.

The great topic was the concert, at which Lord and Lady Kilmorey,[1] and Lord and Lady Arthur Hill[2] were to be the principal performers. We went in to the second part, Father being attracted by the prospect of hearing Lord Arthur Hill sing the 'Clown's Song', and being then able to tell him of the fact on the floor of the House afterwards.

After music we took to cards, and resumed the game of whist we had begun before going to the concert.

30 Oct., Sun.

A brilliant frosty morning, cold, but with a cloudless sky—only a veil of morning mist hanging over the water, pierced by the masts of the small ships lying in the Lough. Left the hotel at 9 in an outside car, and after driving $\frac{3}{4}$ of an hour, sent back our wraps and started to walk over the heath and bogs of the Mourne Mountains, to the top of the Eagle Mountain, the highest summit[3] within easy walking distance of Rostrevor. Reached the top soon after 12, after a pleasant leisurely walk, which Father greatly enjoyed: a fine view from here over the dark sides of the Mourne Mountains on our right hand and on our left; behind us the plains of County Down, faint coloured and bright under the cold sunny sky; in front the sea and the mouth of Carlingford Bay, and far in the distance the Head of Howth and Lambay Island.

The silence and solitude amongst these heaths and bogs was even more profound than amongst our Westmoreland mountains—no highland sheep nibbling amongst the rocks, no streams tinkling over the stones—plenty of

[1] Charles Francis Needham (1842–1915): 3rd earl of Kilmorey; M.P. for Newry, 1871–4; representative peer for Ireland; of Mourne Park, Rostrevor.

[2] Arthur William Hill (1846–1931): 2nd son of fourth marquis of Downshire; conservative M.P. for Co. Down, 1880–85; for Down W., 1885–9, 1907–8.

[3] 2,084 feet.

water, but moving noiselessly through the soft beds of peat, and grassy tussocks, and little clefts and valleys in the heather—not a living creature to be seen for hours, till in coming homewards in the afternoon we met a shepherd with his collie dog, and Rob disturbed some hares and a few grouse.

This shepherd was a very civil friendly man, warned us to look out for Robbie, as poison had been put about the moors by the gamekeepers, and gave us advice about our road.

We had also some amiable conversation with three men whom we came upon spending a quiet afternoon on the mountain side with their two dogs; a little talk as to the coming Land Court, information about the names of neighbouring landlords, and again advice and directions as to our road back to Rostrevor.

The bluntness of manner, and Scotch accent of these Ulstermen strike one very much in coming straight from the Co. Dublin.

About 4 o'clock we came off the little Mountain road we had been following down for some time, on to the highway leading along the edge of Carlingford Bay, and finally reached the hotel a little after 5—the last 4 miles along the road seemingly to me very long, though the way was beautiful with the mountains on one side, and the bay on the other.

We dined at half past 5, and half past 6 drove to church, walking back the ¾ of a mile to the hotel under the moon and stars, which were reflected in the water, so that the end of our day was as beautiful as the beginning.

In the evening Father, Mr Cullinan, and Oakel went down into the smoking room, and were entertained by an elderly gentleman who undertook to enlighten Father on current events in Ireland—'Now I'll just explain to you what they mean by "Boycotting"' he said—going on afterwards to speak of Mr Clifford Lloyd, and giving Father the information that he was a man who had been much attacked in the House.

31 Oct., Mon.

Left Rostrevor at 7.10. Warren Point 7.40. Changed at Goragh Wood and at Newry,[1] where we had a passing interview with Mr Richardson, M.P., and reached Dublin at 11.

The worst news in the papers this morning, an account of an affray between the police and the people in Co. Mayo, near Belmullet. The police in defence of a process server (for poor rates) on the estate of a Mr Walter Bourke, were attacked in a narrow roadway by the people, with stones and sticks—after several times trying to clear the way by charging, they fired, and, as usual in

[1] Florence has got the order of these two places wrong; read 'Newry and Goraghwood'.

these cases, it was the women who suffered. Two mortally wounded, and others very seriously.[1]

It is one of the saddest things of the kind that has happened for a long time, and one feels anxious to know how far the police were justified in firing when they did.

Archbishop McCabe's pastoral appears in the papers to-day. Its language condemning the Land League doctrine, and the 'No Rent' Manifesto, was too strong for some of the congregations to whom it was read. In Marlborough St Cathedral a body of 100 young men got up and went noisily out of the church when this part of the Pastoral was read. This it is thought was an organized demonstration, portions of the Address having been published the night before in an evening paper, and this form of protest having been arranged beforehand.

On reaching Amiens St station, Father, Oakel and Mr Cullinan went straight to the Castle, and Rob and I returned home.

A quiet, lazy afternoon in the house. Mother and Edith drove into Dublin. Called to ask for poor Carpenter; he was unconscious, and not expected to live much longer.

He died two hours later.

We shall all miss him, and regret him sincerely. From the very first time we came here we have liked and respected him, and felt that he was a thoroughly honest and faithful man. It is a most terrible and unexpected blow for poor Mrs Carpenter and Kathleen—indeed they were all a most affectionate family, and devoted to their father.

Edward returned this evening from his two days visit to Major Neild in Leitrim: he had been much interested in his experience of a really bad corner of 'disturbed Ireland'.

Major Neild and his wife are living in lodgings, and the lodging house keeper did not at all relish having Edward for an inmate.

Somehow or other his name became known in the village, and it was thought better to put on an extra police patrol whilst he was there, outside the house, and to follow them in their drive across the desolate country.

The principal landlord in the neighbourhood—Capt. (Mr ?) White,[2] was a victim to 'boycotting'—and from all accounts never did a man less deserve ill of his tenants.

But in all this 'land war' (as the Nationalist papers like to call it) nothing is sadder and more disheartening to those who would be ready enough to make allowance for the Irish peasantry in this crisis, than their remorseless, cruel personal injustice towards old friends; there may easily be too much talk about 'gratitude' and so forth—perhaps in some cases the kindnesses of good landlords towards their tenants may have had in them too much of patronage to

---

[1] Florence's account agrees with that in the *Irish Times*, 31 Oct., which adds that several police were injured and over twenty persons arrested.

[2] Captain George White owned 6,152 acres in Co. Leitrim, valued at £2,292.

constitute a bond of goodfellowship, solid enough to resist the strain of a movement like the present—but, on the other hand, I believe that there are many
cases in which not only in outward act, but in feeling, the landlord has been a
true friend to the people amongst whom he lived—thinking for them, working
for them, helping them through bad times, not like a paternal despot but like a
kind-hearted man using his advantages of wealth and influence for the benefit
of his poorer neighbours.

And now just because those neighbours are his tenants, they seem to have no
hesitation in becoming his bitterest enemies, or at any rate in allowing themselves to act as though they were so.

Not a spark of loyalty or faithfulness to old friends—they are either so fickle,
so selfish, and so ungenerous, that they do really forget and disregard old ties,
or they are so cowardly that they will profess to.

In either case it seems a poor prospect for the future social relations of Irishmen: even if landlords are abolished, and the Irish people cease to be tenants,
they cannot help being men; and men who have behaved to their countrymen
as some of them have done will do little credit to a United Ireland of peasant
proprietors if that Utopia should ever become realized.

The best friends of the people say that they are only misled, and have not
really become demoralized, and I fervently hope that is the truth.

A dinner party here in the evening—Lord Clarina, Col. and Mrs Julian Hall
(Coldstream Guards), Col. and Mrs Montgomery Moore, Mr and Mrs
Haughton (he, one of the Sub-Commissioners, just starting with two colleagues, and his wife for Mayo), Mr and Mrs Porter (Mr Porter was meant to
have been an eminent Q.C. of that name, but by a mistake of mine in addressing the invitation he turned out to be a doctor, Surgeon to the Queen; I only
found this out in the middle of dinner, and meantime the poor doctor had been
treated by us all—Herbert Gladstone included—as a lawyer, and talked to
accordingly, which must have puzzled him), Mr Le Fanu, Dr Hatchell, and Mr
Papillon, and Dr Molloy.[1]

A pleasant evening—company self-acting.

Circumstantial rumour of Mr G's resignation. Father announced the fact to
Herbert Gladstone at breakfast: who remarked that it was the first he knew of it.

1 Nov., Tu.

Another cruel outrage in Cork, a man dragged out of his house at night and
shot (it is feared fatally) by a band of armed men for refusing to give them
arms.[2] These sort of crimes are the most impossible for the Govt to prevent—

[1] Julian Hall (1837–1911): O.C. 1st Battalion of the Coldstream Guards. George Hornidge
Porter (1822–99): F.R.C.S.I.; the man who should have been there was Andrew Marshall Porter,
Q.C., solicitor general.
[2] At about midnight on 30 Oct., Peter Kelleher, a farmer, was visited by moonlighters who took

as Father says, 'The police cannot be everywhere'. The patrols are easily evaded by the band of ruffians who visit isolated farms at midnight, for the purpose of intimidating and ill-treating their defenceless inmates.

A speech by Lord Randolph Churchill at Hull, reported this morning. A remarkable piece of political Billingsgate, unusually violent in its statements even for Lord R. Churchill.

Drove in the afternoon with Mother and Edith through Chapelizod and back by Inchicore, and Kilmainham. A showery afternoon with a gleaming wet sunset throwing a magical brilliancy over the towers and spires of Dublin—the pillar of steam from over the Inchicore Ironworks, shining like gold against the dark rain-clouds.

Miss Burke and Mr Herbert Murray and his daughter to tea. Apropos of visitors, it is amusing to notice how the 'beau monde' in these parts has begun to take notice of the Ch. Sec. since the Govt policy has been more deserving of their approval. This year people come to write their names in our Visitors book, who last autumn combined to 'boycott' the representative of Mr Gladstone's Government.

A small family party at dinner—Father whispered to me—'We've let out Sexton'.

This is on account of his health, and is a great satisfaction to Father. I believe that poor Mr Sexton is engaged to be married, and I hope now that nothing will interfere with this.

Chess playing in the evening between Herbert Gladstone and Father.[1]

2 Nov., Wed.

This morning's papers contain the first decision of the New Land Court. The Sub-Commissioner[s] at Castle Blaney after two days careful examination into an application for fixing a judicial rent, have given their judgment which involves a reduction of the rent by 50%.[2]

Within the last few days it has become quite clear that the Court will not be a failure from want of applicants, but will run the risk of breaking down from the extraordinary amount of work that is being heaped upon it; the Land League papers, which a fortnight ago were publishing cartoons representing the unfortunate tenants being dragooned into Court by the Govt and hanging back on the plea that 'their best friend Parnell' had warned them not to go in, will have to choose a different theme for their illustrations.

From all parts of the country the tenants are applying to the Court in shoals,

his gun, asked him to produce his league membership card, questioned him about a farm he was interested in, and then shot him in the leg. A man was arrested, but at the spring assizes the crown entered a *nolle prosequi* (S.P.O., I.C.R., Returns of outrages, Oct. 1881).

[1] A common practice—on this occasion, Forster won twice.
[2] This should read '30%'; the rent was reduced from £8. 16s. 2d. to £6. 6s.

and the great danger now is that, considering the judgment of the Commissioners must in many cases be adverse to the tenants, the reaction will be proportionately great.

'I confess', Lord Monteagle writes to Father, 'I am apprehensive of anarchy extending, if the tenants are disappointed as largely as I should expect by the decision of the Commissioners.'

As to the landlords at the present time, they are on the whole behaving very well, and Father does not expect that their objections to the decisions of the Court, even when against themselves, will be a cause of trouble.

The ill-feeling towards the Court from that side, is shown more in such papers as the *Express* and *Mail*, who gloat over the prospect of the machinery of the new system collapsing under the tremendous pressure of the moment, and calculate with malicious satisfaction, the number of years that must elapse before all the cases brought forward can be decided upon: if the length of time occupied is to be reckoned by the time spent over one case at Castle Blayney.

As usual extremes meet, and this is the line of depreciation which the *Freeman* is also inclined to adopt. 'The crowd of applications to the Court is so great that what will become of the poor tenants who want a hearing and will have to wait so long for their chance?'

As to this the Commissioners themselves think that pressure will not be really so great as it seems, since many of the cases will probably be arranged before they come before the Court, and in many hundred applications coming from the tenants of the same estate one decision will be a decision for all.

Persistent rumours again of Mr Gladstone's resignation.

Also numerous reports of an apprehended rising in Co. Cork, the military confined to barracks, guards doubled etc.

Edward has gone down for a two days visit to Cork, so he will come in for a time of excitement there. Of course the military authorities are bound to take precautions when they receive warning of intended attack upon isolated barracks and so forth, but I believe that there is no expectation of anything to be called a 'rising' in Cork or anywhere else.

Father, Mother and Francie called at the V.R. Lodge to ask Lady Cowper whether it was true that there had been a 'scene' at the theatre last night, as reported in one of the papers—there had been some hissing from the gallery, as there generally is, but this had been quite drowned in the counter cheering, which had been more hearty than usual. Altogether the 'scene' had not been very much.[1]

Walked with Oakel part of the way through the Park.

I believe I was mistaken in my suppositions about Dr Kenny. As things are I cannot help being sorry it was thought necessary to dismiss him from his

[1] The *Freeman's Journal* (2 Nov.) reported cheers for Parnell at the close of a performance of 'Heartsease' at the Gaiety Theatre.

doctorship, which seems to have so little to do with politics, but I suppose it had to be.[1]

Called on Mrs Carpenter and Kathleen.

Mother and Edith drove into Dublin in the afternoon—Mother calling at the Castle with a message for Father, who was found as usual overwhelmed with work, receiving deputations (one from the Sunday Closing people), hearing statements from country police inspectors, and sending our warrants for arrests.

Lord F. Cavendish arrived by the evening Mail. Some quiet talk over the present and future between him and Father.

On the whole a good deal of rent is being paid, in spite of the Manifesto—but on many estates the tenants refuse in a body. What is to happen then? The Govt must enforce payment with a strong hand—going systematically to work—taking a small district at a time, and accumulating sufficient force there to carry out the law—beginning if possible with the estates of rich landowners who can afford to take the consequences of having their farms thrown on their hands.[2]

The worst county at present is Clare—where the farmers are by no means poor, but where matters between landlord and tenant have come almost to the state of a 'servile war'.

3 Nov., Th.

Father went into Dublin early with Lord Frederick. Sir Ralph Lingen was to arrive in Dublin also by this morning's mail, and a long day be spent over Treasury business.

I have been kept so hard at work over our all-absorbing Irish experiences, that my Notes have lately contained no record at all of other matters that a year or two ago would have interested me deeply.

The death of Baron Haymerle,[3] the demonstrations of friendship between Russia and Austria, thereby re-establishing the famous Triple Alliance—the Meeting of the Delegations and the Emperor's speech to them—the visit of the King and Queen of Italy to Vienna, and the consequent inference that Italy has joined the Triple Alliance—estranged from France by the Tunis affair—the defeat of the Ministerial candidates in the recent elections in Germany—the imminent break-up of the present French Cabinet and the entrance of M. Gambetta into the coming Government—the probable return to office of my once familiar friend Count Andrássy[4]—all these things I now read of merely

---

[1] Above, p. 294. The government was eventually obliged to reverse this dismissal.

[2] According to Herbert Gladstone's diary, Forster had proposed this course on 19 Oct. in discussion with Lords Courtown and de Vesci (above, p. 281). Forster announced it to the prime minister on 20 Nov. (B.L., Add. MS 44159, ff 102–5).

[3] Karl von Haymerle (1828–81), chancellor of the Austro-Hungarian empire and minister for foreign affairs.

[4] Gyula Andrássy (1823–90): Hungarian statesman; formerly Hungarian premier and foreign minister of Austria-Hungary; resigned 1879, and did not return to power.

in large type paragraphs from time to time, and could no more write of in detail than I could of compound arithmetic.

Mother, Edith, and Francie went in the afternoon to visit the Meath Industrial Home[1]—the Protestant parallel to Artane. Mother was received with great ceremony by Sir John Lentaigne, Lord and Lady Bangor,[2] Mrs Vernon and others, and after inspecting the Institution most conscientiously they went to have tea with the Vernons at their beautiful place Mount Vernon.

Mr Vernon, Judge O'Hagan, Mr Litton, Lord F. Cavendish and Sir Ralph Lingen dined with us here, and there was naturally a world of talk (lasting without intermission till 2 a.m.) between the Ch. Secretary, the three Commissioners, and the two representatives of the Treasury.

4 Nov., Fri.

The appointment of Mr Law as Lord Chancellor is now a public fact: Mr Johnson will succeed him as Attorney General.

Another bad murder this morning—a young man named Doherty shot dead in Co. Galway, by a band of armed men at night—on the pretext it is supposed of his having at some time taken land from which another had been evicted.[3]

A letter[4] again in the *Freeman* from Archbishop Croke—'hedging again', says Father—this time Croke, after abusing the Govt, he [*sic*] advises the people to offer their landlords a 'fair rent', and if they will not accept that, to let the responsibility of refusing, and of the consequences, be on their heads.

A more satisfactory feature in the morning papers—now coming every day into greater prominence—is the Land Court and its decisions. Its enemies prophesy with delight a 'deadlock' from over press of applications, but the Govt are determined it shall not break down if they can help.

Lord F. Cavendish and Sir R. Lingen, say the Commissioners, will have reason to remember the days they have spent over here being sued for money— but at any rate the result of these long personal interviews with the Treasury seem to have been satisfactory. There are going to be 9 more Sub-Commissioners,[5] and the choice of men will soon begin.

Walked with Father and Oakel to the Park gates. Father suggested laughingly that he should take a peerage, and remain here as Lord Lieutenant— letting the Parnellites slang him at their pleasure in Parliament.

[1] Carysfort Avenue, Blackrock.

[2] Henry William Crosbie Ward (1828–1911): 5th Viscount Bangor, of Castleward, Co. Down.

[3] At about 9 p.m. on 2 Nov. Peter Doherty was shot dead outside his house; shortly afterwards the house of his uncle John (the intended victim) was fired into. Two men were arrested under the P.P.P. act and held for nine months. In the next three years several arrests were made, and at the spring assizes, 1884, two men (one a former R.I.C. constable) were sentenced to penal servitude for life (S.P.O., I.C.R., Returns of outrages, 1885).

[4] Not a letter, but a report of Croke's reply to a deputation from the Ballingarry branch of the league, which had visited him the day before (*F.J.*, 4 Nov. 1881).

[5] To fix fair rents under the land act.

'Seriously', he said, 'I think the best thing would be for me to give up altogether, and let Spencer come here with a new Chief Secretary'. He would be a bold man, I suggested, who would like to step into your shoes just now—'Oh, Shaw-Lefevre thinks he could do it', was the answer—'I suppose this is likely to be the arrangement next year'.

Drove in the afternoon with Mother and Edith to St Helen's to call on Lady Gough.[1] On our return found Miss Jephson arrived—come to dine and sleep.

Edward returned from Cork and Queenstown where he had been most kindly received by the various naval and military authorities, and, thanks to a card of Father's, had also been shown over the Convict prison on Spike Island, to which no naval or military introduction was found to admit him.

Mr and Miss Jephson, and Mr Henry Robinson to dinner. All the party (with the exception of Father, Oakel, and myself) going to a concert at the V.R. Lodge.

I wrote to Mrs Dugdale, in answer to enquiries as to the 'state of the country' and our own position.

5 Nov., Sat.

Other decisions of the Sub-Commissioners reported from Ulster—again greatly to the advantage of the tenants, the landlord in this case being an Absentee clergyman in Australia, whose rents had been gradually raised on the strength of improvements, shown to have been made by the tenants alone.

Father drove into Dublin early having an appointment with Lord Drogheda.[2]

We spent most of the morning entertaining Miss Jephson, and after her departure, I read the Sedition papers—duller than usual but with the same monotony of abuse.

A perfectly heavenly afternoon—everything basking under mild bright sunshine and blue sky. There can be no doubt that Irish weather—at all events—is much maligned.

Francie and I with the two dogs walked with Herbert Gladstone to the Park gates, and home by the Magazine Hill and the Fifteen Acres.

Edward left us by the evening boat to return to Burley.

Herbert Gladstone, Edith and I dined early and went to the Gaiety theatre, where the Jephsons had kindly offered us places in their box. The last night of Mme Modjeska who appeared with Mr Forbes Robertson in *Romeo and Juliet*. The house was a pleasure to see, crammed from floor to ceiling with an enthusiastic audience who insisted on calling Mme Modjeska before the curtain at the end of every scene.

[1] Jane, née Arbuthnot, 2nd wife of George Stephens Gough (1815–95), second viscount. St Helen's (Booterstown, Co. Dublin) was their Dublin residence.
[2] Henry Francis Seymour Moore (1825–92): 8th earl and 3rd marquis of Drogheda; owned 16,609 acres in Kildare and 2,688 acres in Queen's County, worth a total of £10,466.

6 Nov., Sun.

A pleasant quiet Sunday. Father went with us to church at the Hibernian. After luncheon he and Mother went for a walk round the Circular. A beautiful afternoon.

Oakel and I called on Miss Burke for him to make his adieux. We found there Sir W. Gordon Cumming, a disconsolate and indignant Guardsman—bewailing the hard fate of himself and his brother officers—especially the younger ones—'men with lots of money, and taste, and plenty of houses to go and stay at for shooting and hunting'—condemned to spend three days out of the week on guard at Kilmainham for 24 hours together—and then with all this 'no chance of promotion', 'a young fellow might as well hope to become a field-marshal as a lieutenant colonel'—10 or 12 of the young officers have already been driven to throw up their Commissions—and Sir W. Gordon Cumming seemed to think that if the rumour was true that the Scots Guards were to be kept on in Dublin till March, the battalion would dissolve altogether.

Oakel left us by the evening boat for London. We shall miss him more than I can say.

A visit later in the evening from Mr A. Burke, just returned from Galway. His cousin Mr Christopher Redington is very much depressed, and despairs of getting his rents.

Mr Burke (our Mr Burke) on the contrary has been paid in full on his Galway estate. Mr Redington is very unhappy about the disposition of the people round him, which I fear[1] is still very bad and sullen. The murder of Peter Doherty was in his neighbourhood; it is believed to have been a judicial assassination, planned and executed by a secret society which had sentenced the man to death.

What can be done to prevent such crimes as these? The law is simply power-less, and the people are either unable or unwilling to combine amongst themselves in Vigilance Committees such as suppressed the murdering Associations of the United States. As usual in this case of Peter Doherty, no evidence is forthcoming, and if there were no jury would convict upon it.

A small party at dinner—in the evening Father read aloud Tennyson's 'Two Voices'.

7 Nov., Mon.

Herbert Gladstone left by the morning boat for Hawarden; he returns at the end of the week.

An early visit from the pretty Mrs Dalrymple and her black poodle 'Dinah'.

Walked with Father and Mr Jephson to the Park gates, Mother overtaking us in the carriage and going on with us into Dublin.

[1] The TS reads 'the people, which I fear round him'.

Father's principal trouble this morning is from violent priests—one or two of whom have been making speeches containing downright incitement to murder. There is every reason for wishing to avoid arresting a priest at this juncture, much as some of them evidently desire it, and yet while men are being arrested for less offences under the Coercion Act, a priest cannot be allowed to go on for ever speaking with impunity.

Father had been half inclined to write himself to the Bishop to whose diocese the worst offender belonged—but there are grave objections to thus officially seeking the assistance of the Catholic ecclesiastics—with the possibility of its being refused—and it is felt that the precedent might be too dangerous.

However, fortunately the Bishops as a rule are becoming much more outspoken on the side of law and order. The notorious Father Conway of Clonbur has been removed from his parish, and the papers of this morning contain two more speeches (or sermons) against the No Rent doctrine—one from the sturdy Archbishop McCabe, the other from the Catholic Archbishop of Armagh (Dr Gettigan?).[1]

On the other side there is published this morning a fresh 'Manifesto' from the No Rent party, urging the people—'to stand firm, to shun the Land Court, to pay no rent, etc.'

This placard is being posted extensively in the South, and is said to be the work of the indefatigable Mr Patrick Egan, and to be issued from Paris with all the remaining authority of the Land League—the *Freeman* however throws doubt upon this supposition.

The 9 new Sub-Commissioners have been appointed (these appointments being only for a year), the only two friends we have amongst them this time are Mr Edward O'Brien and Mr Gerald Fitzgerald (our Chamonix acquaintance).

Mr Law will be succeeded as Attorney General by Mr Johnson, and Mr Johnson by Mr Porter, Q.C. who will stand for Derry in place of Mr Law. Lord O'Hagan is to become a Knight of St Patrick—an arrangement which seems to give general satisfaction.

After leaving Father and Mr Jephson at the Castle, I went with Mother to Chancellor's, where they made many attempts to take her photograph—some at least it may be hoped will turn out successful.

Rode in the afternoon in the Park with my dear Puck.

A dinner party in the evening, Roberts, Monahans, Harmans, Barbours, Stotherds, Mr Godley, Mr A. Dillon, Mr Ball Greene, Mr W. Cullinan. Mr Ball Greene (son-in-law of the famous Sir Richard Griffiths, and himself Commissioner of Valuation) told Mother that he quite agreed with the judgment of the Castle Blayney Sub-Commissioners in their estimate of a fair rent

[1] Daniel McGettigan (1815–87): archbishop since 1870.

on the particular cases submitted to them. But he appeared to be rather alarmed at the principle apparently laid down by Mr Baldwin[1] (apropos of this Crawford estate)—that the rent to be paid in future was to be what the tenant could afford to pay after he had allowed the land to deteriorate, not what the land would be worth under proper cultivation.

8 Nov., Tu.

Miss Dixon to breakfast. She too hears from her brother and other agent connections that rent is being paid—in one case she heard of the tenants were coming to terms with their landlord for fear he should take them into Court.

Mr Egan in a telegraph to the *Freeman* has claimed full credit for the last 'No Rent' Manifesto, 'which was issued with the approval of all our imprisoned friends'.

Walked with Father, Mother, and Miss Dixon to the Park gates, going on with Father in the carriage to the Castle. Brought back with me the *Illustrated London News* containing the pictures headed the 'Crisis in Ireland'—one the 'Arrival of Mr Forster' at the Castle—driving up in an open carriage with a mounted escort before and behind, a regiment of the Guards presenting arms in the Court yard, and a large cannon in the foreground—the second picture is of this house, with two policemen and an officer confabulating outside the drawing room window.[2]

A mild pleasant afternoon. I rode to Lucan and back on the other side of the river, accompanied by my dear Puck. Mother drove into Dublin to see Father who was to leave for London by the evening mail.

A quiet evening, only ourselves and Miss Dixon.

9 Nov., Wed.

A letter from Oakel—he had crossed with Mr David Plunkett, whom he found much alarmed at Mr Baldwin's decision.

Miss Dixon left us.

Spent the morning over the Visitors Book, and writing invitations—three dinner parties on the stocks—the Vice Regal people and other notables due on the 15th, more people on the 16th, and 17th.

In the afternoon Mother and Edith took the little boys to Sandymount for them to see the sea and pick up shells. I spent the afternoon in Father's study, cutting out newspaper extracts, and gumming them into the book which Oakel has bequeathed to my care.

---

[1] Thomas Baldwin, M.R.I.A., asst commissioner, Irish land commn.
[2] *Illustrated London News*, 5 Nov. 1881, p. 440.

10 Nov., Th.

Reports in the papers of the speeches at the Guildhall, notably Mr Gladstone's. His allusion to Ireland—to the Land Commission—and the acceptance of the Act by the people—considered 'disappointing' by the *Freeman* 'prudent—or at least not as imprudent as usual' by the *Irish Times*.[1]

Mr Gladstone's references to the need for all parties to unite in reforming the procedure of the House of Commons, is received with much interest, as foreshadowing sweeping changes to be proposed by the Govt next Session.

This morning's papers announce another startling decision of the Land Court: The Sub-Commission at Limerick have given judgment in the case of Enright, an un-improving, apathetic tenant, against Ryan, his equally un-improving apathetic landlord. After a long examination of witnesses, and a personal inspection of the land in question, the Commissioners have reduced the rent from £19 to £9. The sensation caused by this decision (against which the landlord has appealed) is very great. Even the Moderate *Irish Times* seems staggered at this sweeping reduction, and inclined to sympathise with those who say that if the landlords are to be thus suddenly docked of one-half of their incomes through the inevitable operation of the new Act, they will have a right to claim compensation from the State for the injury inflicted on them in the public interest.

In fact there is no doubt that the Conservatives' opposition to the Act is growing fiercer with each new decision, though the opposition and criticism is mainly expressed in the newspapers and not by the Irish landlords as a body.

They for their part are treating the new Tribunal with perfect fairness, and seem disposed to give the tenants full opportunity to take advantage of it.

It is said that the good landlords are not afraid of being hit by it, and recognize with equanimity that the rents so suddenly brought down have been in reality rack rents.

Spent the morning amongst the Rebel papers and others, cutting out and gumming in extracts. Mr Jephson to lunch. In the afternoon with Mother and Francie to see over the Alexandra College for Girls, where we were met by Dean Dickenson,[2] Mr and Mrs Graves, and Miss La Touche, the Lady Superintendent.

Afterwards left cards in Merrion Square, shopped in Grafton St, walked through the New Markets in Henry [*recte* George's] St and bought the latest caricature of the Ch. Sec. at one of the stalls, and called on our way home at the V.R. Lodge, but not finding Lady Cowper at home.

A quiet evening over the London papers—all reporting in various forms the hearty reception given to the Ch. Sec. at the Mansion House—'loud plaudits'

[1] 'If without much substance, it is not a new mischief' (*Irish Times*, 10 Nov. 1881).
[2] Hercules Henry Dickinson (1827–1905): vicar of St Ann's, Dublin, since 1855; helped to found Alexandra College, 1866; dean of Chapel Royal since 1868.

cries of 'bravo' and prolonged cheering when he walked up the room, and when his name was mentioned by Mr Gladstone and Lord Granville in their speeches.

11 Nov., Fri.

The papers full of the proceedings of the various Sub-Commissioners.

In foreign news the great fact is the resignation of the French Cabinet, and the advent of M. Gambetta to power as Prime Minister.

Spent the morning over the extracts. In the afternoon rode with my Puck to Mount Jerome Cemetery, where there is I believe a statue of Thomas Davis.[1]

Mother and Edith went for a drive.

Mrs Dickenson (née Miss Kennedy) brought her two children to pay a visit to Del and Vernon, by whom they were most graciously received. Later in the evening a call from Mr A. Burke and Mr Redington and Lady O'Hagan.

Finished the first volume of Grandpapa's *History of Rome*. I feel as if it were quite an event to have read through anything that is not the newspapers these days.

Apropos of the papers, *The Times* is every day full of letters on the subject of the Sub-Commissioners decisions, and the *Standard* fulminates indignantly in its leading articles. The cry of confiscation and the demand for compensation are reviving in full force.

Meanwhile the Land League papers abuse the Govt and the Land Act on different grounds but with harmony of intention.

Mr F. H. O'Donneil sends 2nd elaborate letter to the *Times* to show that whereas the rents are being so enormously reduced, Mr Gladstone turns out to have deceived both the landlords and the Land League—the former were refused compensation on the ground that rents would practically remain unchanged and that therefore there would be no confiscation of the landlords' property: while the latter, and especially Mr Parnell, were first tempted on false pretences needlessly into taking a hostile or rather a cautious attitude towards the Act, and were then thrown into prison for doing so.[2]

The Land League papers on the contrary, so far from echoing Mr O'Donnell's complaint that the landlords are being unfairly treated by the unexpected reductions of the Sub-Commissioners, are busied with pointing out with all the assistance in the way of emphasis that can be given by large type and sensational headings, that the Act is a failure and a disappointment for the unfortunate tenants. 'Great Promise and small Performances'. 'The Tenants Improvements rented as before'. 'A Heavy Rent for 15 years and costs against the Tenants' etc. etc.

[1] Now in the City Hall, Dublin.
[2] *The Times*, 11 Nov. 1881; printed under the heading 'Audi alteram partem'.

12 Nov., Sat.

The contest in Londonderry will be a sharp one. Mr Porter is to be opposed by
Sir Samuel Wilson (Conservative) and Mr Dempsey, a Newspaper editor and
Parnellite, under the patronage of Mr Harold Rylett and Mr O'Donnell.[1]

Further long reports in all the papers of the Land Court proceedings. In
several instances landlords and tenants have come to an amicable settlement
(on the basis of a large reduction) before coming into Court.

Another beautiful day. In the afternoon Mother and I drove to Somerton[2]
and home by Castle Knock—the carriage open, and beautiful views, through
the wooded lanes, of our favourite Wicklow mountains.[3]

Francie and Edith to lunch with Miss Guinness and afterwards to a lecture
on the Prayer Book by Canon Smith at the Alexandra College.

Our quiet week is now over and this evening we are expecting Mr Cropper
and May, and Agnes Holland. Herbert Gladstone is also to return to-night,
and Father and Mr West to-morrow morning.

Mr Cropper and May, and Agnes Holland, and Mr H. Gladstone arrived by
the evening mail.

13 Nov., Sun.

Father and Mr West arrived by the morning boat. Went to Castle Knock
church—Father, Mr Cropper and I walking.

A quiet afternoon. Walked with May Cropper round the Circular—helped
Father make up his journal.

14 Nov., Mon.

A strong attack on the Govt by Lord S[alisbury] speaking at the Colston
dinner,[4] reported in this morning's papers. As before, comparison or rather
parallel drawn between Mr Parnell and Mr Gladstone, as equal instigators to
public plunder.

The Sub-Commissioners continue to give judgments reducing rents—sometimes only by a few shillings, sometimes by pounds, and as might be expected
corresponding indignation and consternation finds expression in the Conservative papers.

[1] Samuel Wilson (1832–95): born in Antrim; prominent in Australian politics up to 1880; now
tenant of Hughenden Manor, Bucks.; knighted 1875. Charles J. Dempsey, proprietor of the Belfast
Ulster Examiner. Rev. Harold Rylett had been the unsuccessful home-rule candidate at the recent
Tyrone election (above, p. 240).

[2] The house of the Brooke family, near Castleknock, west of the Phoenix Park.

[3] Actually the Dublin mountains.

[4] The dinner of the conservative Dolphin Society at Bristol on the annual commemoration of
the philanthropist Edward Colston (1636–1721).

Some incidents in the proceedings of the Sub-Commissioners, however, have been regretted by their friends, and there is a general desire that the Chairman of the different Commissions should not fall into the snare of 'speechifying' which would give an opening for unguarded statements and generalities that may have to be disavowed subsequently by the Chief Commissioners.

Walked with Father to the Park gates, afterwards going on with Edith in the carriage to Chancellor's, where very good photographs of my dear Puck were taken, also of myself.

The Croppers and Agnes went to Bray. I rode in the afternoon. Call from Lady C[owper], and Lady S. Spencer.[1] Mr Cullinan and Mr Fitzgerald to tea. Miss Burke and Mr A. Burke, and Mr [T. H.] Burke 'of ours' to dinner.

15 Nov., Tu.

Report in the morning papers of an attempt last Sunday to shoot General Meares whilst driving home from church, with Mr and Mrs [J. F. H.] Lowry. The General pursued the men, who had fired from behind a hedge, for some miles, but did not overtake them.[2]

Walked with Father to the Park gates.

Went with May and Agnes to the Royal Hib. [should be 'Irish'] Academy, where we were also taken over the library and introduced to the 'Book of the Dun Cow'. It was pleasant to hear the enthusiasm with which the librarian spoke of Uncle Matt's book on Celtic literature.

Lord de Vesci and Mr Edgar Vincent to tea—the latter just returned from Thessaly where the International Commissioners have been establishing the Greeks in their new territory.

The Vice Regal party to dinner in the evening. Their Excellencies, Capt. Dease, Mr Law (the new Lord Chancellor), Lord O'Hagan, the Lord and Lady Mayoress, the Lord Chief Justice and Miss May, Lord and Lady Kilmaine, Baron and Miss Dowse, the Archbishop and Miss Trench.

I sat at dinner in exactly the same place as I did last year on the same occasion, and also with the Lord Mayor of Dublin by my side—but a very different Lord Mayor. I must own that the eminently respectable, law abiding Conservative Mr Moyers was not as interesting company as the in every way reprehensible Mr Gray[3]—but my neighbour on the other side, Baron Dowse,[4] quite made up for his deficiences.

We had a great deal of very lively conversation, and I felt that I quite understood the Baron's reputation for having been one of the most amusing men in

[1] Sarah Isabella, sister of Lord Spencer.
[2] Florence's account agrees with S.P.O., I.C.R., Returns of outrages, Nov. 1881. The attack occurred at Ballymore, Co. Westmeath.
[3] See above, pp 34, 42.
[4] See above, p. 36.

the House of Commons. He was anything but complimentary about his fellow countrymen, especially the Parnellite members—expressing his opinion that Healy in particular could not have been such a blackguard by nature—he must have taken 'great pains' with himself to become what he is.

As to the possibility of a Home Rule Parliament, he was very contemptuous, declaring that if England gave the Irish a Home Rule Parliament and turned the key on them for a year, there would be no members left at the end—they would all have destroyed each other.

As to the recent Convention, which I suggested as an example of how decorously they could manage an assembly if they liked, he remarked that of course they could if they were all on one side as were the members of that Convention.

However, if Baron Dowse was inclined to be severe on his own countrymen (assuring me that deep down in the mind of every Irishman was the longing for a place—every patriot now in Kilmainham—not to speak of Mr Healy—had visions of getting something someday—if it was only the governorship of a Colony) he was anything but a 'Philo Saxon'.

'To speak frankly, and I generally do speak frankly' he informed me, 'I shouldn't mind hearing to-morrow that England had gone to the bottom of the sea, if it were not that I thought I should have my own throat cut over here'— 'but it is with us as Carlyle said of the American Republic—"anarchy plus a policeman"—England is our policeman'.

Apropos of England he discoursed half in fun and half in earnest on the irritating effect of the English tone about Ireland and Irishmen generally— quoting special instances from the *Athenaeum*—*Saturday Review* etc., and even from Mr Gladstone, who it appears had once confided to Mr Baxter his opinion that 'No Irishman was financially sound'—a remark which Baron Dowse had heard Mr Baxter refer to in private conversation in the House, and which he had never forgotten.

'Englishmen seem not to know that there are Irishmen who are as much educated gentlemen and loyal subjects as themselves—why even the boy who begs a penny of you in the street thinks himself infinitely your superior if you are an Irishman'.

As to Englishmen not taking sufficient account of the good, loyal Irishmen in the country, Baron Dowse acknowledged that it was to some extent their own fault for putting themselves so little in evidence in comparison with the ever talking agitators; and he agreed most emphatically with the remark that in no country were there two such unfortunate extremes of over-talking and over-silence.

'But the truth is' he said, 'there is no public opinion in Ireland to support a man!'—a truth which the Chief Secretary has long ago found out to his cost.

Like Mr Naish and Judge O'Hagan, Baron Dowse was not sanguine as to the suppression of the agitators so long as they are supported as they are, on the

American money—'How can they be expected to give up their profession? it is what they live on'.

The evening altogether went off very pleasantly, Mother's only affliction being that people would not talk sufficiently to their Excellencies, who in the nature of things cannot circulate freely themselves, and are therefore dependent on the politeness of others.

Lord Cowper spent most of the evening tête-à-tête with Francie with whom he has much affinity, and who cordially likes him.

The Cowpers are going to make a tour in Ulster staying with Sir T. Maclure and attending festivities at Belfast. It is edifying to see how eagerly the Lord Lieutenant and Lady Cowper catch at any opportunity given them for doing good and being useful at any sacrifice of their own natural tastes and proclivities.

16 Nov., Wed.

Mr Gibson has been speaking at Huddersfield on Ireland and the Govt. The Conservative cue at this time, is to express a magnanimous intention to support the Queen's Govt in the present crisis, and at the same time to abuse them roundly for all they have done, and left undone in their dealings with Ireland— to criticize with amazed indignation the proceedings of the Commissioners, and finally to hint very plainly at the necessity of compensation for the landlords.

Walked with Father, Agnes and Francie to the Park gates. A call in the afternoon from Lady Steele and the pretty Miss Steele.

Mr Edward and Mr Murrough O'Brien to tea. The former painfully anxious and apprehensive as to the difficulties before him as Sub-Commissioner in Donegal—much alarmed too at the sweeping decisions being given by the other Commissioners, and depressed with the perplexity of having to decide on a 'fair rent' with no fixed standard to go by, and the principle of competitive value excluded.

Edith and the four dear little children left us by the North Wall boat to return to Cathedine; the boys are greater darlings than ever, and Iris is becoming so in her own determined little way. We miss them much.

Mr and Mrs [Thomas] Hamilton (from the office) Major and Mrs Fitzgerald (the new Adjutant at the R.H.M. School),[1] the Dean of the Chapel Royal, and Lord William Compton dined with us.

Gathered from Father and Mr Hamilton that things were getting very bad again in the matter of outrages.

[1] Joseph William Fitzgerald (1839–93): appointed adjutant on 25 Sept. 1881.

17 Nov., Th.

Spent the morning over the Newspaper book. Calls in the afternoon from Mrs Wade and Mrs Monahan. Went for a walk in the park with Agnes Holland and the two dogs.

A dinner party in the evening, Judge and Mrs and Miss Fitzgerald, Eardley Willmotts,[1] Dr and Miss Salmon,[2] Dr and Mrs Hancock, Mr E. O'Brien, Colonel Gipps, Mr Fred Romilly,[3] and Mr G. Fottrell. This last is a Dublin solicitor—recently appointed Clerk (or secretary) to the Commission, and I believe a great friend of Mr Dillon's. He is said to be 'smart', but is certainly not an attractive young man—vulgar, I thought—'a snake in the grass' Father says, but this of course I had no means of judging.

Judge Fitzgerald, Mother and I thought charming—'just like an old English gentleman'—was her criticism on his looks and manner, and a very high compliment from her.

18 Nov., Fri.

Father received at the Castle a deputation of Quakers from Ulster introduced by Mr Richardson, M.P. for Armagh. They came to express their satisfaction with the Land Bill, and each one made a separate little speech to that effect.[4]

Read the Sedition papers. In the afternoon Mother took May Cropper and Agnes to Trinity College. I rode in the Park with Puck. May Cropper left us by the North Wall boat to return to England.

Father brought Major Neild (Edward's friend the R.M. at Leitrim) back to dinner with him.

I had known that of lately things had been going very badly, but this evening the state of the country seemed to be fearfully brought home to one. A few words from Father made me see that he had had a bad day, and just as we were going in to dinner I heard from Mr West that a bailiff had been murdered—the news had just come to the Castle before they came out.[5]

The picture Major Neild drew of the state of things round him in Leitrim was dark and disheartening to the last degree, and taken in connection with

[1] Major William Assheton Eardley-Wilmot (1841–96): deputy assistant adjutant-general of the forces in Ireland since 1879.

[2] George Salmon (1819–1904): mathematician and divine; Donegall lecturer in mathematics, Trinity College, Dublin, 1848–66; regius professor of divinity, 1866–88; provost, 1888–1902; author of *Non-miraculous Christianity* (1881), *The infallibility of the church* (1889), and many other works.

[3] Frederick William Romilly (1854–1935): captain in the Scots Guards.

[4] The six members of the deputation stressed the importance of security of tenure in encouraging development (*F.J.*, 19 Nov. 1881).

[5] Luke Dillon, bailiff on an estate near Logboy, Co. Mayo, was found shot dead on the road on the morning of 18 Nov. He was thought to have been responsible for his employer's refusing to reduce rents, and was on bad terms with the local league (S.P.O., I.C.R., Returns of outrages, Nov. 1881).

the Land League papers I had been reading in the morning it seemed all the more so. The boy shot down and maimed for life simply because his father was a bailiff—the woman insulted in her home and her husband half beaten to death on the road, screaming for help to the neighbours, but with no one to come to their rescue because, as the woman told Major Neild, 'she and her husband were bad Land Leaguers'—the landlord, who in former days had done all he could for the people as their friend, now living in complete isolation and obliged to go about armed, and under police protection—everywhere sullen hostility, and deadly fear and suspicion.

All this seemed just the practical illustration and explanation of the teaching of *United Ireland*.

As for the Land Courts, the people in that part of the country were following Mr Egan's advice and refusing to go in—preferring to maintain as long as possible a total strike against all rent—a strike enforced by terrorism.

The impossibility of protecting the unfortunate 'bad Land Leaguers' against the armed ruffians who enforce Land League principles by easy cruelties upon old men, women and children is one of the most serious difficulties the Govt have to deal with.

Crime of every description (provided it is or appears to be agrarian) can be committed with absolute impunity, from the double obstacle to a conviction, fear on the part of witnesses, and fear on the part of the jury.

In the first impulse the victims will sometimes promise to give the needful evidence (for in 9 cases out of 10, they know perfectly well who has attacked them), but 24 hours later no persuasion, no promise of protection by the magistrate who takes their deposition will induce them to identify their assailants.

They know that they would be marked men ever afterwards and they prefer to suffer once rather than twice.

As may be supposed, the talk at dinner and after dinner was of little besides the state of the country. Every one seemed sober and silent as well they might.

'It's a tremendous battle', I heard Father saying to Mr Cropper, as they stood over the fire together, 'I don't know that I shall be able to get on without doing what will need a Bill of Indemnity'.

'What do you consider would require that?'

'Oh the introduction of some sort of Martial law—you see we have lost the great lever of government and law, the power of punishment. We have to keep patrols all over the country by way of a preventive measure—but a single case of punishment would be the only real preventive. What between the people who sympathise with the crime, and the people who are afraid, there is no backbone of resistance anywhere.'

Mr Cropper is deeply interested in the new lights he is getting on Irish matters over here, and is constantly wishing that some of the theoretical Radicals, especially Mr Jesse Collings, could have the same advantage.

19 Nov., Sat.

A very black list in the papers this morning. 'A bailiff murdered', Luke Dillon, on the property of a Mr Farrell in the Co. Mayo. 'An agent shot', Mr Digby, cousin and agent to Lord Digby in King's Co., fired at and wounded whilst walking back from the Rent Office in the evening.[1] 'A Farmer shot', an old man named McManus in Kerry, visited at his house by a party of armed men and fired into for having paid his rent.[2]

Even the *Freeman* ceases to talk about 'manufactured outrages', and at last calls out that such crimes as these injure the good cause.

Mr Cropper left us to stay with Mr Richardson at Bessbrook.

Gummed extracts in the morning.

A visit to Father from Mr Burke in re a letter to the Sheriffs.

In the afternoon with Mother and Agnes Holland to see the Drummond Institute, a home for Soldiers' orphan girls, as the Hibernian R.M.S. is for boys.[3] A very nice home-like institution, and a very pleasant looking set of girls. Afterwards went with Agnes to have tea with Lady and Miss Steele at the Royal Hospital.[4]

A small party in the evening—whist playing with Father, Agnes and Mr West.

20 Nov., Sun.

A week or more ago Father had talked of a walk to-day in the Wicklow Mountains, but now this was quite out of the question—things much too anxious for him to be away.

To church in the morning at the Hibernian, without Father. Mother and Agnes to church at St Patrick's in the afternoon. A visit from Mr E. O'Brien, and afterwards a walk with Father in the Park, attended at a respectful distance by the inevitable gentleman of the G Division,[5] whom Father has not yet identified.

Mr O'Brien very anxious and depressed—both about the outrages, and about the decisions of the Commissioners. Apropos of the former, he told me that his father had described to him the way in which an organized system of nightly outrages had been put down in his day. The gentry and the loyal farmers of the district patrolled the country themselves—30 of the midnight

---

[1] At 4.30 p.m. on 18 Nov., William Fitzgerald Digby (1844–98) was shot in the back, but received only a flesh wound and was able to chase his attacker. For later developments, see below, p. 334.

[2] 'Kerry' is a mistake; Patrick McManus lived near Mullingar in Westmeath.

[3] The institute was founded in 1864 at Mulberry Hill, Chapelizod, through a bequest of £20,000 from Alderman Drummond.

[4] Royal Hospital for Ancient and Maimed Soldiers, Kilmainham (the Irish Chelsea). As commander of the forces in Ireland Sir Thomas Steele was Master of the hospital and had his residence there.

[5] Detective section of the Dublin Metropolitan Police.

raiders were taken and sent for trial to Ennis, where they were convicted, sentenced, and despatched straight from the dock at Ennis to penal servitude in Australia.

This sudden and absolute disappearance of the prisoners struck the imagination of the people, and such was the impression made, that the outrages entirely ceased.

I pricked up ears at hearing of the volunteer patrolling, and combination of the law-abiding inhabitants of a district, and was beginning to wonder why outrages might not be met in some such way nowadays, but Mr O'Brien explained that everything was quite different, the farmers sided with the gentry because the offenders were to a great extent of the labouring class who had a grudge against the farmers, and as to the conviction, that was the result of having a 'packed jury' composed of Magistrates who were not afraid for their lives to do justice on a criminal.

As to the Commissioners Mr O'Brien evidently looks with dismay on the work they are doing, and in which he will have to take part.

I showed him Mr Egan's No Rent Manifesto, which he had not seen and was interested in reading—but he thought that the landlords have much more cause to be afraid of the Commission than of these No Rent Manifestoes.

Helped Father make up his journal, and copy a letter to Mr Gladstone in answer to an enquiry about how the Govt here is to be reinforced when the Ch. Sec. goes over to London.[1]

Father's answer explained amongst other things his wish to leave Ireland as soon as he could do so without seeming to shirk present difficulties. If these could be met he thinks the best régime would be Lord Spencer and Mr S. Lefevre—or better Mr Shaw as Secretary. Lord Cowper would almost certainly resign when he did.

A quiet evening. Mr West dined in Dublin: Father read aloud to us in the evening Wordsworth's 'Cumberland Beggar'. I think this poem was never done more justice to in the matter of reading.

21 Nov., Mon.

The Conservative candidate (Mr Salt) has beaten the Radical working man's (Mr Howell) at Stafford [(Borough)], by a considerable majority.[2] The *Freeman* in great satisfaction over the result as a Parnellite victory. The Conservative papers equally jubilant over it as a snub to the Govt on general grounds.

From all accounts Mr Salt was decidedly a good candidate and will be a good man to have in the House. The Irish influence does not seem to have been

[1] B.L., Add. MS 44159, ff 102–5; quoted at length in Reid, *Forster*, ii, 366–8. As Law had become lord chancellor, Forster thought Cowper need not be replaced: 'much is due to his devotion and self-sacrifice'.

[2] 1,482 votes to 1,185. Thomas Salt (1830–1904), a director of Lloyd's bank, had been M.P. for Stafford 1859–65, 1869–80.

so potent in this election as the *Freeman* would wish to make out, the number of Irish voters in Stafford being small, but there is no doubt that the withdrawal of the Irish vote will lose many Liberals their seats at future elections.

Moreover the Conservatives will reap the advantage of this transference without the necessity for making important promises to obtain it—which will be a great convenience to them—and also good for the country, putting the issues of divisions on Irish matters in the House in its true light.

Walked with Father through the Park, afterwards driving with him to the Castle, and doing some shopping in Grafton St.

In the afternoon took Agnes to the National Gallery, where Mr Doyle went round with us, and pointed out the new pictures which have been added since I was last at the Gallery—a Van Hals, and a beautiful landscape 'Le jeune Pecheur' by the brothers Both.

A call from Miss Burke. A dinner party in the evening—very uphill work, at least I found it so on coming in after dinner—present: Mr Justice and Mrs Harrison (she a beautiful and stately woman—quite different to the average Dublin ladies in appearance), Mr and Mrs Wallace, Canon and Mrs Sadlier of Castle Knock, Dr and Mrs Gordon, Col. and Mrs James, Capt. Darcy Irvine, and Commander Pipon from the *Penelope* now the guardship here in place of the *Belleisle*.

Judge Harrison very gloomy about the state of things, telling Mother that he should never see it any better in his time.

'After all', I said to Father, as he sat over the fire in my room, where he had come to say good night to Francie and me,

everything that is happening now is what you had foreseen would happen. You said that there would be a great deal of secret crime and outrage, and that November would be a particularly bad month, and as to the necessity for some system of eviction to meet the obstinate refusal of rent, you were planning it out and talking it over with Lord Frederick the last time he was here.

'Yes' said poor Father, 'but talking about a thing in prospect and realizing it are very different'.

He certainly is having a very anxious and distressing time just at present; but he sets his teeth and works hard without wasting words over lamentations, and with so much zeal and energy as though he did not feel the gloom and oppression of the dark horizon.

I spoke to him about *United Ireland* and its 'No Rent' propaganda: he does not think so much of this—the circulation of the paper, Mr Johnson tells him, has fallen off by one half, and a prohibition or prosecution would only give it a new lease of life. As to the outrages, Father thinks 'that the word has gone out to murder'; one thing is certain, murder is not discouraged by the present leaders of the agitation—witness their organ *United Ireland* in which every fresh cruelty committed against an unhappy man—whether landlord or bailiff—or farmer, is entered under the heading—'Incidents of the Campaign' or 'Spirit of the Country'.

22 Nov., Tu.

Report of Lord Monck's meeting of Dublin Magistrates.[1]

French accounts in the papers this morning of outrages upon farmers suspected of having paid their rent, and mutilation of cattle: in one case 52 head of cattle belonging to a priest beaten to death, because their owner had condemned the 'No Rent' Manifesto.

Mr Burke to see Father in the morning.

Walked with Father and Mr West to the Park gates. Francie and Agnes went thoroughly over the Hibernian [School] with the new Adjutant Major Fitz-Gerald.

A call in the afternoon from Miss Trench. In the evening with Major and Mrs Fitzgerald, Agnes Holland, Mr West and Mr Jephson to the [Gaiety] theatre 'Cloches de Corneville'.

Mr Naish dined here.

23 Nov., Wed.

Mr Holland arrived by the mail boat, coming fortunately just too late for the fearful gale which raged here on Monday night. We lost two more trees, but from the trees' being without their leaves there was less destruction in this respect than in the last storm.

Lord and Lady Cowper who left on Tuesday morning for Belfast seem to be having a really good reception.

Worked at the newspaper book in the smoking-room most of the morning. Mr Holland and I started to walk with Father through the Park, but were driven back by a storm of rain and hail.

Drove in to Dublin in the afternoon with Mother, Agnes and Mr Holland to the Land Court (which was not sitting) and afterwards to the National Gallery.

Mr Vernon and Mr Jephson to dine and sleep—much business done and much talk between Father and Mr Vernon over Land Court difficulties, which are legion.

Mr Jephson, Mr West, Agnes and I played whist in the evening, but it was impossible not to hear at the same time the talk going on at our backs, over large sheets of paper covered with figures—I believe comparative tables of rents, old valuations and new decisions.

[1] A meeting of the J.P.s of the county of Dublin, summoned by Lord Monck as lieutenant of the county, was held in the grand-jury room at the Four Courts on 21 Nov. 130 magistrates attended and passed resolutions of support for the government, although a few tentatively admitted sympathy for home rule (*Irish Times*, 22 Nov. 1881).

A very severe letter from Lord Doneraile[1] read aloud by the Ch. Sec. on the delinquencies of the Sub-Commissioners and the special unfitness of one man (Mr Rice) for his present place, owing to his large family connection in the neighbourhood where he and his colleagues were sitting. Both Father and Mr Vernon are evidently very anxious as to the proceedings of the Sub-Commissioners. Father is inclined to think that in almost every case, even in those which seem most startling at a distance, the decision can be justified on a full knowledge of all the circumstances; and a letter he had received from Lord Waveney[2] on the decisions in his immediate neighbourhood had confirmed him in this belief.

But the decisions in Lord Clarina's case, and in that of Enright v. Regan[3] at Limerick, did surprise him.

Both he and Mr Vernon seem to feel that the Commissioners should have some principle on which to act—how can such an intimation be conveyed to them? A letter from Mr Vernon to the Sub-Commissioners is proposed, suggesting this on the ground that their proceedings will have to be defended in Parliament, and that the Ch. Sec. must know what their line has been.

Another difficulty is evidently the question of Valuators—more officials, however necessary, means more money from the Treasury. In fact there seems to be perplexities all round, and the Ch. Secretary is very hard beset and anxious.

24 Nov., Th.

A subscription Fund opened in the *Freeman* this morning for the benefit of the 'suspects' in Kilmainham, who had expressed their intention to submit [subsist] for the future on prison diet instead of on the food supplied by the Land League funds from America. To prevent them having to suffer from their resolution the *Freeman* has opened this subscription on their behalf, declaring in a very effusive and touching leading article that such a question as this 'is above politics'.

Report in the papers of Lord Cowper's speech at Belfast—very spirited and outspoken, and very loyal to his political colleagues.

Spent the morning over newspaper cuttings. Father very busy with a letter to Lord Hartington, who is going to make a speech and requires information, and if possible some reassuring facts about the Commissioners—whose proceedings are very naturally very trying in some cases, and very inexplicable to such members of the Cabinet as Lord H. and Lord Selborne.

Father drove to the Castle at 12.30, very much absorbed and I fear worried.

[1] Hayes St Leger (1818–87): 4th Viscount Doneraile; owned 14,958 acres in Cork and Waterford, valued at £13,738.
[2] Robert Alexander Shafto Adair (1811–86): cr. Baron Waveney, 1873; M.P. for Cambridge, 1847–52, 1854–7; A.D.C. to the queen; owned 6,546 acres in Antrim, valued at £6,810.
[3] A slip for 'Ryan'; see above, p. 308.

I believe that more Sub-Commissioners are going to be appointed. They will be bold men to undertake the office.

The truth is that talking about things in theory, and seeing them carried out in practice are, as Father said the other night, very different.

The principle of a Court of Arbitration (when one heard it discussed in the House) for the fixture of rents sounded much like any other strong and novel measure of reform, but when one sees the actual and inevitable working of the Court in Ireland, one feels as though one were assisting not so much at a reform as a revolution.

The absolute and legitimate power of these Sub-Commissioners to reduce by one half the income of one man, and to ruin another, cannot but strike one as something quite outside one's ordinary political experience, and it is very needful from time to time to take a general view of the situation, and remind oneself of the true position of the Commissioners and of the antecedent causes which have made them and their strange functions a public necessity.

After a morning over the newspapers, went out to lunch with Miss Burke— meeting Lady Constance Bellingham and a Miss Fitzgerald.

Mother, Mr Holland, Agnes and Francie to a Bazaar for the Orthopaedic Hospital. A prominent feature of this was a stall of Irish Manufactures— including apparently, packets of tea, ham, biscuits, a broom, and a stamped woollen table cloth.

Dr Salmon to dinner. He was invited for the purpose of talking to Mr Holland about the Irish Church, but instead of this, both he and Mr Holland spent the evening superintending a game of whist between Father, Agnes, Mr West, and me.

25 Nov., Fri.

Father read aloud to us at breakfast a letter or statement he had received from Mrs Lalor,[1] the courageous lady who is being most cruelly boycotted by her tenants, and is meeting her difficulties with great spirit and good sense.

Her letter was most admirably written—concise, calmly expressed, and perfectly clear and straightforward, and as she has the right in this case I believe entirely on her side, one can sympathise unreservedly with her pluck and determination—refusing to be frightened or worried out of the country, declining to come to a compromise with the bullying tenant who is trying to defraud her, standing by the labourers who are 'boycotted' for refusing to leave her service, and opening a store for them at her own house, etc.

As the ringleaders in this very flagrant case seem to be well known in the district, the Ch. Sec. will probably have them arrested under the Coercion Act.[2]

[1] Mary Frances, widow of Edmund James Power-Lalor (1817–73) of Templetouhy, Co. Tipperary. The estate was of 7,311 acres, valued at £2,841.
[2] Thomas Collier, publican and farmer of Templetouhy, was arrested on 17 Jan. and imprisoned at Clonmel until 6 Apr. (S.P.O., I.C.R., P.P.P. Act, lists of arrests).

Read the Sedition papers. *United Ireland* as usual occupied mainly with vilification of the Land Courts and their decisions, general abuse of the Govt, and eager triumph over every case of non-payment of rent, and outrages conducive to this end.

Walked with Father and others to the Park gates.

Through the V.R. grounds in the afternoon, with Mr H[olland], Agnes, and Francie. A perfectly beautiful afternoon, level sunshine over the green tract of the Fifteen Acres, and a clear wind-swept sky.

Mr Holland and Agnes left us by the evening boat to return to London. Agnes has been a charming visitor and we all miss her—down to Puck and Yarrow, to whom she was very cordial and attentive.

A dinner party in the evening, Mr and Mrs North Dalrymple, Judge Barry, Sherlocks, Deputy Commis. General Murray and Mrs Murray[1] (just arrived in Ireland from Nova Scotia) Mr and Mrs Ulick Bourke (he one of the 2nd batch of Sub-Commissioners, going off on Monday to Donegal), Mr Vincent, Mr Lentaigne, and Mr Moyers (son of the Lord Mayor).

26 Nov., Sat.

The Municipal Elections in Dublin have not been the triumph for the Parnellites which the *Freeman* had meant them to be, and in Cork 4 out of the 5 extreme men have been defeated—a surprise it is said to all parties.

The labourers are being brought forward more of late in connection with the working of the Land Act. On Friday a notice from the Land Commissioners was published, reminding labourers of the claim they are entitled to make on the farmers when the latter have their judicial rent fixed, and in several of the papers letters and leaders have appeared complaining that the labourers were not being sufficiently considered.

A curious incident was reported also in Friday's papers—namely, that a body of labourers on the estate of a Mr Urquhart in West Meath, who had been turned off by their employer, came to the agent requiring to be taken back to work again; the agent explained that so long as no rents came in the landlord could not employ them, being unable to pay their wages; on their being assured that, if the rents were paid Mr Urquhart would take them into work again, the labourers informed the agent that if the rents were longer withheld 'there would be bad work'—and then proceeded to threaten the farmers with the object of making them pay up.

We walked with Father to the Park gates. Another gale began. Arrival of flowers from Fox Ghyll. An afternoon indoors, the weather outside being wild and rainy.

Mr Robin O'Brien to 5 o'clock tea. He had been dining the evening before with Judge O'Hagan, whom he had found 'very low' about the state of things.

[1] J. W. Murray, deputy commissary-general of the Dublin military district.

Mother rather alarmed at this report, but reassured on finding that Judge O'Hagan's despondency came in great part from his dislike of adverse criticism—Lord Emly calling him Chief Confiscator, etc.—to which Irish Judges are apparently not so hardened as English politicians have every reason to be, especially if they have anything to do with Ireland.

Father and Mr West dined in the evening at the Richmond Barracks with Col. Hall and the Coldstreams—meeting Mr Gibson, Judge Barry, Col. Bruce, Sir Thomas Steele, and Mr Mahaffy.[1]

27 Nov., Sun.

Advent Sunday. A wild stormy day—the gale which had been blowing all night continuing in full force.

Drove to church at the Hibernian—the wind over the Fifteen Acres making walking almost impossible—not to speak of the sweeping showers.

Mr Reeves Q.C.,[2] the Chairman of the Limerick Sub-Commission, to lunch—a smooth-shaven, carefully-dressed man, evidently priding himself on his familiarity with French, his musical attainments, and his general acquaintance with cultivated and elegant society—in face and manner reminding us of the Dean of Durham.

One of the strange indirect results of the present revolution has been to place this gentleman in his present position—shut up night after night at an inn, good, bad or indifferent—in South West of Ireland—with a worthy professor of chemistry, and a tenant farmer for his inseparable, and only companions—with the exception of his registrar Capt. Mc Causland—Mr Rice and Mr O'Keefe[3] these two other Sub-Commissioners are both, it seems, excellent men, and by all accounts well qualified for their business—but one could understand Mr Reeves's rueful though good-humoured description of the long evenings passed exclusively in their society—for the Sub-Commissioners are strictly forbidden to avail themselves of any private hospitality whilst on their mission.

Mr Reeves being such a man as he is, connected by taste and association, and family with the landlord class, and feeling keenly the abuse and indignation poured upon him by his friends of the Kildare St Club—one was all the more impressed by his perfect confidence in the needfulness and justice of the work he was doing.

It was very interesting to hear his description, half humorous, half pathetic, of the scenes in Court: the eager anxiety of the farmers, without a spark of the old liveliness and wit, absorbed only in the excitement of being allowed for the first time in their lives to lay before the public every detail of their special history and special grievances—the self-satisfaction of complacent witnesses,

[1] See appendix.
[2] Robert Reeves (1833–89): Q.C., 1880; appointed legal assistant commissioner, 22 Sept. 1881.
[3] John Rice; Cornelius O'Keeffe.

the quaint and graphic expressions of the people in describing to 'My Lord', as they call the Legal Commissioners, the physical peculiarities of their particular holdings, and the special decision which had given such umbrage—e.g. Enright v. Ryan—and the Town parks decision. Mr Reeves was quite prepared to justify them, and I believe reassured both Father and Mr Vernon in their qualms on this subject.

A wild stormy afternoon. Walked with Father to the Burkes', and struggled home against a raging wind and in torrents of rain.

Went into the study after tea to help Father make up his journal. We spoke of Mr Pigott's article on Ireland in the December *Mc Millan*, which is making a considerable sensation.[1]

[Two pages were missing from the original typescript.]

if not an editor of a Land League journal.

Lord de Vesci to dinner. It was pleasant and edifying to hear the calm, kindly spirit in which Lord de Vesci talked about his hopes and plans for the future— discussing the possibility of Irish School Boards—asserting his belief, in spite of unfavourable examples, in the capability of middle-class Irishmen for local self-government, and for filling the office of Guardians and School Board Members, etc.—not a trace in all he said of bitterness or despondency, or vindictiveness—not a word betraying the soreness and angry disappointment which are naturally so common in these times, and which would seem especially natural in a man who has been treated as Lord de Vesci is now being treated by his tenants.

It seems however, that the virtues of a good landlord are hereditary, and perhaps ineradicable in the de Vesci family, for the present Lord de Vesci is at this moment joint owner with Lord Longford of a property which was left to the great-grandfather of the former, and the grandfather of the latter, by a Mr Dunbar—a complete stranger, who in his will assigned all his large property to these two noblemen, on the ground of their being the two best landlords in Ireland.

Some talk in the evening of a book I had just received from Pesth, Déak's Speeches about Austria–Hungary and Home Rule—of the difference between the Magyar nation, and the sort of Irishmen who agitate for Home Rule in this country (i.e. Mr Dawson etc.).

---

[1] Richard Pigott, 'The Irish question' in *Macmillan's Magazine*, xlv (1881–2), pp 165–76; the article praised the land act, condemned the league, judged Fenianism extinct, and considered it the duty of Irish patriots to support the government and the union. The author had been editor and proprietor of the *Irishman*, the principal organ of Fenianism till Aug. 1881; he was exposed in Feb. 1889 as the forger of letters which *The Times* had published in Apr. 1887, intended to incriminate Parnell.

The mass of educated men—the Irish gentry—take far less part in the present Home Rule agitation than they did for instance in '48.

'But even if you did wish it' (Home Rule), said Father to Lord de Vesci,

you would never get it—because it would not suit us to give it to you. Look what it would involve—it would mean a return to personal rule in England. In Austria–Hungary they settle their affairs by means of two delegations. A plan which seems to work well enough.

But what is the consequence—before I made my speech (about Home Rule) I went to Beust[1] to ask him about it, and said I suppose if there is any question in which the Delegations can't agree the Emperor himself settles it?

He said, you are perfectly right, that is how the system works.

So if the Imperial Parliament once ceases to be supreme, it becomes necessary to have this sort of personal government, or to give the power of final decision into the hands of a body of lawyers, as is done in the United States. Home Rule would mean asking us to set aside our present Constitution, in favour of a paper constitution which would have to be manufactured to suit the new order of things.

(I think this is a fairly correct version, though certainly not verbatim.)

28 Nov., Mon.

The storm abated, and Mother resolved to keep to her intention of going over to London to superintend papering and painting at No. 80 [Eccleston Square].

Report of Lord Hartington's speech at Blackburn.

Worked at the Newspaper book, and wrote invitations.

Walked with Father and Mother and Mr West through the Park. Calls in the afternoon from Julia O'Brien, and Mrs Ulick Bourke—both mourning their respective husbands who had gone off that morning to Donegal as Sub-Commissioners—also from Mrs Crofton and Lena, on their way to England from Co. Sligo—the Crofton tenants decline to pay their rents but are not personally offensive—in fact, at a dance and other festivities given in celebration of the birth of Sir Malby's son,[2] the tenants insisted on appearing in great force, and seemingly as amiable as if there were no Land League in existence.

A call also from Lady Burke who chattered on endlessly on reminiscences of the Marlboroughs—state of the country—great distress (this apropos of the Distressed Ladies Asst.) sad cases—but after all what could you do—people would have to resign themselves to having smaller incomes—years ago Sir Bernard used to get himself into trouble by saying to the landlords when he

[1] Friedrich Ferdinand von Beust (1809–86): foreign minister of Saxony, 1849–53; minister for internal affairs and minister-president, 1853–66; subsequently minister-president and foreign minister of Austria–Hungary, taking a leading role in the *Ausgleich* settlement (1867) and internal liberalisation; ambassador at London, 1871–8; at Paris, 1878–82.

[2] Malby Richard Henry Crofton, born 18 Sept. 1881, son of Sir Malby Crofton, owner of 3,422 acres, valued at £1,440, in Co. Sligo.

stayed with them at their country houses—'you're getting too much out of the land', 'the rents are too high'.

Dear Mother went off by the evening boat intending to sleep at Holyhead, and go on to London the next day.

Father home to dinner. A game of whist in the evening with Dummy—Mr West having gone to the theatre.

29 Nov., Tu.

A telegram from Mother telling us of her good passage.

The newspaper book. Father and Mr West amused themselves with firing their revolvers at a mark in the kitchen garden. Drove into Dublin with Francie, first taking Father and Mr West to the Castle.

Rode Paris about the Park in the afternoon; a perfectly lovely day. Miss Burke to tea. A long quiet evening; Father at the last moment sending word that 'he had been deluded' into stopping to dine at the Kildare St Club (and playing whist afterwards at the Cavendish).

30 Nov., Wed.

Received the *N. American Review*, containing O's article on 'Ireland'.[1]

A wet grey morning. Attempted to walk with Father, but were both of us driven back by the rain and he had to take to the carriage.

A deputation of Licensed Vintners to Father.

Francie and I called in the afternoon on Mrs Stotherd at the Mountjoy Barracks.

Another quiet evening, Father again dining in Dublin, this time by previous arrangement, so Francie and I could subside comfortably into a meat tea, instead of eating through a dinner of 6 courses with three servants standing round staring at us.

Heard through a letter from Lady Buxton of Sydney's engagement to Constance Lubbock. He is a very fortunate man.

A long attack in the *Standard* by their 'Special Commissioner' on Mr Evelyn Ashley for his conduct on his Sligo estate—everything taken down as gospel that was told by the hostile priests, and direct charges of harshness and cruelty alternated with insinuations to the same effect. Finally the statement that probably Mr Ashley refused to make just abatements because, being in the confidence of the Govt, he knew that they intended compensating landlords whose rents had been reduced by the Courts, and was therefore waiting to have his reduced by compulsion.

[1] H. O. Arnold-Forster, 'The Gladstone government and Ireland' in *North American Review*, cxxxiii, no. 301 (Dec. 1881), pp 560–77.

Apropos of this, a leading article urging the necessity for compensation—a very favourite topic at present.

1 Dec., Th.

A long letter to Father from Lord Monteagle explaining the extent (a very large one) to which the *Freeman* had told falsehoods about the proceedings of his tenantry. Most of them have paid and all will probably do so in time. Nevertheless Lord Monteagle tells Father that he was never more sad about the state of the country—the intimidation and terrorism everywhere, the 'land reeking with blood' from the almost daily murders and outrages, the perpetrators of which can never be brought to justice.

Walked with Father, Francie and Mr West to the Vice Regal. His Ex. at home, but Lady Cowper not, so Francie and I wrote our names and returned.

An interview with McKenna the new gardener.

Miss L'Estrange and Miss Jane Lee to lunch—Francie having made their acquaintance at the Trenchs. Miss L'Estrange, very handsome and interesting and altogether attractive: Miss Lee[1] knows 14 languages including Sanscrit, and seems very amiable. After lunch Francie drove with these ladies into Dublin, going to a service and a sermon by the Archbishop at Christchurch, and afterwards to tea at the Palace.

I rode Mr West's pony in the Park—Puck accompanying us. The pretty Lady Kilmaine and her cousin Miss Brownlow to tea. Lord Kilmaine has got his rents.[2]

Mr Evelyn Ashley arrived to stay for the night—Father and Mr West home to dinner.

Evidently it had been a black day and the Ch. Sec. was very tired; had ordered the arrest of 7 people from one district—this is for the cruel outrage upon poor Galvin in Co. Kerry.[3]

Heard from Mr Ashley at dinner some of the truth about the incidents mentioned by the *Standard* correspondent. He has written a letter which I suppose we shall see in the *Standard* to-night.

A short game of whist in the evening. Father told us of one amusing incident that had occurred during the day—a visit from the O'Gorman Mahon.

This veteran duellist (who simply by dint of living, says Father, has come to be considered quite the venerable hero and man of honour) is fond of offering himself as intermediary between his friends in Kilmainham and his friend the Ch. Secretary. To-day he came to request that certain of the 'suspects' might be

---

[1] Jane Lee (d. 1895), daughter of William Lee (1815–83), archdeacon of Dublin since 1864; later vice-principal of Newnham College, Cambridge.

[2] Kilmaine owned 18,765 acres, mostly in Mayo, valued at a total of £8,906.

[3] Seven men from Castleisland district (including four who had previously been arrested but were released when Galvin refused to identify them) were arrested on 9 Dec. under the P.P.P. act and held for six to seven months (S.P.O., I.C.R., Returns of outrages, Dec. 1881).

let out, assuring the Ch. Sec. that Mr Parnell would give an undertaking for their good behaviour if released.

The objections to taking the undertaking of one suspect about another was pointed out to him, on which the O'Gorman Mahon exclaimed: 'Then I'll give you my own word of honour'—an arrangement which seemed to him absolutely satisfactory.

Father, not at all embarrassed, explained that he would be quite willing to take the O'Gorman's word of honour as a guarantee for anything, if only he could be sure of his being able to make his friends keep to their part of the bargain. 'But if they did not Sir, I would shoot them!' was the O'Gorman's most reassuring and conclusive answer to this objection.

2 Dec., Fri.

A morning in the smoking room over the Rebel papers and others. By the way, Mr Killen, acting editor of *United Ireland*, has been arrested. Considering that the paper was one broadsheet of direct 'incitement not to pay rent' it was not surprising that the authorities felt bound to take notice of him.

Walked with Father and Mr West to the Park gates. Read Mr Pigott's article on the way back. Arranged Fox Ghyll flowers, and a call from Mrs Eardley Wilmot in the afternoon.

We dined at 7 and went with Mr Evelyn Ashley to the theatre to see Dion Boucicault in 'The Shaughraun'.[1]

His acting as 'Con the Shaughraun' and that of Mr Shiel Barry[2] as the informer 'Harvey Duff' were really fine, and quite worth going to see. A crowded house, appreciative, and indeed enthusiastic, but not politically excited. Called after leaving the theatre for Father, who had been dining with Mr Mahaffy and the Fellows of Trinity. He had enjoyed his evening, and told us he had been well cheered by the students in hall.

But nothing, however pleasant can distract his mind for long from thoughts connected with his great task, the government of Ireland under the present hard circumstances.

He told us he had been seeing Mr Ashley's friend, Sir Henry Gore Booth,[3] and also a man who came from the very heart of the bad country—Lord Dunsandle.

'It is quite clear that the landlords will do nothing till January'—a remark to which Mr Ashley fully assents. He himself has been busy all day with his agents in Dublin (Stewart and Kincaid) arranging their plan of campaign—Writs are

---

[1] Dion Boucicault (?1820–90): born in Dublin; actor, theatre manager, prolific dramatist, and champion of home rule. 'The Shaughraun' was first produced in 1875.

[2] Shiel Barry (1841–97): specialised in Irish parts until 1878; he then played Gaspard in 'Les cloches' almost continuously until 1889.

[3] Henry William Gore-Booth (1843–1900): 5th baronet; owned *c.*32,000 acres in Sligo valued at £16,774; father of Eva (d. 1926) and of Constance (d. 1927), the future Countess Markiewicz.

to be sent down, and Mr Ashley hopes that with the beginning of strong measures (which have now become quite necessary) the 'anti-rent' movement on his estate will collapse.

It is I believe Father's opinion that the 'No Rent' agitation is spreading, but that to a great extent it is hollow; and meantime, of course, the prolonged inaction of the landlords in asserting their claims increases the difficulty of the Govt by increasing the people's confidence in their own power of resistance to the law.

On coming in read the papers in the smoking room—a very good and satisfactory letter of Mr Ashley's in the *Standard*.

In the first *Times* leader a nice allusion to Mr Arnold-Forster's article in the *N. American Review*.

3 Dec., Sat.

Mother returned from London bringing Lucy with her. Spent the morning over the Newspapers and Visitor's book in the smoking room. Mother walked with Father. He is greatly oppressed and over-worked at present, and has told Mother, incidentally, that at times during the last day or two he has fallen asleep for a few moments in his chair, even in the midst of some interview or conversation that was really interesting to him.

This particular morning his depression I think was increased by the report in the *Freeman* of the behaviour of the Members of the Kildare Hunt, at a meeting at Naas.

This meeting of the farmers of the county was convened by the gentlemen of the Kildare Hunt with the object of ascertaining how far hunting would be allowed to proceed, and if possible of coming to some amicable agreement on the subject with the farmers.[1] The result of the meeting, at which several gentlemen—Lord Drogheda, Lord Clonmell, Baron de Roebuck, Mr Mansfield,[2] were not only present, but took part—was that a resolution was proposed and 'carried unanimously' in which,

we the undersigned inhabitants of Kildare, Magistrates, farmers, artisans and labourers, petition the Govt to release the political suspects now detained in prison; and do hereby

---

[1] The gathering of crowds to obstruct the hunts, or to conduct 'Land League hunts', amounting to massive poaching expeditions, became common during the winter of 1881–2, and on 24 Dec. a circular was issued to constabulary officers and R.M.s, drawing attention to the power to disperse such gatherings as illegal assemblies. Where circumstances permitted, however, a formal proclamation was issued, on similar lines to the type devised in June; see above, pp 160, 163.

[2] Lord Drogheda, as well as being vice-admiral of Leinster and ranger of the Curragh of Kildare, was lord lieutenant of Kildare. John Henry Reginald Scott (1839–91), 4th Earl Clonmell, owned some 21,000 acres, over half in Tipperary, valued at a total of £13,977. John Henry Edward Fock (1823–1904), 4th Baron de Robeck, owned 1,838 acres in Kildare, 2,638 in Wicklow, and 1,660 in Dublin, valued at a total of £5,110. George Patrick Lattin Mansfield (1820–89) owned 4,542 acres in Kildare and 1,097 in Waterford, valued at a total of £4,417.

declare that their incarceration and the Act under which this county is proclaimed is no longer necessary for the peace and preservation of property in this county; on the contrary, it is tending to create more disunion and discord; and if this resolution is subscribed to, we hereby pledge ourselves to give everyone facilities to hunt.

The meeting finally ended with a resolution stating that Mr Forster might be allowed to continue hunting 'till we see what way things will turn out'.

Walked with Lucy and Francie round the Circular in the afternoon: a call from Mr Percy Joy, a friend of Hamlet Philpot's, just entered the R.I. Constabulary.[1]

A short game of whist in the evening, but Father could think of nothing but the Naas meeting. 'What can you do for people like this?' he says; 'even the violent little Tory paper the *Dublin Evening Mail* has a very fierce and indignant article on the conduct of the Kildare gentlemen, who for the sake of their hunting will consent to increase the difficulties of the Govt at a time like this'.

4 Dec., Sun.

To church in the morning at the Hibernian. Father hard at work and quite unable to go.

The three Commissioners and Mr Jephson to lunch. The conversation not of a very sanguine character. Mr Vernon especially grim about the prospect before the Commission—what with all the cases coming before the Sub-Commissioners, and the appeals before the Dublin Court, he does not see how the work is ever to be got through, and hardly likes to face the outlook before us.

Certainly intelligent Irishmen are not subject to illusions about their own countrymen. No one who knows them can say that either Mr Burke or Mr Vernon is a narrow-minded or prejudiced man, incapable of sympathy with a national and liberal idea, and yet both of them have the same utter disbelief in the possibility of governing this country successfully under the British Constitution.

'The worst of it is we are neither fit for freedom nor for slavery' said Mr Vernon.

'Certainly not for freedom' was the immediate comment of another Irishman.

The whole live-long afternoon spent by the Ch. Secretary, the three Commissioners, and two private secretaries, shut up together over the appointments of new Sub-Commissioners.

The only man of the party left at liberty was Mr Evelyn Ashley, with whom Mother had a good deal of talk after lunch.

[1] Percival Holt Joy, a third-class sub-inspector awaiting assignment to a district.

As to the question of compensation to landlords—which is so much being talked of now—Mr Ashley thinks that the practical difficulty in the way of doing this fairly will make it quite impossible. 'Why should rack renting landlords, who are now chiefly suffering from the Land Court reductions, be compensated, and nothing be done for those who have voluntarily reduced their rents? Would not a more feasible system of compensation be for the State to engage to purchase the estates from those landlords who wish to sell?'

As a matter of fact he does not think that there would be many applications, and believes that the State would find itself completely reimbursed by the tenants' payments.

A hard afternoon's work for Father. About 5 o'clock he came wearily into the drawing room, depressed not only by work but by bad news.

'Just as I was hugging myself on my Outrage returns being better, there is another brutal murder'. A process server named Rogers (a one-armed man) battered to death by a party of men in the King's [should be Queen's] County.[1]

'It's sickening!' I hear Father say to himself, and he looks regularly worn out. Mr Ashley left by the evening Mail.

A short walk in the dark and rain with Father and Mr West, even this amount of air being better for him than nothing. Mr G. (Detective) prowling after us as usual.

5 Dec., Mon.

Newspaper book. Mr Burke to see Father. Walked with Father. With Mother and Lucy. Dinner party—Sergeant Hemphill, Dr Ball, Mrs and Miss Brooke,[2] Capt. James, Col. Smith, Mr F. Cullinan.

6 Dec., Tu.

Mr Burke to see Father. Walked to the Park gates. Father, Mother and Francie dined at the Trenchs.

---

[1] Martin T. Rogers, solicitor's clerk, was found beaten to death with stones at about 1 p.m. on 3 Dec., after he had been serving writs for recovery of rent. Five men were arrested; at the spring assizes one was acquitted and the rest discharged (S.P.O., I.C.R., Return of outrages, 1881, 1882).

[2] The Brookes are probably Henrietta (d. 1911), daughter of the 3rd Viscount Monck and widow of Francis Richard Brooke (1817–67), and her daughter Grace Agnes.

7 Dec., Wed.

Uncle Tom arrived. Newspaper book. Walked through the Park. L[ucy] and I lunched with Miss Burke. Mother, F. and L. to a Bazaar. In the afternoon I rode Comet in the Park. Telegram announcing the Derry election.[1] Dined at the V.R.

8 Dec., Th.

Walked with Father, returning with Mrs Dalrymple and her dogs. Rode in the afternoon. A party in the evening, Col. and Mrs Dease, Judge and Mrs Warren, Lady and Miss Wolseley, Mr Gilbert D[   ] and Mr Naish.

Mr Ross of Bladensburg[2] to dine and sleep.

9 Dec., Fri.

A black and dreary morning. Letter to Father from Lady Emly 'things almost intolerable'; as bad as they can be. Pigott letters. Walked with Lucy. Spent the afternoon in Dublin. Tea with Miss L'Estrange. Cold beginning. Mr Ross, Lord M[onteagle] and Mr C. Lloyd to dine and sleep. Collapse of Irish Indus[tries] Ex[hibition] on the question of the Queen as President.

10 Dec., Sat.

Walked with Father and others in the Park—fiercely cold—an afternoon at home—the visit to the Observatory having to be given up from the mist.

Mr Lloyd, Lord M[onteagle] and Mr Wilfred Lloyd, R.H.A.,[3] at dinner.

A riotous game of whist—Mr Lloyd in high spirits at his temporary escape from Kilmallock: his brother declaring that he had never seen him in such a state of exuberance. Father has thorough confidence in this man—if all Resident Magistrates were of his pattern Ireland would not be in the condition it is now.

Mr [Herbert] G[ladstone] returned at 10 o'clock from the west.

11 Dec., Sun.

A brilliant frosty day, every tree crystallized in white. To church at the Hibernian. Walk with Lord Spencer and Father—riotous behaviour of the junior 'Harvey Duff' capering and laughing.

---

[1] Porter was elected by 2,701 votes to Wilson's 2,054; no return of votes for the home-ruler Dempsey is available.

[2] See appendix.

[3] Wilford Neville Lloyd (1855–1935): Royal Horse Artillery; brother of Clifford Lloyd.

12 Dec., Mon.

Conviction by Cork jury.[1] Walked to the V.R. Copied Lord O'Hagan's letter concerning the Pope and the Archbishops. Mr Lloyd left. Lady Burke and Miss Crofton to dinner—Sir H[ubert] Miller and Mr Jephson. Letter from Pesth.

13 Dec., Tu.

Walked with Father. Called on Miss Burke. Wrote for Father his Memorandum on R.M.s.[2] Mr H. Gladstone, Lucy and Lena drove into Dublin. Col. Hillier to be informed of the new scheme. No one to dinner. Telegram—Lord Boyle.

14 Dec., Wed.

Mr and Mrs A. Johnston[3] arrived. Lena C. left us. I lunched at Killiney. Message from Mr Murrough—'When are you going to release the political prisoners?' Invitation to come and see him in his room at the Land Court. Called on Julia and returned with her and her girls—heard of Charlotte's [Charlotte O'Brien's] projected good work at Queenstown, and of the help she has already been to emigrants in distress. Mahaffys, Mr Kindersley, and Mr Jephson to dinner. A note from Father—'alas another murder!'[4]

15 Dec., Th.

H. Gladstone left. A morning of ball invitations. Julia O'Brien left us. A few moments talk with Father in the carriage drive. To the Bazaar in the afternoon. The Seebohms arrived. Mr Ross of B. to dine and sleep. Heard that *United Ireland* had been seized. Father very much absorbed.

---

[1] On 12 Dec. a Cork city jury at the Cork winter assizes convicted seven men of attacking the house of a woman who had given evidence, near Listowel on 26 Nov.

[2] On 11 Dec. Forster had written to Gladstone announcing his intention of introducing a system of decentralising executive work under 'say six' temporary commissioners, each 'responsible to me for the peace of his district, and for the use of all the powers which the executive possess [*sic*]'. Gladstone replied (12 Dec.) that it was well worth trying (B.L., Add. MS 44159, ff 131–2, 134). The scheme had been devised in consultation with Spencer and Lloyd. See also Lloyd, *Ireland under the Land League*, p. 227.

[3] Andrew Johnston (1835–1922), grandson of Sir Thomas Fowell Buxton; liberal M.P. for South Essex, 1868–74.

[4] Probably the murder of James Brennan, farm labourer of Co. Roscommon, shot dead at about 7 p.m. on 13 Dec. because his brother Michael had paid rent (S.P.O., I.C.R., Returns of outrages, 1881).

16 Dec., Fri.

Mr C. Lloyd, and Capt. Plunkett to breakfast. Mr S[eebohm] and Mr Johnston to Artane. A morning over invitations. Mr Lloyd, Mr [H.] A. Blake, and Capt. Plunkett[1] all to lunch. Walked with them afterwards and drove with L. into Dublin. No one to dinner. Wished success to H. Gladstone speaking this evening at Manchester on Ireland.

17 Dec., Sat.

Johnstons left—Seebohms going with them to ? Invitations and Newspapers. Father's journal. To Dublin and R. Hospital with Lucy. Father and Mother to Abbeyleix—(well guarded). Miss L'Estrange and Baroness Prohasseka to tea. Uncle Tom and the Seebohms returned, one from King's Co. the other from Cavan.

The man who had shot, and known to have shot Mr Digby, acquitted from absolute witholding of all evidence.[2]

The impression in both places of perplexity from the sullen, passive opposition of the people, either from ill-will or fear, to the payment of rent, which will all the same be paid on the application of strong measures.

18 Dec., Sun.

The Seebohms, Lucy, Francie to church at St Patrick's—I to the Hibernian, driving home with Lady C[owper]. Walked in the afternoon with Lucy and the Seebohms. Mr S. called on His Ex[cellency]—an old Hertfordshire neighbour.

19 Dec., Mon.

Ball invitations. A call from Miss Burke. Uncle Tom and Mr S. to Dublin. Went to meet Father and Mother at Kingsbridge at 1 on their return from Abbeyleix. An embrace and a few words with Father on the platform before he vanished in the brougham to the Castle.

Heard from him that there had been another murder reported to him that morning at Abbeyleix. It turns out however that this was more in the nature of a family quarrel than an agrarian or 'No rent' crime.[3]

[1] Thomas Oliver Westenra Plunkett (1838–89): second son of the 12th Baron Louth; R.M. since 1866; now stationed at Belfast following Lloyd's transfer to Longford and Kilmallock. It was on this day that the three future special R.M.s were first briefed for their task.

[2] Above, p. 316.

[3] Patrick Dunne, an elderly small farmer, was found stabbed to death in his house on 18 Dec.; he had been dead for a week. His brother Timothy, a 'returned Yank' who had quarrelled with him about the farm, was suspected of the crime, but absconded and was later found drowned (S.P.O., I.C.R., Returns of outrages, Dec. 1881).

The visit to the De Vescis had been pleasant, but somewhat sad. Lord Spencer there, Mr Mahaffy, Lady S. Spencer, and others.

An afternoon at home. The Seebohms left us by the evening Mail. Dinner party in the evening, Solicitor Gen. and Mrs Porter, Lady W. Seymour, Col. and Mrs Wray, Col., Mrs and Miss Bruce, Mr Ch. Trench, and Dr Newall.

Father evidently much absorbed and worried, talking almost entirely to Col. Bruce, of the Constabulary—there are endless difficulties rising up in connection with the new scheme for relieving the R.I.C. by enlisting retired soldiers and others to assist them in their duties.[1]

'Well, this *is* a country', says Father, after the guests have departed, and he settles down to the evening papers—'I think things get more difficult every day'.

Heard also this morning that the Ladies Land League is to be proclaimed.

20 Dec., Tu.

A Circular signed by Col. Hillier in the morning papers, explaining that the illegality of the men's Land League applies to the Women's also. 'Females' taking part in illegal meetings etc., will incur the same risks as men.[2]

Ball invitations. Walked with Father and Mr West to the Park gates—a bitterly cold morning.

Heard from Father that Mr Dillon and Mr Parnell's grievance, displayed so elaborately in the *Freeman* last week, was not quite so bad as it appeared. They had never been compelled to move into other and more objectionable rooms at all, the plan had only been talked of, and the object was to give them rooms which it was thought were healthier and more convenient.

An afternoon in-doors. Mr C. Lloyd to 5 o'clock tea—also by his own invitation to late tea with Lucy and me—Father, Mother, and Francie dining at the V.R.

Mr Lloyd very eager about this new plan—appointing him and 2 or 3 others head-men over a certain district for the pacification of the country and suppression of outrage—very indignant with Mr Johnson,[3] who it appears has been demurring, declaring that such a delegation of authority from the Castle will be an avowal of weakness on the part of the Govt, and moreover they have not legal powers to do it. 'Red Tape' says Mr C. Lloyd furiously.

He hopes great things—probably too much—from what such men as he and his friend 'Tom Plunkett' could do, by personal vigour and influence and authority, in stirring up and wisely directing the decent loyal people of all classes, even in the bad districts.

[1] Recruiting for an auxiliary force had begun on 15 Dec.

[2] Law had decided on 29 Oct. that the Ladies' Land League could be suppressed under the proclamation of 20 Oct. but that it would be inexpedient to do so. The circular was drafted on 12 Dec. and issued on 16 Dec., considerable care being taken to preserve secrecy during its preparation.

[3] Attorney general 17 Nov. 1881–3 Jan. 1883.

An article from the *Times* read aloud by Mr Lloyd, and 'Patience' in the evening.

A seance in Lucy's room of all the family after the return of the others from the V.R. Father in better spirits than I had expected.

21 Dec., Wed.

Oakel arrived from London. He had been speaking the day before at Bridport, on Ireland.

Ball invitations. Mother drove with Father into Dublin, thinking him much oppressed and over-taxed.

The scheme as originally planned can hardly be carried out. Sir H. Miller to lunch. Drove with Mother into Dublin. Mr Vere Forster, of emigration fame,[1] to dinner. Whist.

22 Dec., Th.

A cold frosty morning. Father walked with a large detachment of the family to the Park gates. An interview at 1 with the anxious R.M.s. Drove into Dublin in the afternoon with L[ucy] and O. The shops alive with people—no signs of distress in Grafton St.

Mr Kinder[s]ley and Capt. Bunn to tea. A family party at dinner. Whist in the evening.

23 Dec., Fri.

Report of 1st Landlords' Meeting,[2] and [Irish Manufactures] Exhibition Meeting. The Exhibition given up.

Rumour in the *Freeman* of proposed appointments (Mr C. Lloyd etc.), 'Can it be true?' The *Freeman*, always charitably willing to think the best of their abandoned Govt, refuses to believe the report. Newspaper book. Walked with Father to the V.R. to enquire for his Ex[cellency] who has been unwell.

Mansion House controversy still continues. Arranged flowers. Yarrow had a fit. Mother and Francie drove into Dublin. I wrote. A family party and whist in the evening.

---

[1] Vere Foster (1819–1900): since 1848 assisted (chiefly at his own expense) the emigration of nearly 25,000 young women from the congested districts, and the building or equipping of 2,200 national schools.

[2] Nearly three hundred landowners attended a poorly-organised meeting in the Rotunda, Dublin, on 22 Dec., and passed resolutions including a demand for state purchase of the lands of those who could not accept the effects of the land act. A further meeting was arranged for 3 Jan. (*Irish Times*, 23 Dec. 1881; see below, pp 342–3).

24 Dec., Sat.

A wet morning—newspaper book and invitations. Drove with Father to the Castle—lunched with Miss Burke—Lord W. Compton to tea—ourselves alone to dinner.

25 Dec., Sun.

Christmas Day. To church at the Hibernian, but Father not able to come. A moist rainy afternoon. Walked with Oakel to Castleknock. Francie and Lucy to St Patrick's. Miss Burke and the brothers, and Mr Redington to tea. Dr Smyley[1] to see Father, he having a slight chill and feeling rather unwell—partly exhaustion showing itself the first opportunity there was leisure for it to do so. Mr Burke to see Father.

26 Dec., Mon.

Father did not go to the Castle: his chill better after a good night. Mr Jephson to lunch. Final applications for ball invitations etc. to be attended to. A call from Mr Mahaffy and Mr Wilson King, once American Consul here, and now at Birmingham. Father, Mr M. and Mr K. walked with us to the Racquet Court where O. and Mr West were spending the afternoon.

Mr King is a thin, agreeable American, bearing a marked likeness, he considers, to Sir M. Hicks Beach. He is much interested in finding himself again amongst his Irish friends, and notices little in society to make him realize the state of things, except that each person he meets tells him in the course of conversation some story of distress or outrage worse than the last; coming straight from amongst the Radicals of Birmingham, these stories of personal experience bring home to him the reality of a condition of things to which his surroundings there had begun to make him callous. He is struck with one parallel to the French Revolution in the present Irish agitation—the change in the relation of men and parties which has taken place since he was here last. As the extreme men at the beginning of the French Revolution became by comparison the Girondists and the Moderates, so the men who four years ago were regarded as the extreme politicians here are now completely left behind.

Mrs Mahaffy and her two boys[2] to tea, to meet Mr Mahaffy and his friend.

An early dinner in the smoking room, and afterwards to the Pantomime with Oakel, Mr West, and Lucy.

Herbert Gladstone and his sister arrived from England. Mr Murrough O'Brien to dinner. He has been appointed assistant Valuator to Mr Gray—an

---

[1] Philip Crampton Smyly (1838–1904): surgeon in ordinary to the lord lieutenant.
[2] Frances Letitia (d. 1908), née MacDougall, who married Mahaffy in 1865, and their sons Robert and Arthur.

impartial man of great experience who has been appointed Assessor in Chief to the Commission, for the purpose of deciding in appeals as to the valuations of the Sub-Commissioners.

May and Madge Benson arrived from South Wales by the North Wall, having left home at 5 in the morning.

27 Dec., Tu.

A morning of ball lists, and battle-door and shuttle-cock. A beautiful afternoon, the mountains and park shining under the sun.

Visit from Miss Trench. Lord and Lady Monteagle arrived. Mr Jephson to dinner, otherwise a family party.

Unanimous decision of the Judges with regard to service [of writs] by post.[1]

28 Dec., Wed.

Circular to the new R.M.s, explaining their functions. The *Freeman* indignant at the action of the Privy Council in the matter of writ-serving—'arbitrary', 'despotic', 'removing safeguards' etc.

Walked with Father to the Park gates, talked of Mr Wilson King and the American Constitution. Mr Redington to lunch—made him promise to come to the ball in the evening. Drove into Dublin to have my ball dress tried on. Took Lady M[onteagle], Helen Gladstone and May Benson to the R.I. Academy, where we were joined by Mr Gilbert, Mr McSweeney, and Major MacEnery—the Chalice of Ardagh was taken out for us to see the beautiful decorative work beneath the foot of the cup—the brooch of Tara was also taken out and I was allowed to take it in my hand to examine. Certainly the Irish of those days were not a barbarous people, at any rate as far as art was concerned.

Harry Benson arrived from Cashel.

First Ball.

29 Dec., Th.

Mr Drawith [Drewitt] arrived. To the Mountjoy Barracks to see the making of the Ordnance Map for Ireland. Hard at work all the afternoon over ball list for the papers.

Important arrest announced in the morning papers of a man named Connell—supposed to be the 'Capt. Moonlight' whose gang had committed so

[1] On 10 Sept. the Irish judiciary had revised the rules for service of processes so that, in cases where resistance was expected, a process could be served by postal delivery. On 5 Dec. the inspector general had issued a circular reminding the constabulary that in view of these rules they were no longer obliged to give protection to process-servers in dangerous cases. Florence's remark here refers to recent judicial decisions to facilitate the serving of processes by post by cutting out court preliminaries; see *Irish Times*, 26 Dec.; C.S.O., R.P. 1881/37171, 43537.

many outrages near Millstreet, Co. Cork—papers found in his possession, and a stolen watch.[1]

Call from Lady O'Hagan. Mr D'Eyncourt, a barrister and friend of Oakel's, arrived.

Second Ball. His Ex[cellency] not able to come either night from slight attack of gout—she very gracious. All persons represented, landlords, Sub-Commissioners, Judges, doctors, Aldermen, Guardsmen, professors, etc., etc. Balls pronounced a success. Father playing whist, and to use his own expression 'buzzing about'.

30 Dec., Fri.

Article in the *Freeman* on the R.M. appointments, talking severely of 'almost Martial law', but giving wholesome warning to the people to try and avoid collisions with the night patrols. Up to the present 5 men have been appointed[2]— all first-rate for the purpose, and acknowledged to be so.

Father had an interview at the Castle with Mr Dawson, the Lord Mayor elect, who came to apologise for having spoken of the Ch. Secretary as 'Buck-shot Forster'.

Drove with Lucy and the Bensons.

The Gladstones, Monteagles, Oakel and I dined at the V.R. Lodge; Lady Cowper gave Herbert Gladstone a 'blowing up' as he said for his speech, or at least for what he had said about the landlords. She appears to have told him that though she agreed with what he said, she thought his saying it at this time only did harm—irritating the Liberal landlords, and not improving the others.

It is certainly a fact that in Ireland under present circumstances a truth sometimes has done as much harm as a lie—that is to say in the effect it produces.

Mr Walpole one of the S.C.[3] dined here. A plain, sober man, very gloomy about the demoralization of the people, which it will take a generation to [? cure]. 'The lying in Kerry something fearful.'

31 Dec., Sat.

The Monteagles left us, having, I think, enjoyed their visit, and the opportunity of meeting old Dublin friends. They are both most loveable people, and the Irish tenantry and their present leaders will not be in any way the better for driving them out of the country, if they succeed in doing so.

[1] See below, p. 345.

[2] Florence has not previously mentioned Captain Owen Randal Slacke (1837–1910): R.M. since 1868, stationed at Carrick-on-Suir; and Captain Antoine Sloet Butler (1823–1901): R.M. since 1853, stationed at Athboy, the fourth and fifth special R.M.s, appointed on 28 Dec. 1881. See also above, p. 334.

[3] Presumably Thomas Walpole, a sub-commissioner.

The Raid on hunting,[1] as the *Irish Times* calls it, still continues; the Galway Hounds have been stopped, and Mr Brooke (near here)[2] having been requested to get rid of three obnoxious members of the hunt at the last Meet, refused to allow them to leave, and withdrew the hounds.

Read the papers in the study and walked with Father to the Park gates— driving afterwards with Lucy into Dublin for shopping, etc. In the afternoon with a large party into Dublin to tea with the Ormsbys and Lees.

Mr Van Wagner to dinner. The whole party here in the evening to the V.R., to see Dumb Crambo[3] and acting by the party there.

1 Jan., Sun.

'Mine's a more modest wish' said Father, when somebody wished him a 'happy New Year'—'that it may be a less bad year than the last'.

To church in the morning at the Hibernian. I walking round by the road with Father, and Mr West. The whole party in the afternoon to St Patrick's with the exception of Father, Mother and me.

His Excellency to see Father, and a call on Mother from Lady C[owper]. She had just been seeing Lady Kenmare[4] (passing through Dublin on her way to England) and hearing her indignant and angry story—the utter impossibility for the Commissioners to arrive at the truth on which to found their decisions—everyone in the pay of the tenants including the valuators, etc. etc.

Lady C[owper] had been suggesting as strongly as she could that they should engage an impartial valuer from England, but it appears that Mr Hussey, the agent,[5] would object to this, and for some reason or other this Mr H. has such control over the property that the Kenmares dare not oppose him.

Lady Cowper's scornful indignation over such a state of relations between landlord and his agent was very characteristic.

At 5 o'clock tea we had several visitors—Miss Burke, Col. Burke, and Mr Redington, Lord de Vesci, and Mr Penrose Fitzgerald come up to attend the Great Landlords' Meeting on Tuesday.

Spent an hour in the study before dinner helping Father make up his arrears of journal, and talking.

---

[1] See above, pp 329–30.

[2] George Frederick Brooke (1849–1926): of Somerton; son of the Hon. Mrs Brooke (above, p. 331); high sheriff of Co. Wexford, 1882.

[3] A word-guessing game involving two sets of players acting in turn in dumb show.

[4] Gertrude Harriett, née Thynne; wife of Valentine Augustus Browne (1825–1905), 4th earl of Kenmare, liberal M.P. for Kerry, 1852–72, and owner of 91,080 acres in Kerry, 22,700 in Cork, and 4,826 in Limerick, worth a total of £34,473.

[5] Samuel Murray Hussey (1824–1913): high sheriff of Kerry 1868; unsuccessful conservative candidate for Tralee, 1880; owned 4,272 acres, valued at £1,590; supervised 88 estates with a rental of £250,000; author of *The reminiscences of an Irish land agent* (London, 1904).

The murder of a woman at Mullingar on Saturday does not appear to have been agrarian.[1]

Two at least of the New Superintendent R.M.s have got to work; Father showed me the letter[s] to Mr Burke from Mr Clifford Lloyd and Mr Butler which looked like a promising beginning—in both came the demand for more men—the system of night-patrolling is to be carried out vigorously.

After dinner, Uncle Matt's poem on Dean Stanley in the *19th Century*[2] read aloud by Father to the assembled company, still 13 strong; afterwards hymn singing, H. Gladstone playing the accompaniments.

Later in the night extensive skylarking in the garden and other 'ballyragging' in which as usual the Member for Leeds[3] took a prominent part.

2 Jan., Mon.

Spent the morning chiefly in the study and smoking room over newspaper cuttings. Oakel to Dublin to see the Lord Mayor's Show. Father at home to lunch. Mr Gerald Fitzgerald, one of the Sub-Commissioners, to lunch, before returning on the following day to his duties in Tyrone.

Oakel, Mr D'Eyncourt, H. Gladstone, Lucy, the Bensons and I to the Zoological [Gardens]. We were admitted to a private interview with 5 sweet little lion cubs, born seven weeks ago in the gardens.

A wild rainy evening, and many vacillations in the family plans up to the last moment; finally the two Bensons and Lucy determined to brave the elements and left us by the North Wall to return to England—Oakel and Herbert Gladstone escorting them to the steamer.

Father dined at Woodlands to meet Archbishop McCabe; Oakel and H. Gladstone in Dublin with Mr Cullinan.

Lucy's departure is very sad; she has been a month with us, and is more endearing than ever, not to say prettier and more attractive—a fact which someone outside Lucy's family was evidently not blind to.

3 Jan., Tu.

No special outrage reported in the morning papers, but still it was clear from Father's face and manner at breakfast that something was seriously amiss. Half an hour later Mother coming out of the study said to me with a grave face 'Did you see what Herbert Gladstone has been doing—writing to the papers from here, without even consulting Father or showing him his letter'.

This was a letter appearing both in the *Irish Times* and *Express*, from Herbert

[1] Esther Cregan, farmer's daughter, was shot by an intruder in her parent's house at about 8.30 a.m. on 31 Dec., and died a quarter of an hour later (S.P.O., I.C.R., Returns of outrages, Jan. 1882).

[2] 'Westminster Abbey: July 25, 1881' in *Nineteenth Century*, xi, no. 59 (Jan. 1882), pp 1–8.

[3] Herbert Gladstone.

Gladstone to the Chairman of the Town Commissioners at Ennis, explaining in elaborate terms why he had declined a public interview when passing through Ennis, and ending with the statement 'I am glad that I can reliably inform you, from official information obtained since my return to Ireland, that crime is decreasing in the proclaimed districts, and that the authorities look with sanguine expectation to the time—not far distant—when the repressive measures now in force can be abandoned'.

There were leading articles on the letter in both papers, and Father was much annoyed at the whole affair. Herbert Gladstone received a summons to the study, and a few minutes afterwards Father appeared in the drawing room to announce—'He never wrote the letter at all'.

The whole thing was a hoax, and till Father showed it him, H. Gladstone had not even seen the letter, having been reading the *Freeman* in which it was not published.

Walked with Father, Mr Drewitt, and Mr Gladstone to the Park gates, driving on afterwards into Dublin.

Charlotte O'Brien to lunch, a strong proof of affection on her part, considering how cordially she disapproves of us officially. She had thought it necessary to warn Mother that she should probably become a Member of the Ladies Land League, but happily, while she was here, she quite eschewed 'burning questions', and only talked about her now absorbing interest of emigration, Father Nugent, and her scheme for a Lodging House at Queenstown, which she is going to keep herself—quite giving up her beloved country life, and her pretty little house and garden on the Shannon.

She had been delighted with H. Gladstone's apocryphal letter, which she said seemed to give a gleam of hope, and I felt almost sorry to have to shout into her ear that he had never written it.

Mother and Helen Gladstone for a drive. A quiet afternoon at home. Mr Drewitt left us by the Mail. Father dined at the Stephen's Green Club—Oakel and Mr H. Gladstone with the Ormsbys. We, including Mother, Helen Gladstone, Mr West and I, dined early at home, going afterwards to see some good private theatricals at Castleknock, by various members of the Brooke and Fitzpatrick families.

Heard from Mr West that the landlords' Meeting in the Exhibition Palace that afternoon was considered to have been a great success—moderate, unanimous, and very largely attended, 3,000 present. Mr Penrose Fitzgerald said to have made the most vehement attack on the Sub-Commissioners—Lord Waterford's speech the nearest approach to a political attack on the Govt, Mr Mahony's pathetic, as I can well believe, and bitter.[1]

The Corporation have also been holding a Meeting, and conferring the Freedom of the City on Messrs Parnell and Dillon by a majority of 7.[2]

---

[1] Mahoney foretold the expulsion of the working landlord and his replacement by the gombeen man (*Irish Times*, 4 Jan. 1882). [2] Above, pp 287–9.

4 Jan., Wed.

Full reports in the papers of the Landlords' meeting, and also of Mr Bright's and Mr Chamberlain at Birmingham. No allusion this time to 'force being no remedy'—on the contrary, so vigorous an endorsement by Mr Bright of the strong measures taken by the Govt in Ireland, that the *Freeman* declares he may well disclaim as he does the name of 'democrat'.

The landlord Meeting seems to have been successful and impressive; the Resolutions studiously moderate, and the speeches on the whole sensible and spirited, by no means justifying the stereotyped charges of class selfishness, blindness, imbecility, avarice, etc., which it is the custom in some quarters to make against any landlord who points out what he considers to be defects or mistakes in the administration of the Land Act.

Judging from the reports one would say that the Duke of Abercorn's[1] was the speech most requiring the serious consideration of the Govt, but Lord Waterford's was evidently the one which roused the enthusiasm of the audience at the time.

Amongst the Herculean labours of the poor Chief Secretary during the coming Session will be the championship of the Sub-Commissioners, for whom he is of course personally responsible. All their sins he says will be laid on his shoulders—though for that matter, as Helen Gladstone truly observes, 'everybody's are'.

At 10 o'clock Father and Oakel went off to the Richmond Barracks to accompany Sir Thomas Steele on his inspection of the troops, according to an arrangement made with Sir Thomas the night before.

Helen Gladstone left us in the afternoon for Kilruddery, to spend two days with the Meaths.[2] Called on Mrs Carpenter and Kathleen. Mother with Miss —— to the St Vincent's Refuge. Father home to dinner after a long day at the Castle.

It is feared that a bailiff on Lord Ardilaun's property at Cong has been murdered. He went out alone with his grandson to serve writs in this dangerous part of the country, and has never been seen since, though some of the writs have been found scattered about the road.[3]

5 Jan., Th.

Father left by the Mail for London, intending to travel up from Chester with Mr Gladstone.

A morning over the newspaper book. A speech of Lord Derby's reported—

[1] James Hamilton (1811–85): 1st duke of Abercorn; lord lieutenant of Donegal; lord lieutenant of Ireland, 1866–8, 1874–6; owned 15,942 acres in Donegal, and 47,615 acres in Tyrone, valued at a total of £35, 802.

[2] William Brabazon (1803–87): 11th earl of Meath. Kilruddery, near Bray (Co. Wicklow), was one of his houses; he owned 14,717 acres in Wicklow and 36 in Dublin city and county, valued at a total of £7,945.   [3] See below, p. 363.

for the first time in the character of an avowed Liberal to a Liberal Meeting. His remarks on Ireland not exactly sanguine, but less hopelessly gloomy than in his article in the *19th Century*,[1] and a good word for the Govt.

Proposal from Mr Dickson and Mr Givan to hold a great 'Tenant' meeting, to protest against the landlords.

Drove with Oakel in the afternoon to Woodlands, and to tea at Somerton with the Brookes.

A small party at dinner, only our 4 selves, the Occidental and Herbert Gladstone.

Whist in the evening.

6 Jan., Fri.

To Dublin in the afternoon with Mother for shopping, etc. Helen Gladstone returned from Kilruddery to spend the night with us before going over to England. A scattered party in the evening, Oakel dining at the O'Hagans, Mr West and H. Gladstone in Dublin, and Mother and I at the Steeles'. Miss Steele looking bewitchingly pretty in black, with white lace in her dark hair, but the party not particularly amusing. Mr Mahaffy asked me eagerly if I had read his article (on Irish Landlords in the *Contemporary*)[2]—I said as yet only what I had seen in the papers.

'Oh, don't judge from those, they tell lies, they are garbled extracts—lots of people have told me after they had read the article in full that they agreed with every word I said.'

This may be, but certainly a great many people dislike the article in full as much as they could the extracts. His diatribe against the Irish landlords (especially coming just at this time) has created furious indignation, and the *Irish Times* is full of letters protesting against Mr Mahaffy's calumnies.

Sir Thomas Steele and I had a little talk about Mr Clifford Lloyd, with whom he had just been making personal acquaintance. As might have been expected the two seem to have hit it off very well—Sir Thomas Steele had been much impressed with Mr Lloyd's vigour and capacity, and had willingly given him the men he asked for.[3] A hundred of the Scots Guards under charge of Mr Romilly had gone down that day [6 Jan.] to Co. Limerick to be billeted about the country in parties of two for the purpose of giving protection to individuals,

---

[1] 'Ireland and the land act' in *Nineteenth Century*, x, no. 56 (Oct. 1881), pp 473–93. Derby's speech at Liverpool affirmed that in the interests of the empire the will of the Irish majority favouring home rule must be outvoted by the majority in the United Kingdom (*The Times*, 5 Jan. 1882).

[2] Mahaffy's article, 'The Irish landlords' in *Contemporary Review*, xli (Jan. 1882), pp 160–76, accused the landlords of inactivity, lack of public spirit, and (to some extent) illiteracy.

[3] This is notable in view of the caution, and sometimes apprehension, with which Steele, and the military authorities in London, responded to the demands of the Irish executive for military aid; see Richard Hawkins, 'An army on police work: Ross of Bladensburg's memorandum' in *Irish Sword*, xi, no. 43 (winter 1973), pp 75–117.

and setting the Constabulary free for more efficient night patrolling. A hundred of the Coldstreams under Capt. Fortescue have also been despatched to Clare and Limerick for the same purpose.

7 Jan., Sat.

Helen Gladstone left us to return to England, Francie going to see her off at the North Wall.

Oakel and I left Kingsbridge at 10.15 for a two days visit to the Monteagles.

The newspapers on the way down gave us a good deal of reading. A full report in the *Irish Times* of the Property Defence Meeting at the Mansion House, at which Mr S. Morley,[1] Mr Chaplin, Lord G. Hamilton[2] and others spoke.

The affair seems to be now at last put on the right (i.e. non-political) footing, and it is to be hoped that money will be largely forthcoming. At present I believe £16,000 has been raised, and Mr Morley is of opinion that £50,000 is required. I believe that the very sensible and reassuring action taken by this highly orthodox Liberal with regard to the P. Defence subscription is in great part due to Mother who wrote him a full reply to some enquiries he had privately made as to its aim and character.

The papers of this morning also contained further particulars of the 'Capt. Moonlight' affair, and the evidence against Connell at the Cork Assizes.[3]

Judge Fitzgerald, Mr Peter O'Brien Q.C., and the carefully selected Cork jury still combine to prevent the old custom, of punishment following crime, from becoming quite obsolete in Ireland; one or two more convictions have been obtained, and justice at Cork does not seem to be a mockery.

Oakeley and I having three hours to spend in Limerick, went to Cruise's Hotel in George St., and ordered lunch. Meantime Oakel had sent up his card to Mr Clifford Lloyd, who is staying at this hotel, and greeted us in a very friendly manner.

We went up with him for a few moments to his room—already looking like a Government office, the tables and chairs covered with papers, and two of the faithful Royal Irish Constabulary in constant attendance in the passage outside.

We spent the afternoon partly in the streets, and partly over the fire in the Coffee room, and soon after 5 had a second short interview with Mr Clifford Lloyd who came down to talk to us while we had our tea. He looked ill, which is not surprising, as he has to struggle through his hard work in face of an attack of

[1] Samuel Morley (1809–86): member of one of the largest textile manufacturing concerns in Britain; liberal M.P. for Bristol, 1868–85.

[2] George Francis Hamilton (1845–1927): 3rd son of the duke of Abercorn; conservative M.P. for Middlesex, 1868–85.

[3] Connell and his associates were not in fact before the assizes but a special petty sessions at Macroom. See below, pp 361–2.

ague, the relics of a 'jungle fever' caught in India. However he is full of zeal and on the whole I think hopeful of being able to do real good under his new circumstances.

I believe that apart from other reasons which make him anxious to succeed, Mr Lloyd has a sincere desire to help the Chief Secretary, for whom I think he has a strong personal feeling. His position is not without considerable risk which has probably been increased by his becoming more conspicuous.

He told Oakel and me that on the previous day as he was riding out, followed as usual by two Mounted Constables, they saw a man in a field by the roadside, hastily burying a gun, which turned out to be loaded; the natural supposition is that if the mounted police had not come in sight, the man with a loaded gun would have used it against Mr Clifford Lloyd.

At 6 o'clock Oakel and I met Lord Monteagle at the station and went down with him to Foynes, an hour and a half's distance.

Mr White, a friend of Lord Monteagle's, who travelled part of the way with us, enquired quietly of the guard as we stopped at a small station, whether it was true that an attempt had been made a day or two ago to upset a train on this line, by placing large stones on the rails.

'Yes, quite true, the only wonder was how a bad accident had been avoided.'

Capt. Plunkett, the newly appointed Superintend[ing] R.M. for Kerry [and Cork W.R.], had been in the train, which perhaps accounted for the attempt.

We reached Mount Trenchard about 8 o'clock, and were most cordially and kindly received by Lady M. A picture of a peat fire burning in the cosy little library—now lined with books, and looking, as did the house generally, more thoroughly liveable and snug than when I was staying in it 4 years ago.

The Monteagles, like so many other Irish landlords, are very poor at present, and from the wish to pay off before everything else the unusually heavy charges upon the property are reducing their personal expenditure to the lowest possible point—but all this did not prevent their treatment of us (I believe the only guests they have had this autumn) from being most hospitable, and their house very comfortable.

Their staff of servants is very small, but they are blessed with a most amiable set who seem to have no objection to doing each other's work if necessary. The pretty Irish girl (Joanna) who did duty as parlourmaid and housemaid combined was apparently a host in herself, for everything went as smoothly as if we were waited on by the regulation number of housemaids and footmen.

8 Jan., Sun.

A wild grey morning. Read the morning service in the library, the morning service at the church being only on alternate Sundays.

Before lunch we all four went for a walk in the woods—very pretty, but very muddy, owing to their having lately been drawing timber down the paths.

The Monteagles and I to church in the afternoon, through the rain which had set in steadily. A larger congregation than usual, two men having come from Foynes, in addition to the Monteagles, their English maid, the clergyman's two children, and the daughters of a Protestant gentleman farmer in the neighbourhood.

At 6 o'clock after tea was over and the letters despatched, the Monteagles adjourned to the large unfurnished drawing room, and held their usual Sunday singing class for 12 or 14 of their labourers' children—ranging in age from big shy boys of 17 or 18, down to small children of 9 or 10. The singing used to be of sacred music, but this was objected to, and now the repertory includes all sorts and kinds of songs, German, English and Irish.

It was a pleasant sight—the boarded floor and stone walls of the beautiful room (still bare of furniture and ornaments for want of money to furnish it) lighted by one lamp and the blaze of a splendid peat fire, Lady Monteagle at the piano with Stephen perched beside her, quite absorbed in silent interest in the proceedings, the little one-year-old baby sitting on its nurse's knee by the fire, and expressing her delight at the singing in most audible crows and shouts—Lord Monteagle standing before a half circle of boys and girls who gazed on him with fixed and smiling attention whilst he sang song after song with great spirit and action—each having a lively chorus in which the children chimed in lustily.

A good many of the Songs were from the Harrow Glee Book,[1] and it had a funny effect to hear these little Paddies in the County Limerick, joining fervently in the chorus of 'There lies Harrow, as it ought for to be', and other Public School songs, concerning the glories of Football and Cricket at Harrow.

9 Jan., Mon.

No morning papers. At 12 Oakel and Lord Monteagle started for a long walk, the weather having decidedly improved. Lady Monteagle and I spent a quiet morning with the children, and after lunch drove to Glin where Lady M. had two arrears of calls to pay. The carriage horses proper have long since had to be dispensed with, but a very fair pair of horses, whose ordinary walk of life is the plough, are pressed into the service on the rare occasions when Lady M. wishes to go for a drive, and a man who was formally employed in some humble capacity about the stables and garden makes a most efficient coachman.

Our road lay along the banks of the Shannon, through the villages of Loghill and Glin to a house some 7 or 8 miles off inhabited by an old Mr and Mrs Fitzgerald.

Mr Fitzgerald (a distant relation of the Knight of Glin) is a Protestant clergyman of strongly marked opinions, but so popular (or at least so generally

---

[1] E. E. Bowen (1836–1901), writer of many Harrow songs, came of a Mayo family.

tolerated) in the neighbourhood that he scatters Protestant tracts broadcast over the country without arousing the least opposition or ill-feeling towards himself.

At present the old clergyman (whose habits it appears are often somewhat eccentric) has suddenly and relentlessly taken to his bed. He is not ill, but nothing will induce him to leave his bed, and poor Mrs Fitzgerald, a stout lady with dark curls on each side of her forehead, gave Lady Monteagle a melancholy account of his condition. He will not allow a ray of light to be admitted into his room, he will not read or talk, or allow himself to be read or talked to, but lies all day long in absolute retirement, with no occupation but that of taking his meals for which he has a good appetite.

Life on this remote bank of the Shannon with the flat ugly shores of County Clare opposite must be quiet under all circumstances, but under such circumstances as these it must be deeply depressing.

On our way back we called and had tea at Glin with Mrs Fitzgerald wife of the Knight of Glin, and Mother of the lovely Nesta Fitzgerald, whom I was cruelly disappointed not to see; she had just gone off with her young brother to Tralee to stay with the Mother of her fiancé, Mrs Arthur Blennerhasset, the head of all the Blennerhassets of Kerry.[1]

Mrs Fitzgerald a handsome spirited woman and very proud of her daughter, whose engagement has evidently been a pleasant and exciting break in the mournful circumstances of their present life. The Knight of Glin is now entirely estranged from his people, who used to look up to him as to the head of an ancient clan, and would bring all their quarrels before him for arbitration rather than take them into the County Court.

Now the occupation which this gave him is entirely gone, and if he roams about his property he has to go armed for he has received several threatening letters, and though his wife is clearly not a woman to be easily or needlessly frightened, she owned to Lady M. that she now becomes very uneasy if he is out late at night.

They are extremely poor, and are likely to remain so for the Knight's rents have just been ruthlessly cut down by the Sub-Commission which has been sitting at Glin.

Everywhere one hears the same lamentation and wringing of hands over the ruin being wrought by the Commissioners—one poor lady asking me earnestly whether I thought the recent Landlords' Meeting in Dublin would do any good 'by stopping the Sub-Commissioners going on as they were'?

As things are at present (that is before any authorised scheme of compensa-

---

[1] 'Nesta' was Clara Nesta Richarda, only daughter of Desmond John Edmund Fitzgerald (1840–95) and his wife, Isabella Lloyd, née Apjohn. Her fiancé was Arthur Blennerhassett (1856–1939), son of Charles John Allanson Winn Blennerhassett (1830–59), and his wife Barbara, a Mahony of Dromore. Arthur, head of the senior branch of the Blennerhassetts, owned 12,621 acres, worth £4,157; other branches of the family owned some 22,000 acres, worth about £5,000, in Kerry alone, as well as land in Limerick and Cork.

tion in some form or another has been proposed) the just dealings of the State—as represented by the Sub-Commissioners—do seem to involve the most cruel injustice to one class, and one class only within the State.

It may be said that *pour faire une omelette il faut casser des oeufs* but surely legislation should not be conducted on the principles of warfare, with the understanding that a benefit for one class must—like a victory—be obtained at the direct cost of the other.

While we were at Mrs Fitzgerald's, one of the officers from the *Valiant*, the guard ship now stationed at Glin, came in. Certainly life on board the *Valiant* cannot be lively, and Captain Regnier's[1] account of his and his fellow officers' miseries was very melancholy—the weather is generally too rough and stormy for them to go ashore, and when they can it is so dull that they do not care to go.

Found Lord M. and Oakel had returned from their walk when we got back. They had been round by Shanagolden, the chief centre of the Land League in this part of Limerick, and the headquarters of the ill-conditioned priest[2] who for some time past has been doing more harm than any other man in the district.

Being angry with Lord M[onteagle] for refusing to allow him the Management of the Schools at Shanagolden, he had them 'boycotted' and set up a so-called school of his own, appointing as Master a man who had been formerly dismissed on the ground of drunkenness.

The priest is trying to make the farmers believe that he will induce the National Board to recognize and support his school instead of Lord M[onteagle]'s (which the Board of course has no intention of doing).

Meantime, the school master, having at the instance of his patron, the priest, been supplied with a few shillings in the way of fees by the Land League farmers, spent his earnings in again becoming drunk. The school has consequently fallen somewhat into discredit, and many of the farmers would gladly send their children back to Lord Monteagle's school if the priest would only give permission—this he refuses to do, and so the matter stands at present, to the great detriment of everyone concerned, but above all the children.

Apropos of priests it is pleasant to record that I have heard of another good one. This man—whose parish is a few miles lower down the Shannon—has steadily refused to join the Land League; at first he was punished for his independence in the usual way by the withholding of dues, but now the people have become reconciled to him and his influence amongst them will probably be stronger than it was before.

This makes now the seventh good priest that I know of—by which I mean a man who has the courage to hold and to assert opinions different to those of the popular party.

---

[1] Commander John H. Rainier of the 6,713-ton armour-plated H.M.S. *Valiant*.
[2] Very Rev. James Mulqueen, P.P. of Shanagolden, Co. Limerick.

Archbishop McCabe, Bishop Giloolly, Canon Griffen, Canon Denelty, Father Hewson, and Father Flanagan.

At 6 o'clock the labourers' boys and girls again assembled in the empty drawing room, this time for dancing. We had the satisfaction of seeing some elaborate jigs performed, and ourselves (Lord M[onteagle], Oakel and I) took part in a vigorous square dance or set, something like a lively and more complicated combination of quadrilles and 'Lancers'.

10 Jan., Tu.

Oakel and I left Mount Trenchard at 8 o'clock having arranged to pay a visit to Mrs [O']Brien of Oldchurch on our way back to Dublin.

We reached Limerick about 10 o'clock, Oakel going to call first to Cruise's Hotel to try and see Mr Clifford Lloyd (who was 'just after taking a car' and starting for New Pallas) and I driving straight to Oldchurch, where I was kindly received by Mrs O'Brien and her daughter in spite of the unconscionable hour of my appearance.

Mr Robin O'Brien had gone off for a week to Ennistymon where the Sub-Commissioners were holding a Court. Mr O'Brien I gather is very irate with the proceedings of the Sub-Commissioners (the Forty Thieves as he calls them), considering that the Limerick Sub-Commissioner especially is quite unjustified in reducing old-established rents as they have been doing on several properties in this County.

He appears also very anxious that the Ch. Sec. should be quite 'kept up to the mark' as regards a full understanding of the bad state of things in Clare— every gentleman in the Club at Ennis obliged to go about armed—lawlessness if not open outrage everywhere, and (worst of all) as much difficulty in obtaining payment of the 'judicial' rent as of the old so-called rack rent.

In the course of conversation with Mrs and Miss O'Brien, I enquired if Herbert Gladstone had been to see them when he was in Limerick. He had not, and perhaps on the whole it was just as well, for the Member for Leeds is quite the *bête noire* of the Irish gentry at present, as I now found from various remarks that were made about him; he is thought whilst on his journey in the South West and on other occasions to have spoken unadvisedly on several matters, and to have enlightened his ignorance about Irish affairs from one side only.

'Is he a friend of yours?' said Miss O'Brien, evidently prepared to express her views very strongly—and on my declaring that he certainly was, the subject of his delinquencies was suppressed for the time being.

The O'Briens gave us an early lunch, and at half past 1 we left Limerick for Dublin.

Amongst our fellow travellers the 'state of the country' was of course the inevitable topic, this time chiefly in its sporting aspect, for the gentlemen in the carriage were hunting men, discussing the exodus of Irish hunters and hunting men to England—chiefly it appears to Rugby.

There was also an elderly clergyman from the Co. Cork—full of satisfaction at the appointment of Capt. Plunkett, and at the arrests so successfully accomplished at Millstreet under his direction the day before.

Certainly as far as one can judge from stray expressions of current opinion, the appointments of the Superintend[ent] R.M.s, are considered highly satisfactory, and much is hoped from their vigour and experience.

Reached home about 6 o'clock, and found to our disappointment that Father was detained (by some interview I believe with Mr Childers) and would not be back till the next morning.

Lord Lifford and the Burkes to dinner—Lord Lifford disappointed at not seeing the Chief Secretary—having come up to Dublin for that purpose—but bearing up like a courteous old Tory gentleman that he is.

11 Jan., Wed.

Father returned by the morning Mail, well and on the whole in good spirits—he had had a pleasant visit to Osborne on Sunday, and a long talk with the Queen—more like old times than for some time past. She had begun by violently attacking the Sub-Commissioners, but he had stood up for them 'like a brick' he told me.

I do not know of course what line he and Mr Gladstone are going to take in the House about this very burning question, but as a matter of fact I believe that both feel confident in the success of their defence.

Amongst other things the Queen talked to Father of Uncle Matt's poem on Dean Stanley, which she had not yet seen; consequently he sent her the *Nineteenth Century* for which she has since sent him through Lady Ely[1] a message of thanks, and to say that 'she admired the lines so much'.

Walked with Father through the Park, and gave him my report of Limerick and Clare.

An afternoon at home, arranging flowers etc. Mrs Henry Doyle to tea. Miss Crampton and Mr Richard Dixon to dine and sleep—Canon Bagot, Mr and Mrs Ross of Bladensburg, Mr George Coffey and Mr Jephson to dine and sleep.

Mr Ross of Bladensburg is now finally installed at the Castle under the title of [Temporary] Asst Private Secretary to the Chief Secretary. The name of Military Secretary would have better described his position, but this was thought to sound too warlike.[2] He again seems to be a case of the right man in the right place.

---

[1] See appendix.
[2] It would also have invited confusion with the office of assistant military secretary, at military headquarters.

12 Jan., Th.

Mr Richard Dixon left quite early. Of all the quaint and curious visitors we have ever had he is about the quaintest. He belongs to a large agency firm in Dublin, and in this capacity (as I believe in every other) he is intensely gloomy about the present state of the country. In his experience rent is *not* being paid anywhere, everyone is poor—will be poorer—and in the meantime over-spending to a fearful extent.

Many persons, who are living just as they used to, ought—according to Mr Dixon's knowledge of their circumstances—to eat meat only once a week, and do all their household work themselves.

Like many other people Mr Dixon had a suggestion—a simple remedy to propose to the Govt for meeting the difficulties of the situation. His was imprisonment for debt—to be enforced wholesale all over the country.

'Yes', said the Ch. Secretary, when the advantages of this procedure were fully set out before him, 'I have had many suggestions made to me—another is that we should set up State bloodhounds'.

'No' said Mr Dixon, thoughtfully, 'I should not approve of that, it would be cruel'.

Mr Dixon's appearance was as interesting and perhaps as grim—or at least austere, as himself, even his clothes were quite unlike other people's.

'Your invitation', he informed Mother, 'has done good indirectly to my wardrobe'—on which he explained that his evening clothes had not been worn for 25 years, and that on being obliged to examine them (preparatory to wearing them on the extraordinary occasion of dining at the Chief Secretary's Lodge) he had found them so covered with mildew that he had feared it might be 'dangerous' to attempt wearing them.

Had a few more years elapsed the consequences might have been quite fatal; happily, as it was—thanks to Mother's timely invitation—the mischief was discovered in time, the mildew was successfully removed, and the venerable garments appeared in the world again with great éclat. At the end of his long history, Mr Dixon came over to Mother to exhibit himself, remarking with just pride, 'You don't often see a coat like that nowadays'.

Mother was interested in noticing that it was just like what Grandpapa used to wear.

The three Land Commissioners have begun hearing appeals, the first Court being held at Belfast.

Spent most of the morning entertaining, or rather being entertained, by Miss Crampton. She is a most wonderful and vivacious old lady, with a strong manly voice which she seems never tired of using; we could [not] believe (what we found out afterwards) that she is over 80.

She had been intimate in her youth with the Edgeworth family, and spoke in the warmest and most affectionate terms of Maria Edgeworth.

Her sweet temper and amiability must have been unfailing—this side of her character was strongly shown in her relations with her successive step-mothers. One after another she devoted herself to them, tended them through their last illness, and was then prepared to receive the next with equal goodness and affection. Her father was the hero and centre of her life, she believed in him implicitly, and allowed him to injure (as Miss Crampton thinks) most of her novels by his collaboration. *Helen*, the best of all her stories, was written after his death.

He appears to have had very strong and definite theories on the subject of education, which he held to be all powerful in the formation of character.

Miss Crampton described his dining with her father Sir Philip Crampton[1] on one occasion, and holding forth on his favourite subject—saying apropos of Sir Philip's children who were in the room—'Now you consider that child to be a born musician, and that to have a natural turn for mathematics, but by dint of education I could reverse those characteristics as easily as I can change the labels on these bottles'—pointing to the wine decanters—on which Sir Philip remarked, 'Yes, but by doing that you don't change the wine in the bottles'.

Miss Crampton promised to lend Mother Maria Edgeworth's letter—printed for private circulation—she having expressly forbidden the publication of any Memoir or letters connected with her.

Walked with Father and others to the Park gates. Rode Paris about the Park in the afternoon. Lady Cowper called. A quiet evening. Whist.

13 Jan., Fri.

Mother, Francie and I went to Christ Church to the Special Service for the state of the country, appointed by the Irish Church for this day.

The Archbishop preached a beautiful New Year's Sermon, but one wished it had had more obvious connection with the service for which people had come together. At all the churches in Dublin the special Service for the day was well attended, and in no case, I believe, was there the least display of party or political bitterness by the preachers.

An afternoon at home with Oakel in the smoking room. A call from Mr Ross of Bladensburg. Oakel left us by the evening Mail to return to London. Father home to dinner very tired—having been too busy all day to get his usual half hour of whist. He had been seeing Lord Dunsandle, and hearing his history from Mr Burke with whom he drove home.

14 Jan., Sat.

A morning in the study over the newspaper book—heard Father's Mem. to Mr Gladstone, concerning the vacant Judgeship (by the death of Judge O'Brien) and possible changes amongst the law officers. Mr Johnson would have a

[1] Philip Crampton (1777–1858): cr. baronet, 1839; F.R.S., surgeon to the queen.

natural claim which would in itself, like the change, mean also the promotion of Mr Naish—but this would involve a contest and probable loss of the seat at Mallow, and Mr Johnson is very considerate in his wish not to be the means of embarrassment to the Govt.

At the same time the Ch. Sec. was in favour of the offer being made to him—he would not mind the Solicitor not being in the House, so long as the Govt have a good Attorney—much is hoped from Mr Porter.

Lord William Compton called to see Father and tell him that a small gentleman farmer, to whom he had spoken on the platform of one of the stations (Monasterevin) coming from Abbeyleix, had been boycotted for his supposed intimacy with the Chief Secretary—the story having got about that Mr Forster had been to see him at his house—whereas all Father had done had been to enquire, with his natural wish for information on such matters, who lived at a certain large farm house which he had passed in driving to the station, and which it turned out was the abode of the same man whom he chanced to say a few words to on the platform.

Walked with Father. Rode Comet in the afternoon, accompanied by Puck. A mild lovely afternoon, with a fresh breeze over the Fifteen Acres. The climate here is certainly enough to spoil us for any other part of the United Kingdom.

Father, Mr H. Gladstone, and Mr West dined with the Lord Chancellor.

15 Jan., Sun.

To the Hibernian in the morning, Father going with us, and walking back with His Ex[cellency]—partly I believe for the purpose of being coached for the St Patrick's Ceremonial on Tuesday.

Walked with Father and Francie in the afternoon, and heard from Father of his interview with Mr (Dr) Kenny the day before.

Mrs O'Hagan to call on Mother, Judge O'Hagan to see Father in the study, combining at tea.

At 7 went into the study to help make up the journal.

The report of the Govt valuators (Mr Gray and Mr Murrough O'Brien) will be produced in public the next day (as desired by the landlords' Counsel) but to the probable surprise of everyone it will appear that their valuation is on the whole lower than that of the Sub-Commissioners.

16 Jan., Mon.

Morning in the study. Walked with Father. In the afternoon with Mother to the School for Daughters of the Clergy, where we were met by Mrs Trench, Mrs Smyly and others. Called on Dean and Miss Dickenson.

To tea with Miss Burke. For the first time within my recollection she voluntarily told me of a landlord who has just been paid his rent. This was near Gort and was the consequence of the landlord having presented each of his tenants with a writ, when they came to his office to inform him that they should pay no rent till the 'suspects' were released.

Only our own party at dinner. Whist.

17 Jan., Tu.

Morning over the newspaper book in the study. Father anxious and annoyed about a bad case of wholesale eviction in Galway—on the Berridge estate.[1] He hopes that the six months redemption clause in the Land Act will come to the relief of the tenants, who appear to have had a cruelly hard bargain made with them by their landlord.

Walked with Father and Francie—he practising with his umbrella for the Sword of State ceremony in the evening.

Drove into Dublin, having both Yarrow and Puck in the carriage with us. Rode Paris in the afternoon. Father and Mother dined at the Vice Regal. We, i.e. Francie, the occidental, Herbert Gladstone and I joined them in the evening to see the installation ceremony.[2]

A small evening party assembled in the drawing room; when we arrived the Banquet over, but a considerable interval to wait whilst the Knights were robing: distant glimpses through an open door of the Chief Secretary struggling to unsheathe the Sword of State.

Half an hour later, the party headed by Lady Cowper, Lady Drogheda, Mrs Forster, Lady Steele, Miss Trench and others adjourned to the ball room, in the centre of which was a large table covered with a light blue cloth, and set round with chairs.

We ranged ourselves round the room, and in a few moments—enter the Procession, half a dozen gentlemen in Windsor uniform, Ulster King at Arms in red robes, the Grand Master (Lord Cowper) with two blue and white pages carrying his blue train, the Archbishop of Dublin and the Dean of St Patrick's, the Chief Secretary carefully bearing in both hands the Sword of State—an immense gold-hilted weapon, in a red velvet sheath, 5 Knights of St Patrick, in blue robes—Lord Drogheda, Lord Granard, Lord Listowel, Lord Cork, Lord Powerscourt.

Lord Cowper, seated at the head of the table with the two ecclesiastics on either side, was asked by the Ulster King at Arms, after he had with a beaming

---

[1] Richard Berridge (?1808–87): of Ballynahinch Castle, Co. Galway; purchaser of the Martin estate from the Law Life Insurance Co.; owned 254 acres in Galway city, 159,898 in the county, and 9,965 in Mayo, the largest estate in Ireland; but of a total value of only £8,742.

[2] Of Lord O'Hagan as a knight of the order of St Patrick. Founded in 1783 and enlarged in 1833, the order at this time consisted of the queen, the lord lieutenant of Ireland, four members of the royal family, and twenty Irish peers (all large landowners), O'Hagan becoming the twenty-first. The officers of the order were headed by the two protestant archbishops and the dean of St Patrick's.

face read out the title of the Knights, whether it was his pleasure that Lord O'Hagan should be summoned to his presence.

Presently the Knight elect shuffled in and was solemnly initiated and sworn in by the Archbishop, Knighted by the Lord Lieutenant as he knelt before him, dressed up in his new blue robe by the two junior Knights of the Chapter, shaken hands with by each of his companions, and allowed to take his seat with them at the august blue table. A flourish of trumpets, a waving of the Banner of the Order till half the lights in the chandelier were put out, and then the whole Chapter—Grand Master, Knights, Ulster King at Arms, pages, household, and the Chief Secretary with the Sword of State filed out in procession—soon to re-appear amongst us as ordinary gentlemen, highly amused at the performance they had been going through—the 'pageant' as Sir Bernard Burke says, the 'tomfoolery' as Mrs Forster calls it.

18 Jan., Wed.

Father looked over my newspaper book, and gave his approval. He showed me a letter he had received that morning from America—the editor of the *Pittsburgh Dispatch*, writing on behalf of his brother lately arrested under the Coercion Act; judging from this, and from other family letters on the subject which he enclosed, this poor Mr O'Neill is just one of the numerous Irishmen who have allowed themselves to be dragged by the Land League further than they wished to go and have had to take the consequences.

Walked with Father and Herbert Gladstone to the Park gates. Mother and Francie to the Drummond Institute. Drove with Mother into Dublin in the afternoon. We talked over the special perplexities of the moment; amongst these first and foremost is the question to be decided by the Commissioners as to the final definition of 'Healy's Clause'—How far does the Land Act when legally interpreted deprive the landlord of the value of all previous improvements made on his property by tenants who have already received 'compensation' for these (or their predecessors') improvements in the form of a low rent—a rent that is below a 'fair rent'?

On the one side it is said that if this interpretation is put upon the clause by the Commissioners, they might as well accept Mr Parnell's theory of the 'prairie value' of the land being all that the landlord is entitled to.

On the other hand it is asserted (in the *Freeman* and elsewhere) that if any other interpretation is given, the Land Act will be proved a failure, and the tenants might as well give up going into Court altogether.

The whole question is full of legal difficulties on which much disagreement is possible.

Mr Vernon, Mother told me, would probably go out of the Commission altogether if the *Freeman*'s interpretation of 'Healy's Clause' (which it sustains by quotations from Mr Gladstone's own speeches) was finally accepted.

I heard also that the Cowpers will probably not be here very much longer.

Mr and Mrs Moore (née Bessie Wale) to dinner. Letter from Lord Grey[1] in the *Times* announcing his secession from the Liberal party apropos of the election now proceeding in the North Riding—Mr Guy Dawnay against Mr Rowlandson, a large tenant farmer. It is thought that many of the great Whig landowners will leave Mr Gladstone's party in fear of what he may do in the matter of land reform in England.

19 Jan., Th.

Judge O'Hagan has given an elaborate and carefully argued judgment in the first case brought before the appeal Court at Belfast, which has the effect of sanctioning the popular interpretation of the Improvements Clause. Mr Vernon signified his dissent from the interpretation but has as yet taken no stronger course.

Walked with Father, Mother and others to the V.R. Lodge, where they went in to call on their Excellencies, and Francie and I walked on with the dogs.

Read an interesting letter from Mr Blake R.M. to Father. Canon Bagot called. Only our four selves at dinner—quite a phenomenon. Heard from Father on the intended visit of the Lord Mayor in State to the Lord Lieutenant, to demand the release of the 'Suspect' M.P.s. Sir Bernard Burke had been consulted as to whether it was necessary for the Lord Lieutenant to receive Mr Dawson in State, and had given it as his opinion that precedents were in favour of doing so, the coming in state being a piece of politeness on the part of the Mayor and Corporation which it would be seemly for the Lord Lieutenant to return in the same manner.

Sir Bernard was much relieved to find that the Ch. Sec. quite agreed with him in this opinion.

Previous however to the Lord Lieutenant agreeing to receive them, an assurance had been secured from the Town Clerk that the occasion would not be seized for political speech-making.

The deputation are to read the Petition, the Lord Lieutenant will read his reply, and the ever-eloquent Mr Dawson will not make a speech—such at least is the understanding.

Amongst people whom Father has seen at the Castle to-day have been Dr Kenny's uncle, and Captain Slacke, one of the 5 Superintendent R.M.s. I believe these appointments are really proving a success; even Mr Burke, Father tells us, acknowledges this, and he was by no means in favour of the scheme at first.

[1] Henry George Grey (1802–94): 3rd earl; secretary of state for the colonies, 1846–52; his article 'Ireland' in the *Nineteenth Century*, xi (June, 1882), pp 977–1012, is an interesting whig criticism of the P.P.P. act.

20 Jan., Fri.

News in the papers this morning of Gambetta's defeat: the Bill for the Revision of the Constitution, including his favourite project of the *Scrutin de Liste*, on the acceptance of which he had staked his Cabinet, has been rejected by an enormous majority of Committee-men elected by the various Bureaux of the Chamber to consider the Bill. There has been a financial panic, and the greatest excitement prevails in Paris.

Foreign affairs altogether are very disquieting at present. Austria–Hungary is engaged in the suppression of a rebellion in Dalmatia and the Crivoscie which may lead to the reopening of the whole Slav Nationality question in Eastern Europe, and eventually to the long-foreseen war between Russia and Austria.

In Germany, the Emperor under the inspiration of Prince Bismarck has issued a Royal Rescript which virtually extinguishes Constitutional Government, and replaces it by the authority of the sovereign.

Our own troubles in Egypt seem on the increase. I have followed things so little of late (out of Ireland) that I cannot even profess to understand the complications which have been going on there for some time past. But a crisis seems now to have arisen from the issue of a Joint Note by France and England, calling on the Egyptian Govt to reform itself in a way which only force will induce it to do. The idea of applying force is embarrassing and might have the further effect of embroiling us not only with the Sultan (who resents our interference in Egypt) but with other European Powers.

Altogether, what with Egypt, the Bradlaugh question, and Ireland, Mr Gladstone's Government have enough rocks ahead in the coming Session to make their shipwreck quite within the bounds of possibility if not probability.

The Conservatives are in proportionately good spirits, and are protesting loudly that they will not allow the Govt to 'trample on the rights of minorities' by any reform of the House, which shall include the introduction of the Clôture. Evidently there is going to be a fighting alliance between the Fourth Party, Conservatives, and the Parnellites, who it is now discovered did not 'obstruct' at all last Session more than was reasonable and legitimate.

Mr Shaw Le Fevre (our probable successor) arrived by the morning boat.

Walked with him and Father to the Park gates. Talk over Compensation possibilities (or impossibilities); can anything be done to relieve landlords from the weight of charges and mortgages—the State in fact becoming the Mortgagee. As to the vexed question of arrears, the Ch. Sec. seems inclined to think that it would not be desirable for Legislation to attempt anything further in this direction.

For the State to promote the cancelling of all present arrears would mean in most cases to abet robbery—for the greater part of the arrears now due have been contracted of malice prepense during the past year of agitation by tenants well able to pay; most of the cases of real hardship—arrears from inability to pay—have been already settled between the landlord and tenants without the necessity for State intervention.

Apropos of some question of Mr Le Fevre about the troops, Father told him his impression (formed since he has had so much to do with the Military authorities) of the total inadequacy of the present system at least in its present stage. He told him of his going with Sir Thomas Steele on one of his inspections, and of the skeleton condition of some of the regiments—'Why one regiment was all boys'—and there were none of them, he explained with a force of expression, worthy of this country.

Rode Comet in the Park in the afternoon.

Francie dined at the V.R. and went afterwards with Lady C[owper] and Mrs Dalrymple to hear the 'Creation' at St Patrick's.

The O'Conor Don, the Lord Chancellor[1] and the Solicitor General[2] to dinner here. Of all our official friends Mr Law is the most amiable. We shall miss him greatly during the coming Session, as a man even more than a politician, and in this capacity too, he was very helpful to the Govt.

21 Jan., Sat.

Walked with Father, Mr Le Fevre and Francie to the Park Gates. Mr Le Fevre enquired about the probability of any open rising, he supposed that such a thing was quite out of the question.

Well, I don't know about that—you saw what Blake said—there is certainly a sort of feeling of expectation running all through the West—if there was anything we should put it all down in a week, and this would break up the whole movement.

'Would it not be desirable that some such crisis should come?' suggested Mr Le Fevre.

In some ways, yes—but it would mean considerable loss of life—and after all, I can say that up to now I have got through with hardly any loss of life.

Full reports in this morning's papers of the Tenant Right Meeting at Belfast. Speeches by Mr Givan, Mr Findlater, and Mr C. Russell—good in tone, and likely to be useful as a contribution to rational discussion of the Land Act, and Sub-Commissioners.

Miss Trench and her cousin Miss Prittie (daughter of Lord Dunally) to lunch. In the afternoon Mother, Francie and I to a tea at Lady Ferguson's—a literary and musical gathering—Mr Mahaffy greatly annoyed at the musical interlude as an interruption to conversation.

Father received a long deputation from the National Teachers.

Mr and Miss Burke and Mr Blake R.M. to dinner.

---

[1] Hugh Law.   [2] A. M. Porter.

22 Jan., Sun.

To church in the morning at the Hibernian, without Father. Mr Shaw Le Fevre conducted round the Kitchen gardens and houses by Mother, with a view to giving him information that may be useful to him in the future. He will not be sufficiently enthusiastic about our lovely park and the Dublin mountains, which were looking unusually beautiful under the rays of sunshine, as we walked to church across the Fifteen Acres.

Mr Hambro, a friend of Mr West's, to lunch. Walked with Father in the afternoon. A call from the Lord Chancellor. Mr and Mrs Blake, Mr A. and Miss Burke, and Mr Mahaffy to tea. A consultation in the study afterwards between Mr Blake, the Ch. Sec. and Mr Burke.

Mr Shaw Le Fevre left at half past 6 for the West, very anxious to preserve his incognito, which he is assured is impossible, as in a quarter of an hour after his arrival at Loughrea, Tuam or wherever it may be, everyone in the district will have found out, first that he is a stranger, and secondly what particular stranger.

After dinner Mother read aloud out of Miss Edgeworth's Memoirs, letters written by herself and her stepmother during the Rebellion of '98. Father was much interested; in some ways things were worse then than they are now, but what struck him most was the fact the people on the whole seemed to have been on the side of the authorities and of the law.

'We couldn't have yeomanry now', he remarked, as we read of Mr Edgeworth commanding a troop of yeomanry in the neighbourhood of Mullingar.

At 10 o'clock I went into the study professedly to help Father arrange his papers, but was not much more than a spectator; however we had a pleasant time. 'There' he said as he pointed to a cupboard in which he stowed away another packet of letters, 'these are the materials for my life. If you ever write my life—as you very likely will—make it short.'

Amongst the papers and memorandum he was arranging was a copy printed for the Cabinet of his letter to Mr Gladstone of the 11th of October.[1]

'It was upon that, that Parnell was arrested' he remarked.

I said—'I see that amongst the alternatives you suggest in this letter, you go on the supposition that the Land League could only be suppressed by Act of Parliament'.

Yes, at that time the Law officers had not been screwed up to the point. It takes a very great deal to do that. That act—the suppression of the Land League—was entirely my own doing, about the most important step that was ever taken by a man on his own responsibility without consultation with his colleagues.

---

[1] This probably refers to his memo. of 9 Oct. 1881, printed for the cabinet on 11 Oct. together with the law officers' opinions on legal resources against the league (P.R.O., Cab. 37/5, 22; B.L., Add. MS 44627, ff 85–8); see also his letter to Gladstone, 9 Oct. (Add. MS 44159, ff 58–9), quoted in Reid, *Forster*, ii, 352–3. Cf. above, p. 263.

'The Lord Chancellor said to-day, that he thought things were better', I told him. 'So they are, and will be before Parliament meets.'

23 Jan., Mon.

Our last day here.

Walked with Father, Francie and the occidental to the Park gates—tried to modify by argument the strongly anti-Irish sentiments of this last, but I fear made small impression.

Drove on with Mother into Dublin, and was photographed at LaFayette's. A quiet afternoon at home: the Fifteen Acres, cheerful and serene under the bright afternoon sunshine. I fear we shall leave this cheerful weather behind us when we cross the Channel to-morrow.

Our four selves at dinner—heard from Father of the two Deputations he had been receiving to-day—the South Dublin Ward on Poor law Relief—and a deputation of poor law doctors on superannuation pensions. These latter were informed that the Govt through 'my friend Mr Gladstone' who was present at the interview, were going to introduce a Bill giving them all, and more than all, they asked for.

In the course of dinner a telegram was brought in from Capt. Plunkett, R.M. announcing that the Twohig brothers prominent in 'Captain Moonlight' raids had been convicted and sentenced to 7 years penal servitude, the Judge declaring that the case was one of vast importance as showing the existence of a Fenian conspiracy.

Tomorrow morning Francie and I leave by the morning Mail for Fox How. The last time I was there was during the General Election in April 1880, and it was as we walked down the Birch Copse hill on our way to Ambleside with Aunt Fan that Father first mooted in my hearing the idea of his taking the Irish office.

I jumped eagerly at the notion—not foreseeing, with the wonderful and painful clearness that Mother did, all that would come upon him in such a position. It is not yet two years since then, but it seems more like five.

It is more than four months now since I have set foot out of Ireland.

In spite of everything that has happened I must confess that personally I am much attached to this place—even I may say to Dublin—and shall be sorry to leave it for good.

I do not suppose that I am actually leaving it now for the last time, but I do suppose that I shall never come back to spend four months here again as though it were my home.

Mother expects to join us at Fox How at the end of the week, when Father will go to London.

We shall hope all to meet at No. 80 in time for the opening of Parliament, when a fresh chapter in the troubles of an Irish Secretary will begin.

24 Jan., Tu.

Francie and I left the dear C.S. Lodge on a lovely starlight morning—an aspect under which I had never seen it, having never before crossed by the Morning Mail. A beautiful passage—sunrise over the sea.

Read the Irish papers. 600 lbs of dynamite stolen from a Store at Limerick; fresh threatening placards against Mr Clifford Lloyd, offering a reward for shooting him; full report of the Millstreet trial, Connell's evidence, Judge Fitz-gerald's charge.[1] One is almost inclined to regret that he should have con-nected the cowardly outrages of the Moonlight gang (for which the perpetrators were in the habit of receiving either money or a 'Parnell medal for bravery') entirely with Fenianism and not with Land Leagueism in its present phase. Surely these crimes have more connection with the 'No Rent' policy than with any political scheme of an 'Irish Republic'.

Reached Fox How about 7.30. Aunt Lucy and Lucy staying here.

25 Jan., Wed.

Heard from Mother that the Lord Mayor's deputation to the Lord Lt had gone off very quietly—'but I think His Excellency did not put on quite sufficient state for the occasion, his servants were not up to the mark, Lady Cowper says, through some mistake in the order, and His Excellency much annoyed'. Both the *Freeman* and *Express*, she adds, 'are angry with Father for his answer to the Deputation' (on Intermediate Education).

Defeat of the Liberal in the North Yorkshire election—Mr Rowlandson the tenant farmer being beaten by a majority of about 300 by Mr Dawson [Dawnay].[2] A great disappointment to the Liberal party—but at any rate not an Irish question—so long as the triumph is not to the Parnellites, I personally can bear it with philosophy.

Father and Mother dined to-day at Lord O'Hagan's to meet Their Exes. 'We had an escort of three mounted Constabulary', Mother writes, 'with drawn swords at each carriage window, and one behind'

It made such a fearful clatter in driving through the lanes that it made me quite nervous, the Park roads too were lined with police. Dear Father has loads of worries; a grand swoop which was planned on a nest of assassins at Loughrea is in danger of miscarrying through some stupid man at the office sending an open telegram with orders. Mr Le Fevre brought word of this from Mr Blake. Then all parties all round combine to be furious with Father's refusing money to the Deputation (Intermediate Education); even Lord O'Hagan was hardly civil: that is certainly a panacea for uniting Irishmen, to refuse them State money.

[1] See above, pp 339, 345. Connell having turned queen's evidence, two members of the gang were convicted at the Cork assizes on 23 Jan. 1882 for an attack on a dwelling on 7 Dec. 1881.

[2] Dawnay beat Rowlandson by 8,135 to 7,749, the poll being held on 24 Jan.

Francie, Lucy and I had tea with Miss Quillinan, and played round games of cards for two hours.

26 Jan., Th.

Resignation of M. Gambetta and his Cabinet—the Chamber having definitely refused to agree to a Limited Revision of the Constitution in which the chief item would be *Scrutin de Liste*; this may be a wrong statement of the case but the point at issue is very difficult to understand, and I have in no degree mastered the situation. There seems to be an impression that Gambetta owes his fall more to intrigues within the Chamber, and objections of a transitory kind, than to any real lack of confidence in the country; it is possible that he may return to power at no long time hence, the stronger for his defeat.

27 Jan., Fri.

News in the papers of another Murder in Co. Clare. This time a land Steward of 80 shot whilst sitting at his fireside, for having refused to leave the family of his employer Mrs Morony of Miltown Malbay, with whom he had lived for 50 years.[1]

The bodies of the two men supposed to have been murdered in Galway (a bailiff named Huddy and his nephew aged 17) have been found in the lake near Cong. They had been treated exactly as Mr Dillon (speaking in the House in May 1881) intimated he should himself treat persons who came on such a duty, as [did] these unfortunate men. Their bodies were riddled with shot, and blood-stained clothes and implements have been found in the house of a man named Kerrigan.[2]

There is every reason to suppose that all the neighbourhood are fully acquainted with the particulars of the murder, but of course they all share Mr Dillon's feelings on the subject of killing a bailiff, and reserve their sympathy for the Kerrigans who have been arrested on suspicion.

28 Jan., Sat.

Father and Mother arrived about 1 o'clock having left Dublin on Friday night and slept at Chester.

As they were just leaving the Station at Kendal, a man (a total stranger) came

[1] John Lennane (77), described as 'labourer' in the outrage return, was killed at about 7 p.m. on 24 Jan. by a shot fired through his window. The murder was also probably intended to induce Mrs Morony to come to terms with her tenants. Three men were arrested, discharged for want of evidence, rearrested under the P.P.P. act, and held for five months (S.P.O., I.C.R., Returns of outrages, 1882).

[2] Joseph Huddy (70) and his grandson John (17) were shot dead on 3 Jan., and their bodies found on 27 Jan. Three men were arrested, and were hanged in January 1883 (S.P.O., I.C.R., Returns of outrages, 1882).

up to the carriage window and said: 'God bless you, sir, and your work'—a pleasant welcome back to England for the Irish Secretary, and a good omen for the Session.

Spent two hours with Father going over the Fox Ghyll woods and intacts,[1] the faithful Robins at his heels in great felicity. Father much pleased with the flourishing condition of his young trees, some of which are nearly 12 feet high.

Uncle John arrived from Beeston. A pleasant family dinner party—quite like old times at Christmas. Father in cheerful spirits—read aloud to us the latest abuse of himself in *United Ireland*, and a poem in the same paper, which he thought very spirited, and which was certainly an improvement in a literary point of view on some of the productions which have lately been appearing in the 'sedition papers' under the head of poetry.

29 Jan., Sun.

A cold, gloomy, grey day; but very peaceful and pleasant for the Chief Secretary, who is supposed by the papers to have gone straight from Dublin to London on Saturday.

To church at Rydal in the morning. An afternoon indoors—Father asleep a good part of the time on the drawing room sofa—having leisure to feel thoroughly and comfortably tired.

All the party except Father and me to Ambleside church in the evening to hear Mr Chase the new clergyman take his first service.

Father read Mr Childers on the Army, which he had not had time to do before, after which I was summoned as usual to assist at the making up the Journal and noting for Grillion's.

After Fox How tea, and a quiet evening over hymns, talking, and prayers (at which Father was called upon to read the chapter 40), he left this peaceful haven at half past 10, driving to Oxenholme, and going on by the night Mail to London for the Cabinet on Monday.

30 Jan., Mon.

Uncle John left early in the morning. I dined at the Hall.

31 Jan., Tu.

A de Freycinet Cabinet formed in Paris.[2]

A letter from Father to Mother—very tired with a sleepless journey and the Cabinet after it—always in itself a serious strain.

[1] Should read 'intakes', a north of England usage for land reclaimed from moor.
[2] Charles Louis de Saulces de Freycinet (1828–1923): chief of military cabinet under Gambetta, 1870–71; minister of public works, 1877; president of council and minister of foreign affairs, 1879–80.

Finished Burke's *Some Observations on the conduct of the Minority*.
In the afternoon to tea at Mrs Benson Harrison's.

1 Feb., Wed.

Aunt Lucy and Lucy left. Called with Mother and Aunt Fan on Mr Irving and
Miss Reynolds.

The valley still buried in fog, nothing visible of the mountains. Mrs Benson
Harrison and Kitty to tea. Finished *Elsie Venner*.[1] Morley's *Life of Cobden*[2] read
aloud by Aunt Fan in the evening.

2 Feb., Th.

A letter forwarded to us by Edward from Major Neild, R.M. at Mohill, Co.
Leitrim. On the whole a cheering report—the demeanour of the people
changed decidedly for the better, and some rents beginning to be paid.

Remembering vividly the last time we heard from Major Neild—that dismal
evening at the C.S. Lodge[3]—this more hopeful account of his present experience in the same district gave one acute pleasure—more no doubt than was at
all justified by the actual facts.

3 Feb., Fri.

A day of still more impenetrable fog and mist. Spent half an hour at Fox
Ghyll—talked over the political situation with Robins in the potting shed. Poor
Robins' feelings about Mr Forster, and about the Irish, are almost too deep for
words, but it is a pleasure to him to express himself sometimes on the subject,
and when he does talk it is very good sense.

More of *Cobden*. Our last evening with Aunt Fan.

4 Feb., Sat.

From Fox How to London. Francie remaining at Rugby to spend the Sunday
with the George Macauleys.[4] Reached No 80 about 6 o'clock, just in time to
escape the great fog which a few minutes later descended upon London.

Father and Oakley to dinner.

[1] *Elsie Venner: a romance of destiny*. By Oliver Wendell Holmes. Boston, 1861. Many later editions.
[2] Published at the end of 1881; Morley's most successful book up to this time and decisive both
in establishing his reputation and moulding his own thought.
[3] Above, pp 314–15.
[4] G. C. Macaulay (1852–1915): fellow of Trinity College, Cambridge, and assistant-master at
Rugby since 1878, when he married Grace Mary Conybeare; published selections from the poetry
of Matthew Arnold.

5 Feb., Sun.

To church with Mother in the morning at St James the Less. Oakel in bed with a heavy cold, but full of his 'seditious extracts'—selections from speeches by the Land League leaders, showing their intimate connection with the crimes committed during the 'constitutional agitation'.

He has shewn these to Lord Monck who was much struck with them, and encourages him to publish them in a pamphlet form.[1]

Mr Johnson (Attorney General) and Mr Jephson to lunch. The latter, by no means inclined generally to a sanguine view, acknowledged that the state of things in Ireland seemed rather improved—such at least is the general impression, though not always derived from definite facts.

Mr Johnson had heard the day before from a cousin of the O'Conor Don's that some rents were being paid in Roscommon.

Called with Father in the afternoon on Mr Algernon West and Lady Ely.

After supper stayed up with Father in the library till he had finished arranging the rough notes for his speech—half past 12.

It will have to be a two-sided defence against the Red and the White enemy so to speak, on one side he will be attacked by the Land League, and on the other by the Landlords, whose cause will be represented in especial by Mr Gibson; it is uncertain who will take Mr Parnell's place as Chief of the Land League section.

6 Feb., Mon.

Mr Justin McCarthy is to bring forward the principal indictment against the Irish policy of the Govt, but Mr Gray is to be the leader in place of Mr Parnell.

A call from Miss Dixon. Father to General Dodgson[2] to lunch. Calls from Nelly—Lady Reay.

Met Francie at Euston on her return from Rugby.

Father dined with Mr Gladstone—Mother, Francie, Oakel and I to the party there in the evening. Very pleasant, cordial greetings, and much agreeable chatter.

7 Feb., Tu.

A conspicuous paragraph in the papers this morning headed 'Attempt to injure Mr Forster'.

This was the first I knew of the escape he had had, Mother and he having kept the fact to themselves until it was allowed to become public.

An envelope marked O.H.M.S. and directed in a bold educated handwriting

---

[1] They were published on 1 Apr. 1882 as *The truth about the Land League*.
[2] David Scott Dodgson (1821–98), major-general in the Indian army.

to Mr Forster was received at the Castle last Wednesday. Steele (the office keeper) noticed that something was oozing out of the envelope, which was also stained dark by something inside it. Instead of forwarding it direct to Father with the other letters he took it to Mr Burke, who, seeing that the envelope contained some curious substance sent it to be chemically examined at a laboratory.

It turned out to be filled with iodide of nitrogen, which is used I believe in charging bombs.

As soon as it was dry the whole thing exploded on being touched with a feather—some of it going off by itself. The sender of the letter had been obliged to wet it to prevent it going off when stamped in the post office, and his calculation had evidently been that it would have become dry enough to explode by the time it reached the hands it was intended for.

As it turned out the calculation was wrong by about an hour—not to speak of the fact that it would have been Mr Burke or Steele who would have been injured instead of Father.

Copied *Irish World* extracts for Father in the library most of the morning. He to the Cabinet at 12. Aunt Neda and W.H. to lunch. Oakel to Mr Playfair to show him the blotting paper in which the explosive letter had been sent.

On holding it to the light it was found to be written over with chemical symbols—shewing that the concoction had been made up by some one familiar with scientific chemistry—and at one of six places in Dublin—so said Mr Playfair, who gave Oakley at the same time some interesting information about various explosives and the best way of treating them.

Walked with Francie in the afternoon: Uncle Walter and Mr Rutson to tea. Explanations from the latter as to the causes of the Liberal defeat in the North Riding—Bradlaugh, and the proposed abolition of the law of Distress.

Father not home to dinner.

Queen's Speech in the *Pall Mall Gazette*—mild and lengthy.

Mr Bradlaugh finally disposed of for the present. Came up to the table to take the oath. Motion to prevent him doing so by Sir Stafford Northcote, speeches by Sir W. Harcourt and Mr Newdegate. Moderate speech by Mr Bradlaugh offering to consider the oath binding on his conscience, and to resign his seat and take the chance of re-election if the House would bring in and pass an Affirmation Bill. Division: Govt beaten (as was expected) by a majority of 60—even such good supporters as Mr Cropper voting against them, and many others staying away.[1]

Mr Bradlaugh, being requested by the Speaker to withdraw, did so under protest and the 'affaire Bradlaugh' will now pass from the constituencies to the Law Courts.

Question of the imprisoned M.P.s, brought forward as one of 'Privilege' by Mr E. D. Gray. The Govt., backed by the authority of the Speaker, declined to

[1] The division was 286:228.

be drawn into a debate on the whole subject of their Irish policy on this occasion, though they fully acknowledged the importance of the question, and
suggested that it should be brought forward in the proper form as an Amendment to the Address.

Indignation on the part of Mr O'Donnell, Mr Gray, etc., but no prolonged
debate allowed by the Speaker.

The proposed new Rules of Procedure laid on the table of the House by Mr
Gladstone.

8 Feb., Wed.

Walked with Father to the office, bringing back a sheaf of papers—*Irish World
United Ireland* etc.

We talked of the pamphlet published by the Land Commission which is
making such a sensation. A pamphlet entitled 'How to become Owner of your
Farm' (appearing originally in the *Freeman*) has been published with the
authority and by the sanction of the Secretary to the Land Commission, Mr
Denis Godley. A good deal of the contents are useful and harmless, but
certain portions, extolling the Land League and that 'far-seeing man',
Michael Davitt, and exulting in the ruin of the landlords, have given deep
offence, and caused very natural astonishment, as appearing under the
authority of a Govt which has thought it right to suppress the Land League
and imprison its leaders.

Mr Godley has written to Father to explain that he took the pamphlet on
trust, having been assured by the Solicitor (Mr Fottrell) that it was such as the
Commission might reasonably publish in their official capacity; he thinks that
having received this assurance from the official Solicitor to the Commission, he
(Mr Godley) is in no way to blame for having allowed the publication of the
pamphlet without further enquiry as to its contents.

Father has written an official letter to Judge O'Hagan calling his attention to
the matter (which is being complained of in the H. of Lords and in the Press),
and also a private letter telling him of Mr Godley's lame explanation, and
suggesting whether the Commission will think it desirable to retain Mr Fottrell
in the position of confidential Solicitor after what has happened.

This Mr Fottrell, whom [*sic*] Father privately suspects is the author of the
objectionable part of the pamphlet, was recommended to him by Mr C. Russell, and also received a character from Mr Gibson. When he was appointed
Father was told that he was not mixed up with the Land League, except in so
far as he had once or twice been consulted by them in a professional capacity; it
was not mentioned, what Father has since found out, that he was consulted by
them on the question of the purchase by the League of the *United Ireland* newspaper; this however is a secret.

Drove with Mother and Francie in the afternoon: Francie to Hatchard's to enquire about the publication of her book.[1]

To the House, a friendly meeting with Wilson of the Ladies Gallery, who was full of regret that we were too late to hear Mr Gladstone's answer to Sir Stafford. Mr P. J. Smyth speaking on a Home Rule Amendment. I came in just in time to hear him citing the example of Deák, who had done for Hungary what O'Connell wished to do for Ireland; he was followed by Mr O'Connor Power—in both their speeches a very different tone from that with which the Parnellite patriots have accustomed us.

We shall have plenty of this very soon when Mr Justin McCarthy's Amendment comes on.

To tea at Lady Victoria Buxton's, and at No 7, Mary and Humphry Ward to tea here.

The *Pall Mall* furious at last night's division on Mr Bradlaugh—'malignant faction'—religious people 'sacrificing their principles for the sake of gratifying a personal aversion' etc., as if to some people (however misguided) religion might not involve principles as well as politics.

Lord Monck, Mr Gray (Valuator to the Commission), Uncle Walter, Aunt Neda, Mr Hayes and Arnold to dinner.

In the evening to Lady Granville's and Lady Tenterden's—everyone full of Mr Gladstone's speech—said to be one of the finest he has ever made. Father had said to him when he sat down—'Well, I don't know what sort of speech you will make when you are ninety, for you seem to get better and better as you grow older'.

9 Feb., Th.

Father at home all the morning finishing off his speech. Uncle Matt to lunch.

Walked with Father to the office—Mr Fottrell has resigned.

Drove with Mother and Francie at 6 o'clock to the House. The debate on Mr P. J. Smyth's Home Rule Amendment[2] still going on, and the prospect not favourable for getting to Mr Justin McCarthy's on which the Ch. Sec. was to make his defence.

Moderate speeches from Mr Molloy and Mr O'Sullivan demanding Home Rule in a reasonable and argumentative manner—when considered from the rational Irish point of view only.

Mr Gladstone in his reply was evidently answering the reasonable Irish Home Rulers only, and ignoring for the time the use that might be made of his words by the irreconcilables.

His speech consisted of two parts; in the first he confined himself entirely

---

[1] See below, p. 402.
[2] Amendment to the address moved by P. J. Smyth on 8 Feb. and defeated on 9 Feb. by 93 to 37 (*Hansard 3*, cclvi, 195–216 (8 Feb.), 250–75, 1033 (9 Feb.)).

and unmistakably to the question of local self-government, such as might conceivably be extended in Ireland as well as in England and Scotland.

In the second he dealt with Home Rule as understood by such Home Rulers as Mr Molloy and Mr Sullivan, and showed the impracticability of conceding it mainly on the ground of the impossibility of distinguishing in practice between 'Imperial' and local matters, and of the necessity that would arise, in case such a system were ever adopted, of establishing some supreme deciding authority independent of Parliament.

He declared that the burden of proving the possibility of working such a system without injury to the United Kingdom must rest with the Home Rulers themselves, and pointed out that hitherto no two of them had ever agreed in a practicable scheme.

Mr Gladstone was followed by Mr O'Donnell, who took an ingenious line in pointing out that all the Premier had done was to state the difficulties in the way of a Home Rule system, whereas difficulties attended every project of reform (e.g. London Corporation reform); it was patent that the objections to the present relations beteen England and Ireland were great, and it might be worth running the risk of other objections in the future, for the sake of removing these in the present.

We left the House about half past 7—Father having come up to tell us that there seemed every possibility of this Home Rule debate going on all night, thereby preventing him from making his speech.

In the middle of dinner we received a note from Father to say that the division on Mr P. J Smyth's Amendment had been taken, and Mr Justin Mc-Carthy's had come on—he would probably speak about 9 or ¼ to 10. When we reached Lady Brand's Gallery at half past 9 he had already begun, and was engaged in describing to the House (rather a thin one) the Boycotting system and its patronage by the Land League leaders.

As he went gradually through the successive Acts of his five months' administration in Ireland, describing what had been done, justifying his action, producing documents and stating facts in support of it, the House—now gradually filling—followed him with unflagging attention; an element of liveliness was imported into the scene by the angry shouts and interruptions of the Parnellites, who frequently vented their deep irritation at some of the quotations read by the Ch. Secretary from their own writings and speeches by flat denials of very palpable facts.

They loudly disclaimed for instance any connection with, or knowledge of the 'No Rent' Placard, in spite of the fact that Mr Egan himself had telegraphed to the *Freeman* in November to vouch for its authenticity, and that the *United Ireland* (organ of the Land League) had referred to it with fond pride as the 'irrepressible Manifesto'.

The Ch. Secretary spoke all through with the leisurely deliberation of a man who is conscious of a strong case, and relies on his facts duly marshalled and brought forth to produce a sufficient effect, without the aid of much oratorical display on his part. Every now and then however he spoke out with a vigour and concentration which were very impressive, and in his short description of the tyranny which the Land League would have finally established over the country, if the Government of the Queen had not asserted itself by strong measures, he carried the House with him most emphatically.

The second and shorter part of his speech was devoted to a defence of the Sub-Commissioners, for whose appointment (but not for whose judicial decisions) he acknowledged himself to be entirely responsible.

Before closing he declared in sober and restrained language his belief that the state of the country did show signs of improvement; he did not wish to take too sanguine a view, and acknowledged that, in some parts of the country especially, outrage and lawlessness still prevailed, but yet it was his conviction and hope, judging from the outrage reports, from the confidential reports received, from the return in many cases to the payment of rent, that things were rather better than they had been, and that the strong powers entrusted to the Irish Executive had not been used in vain for the restoration of order, and the security of life and property.[1]

After Mr Forster's speech, which lasted a little over two hours, the adjournment of the debate was moved by Mr Redmond—who all through the Ch. Secretary's defence had seemed in a high state of excitement, as did also Mr Sexton and Mr Dawson.

Mr Justin McCarthy, the wary Mover of the Amendment, had been out of the House most of the time, greatly to the indignation of the Ch. Sec., who amused us by his constant cry for the Member for Longford—'Is not the hon. Member for Longford present?' 'If the hon. Member for Longford were in his place', etc.[2]

Mr McCarthy, on meeting Father in the Lobby afterwards, appears to have volunteered the statement that 'he was sorry he had not been in the House, as he understood that he (Mr Forster) had been making some allusions to him'—certainly a mild way of describing the vials of wrath and indignation which the Ch. Secretary had just been pouring on the virtuous head of the gentleman who aids and abets by money and tacit sanction the most violent teaching of the most seditious press, and then goes off to enjoy himself in Greece, regardless of possible consequences in Ireland.

Father did not get home till late, Mr Sexton having brought in a Bill for the Repeal of the Coercion Act, which he had felt bound to oppose even in this initial stage—a proceeding that had given offence not only to the Parnellites but to some of the English Radicals.

---

[1] *Hansard 3*, cclxvi, 286–325 (9 Feb.).
[2] McCarthy had made frequent use of this tactic against Forster.

10 Feb., Fri.

The papers much exercised over Mr Gladstone's speech, both *Times* and *Standard* taking the line of Mr Plunkett (who had spoken after Mr O'Donnell the previous evening) that it was in a high degree mischievous and might be construed into an invitation to a fresh agitation in Ireland.

By the Conservatives it is believed (or rather stated) that Mr Gladstone, knowing a Dissolution to be impending, spoke as he did about Home Rule for the purpose of bribing the Irish Members into supporting the Govt.

A friendly article in the *Standard* on the Ch. Secretary's defence of his policy.

Gummed extracts into the Newspaper book. To Lillington Street. In the afternoon with Mother to Burlington House to see the Old Masters Loan Collection—amongst them the Tintoretto from the Irish National Gallery, who followed us round with his grave dark eyes, as if he recognised Dublin friends.

Father home to dinner. Mr Gibson had made a good speech, gentlemanlike and moderate—the main ground of attack that the Govt had not done what they did do, much earlier.

In the evening with Mother to Lady Victoria's, to meet Lord Roden, Lord Waveney, the Treve[lyan]s, Kirks etc. Lady Kirk—wife of our Consul at Zanzibar—(formerly Dr Kirk) told me a great deal that was interesting about the heroic Captain Brownrigg, and about the Universities Mission at Zanzibar, and in the interior—but otherwise the evening was as dull as I had expected.

11 Feb., Sat.

The debate had been continued last night by Lord Randolph Churchill, Mr Porter, etc. The Solicitor General a decided success, and congratulated heartily by Mr Gladstone and the Ch. Sec. when he sat down.

Visit from Aunt Fanny Lucy and Lucy in the morning. Walked with Father to the office. To Kensington Gardens with Oakel and Rob in the afternoon; a pleasant day fresh and mild, with just breeze enough to carry the toy ships in fleets across the Round Pond. Oakel and I spent a long time sharing in these peaceful delights, watching not only the various boats but their various owners, from elderly artizans down to smartly dressed little girls, all following the proceedings of their respective craft with the most anxious interest and absorption.

Aunt Mala, Arnold and Louis to dinner; played a new form of the old Historical game which Father entered into with great zest.

Later, he and I to Spencer House—a pleasant party as they always are at this house. On our way home stopped at the Reform Club for Father to see the provincial papers on his speech. He is glad to find that it seems to have produced just the effect he intended—even the Radical *Manchester Examiner* after a careful article upon the speech comes to the conclusion that the verdict of the country with respect to the dealings with Ireland must be given in favour of the Govt.

Every one we meet in Society is very cordial and friendly about Father; his vindication of his proceedings during the hard five months in Ireland, during which he has had to take his abuse in silence, has made a very good impression. Even the Irish Tory papers are respectful towards him personally, and my favourite *Irish Times* sticks by him as though he were a brother Irishman instead of an English Minister.

12 Feb., Sun.

To church at St James the Less. A visit from old Sir Harry Verney to congratulate Mother on Father's speech. Aunt Mala and Arnold and Louis to lunch. Walked with Father to Lady Ely's, and to church at St Michael's.

A visit from Mr Bevan Braithwaite in the evening. Copied extracts from the *Irishman* and *Freeman* showing the contrast between the language of a Land League M.P. in America (Mr T. P. O'Connor) and a Land League M.P. in the House (Mr Redmond).

13 Feb., Mon.

Next to Ireland the most prominent crux at present is the New Rules. There is a great agitation against the 'tyranny of the government' in proposing to make the question of the Clôture (the First Rule) a question of confidence.

One or two Liberals have given notice of Amendments, and there has been great hope amongst the Opposition that by dint of a coalition between Tories, Parnellites, and recalcitrant Liberals, the Government may even be defeated. Father, however, does not think this probable, and within the last day or two it has seemed less so.

A telegram to Father this morning announcing that Mr Wilford Lloyd—Mr Clifford Lloyd's brother—had been (in mistake for a neighbouring landlord) shot at, and a policeman with him wounded in the chest. Several shots were fired back, but it is feared that in the dark none took effect.[1]

Lord Kenmare and his solicitor to see Father.

I with Mother to Miss Wood's. Drove with Mother in the afternoon. Sir John and Lady Smale to tea.

Dined with Oakel at the Humphry Wards' in the evening.

---

[1] Lloyd, who had been appointed temporary R.M. in Dec., and Lt Walter Besant of the 9th Foot (Norfolk Regiment) were being driven from Scariff to Tulla by Sub-Constable Thomas Mills when they were fired on; Mills was not dangerously wounded. The intended target was thought to be Col. John O'Callaghan, owner of 4,842 acres in the county (Clare), worth £1,919, whose estate remained disturbed for years (S.P.O., I.C.R., Returns of outrages, 1882).

Father returned to dinner here—Lady Ely, Mr Porter, and Herbert Gladstone to dinner—Mother going down to the House afterwards with Lady Ely.

Mr Plunkett made a fine speech as usual, but ending with a very gloomy prognostic for the future—anticipating fresh agitation, 'Prairie value and Home Rule' and non-payment of the judicial rent; he was followed in the course of the evening by Mr Chamberlain, Lord G[eorge] Hamilton, Mr Shaw LeFevre, and Mr E. D. Gray.

Mr LeFevre's speech a defence of the Land Act, and a vehement denunciation of the League—signs in it I thought of his sojourn with Mr Blake, R.M.[1]

14 Feb., Tu.

Mr Edward Wade of Ilkley to breakfast.

Mother walked with Father to Jermyn Street. Uncle Matt to lunch. Drove with Mother in the afternoon. Mr Cropper to tea, leaving Mr Sexton speaking at the House.

Father home late to dinner, bringing Mr Pell with him. The Debate at an end, Division taken and the Address finally passed. A most sudden and unexpected finale.

Mr Sexton had spoken for two hours—'a very clever speech' Father said, 'but stuffed as full of lies as it could hold'—when he ended, the Parnellites (evidently by prearrangement) refrained from continuing the Debate, the object being to force Mr Johnson or Mr Gladstone to reply in the dinner hour, which it was hoped might be disagreeable to the Govt. Instead of this Ministers also refrained from speaking, upon which the Division—thirty to ninety—was taken, only about half the Cabinet being present.[2]

We heard from Oakel who came home about 11 o'clock after a hard day of Meetings and arrangements with his Liberal Union, Municipal Reform Asstn etc., that the 'score' as it was intended to have been, was arranged by Lord R. Churchill.

15 Feb., Wed.

Curious article in *The Times* on last night's Debate, so anti-Government in tone as almost to look like the beginning of a complete reversal—exhausting itself in laudation of Mr Sexton's 'brilliant and able' speech, and winding up with pointing the moral of the necessity for no concession in Ireland—this being an allusion again to Mr Gladstone's speech of last Thursday.

A long letter from Mr G. Fottrell to the Commissioners, explaining to his own complete satisfaction, his connection with the pamphlet scandal (he is the

---

[1] In his *Incidents of coercion* (London, 1888), Lefevre wrote that this visit 'opened his eyes' to the failure of coercion and Castle government.

[2] The division on McCarthy's amendment was 30 to 98 (*Hansard 3*, cclxvi, 680).

author of it), and complaining that all would have gone well if the Commissioners had not allowed themselves to become the 'inquisitors' of a Minister who had not, as Mr Fottrell fears, sufficient regard for their dignity.

However, the long and short of the matter is that Mr Fottrell's resignation has been accepted, and that all the solicitors in Dublin are applying for the vacant post.

Father to the House at 12 o'clock. Uncle John to lunch. Spent most of the afternoon indoors with Oakel, who is trying to give his long cold a chance of being cured. Helped him with the Land League pamphlet which he is preparing.

The *Pall Mall* and in fact all the papers full of speculation about the Procedure Debate, which begins to-morrow.

Father and Mother dined at Mrs Jeune's (ex Mrs John Stanley)[1] and afterwards to Lady Harcourt's, Father afterwards to the Cos.

16 Feb., Th.

A Debate on Report having sprung up, the Debate on the New Rules will not begin till Monday.

Walked with Father and Mr West to the office.

Ted, Mary Cropper, and Uncle Matt to lunch.

Uncle Matt is amused and pleased to see that his note to the *Pall Mall* on 'Closure' as against 'Clôture' has produced such effect with his complaisant friend, Mr Morley, that the *P.M.G.* has already adopted the new word in every instance where it occurs all through the paper.

Drove with Mother in the afternoon. Sir Thomas Acland, Lady Buxton, Mr Edward Buxton, Kitty Buxton, Mr Rutson, Mr John Penrose, and Mr Davidson (our Chamonix acquaintance) to dinner. Father and Sir Thomas returning to the House immediately after.

The Liberal, Lord Kilcoursie, beaten at Taunton by 227 by Mr Allsop.[2]

17 Feb., Fri.

Mr Lowther spoke last night, also Mr Johnson and Mr Gladstone—the Premier in vindication and explanation of the Home Rule speech which caused such excitement. He still maintains that he is and always has been in favour of decentralisation, and would be willing to give such amount of local self-government to Ireland as might be safely granted to Scotland if she chose to ask for it.

Deputation to Father from Trinity College.[3]

[1] See appendix. [2] Allsop 1,144, Kilcoursie 917.
[3] The deputation was of middlemen holding tenancies from T.C.D., seeking protection against rent increases. Forster declined to intervene, but advised them to secure the support of a private M.P. (*Irish Times*, 18 Feb.).

A bad report this morning from Ireland. A constable (Kavanagh) shot dead at Letterfrack, Co. Galway.[1]

Walked with Father to Lady Ely's—at 2.30 with Mother to the Drawing Room. The Queen very gracious, shaking hands with Mother, as also the Princess which they have not done for some years.

Mrs Buxton, May, Chenda, and Nelly (Arnold) to 5 o'clock tea. Father home to dinner for an interval in the middle of 'agricultural depression', the Debate on Report of the Address having now taken this form.

The House sat till three, and Father has decided to go over to Dublin on Sunday night—various things are being done in a way that does not altogether satisfy him both as regards arrests and releases, and he is glad to take this opportunity of going over.

I was enquiring again to-day about the Mr O'Neill, whose brother of the *Pittsburg Dispatch* wrote to the Chief Sec. about his arrest shortly before we left Dublin. Unfortunately the facts when referred to again by those who know do not seem in favour of his being let out.

18 Feb., Sat.

The newspapers this morning full of the very important Debate on the Land Act in the House of Lords last evening, and of its still more important result.

By a majority of 42 the Lords have accepted Lord Donoughmore's proposal to appoint a 'Select Committee' to enquire into the working of the Act.[2]

The full significance of this is pointed out in impressive and complacent words by the *Standard*; it means a repeal of the Land Act on the ground that the Govt have failed to redeem the pledges as to its scope and administration which they gave last year by way of inducing the House to pass the Bill.

The Select Committee will have the power to summon any witnesses it likes, to put and exact an answer to any questions however inconvenient, to summon the three Chief Commissioners to London to give evidence, in short to impede if not entirely to put a stop to the whole working of the Act as at present in force. Lord Spencer, Lord Emly, Lord Carlingford, and Lord Selborne spoke strongly against Lord Donoughmore's Motion—Lord Waterford, Lord Kilmorey, Lord Dunraven,[3] and above all Lord Cairns in support of it.

[1] Constable John Kavanagh, who had been active in securing an arrest in the Lydon case (above, p. 126), was shot dead near Letterfrack barrack at about 10.30 p.m. on 15 Feb. Two men were arrested and discharged for want of evidence; one was later rearrested, convicted, and sentenced to death, commuted to penal servitude for life (S.P.O., I.C.R., Returns of outrages, 1882).

[2] John Luke Hely Hutchinson (1848–1900): 5th Earl Donoughmore; owned about 12,000 acres, chiefly in Tipperary, Waterford, Cork, and Wexford, valued at £10,466. His proposal was accepted by 96 to 43.

[3] Windham Thomas Wyndham Quin (1841–1926): 4th earl of Dunraven and Mount-Earl; A.D.C. to lord lieutenant, 1868; *Daily Telegraph* war correspondent, 1870–71; author of *The Irish question*, 1880; owned 14,298 acres in Limerick, 1,005 in Kerry, and 164 in Clare, valued at a total of £11,033, as well as large estates in Britain.

The speaking all through was good, the most impressive speeches being Lord Spencer's and the ex and present Lord Chancellors'.[1] Considering the extremely moderate views which Lord Selborne has been known to hold on the Land question, his thorough-going and vigorous vindication of the Land Act and protest against interfering with it after only 4 months trial, was all the more valuable.

However, whatever the arguments against interference with the working of the Commissioners, it was not likely that the landlords, having at last got a favourable opportunity for asserting their grievances, would refrain from doing so in the most effectual manner they could devise.

As to the importance of what they have done and all the consequences that must result from it, 'the *Standard* is quite right' says Father. He was profoundly gloomy and annoyed over what had happened, and if some of the Conservative peers could have seen his vexation and anxiety as he looked through the morning papers, they would no doubt have felt well satisfied with the success of their last move.

At 12 he went off to see Mr Gladstone—afterwards to the Cabinet.

Drove with Mother in the afternoon—called on the Charles Bucklands, Mr Spring Rice, etc., the Humphry Wards, Balls, and Bernard Holland. Mr Holland is in the same Chambers with a brother of Mr Dillon's[2]—professedly moderate and indifferent as regards politics, but turning into an ardent Nationalist as might be expected when talked to.

Mother, Francie and Oakel to the Admiralty; Father to bed—tired out and looking as he used to do after a bad day in Ireland.

19 Feb., Sun.

A depressing article in the *Observer*, complaining that the Land Act had quite failed to do what even those who disapproved of its principles had hoped that it would do, namely, extinguish the political agitation—then followed apropos of this with a further lamentation over Mr Gladstone's Home Rule (or Local Govt) speech.

It is much to be feared that in thinking of Mr P. J. Smyth, Mr Shaw, Mr Morley, Mr O'Connor Power, and a few other Irish politicians by whom perhaps reasonable propositions for the establishment of Irish local government would be met in the honest and friendly spirit in which they were put forward, Mr Gladstone quite left out of mind the overpowering majority of Irish politicians, by whom any concession in this direction would be used as a leverage ground against our country.

However much there may be to be said theoretically in favour of giving a fair hearing to Home Rule demands, it is hard to believe that in practice, and under

---

[1] Lord Cairns, Feb. 1874–Apr. 1880; Lord Selborne, Apr. 1880–June 1885.
[2] William, John's senior by a year. For Bernard Holland, see above, p. 74.

present conditions, such a way of dealing with the subject can do anything but harm; this is especially the conclusion one comes to after reading the Irish papers, and seeing the honest regret of such a thoroughly Irish-minded paper as the *Irish Times* at a fresh incentive being given to agitation, and the exultation of the *Freeman's Journal* over a concession which is evidently the result, it points out, not of the moderate tactics of past Home Rulers, but of the violent system of the present day.

What good can ever come out of any possible arrangements for an amicable definition of Imperial and Local questions, which is contemplated in such a spirit as this?

To church in the morning at St James the Less. Father followed us later, having been detained by a visit from Mr Escott of the *Standard*.

Mr Jephson and Mr West at luncheon. Calls in the afternoon from Mr D'Eyncourt and Mr J. G. Butcher. At 5.30 walked with Father to 7 Grosvenor Crescent. He told me of his interview with Mr Escott—a man 'who is at heart a Radical' says Father, but writes Moderate articles for the *Standard*. He had come professedly to give information, but also to try and extract it. He told the Ch. Sec. amongst other things that the Lords' great coup had been arranged at Hatfield[1] some little time back, and also gave him to understand that a Resolution to the same effect as that passed in the Lords would be brought forward by the Opposition in the Commons.

This certainly seems rather surprising, considering that a division there would mean a defeat, but Father supposes they would hope to detach many Whig Liberals and some of the Irish—and so I suppose by diminishing the Govt majority make a sufficient demonstration to enhance the effect of the Lords' decision.

We dined at 7 to suit Father who left for Dublin by the night Mail. Before going he read us part of a letter just received from Captain Talbot concerning the explosive letter (of course strictly private). It began with a categorical denial one after another, of the statements made on the subject by the *Freeman*, which had professed to 'know' that the contents of the letter were not such as to have done serious harm—that the envelope was addressed in a school-boy hand (implying that the whole thing was a practical joke) etc., etc. Captain Talbot then informed him that the Police had every reason to believe that the letter emanated from the Ladies' Land League, and that the sister of Mr Walsh[2] (one of the worst of the agitators now in Kilmainham) assisted by two young men (also known to the police) was responsible for it.

Various reasons were given explaining this supposition, but Captain Talbot added that it was not likely this charge, like so many others, could ever be publicly proved, from want of the necessary evidence.

[1] Lord Salisbury's residence.
[2] John W. Walshe, Fenian and Land League organiser. His sister, Beatrice, one of the founders of the Ladies' Land League.

There were 50 grains of iodide of nitrogen in the packet—much more than sufficient for the purposes of a harmless practical joke.

20 Feb., Mon.

Father had a good passage. He is staying this time at the Castle with the Cowpers.

A call this morning whilst at breakfast from Mrs Redmond, Mother of Mr Redmond, M.P. and of his brother, now a suspect. Oakel went out to have an interview with her. She was very polite, and will write to Father on the subject she came about, the removal of her son to another prison.

To a Meeting of the C. and S. in the morning.

Maud Goschen and Lucy and Nelly to lunch. Drove in the afternoon, but not with Mother who was kept to the house with a bad cold.

A quiet evening—Oakel at his Debating Society where he found himself one of a minority of 3 in defending the Govt on the New Rules of Procedure.

A long and interesting talk with Mother in her bedroom over Ireland, and the future; she has quite given up all hope of seeing any visible improvement in Father's time.

21 Feb., Tu.

Having spent all yesterday in primitive ignorance of everything that was taking place at the House, we were doubly interested in the news this morning.

Public excitement over Mr Gladstone's speech on the New Rules had been almost swamped in excitement over a Motion of which he had given Notice for Monday to the effect that any Parliamentary enquiry at present into the working of the Irish Land Act tended to defeat the operation of that Act, and must be injurious to the administration of good government in Ireland.[1]

This notice appears to have been received with loud cheers by the Liberals, as was Sir W. Bartelott's[2] angry outburst against the Govt for 'gagging the Commons' and collaring the Lords, by the Opposition.

The *Times* is in a high state of indignation with Mr Gladstone for this move, the *Standard* excited and calling for a compromise, to avoid a conflict between the Houses, etc.

The *Times* is furious with the Govt (professedly) for provoking 'heated discussion' on the Land Act just at the time when they profess to need all the time and attention available for the Procedure debate; but if what Mr Escott said is true, the debate would have arisen in any case, and all the Govt have done is to assume the offensive instead of waiting to be attacked. One thing

[1] *Hansard 3*, cclxvi, 1107.
[2] Walter Barttelot (1820–93): conservative M.P. for West Sussex, 1860–85; baronet, 1875; C.B., 1880.

must at any rate be allowed, and that is, that from the point of view of the Government—responsible for the actual administration of Ireland from day to day—Ministers are justified in taking any measure however drastic that may tend to stop such a dangerous proceeding as the Lords have initiated. If the Upper House have brought in and carried their Resolution for a Select Committee merely for the purpose of expressing their censure of the Sub-Commissioners, and with no intention of carrying their proposition into execution, it is for them to talk of compromise, for them to explain away what they have done, and not for the Govt, as the *Standard* is good enough to suggest.

The Conservative critics of the Land Act may be right, or they may be wrong, but in any case, what right have they to complain if the Govt chooses to meet their attack with as vigorous a retort. It is all very well to write as the *Times* does this morning of Mr Gladstone sending 'a message of war' to the Upper House, but under the circumstances, and in face of the solemn protests of Lord Spencer and Lord Selborne—responsible Minister of the Crown—the appointment of a Select Committee could hardly be described as a Message of conciliation.

A letter to Mother from Father this morning—very hard at work, difficulties looking somewhat less when actually faced.

Arnold and Julia to lunch. To the Grosvenor Gallery (Watts Collection) in the afternoon. Uncle Matt, Aunt F[anny] L[ucy] and Lucy to dinner. Oakel and I in the evening to Private theatricals at Lady Collier's—amusing as they usually are here, and Mrs John Collier very clever—but an English attempt at the brogue, which was necessary in her part, seems very unsatisfactory to those accustomed for five months to the real thing.

The talk of the evening amongst the audience (which included many M.P.s and such like) was of Mr Bradlaugh, who it appeared had suddenly rushed up to the table from behind the Speaker's Chair, taking his own Testament with him, sworn himself in, written his name and then professed to have duly qualified himself by this extraordinary proceeding to take his seat in the House. He had entirely 'done for himself' now was the general opinion, and would probably be expelled from the House.[1]

22 Feb., Ash Wednesday

The papers this morning full of the 'Extraordinary Scene in the House'—the 'Bradlaugh Outrage' etc. The question of what was to be done by the House in the assertion of its own dignity, in face of this flagrant disregard of the recent Resolution, to be decided to-day.

To church at St Peter's in the morning. Drove with Lucy and Francie in the afternoon, Mother not going out on account of her cold.

[1] *Hansard 3*, cclxvi, 1251–2.

Sent out for an evening paper to see what had happened about Mr Bradlaugh. On a Motion of Sir Stafford's (Mr Gladstone still declining to take any initiative in the matter) Mr Bradlaugh has been expelled the House. A fresh election will take place for Northampton; Mr Corbett[1] stands for the Conservatives, and it is to be hoped that many Liberals will vote for him, and so shelve the Bradlaugh difficulty effectually for the present, by keeping him altogether out of Parliament.

23 Feb., Th.

Drove with Mother and Lucy in the afternoon to the Grosvenor Gallery, and afterwards to tea with Louisa Childers at their new house in Piccadilly.

Mother met Father at Euston and took him straight to the House where some of the Irish Estimates were to be discussed in Committee.

After dinner Lucy and I went down to the House and spent 2 hours in Lady Brand's Gallery—Lucy, who had never been before, came in for a most characteristic evening; we arrived just in time to hear Mr Redmond call the Chief Secretary 'a dishonest politician' an expression he was made to withdraw; Lord Randolph was in great force—kindly endeavouring to do the Govt 'a good turn' as he remarked, by informing the Ch. Secretary that he was generally supposed in Dublin to have urged on the landlords to evict, quite regardless of whether their tenants were dishonest, or poor, and unable to pay their rents.

This attack was eagerly followed up by Mr F. H. O'Donnell; Lord Claud Hamilton and Mr McCartney[2] on the other hand, disapproving of Lord Randolph's abuse of the Ch. Secretary, who they considered did not deserve this at a time when he was showing himself thoroughly alive to his duty.

There were numerous personal episodes of this kind all through the evening, the remarks turning more or less on the character and crimes of the Chief Secretary, who meantime sat on hour after hour, looking rather tired, as was not unnatural considering he had been travelling all day, but serenely indifferent to the denunciations levelled against him and rising every now and then to make an explanation, or defend his conduct with the most perfect courtesy and patience, as though the discussion were being conducted generally in this spirit.

Before Lucy and I left, we had heard many familiar names and subjects talked over. Mr Penrose Fitzgerald, Ross of Bladensburg, Dr Kenny, Colonel McKerlie,[3] etc., and by the end of the evening three of the principal votes had been passed. We saw Mr T. Healy received safe home from the States.

---

[1] Edward Corbett (1817–95): who had sat for South Shropshire, 1868–77.

[2] John William Ellison Macartney (1818–1904): liberal-conservative, later conservative, M.P. for Tyrone County, 1874–85.

[3] John Graham McKerlie (1814–1900): Royal Engineers; commissioner of public works in Ireland since 1855, and chairman of the board of public works since 1862; C.B., 1870.

24 Feb., Fri.

Walked with Father to the office. We talked of last night, and of his time in Dublin, where he had been worked from morning till night, never getting a breath of fresh air; he agreed that his staying at the Castle is not a good plan, and that on the whole it is better for him to go out to the C.S. Lodge.

He had seen Mr Clifford Lloyd who was staying at the Castle; at first he was deeply depressed, but his spirits—if not the state of Clare—appear to have improved before he left. On the whole, of all the five Superintendent R.M.s, Father is inclined to think Mr Plunkett is the best for his work. With all his vigour Mr Lloyd is a little too impulsive, too much up and down, and Father finds that it does not do to quote him too quickly—unfortunately he spoke too soon about the Milltown Malbay boycotting which has not yet been put down.[1]

As to the Commissioners, Mr Vernon—the only one whom he saw—did not seem as much depressed as might have been expected, especially with Mr Vernon.

They (the Commission) do not appear much alarmed at the prospect of the Select Committee enquiry—could arrange amongst themselves so as not to be inconvenienced by it, etc. (Does not this throw rather a different light upon Mr Gladstone's much dreaded Motion—at least upon the necessity for it as regards administration in Ireland?)

Lunched with Francie and Lucy at the H[umphry] Wards', going afterwards with them to the British Museum.

Uncle Matt and Aunt Fanny Lucy, Louisa and Mr Spencer Childers,[2] Mr D'Eyncourt, and Herbert Gladstone to dinner. Father unable to come, the House being again in Committee on the Irish Estimates—this time the Constabulary.

25 Feb., Sat.

A terrible agrarian murder reported this morning at Ballyhaunis in the Co. Mayo. A young man named Frealing dragged out of his bed by a party of armed men, who broke into the house shouting for the 'traitor who had paid his rent'; the man in question was Frealing's father (formerly a member of the L. League) but nevertheless the young man was dragged outside the house, beaten and ill-treated, and when he escaped back into the house, pursued, dragged out again, and this time shot dead.[3]

[1] For Lloyd's opinion of the Superintendent R.M. system see his *Ireland under the Land League*, pp 227–49.

[2] Edmund Spencer Eardley Childers (1854–1919): served with Royal Engineers in Afghan war, later in Egypt; since 1880 assistant private secretary to his father, H. C. E. Childers, at the war office.

[3] Patrick Freely was shot dead by moonlighters at about 10.30 p.m. on 23 Feb. Thirteen men were arrested, but eleven of these were discharged for want of evidence; one was discharged at the spring assizes of 1883, and the last at the winter assizes (S.P.O., I.C.R., Returns of outrages, 1882, 1883).

This hideous murder is the direct and evident result of the 'No Rent' Manifesto, and the No Rent agitation which is kept up mainly by the paper which belongs to Mr Justin McCarthy and his friends.

Such deeds as these are the natural outcome of the 'constitutional agitation' which Mr Parnell and the principal Land League chiefs have allowed to be carried on in Ireland during the past year and a half.

Walked with Father to the office, stopping on the way to examine some of the numerous caricatures of him which abound at present.

Most of the Irish Estimates have been carried; the rest stand over for the present. Apropos of the Estimates and the Parnellites, Father had heard a pleasing anecdote concerning Mr Callan's opinion of him. Someone having asked the Member for Louth why he did not once for all give up his present line, square it with the Govt and apply for a place, Mr Callan replied 'Sir, the Chief Secretary is not a man whom any Irish gentleman can approach with confidence'.

Father dined in the evening with Lord Spencer to prick the Sheriffs.[1] Mother, Aunt F. L., Francie, Lucy and I to see the 'School for Scandal' at the Vaudeville. A strong cast. Ada Cavendish, Lady Teazle; Mr Farren, Sir Peter, Henry Neville, Charles Surface[2]—I am glad to have seen this classic,[3] but do not particularly wish to see it again.

26 Feb., Sun.

To church in the morning at St James the Less.

Mother to St Peter's. Father at work all the morning with Mr Porter. Mr Porter, Mr Jephson, Willy and Mr Charles Buckland to lunch. Father afterwards to Lord Granville's, Mother walking with him. Lucy and I to church at St Peters, and afterwards to [14] Grosvenor Crescent. Mrs Buxton anxious to know what was going to happen on Monday, and expressing her strong dissatisfaction with Mr Gladstone for his unnecesary challenge to the House of Lords. Sir H. Holland had been informing her that a protest from Lord Granville in the Lords, and the abstention of the Liberal Lords from the Committee would have done all that was needed to prevent the bad effect of Lord Donoughmore's Motion.

She was all the more sorry to disapprove of this, as the Govt had already done other things which she could not agree with: for instance the Clôture—why did they insist on a bare majority? Would not a two-thirds have been enough to stop the only real obstruction, that of the Parnellites? etc.

[1] i.e. to appoint sheriffs of counties.

[2] Ada Cavendish (1839–95): prominent actress in light and comic drama; recently returned from three years in the U.S.A. William Farren (1853–1937): fourth generation of an acting family. Henry Neville (d. 1910): first appeared in London in Boucicault's 'Irish heiress'; lessee and manager of Olympic theatre, 1873–9; writer and dramatic teacher.

[3] By Richard Brinsley Sheridan; first produced in 1777.

There can be no doubt that Mrs Buxton's opinions are those of a good many people in London at present: the Govt is thought to have made rather a mess of things; and once there is disapproval in the air, all doubtful points are judged to be defects, and people fall naturally into the attitude of shaking their heads half in sorrow, half in anger over the blunders of Ministers and above all of Mr Gladstone.

As for the Irish sedition papers (and above all the *Freeman*), they are in high delight over the situation which they describe in large letters as the 'Muddle', and congratulate Ireland, 'brave little country', on being the main cause of the difficulty. No doubt this is true, though it is not easy to see where the 'bravery' comes in.

A number of people to call and have tea in the afternoon. Mr Cropper, the Frederick Verneys, Mr George Russell (to see Aunt Fanny Lucy), Mr Baden Powell, Sir Fowell Buxton, Mr Percy Fitzgerald. Mr Russell lamented that for the second time this Session, his Sunday—which ought to be a quiet day—had been agitated by political events. This time he had been perturbed by the summons of his leader to a meeting of the Party on the following day at Downing Street. This is for the purpose of discussing the propriety of Mr Gladstone's Motion on the House of Lords. Mr Russell agreed with Father (who came in before he left) that it was a wise step, and would be likely to please people.

At 7 o'clock after all the visitors had departed, and before Father had left us to plunge into an evening's work in the library, a telegram was brought up to him, just left at the door by Mr Jephson.

'I hate the sight of these things' said Father, as he took out the closely written pink sheets—Another murder. This time in Dublin, of a man who had informed the police of the Fenian arms and ammunition found by them in Kevin St at the house of the Whelan brothers. The man (Bernard Bailey) had been living for weeks under police protection, but having at last ventured out alone in his old haunts he had been shot dead in one of the streets behind the Quays opposite the Four Courts.[1]

An hour spent by Father and Mother tête-à-tête in the library resulted in the despatch of a letter from Father to Mr Gladstone. In this he first regretted having heard from Mr Hamilton that Sir Stafford would not agree to the proposed arrangement (from which I gather that attempts at a compromise between the two Houses had been going on during the day); and then wrote on the question of his being summoned as a witness before the Lords Committee. On thinking it over he was inclined to believe that Harcourt might be right and that it would not be becoming for a Cabinet Minister to be placed in this position. Not from any feeling about his own personal dignity—this had not been in his consideration at all.

[1] At 11.00 p.m. on Saturday 25 Feb., the body of Bernard Bailey, shot twice in the head, was found in Skipper's Alley, off Merchant's Quay (*Irish Times*, 27 Feb.).

These were not by any means the words, but the main drift of the letter.
Helped Father make up his journal—a fortnight in arrear.

27 Feb., Mon.

Very bad accounts from Ireland—especially Clare. I heard from Mother that it was possible Father might decide to go back there again—perhaps indeed that we might all go and settle down there.

Father off early to see Lord Hartington. Meeting of the Party at Downing St at 3—the Irish Secretary received with applause.

Lunched with Edith Cropper[1] at Lady Holland's. Uncle Walter to tea. Father home to dinner, late, and full of news.

'Well, it has been a fiasco!' was his first piece of information (after having ascertained, much to his annoyance, that Oakel was not at home, having gone to his Debating Society). We were rather alarmed—being so accustomed to gloomy news at present that to hear of a fresh fiasco seemed quite natural though disagreeable. For once however, the fiasco was not on our side but the other, and it was pleasant and cheering to hear Father's animated and detailed account of all that had been happening during the day—the Meeting at Downing St (a great success, everyone unanimous in support of the Government)—and the scene in the House, Sir Stafford's half-hearted speech in favour of his own Motion[2] (to prevent the Govt from bringing in their Resolution in the House of Lords in place of the Procedure debate)—Mr Gladstone's spirited reply—the evident wish of the Conservatives to evade a division on the point their leader had raised—the embarrassing determination of the Parnellites to divide by way of demonstration against the Govt, with the strange result that the Conservatives were finally obliged to follow the Parnellites into the lobby with Mr Redmond and Mr Power acting as whips, and a majority against them of nearly 2 to 1.[3]

After this preliminary affair, which—taken together with their happy Meeting at Downing St—seems greatly to have raised the spirits of the Liberal party, Mr Gladstone brought forward his Motion in a Speech which, like so many of his previous speeches during this and last Session, is said to have been one of the finest he ever made in the House.

Towards the end of dinner we were astonished by Father's quietly intimating that he was going the next morning to Dublin and wished to take Oakel with him, as he should probably go down into Clare and should want somebody with him who (in addition to other things) knew a little law. Clare is just on the verge of what may become downright civil war.

---

[1] Edith Emily (née Holland), wife of Charles James Cropper; see appendix.

[2] Northcote had not brought in a formal motion, but had declared on 21 Feb. that he would oppose Gladstone's resolution (*Hansard 3*, cclxvi, 1224).

[3] The division was 300:167.

That very day information had been received of another vile outrage. Again the victims were farmers and their families who were suspected of having paid their rents. A gang of men forced their way into a farmer's house near Feakle in the Co. Clare, ill-treated his sons, and shot him deliberately through the knees, so that amputation at least would be inevitable.[1]

Father was not positive whether he should go down to Clare, but was determined at any rate to go to Dublin. 'It is impossible', he said 'to govern Ireland at the end of a telegraph wire'.

A message was sent to Oakel at the Debating Society to prepare him for this unexpected departure. Aunt Fanny Lucy and I went back with Father to the House. A dull evening—various minor lights discussing with more or less relevancy on Mr Gladstone's Motion, and the desirability or not of censuring the Upper House for appointing a Select Committee at the present juncture. Mr O'Donnell who absorbed the greater part of the evening made a violent attack on the Land Act which he described as a 'dismal failure'. Scarcely any Members spoke from the Liberal side, a fact which, combined with the remembrance of the 'unholy alliance' they had been forced into earlier in the evening, was apparently somewhat exasperating to the Tories.

The Debate was adjourned at 12.30 o'clock to Thursday—private Members refusing to agree to Lord Hartington's suggestion that it should be continued on the following day.

Father home at 1 o'clock, and at work in the library till 2.

28 Feb., Tu.

Father and Oakel left by the Mail for Dublin.

With Aunt F[anny] L[ucy] and Uncle Matt to the school in the morning— with Mother to Lowndes St for her to see Dr Hutton—afterwards to Lillington St. Uncle Matt to lunch. Uncle Matt and Aunt Fanny Lucy at dinner. Telegram from Father—'a fine passage' (a dinner party of 70 at the Castle and a ball afterwards).

1 Mar., Wed.

A Davitt debate in the House last night concerning the issue of a new writ for Meath.

Mr Davitt has been elected for Co. Meath in place of Mr A. M. Sullivan, but

---

[1] Michael Moroney was shot in the left thigh by a large band of moonlighters at about 8 p.m. on 25 Feb.; he died on 4 Mar. after amputation. One man was arrested and discharged for want of evidence; three others were arrested under the P.P.P. act, and held for five months (S.P.O., I.C.R., Returns of outrages, 1882).

is disqualified from taking his seat by reason of having been convicted.[1] Mr Egan, who was nominated at the same time, will, it may be supposed, take his place eventually in the House, but at present he does not push the matter as he prefers to remain in Paris.[2]

Morony, the farmer who was shot at Feakle, Co. Clare, has died of his wounds.

There is said to be great indignation amongst the Land League Members in consequence of the report that Mr Parnell has been suffering 7 days 'solitary confinement' (i.e. prohibition from receiving visitors) for having tried to bribe a warder to carry a letter out of Kilmainham for him.

Spent the morning walking with Lucy. Was surprised to meet Sir Thomas Steele who enquired if it was true that Mr Forster had really gone over to Dublin yesterday. The Commander of the Forces crossed to London the same day, and will remain here with his family for a month.

Uncle Tom and Aunt Julia to lunch. Drove with the latter and Aunt F. L. in the afternoon. Mother not being well enough to come out. A quiet evening alone. Began reading aloud a new novel much more promising than our last— *Democracy*[3] a political-social novel of American life—scene laid in Washington.

(Father and Oakel with Mr Ross of Bladensburg went down to Limerick this day[4]—going to Mr Clifford Lloyd's lodgings in the High St. 'So far all has gone well', says Oakel, 'and there has been some cheering news about rents. We go on shortly to Tulla'.

2 Mar., Th.

Letters from Father and Oakel this morning.

The newspapers full of Mr Forster and his movements—'Mr Forster in the disturbed districts'. 'Mr Forster and Lord Cairns'—'Mr Forster and the Select Committee', etc. etc.

A curious change has come over the language of the Conservatives on the subject of the Lords' Committee since last Saturday week, when the *Standard* asked triumphantly 'what will the Government do in the face of this rebuff?' and enumerated complacently the various embarrassing results that must follow from the acceptance of Lord Donoughmore's Motion.

Now the tone is one of remonstrance with the Govt not to press the advantage which their undoubted majority in the Commons would give them to

[1] A. M. Sullivan having resigned his seat owing to ill health, Davitt, then in Portland prison, was elected unopposed on 22 Feb., but on 28 Feb. the house of commons declared him incapable of being a member (Moody, *Davitt*, pp 500–01).

[2] Egan was nominated on 14 Feb., but his nomination was withdrawn on 22 Feb. when it was certain that there would be no third candidate (ibid.).

[3] *Democracy: an American novel*. New York, 1880. Published anonymously, but attributed to Henry Adams in the *Dictionary of American biography*.

[4] For Forster's journey in Limerick, Clare, Galway, and King's County, 1–6 Mar., see Reid, *Forster*, ii, 390–404.

carry Mr Gladstone's Motion of Censure—they are assured that the sting of the offence has been removed by the Lords' concession that no enquiry should be made into the 'judicial working of the Act', and it is pointed out that Lord Cairns (the Chairman of the Committee) in his letter to Mr Forster inviting him to appear as a witness has expressly defined the limits within which the Committee intend to confine their enquiry.

It is not yet known whether or not Govt and the House of Commons will refuse Mr Forster leave to appear before the Lords' Committee, but if they do they will incur the displeasure of the *Times*, which is urgent for a 'compromise', and entreats Mr Gladstone to begin by withdrawing his Motion, and requesting the Chief Secretary to submit to examination by the Committee on the terms offered by Lord Cairns.

Meantime the Liberals—cheered up by their successful move on Monday—seem less inclined than ever to countenance in any way the idea of a Committee of Enquiry under the present circumstances; whilst the *Pall Mall Gazette* finds daily congenial occupation in retorting upon the *Times* and pouring scorn and derision on the House of Lords.

The election proceeding this day at Northampton, great hopes that Mr Bradlaugh may be beaten, but a stubborn contest expected; since the last election many new voters have been put on the register, of a kind likely to favour an extreme Radical.

Uncle Matt to lunch—calls in the afternoon from Eva Gurney, General Dodgson, Mrs Conybeare, and Mr Wyvill. Uncle Matt and Aunt Fanny Lucy to dine and sleep. Uncle Matt had been hearing various forecasts as to Northampton—chiefly in favour of Mr Corbett.

Mr Chenery (the *Times*) very gloomy about the outlook for the present Govt—convinced that on all sides a strong revulsion had set in.

Newspaper Ghouls bawling in the street while we were at dinner. Sent out for a paper—bad news from Northampton. Bradlaugh 3798. Corbett 3687. The only consolation (in my mind) is that Mr Redmond went down to speak for Mr Corbett and denounce Mr Bradlaugh—not for being what he is—but for being a supporter of the Govt in their Irish policy; *ergo*, Mr Redmond will find that his eloquence has failed, and that the 'Irish vote' cannot always accomplish the wonders he boasts of in the way of deciding English elections.

The Northampton election was not the only news this evening. The Queen shot at. A man named McClean who professed to be starving, but was provided with a revolver of the newest make, fired into the royal carriage as the Queen and Princess Beatrice were driving out of the station yard at Windsor. Mercifully no one was hit, and the Queen seems to have behaved with her usual spirit, and not to have suffered in mind more than in body from the shock of this frightful attempt on her life.

The debate on the Motion of Censure continued in the House of Commons; adjournment moved by Mr C. Russell.

I went in the evening with the Uncle Matts to a party at Lady Bowen's—mainly Colonial—Racino's Band. Mrs Walter almost in tears over the Northampton election, everyone disgusted. At any rate in London.

Father and Oakel having spent the night—Wednesday—at the hotel, or rather small inn kept by 'the only loyal man in the district' an Orangeman from Derry, in Tulla[1]—spend this day (Thursday) in visiting different places in the district. The Ch. Secretary had a long interview with Mr W. O'Hara, R.M. He made a speech to the people in the market place at Tulla, 'advising them to assist the Executive in restoring order to Ireland'. 'He alluded to the Measures which the Govt had carried towards ameliorating the condition of the Irish people, pointing out the benefits which must accrue to the country by the working of the Land Act, and concluded by stating that while the Govt would continue to advance the interests of the country and consider fairly any proposition brought forward, they would nevertheless repress crime and outrage wherever it was found to exist'.

This is the account of his doings in the Newspapers. Other very interesting details have been given by Father and Oakel in their letters—the former received on Friday night, the latter on Saturday morning.

After seeing inspectors and R.M.s at Tulla in the morning, inspecting the 50 soldiers, speaking a word of encouragement to the Constabulary at the Court house and to the policeman who was shot when with Mr Wilford Lloyd, and making a little speech to some men who were standing about the door of the inn under a shed, Father and Oakel went for a drive (with an escort insisted on by Mr Lloyd) first to the Workhouse to see poor Morony (who has not yet died) then to call on Colonel O'Callaghan,[2] a boycotted landlord, whose rents are undoubtedly high, and who is consistently under the protection of the Scots Greys; and afterwards to the dispensary doctor and to the parish priest and his curate. From them he heard the other side ('there is another side' says Father) and at the same time took the opportunity to speak his mind to them about the outrages and their responsibility and duty.

At 5 o'clock they drove from Tulla to Ennis where they are being hospitably entertained at the Clare Club, by Mr Clifford Lloyd.

Whist in the evening.

3 Mar., Fri.

Newspapers full of the attempted assassination of Her Majesty. There seems every probability that McClean was a lunatic. The event has done good in provoking a genuine outburst of loyalty all the stronger from admiration of the Queen's courage and equanimity. Foreign powers too are very attentive in their congratulations, and in America, where the Queen's sympathy with Mrs Garfield is remembered, the expression of feeling is very warm and cordial.

[1] Co. Clare. [2] See above, p. 373.

Drove with Mother in the afternoon; called to enquire after H.M. and were informed that the Duke of Albany[1] had received a message at 12 o'clock saying that the Queen was quite well.

To tea at Lady Midleton's. Mother and I dined in the evening at the Shaw LeFevres'. Present the Whitbreads, Peases, Mr Froude, Lord O'Hagan, Mr Arnold Morley,[2] etc. The latter took me in to dinner and made himself pleasant; we had a good deal of talk about the Parnellite members. Like every one else this Session he was much impressed with Mr Sexton, and thought Mr Healy more offensive than ever since his return from America, however he had a long conversation with him in the Underground the other day about America, and had found him very intelligent and not disagreeable.

After dinner I had some talk with Lord O'Hagan. He is inclined to think that so far as the payment of rent goes, there are some encouraging symptoms at present in Ireland.

After all there is no surer test than this of the return of law and order to a district, or at any rate the suppression of actual intimidation and outrage on behalf of the 'No Rent' policy of Mr Parnell.

The House occupied for 3 quarters of an hour with a question concerning the warrant said to be impending over Mr A. [O']Connor if he should return to Ireland. He and Mr Healy claimed privilege as Members, and asked that if this warrant existed it should be laid on the table of the House. Mr Gladstone obliged to decline this request, explaining that the conditions under which warrants were issued applied to Members of Parliament as much as to other persons, and that the Govt could not undertake to do in one case what they should not do in another.

After this Baron de Worms, Mr Slagg,[3] Sergeant Simon and Mr Gladstone on the persecution of the Jews in Russia. Baron de Worms' Motion withdrawn without a division.

On our return from the LeFevres' Mother found a letter from Father.

3 Mar., Fri. [*sic*]

Father, Oakel and Mr Ross went from Ennis to Athenry in the worst part of Galway, where they were met by Mr Blake. It being a Fair day Father went out and walked about amongst the people—'Blake most kindly allowing me to go about without police'. He heard from Mr Blake of the attack upon the Queen, and at once telegraphed his congratulations to Her Majesty upon her escape.

---

[1] Leopold George Duncan Albert (1853–84): eighth child of the queen; cr. duke of Albany, 24 May 1881.

[2] Arnold Morley (1849–1916): liberal M.P. for Nottingham, 1880–1900.

[3] John Slagg (1841–89): Manchester merchant, liberal M.P. for Manchester, 1880–85.

4 Mar., Sat.

Father and Oakel left Ennis at 8 this day for Portarlington. After breakfasting at Limerick, they went on to Limerick Junction where Father took part in a long conference of the Five Special R.M.s—Mr Clifford Lloyd, Captain Plunkett, Captain Slacke, Mr Butler, and Mr Blake.

At Gort station a crowd of about 10 persons was assembled headed by the priest of that district—a notorious Land Leaguer—groans and hoots, and cries of 'Buckshot' as the train went out of the station. This is the only place where the Chief Secretary has been met with personal insult.

4 Mar., Sat. [*sic*]

Mother received a long and interesting letter from Oakel written in the train between Ennis and Athenry.

Read the rebel papers of this week.

Alice and Maud Wyvill to lunch. Apropos D'Arcy Wyvill, like many others connected with the land, has lately gone over to the Conservatives.

Edward and Edith arrived to spend Sunday with us on their way to join the Turnbulls at Mentone. Colonel and Mrs Drury, Mrs and Fred. Delamaine, Colonel Johnson, and Bernard Holland to tea here—a fearful medley.

A letter from Father in the evening sent from Ennis. Mother and Francie to Lady Harcourt's in the evening—everyone full of enquiries after the Ch. Secretary. Dr Lyons anxious that Mother should be in the House when he re-appeared there as he would receive a very good reception.

5 Mar., Sun.

To church in the morning at St Peter's. A short letter from Father—some rents being paid and some of the worst ruffians bolting—more encouraged than he had been since he came down.

In the afternoon with Mother to church at St Peter's, Lucy returning with us to tea. General Dodgson, Mr Rutson, Lord and Lady Monteagle and Mr Ball. Edward and Edith had heard from Mr Jephson, whom they met in the Park, report had come of an outrage committed, just after the Chief Secretary had left Tulla. No details, but the mere fact was enough to cloud over the day which had been brightened in the morning by Father's letter.

(Sunday. Father and Oakel spent this day at Portarlington, with the Blakes. Mrs Blake a delightful hostess. Mr Ross of Bladensburg sent on to Tullamore to see the priest there, and arrange if possible for Mr Forster to hold a meeting there the next day.)

Edward and Edith left at 9 o'clock for Mentone.

6 Mar., Mon.

The outrages near Tulla had been midnight visits to farms, threats, shots fired—mercifully no injury done by the Moonlighters this time.[1] On the other hand at Boyle an unfortunate rate collector (employed in collecting the money due for the Seeds loan) was murderously attacked whilst on his way to Mass, by three men who were allowed to fire deliberately into him though he was in the midst of a crowd of about 50 people.[2]

Letter from Oakel written from the Blakes' at Portarlington, sending at the same time a small box of sweet white violets which he had begged from Mrs Blake as a 'sign that they were returning to civilization'.

Mary Ward and her children to lunch. To the S. Kensington Museum in the afternoon and afterwards to tea with Mary in Russell Square.

On my return found that Mother had received a telegram from Father at Tullamore—'We are leaving here after a pleasant and successful visit'.

This was a great comfort, as we had known that he meant to dispense entirely with all police precautions at Tullamore and take the chance of his reception there.

Uncle Walter to tea. Francie with Mrs Fred. Verney to the Monday Pop. Mother and I had a quiet evening alone and went on with our novel *Democracy*. A very clever and enlightening book; there are rumours that it is written by Mrs Henry Adams, but the extreme familiarity with political intrigue and the details of political machinery behind the scenes which forms a main characteristic of the book, would seem more natural in a man than a woman, however clever and socially well-informed she might be.

6 Mar., Mon. [*sic*]

Father and Oakel arrived this day at Tullamore about noon, and called on the priest, examined and went over a Convent school, and after lunching at Hayes' Hotel, the Chief Secretary made a speech to the crowd (numbering about 300) which had assembled in the street ouside. Later in the afternoon he went on to Dublin going to the Chief Secretary's Lodge.

7 Mar., Tu.

An eventful and memorable morning for us, for we read in the papers a full report of Father's speech at Tullamore. For a year and a half past the Chief Secretary has been longing for an opportunity to come face to face with the

---

[1] A house was fired into near Tulla on the evening of 3 Mar. Ten or twelve similar incidents occurred in Clare during Feb.–Apr. (S.P.O., I.C.R., Returns of outrages, Feb.–Mar. 1882).

[2] Laurence O'Hara was fired at and wounded by three disguised men, who cheered and departed in a leisurely manner, at about 11 a.m. on 5 Mar. One man was later arrested and discharged for lack of evidence (S.P.O., I.C.R., Returns of outrages, Mar. 1882).

Irish people, to be able to speak his mind to them, to let them hear for once something besides the violent one-sided statements, the deliberate or unintentional falsehoods and misrepresentations, the open or veiled incitements to dishonesty, sedition and murder which have been dinned into their ears from the 'national' platform or through the 'national' press without cessation since the opening of Mr Parnell's constitutional agitation last August year.

The newspapers and the speakers who week after week and day after day, edified the people by enlarging on the gratuitous wickedness of the English Govt, on the tyranny, the cruelty, the injustice of the Ch. Secretary and all those responsible for the administration of the law and the suppression of crime and outrage in Ireland, have been for two years past the only leaders whose words have reached the people.

Every now and then a letter putting something like the fairer view of things has found its way into the *Freeman*; or some County Court Judge or City Recorder, or one of the Judges on Circuit has drawn a true picture of the condition to which the people have allowed themselves to be brought by carrying out Land League doctrines to their full extent, but as a rule no one has been heard who did not utter the regulation platitudes of envy, hatred, malice and all uncharitableness.

The Chief Secretary's speech at Tullamore on Monday was an experiment, but as far as one can judge at present, it has been a successful experiment; at any rate it cannot do harm for the Irish people—as distinguished from the Land League M.P.s, and newspaper writers—to gain a new and more truthful idea of the English Minister whose every motive and action they have been taught to distrust and condemn, whose name they have been taught to curse, whose very outward appearance they have been made to believe was something between that of an ogre and an idiot.

However little permanent impression his words may have made on the crowd at Tullamore, they must at least have seen that personally 'Buckshot' was not all that he has been painted to them.

Amongst all the incidents of Father's public life, there is none at which I would rather have been present than at this speech at Tullamore.

The circumstances under which it was made, the remembrance of all that had gone before, and above all the words themselves were such as to touch one's heart, and make one feel very proud of the speaker—an Englishman, and my dear Father.

It was pleasant to think that Oakel was with him to represent our ears and mind on this occasion.

In spite of occasional interruptions which do not seem in the least to have disconcerted him, Father was heard not only with attention, but with goodwill, and one or two of the interpolations on the part of the audience were anything but unfriendly in their character. The great point and object of the speech was to enlist the people themselves against the outrages which are disgracing their country. He told them what he had just seen and heard at the bedside of the murdered farmer in Clare; that this would stick in his memory, as an eviction he had seen 30 years ago would stick; that as he had done his best to make evictions impossible for the future, so he should do his best to make such a scene as that he had witnessed in Clare impossible.

He ended his speech by saying: 'Well, I have been heard, and I am very much obliged to you. I will just end with three words—words with which I have seen many speeches in many towns in Ireland have ended, and words with which many letters that I receive end—'God save Ireland'. (cheers) (a voice 'Is that from your heart? Why not let out the suspects?')

'Sometimes when I have read a letter telling me that I must have a bullet through my head, or that I must go to a place that is rather warmer than we are in now (laughter) I regret to find that it is signed 'God save Ireland'. However, you may be sure that that is the feeling which the Govt has, which Mr Gladstone has, and which I have. God save Ireland from enemies outside her borders, and from those within. God save Ireland from cruel men, of whatever class be they, and I trust there are very few—grasping landlords and rack-renting landlords, or be they dishonest tenants or midnight marauders. God save Ireland from the pestilence that walketh at noon, and the terror that stalketh at night; and I believe that God will save Ireland, for with all her faults there is that amount of virtue amongst the Irish people, that love of their country, that love and devotion of men to their families, that willingness to sacrifice for them, which are abiding and homely virtues that do much to save a country and to enable God's laws to be respected. And with the earnest desire that God may save Ireland, I thank you for having heard me'. (applause)

Afterwards a question was put to him about the suspects to which he answered that 'as soon as we can fairly say that outrages have ceased in Ireland, and that men are not ruined, are not maimed, and are not murdered for doing their duty, or doing what they have a perfect right to do, the suspects will be released'.

At the close of the Meeting the crowd quietly dispersed and Father, Oakel and Mr Ross of Bladensburg returned to Dublin.[1]

The Tullamore speech, of which the *Times* gave a long and spirited report in its Irish Correspondence, has created very great interest both in England and Ireland, where the papers are full of comments, and private friends full of congratulations.

On the whole there is genuine sympathy and admiration, with earnest hope (which may seem, alas, this time six months like bitter mockeries) that the Chief Secretary's visit to the West and his speech in the King's County may

---

[1] Ross's own account of the tour, full of animus against nationalists generally, was published five years later in his article 'With Mr Forster in Ireland in 1882' in *Murray's Magazine*, ii (Aug. 1887), pp 165–86.

produce a good moral effect, and prove a fresh departure in the history of Irish administration.

The *Times*, *Standard*, *Express*, *Irish Times*, even the *Freeman* are all more or less friendly and respectful. Only the *Pall Mall Gazette* finds in the Chief Secretary's last effort, fresh subject for a sneer—irritating at first sight, but of course natural in that quarter and only to be expected. However, as the *Irish Times* truly remarks, Father did not spend a word of his speech in abusing his political opponents, and it is nasty of me even to think of minding what they say of him; but the real truth is that one cannot help feeling as if in the *Pall Mall* criticisms on the Chief Secretary there were something more malignant than ordinary political opposition. A suspicion of personal rancour and unfairness, which one is quite accustomed to in a certain class of Irish pressmen, but which is disagreeable to find in an English Liberal journal.

The Bradlaugh difficulty is still in its prime. The Conservatives on Monday night succeeded in defeating the proposition for a compromise in the shape of an Affirmation Bill to be brought in by Mr Majoribanks,[1] and Sir Stafford's Motion re-expelling Mr Bradlaugh from the House was again carried, with great cheering—most of the Irish and a few Liberals voted with the Majority— no Conservatives with the Minority.[2] Meanwhile Mr Bradlaugh is supposed to be meditating a fresh coup de main, and many scrimmages may be anticipated in the immediate future.

Debate on Mr Gladstone's Motion continued.

A letter from Father—pleased with the success of the Meeting at which the people had given him a quiet hearing 'though he had not minced matters with them'.

Uncle Matt to lunch. Mother in the afternoon with Mrs Buxton to the Lady Mayoress' reception. The Lord Mayor came up to express to her with solemn cordiality on behalf of himself and his fellow townsmen their admiration of the Chief Secretary.

I went to tea with Dolly Yates Thompson. Mr Thompson began at once to speak of the Tullamore [speech], and expressed emphatically that '*he* did not think it had come too late to do any good'.

A reference I imagine to the 'Occasional Notes' in the *P.M.G.* of that evening which I had been reading just before I came.

A call from Herbert Gladstone and from Arnold. Heard from Herbert Gladstone that Mr Gladstone had dispensed Father from the necessity of coming back for the debate on Thursday.

Lucy and Nelly to dinner. They are expecting Dick[3] home from Australia on Saturday.

[1] Edward Marjoribanks (1849–1909): liberal M.P. for Berwickshire, 1880–94.
[2] The division was 257:242.
[3] Richard Penrose Arnold (b. 1855), 3rd and only surviving son of Matthew Arnold; brother of Lucy and Nelly.

Mother and I in the evening to Lady Trevelyan's. One person after another coming up to shake hands cordially with Mother, and congratulate her on the Tullamore speech—Mr Philips M.P., Sir Alexander Wood, Sir Fowell Buxton, Lord O'Hagan, Sir Garnet Wolseley, Mr Leveson Gower, etc., etc.

There was something unique and personal about this speech of Father's which has made a great impression on people, and drawn forth expressions of evidently sincere admiration and sympathy from very different sorts of people.

7 Mar., Tu. [*sic*]

Father spent the whole day at the Castle overwhelmed with work, 'after all' he says 'nothing is such hard work as the Castle'.

8 Mar., Wed.

Prince Milan has become King of Servia, with the amicable consent of his great but at present much embarrassed neighbour Austria.

The revolt in the Herzegovina continues; it is said that the Empire is getting the better of it but the difficulties are great, and the actual fighting severe.

Mr Arthur Evans has at last been suppressed by force. The Austro-Hungarian Govt gave him 24 hours in which to leave the country; at the end of that time, being still on the spot, he was put under arrest, where he still is.

A morning indoors. In the afternoon drove with Mother—calling (amongst others) on the Verneys, Kennedys, and Monteagles.

It is really touching to see the delight—I might almost say gratitude—of our Irish friends over the Chief Secretary's journey and his speech. They feel that such an appeal marks a new departure in the relations between an English Minister and the Irish people, and hope that not only in itself, but in the example given, it may do good.

There is too in Father's manner of thinking and speaking about Irish matters and to Irish people, an entire absence of British superciliousness and patronizing good-will, which is felt and appreciated by Irishmen.

But then, as poor Mother says, with a resigned sigh of astonishment, 'you see, he *likes* them'.

A telegram from the Castle announcing Father's return the next day.

9 Mar., Th.

With Francie in the morning to the Press Agency to enquire about Oakel's Land League pamphlet, as he is not coming back for a few days. Have sent him the Extract book which he needs in writing his chapter on the 'No Rent' agitation.

Afterwards with Francie to the Church Missionary Society's office, and to the Propagation of the Gospel Depot: in all these haunts Francie is well known, and treated with great distinction and cordiality by everyone concerned, from the Rev. Eugene Stock[1] to the Commissionaire at the door.

In the afternoon with Mother to the Hospital: to tea with the Bruces in Queen's Gate.

Between 6 and 7 I went down to the House expecting to see Father there. However I only came in for a personal episode between Mr C. Lewis[2] (M.P. for Londonderry) and Mr Porter, in which I am glad to say our Solicitor got entirely the best of it.[3]

On coming in from the House a few minutes before 8 I found Father sitting peacefully in the drawing room toying with a newspaper, like any gentleman of leisure.

Oakel is staying on with Mr Clifford Lloyd, partly I believe on account of his health which is suited by the out-of-door life he is leading there.

We had a pleasant family dinner and heard a great deal that was interesting about the journey in the West, and things in general. The Meeting which turned out so successful an experiment had been on the verge of going quite the other way. On Sunday Mr Ross of Bladensburg had been sent on to arrange with the priest—an old man of 80[4]—about the possibility of a meeting. He promised that he would himself make it known amongst his flock, engaging not to do so till after 9 o'clock on Monday morning, so that Land League emissaries might not be sent down from Dublin to interfere, as they would certainly have been if they had had the chance. However, when it came to the point, the priest changed his mind, or his courage failed him, for he never gave the promised notice, and when Mr Forster arrived in Tullamore on Monday morning with Mr Blake and Oakley, they found that nothing had been done in the way of advertising the meeting. Consequently the Chief Secretary had to advertise it himself by walking about the town, going over the Goodbody's Tobacco Factory, visiting the Convent School escorted by the priest, his curate and a number of Sisters. He ordered luncheon at the hotel (kept by a Land Leaguer) and enquired if there was any place from which he could address the people if he wished to do so. He was shown a window in the front of the hotel from which he was told electioneering talk used to be done, and when he came forward to speak between 1 and 2 o'clock he found that in preparation for a speech the window frame had been removed, and a crowd of about 300 men was assembled outside.

For the first 10 minutes, Mr Blake told Father he was afraid the affair might

---

[1] Eugene Stock (1836–1928): in mercantile life until 1873; since then, secretary of the Church Missionary Society and editor of the society's publications.

[2] Charles Edward Lewis (1825–93): born in Yorkshire; conservative M.P. for Derry city, 1872–86; for Antrim N., 1887–92; author of *The election manual for England and Wales* (1857).

[3] Lewis had maintained that Porter's election agent had publicised rent reductions under the land act in a manner tantamount to attempted bribery of the Londonderry electors.

[4] Very Reverend Mathew M'Alroy, V.G.

be a failure, but at the end of that time he saw that he had entirely got hold of his audience—'he had them in the hollow of his hand, and could do what he liked with them'.

After it was over Mr Blake went out and mixed amongst the crowd overhearing their comments which were not unfriendly.

In the course of the afternoon Father had seen both the Mr Digbys who came to call on him at the hotel. One of them (the one who was shot at in the autumn)[1] is a vigorous but unwise man with a reputation for hardness, and so fiercely unpopular that Mr Blake is of opinion that he is quite certain to be shot again some day. However he has just succeeded in getting all his rents in a bad district (Croghan) where the tenants had been for long past defying their landlord without the smallest justification.

Captain L'Estrange the R.M. at Tullamore is also very unpopular, it is to be feared with some reason, and the Ch. Sec. thinks it may be best for all parties to remove him elsewhere.[2] Apropos of R.M.s, Father seems to have come back more impressed than ever with the utter worthlessness of some of the County Magistrates.[3] One gentleman had nervously and persistently refused to come near the Chief Secretary when he was in his district, declaring that he was sure that if anything bad were to happen it would be said to be all his fault. This same gentleman was being refused his rents, and when asked if he meant to take proceedings against his tenants explained that he should wait to do so tll he got a new agent, that he might 'divert the odium on to him'.

The Five Special R.M.s seem to be really doing the work they were appointed for, and the Sub-inspectors serve under them with zeal and satisfaction; the people who object to them—naturally enough—are the nominal R.M.s in their respective districts, and as for the head department—'it is just as much as Hillier can bear', says Father. However he does bear it, and up to the present there has been no breakdown between the different authorities, though I gather that at one time there was near being an awkward collision with the War Office which it was very fortunate could be averted.

No doubt this is in great part thanks to Mr Ross of Bladensburg, who seems to be a thorough success, and quite to answer the purpose for which he was appointed.

Another subject for anxiety which evidently weighs on Father's mind a good deal, is the evictions—there are some very bad cases—above all on the Berridge estate, where the landlord seems to be a specimen of the worst type of rackrenter, and the tenants genuinely poor and unable to struggle against their arrears of rent.

It will not be Father's fault if Mr Berridge does not know his opinion of his

---

[1] Above, pp 316, 334.
[2] Champagné L'Estrange (1832–1900): captain, Royal Artillery; R.M. since 1873; in Mar. 1879, suggested the issue of buckshot to the constabulary for use in riots in place of ball.
[3] i.e. the unpaid justices of the peace, not the R.M.s.

proceedings, for there is not a landlord he has spoken to on whom he has not impressed it very strongly.

On the whole his impression of the state of the country is just that of Mr Burke who says that some things are distinctly better, and others distinctly worse, during the last month or two. Certainly Father does not make his life more tolerable by indulging in illusions about the condition of Ireland at the present time.

Mother and I went back with Father to the House after dinner. Found Mr Chaplin in the midst of an effective speech on the injustice done to the land-lords by the Land Act, and the need for an enquiry. Whilst he was in the middle of a sentence, assuring the House 'that he could if necessary bring proofs of what he stated', etc., he was interrupted by a cheer from the Liberal benches which evidently astonished him, and he was beginning to remonstrate at these 'ironical cheers' from hon. Members opposite, when a general laugh from all parts of the House, and the sight of the Chief Secretary once more in his place on the Treasury bench, explained their meaning.

On realizing the situation, Mr Chaplin remarked very prettily that if 'he had not been so absorbed with the question he was trying to bring before the House, he should have been the first to join in those cheers'.

Mr Chaplin was followed by Mr P. J. Smyth in a short speech attacking the Land League, and then by Mr Lowther, whose speech was one of the worst possible specimens of a party attack, at once mischievous and stupid, that I have ever heard—mischievous, from its playing into the hands of the Parnellites, and stupid, from the commonplaceness and irrelevance of its arguments. Lord Hartington and Sir Stafford wound up the debate, the latter having decidedly the best of it from the point of view of debating effectiveness.

The majority was larger than had been expected, 84 for the Govt on the 'previous question' when the Parnellites voted with them, and 68 on Mr Gladstone's Motion when they did not.[1]

Everyone had got thoroughly tired of this debate, which was wasting time and exhausting everyone's patience, without any visible good result to either side.

10 Mar., Fri.

Mr Shaw to breakfast—a man who gives one the impression (I don't say how far it is a true one) of being honest and fair-minded, with a considerable knowledge of men and things in Ireland, and a habit of talking about what he knows, with coolness and common-sense.

He told us several interesting facts concerning estates, agents and tenants in his own neighbourhood—as for the famous Mr Hussey,[2] he was very emphatic in describing the evil he had wrought by his hard, tyrannical behaviour.

'For years' said Mr Shaw, in his deep bass voice and quiet unsensational

---

[1] The divisions were 303:219 and 303:235.   [2] See above, p. 340.

manner, 'that man has been accustomed to spread terror among the people round him, and now he goes about himself as terrified as any frightened dog.'

This is emphatically one of the cases in which it is the agent and not the landlord who has done the mischief. Lord Kenmare himself, says Father, had been quite ignorant of the existence of those unjust leases, which have just come before the Sub-Commissioners, and have been made the text of violent homilies on the rapacity of landlords.

Archbishop McCabe has just been made a Cardinal or rather the announcement of this fact is now made public. According to Mr Shaw, who had lately been summoned to an interview by Cardinal Manning, the latter is not at all pleased with the proceeding, nor with the position in which his attitude as regards Irish agitation is supposed to have placed him at Rome. He had evidently been got at by Archbishop Croke, Mr Shaw said, and in consequence had been induced to take a line about Irish affairs of which he now finds the disadvantage—much to his annoyance apparently.

Mr Tuke and Mr Whitbread called on Father in the morning to consult about some scheme for improving the prospects of emigration; it is to be feared that the Emigration clauses in the Land Act are proving inoperative, and that if anything effectual is to be done it will have to be by private effort.

Walked with Father to the office. I was amused by hearing of the old O'Gorman Mahon who came up yesterday to the Chief Secretary to express his approbation of his proceedings in the West of Ireland, adding—'There is only one thing I don't like about it, and that is that you did not let me know you were going, so that I might have come with you'.

Francie with Mother in the afternoon to Lady Pelly's—Alice and Freddy Spring Rice to tea here.

Mother received this afternoon a most enthusiastic letter about the Tullamore speech from Lord Blachford—written, as he pointed out—'after 48 hours cooling down'.

Father not home to dinner being kept at the House in expectation of Irish Estimates coming on. Mother and I went down to the House about half past, Father coming up to see us in Lady Brand's Gallery, which we had quite to ourselves.

At that moment a dull discussion on the State purchase of Railways in Ireland was going on—one of the many Miscellaneous Motions brought forward on going into Supply. Earlier in the evening the Chief Secretary had been attacked by the Parnellites, apropos of the arrest of Mr Rourke, Mr Egan's partner in Dublin.[1]

Each one after the other had taken this opportunity to make their various criticisms on the Ch. Sec.'s speech at Tullamore. 'Biggar having outshone

[1] James Rourke (described as uncle to Thomas Brennan) had been assisting Patrick Egan as league treasurer, was arrested on 9 Mar. and was released on 15 May (S.P.O., I.C.R., P.P.P. act arrests, no. 862). He was co-proprietor with Egan of the City Bakery, Dublin.

himself', as Father said, by suggesting that Mr Forster had gone down to the West of Ireland in the famine year in order to gratify his love of seeing human suffering.

The Speaker marked his sense of this remark by requesting Mr Biggar to withdraw it, which he did, and was probably a happier man for the rest of the evening in consequence of this distinction.[1]

The power of suspending a Member for offensive language, frequently indulged in, has not been exercised this Session, which seems a pity. Mother and I left the House a little before 12, thinking that there would be no chance of the Irish Estimates coming on that night. However, they did, and by dint of sitting till 3 o'clock the Land Commission estimates were got through.[2]

A letter from Oakel this evening written from Tulla where he is staying with Mr Clifford Lloyd. He says

The country here is now in quite a state of siege. In this little hole there are 50 soldiers, extra police, a number of army reserve volunteers, and some of the Emergency police as they call them. Of course they are not all wanted in the place itself, but are scattered in huts and houses throughout the neighbourhood. I think the measures taken are already having good effect, and from the number of scoundrels in prison or on the run, the outrage classes must be getting very seriously diminished.

11 Mar., Sat.

Heard from Father that there had been a disagreeable wrangle late last night in the House.[3] Mr Gorst had made a speech on the state of Ireland which had been so exasperating and bad in its tone as to cause Father to lose his temper— a most unwonted occurrence, for which poor Father seemed very remorseful. However he appears to have had sympathy in his irritation from Lord Hartington, who had been moved to equal wrath by Sir Richard Cross, who followed in the same vein as Mr Gorst. Lord Hartington in fact confessed to Father that, as for Cross, he felt a strong desire not so much to answer him but to take off his boot and throw it at him.

This very marked expression of disapproval coming from the most impassive Minister on the Treasury bench would certainly have surprised the House.

Read the sedition papers this morning—'Forster on the stump'—'An impudent Foreigner' etc.—evidently great anxiety to counteract any possible effect from the Chief Secretary's visit and speech, and strong recommendations that he should not be allowed to be heard a second time.

Walked with Father to the office. He told me of an interesting paper he had received that morning—the copy of his own letter written in 1847 describing his

[1] *Hansard 3*, cclxvii, 621. Biggar used this attack subsequently on 13 Mar. (ibid., 804); and see below, pp 403, 405.

[2] *Hansard 3*, cclxvii, 706, records it as 2.45 a.m.

[3] The short debate is in *Hansard 3*, cclxvii, 667–84. T. D. Sullivan wound it up with a renewed dig at the standard of crime in England, and the role of the P.P.P. act in producing crime in Ireland.

personal experiences when acting for the Society of Friends during the famine.[1]

This had been sent him by Mr Langley—a man whom he has never seen, but who has always taken a warm and friendly interest in Father since the day when, on Mr Carlyle's introduction and at his request, Father subscribed towards some literary work which Mr Langley was too poor to continue without pecuniary assistance. Mr Langley had found Father's letter in full (not extracts as in the Report which we had seen before at the British Museum) and now sent Father a copy.

'If ever any sketch of me is made,' said Father 'this will be interesting.'

Curiously enough the letter describes the state of things on the very estate (Mr Berridge's[2] estate) which is now giving the Chief Secretary so much anxiety; the landlord of those days (one of the old Martin family) seems to have been far less to blame personally for the misery of his tenants than the present hard, evicting landlord.

I heard also from Father that Mr Shaw had come as I expected about the Arrears question, to talk it over and see if anything could be done—he is not very sanguine—'But I have a sort of plan in my head' says Father.

Poor darling Father! if all the plans he has in his head for the benefit of the Irish people could be carried out, things would be very different.

We talked amongst other things of the recent debate, and had a few confidences on the subject. As it turned out, Father thinks it was perhaps a pity they did not content themselves with protesting against the Select Committee in the Upper House and refusing to have anything to do with it. Why? Because, as it appeared afterwards, the bad effect in Ireland of the proposed Committee, was not as great as they had expected when they took such a strong measure as the Vote of Censure?

'Yes, mostly that, and then, how they could have been such fools as not to foresee the length of time it would take up—however, considering all things the debate was got through quicker than might have been expected.'

There is a good deal still to come unfortunately before the House can get to the Procedure Debate, Army and Navy Estimates at the beginning of next week, and the worst of the Irish Votes—(Special Magistrates' salaries) at the end.

Francie went down to Weybridge to spend Sunday with Mrs Conybeare.

The first proofs of her book *Heralds of the Cross* arrived from Hatchard's to-day.

Mother called for Father at the office, and after waiting patiently for some time, persuaded him to go with her to see the Watts Exhibition at the Grosvenor Gallery. On the way he read her an interesting letter sent on to him

[1] The date in the TS is 1837 but this is clearly a slip, for the 'paper' referred to is Forster's report of Jan. 1847, on the distress in the west, to the central relief committee of the Society of Friends (*Transactions of the central relief committee of the Society of Friends during the famine in Ireland in 1846 and 1847* (Dublin, 1852), app. III, pp 153–60.

[2] See above, pp 355, 398–9.

by Lord Spencer, from an agent (Mr L. Morrough) describing his own impression of the good effect the Chief Secretary's visit had done, and enclosing at the same time a letter to him from a tenant farmer near Tullamore, to the same effect—but this especially in connection with the speech.

From all I have learned since his (Mr Forster's) visit I believe that the most ardent politicians in the town and locality are almost reduced to silence, he so fully exposed the phantom that has so long and so terribly distracted the poor unthinking—but well-meaning—tenant farmer. He dashed to the winds the teaching of the professional agitators without condescending to name them.

No doubt this is to some extent exaggerated, but still as being written by a man who had no particular object in romancing, and no reason to suppose that his letter would come round to the Ch. Sec., it is not without interest.

I stayed at home this afternoon, and wrote to Oakel. Father and Mother dined at Mrs Buxton's—I had a solitary meal, cheered by the Tullamore farmer's letter, and a good article on Mr Forster in the *Saturday Review*.

Amongst the people dining at Grosvenor Crescent was the *19th Century* Mr Knowles, who informed Father that Cardinal Manning had said that the Tullamore speech had reminded him of Socrates. 'I only hope he'll lay it to heart then', said Father, remembering the line His Eminence has been inclined to take about Irish affairs.

To Lady Spencer's in the evening. A little knot of the Ch. Sec.'s Cabinet colleagues, chaffing and condoling with him on Mr Biggar's amenities, and his 'delight in human suffering', etc. 'Well, Forster, I sent you an antidote this afternoon', says Lord Spencer, from his post of duty in the doorway, alluding to the agent and tenant farmer's letter from Tullamore.

I should think there were few men living who took a more sincere pleasure in doing a kind and friendly action than Lord Spencer—though no doubt Mr Biggar would not think so.

On our return home we found a letter from Oakel enclosing Father's speech printed in paragraphs as a broadsheet; Oakel has had this done in Limerick and intends to try if he can get copies circulated amongst the people.

12 Mar., Sun.

Mother and I to church at St Peter's. Father at work all the morning with Mr Jephson over arrears of office business. Lord Spencer to lunch—some cheerful pleasantry between him and Father—in fact for one half hour an oasis in the desert of Irish discussion.

It has been settled that Lord Spencer goes to Mentone as Minister in attendance on the Queen. Father went out with Lord S. immediately after lunch.

A visit from Sydney and Conny Buxton—the first time I had seen her since her marriage. Mother and I to the Bible reading at St Peter's.

Sir Fowell, Mr Ball, and Mr Tennant to afternoon tea. Father, who came in early today had much interesting talk with Sir Fowell, chiefly about the emigration problem. There is some thought of getting up a Meeting on the subject, with the Duke of Bedford[1] in the Chair. Father gave a graphic description of the condition of the evicted tenants in Connemera—for whom there is absolutely no hope but emigration—for which they themselves would be willing. There is also a bad corner on the confines of Tipperary and Roscommon[2] which is giving him much anxiety just now. The people there have been in the habit of supporting themselves and paying their rents by coming over to harvest work in England. But now they are beginning to open their eyes to the fact that this means of livelihood may fail (owing to agricultural depression in England), and since the agitation have steadily refused to pay any rent at all. They are sullen in temper, and as there is reason to believe that they have a good supply of arms amongst them there are grounds for anxiety.

In the course of his intimate friendly talk with Sir Fowell, Father suggested laughingly that he (Sir F.) should induce his Uncle—Mr Fowell Buxton—to give him a hundred thousand pounds for the pacification of Ireland. 'If I had £100,000 to spend as I liked in Ireland, I could get peace for six months—and I know who I would get to do it—he would [so] thoroughly enjoy the work that he would do it for nothing—Labouchere.'

'How would you do it—do you mean by bribing Parnell?'

Oh, not Parnell—I couldn't bribe him—but most of the leaders—it would put a stop to the whole affair—for a time. But it would only be for a time, there is really nothing so unwise as a policy—the only result is that you make six fresh agitators for the one you have pacified—partly because every man sees an opening for being pacified in the same way himself.

A quiet evening—a long talk tête-à-tête between Father and Mother in the library. Father brought his journal up into the drawing room to write up his arrears, telling us in the intervals many interesting details about his experiences during the past week.

13 Mar., Mon.

Father went out early to the Turkish Baths. A call from Dick, just returned, after three years in Melbourne—quite unchanged himself, and surprised to find his family so little changed also.

A long and sad talk with Mother about Father, and the gloomy, almost hopeless prospect before him. There is some idea of Lord Cowper's resignation

---

[1] Francis Charles Hastings Russell (1819–91): liberal M.P. for Bedfordshire, 1847–72; 9th duke since 1872; K.G, 1880; president of the Royal Agricultural Society; owned no Irish estates.

[2] These counties are nowhere contiguous. Tipperary is probably a mistake for either Mayo or Galway.

being accepted, and Lord Spencer's going to Ireland. Of course this is a matter of the strictest privacy, and is still only a possibility for the future; but there seems reason to believe that Lord Spencer would be willing to go, and Mother thinks that his doing so might make the possibility of Father's retiring a stage nearer.

Poor darling Mother is very much cast down; she feels that Father is struggling on under a sense of oppression and disappointment—that he had hoped more (though he never exactly says so) from the appointment of the Special Magistrates—and that on every side encouragement and support seems failing him in the thick of his hard battle.

No one, not even his closest friends and acquaintances, can have any idea how hard and how painful it is.

Lunched with Mrs Ball—going afterwards with her to the S. Kensington Museum Library to read M. Daret's article in the *Gazette des Beaux Arts* on the Dublin National Gallery and Mr Doyle's merits as Director.

To tea at Mrs Percival's—Mother back between 6 and 7, having been down to the Ladies' Gallery to look at Father and see how he was getting on. Had left the House launched in an angry wrangle produced by the irritation of the Conservatives at Mr Gladstone having gone out of his way to remark that the state of business was 'discreditable'. Mr Gorst had moved the adjournment, and the prospect of the Army Estimates being brought on at any reasonable hour seemed very doubtful.

(Mr Redmond on the 'suspects'.[1])

14 Mar., Tu.

For four hours last night the Parnellites 'in full cry after Mr Forster' as *The Times* put it. The subject was the suffering of the suspects—which afforded an opportunity for the most virulent abuse of the Ch. Secretary, from every member of the Parnellite faction, Mr Biggar expressing it as his opinion 'that the right hon. gentleman felt the most intense delight in having to administer the Coercion Acts, and that he took the greatest pleasure in the sufferings of those persons to whom the coercion was applied'.

The Speaker called Mr Biggar to order for imputing unworthy motives and intimated that if he persisted in that course he should have to take summary proceedings against him.

As usual on occasions of this kind, a Conservative member was forthcoming (Sir John Hay,[2] this time) to make party capital out of the affair by joining in the Parnellite chorus, as did also Mr Caine, a Liberal from below the gangway.

[1] Redmond initiated a debate on the conditions under which the suspects were held (*Hansard 3*, cclxvii, 785–815).

[2] Sir John Charles Dalrymple Hay (1821–1912): admiral with a distinguished naval record; M.P. for Wakefield, 1862–5; for Stamford, 1866–80; for Wigtown Burghs, 1880–85.

On the other hand, the only man who stood up to suggest that the Ch. Secretary was not altogether the inhuman monster he was painted was a Conservative gentleman, Mr Onslow.

As to the truth or falsehood of the complaints made of the prison treatment, this would probably have been owned by the speakers themselves to be a matter of secondary importance. The main object, as Mr Healy plainly declared, was that the statement of himself and his friends should be reported in America—'and other foreign countries', which probably means, that Monday night's attack and vilification of the Ch. Secretary was meant as a 'Charity Sermon' to draw fresh funds from the Irish in America.

The Army Estimates were got through last night at a very late hour, the House not rising till 4.

A letter from the Queen to the nation published in this morning's papers, thanking all those from the highest to the humblest who have shown such sympathy and devotion on the occasion of the attempt on her life.

A perfect and most Queenly letter, beautiful and simple both in feeling and expression.

Walked with Father to the office—he tired and depressed this morning, but listening pleasantly to all the miscellaneous chatter which I inflicted on him; the morning was lovely, and we walked inside the park, and avoided all reference to politics.

Aunt Fanny Lucy to lunch. Mother and Francie out in the carriage. I at home searching everywhere for a suitable heading to one of Oakel's Land League chapters, of which he has sent me the MSS to complete.

The *Pall Mall Gazette* of this evening continues its crusade against the Ch. Secretary and the Coercion Acts, and undertakes to refute a letter from Mr Goldwin Smith in its own columns. In this letter Mr Goldwin Smith puts the question of the necessity for Coercion on the right ground.

For what is Coercion—odious and painful as it is—an alternative? If the Land League had been allowed to go on unchecked a rebel government would have been set up all over Ireland: this state of things, this successful defiance of the law, had to be stopped; it was stopped without bloodshed. Which would be the worst, to keep the Land League leaders under restraint, or to have to fire on the people? Are you [says Mr Goldwin Smith] prepared to accept the dissolution of the Union, for this and nothing short of this, is the aim and object of the men and of the organization against whom the Govt has taken the strong measures known under the name of Coercion.

To this the *P.M. Gazette* replies by declaring that Mr Goldwin Smith puts the whole matter in too high a key, that there is no question of the dissolution of the Union in the case, and that the Land League is nothing more than an agrarian association, with an extreme as well as a 'Moderate' section belonging to it.

According to the *P.M.G.* the Moderate section was in the ascendant until the

Govt, by their unwise and uncalled-for severity, exasperated all parties and threw the country into the arms of the extreme Nationalists.

This is a very plausible theory, and quite credible by those who also believe that the Land League agitation during the Autumn of 1880—before the passing of the Coercion Act—was of that harmless 'constitutional' character which Mr Parnell was sometimes pleased to attribute to it.

Uncle John to dinner, Father back from the House bringing Mr Fry with him. Father dog-tired and exhausted—not having touched food since his meagre breakfast in the morning.

Oppressed also, and anxious. The actual difficulties of coping with crime and lawlessness—almost rebellion—in Ireland, will become almost insuperable if the Minister responsible to this country for the government of Ireland has not the full support of the country.

It seems that amongst the Radicals a feeling of impatience with the present system is springing up—an impatience which for different reasons is fostered upon different quarters. Quite apart from motives of hostility to the Govt, this disappointment is natural—judging from a surface view of the situation. Bad outrages—midnight attacks and attempts to murder—are still reported daily from Kerry and Clare, and the Judges' Charges at the Spring Assizes have been very gloomy—crime seems more rife, and convicted criminals even fewer than in the autumn.

But on the other hand, it can truly be said that there has been an improvement—distinct improvement—in some counties, and that, throughout Ireland, the adoption of the Coercion policy, now looked on with disfavour, has been the means of checking the triumphant establishment of Land League law in place of the law of the country. This may not be Mr Morley's opinion, but it is the opinion of men who have watched the progress of events in Ireland, from a nearer point of view than Northumberland Avenue; and who have had wider opportunities for knowing the true bearing of measures and the character and aims of men in that country than is afforded even by personal acquaintance with the Land League M.P.s in London, and a close study of the *Freeman's Journal*.

For instance, it is the deliberate opinion of Mr Naish (expressed the other day to Oakel in Dublin) that bad as things are, especially in the matter of unconvicted crime, they would be ten times worse if it had not been for the Coercion Act, and the exceptional powers (arrests etc.) with which it armed the Govt. If things had been allowed to take their course in '81 as they did in '80, Mr Naish believes that Land League Courts would have been in full swing all over Ireland, owning no authority but that of Mr Parnell and the Land League, and placing the Queen's government entirely in abeyance.

The crime and outrage which the Coercion Act has not been able to suppress, are patent to everyone—the evils, threatening the very existence of society and law in Ireland, which it has in great measure been able to suppress, are forgotten or ignored.

Meantime there is cause for grave anxiety in the future. The Coercion Act expires at the end of this Session:[1] and what is to happen then? Will the Govt ask to have it renewed in its present form (a dangerous request if the present signs of Radical discontent increase), or will they adopt some fresh means of [af] forcing the ordinary powers of the law? One thing seems certain to those who are responsible for the preservation of peace and order in Ireland, and that is that a simple reversion of the coercion policy would mean anarchy.

As for want of support in the country and in the House, I believe that a plain statement of facts from the Chief Secretary would at any time restore confidence in the Govt policy however distasteful in theory to the mass of their supporters. Of course there would be strong differences of opinion, and a certain number, perhaps an increased number, would oppose it steadily as they did the Coercion Act itself. But I do not expect that the *Pall Mall Gazette* will as yet succeed in arranging a large Radical Opposition against the Chief Secretary.

The House counted out at half past 8 this evening—a private Member again quenched by the indifference of his compeers—the second time this has happened.[2]

15 Mar., Wed.

Mr Tuke to breakfast to talk about emigration. The D. of Bedford will take the Chair at a private meeting. Father gives £200.

Mother walked with Father to the office. Drove with Mother in the afternoon. In the evening with her and Lady Ely to the Lyceum to see Mr Irving and Miss Terry in 'Romeo and Juliet'.

Father dined with the Duke of Cambridge—a large Ministerial dinner—afterwards to the Cos.

Father made two short speeches in the House this afternoon—one of Extension of Municipal Franchise in Ireland, the other on a scheme—supported by all the Ulster Liberals—for making the working of the Land Act more effective and rapid.

16 Mar., Th.

Looked through Lord [John] Russell's *Recollections*,[3] in search of a heading for one of Oakel's chapters. What he says about Ireland might every word of it be said by Father writing about the same subject to-day.

[1] Clause 4 of the act provided that it should expire not later than 30 Sept.

[2] The house was adjourned for lack of a quorum while a resolution on the Metropolitan fire brigade was being introduced by Sir Henry Selwin-Ibbetson (1826–1902), conservative M.P. for S. Essex, 1865–8; W. Essex 1868–85; Essex (Epping) 1885–1902. A similar event had occurred a week previously. The time was 7.30, according to *Hansard 3*, cclxvii, 916. Selwin-Ibbetson had been under-secretary to the home office, 1874–8, and parliamentary secretary to the treasury, 1878–80, and had declined the governorship of New South Wales in 1879.

[3] Lord John Russell, *Recollections and suggestions of public life, 1813–1873* (London, 1875).

Mother walked with Father to the office—I being sent there afterwards to take him his sandwiches, was summoned up into his room in the midst of an interview with the Law officers—rather I should think to their surprise.

A long visit to Mother from Miss Tod of Belfast on Women's Education, and a forthcoming bill of Mr O'Shaughnessy's.

Uncle Matt to lunch. At 4 o'clock Mother and I called for Father at the Irish office and took him down to the House, going up first with him to see his private room, and then to Lady Brand's Gallery.

Amongst the numerous questions to the Chief Secretary, two required specially full answers. One, a series of charges, and insinuations about his speech at Tullamore—'that the Govt. had paid a reporter to report and circulate the speech—that the town had been filled with soldiers and police—that a man had been threatened with arrest for shouting 'Release the suspects' etc., etc.—a string of trumpery falsehoods, showing plainly how deeply irritated and annoyed the Parnellites have been at the effect produced by the Ch. Secretary's speech and the quiet hearing accorded him at Tullamore.

The other question by Sir Arthur Otway as to the treatment of the suspects, and the possibility of giving them greater indulgence, also received a full and detailed reply and explanation—apparently to the satisfaction of the House.

After the questions—not over till 6 o'clock—came various Motions, settling down into a long affair over the Major Bond grievance. Mr Callan made a long droning attack—the House emptied—the Chief Secretary replied—the Parnellites followed one after another, Mr Porter spoke for the Front Bench, and finally a division was taken in which the minority numbered 14 as against 60.[1]

Father was prevented by this affair from coming home to dinner. Mr and Miss Mundella, the Easeneze Buxtons, Mr Fison, and Mr Jephson dined here.

In the course of the evening Father had again to contradict the identical string of lies about his Tullamore speech—this time retailed by Mr Sexton in the form of a Motion instead of by Mr O'Donnell in the form of a question.

Mr Trevelyan could not make his Statement, and the House get to the Navy Estimates, till 12.

17 Mar., Fri., St Patrick's Day

Oakel returned this morning from Ireland. He has been most hospitably entertained in Cork by Mr O'Sullivan, High Sheriff and ex-Mayor, and brings back on the whole an [a more] encouraging report from that part of the country than might have been expected.

A spirit of independence of Parnellite coercion seems on the increase in the city of Cork, and the state of the country generally has improved. This was the testimony, amongst others, of Mr Horace Townsend, the agent, who has been getting his rents in without difficulty.

[1] The division was 78:14.

According to Mr O'Sullivan and others, Mr Shaw would not have a bad chance of getting in for Cork City if he did not venture to contest the County—provided, that is, that a dissolution does not take place very soon. All were agreed that this would be fatal to the chances of the Moderate party in Ireland.

As for Mr Clifford Lloyd, whom Oakel has seen so much of, he comes away with a high impression, not only of his vigour and courage, but of his judgment in dealing with the people. He has done wonders in Limerick where the worst districts have been reduced to order, and even in the immediate neighbourhood of Tulla[1] he seems to be making some impression. At present he is recommending the release of all the suspects from New Pallas, because that part of Limerick has become orderly, and he is anxious that the recognition of this should be at once given in a wholesale release; on the other hand he would on no pretext whatever have a single man released from the Tulla district until a better state of things has been established. Clare is still in a very bad condition.

Mr Fison to breakfast. Walked with Father to the office—we talked a little over last night; 'he thought he had got through the Major Bond affair better than he had expected'—at one time it had looked as if it might be very awkward: 'the fact is he had made a great mistake in appointing him without first writing to people at Birmingham—he ought not to have done so'.[2]

'Well at any rate', I said, 'you told the whole story, and didn't leave anything behind for them (the Parnellites) to find out afterwards; you certainly go on Prince Bismarck's plan in diplomacy, of perfect truthfulness.'

'Yes, that is one thing that so disgusts them—what they call "my lying frankness".'

Father to the City.

Drove with Mother and Francie in the afternoon, calling on Lady Collier and Lady Holland.

Father home in time to dress and go with Mother and Francie to dine at the Alfred Taylors'—to meet the Harrisses and other old Bradford friends.

Borneo debate in the House; at 12 the last of the Irish Estimates—Special Magistrates' salaries—came on, and to our surprise was got through with very little difficulty—only 6 Parnellites staying to vote in the minority.[3]

At the Conservative meeting of the party held at the Carlton to-day, the course of action with regard to the New Rules was agreed upon. Amongst other subjects, it was urged that Conservatives 'should not go out of their way to praise Mr Forster and the Irish Govt', or fall into the other extreme of sympathising with the 'suspects' and their friends, and lending countenance to the Fenian Movement.

[1] In Co. Clare.

[2] Edwin Edmund Brutton Bond (1835–92): served in the Bengal army, 1852–71, and was chief constable of Cardiff, 1873–6, and of Birmingham, 1876–27 Dec. 1881, resigning from the latter post after his conduct of a case had been censured. He was appointed a temporary R.M. on 3 Jan. 1882, and was stationed at Lough Mask (Co. Mayo). After leaving Ireland, he organised the Cairo police.

[3] The division was 124:6.

Lord Monck to breakfast. Father much cheered by the feeling of having finished his Parliamentary battles for the present.

A visit from Lord Monteagle.

Walked with Father to the office: joined on the way by Lord Morley,[1] who has just been sent over to Dublin by the War office to enquire into the Royal Hospital and Hibernian Military School. Consultation between him and Father over the merits and the grievances of Dr Carte, who is well known to the Ch. Secretary from his connection with Kilmainham.

Drove with Mother in the afternoon to the Dudley Gallery and tea at Mrs Stair Douglas's.

Francie to Lillington St[2] to take her Missionary Working Party, which she has established with great success.

Report in the evening *Pall Mall* of the capture of four 'Moonlighters' by a large patrol force in the Co. Kerry near Tralee. Copies of the 'No Rent' Manifesto were found in their possession.

It seems a curious state of things in which the sight of such a paragraph as this in the newspaper should distinctly raise one's spirits, and give one a sense of personal pleasure.

18 Mar., Sat.

Father, Mother and Francie to the Haymarket to see 'Ours' in which Mrs Langtry[3] is acting.

I dined at the George Trevelyans'—meeting there the Garnet Wolseleys, George Howards, Mr and Lady Catherine Milnes Gaskell, etc.

Mother and Francie in the evening to Lansdowne House which has been taken by the Roseberys.

19 Mar., Sun.

Father and Mother to church at the Savoy—Oakel and I also, but failing to find room took refuge in St Martin's, Trafalgar Square.

Father in the afternoon to the Turkish Baths, and to call on Lady Ely. Lucy to lunch. Mary and Humphry and Sir Fowell to tea.

Spent an hour in the library after supper, looking through the rebel papers, etc. They are chiefly occupied this week with violent attacks upon various 'traitors' i.e. non-Parnellite Irishmen—Mr P. J. Smyth, Mr O'Connor Power, Mr McCoan, Mr A. Moore, the Corporation at Drogheda (who have refused by 10 to 8 to re-elect a Suspect as Mayor)—all come in for abuse and denunciation.

[1] Albert Edmund Parker (1843–1905): 3rd Earl Morley; under-secretary of state for war.
[2] St James the Less, church and school. See appendix.
[3] Emily Charlotte le Breton (1852–1929): the 'Jersey Lily'; in 1874 married Edward Langtry (d. 1897); created a sensation in 1881 by being the first London society woman to go on stage.

The small number of the Parnellite Members forthcoming in the recent debates is also a subject of lament.

Read two very interesting letters to Father from Mr Ross of Bladensburg describing the state of things in Roscommon and Mayo—especially on Lord Dillon's estate. Passive anarchy—the people have found that no rent is better than low rent, and have remained so long masters of the situation that it will probably require a display of force to make them recognise the fact that the law is not completely in abeyance even in Roscommon.

A circumstance which may set a good example in other parts, has been the Meeting of a large body of the gentry and principal farmers convened by Col. King Harman[1] the L. Lieutenant of the County—to organize combined resistance to an agitation which has just been started amongst the shepherds on the grass farms of Roscommon.

It has long been strongly and painfully felt by the Irish government that it is only by this sort of defensive combination amongst the resident gentry that illegal and aggressive combination can be fairly coped with.

It is point blank impossible for the authorities civil or military to be successful in the establishment of law and order if those who should be the natural champions of order in a district remain simply passive—waiting for the Govt to take every conceivable measure for their personal protection, and then satisfied to take no further part in any general measures for the public good.

Even in the matter of personal protection there are some who think that the Govt undertakes what might be more profitably done by the individuals themselves—judging from a letter sent on by Mr Ross, General Torrens[2] is decidedly of the opinion that people should be encouraged to fight their own battles (even at the risk of some approach to civil war) rather than depend always on the protection of soldiers and police.[3]

20 Mar., Mon.

Walked with Oakel to the Admiralty, where he was anxious to make some enquiries of Mr Trevelyan concerning the new ship, the *Polyphemus*.[4]

Drove with Mother in the afternoon. Mother and Father went down at 7 o'clock with a large party including the Gladstones, Goschens, Wolseleys,

---

[1] Edward Robert King-Harman (1838–88): conservative M.P. for County Sligo, 1877–80; for Dublin County, 1883–5; honorary colonel of Roscommon militia; owned 29,242 acres in Roscommon, 28,779 in Longford, 12,629 in Sligo, 1,239 in Westmeath, and 1,024 in Queen's County, valued at a total of £40,105.

[2] Henry D'Oyly Torrens (1833–89): C.B., 1867; G.O.C. Belfast military district, Jan. 1880–Sept. 1881; G.O.C. Cork military district since Oct. 1881.

[3] From the beginning of 1882 the Irish executive showed an increasing tendency to support this view.

[4] H.M.S. *Polyphemus*, completed in Feb. 1882, a 'torpedo ram' of 2,610 tons, conspicuous for heavy torpedo armament and high speed.

Arthur Russells,[1] Mr Hayward, the Tweeddales etc., etc. to the Crystal Palace, where they were shown over the Electric Exhibition and entertained at dinner by Mr Pender M.P.[2]

The place was thronged with people through whom the 'distinguished party' had slowly to make their way—escorted by four policemen, from the Low Level station to the Palace; next to Mr Gladstone the Irish Secretary came in for the most cheering, Mrs Goschen (who was walking with him) and Mr Hayward telling Mother that he received quite an ovation.

Mr Hayward also took the opportunity at dinner to tell Mother, from his experience of club and society talk, how friendly is the general feeling towards Mr Forster with respect to his present management of the Irish troubles.

On returning from the Crystal Palace, Mother took Father down to the House, where the Procedure Debate was going on—Mr Raikes and Sir Richard Cross the chief speakers on the Opposition side, Lord Hartington, Mr Fowler and Mr Bryce on ours. Lord Hartington, in a vigorous speech, gave it clearly to be understood that the Govt mean to stand or fall by their proposal of the Closure—without which they declare themselves unable to carry out the legislative measures for which they made themselves responsible to the country when they took office.

If there are others who think that without these changes they can carry on the business of the country and can persuade the House of their capability to do so, we shall cheerfully resign our functions. But so long as we are responsible for the business of the country we must appeal to the House to give us those powers by which alone we believe that business can be effectually performed.[3]

Francie and Oakel dined at the F. Hollands'.

21 Mar., Tu.

Another murder reported this morning from Dublin, which it is feared may be again the work of a secret society, or rather of Fenians, as was that of Bernard Bailey.[4]

There have been several bad outrages within the last few days. On Thursday Mr Shaen Carter, a landlord near Belmullet in the Co. Mayo, was shot at in his car from behind a hedge, and so badly wounded that his life is considered in danger.[5] On Monday a sub-inspector, a Mr Doherty, was shot at and wounded,

---

[1] Arthur John Edward Russell (1825–92): senator of London University; liberal M.P. for Tavistock, 1857–85.

[2] John Pender (1816–96): Glasgow textile merchant, telegraph entrepreneur and chairman of London electricity supply company; liberal M.P. for Totnes, 1862–6; for Wick, 1872–96; author of *Statistics of the trade of the United Kingdom* (1869).

[3] The wording of the passage diverges slightly from that in *Hansard 3*, ccxvii, 1337.

[4] Above, p. 384.

[5] George T. Shaen Carter was shot in the knee while driving home at about 8 p.m. on 15 Mar.; he had evicted tenants two weeks previously (S.P.O., I.C.R., Returns of outrages, Mar. 1882).

as was also a lady who was in the same car.[1] A boy of 17 named Gibbons, son of a gamekeeper in the service of Lord Ardilaun at Clonbur, has been attacked and killed with stones on the public road, the boy's mother being also savagely beaten for daring to come to his rescue.[2]

It seems as though the word has gone round to murder, and this is I believe Father's opinion.

A feeling is again finding expression as to the unfitness of the jury system for Ireland. Even where evidence is forthcoming—as was the case at the Limerick Assizes the other day—the jury evade the natural conclusion by persistently combining in one case after another to disagree. Various suggestions are being put forward in very different quarters—the *Spectator* proposes that when, after the Assizes have been gone through in the usual manner with an ordinary jury, the ends of justice shall be seen to have been frustrated not from want of evidence but from the dishonesty or timidity of the jury, the prisoners shall be tried again before a Commission empowered to convict and sentence on its own authority alone.

This suggestion is quoted with approval by the *Express*, and is practically the same remedy which is proposed by Mr Goldwin Smith, and resisted by the *P.M. Gazette* on the ground that the non-conviction by juries is invariably due, not to any fault in the jury, but to the total absence of evidence, without which no tribunal could venture to convict or pronounce sentence.

Another suggestion of another kind, but with the same object—viz the suppression of agrarian outrages—is again coming to the fore. This is the imposition of what Mr Ross calls a 'blood tax' on a district in which an outrage has been committed. The power to levy a fine of this nature was given by the Peace Preservation Act and has never been revived since that Act expired in 1880.

I believe that Mr Blake, and others who have had close and long experience of the people, are of opinion that this fine has a most salutary effect on people who can be made in no other way to suffer from their acquiescence, if not actual participation, in crimes against the unpopular party in a district.

Miss Tod to breakfast to talk about Intermediate Education—more money wanted.

Walked with Father to the office: heard that our going over to Dublin was postponed to Wednesday night, neither the Solicitor General nor Herbert Gladstone wishing to undertake the responsibility of some questions about the Queen's University, which were to come on Wednesday afternoon.

[1] Sub-inspector James Doherty, of Tubbercurry, Co. Sligo, and Lizzie Conroy, daughter of a J.P., were wounded at about 10 p.m. on 19 Mar. Eight men were arrested but later discharged for want of evidence (S.P.O., I.C.R., Returns of outrages, 1882).

[2] At about 6.45 p.m. on 17 Mar. Thomas Gibbons, while walking with his mother, was attacked and beaten by three men, receiving injuries from which he died in the early hours of 19 Mar. Four men were arrested; one was discharged for lack of evidence, the other three each being sentenced to 20 years penal servitude at the Connacht summer assizes in 1883. The official returns give Gibbons's age as 24 and his father's occupation as woodranger to Lord Ardilaun (S.P.O., I.C.R., Returns of outrages, 1882, 1883).

Drove with Mother in the afternoon. Father home to dinner. Had been having a talk with Sir Walter Bartelott, a friendly old Tory. 'Can't you stop Hay?' Father had asked him—alluding to Sir John Hay's Motion about the Suspects.[1] 'I have been doing everything I can' was Sir W. Bartelott's answer, who further gave the information that pressure to the same effect had been put on at the Carlton meeting the other day.

After all, the number of Conservatives who relish a close alliance with Mr Healy and Mr O'Donnell, even for the purpose of annoying the Govt, is limited.

Father in high indignation with Judge Barry who has written to him in the character 'not of a judge', but of a citizen of Limerick, to intercede on behalf of Miss McCormack, who remains in prison, because she prefers to defy the law and refuses to give surety for her good behaviour if let out.

Judge Barry is of opinion that to condone her offence, and yield to her desire to triumph over the law, will 'strengthen him in his judicial capacity'. Father has written to Judge Barry expressing his surprise that he should think that this will be the result, and his fears that the general public would find it difficult to discriminate between the acts of Mr Justice Barry as a Judge of Assize and as a Limerick man.

'How are you to get on when you have people like this to do with?' exclaims the Ch. Secretary, not for the first time since he has had to deal with Ireland.

The House occupied with discussing County Govt—debate adjourned.

22 Mar., Wed.

Report in the morning papers (which we had heard from Father the evening before) of an attempt to blow up the house occupied by members of the detective police in Dublin. A loud explosion but happily no one injured.

The Parnellite Members are in a state of the most feverish excitement about the Closure Resolution—holding parliamentary meetings—issuing fervent, menacing and entreating 'whips', and causing leading articles to be written in the *Freeman* commanding all Irish members to vote against the Govt under pain of being considered (by the *Freeman*) to have acted 'against Ireland'.

One result of this violent abjuration has been a letter from Mr P. J. Smyth to the *Freeman* in which he announces his intention of voting for the New Rules, explains his reasons for doing so, and hopes that other Irish members will do the same.

The beautiful weather has entirely departed, and to-day we have a furious wind with blasts of snow and cold rain. A pleasant prospect for our crossing to-night.

Mother walked with Father to the office.

[1] There is no evidence of such a motion in *Hansard* or *F.J.*

Father home to dinner at 7, having made his speech on Mr Corbet's[1] Motion about the Queen's Universities; had been having a few private words with Sir Stafford about the Conservatives' action with regard to Coercion—impressing on him the harm done in Ireland by any supposition however faint that the Opposition were ceasing to support the Govt in this matter.

Sir Stafford appears to have taken the same line as Sir Walter Bartelott, and intimated plainly that Sir John Hay was not acting on behalf of the party generally.

Father and I left by the Mail at 8.25; to our amazement we had a perfectly smooth passage and a good night.

23 Mar., Th.

Reached the C.S. Lodge about half past 8, and found the dear dogs well and thriving under Kelly's care, and delighted to see us.

A pleasant leisurely breakfast, and talk over various plans and possibilities for the future. In considering the matter of Lord Cowper's successor with Mr Gladstone lately, several names were suggested: Lord Carlingford, Father had thought, would not take it, besides the fact of his being an Irishman would make it difficult for him to be severe enough, which in these times is very necessary; Mr Goschen raised to the peerage—'a very good man'; but why not Lord Spencer? 'Gladstone is very unwilling to lose him as Lord President—a post which requires to be filled by some very leading grandee—though, as I reminded him, Aberdeen was once Lord President for a time.'

Then it appears Father had actually mooted to Mr Gladstone the suggestion which I have heard him make before—though he has never propounded it to Mother even, as 'she would think it so dreadful'—namely that he should himself be made Lord Lieutenant, with the stipulation that it would not oblige him to take a peerage—which would be 'a great blow', as Mr Gladstone freely admitted.

It is easy to see the attraction there is to Father in the idea of being freed from the embarrassments of his present double position, with all the duties and responsibilities of an irresponsible governor on one side of the Channel, and all the duties and responsibilities of the Parliamentary head of the department on the other.

At the same time I do not think there is much chance of his escaping from his difficulties in this way; nor do I at all believe that when it came to be a reality, instead of a dream suggesting itself from time to time as a possible means of

---

[1] William Joseph Corbet (1825–1909): chief clerk of Irish lunacy office, 1853–77; home rule M.P. for Wicklow County, 1880–85; for Wicklow E., 1885–92, 1895–1900. For his motion on the second reading of the University Education (Ire.) Bill, see *Hansard 3*, cclxvii, 1560–1620; the motion was defeated by 214 to 35.

disconcerting the irrational wickedness of the Parnellite Members, that he would at all like the position himself.

One result would probably be (and one objection), and to this he agreed, that such an arrangement would mean an extra load on Mr Gladstone's shoulders, for it is quite certain that Parliament would not be satisfied with any vindication or explanation of affairs in Ireland that could be offered by the minor officials who now answer for the Ch. Secretary during his temporary absences.

Mr Burke to see Father at 11 o'clock—walking with him afterwards to the Castle.

A quiet day in the house—called on Mrs McKenna, sent off and arranged flowers, wrote to Mother, etc.

Father home at 8 to dress and go with me to the Burkes', where we dined and spent a pleasant evening. Mr Burke in rather better spirits, Father thinks, than when he was over here before.

'Things do not look so bad when I come over' says Father, who is certainly getting more and more to dislike 'governing Ireland at the end of a telegraph wire'.

Received a telegram from Mother announcing their safe arrival at Wharfeside.

24 Mar., Fri.

A stormy morning—drove with Father to the Castle—Puck accompanying us in the carriage.

Lunched with Miss Burke, meeting there afterwards Mrs Ross of Bladensburg. Both ladies very anxious that Cardinal McCabe may return from Rome in the character of Papal Legate. The last Legate was Cardinal Cullen, and if it had not been for his influence, says Miss Burke, things would never have settled down as they did after the Fenian affair.

A quiet evening—finished translating from *Gazette des Beaux Arts* on the Dublin National Gallery, read the papers, and nearly finished *Sylvia's Lovers*[1]— a beautiful story but almost too sad to read in solitary state.

A talk with Father in my room on his return soon after 12. Heard the satisfactory news that a party of 'Moonlighters' in Tipperary whilst in the act of attacking a farmhouse had been fired into and dispersed by a patrol in ambush, and one of their number left behind badly wounded.[2]

---

[1] By Mrs Gaskell, first published in 1863.

[2] At about 11 p.m. on 23 Mar., some thirty men attacked the house of Jeremiah Ryan, schoolmaster and farmer of Drumbane, in the north riding of Tipperary, firing twenty shots into it; Ryan had paid his rent. The wounded attacker was arrested and pleased guilty at the spring assizes, 1883, when he was released on his own recognizances (S.P.O., I.C.R., Returns of outrages, 1882, 1883). See below, p. 420.

25 Mar., Sat.

A pleasant sociable breakfast, before the arrival of papers and letters. No specially bad news in the papers—but evidently some rather perturbing letters. Father standing before the fire with his hands behind him, silent—clearly something on his mind. 'Anything horrid?' I enquired.

'No, not horrid—but, well it just shows how people can lose their heads. However, I have got the matter in my own hands.'

He then read me a letter from Mr Gladstone, the purport of which was that Lord Richard Grosvenor's reports as to the prospects of the division on the Closure were disquieting—that the great obstacle in the minds of Irish Liberals and their friends was the use that might be made of the New Rules for facilitating further Coercion—and suggesting that perhaps with the improvement perceptible in Ireland (payment of rents etc.) some modification of the Coercion Act might be possible—a possibility which the Chief Secretary might convey to Mr Shaw, who at present seemed inclined to show great reluctance to support the Govt.

The day before, Father had received a cypher telegram from Mr G. desiring him to be ready to see Mr Shaw the next day if he thought desirable, and accordingly—though without at the time understanding for what reason—he had made arrangements for Mr Shaw to come and see him at the Castle.

However, his mind was at once made up *not* to speak to him about the subject of Mr Gladstone's letter—there were various other matters which would serve as an excuse for the interview. Whatever he were to say to Mr Shaw on that subject could only be tantamount to a Government intimation of their intention to relax their present energy in Ireland—'and what a moment to choose for doing this!' says Father.

'As far as I can make out', I say, 'they want to make a bargain and you are to pay for it'.

'Yes, but I shall not do it', says Father quickly. He is quite clear that to carry on the government of Ireland after such an arrangement as is hinted at would be impossible—at any rate he would not attempt it—to this extent he certainly 'has the matter in his own hands'.

At the same time he is very fully awake to the dangers of the situation—a small majority on the Closure Resolution might involve a dissolution, and hardly anything could be worse for Ireland at the present time than this.

He will send a letter to Mr Gladstone to-day—a letter which will require a good deal of consideration.

In spite of these troubles Father and I had a cheerful walk to the Park gates, writing our names at the Vice Regal, and driving on afterwards to the Castle—both the dogs in the carriage with us.

Returned to lunch. Drove into Dublin in the afternoon, calling first (by Father's desire) at the Castle to enquire if he wished to see me.

After waiting in the carriage for ten minutes and seeing a constant succession of people pass silently in and out of the Chief Secretary's office, I was summoned upstairs and shown into Mr Jephson's room where we were joined by Mr Ross of Bladensburg.

Apropos of Oakel and his visit to Cork (where he had thought some independent anti-Land League spirit was springing up), Mr Ross told me that near Millstreet some farmers had ventured to take land from which former tenants had been evicted, and were now banding themselves together in self-defence for protection against the Land League and the Moonlighters.

In other parts too, the farmers are beginning to think of defending themselves, and in some cases the authorities are providing them with arms for the purpose—Major Traill R.M. in (I think) Galway going further, and teaching a man to shoot—greatly to his satisfaction.[1]

Presently Father came in to see me, looking flushed and tired in the midst of his hard day's work. He told me that we should probably have to go back on Monday—the Parnellites having set up fierce obstruction on some Supplementary Irish Estimates.

On going down stairs Mr Jephson told me further that, after obstructing for a long time last night, the Parnellites had only been stopped on the condition that they should be allowed to bring the whole matter forward again on Tuesday, when they would discuss the Lord Lieutenant's Household—the Chief Secretary's salary, etc., etc.

I cannot quite understand how the matter stands; the only thing clear is that Father is much annoyed, and that he will have to return to another long spell of the useless, irritating, disheartening Parliamentary badgering, which is so specially trying to him at a time when he is anxious to be spending all his available time and energy in practical work in Ireland.

After leaving the Castle, I called on Mrs Trench whom I found at home; she and Miss Edith Trench were both very kind and friendly, and lent me a charming book—the Memoirs or rather Journal of Mrs Richard Trench,[2] the Archbishop's most beautiful Mother—to judge from Romney's portrait of her, and also a miniature which they showed me.

Having written my Notes up to date, my Puck and I must now go and prepare for our solitary 8 o'clock meal.

A quiet evening over Mrs Richard Trench's *Remains*—a most lively and companionable book in which I read on and on till nearly 12, when I went upstairs hoping that Father would soon come in and pay me a visit. However he did not reach home till half past 2, by which time I had contrived to work

[1] Traill, like Lloyd, was convinced that the majority in Ireland would be peaceful and loyal if the effects of intimidation were nullified. He made a series of trials in instructing the people in defending themselves and their homes. The results did not lead to a general adoption of the principle (S.P.O., R.P. 1886/1549).

[2] *The remains of the late Mrs Richard Trench, being selections from her journals, letters, and other papers: edited by her son, the dean of Westminster* (London, 1862).

myself up into a high state of imaginative alarm. Nothing worse had befallen him than to stay late at the club, and then find some difficulty in getting a cab to come home in.

26 Mar., Sun.

At breakfast Father read me the Sub-inspector's report of the Moonlight capture in Tipperary. The patrol it appears consisted only of three men, who behaved very well in at once attacking the Moonlighters—a gang of about 30 men—well armed. They will be rewarded as they deserve.

After breakfast Father read me his letter to Mr Gladstone—in this he explained his telegram in which he had told Mr Gladstone that he should not make the proposed suggestion to Mr Shaw. This would have meant a Government declaration of an intention to give up a renewal of the Coercion Act; if it were thus undertood, it would be impossible to resist the demand for the release of the suspects at once; this would make Ireland ungovernable, unless equally strong measures were passed in a different form, and this would take up more time. Moreover, he (Mr Forster) did not think the Govt ought to pledge themselves even for the future. If the Act were prolonged for another year— perhaps for less—it might be possible on the occasion of doing this to release all the suspects now in prison. But an abandonment of the policy at the present juncture would be most dangerous just now—that is, when there are signs that the conspiracy is breaking up. The power of arrest conferred by the Coercion Act cannot be given up—it is a valuable weapon in dealing with the Secret Societies and the 'No Rent' conspiracy, and in such places as Loughrea and the neighbourhood wholesale and summary arrests have been the means of preventing murder.[1]

As to the division he (Mr Forster) did not underrate its importance, but he did not think it would be wise to buy votes by any concessions to the Parnellites. Judging from his conversation with Mr Shaw, he believed that he would vote with the Govt probably Col. Colthurst also.

Before ending, Father expressed his regret that Lord Richard's summons for Tuesday would oblige him to leave the useful work he was engaged in over here (examining into the claims of the New Sub-Commissioners, etc.) and come over to take part in 'sham debates and sham divisions'.

(I think this is a fairly accurate though clumsy version of this letter.[2])

To church alone at the Hibernian. The Lord Chancellor and Mr Jephson to lunch—a consideration of new Sub-Commissioners.

Heard from Mr Jephson of an attempt made last night to blow up the house

---

[1] Up to this date, 57 arrests had been made under the P.P.P. act in Loughrea district (as well as many in adjoining districts), 25 of them since the beginning of 1882 (S.P.O., P.P.P. act 1881, List of persons in custody).

[2] Extracts in Reid, *Forster*, ii, 407–8.

of Mr Ross Mahon, a landlord in Co. Galway—no one was hurt, but a good deal of damage done.

Walked with Father through the gardens and afterwards to the V.R. Lodge. While we were going with McKenna through the vinery, a telegram was brought Father—from Mr Gladstone to say that from everyone being out of town there was difficulty in arriving at an exact knowledge of the position in which matters had been left, but that he (Father) should not be made to come over for Tuesday unless absolutely necessary.

Their Ex[cellenci]es not home from Christchurch, so Father and I returned to spend a quiet evening together—he seemed bodily tired and languid, as is often the case when for a few hours the long strain of the week is relaxed, and he has leisure to feel tired.

A call from Mr and Miss Burke about 6 o'clock, marked by the usual three stages—the first five minutes in which Father and Mr Burke observe the customs of an ordinary visit of society, and take part in general conversation; the *next* ten minutes during which they talk exclusively to each other; and the last quarter of an hour which they spend closeted together in the study to which Father has hurried off his visitor.

A pleasant tête-à-tête dinner and long evening with Father, during which we talked over many things, past, present and future—the Tithe troubles, when the same horrors, and worse, seem to have gone on as now, the Jury system, the Law officers, the Special Magistrates, the Lord Lieutenancy—a subject which is very much in Father's mind at present. Sir Bernard Burke has drawn up a list of all the Lord Lieutenants who have governed Ireland. It appears that no commoner, with the exception of Richard Cromwell, has ever held the office.[1]

I received this evening a note from Mr Edward O'Brien enclosing a letter from a man on his estate at Cahirmoyle speaking of the interest that had been felt by the farmers round him in the Chief Secretary's speech.[2] He had distributed a good many copies that had been given him by Mr Donough O'Brien, and could find many more that would like to have them if they could.

This shows again that Oakel's idea of publishing the speech was a good one.

Copied a note from Father to the Duke of Bedford, who has offered in a very friendly manner to take up this Emigration scheme, which he understands has Father's approval. A private Meeting is to be held at his house on Friday, and he is anxious that Father should be present. It is not certain whether he will do this, as it might be thought to give too much a government aspect to the affair, but he will certainly write a letter.

---

[1] 'Richard' is an error for 'Henry' (lord lieutenant, 1658–9); and, in fact, several other commoners, including Oliver Cromwell (1649), the father of Henry and Richard, held the office.
[2] At Tullamore, on 7 Mar.

27 Mar., Mon.

Again a sociable and ante-postal breakfast. The Lord Lieutenant question still in Father's mind—much talk over the pros and cons, and various possibilities discussed. At one moment even that of a peerage—'at my time of life a thing to be thought of', says Father—'they might make me an Irish peer—so that I should not have to leave the House'. However this is only a passing idea like others which come before us. 'Well, I see that what it will probably come to', he says finally, 'will be Spencer if I can have him, and failing him Carlingford'.

A letter to Father this morning from Mr Gladstone in answer to his of Saturday. Mr G. would be most willing to see Mr Shaw (as Father had suggested); quite agreed that they could not make any agreement even with him; thinks that Parliament will not, and probably ought not [to], consent to a renewal of the Coercion [Act] except for present necessity.

Father seemed well satisfied with this letter. As to the last phrase—'there is a good deal in that', he says to me, explaining (so far as I could understand) that it pointed to a difficulty which his proposal—namely the renewal of the Act simultaneously with the release of the suspects and the enactment of other measures—had not sufficiently taken into account.

It seemed certainly probable that the House might refuse to renew the Coercion Act except 'for a present necessity'.

An angry article in the *Freeman* this morning on the committal of a priest (Father Feehan) to prison for refusing to give bail for good behaviour after having made a violent speech for which he had been charged before Mr Blake and other magistrates.

The Bishop of the diocese has suspended Father Feehan during his imprisonment: there have been several signs lately that the Bishops and priests generally are beginning to take a more satisfactory line in discouraging violence; it will be a case of better late than never if they do.

Drove with Father and the dogs to the Castle, going in with him to see if any message had come from London which would settle whether we were to return that night or not. However nothing had come, and Father promised to send out word to me later.

Lunched with Miss Burke, who is very kind and friendly to me and Puck. On returning to the C.S. Lodge found a note from Mr Jephson to say that we were to go that night.

Spent the afternoon collecting flowers to take back with me. A violent wind blowing causing unpleasant forebodings about the passage.

Father joined me at Westland Row, looking tired and harrassed. An interview at the last moment with Captain Barlow, who sought him out on the platform and delivered a document just before the train started.

Contrary to our expectation we had a perfectly quiet passage. I have now made the journey 16 times and only once had a bad passage, and that was in going over to London in November 1880.

As usual I slept like a dormouse both on the boat and in the train, but poor Father with a hard day's work behind him and before him scarcely closed his eyes.

Between Chester and Crewe he showed me the document Capt. Barlow had brought him—the request of the three Members in Kilmainham[1] to be released on parole for the purpose of coming to vote against the Govt in the important division on Thursday. Mr Gladstone has already declined this request, so Father will only have to refer to his refusal.

28 Mar., Tu.

Reached No. 80 about half past 7. Mother and Francie had arrived from Wharfeside the evening before—Mother with a bad cold and cough.

Spent a long morning arranging the flowers. Father after 2 hours sleep to the office (Mother walking with him), and afterwards to the House for the Morning sitting to which he had been summoned back to please the Parnellites.

I came down to put a flower in his buttonhole when he started—'Yes, let me go in smiling' he said, looking down at my work of decoration with a comic mournfulness.

'You'll come out smiling too', I said—a cheerful prediction which came true.

Drove with Mother in the afternoon, going down about half past 5 to the House. 'The Irish Members are very troublesome this afternoon' said our sympathising friend Wilson as we went in to Lady Brand's Gallery.

Father was speaking—or rather at that particular time he was sitting down while Mr Callan tried without success to make the Speaker call him to order for some expression he had just used which had evidently been too strong to be pleasant for the Parnellites.[2]

He was soon on his feet again and speaking with a vigour and strong current of expression that seemed very unlike a tired-out man, or one dispirited by an afternoon of vexation and abuse. In plain straightforward words he acknowledged and answered the complaints against the failure of the Coercion Act which have been more or less expressed in various quarters of late. He explained in what respect and for what reason the Coercion Act had not succeeded as the Govt had hoped, and also to what extent it had most answered the purposes for which it had been passed—the authority of the Queen's government, as distinguished from the govt of the Land League with its unwritten law, had been re-established, the murderous power of Secret Societies

[1] Dillon, O'Kelly, and Parnell.

[2] Forster, asserting that outrages were the natural result of speeches by the Irish members, used terms that suggested that he accused them of direct incitement (*Hansard 3*, cclxviii, 198).

had been checked, the 'No Rent' policy had been defeated, in spite of the efforts of some honourable Members opposite rent was being paid.

In a few effective sentences he brought before the House the close connection between the authors of the No Rent Manifesto and the crimes committed to enforce its observance—a point which was fully appreciated.

Towards the end of his speech (which had been unprepared) he declared that the Govt considered it to be its chief duty to prevent if possible a continuance of these crimes, and that if it should become necessary they would take stronger measures for the purpose.

As Secretary to the Lord Lieutenant, with a responsibility as much as man can have for the maintenance of law and order in Ireland, my business is to maintain it and to stop outrages (cheers) and that is the business of this House also (renewed cheers). We cannot look forward to the future. Signs of improvement may be much greater than they are, but it may turn out that in order to maintain law and order, and to stop these murders and outrages which are a disgrace to our country and to humanity, that some stronger measures even yet may have to be passed (loud cheers). And if the House of Commons is convinced of the necessity, it will mind its business and pass them (renewed cheers).[1]

It was very interesting to see how greatly this speech 'told' on the House—by the silence as well as by the cheers which seemed to come from all parts of the House, it was evident that the Chief Secretary was being listened to with attention and approval.

The effect on the Parnellites was seen in the tone of Mr Sullivan's speech who immediately followed—instead of being hectoring and insulting it was rather deprecatory, and evidently constructed with the object of doing away with the impression made below the gangway by the Chief Secretary's outspoken denunciation of the No Rent policy and its results.

Mr Sullivan was followed by Mr Daly[2] who spoke in praise of 'boycotting', vindicating it as an old Irish custom, and was replied to by Count Moore and Mr Mitchell Henry.

Mr Gorst got up to demand an explanation of the 'change of policy' implied in the Chief Secretary's reference to the possible necessity for stronger measures—this he construed as an announcement that the Govt were declaring their intention to propose further coercion, an explanation of his speech which Mr Forster at once got up to disavow.

Sir Stafford in a few words closed the discussion, declining to take up Mr Gorst's arguments; and after Mr Biggar had frightened the House by launching into a speech which threatened to talk out the debate, the Motion was put, a division declined, and the sham fight over the Supplementary Estimates and

---

[1] The wording, but not the sense, diverges somewhat from that in *Hansard 3*, cclxviii, 202.

[2] John Daly (1834–88): merchant, of Cork city; mayor, 1871–3; home rule M.P. for the city 1880–84; chevalier of the Legion of Honour.

the grievances of the three Kilmainham Members was well over before 7 o'clock, to the great satisfaction of everyone.

Father came up to us in Lady Brand's [gallery], much relieved at having had the opportunity of speaking his mind.

We went down with him through the House—actually walking in from behind the Speaker's Chair, right down the floor of the House and out into the Lobby, still swarming with Members.

Several of them came up to speak to us, and tell us of the impression the Chief Secretary's speech had made—Mr George Howard shaking hands cordially and saying to me 'your Father was splendid to-night'.

Father, Mother and I walked home together from the House—a most unwonted experience.

At dinner, in the course of talking over things, Father told us of a pleasant interview he had had with Mr Goschen. Mr Goschen wished him to know that there was a strong desire amongst Liberals behind the Front bench to make some protest against the incessant Parnellite abuse and falsehood, and that he and others would be prepared to speak on Friday (when another Irish row was expected) if Father should think advisable.

A count-out expected but Father obliged to go back to the House in order if possible to see Mr Gladstone and arrange with him about seeing Mr Shaw next day—it appears that Mr Shaw had taken alarm at the passage in the Ch. Secretary's speech about the possible necessity for stronger measures. Evidently this has caused some perturbation—Sir William Harcourt much annoyed at the possible effect, saying to Father, 'In short, you have sacrificed the majority'.

The House counted out immediately after Father got down, so he saw no one that evening.

Oakel and I in the evening to Lady Holland's. Mr Jephson whom I met here, told me of a conversation he had had with Mr Dwyer Gray on the boat last night. 'He was very despondent about the future—things couldn't go on as they were now'—'we can't go on like this—and no more can you'—as for Mr Forster, he believed that 'he had tried to administer the Coercion Act conscientiously'.

Certainly one would not gather from the *Freeman* that this was Mr Gray's impression—but it would seem that every Irish politician is two-sided in the sense of having a public and a private opinion which are kept quite distinct and seldom allowed to interfere with each other.

It was only on Saturday that Mr Maurice Brooks came to the Chief Secretary with a deputation protesting against the recent arrest of Mr Rourke (Mr Egan's partner).[1] This was in his capacity of Member for Dublin—privately he had given it to be understood that he was by no means so indignant over Mr Rourke's fate as the deputation represented.

---

[1] See above, p. 400.

29 Mar., Wed.

A note to Father this morning from Mr Gladstone, very courteous and friendly but expressing some uneasiness at the effect which seemed to have been produced by the sentence about future coercion in his last night's speech.

Father sent him the correct report (from the *Standard*) and calling attention to the fact that what he said had been in connection with Mr Brand's speech (on the inefficiency of the Coercion Act) and further to his interruption and contradiction of Mr Gorst when he had sought to misunderstand his words last night.

Lord Monck to see Father—afterwards to Mr Gladstone's. Uncle Matt to lunch.

We dined in the evening at the Hargreaves Browns'—kind and rich, but very dull. I sat next Mr Cotes, the Whip, who made himself pleasant enough but not so as to alter my general impression of dulness. Everyone in great excitement at present over the prospects of the division—Mr Cotes told me that he thought he knew within three what the figures would be. It would be one of the largest divisions ever known in the House. The 'Whipping' on all sides is very strenuous, and calculations are being made on all sides.

Father puts the probable majority at 25—with a possibility of sinking to 18.

From the Browns' we went on to Lady Granville's, her last Wednesday evening before Easter. Much talk here again about the prospects for Thursday. Met various people—Mr Villiers Stuart, Mr Hayward, Mrs H. Grenfell, Sir James and Lady Paget, Monteagles, etc. Lord Monteagle told me that he had just heard an inveterate old 'croaker' (he didn't tell me who) saying 'I really begin to admire Forster; he is doing his work so well.'

Had a little talk with Mr Lowell about *Democracy*. He seems quite to believe in its being by Mrs Henry Adams—says he feels as though he could hear the very tones of her voice all through. As usual with a satire of that kind he says 'it is a little exaggerated.'

Some business done between Mr Lowell and Father: I believe satisfactory. From Lady Granville's we took Father to the Cos. Heard from him on the way there that after the Thursday division on Mr Marriott's[1] Amendment, the concession would probably be made of a two-thirds instead of a bare majority—Mr Chamberlain very angry on the subject.

Mother and I ventured to wonder much why and how things came to be thus arranged.

Why [says Mother] after dragging your party by main force as it were, up to a certain point, and having taken all this trouble to obtain a majority for a particular object, should it then be abandoned, and concessions made? Surely [says Mother] there has been considerable failure in the tactical arrangements of the Govt this Session; here

[1] William Thackeray Marriott (1834–1903): liberal M.P. for Brighton, 1880–93.

again, as in the affair with the Lords and the Select Committee, they seem to have had the greatest amount of friction with the smallest amount of result.

30 Mar., Th.

Drove with Father to the office, 'Well' he said, alluding to his speech, 'I have committed the Govt after all—at any rate to the extent I wanted. There is no getting out of the effect it has produced in Ireland.'

Mr Gladstone had been very considerate and nice yesterday. I imagine he had been rather alarmed at the interpretation which some people had chosen to put on the passage in question, but he had admitted to Father that when fairly looked at it 'was a truism'.

An afternoon at home. Bertram Buxton called to say goodbye before going to America for 8 months.

Oakel and I dined at the Monteagles. Lord M. had just come from the House—Mr Bright had made a good speech, the first part rather dry and arithmetical, the latter very spirited and eloquent; unusually gracious towards the Conservatives, and severe upon the 'No Rent' party; alluding to Mr O'Connor and Mr Healy's participation in the Chicago Convention, he had declared that honourable members were at liberty to conspire and to rebel, but they were not at liberty 'to make it impossible for this Imperial Parliament to transact the business of the Nation'.

An evening party afterwards, met various people—all talking more or less of the division; for Liberals—at least in London—seem enthusiastic in favour of the extreme Government proposal as opposed to a two-thirds majority, but Mr Marriott's Amendment having been made the ground for a stand or fall division minor objections disappear in the general wish on our side that the Govt may win.

Oakel to the House returning with Father.

May Ward, and Lucy, Mr Errington, Mr Litton and Mr Tuke to dinner at home.

31 Mar., Fri.

The Govt majority last night was larger than had been expected—39. A very full House (largest since 1869)—only 35 members absent; the result received with loud cheers by the Liberals.[1]

The principal speakers had been Mr Bright, Colonel Stanley, Mr Sexton, Mr O'Shaughnessy, Sir Stafford Northcote and Mr Gladstone.

The *Times* furious at the result—in fact quite unbecomingly in a temper. Mr Walter was one of the 5 Liberals who voted with the Opposition.

[1] The division was 318:279.

A murder reported from Ireland this morning, Mr Herbert, J.P., shot dead near Castleisland, Co. Kerry.[1]

Drove with Father to Cardinal Manning's, waiting for nearly an hour in the hansom outside while he had the interview to which his Eminence had summoned him.

On our way to the office he described to me what had passed; he appears to have spoken his mind very plainly about the harm that may be, and is, done in Ireland by such an influence as Archbishop Croke's. It is no secret that Cardinal Manning dislikes the promotion of Archbishop McCabe, but Father's great hope is that he may be induced by such a plain 'exposé' of the situation as he gave him this morning to throw what influence he has in Ireland (probably not much) on to the side of the Archbishop of Dublin and not of Cashel.

On walking down from the Irish Office I met Uncle Matt, and while I was speaking to him he was accosted by a gentleman who turned out to be Mr Tennyson to whom Uncle Matt introduced me.

Walked with Uncle Matt to the Athenaeum, returning from there in a cab.

Father to the Cabinet at 2.

Drove with Mother and Francie in the afternoon. Mrs Ball to tea. Father home to dinner.

Heard from Oakel an account of the private Meeting held this afternoon at the Duke of Bedford's, for the promotion of Emigration from Connemara. The Duke began by reading a letter from Father, and various short speeches followed. £7000 were [?subscribed] in the room by the forty people present.

Mr Tuke will go to Ireland to arrange matters on the spot; the great object is to carry out the plan as quietly and informally as possible in conjunction with the local Boards of Guardians. Sydney Buxton has consented to be honorary secretary.

We heard from Father this evening another amusing instance of two-sided Irish politicians. Mr McCoan came to his room at the House to-day to see Mr Johnson. The Attorney was not there, so Mr McCoan was invited in to speak to the Chief Secretary instead. 'Well' said Father, 'we gave you a licking yesterday'.

'Yes, and I am very glad of it', was Mr McCoan's answer.

'Now don't you think that considering all things you had better have voted with us?'

'I don't know about that—but at any rate I got you a vote.'

This was from Mr Gabbett, one of the Members for Limerick, who had been in doubt up to the last moment and appealed to Mr McCoan. 'Oh vote for

---

[1] Arthur Edward Herbert, land agent of Farranfore, was shot at about 6.30 p.m. on 30 Mar. while returning from Castleisland petty sessions; he was an unpopular magistrate. Four men were arrested but discharged for want of evidence; one was rearrested and allowed bail at the spring assizes, 1883 (S.P.O., I.C.R., Returns of outrages, 1882, 1883).

the Govt by all means' was the advice he had received, probably not knowing when he did so that Mr McCoan himself was going to vote according to his public not his private opinions.

The House counted out soon after 10, as Miss McCormack's case did not come on.[1]

1 Apr., Sat.

A full day for Father. At half past 10 a gentleman to see him in connection with a proposed railway through Ilkley to Skipton. At 11, Captain Mills, the Agent for Queensland, who gave Father some interesting information about the emigration of some Irishmen he has had to do with—farmer's sons implicated in Secret Societies and anxious to get safely away with their lives.

'Just the sort of men' says Father 'by whom the outrages are committed, and whom it is highly desirable to get rid of'.

After Captain Mills, came Lord Kenmare and his solicitor. At 12.30 I drove with him to the office, whence he was to go in a few minutes to meet Mr Lowell at the American Legation.

The Dean of Westminster and Mrs and Miss Bradley to lunch. Drove with Mother in the afternoon—she called at the Irish Office, but found Father quite unable to think of a Saturday half-holiday. Lord F. Cavendish on Treasury business. Lucy, Ada and Mr Cropper to tea.

An interesting event to-day has been the appearance of Oakel's pamphlet, *The Truth about the Land League*, 'by one who knows'—the title insisted upon by the Press Agency who have undertaken the publication at their own risk and are responsible for its circulation.

I cannot but think that this is one of the most effective things Oakel has ever done, and I expect it will attract attention.

Father has not seen a line of it, and we are now not going to show it him till after we have left London.

Father dined at Lord Aberdeen's, going on afterwards to Lady Hayter's. He had been seeing Mr Lowell, who is reported to be in a peck of troubles.

2 Apr., Sun.

Almost every Sunday nowadays is distinguished by some particular worry or hard labour; today the trouble came from America.

Bertram Buxton to breakfast—a call from Mr Lowell in the middle of breakfast, to come again later. To church at St James the Less, Father not being able to come.

Uncle Walter, Mr Jephson and Mr Lowell at lunch. Evidently things have come to a crisis about the American suspects. Mr Lowell, it appears, has been

[1] 9.30 p.m., according to *Hansard 3*, cclxviii, 531.

charged to remonstrate against American citizens being kept in prison without trial, and is not thought by certain persons who have taken up the Land League cause in America to have been sufficiently peremptory.

He tells me that next to my Father he is getting more vituperation at present than any man in Europe: he is accused of 'having been adulated by the lords he has been living amongst' and every day receives newspapers full of violent abuse—a state of things which seems so normal as to be quite in the order of nature for an Irish Secretary but is clearly new and very disagreeable to the American Minister.

Apparently there is some despatch or telegram to be sent to the American Govt about which Mr Lowell and Father are very anxious and which requires much consideration and immediate decision.

Sudden appearance of Mr West at lunch, to inform Father that no one could be found—Lord Granville and Mr Gladstone both gone into the country, and all the private secretaries away too.

'Why, we are left without a government' says Father.

'Happy country!' ejaculated Mr Lowell, probably much oppressed at this moment with the disagreeable evidence of his own government's existence in the form of pressing despatches and injunctions.

It seems that there is more danger—or at any rate cause for anxiety—in this last movement from America than we had quite realized. The agitation is no doubt countenanced by Americans merely for voting purposes, but the serious thing is [that] the German as well as the Irish immigrants are joining in the pressure—'they are very jealous' says Father, 'of any thing that may seem to threaten their own rights of American Nationality', remembering the dangers of conscription in Europe.

Disappearance of Father into the library (I believe to write a letter of consultation to Mr Gladstone) followed reluctantly at an interval by the American Minister, who seemed much to prefer sitting with us round the table discoursing on gout, and old French poetry—of which by the way he has promised to send me a specimen poem.

Sir John Rose to see Father at 3. Calls on Mother from Mr and Mrs Litton, and Mr Cartwright. At 4 went into the library to see if Father could be exhumed and made to go for a walk. Walked with him and Mother to Colbert's—afterwards on with Father to Lady Ely's, where I left him to refresh himself with a call on her.

I to the G.F.S. tea in Denbigh Street.

Mr Rutson at 5.30, greatly pleased at the success of Mr Charles Acland in East Cornwall.[1] The Liberal majority however was smaller than last time, which is a good deal attributable, it is said, to Bradlaugh, and Mr Glad-

[1] Charles Thomas Dyke Acland (1842–1919): eldest son of Sir Thomas Acland (above, p. 92), was elected by 3,720 votes to the 3,519 of John Tremayne (1825–1901), conservative M.P. for the constituency, 1874–80.

stone's support of him. 'Yes, Bradlaugh has certainly been a nuisance' says Father.

At 7 Father vanished again to hard labour in the library. Cabinet box and letter from Mr Gladstone sent up from the Durdans, Epsom, where he is spending the Sunday.

A partial, or rather conditional, consent to the proposed form of agreement arrived at by Father and Mr Lowell—'I think we are unduly hustled' says Mr Gladstone. 'Yes' says Father, 'but hustled by facts, not by the American Minister'.

It appears that a great Meeting is to be held in New York on Monday, for the object of putting pressure on the American Govt for the release of the American suspects, and Mr Lowell is bound to be ready with a communication as to the intimation of our Govt in the matter.

If, as a result of this Meeting, Congress passes a Resolution requesting their Foreign Minister to take active measures, it will make the Irish demand a subject of diplomatic relations between England and the United States, and thereby bring it into quite a new light—and a very undesirable one.

The point under discussion at this time (as far as I can make out) is what conditions shall our Govt attach to the release of the American suspects. To let them out, with liberty to continue their career of agitation in Ireland under present circumstances, would be an impossible concession for the English Govt to agree to, and this, I believe, the Irish Secretary has quite impressed on his colleagues and the American Minister. On the other hand, in their present mood, the American Irish party (headed by General Grant) would protest against their Govt claiming anything short of unconditional release on the ground of American citizenship.

Here lies the difficulty (I believe) in making a satisfactory arrangement between Lord Granville and Mr Lowell, who is evidently much perturbed at the situation.

At 8 o'clock, Father's labours were by no means over. After the letter from Mr Gladstone came a telegram from Lord Granville from Holmbury, agreeing to the proposed arrangement, conditionally on Mr Gladstone doing so—then another note from Mr Lowell, on receipt of which Father drove off to Chesham Place taking with him what enlightenment and instructions he could from his colleagues.

Home at 9.20. At 10 another ring at the bell—this time Lord Granville's private secretary, Mr Sanderson,[1] with whom Father was closeted for ten minutes, to his satisfaction—finding him 'a very shrewd fellow', quite entering into the situation.

This ended the negociations for to-day.

---

[1] Thomas Henry Sanderson (1841–1923): entered foreign office, 1859; private secretary to previous foreign secretaries, 1866–8, 1874–8; to Granville since 1880.

3 Apr., Mon.

A note from the American Minister at breakfast. The negociations in full swing again. Another visit from Mr Sanderson.

Report in the papers that Mr Smythe a landlord in Westmeath had been fired at, and a lady with him hit and wounded but not fatally.

Father to see Mr Gladstone and Mr Childers. Morning sitting at the House.

Francie and I to church at St Peter's, and afterwards shopping. It has been decided that, on Aunt Fan's account, Francie goes to Fox How this Easter instead of with us to Ireland.

The *Pall Mall Gazette* this evening on a new and improved policy for Ireland to be thought over by Ministers during their Easter holidays and acted upon afterwards.

Several suggestions—arrears, alteration of the Land Act, release of the 'political' suspects, but above all the removal of Mr Forster and the substitution of a Chief Secretary who should combine (if such could be found willing to enter the tomb of all political reputations) the characteristics of Mr Cardwell and Sir Michael Hicks Beach.

From Mr Morley's point of view this counsel is perfectly consistent and natural, and a downright attack of this kind is an agreeable change from the malicious sneers and innuendoes which are all that the *Pall Mall* has indulged in hitherto against the Chief Secretary.

Mother home a little before 7. Another note from Mr Lowell—concerning one Michael Slattery claiming to be also an American citizen—an immediate answer required which I was summoned down to copy.

Father received the terrible news this afternoon—made public in answer to a question in the House—that the lady who was shot while driving home from church with her brother-in-law, Mr Smythe, had been killed on the spot, and not only wounded as had been stated in the Morning papers.

Father, Mother and I left for Dublin by the night Mail—a large party including Mr Jephson, and Mr West, two messengers and four servants.

A Coupé lit, and all possible attentions as usual from the Euston officials; but a tiring journey and a wakeful night for Father, haunted with the knowledge of this last terrible tragedy of which some details were given in the last edition of the *Pall Mall*.

A perfectly smooth passage on the *Connaught*.

4 Apr., Tu.

A grey morning, and a gloomy landing in all respects. The papers full of the ghastly crime in Westmeath. Mr Smythe driving home from church with Lady Harriet Monck and Mrs Henry Smythe—a loud report from behind a clump of trees bordering the carriage drive—Mrs Smythe who was sitting on the back seat fell forward dead, her skull completely fractured by a bullet.

The murderer as usual escaped—no clue to him being given by anyone in the neighbourhood.

It is believed that Mr Smythe's life was thus attempted in revenge for his having evicted a family on his estate, who probably employed some member of a Murder Secret Society to do their work for them.

There seems to be no question that Mr Smythe is a good and considerate landlord, and no pretence that this particular family was treated with the slightest harshness.[1]

This outrage is not the only one reported in this morning's papers which are fearfully black reading.

Poor dear Father seemed quite overwhelmed with the burden of difficulty and misery which he has to encounter. As might be expected, the murder of Mrs Smythe, and all the circumstances attending it, have caused such a thrill of horror and fury as no other outrage has yet done.

'Everyone has gone quite mad over it' says Father, after reading the usually sober columns of the *Irish Times*, 'and I'm sure I am not surprised'.

If at this moment the Govt were to ask for Martial law in Parliament I believe they would get it—and I see that even the London correspondent of the *Freeman* acknowledges the same.

Reached the C.S. Lodge about half past 8, and found rather a melancholy reception—no fires and no breakfast, Mother having forgotten to tell Mrs Adams that we should come in the morning instead of the evening. However, Father was much too full of other things to mind whether he had breakfast and fire or not, and for the rest of us it did not matter. Besides in a surprisingly short space of time the drawing room looked warm and cheerful and breakfast was provided there.

A letter to Father this morning from a Kerry gentleman (Mr Hungerford) written beside the dead body of his friend Mr Herbert,[2] charging the Chief Secretary and his Government with the responsibility for this murder, and complaining bitterly that no rewards had been offered to lead to the detection of the murderers.[3]

A kind answer from the Chief Secretary, who feels how natural such anger against him is, though it may be unreasonable.

An article in the *Freeman* this morning exulting greatly over the American

[1] Florence's account is substantially the same as the official return. Seven persons were arrested but discharged for want of evidence; fourteen men (including some of the former) were later arrested and tried for conspiracy to murder at the commission court in Dublin, established under the 1882 crimes act. Five received ten years' penal servitude; four received seven years; one, twelve months; no further proceedings were taken. The Barbavilla case became one of the *causes célèbres* of crimes act administration (S.P.O., I.C.R., Returns of outrages, 1882, 1883, 1884).

[2] See above, p. 428.

[3] The offer of rewards in such cases was almost entirely unproductive, and in the next few years the Castle virtually abandoned the practice.

intervention about the suspects. General Grant has written a letter declaring that if he were President he would know how to assert the rights of American citizens at home and abroad.

Mr Burke to see Father—walking with him afterwards via the Vice Regal to the Castle.

Mother and I spent a very quiet day—continuous rain, so we did not go even into the garden. Chattenooga,[1] who had come over with us, quite recovered from the journey, and settling down here with perfect composure.

Father and Mr West home from the Castle at 20 minutes to 8. Father had had a hard day and was very tired but revived by his dinner.

A short game of whist in the evening. Telegram from Francie safely arrived at Fox How.

An excellent article in to-day's *Times* on the American demand for the release of the suspects, pointing out that, so far as allowing them to leave the country is concerned, this may easily be arranged if the U.S. Govt wishes it; but that on the other hand our Govt cannot give up its rights to subject Americans as well as English and Irish to the law of the land as at present in force in Ireland, and that so long as the Coercion Act exists and the circumstances which make it necessary, it will be impossible for this Govt to allow American any more than Irish agitators to range the country and defy the law with impunity.

In short if they like to leave Kilmainham and Ireland altogether they are welcome, but if they reappear they must consider themselves liable to re-arrest under the law of the land—i.e. the Coercion Act.

5 Apr., Wed.

A gloomy morning. Father much vexed to find that he had been away from the House last night, when, on the Motion for adjournment, Mr Gorst made a formal indictment of the government's Irish policy and demanded what new measure for stemming outrage and disorder the Govt would be prepared to bring before the House after Easter.

To this Mr Gladstone replied without giving any positive indication as to the future, and concluding his speech with a solemn charge against the Land League of complicity with outrage which drew angry but not very impressive rejoinders from Mr McCarthy, Mr Redmond and Mr Healy.

It is a noteworthy fact that the statement that £100 had been paid by the Land League for the defence of Connell's 'Moonlight' gang[2] at the Cork Assizes was acknowledged in so many words to be true by the Land League Members— notably Mr Justin McCarthy.

The debate was closed by Sir Stafford Northcote who deplored the absence

---

[1] The Forsters' cat.   [2] See above, p. 362.

of the Chief Secretary and expressed his great disapproval of the answer which Mr Gladstone had made to Mr Gorst's enquiry.[1]

Father writes to-day to explain to Mr Gladstone his own great regret at not having stayed for this affair: the truth is that, though hearing Mr Gorst give Notice of his Motion he had not heard, or understood, that it was for the following day, and left the House under the impression that the question was not coming up till after Easter.

He also wrote to explain to Mr Gorst the mistake which accounted for his absence.

The *Pall Mall* of Tuesday contains a second attack on the Chief Secretary under the heading 'Facing the Facts'. 'The Chief Secretary has done his best and what he has done has turned out ill. There is no disloyalty nor disrespect then in believing that the time has come for a new diagnosis, a new prescription and a new apothecary.'

The *Pall Mall* at the same time declares itself to be not in favour of attempting to rule Ireland without coercion—'those who, like ourselves, have least faith in one sort of coercion, are most willing that the Executive should resort and even acquire extra powers for resorting to vigorous coercion of another sort.'

It is stated that 60 Members of the Liberal party have met at the Reform Club, and resolved to appeal to the Premier about the state of Ireland and request the removal of the Chief Secretary.

In fact this solution of the Irish difficulty (or contribution towards it) is being freely discussed in the papers at present, with more or less approval. The *Freeman* is under the impression that the attack once having begun will before long be successful, though allowing that 'Mr Forster's personal popularity is undeniable, and that the Prime Minister is supposed to object to the idea of parting with the Member for Bradford'.

Mr Chamberlain or Mr Shaw LeFevre is talked of—in some quarters—as the coming man.

Walked with Father part of the way through the park. The only satisfactory piece of intelligence in this morning's papers was that Father McPhilpin,[2] a very violent and ill-conditioned priest, has submitted to enter into recognisances for good behaviour when summoned before Mr Blake and other Magistrates for a denunciation of the constabulary.

This prevents his having to be sent to prison like Father Feehan which is a good thing in every way. In fact whatever the cause it does seem as though the priests were becoming less identified with the bad part of the agitation.

Yesterday Father pointed out to us as the only good thing reported in the papers—an address by a Father Magee in Roscommon, genuinely protesting

---

[1] Hansard reports Northcote as speaking early in the debate, which was closed by Callan (*Hansard 3*, cclxviii, 730).

[2] Peter McPhilpin, curate at Athenry, Co. Galway.

against violence and outrage, and suggesting that his people should form themselves into a defensive band against the perpetrators of outrage if it should become necessary in their neighbourhood.

A long visit to Mother this morning from Lady Cowper, very despondent about the state of things, which she thought were worse than when Father was over at the Castle three weeks ago.

The de Vescis, who had thought matters decidedly improving at the beginning of the year, are now in as great despair as ever. The bad spirit seems to have settled down amongst their tenantry and neighbours again, and to be making life almost unbearable.

Mother and I spent the afternoon indoors. Mother's cold being unfortunately no better.

Miss Burke to tea—very pleasant, and full as usual of interesting facts and anecdotes—it always strikes me that Miss Burke would have made a very able and effective man: she has great practical ability, administrative power, quick understanding and a clear definiteness both of knowledge and opinion, very different from the vague vehement notions which often do duty with women for political ideas.

Father and Mr West not home till 10 minutes to 8—evidently, from Father's voice as he answered Mother's questions, and from the weary way in which he dragged himself upstairs, he had been having a hard day at the Castle and was feeling dead beat, both in mind and body.

During the first half of dinner he seemed too much dispirited and exhausted to speak a word, but gradually he cheered up a little—outwardly at least—and we played our usual game of whist, and ended the evening rather less mournfully than it had begun. Mr West told me, as showing how he had been, that when they got out of the carriage this evening to walk as Father insisted on doing from the Park gates, he seemed much annoyed at finding that two mounted policeman had been following the carriage. 'What are those confounded fellows here for again—I shall have this stopped—I shouldn't mind if I was shot—everything over here is so disgusting.'

Mr West tells me that he hopes the police escort will not be discontinued— 'Dublin' as he says, 'is full of Fenians, and only this evening as they were driving out of Dublin he caught sight of two men in a side street leaning forward and peering into the carriage as if to make sure who was inside.'

The London papers of this evening contained nothing specially disagreeable. A fair sensible article in the *Times* on Tuesday's debate, and a friendly passage in the Dublin correspondence to the effect that the Chief Secretary was working very hard, and that it was unreasonable to raise an outcry against him for every outrage committed and every mistake and blunder made by persons throughout the country.

The great American Meeting concerning the Suspects has come off, and when seen close the affair seems less alarming than might have been supposed.

The Mayor of New York, who presided, turns out to be an Irishman, as were a large number of those present. The speeches were violent, 'denouncing Mr Lowell's sickening sycophancy' etc., and the comments of the chief newspapers, *Herald* and *Times*, anything but flattering in their criticisms on the motives and the expressions of the speakers.

Meanwhile the American suspects have been released. (No—this is a mistake.)

The statement about the Meeting of Liberals at the Reform Club is categorically denied. There was a meeting to consider Club arrangements—but Mr Forster, Mr Gladstone and Ireland were not so much as mentioned.

Oakel's pamphlet is beginning to be known—Mr Burke spoke to Father about it, and expressed his approval without knowing who it was by—and there have been very favourable notices of it in the *Daily News* and *Chronicle*.

6 Apr., Th.

I do not exactly know, but I rather gather that Father's extreme despondency yesterday had been caused by his disappointment in not finding support and assistance from the landlords and gentry in Westmeath—at present one of the worst and most dangerous parts of the country.

Lord Greville, the Lord Lieutenant of the county, has written to Father and declined to have anything to do with calling a Meeting of Magistrates and taking measures for self-defence, pointing out the risk of Boycotting, and the possible expense which the Magistrates might incur by acting on the Chief Secretary's suggestion. On the other hand Lord Greville suggests that the Govt might send over a contingent of Militia from England which would apparently in his opinion answer the same purpose, and have the further advantage of sparing the resident landlords any responsibility or expense.[1]

The attack on the Chief Secretary continued in Wednesday's *Pall Mall*.

A vigorous and indignant protest in the *Leeds Mercury*[2] against the 'plot' against Mr Forster—in fact so vigorous a denunciation of the *P.M.G.* and its present policy that it will probably not be reproduced in that journal amongst the samples of provincial opinion.

Father received this morning a most delightful and friendly letter from Mr Gladstone, in answer to the letter he had written on Tuesday, apropos of the suggestion for his removal in the *Pall Mall*, placing his resignation in Mr Gladstone's hands if on any ground he should think it better in the public interest to be quit of him.

There is only one strong temptation, Mr Gladstone tells him, to accept his

[1] Fulke Southwell Greville-Nugent (1821–83): cr. baron, 1869; colonel of Westmeath militia; owned 9,783 acres in Westmeath, 3,990 in Roscommon, 1,970 in Cavan, 1,236 in Longford, and 451 in Cork, worth a total of £16,113. Forster had suggested the enrolment of special constables.

[2] Edited (1870–87) by Thomas Wemyss Reid, later Forster's biographer.

resignation, and that is that he would certainly have to go out with him. 'He may rest assured that the idea of his removal has not crossed the mind of one of his colleagues'—nor, Mr G. believes, of any person of note—unless it be John Morley.[1]

Such a cordial, generous letter as this makes one feel inclined to love Mr Gladstone as well as respect him; and the grace and courtesy of the language in which it is expressed are worthy of a statesman of the old school in his dealings with a colleague.

Walked with Father to the Park gates. Mother and Mr West going on with him in the carriage, and I returning with the dogs.

A lovely spring day, and the Fifteen Acres radiant in golden sunshine.

A call from Mrs Maurice Brooks. Mr Ross of Bladensburg and Colonel King Harman to dinner. Father had a visit to-day at the Castle from the Catholic Archbishop of Toronto, about emigration—satisfactory.

7 Apr., Fri.

Mother and I to church in the morning at Christchurch. Father did not go into Dublin at all—wrote to Mr Gladstone in the morning—one of those reports on the present condition of things, and suggestions as to future policy, which will make such interesting contributions some day to the history of these times in Ireland.

Of the most important suggestions were those dealing with arrears, alteration of the jury system with a view to obtain some certainty of punishment of crime—not merely 'tinkering' such as change of 'venue' etc., renewal of the Act for a year, accompanied with release of the suspects now in prison.

(I had only the opportunity of reading this important Memorandum hurriedly just before post time, and therefore may have given a wrong account of it, but from my recollection these were the main points.[2])

The Lord Lieutenant to see Father.

After lunch Father took a tranquil walk with Mother and Yarrow round the Circular Walk. A brilliant but hard afternoon—cloudless sky and a keen east wind.

Visits in the afternoon from Sir Thomas and Miss Steele, and Capt. and Mrs Howard, and from Mr and Mrs Ross of Bladensburg.

Father, Mother, and I alone at dinner—Mr West having gone to Kingstown. Talk over the American affair from which I gathered the following: It is a mistake that the suspects have all been released as stated by Mr

---

[1] Forster's letter of 4 Apr. to Gladstone is in Reid, *Forster*, ii, 411–12; Gladstone's reply is on pp 412–13.

[2] Florence's recollection is accurate enough. For the text, see B.L., Add. MS 44160, ff 77–85; printed, with some minor errors, in Reid, *Forster*, ii, 415–19.

Freylingham.[1] Several American suspects had been let out, but this was before and not in any connection with the recent agitation. Four are still in prison, and therefore the subject for negociation and possible friction still exists, but judging from the tone of Frelingham and the American papers there is a disposition not to make trouble.

We also talked over the personal details of last Sunday's negociations, when Father and Mr Sanderson between them appear to have played the role of Secretary and Under-Secretary for Foreign affairs—being obliged by circumstances and stress of time to despatch telegrams, and undertake responsibilities on their own account.

However it seems as though whatever was done has at any rate not aggravated matters. Our government kept to the ground which it took up at first; the Cooper's Institute Meeting does not appear to have been an important demonstration (Mr Lowell's fear about the Germans' cooperation not being justified), and there is apparently a disposition on the part of the responsible American Ministers and the press to approve of Mr Lowell's action and allow that the British Govt has not acted unreasonably in the matter.

A quiet evening—Father looking over Asst Commissioner testimonials. 'I feel rather less low to-day' he says, 'but I dare say I shall very soon be in the depths again'.

Yesterday's outrage return was a small one.

8 Apr., Sat.

Another brilliant morning, cloudless sky and cold east wind.

A call on Mother from Lord Clarina—Father, who came into the drawing room to see him, took the opportunity to put before him his (and Mr Ross's) idea of a defensive force to be raised in a district for protection against 'Captain Moonlight' outrages. It would be possible, by taking advantage of an existing law (the same under which the 'Auxiliaries' were added to the Constabulary last autumn), for the Lord Lieutenant of a county to enroll and arm young men, farmers' sons and so forth, as special Constables; no amount of additional troops would produce the moral effect which the establishment of such a force would have in a county; 500 men of this class would do more good in stopping the commission of outrages than 2000 soldiers. What did Lord Clarina think of the scheme?

He was not sanguine—in fact hopeless of its success from the fact that the very class of men whom it was proposed to employ, and who had formerly been enrolled in the Yeomanry, could no longer be trusted; the country was so saturated with disaffection that hardly any farmers would be found to accept

[1] Frederick Theodore Frelinghuysen (1817–85): U.S. secretary of state since Dec. 1881, in succession to James Gillespie Blaine (1830–93), Garfield's secretary of state.

the required conditions. Something might be done with gentlemen residents, younger sons and so forth, but farmer special constables would not be possible.

Lord Clarina's own suggestion towards the suppression of outrages was the passing of an Act empowering the police to fine or summon all persons not found within doors after a given time at night.

According to him and his brother (a landlord, I believe, in the Co. Limerick) this would be more effective than arresting people found out of doors at night, and would not be a hardship on respectable people—the doubtful characters likely to be affected and being perfectly well known to the police and to their neighbours.

Walked with Father, Mother and the Occidental to the Kingsbridge, Mother and I with the dogs returning in a cab.

An afternoon at home—calls from Mrs Ormsby and the Duke and Duchess of Leinster.

Their Graces very benignant—Mother surprised at the sudden and marked demonstration of friendliness.[1] I explain it to be the ducal reply to the *Pall Mall Gazette*, signifying that even Mr Forster was a more acceptable Chief Secretary than some who might replace him if the *P.M.G.* had its way.

Spent most of the afternoon reading the Memoirs of Thomas Drummond, Under-Secretary here between '35 and '39.[2]

It would seem as though Ireland had never been served with more devoted, and wise and patriotic ardour than she was by this Scotch official in an English Government, who literally died of over-work in her cause.

Mr Vernon to dine and sleep—Mr Jephson to dinner—Sub-Commissioner appointments discussed in the evening.

9 Apr., Easter Sunday

Mr Vernon left at 11, a little more business having been done since breakfast.

The Chief Commissioner was in decidedly good spirits and very amusing in confidential talk over the different characteristics of his colleagues and sub-ordinates—the very uncultured Sub-Commissioner who distresses his colleagues by his innocence of a pocket handkerchief, the Sub-Commissioner whose principles and theories are appalling but who acts with great sense, the Sub-Commissioner who 'steadily draws his salary' and takes no part whatever in the decisions of the Commission, the Sub-Commissioner who exhibited the eccentricity peculiar to his family in actually desiring to be put on the same Commission with Professor Baldwin, etc., etc.

Mr Vernon was full of the charms of Judge O'Hagan as a companion—knowing everything, with a marvellous memory for poetry, genial, humorous, a good

[1] Cf. above, pp 35–6.
[2] J. F. McLennan, *Memoir of Thomas Drummond, under-secretary to the lord lieutenant of Ireland, 1835–40* (London, 1867).

lawyer, and never letting his sympathies, which were decidedly on the side of the people, influence in the smallest degree the impartiality of his legal decisions, very sensitive, and liable to depression, and keenly alive to all the criticisms made on him in the newspapers.

Mr Vernon told us that he had been much amused to find inserted in the Judge's 'Log Book' which he had taken up one day in mistake for his own, the following caution: 'John O'Hagan, you are not bound to speak, but remember that whatever you do say will be taken down and used in evidence against you'.

Father, Mother and I drove into church at the Chapel Royal—greatly to the delight of the pompous old Verger who had never had the Chief Secretary there before. Mother and I stayed to the Communion, Father going after service to the Castle.

In driving out we overtook him and Mr Burke, and at the Park gates I got out and walked home with them.

Fragments of discussion, evidently begun before, on possible Purchase scheme—'anything that would involve England becoming virtually owners of the land in Ireland, would never be agreed to—the risk too great—No, the Tories would not venture to propose it'.

Mr Burke to lunch. Mother to church in the afternoon at the Hibernian.

On going into Father's study just before post time to see if he wanted any letters sealing, he said: 'I have just got a very perplexing thing', handing me a telegram, at which my spirits sank, for I had thought that for once we were going to get quietly through the Sunday.

'From C. S. Parnell, Kilmainham Jail—Have just heard of the death by typhus of my sister's only child[1]—wish to attend funeral in Paris—will undertake not to take part in any political matters while absent'.

Having sent off his letter Father brought the telegram in to Mother—going over with her to the Vice-Regal Lodge, and sending me to Mr Burke's to ask him to come and consult with him and the Lord Lieutenant.

Judging from Mr Burke's black looks when he found himself thus routed out, and saw the reason why, I thought it looked ill for Mr Parnell's prospects so far as the Under-Secretary was concerned.

Heard from Miss Burke about the open air Meeting which they had been to in the Nine Acres. The object to denounce the City Members, Mr Brooks and Dr Lyons, for their vote on the Closure; the instigator Mr Gray, who it is said wishes to represent Dublin instead of Carlow; the chief speaker Mr T. D. Sullivan.

The speeches as usual violent—Irish virtue, English brutality, outrages caused by the Govt etc., etc.—but the Meeting quite orderly and agreeable. Bands, oranges, and holiday makers attracted by the cheerful weather.

Amongst the thousands whom Mr Sullivan was so proud to see assembled for the righteous purpose of denouncing the Govt and the traitors were

[1] Henry Thomson, only child of Parnell's sister Delia, died in Paris in Apr. 1882, aged 21.

His Excellency and Colonel Boyle, and William and Mrs Crosbie (our Welsh cook). The two latter were treated with great courtesy by the crowd, and room made for them to come up near the platform, where they could hear and see the orators to advantage.

Soon after 7 Father returned, bringing his Ex. with him. They had decided to let Mr Parnell out, and Captain Barlow was coming up to see Father about it.

Just before dinner Capt. Barlow arrived—returning again an hour later after an interview in the meantime at Kilmainham. They were trying to see if it could not be arranged for Mr Dillon to go out at the same time and betake himself abroad—his health gives much cause for anxiety.

As for Mr Parnell he is to go for ten days, giving a written undertaking not to take part in any political demonstration while he is away.

His sister's child turned out to be a young man of 22, which Father thinks makes the plea even more urgent—he believes he was the only member in Mr Parnell's family of the younger generation.

At 10 o'clock a third visit from Captain Barlow. It cannot be managed about Mr Dillon; he will not consent to go abroad—says if he goes anywhere it must be to Ventnor.

It certainly does seem a great risk letting Mr Parnell out under present circumstances, and probably, no one will be more surprised than Mr Parnell and Mr Egan[1] themselves, at having the opportunity for consultation unexpectedly given them. However, as Mother says, the Lord Lieutenant, Mr Burke and Father amongst them may be trusted to know what it is safe to do.

10 Apr., Mon.

Letter to Father from Mr Gladstone—also from Lord Hartington—characteristic and amusing in its brief but sufficiently emphatic expression of opinion: 'Does not agree with the *P.M.G.* and other papers in wishing for a change of Chief Secretary; thinks—compliments apart—that such a triumph for his (Mr Forster's) Land League persecutors would be disastrous. But there ought to be an effective Lord Lieutenant. Why not try the other suggestion of the *Pall Mall* and put the office in Commission?'

Reports in the papers of yesterday's Meeting—and Mr Redmond and Mr Biggar in Scotland—Mr C. Russell's letter to his constituents, etc. The news about Parnell not yet got out.[2]

Mr West has a holiday to-day and has gone to the Fairy House Races— which this year take the place of the defunct Punchestown.

Mr Jephson to lunch and work on Sub-Commissioners. Father at home all day, but in constant receipt of orderly Messages from the Castle.

[1] In Paris as treasurer of the Land League, Feb. 81–Oct. 82.
[2] He was released on the morning of 10 Apr.

Drove with Mother and me in the afternoon to the Knockmaroon gate—walking back across the Fifteen Acres.

A radiantly beautiful afternoon, and the Park and Dublin mountains a vision of sunny tranquility.

Lord Monteagle to tea. Father being in the room, the usual amenities of an afternoon call were very quickly got through, and he and Lord Monteagle deep in discussion over the state of Ireland. Referring back to the 'Coercion Act' of 1833,[1] what was its effect? So far as he can judge from the return of outrages, Father declares it was very small. As for Martial law, Courts Martial did not practically ever sit at all. What sentences were obtained were by juries of the old style—in short, packed Protestant juries.

Lord Monteagle believed that in one county (I forget which) the number of outrages had fallen after the Coercion Act from fifteen hundred to three, but this might only be that crime changed in intensity from one county to another as it does now.

What did most to quiet the country after 1833, says Father, appears to have been Drummond's reorganization of the police—in fact, that beginning of centralization which is complained of now.

As to the measures to be taken now, Father would expect most from the power of making a district pay for the troops quartered in it; to this Lord Monteagle agreed thinking it would be more effective than a 'murder tax'.

But the great question is shall these measures be in addition to the Coercion Act or instead of it? Lord Monteagle would like to have the suspects released and the Act renewed.[2]

The Lord Chancellor to dinner—one of the pleasantest and most congenial of men. A quiet unbusinesslike dinner, and consultation between Father and Mr Law afterwards.

Mr West home at 11—there had not been a row at Fairyhouse, as had been prophesied.

The Vice Regal party both hissed and cheered, but not much demonstration of any kind.

11 Apr., Tu.

The papers this morning in great excitement over Mr Parnell's release on parole—special correspondents, 'leading articles'—statements and counter statements.

Mr Parnell himself appears to be acting honourably and observing not only

[1] 3 & 4 Will. IV, c.4, in force from 2 Apr. 1833 to 1 Aug. 1835. The mention of 'martial law' probably refers to the provision under this act for trying offences by courts composed of military officers with reduced powers of punishment.

[2] The general opinion of the Castle and the special R.M.s favoured renewal for a year, with extensive additional powers; when these were passed, the existing suspects might be released; see below, p. 451.

the letter but the spirit of his parole. In this he justifies Father's opinion: 'It is the one remains of virtue he has left' says Father, 'he'll keep to any undertaking he has given'.

Walked with Father to the Park gates, driving on afterwards with him and Mother into Dublin.

'Rumoured Resignation of the Lord Lieutenant' is posted up amongst other items of news at the *Daily Express* office. 'Very curious' say Father and Mother, from which I concluded that a change at the Vice Regal is now imminent.

Mother and I to the Hibernian Academy—Mr A. Burke's pictures amongst the best there.

Father had a consultation to-day with the Special Magistrates—now 6—Colonel Forbes[1] having been added to the numbers.

A call from Mr and Mrs Doyle, and Mrs Monahan. Wrote to Mr Pulzsky and sent him Oakel's pamphlet.

Father, Mother and I dined at the Vice-Regal Lodge. A banquet—everyone in uniform—the occasion being the investiture of Lord Carlingford as a Knight of St Patrick—the ceremony had been performed quite privately in the middle of the day.[2]

Amongst those present at dinner were the Powerscourts, Droghedas, Ardilauns, Steeles, Burkes, Barnard Fitzpatricks, Lords Monck, Kenmare, Granard, Dartrey, Clarina, O'Hagan, the Archbishop, Lord Chancellor, etc., etc., 37 in all.

Speeches by Lord Cowper and Lord Carlingford.

Lord Monck spoke to me nicely about Oakel's pamphlet.

12 Apr., Wed.

Lord Carlingford and Miss Dixon to breakfast. A call in the course of the morning from Lord Kenmare—very gloomy about the state of Kerry—in his neighbourhood there has been a fresh outbreak of violence.

Secret Societies are trying to enforce the No Rent policy—the tenants are watched day and night to prevent them paying their rent. If a man goes near a bank, or the Agent's office he is in danger—six of Lord Kenmare's tenants have been shot and mutilated for paying, or being supposed to have paid, their rents; one, an old man, has had to have his leg amputated and his life is despaired of.

The last Govt, says Lord Kenmare, sowed the seeds of our present troubles. Lord Beaconsfield was perhaps the only man of his party who foresaw what dangers were impending, but he did not take the measures that might and ought to have been taken at the time of the Dissolution.

[1] William Francis Forbes (1836–99): brother of seventh earl of Granard (above, p. 355); former captain, Grenadier Guards; colonel, Leitrim Rifles; R.M. since 1865; previously stationed at the Curragh, Kildare; now in charge of the north-western division (Mayo, Roscommon, Sligo).
[2] Cf. above, pp 355–6.

As for the Peace Preservation and Arms Act, the Conservative Administration in Ireland had allowed it to remain a dead letter: during the last two years the Conservatives were in office arms were being poured into Kerry, and Lord Kenmare as Lord Lieutenant of the county wrote to the D. of Marlborough on the subject, but nothing was done. It was understood amongst the Magistrates (who were also appealed to) that the Act was not meant to be enforced—a General election was coming on, and it was not desirable to stir up bad feeling.[1]

Thursday's *Pall Mall Gazette* continues the attack on the Chief Secretary, this time apropos of a letter in his defence from Sir George Young.

'The right sort of man for the post', says the *Pall Mall Gazette*, is 'an Englishman who should try as hard as he could to put himself in the place of an Irishman'—and then follows a novel and brilliant suggestion and one that should certainly be 'laid to heart by a Minister' who, according to the *Pall Mall* conception of him, is a mere tool of the Under Secretary, and never consults anyone but landlords and policemen.

He should be ready to listen to as many people as possible; to keep his mind open to suggestions from every quarter; to see everybody who is likely to have anything to tell him. Unless the present Chief Secretary is curiously misrepresented and maligned, he has not followed this course but its opposite. That this should be so is, as we persist in thinking, a failure; and if Sir George Young presses us to call it so, a personal failure.

(I should very much like to know the name of the aggrieved person, on the strength of whose lamentations the *Pall Mall* grounds this particular charge. It is probably some one whose advice on the right course for the Govt to pursue was not received with the consideration he thought it deserved, or who felt aggrieved at receiving an answer to his letter written by Mr West instead of the Chief Secretary himself. One feels sure that if Mr Morley could be examined we should find that it was some very tangible 'he', and not merely rumour, that had so curiously misrepresented and maligned the present Chief Secretary in this matter.)

As before, the *Pall Mall* professes itself to be in favour of a strong 'dose of measures of repression firmly administered'—and for this reason amongst others, it wishes to get rid of Mr Forster, with his 'dishevelled sentimentalism' and substitute a man more of the stamp of Lord Hartington (this is a variety [variation] on the Cardwell–Hicks Beach mixture recommended in a former article), 'a man with more east wind in his composition than the present Chief Secretary has got', whose very virtues do more harm than good.

As for sympathy with the population of Ireland, what is wanted is not sentimental sympathy (an allusion to the Tullamore speech) but an eye for the forces in Ireland out

---

[1] This is not strictly true of general policy; searches for illegally-held weapons had continued, and licences had often been refused or revoked. However, the act was not vigorously applied, and considerable importation of arms (especially old Enfield military rifles) was observed, but not obstructed, by the government.

of which we may hope to build up an ordered Government. We have not detected in any utterance of the Chief Secretary that he has effectively turned his mind to this side of the subject at all. We are not aware of one single constructive suggestion—great or small—unless we are to count the Compensation for Disturbance Bill under this head—for which those who have thought about English policy in Ireland are indebted to Mr Forster.

If Mr Morley had been aware of the secret history of the Land Act and of Mr Forster's share in its construction, I wonder whether he would have said the same.

If the Chief Secretary has a personal antagonist in the *Pall Mall Gazette*, he has an able and most vigorous champion in the *Leeds Mercury*, which takes up the cudgels for him and continues to denounce the conduct of the *P.M.G.* with great spirit.

Miss Dixon staid to lunch.

To Dublin in the afternoon, Mother and I going to a grand Masonic Bazaar and Fancy Fair at the Exhibition Palace. The large building thronged with people—a street of 'Old English houses' kept by various ladies from different parts of Ireland dressed up in costumes of different periods. Very well and prettily carried out, and everyone in a high state of satisfaction—no signs on an occasion like this of distress and national depression.

Dined in the evening again at the Vice Regal—Lord Granard and his pretty young daughter, Lady Sophie Forbes, Lord Carlingford, the Burkes, and four of the Special Magistrates, Mr Clifford Lloyd, Mr Blake, Captain Plunkett and Captain Slacke, and Colonel Dease.

In the course of the evening, all other subjects swallowed up as usual by the everlasting subject 'the state of the country'.

Father the chief speaker—Lady Cowper beside him on an ottoman—not allowing the poor much-bored aide-de-camp to break up the party, even when 11 o'clock had struck and the 'palaver' still continued, Mr Clifford Lloyd and Mr Blake joining in occasionally, and Lord Carlingford with his quiet voice and manner contributing his opinion or experience—Miss Burke, listening eagerly—her brother (who hates political talk or 'shop' after dinner) sitting in a retired corner buried in gloomy silence—Mother on a sofa with Colonel Dease making pretence to keep up a separate conversation, but in reality (Mother at least) listening to what was being discussed in the central group—Captain Slacke a much interested, Lord Granard apparently a passive, spectator; poor little Lady Sophie, finding the last remains of ordinary conversation dying out, and her neighbour Capt. Plunkett being also drawn into the political 'maelstrom' under the chandelier, relapsed into resigned silence, only venturing on a few whispered remarks to me at intervals.

The general tone of the discussion was most depressing—failure of coercion in the past—increase of crime in the present—gloomy forecast as to the future. 'How much longer will England stand the present state of things? What is to be the final outcome—separation, or government of Ireland like a Crown Colony?'

I have seldom heard Father take such a desparing line as he did last night—and I must confess that I did not quite understand it.

It was like a man arguing against himself—determined to put before his mind and look in the face the very worst that could be brought before him by his opponents, refusing almost fiercely to listen to any considerations that might be brought forward on the other side to lessen the blackness and hopelessness of the situation.

It was not till half past 11 that the party broke up.

'Oh me', groaned Father, as we drove back. 'I wish I was out of it—perhaps I shall soon be though—for I doubt whether the Cabinet will agree to my proposals. We will have to guard against the temptation' he added, a minute later, 'of asking for more than is absolutely necessary, for the sake of being out of it all'.

13 Apr., Th.

Mr Parnell is lost! Not only was he too late for his nephew's funeral, but he has never arrived in Paris at all. All his most faithful friends are waiting for him in vain. It is even said that in Paris nothing was known about the nephew's death and funeral, and that Mr Parnell's sister is at Nice, not Paris.

Father suggests that he may have gone to her there—or it is possible that he may be all this time in seclusion in London, as he was once before when he was supposed to be in Paris.

Anyhow, the papers are in a considerable flutter, and Mr Parnell's friends a good deal perplexed by this disappearance of their hero.

Father wrote to Lord Hartington. Mother and I walked with Father to the Vice Regal, Father going on from there with Lord Carlingford. We returned by the Beech Walk—which was looking lovely on this first real spring day.

We talked over last night—and the future. Mother had talked things over quietly last night with Father.

To-day he seems quite like himself again.

A strong speech of Lord Salisbury's at Liverpool in favour of Peasant Proprietorship—reported this morning.

A lovely afternoon—walked across the Park to the Royal Hospital.

Lord Frederick Cavendish arrived. Mr Clifford Lloyd and Captain Slacke to dinner.

Reference was made to a letter by Mr O'Donnell in the *Times* declaring that the whole question at present is the Arrears—'which is not true' is Father's comment, and this is entirely corroborated by the two Magistrates. There are parts of the country (Connemara and Donegal) where the arrears question is really an obstacle to peace, the people there being bona-fide unable to pay, but to sweep away all arrears by legislation, all over Ireland, would be simply a premium on dishonesty.

Moreover, there is a danger that by enforcing compulsory settlements between landlord and tenants in the matter of arrears, you might prevent such a voluntary settlement as that for instance which is now being offered to very poor tenants on the Dillon estate—very much to their advantage.

I could not help thinking during the discussion this evening on various subjects connected with Ireland—Mr Drinkwater and his tramways schemes, the Archbishop of Toronto and emigration, landlords and tenants, farmers and priests—that the *Pall Mall Gazette* might do worse than look at Ireland through the eyes of the Chief Secretary, which it thinks are closed to everything but the reports of the state of the country furnished by the Minions of Dublin Castle.

Mr Parnell has arrived in Paris and is staying with his sister.

14 Apr., Fri.

A letter to Father from Mr Gladstone.

Another speech by Lord Salisbury with a violent attack on the Chief Secretary for not having attended the Lords' Committee—he was afraid, Lord S. thinks, to have his appointments of the Sub-Commissioners looked into, they were so egregiously bad and unfair.

Read the rebel papers, very mild this week.

Drove with Father and Lord Frederick into Dublin. Both of them deeply absorbed in the discussion of possible schemes for facilitating Peasant Proprietorship.

I believe it is as representing the Treasury, the most important factor in all such schemes, that Lord Frederick is over here now. Mr W. H. Smith was over in Ireland making enquiries in the same direction, tending to some proposition respecting State aid for the extension of the Purchase Clauses, to come from the Conservative party.

'The Home Rulers are already beginning to rise to the bait' says Father; it would be very desirable to know what the Conservative proposal is going to be—whatever the Govt bring forward is sure to be flung back in their faces by the Parnellites (who would prefer to make common cause wwith the Tories).

Lord Frederick wishes that the Govt and Opposition leaders could compare notes—agree that this is not a party matter, and refer their respective schemes to a Committee.

Meanwhile Mr W. H. Smith, whose plans had been based on the Church Surplus which Lord Frederick declares is almost nothing in reality, has probably found out by this time that the difficulties in drawing out a fair and workable scheme increase as you get nearer the question.

After leaving Father at the Castle and Lord Frederick at the Shelbourne to meet Mr Welby, of the Treasury, I drove home by the N. Circular Road to try and find the Carpenters. Found *a* Mrs Carpenter but not the right Mrs Carpenter, she and the whole family having gone away from there some weeks ago, and being succeeded by strangers and namesakes.

A cold wet afternoon. A call from Archdeacon Lee and his daughters. Read *John Inglesant*[1]—a most absorbing and attractive book.

Lord Frederick and Mr Welby to dinner.

Played whist in the evening. 'If only we could get the Tories to show us their cards' exclaimed Father in the middle of the game, his mind being never very far away from his work.

A telegram from Oakel to say he would arrive next morning.

15 Apr., Sat.

Oakel arrived—but with most grievous intelligence: our dearest Rob had been lost in Buckingham Palace Road two days ago. He had advertised, and been to the police station, and we can do nothing but wait and hope.

Mr Sheil has been elected for Meath.[2] He was in Parliament before, and only once made a speech, and that not audible, so he is not formidable in the same way as Mr Sexton and Mr Healy.

He is said to be a personal friend of Mr Parnell's; his election is owing to the patronage of Bishop Nulty and the clergy, Mr Egan having expressly written from Paris to protest against his return. In so far as Mr Sheil's election has been got through without excitement, and is contrary to the wishes of Mr Egan, it is a satisfactory circumstance: at any rate it might have been much worse.

Father and Lord Frederick Cavendish to Dublin—Lord Frederick leaving for England in the evening.

Father had an interview in the course of the day with Lord Richard Grosvenor, who called to see him on his way from Abbeyleix.

It seems privately that Lord Richard shared the opinion of the *Leeds Mercury*—that Mr Chamberlain has a good deal to say to the attacks on the Chief Sec. and his policy in the *Pall Mall Gazette*. Mother entirely refuses to believe that Mr Chamberlain has been guilty of this treachery to a colleague.

In the midst of his other business to-day Father sent off a telegram to Mr Anderson[3] at the Home Office about Rob, who he explained 'was a friend of his'.

Mother and I in the afternoon to a musical party at Mrs Palles's, wife of the Chief Baron.

---

[1] By J. H. Shorthouse; first published in May 1881.

[2] Moody, *Davitt*, p. 500.

[3] Robert (1841–1918): brother of Samuel Lee (see above, p. 270); Ll.D. 1875; home office adviser on political crime since 1868; described his work in *Sidelights on the home rule movement* (1906) and *The lighter side of my official life* (1910).

On taking me down to tea Lord O'Hagan surprised me by suddenly enquiring if there had ever been any quarrel between my Father and John Morley—any difficulty about a place?

Mr Bagwell—a good Irish landlord—to dinner—a most indefatigable talker, he never ceased from the moment he appeared to the moment he went away.

16 Apr., Sun.

Mother, Oakel and I to church at the Hibernian—Father hard at work preparing his Memorandum for the Cabinet.

Mr Edward O'Brien, Lord Monteagle, and Mr F. Cullinan to lunch. A call on Father from Mr Lane Joynt, Crown Solicitor, bringing, I believe, an affidavit for Father to sign in the matter of the *United Ireland* action against him. It is alleged that the Govt acted illegally in seizing copies of the paper without payment, and damages are claimed to the amount of £20,000.

Father, Oakel and I walked with the O'Briens and Lord Monteagle to the Park gates. Oakel and I calling afterwards on Miss Burke.

Mr Augustus Burke and Mr Redington to tea here.

Mr Redington spoke to Father about the tenants' grievance which I have heard him dwell on before—the necessity for the tenant, if he is to evade eviction, continuing to pay a rent which the Land Court, when in course of time the case comes before them, will probably declare to be excessive. Mr Redington himself, I believe, meets the difficulty by promising to return to the tenants whatever amount, over and above the judicial rent, they may have paid between the coming in force of the Land Act and the settlement of their particular cases by the Court; but where the landlord does not do this, the tenants have a grievance.

Mr Naish to dinner; he is very anxious that the Chief Sec. should put a stop to the *United Ireland* action by getting a Bill of Indemnity passed, which would cover any technical illegalities that may possibly prove to have been committed in the struggle to maintain or assert the law.

There can be no doubt that *United Ireland* was a violent No Rent placard, and that No Rent placards were being torn down by the police wherever they found them, but a newspaper, it seems, is a difficult [matter] to deal with, and some of the lawyers (notably the Solicitor General) are of opinion that, by strict law, the seizure of the papers cannot be justified.

As far as he personally is concerned Father declares 'that he would rather pay £200 (the claim for £20,000 is as Mr Naish says 'poetry') out of his own pocket than have to carry a Bill of Indemnity for himself through the House.'

When the action comes on (which may possibly not be till November) the Chief Sec. will have to appear as a witness.

After dinner Father read Mr Naish part of his Memorandum. Much talk over the Arrears and Purchase question. As regards the latter the great difficulty seems to be that no one—State, corporate body, or individual—dare guarantee the continuous payment of his purchase money by the Irish tenant, whom it is proposed to convert into a proprietor.

The Irish farmers, it is said, are firmly convinced that if only they wait long enough they will get the land for nothing; and this being so, it seems doubtful whether they will not feel it as intolerable a grievance to have to redeem their land by the payment of an annual sum, in the form of purchase money, as to be called on to pay rent.

In fact, considering the advantages in the way of security and right of sale, which they enjoy under the new Act, as tenants, it is difficult to see what the farmers have to gain by purchase, unless this is offered them on such very easy terms as to amount annually to less than the judicial rent.

If the landlords are to be bought out on such terms as not to be a mere mockery, it will surely have to be by intervention of the State, and not by trusting to the tenants' inclinations to become proprietors.

It is said that this will then be 'compensation to landlords', but I cannot see why this in itself is an objection to the scheme. As for this, Father said himself last night that if the landlords could prove damage (inflicted on them by the State for the public good), they had a right to claim compensation from the State.

The outrage returns very low today—only four.

17 Apr., Mon.

Parliament meets to-day. Great curiosity on all sides to know what the Govt policy is to be towards Ireland; in the direction of improvement of the Land Act—dealing with Arrears, etc.?—or demand for stronger measures of repression and power of punishing crime?

Read Father's Memorandum for the Cabinet:[1] definition of the state of things at present—the hopeful side—the bad side; proposals for future action; one of the chief dangers and evils at present the absolute impunity with which crime can be committed; to meet this the Chief Sec. proposes several minor changes—extension of magistrates' powers of summary jurisdiction, etc.—and appointment of a Commission to try more serious cases without a jury. With such extra powers as these it might be advisable to promise the release of all the suspects, on the expiry of the Act, which however, should be renewed for another year. In spite of the difficulties, fully acknowledged, of getting such legislation carried through the House before the passing of the clôture, Mr Forster was of opinion that it would be very unwise, with a view to the government of Ireland, for the Govt to explain their intentions on the subject of Arrears, Land Act Amendment, etc., without at the same time announcing their proposals with regard to the necessary measures for the repression of crime.

[1] In P.R.O., Cab. 37/7, 29.

Walked with Father to the Park gates—we spoke of the Memorandum. His Memorandum on the Arrears he will have to write to-night.

We were overtaken in the Park by General Harman who rode alongside for some time—discoursing of military matters, the behaviour of certain regiments who have been having a quarrel and consequent riots in Galway, the relations between Mr Blake, R.M., and the soldiers in his district, etc., etc.

The understanding between General Harman and the Chief Secretary seemed to be very friendly and satisfactory; in fact Father does certainly get on well in his dealings with the military authorities, in spite of the fact [that], as he sadly confesses, 'he cannot always tell the difference between an officer and a private'.

An afternoon at home. Calls from Mr J. G. Butcher and Mr Murrough O'Brien.

The latter maintains that the farmers are not only willing but anxious to purchase their holdings when they can get what they consider fair terms; but they are frightened with the idea of American competition and will not offer terms which the landlords are willing to accept.

Again there is the further difficulty that frequently, on a 'townland' which a landlord is willing to get rid of, not all the tenants are able or willing to produce the purchase money at the same time, and the landlord refuses to enter into a transaction which would leave him with a patchy piece of property with the best holdings taken out and the poor ones left.

The Lord Chancellor to dinner. To business with Father in the study at the end of the evening. It appears that Mr Johnson (the Attorney General) missed his train on Sunday night, so there can have been no Irish official at all present to answer questions in the House on Monday.

Mr Parnell, who is still keeping in the strictest privacy, has not yet returned.

A question has been raised on a legal point (and asked by Mr Lewis in the House), as to whether Mr Parnell, having been released on parole under the Coercion Act, can be re-imprisoned without having received a fresh warrant charging him with a fresh offence.

18 Apr., Tu.

Nothing special seems to have taken place in the House last night.

Mother drove with Father to the Castle: a bad outrage return to-day. Deputation to the Ch. Sec. from Ulster Presbyterians concerning the New University,[1] the arrangement of which is causing great difficulties and heartburnings at present on all sides.

Walked with Oakel in the afternoon to the Kingsbridge. A quiet afternoon at home. No visitors. Their Excellencies visible in the distance taking a constitu-

---

[1] The Royal University of Ireland, which, in 1880–82, replaced the Queen's University in Ireland (founded in 1850).

tional across the Fifteen Acres with Osman at their heels. They are in great trouble at present, having just heard of the death of Lady Florence Herbert's eldest boy, Lord Cowper's nephew and heir.[1]

Father sent off his letter to Mr Gladstone on Arrears.[2]

Only our own party at dinner. Some talk over the various Purchase schemes, Father declaring it to be his opinion that the only safe and possible way of getting the money for this essentially Irish object out of the Irish people, is by means of a general tax. This would be favourable to Oakel's favourite suggestion of an extra duty on spirits, by which the revenue would either be increased by payments from the Irish farmers, themselves the chief consumers of spirits, or the cause of temperance would profit by their reluctance to enrich the British Empire.

Another article from the Parnellite point of view in the *Daily News*. On the other hand a strong Resolution in support of the Govt, carried almost unanimously by the Liverpool Liberal 900.

19 Apr., Wed.

A black newspaper this morning. The murder of an Emergency Man, an army pensioner named Roach, reported from near Limerick; and also a savage attack on a 'rent warner' at Castleisland. The man's house was entered by a gang of disguised men who shot him in the legs, he making a violent resistance and tearing the masks off one or two of his assailants.[3]

Walked with Father to the Vice-Regal.[4]

A long visit from Lady Cowper to Mother.

A tempestuous wind blowing and a dismal prospect for our passage to-night, especially as we have just received word that we can get no private cabin, all being already engaged.

A rough passage, but none of us much the worse.[5]

[1] Rolf Herbert (born 1872): son of Cowper's sister Florence Amabel (d. 1886) and Auberon Edward William Molyneux Herbert (1838–1906).

[2] Forster to Gladstone, 18 Apr., in Reid, *Forster*, ii, 427–8.

[3] Richard Roche, aged 61, was battered to death on 17 Apr.; three men were arrested but discharged for lack of evidence. John Culloty was wounded at about 7.30 p.m. on 17 Apr. by a moonlighting party; three men were later arrested, one of whom received thirty years' penal servitude (S.P.O., I.C.R., Returns of outrages, 1882).

[4] On this visit to the Viceregal Lodge Forster proposed that Cowper should take indefinite leave, to be replaced for practical purposes by Spencer as lord justice, a proposal that led to Cowper's resignation a week later (see below, p. 462).

[5] This was Forster's last journey from Ireland; for the sinister background to his departure from Westland Row station see above, introduction, p. xviii.

20 Apr., Th.

Father to the office, and afterwards to a Cabinet.

Call from Mr Bonamy Price to enquire how Father was standing his work. Uncle Walter to tea.

Uncle W. had heard from news at the Club, that there had been a row in the House—Mr Redmond. Details from Father who came home at ¼ past 8, very tired. The attack had been begun by Mr Sexton complaining of a circular sent out by a County inspector in Clare directing the constabulary what measures to take in the personal protection of Mr Clifford Lloyd—to fire on suspicion of an attack, and not wait for him to be actually shot at.

Neither Father nor Mr Lloyd had known of this Circular, the last paragraph of which was certainly unwise.[1]

On this subject, and on Mr Clifford Lloyd's conduct in preventing, on his own responsibility, the erection of Land League huts for the purposes of intimidation under pretext of charity to evicted tenants, the Parnellites became very furious, and so insulting in their language towards the Chief Secretary that once or twice Members on both sides of the House rose to remonstrate; at last the Speaker himself interposed and named Mr Redmond; his suspension was moved by Lord Hartington, and carried by 200 to 12.[2]

The evening had evidently been a very disagreeable one for Father— personal abuse of himself he is well accustomed to, but the difficulties this evening had been increased by his having to make himself responsible for things which he did not entirely approve of. Judging from the report of his speech this morning, it must have been quite a masterpiece in its way, both spirited and discriminating, giving no opening to his enemies by showing himself unconscious of the point of their criticisms, and yet perfectly loyal to his subordinates, as indeed he always is.

Aunt Fan and Francie arrived about ¼ to 9 from Fox How, where Francie has been all the time we have been in Ireland.

21 Apr., Fri.

A visit from Sydney Buxton while we were at breakfast to consult Father in some matter about the Emigration Association, of which Sydney is Secretary. This is really prospering, I believe. Mr Tuke is at present in the West of Ireland, selecting families to emigrate, and one or two Boards of Guardians have agreed to pay their share towards the expenses of persons emigrating from their districts.

[1] On 4 Mar. Henry Smith, county inspector of Clare, issued confidential instructions (not 'a circular') to his sub-inspectors for the guidance of Lloyd's escort. The 'last paragraph' undertook to indemnify any policeman who had shot someone in error. These instructions were issued without reference to Dublin Castle.

[2] The division was 207:12.

Walked with Father to the Office. I asked if anything was known of Mr Parnell. 'Yes', said Father but it's a 'deadly [?secret]'. In fact Mr Parnell is at this moment in London, staying with Captain O'Shea,[1] who communicated the fact to Mr Chamberlain. 'Had he broken his word?' I asked. 'Well, not exactly.' What he is doing is not according to the arrangement he made with the Chief Secretary, which allowed a week or such time longer as might be necessary for him to attend his nephew's funeral. But it appears that Captain Barlow, rather overstepping his powers, asked him when he was leaving Kilmainham, 'how long do you want, a week or ten days or a fortnight?' to which Mr Parnell replied, ten days. He seems, however, to think that the offer of a fortnight having been made him, he is at liberty to take it if he wishes to do, provided he does not break the other conditions of his parole—not to take part in political matters.

Captain O'Shea having said something about Mr Parnell not being well, Father caused it to be intimated to the latter that, if he liked to return to France and apply for further leave of absence on the ground of ill-health, it would be granted him. He declines however, saying that if he stayed away longer he would lose his influence in Ireland, in which Father thinks he is right. Meantime his 'indisposition' does not seem to be anything serious.

Mr Lowell to see Father at the Office at 12.30.

Sir Harry Verney to lunch, having come to express his feelings about Father; 'in all his long experience he has never seen any man treated as Mr Forster is being treated.'

A report in to-day's Bradford papers of a Meeting of the Liberal Four Hundred at which most cordial resolutions were passed in support of the Govt, and very nice speeches made about Father.

Uncle Walter to dinner. Father home to dinner from the House.

22 Apr., Sat.

A wet morning. Father drove to the Office—Cabinet.

Francie and I in the afternoon to Weybridge (Mrs Conybeare's)—she returning at 6, I going on to Cobham for the Sunday.

Mr & Mrs Trevelyan, Captain Mills, and Mr Johnson to dinner here.

23 Apr., Sun.

I at Cobham with the dear Uncle Matts; very pleasant to see Dick at home amongst them again.

A day of hard work for Father. At work all the morning: Mr Jephson and Herbert Gladstone to lunch. Father at work with Mr Jephson till 5 o'clock—'arrears', Mr Healy's bill, etc., etc. A call on Father in the course of the

[1] See appendix.

afternoon from Mr Chamberlain. At 5 to the Club for an hour. From 7 to 9 o'clock supper and work, and again till 11 afterwards.

Todays *Observer* announces that the Dominion[1] Parliament—the Lower House—has passed a Resolution requesting the Queen to grant Home Rule to Ireland and to release all the Suspects. This resolution was proposed apparently by an Irishman, but the extraordinary thing is that Sir John McDonald seems to have supported it—much to Father's amazement.

24 Apr., Mon.

I returned from Cobham early, in time to find Father still in the library. Mother drove with him to the Office.

Helped Oakel with extracts he was making for Father from letters, Mr Clifford Lloyd and others, bearing on the question of Land League huts, showing that charity to the evicted is often less their object than to serve as posts of vantage from which rent-paying tenants may be intimidated. The different light in which things appear, in the ill-written letter from some tenant farmer explaining his own particular case in some disturbed district, and the same state of things described with flowing generalities and valuable reflections at the expense of the Authorities in the columns of a newspaper, is very curious.

Inspector Smith's circular has been withdrawn. He has written a very good private letter about it to Mr Lloyd, expressing his great regret that it should have been the cause of inconvenience to Mr Forster, explaining what had been his object in issuing it, and how carefully he had meant to guard his words, complaining of the unfairness—'even for Mr Sexton'—of trying to make either Mr Lloyd or Mr Forster responsible for the document, which had been known only to himself and the constabulary in his district.

There is certainly much to excuse if not to justify Mr Smith's conduct in the matter of this unlucky document—amongst other things the fact that eight murders and attempted murders (chiefly by shooting from behind hedges) have been recently committed in his district. Under these circumstances it is not surprising that he was anxious to impress on his men the necessity for being more on the alert than is required of the ordinary country policeman in England, who, some people consider, should be in all things the model for the Irish constable.

However, of course, the circular is literally indefensible, and Father has never for a moment attempted to justify it.

Walked with Oakel to the Office. Aunt Mala to lunch. Drove with Mother in the afternoon to the Hospital. Father home to dinner.

Mr Gladstone brought in the Budget. A question had been asked in the House by Mr Healy about Oakel's letter to the *Pall Mall*.[2]

[1] The dominion of Canada.

[2] Healy's question was phrased so as to explore the possibility of 'suspect' league leaders being allowed to reply in print (*Hansard 3*, cclxviii, 1272).

Father had been much touched by hearing from Mr Lowell (whom he had met at the Levée) that when old Mr Adams, who is very ill with softening of the brain, was asked the other day if there were any friends to whom he wished to send messages, he had said 'Yes, to Mr Forster, give him my kind regards'. Father has been very much pleased and touched at this remembrance of him by his old friend whom he has heard and seen nothing of for so many years.

The question of the circular (which has been withdrawn) was brought up again this evening by Mr Sexton, but thanks to a judicious interrogatory as to a point of order from Sir John Mowbray, and the Speaker's reply, Mr Sexton thought it advisable not to force the subject again upon an unwilling House. With regard to the Land League huts he did nothing but read a letter describing a conversation between the Chief Secretary and the priest at Tulla, in which the former had declared that so long as the huts were erected purely as a work of charity and for the benefit of the evicted poor, they could certainly not be prohibited as illegal. It was obvious that there was no inconsistency between this statement and a justification of Mr Clifford Lloyd's conduct in preventing the erection of huts when the object was intimidation not charity.

Debate in the Lords on the Adams v. Dunseath decision.[1]

25 Apr., Tu.

A wet morning. Mr Parnell reached Kilmainham quietly this morning.[2] Drove with Father to the Office—some days since I had had any talk with him.

'I believe a great deal has been going on during the last day or two' I said to him. 'You mean about the Parnell intrigue?'—which, however, I did not, as I had not known about this. 'No, about Lord Spencer.' We had not time for much more talk, for, unfortunately, most of the time had been taken up with a Memorandum of Judge O'Hagan's, and the hansom was now at the Office door. This change will, I believe, soon be made public, and either by coincidence or for some other reason is already being talked of in the *Daily News* and *P.M. Gazette*. The latter had an article yesterday alluding to the possible appointment of Lord Spencer, and adding with its usual amiability that this would of course imply the supersession of the present Chief Secretary.

Aunt Fan and Miss Norris to lunch. A visit in the afternoon from Mr and Miss Baines, the latter bringing a further contribution of £8 for the Distressed Ladies fund.

Aunt Mala and Mr Hayes, and two of our Commissioners, Judge O'Hagan and Mr Vernon, to dinner. The two latter have come over to be examined before the Lords' Committee—an ordeal which they do not seem to have found

---

[1] A case, recently adjudicated by the land commission, in which the issue of the value to a tenant of improvements carried out by him had been examined, and decided by the court of appeal contrary to the 'Healy clause' of the act (*Hansard 3*, cclxviii, 1204–36).

[2] Actually he arrived back 'shortly before 7 p.m.' on 24 Apr. (*Irish Times*, 25 Apr.).

very alarming or embarrassing. They were both in good spirits, and very agree-able, and we had a pleasant sociable evening not overdone with business.

I certainly shall be (personally) very sorry when our connection with Ireland and our Irish friends comes to an end, as I suppose it very soon will now—not that Father's retirement will be simultaneous with Lord Spencer's appoint-ment, as the *Pall Mall* fondly hopes and believes.

Father back to the House in the evening. Lunacy Laws—no special connec-tion with Ireland.

Mother, Oakel, and I to Lady Campbell's.

26 Apr., Wed.

Father down early to the Office and House for a morning sitting.

I walked with Oakel to the end of the Bird Cage Walk. He has again been tantalized lately by having the prospect of a seat in Parliament dangled before his eyes—alas, quite an impossibility for a Man without an income—and as yet work at the bar will not come to him. His name has been sent down amongst 8 others by the Liberal Central Association, as possible candidates for Devon-port. This was done by Mr Wylie without his previous knowledge, and he will have to make them take it off the list.

We have still no news of dearest Rob. Oakel told me that yesterday when he went into Father's room at the House he found him deep in papers and business, but on seeing Oakel his first question was to ask him if anything had been heard of Rob?

Mary and Humphry to lunch—having come from Mr Darwin's funeral at the Abbey.

Father, Mother and I to dinner with the Croppers in James St. Met the Farrer Herschells, Mr Brodrick, Mr Lewis Fry, Lord Ebrington, etc.

The debate this afternoon on Mr Redmond and Mr Healy's Bill for amend-ing the Land Act appears to have been got through very amicably so far as the relations between the Parnellites and the Govt were concerned. Everyone was full of amazement at the moderation and decency of the Parnellite speakers—notably Mr Redmond and Mr Healy. As for the former it was agreed that his speech had been remarkably able and temperate.

Sir Farrer Herschell, however, declares that he suspects the Parnellites the more, the more show of moderation they put on; and as for Ireland generally his feeling about it is one of calm despair—in spite of the fact that just for the last few days things have been a little better.

From the Croppers', Mother and I went on to Mrs Playfair's. A great many Irish Members—Mr Justin McCarthy, Mr O'Connor Power, Count and Mrs Arthur Moore (the former shuffling hastily away when I came up to speak to his wife and introduce Mother to her), the Richardsons, Findlaters, etc. Mr

Findlater spoke with great suspicion of the amiable behaviour of the Parnellites, and said that we had better look out for storms, as he had always
noticed that such unnatural moderation on the part of the Parnellites always
came before a violent outburst.

27 Apr., Th.

The papers rather discontented at having had no more definite statement of
Ministerial intentions apropos of Mr Healy's bill yesterday.

Mr Gladstone declined to enter on the question of possible farther measures
for the enforcement of law and order; he also deferred all explanation of the
Govt intentions with regard to Purchase; he opposed the second reading of Mr
Healy's bill (whilst speaking in complimentary terms of the speeches in
support of it) on the ground that it was not desirable to disturb the working of
the Act in the matter of leases or the 'Healy clause', but promised that with
regard to arrears the Govt would themselves propose legislation, a promise re-
affirmed by the Chief Secretary in a short speech at the end of the debate.

The interchange of amenities on both sides in the course of the debate was
very edifying as a spectacle, and has been made the occasion of effusive leading
articles, and congratulations on the 'New departure' in some of the papers. But
apart from this appearance of amity and moderation on the part of the Extreme
Home Rulers—probably a passing illusion—the satisfactory feature of the
debate was the agreement on the subject of arrears; it would seem as though all
parties, including such Moderate Liberals as Lord Edmond Fitzmaurice, were
prepared to support the Govt in legislation for this object, provided—an
important point conceded even by the Parnellites—that the state money should
only go towards relieving those tenants of their arrears who can prove their
incapacity to pay.

Father went down at 11 o'clock to Windsor for the marriage of the Duke of
Albany to Princess Helen of Waldeck. He was not able to stop down at
Windsor all day, so returned about 3 o'clock for a couple of hours work and
went back at 6 to be present at the banquet in St George's Hall in the evening—
a splendid affair, the Queen herself dining with her guests for the first time for
many years.

Mother went to meet Father at Paddington in the afternoon, and I went in
the carriage with him to the station in the evening. He told me that it was
settled about Lord Spencer—he would go over to Dublin almost immediately;
the fact was not yet public, but it would probably soon get out. He gave me an
amusing account of the way in which affairs of state had been transacted under
difficulties in the very midst of the marriage ceremonial at Windsor. Mr
Gladstone had brought his letters to Lord Cowper and to the Queen with him
in his red box, and Father being very anxious to see them in good time Mr
Gladstone gave them to him in the Chapel. He read what he could, but not

wishing to be shut into his stall and left behind at the end of the service, he was hardly able to get through all, and, even as it was, he was almost the last, and found himself left behind with the red box on his hands, Mr Gladstone having walked on; however, Father hurried on to join him and get rid of the box, explaining that for the Prime Minister to be seen with it would surprise no one, whereas the crowd would certainly imagine if they saw the Chief Secretary with this mark of official work about him that there was some bad news from Ireland.

When they got back to the Castle, an impromptu Cabinet council was held in the Equerrys' Room, an unfortunate equerry who ventured in being apparently much surprised at finding the room taken possession of and himself expelled.

It was at this informal cabinet that Mr Gladstone announced to his colleagues—or rather to those of them who had not been already informed, including Mr Bright [and] Mr Chamberlain—the intended change in the Viceroyalty of Ireland.

An article in this evening's *P.M. Gazette* on the supposed 'New departure' in Ireland apropos specially of Wednesday's debate. To read this curious article one would suppose that the altered and more rational tone of the debate last night had been due to a sudden and tardy repentance on the part of the Govt, who were at last beginning to recognise the necessity of treating the Parnellites like men and brothers, and of acknowledging in fact, if not in word, their error in having even thought of arresting, as dangerous to the public peace in Ireland, a man like Mr Parnell, whose name now appeared on the back of a Bill distinguished by 'judgment, fairness and moderation'.

Considering that Mr Parnell's conduct in October last was certainly not either well judged, fair, or moderate, it must be allowed that, if the present attitude of his party is sincere, the 'new departure' is not only on the side of the Government.

The *Irish Times* in fact construes Mr Parnell's action as a tacit withdrawal of the No Rent Manifesto, and claims to have been a true prophet when it hinted a week or two ago that some such 'new departure' and retreat from an untenable position would signalize Mr Parnell's excursion from Kilmainham and opportunities for conferring with his friends outside.

28 Apr., Fri.

A question of Mr Cowen's to be answered by the Chief Secretary this evening—'whether he will not direct that Mr Parnell, Mr Dillon, and Mr O'Kelly be released from prison?'

As soon as breakfast was over, Father called me into the library to dictate an anwer, the drift of which was that Mr Parnell's case would have to be considered from the same point of view as those of others detained under the Protection Act. The state of the country was not such that Mr Parnell could not endanger the public peace if he chose to do so; and this being so, he could not be released without giving an assurance that he would refrain from using his influence for the same purposes as those with which he had been charged in the original warrants for his arrest.[1]

A call on Father from Mr Clifford Lloyd, who afterwards went down to the House, and was introduced by him to Mr Bright.

Aunt Fanny Lucy, Lucy, Francie and I to the Private view of the Royal Academy. To tea in the afternoon with Lucy at Amy Mulholland's.

Father home to dinner bringing Lord Emly with him—the latter very gloomy about the state of Ireland, and highly indignant at a long letter in the *Pall Mall* of this evening, professing to give a history of Lord Dillon's estate, and crammed with false statements from beginning to end.

Father had not given his answer in the House. Mr Gladstone had replied to Mr Cowen—declining to give an answer at the time, and postponing all consideration of the question till Tuesday when his right honourable friend was to make a statement (apropos of Sir John Hay's Motion) for the release of the Suspects.

Lucy and Dick at dinner, they going afterwards with Francie and Oakel to an evening party at Mrs Buxton's. I with Father and Mother to Marlborough House—a party to meet the King and Queen of the Netherlands.

After the others had gone to the Buxtons', and while we were waiting for the carriage, I had a few words with Father in the drawing room; 'Very likely before next Tuesday is over, I shall be out of office', he told me.

There is no Cabinet to-morrow, but one on Monday, at which I suppose everything will be settled, and then on Tuesday comes the statement to Parliament of what measures the Govt mean to take and to insist upon, for the maintenance of law and order, and the protection of life and property in Ireland.

'Things have come to a great crisis' Father said as we drove to Marlborough House.

'It is not to me you need tell that' answered Mother; adding 'I never knew anything like the way in which things have been allowed to drift'.

A perfect galaxy of royalties and serene highnesses at Marlborough House. The Princess of Wales beautiful as ever, carrying off her elaborate blue and silver dress—the whole front of the body roped and wreathed in pearls—with the air of one to whom fine clothes are natural and becoming. The same could hardly be said of the Duchess of Edinburgh who has grown painfully fat, and whose plain round face looked plainer, though more smiling than ever; nor of the bright little Duchess of Connaught, or the young Queen of the Netherlands, both of whom looked thoroughly amiable but in no way model princesses in the matter of beauty or dignity of deportment.

Prince Teck introduced Mother and me to his wife, who spoke pleasantly to Mother of her hospitality to the former when he was in Dublin; and the Prince

[1] Treasonable practices and incitement to intimidation against the payment of rent.

of Wales and his brothers, and the burly old Duke of Cambridge were as genial as it was possible to be under the rather chilling and stiff circumstances of this royal 'at Home', the Prince condoling with Father good-naturedly on being 'the most unenviable man in Europe'.

The most interesting talk that Father had during the evening was with Count Herbert Bismarck[1]—a tall pleasant-looking young man with thick brown hair standing up all over his head, heavy moustache, and an eyeglass. Judging by the alacrity with which I heard him accept Lord Kenmare's proposal to introduce him to the Irish Secretary, Father's wish to make his acquaintance was reciprocated; and they were soon deep in an animated tête-à-tête over Irish and Prussian land reform. Count Bismarck has promised to get Father some information he wished for about their land system—especially peasant proprietorship—apropos of which he remarked very truly that in Prussia it had taken 40 years to accomplish what the English Government was now being expected to do in a couple of years.

29 Apr., Sat.

The resignation of Lord Cowper[2] and appointment of Lord Spencer announced in the papers this morning. Comments of the different papers according to their kind—all of them occupied with speculations as to how far this portends the 'new departure' and release of the Suspects.

The *Daily News* (which of late has taken entirely the line of the *Pall Mall Gazette* and *Freeman*) insisting on complete amnesty and reconciliation; the *Standard* dwelling with delight on the government 'dilemma', of which an appalling picture was drawn; the *Times* gentlemanly in its dealing with the personal aspects of the change, and very cautious in deductions as to its political significance.

A crisis, a revolution in the Irish policy of the Govt, is evidently looked forward to on all sides; and yet, as Mother was saying a day or two ago, 'it is hard to see what has actually happened in the state of Ireland to account for this sudden agitation of which the result will probably be to break up the Cabinet and to put a stop to that process of 'settling down' and gradual reestablishment of law and order in Ireland which reasonable Irishmen had been so earnestly looking forward to'.

The cause in the first instance no doubt has been the natural—though not very reasonable—impatience of the Liberals and especially the Radicals at the inadequacy of the Coercion Act to pacify Ireland in the space of a year. The evil that has been prevented is either not acknowledged or not considered, and the

---

[1] Herbert von Bismarck (1849–1904): son of Prince Otto von Bismarck, chancellor of the German Empire.

[2] The resignation did not take effect till 6 May, when Spencer was sworn in as lord lieutenant. Cowper left Ireland on 4 May, and Spencer arrived two days later.

good that has been done is attributed to other causes. Then came the Chief Secretary's speech on his return from Ireland just before Easter, with its admission that in one respect the Coercion Act had not been so successful as had been hoped—a single sentence like this, forced from the context, served as a useful text for the *Pall Mall Gazette* when preaching on its favourite subject— the failure of Coercion, and the incompetence of the Ch. Secretary—and the crusade against both was carried on with great vigour and acrimony.

The murder of Mrs Smyth and of Mr Herbert, if they did not tend to strengthen the anti-Coercion argument, at any rate strengthened the general feeling of exasperation and discontent, and set every one declaring angrily that 'something must be done'.

According to the *Pall Mall* and *Freeman*, now joined by the *Daily News*, this 'something' should be the immediate reconstruction of the Irish Executive and the reform of Dublin Castle—'cleaning out the Augean Stable'—as the *Freeman* expressed it.

Discontent with the Irish policy of the Govt being thus loudly expressed by a section of the Liberal press, it was natural that the Conservatives—in good spirits over the Salisbury demonstration at Liverpool—should take advantage of their opportunity. They too have been discovering not only the merits of 'peasant proprietorship', but also the iniquity of Coercion ('500 men shut up in prison without trial').

Whatever Sir Stafford Northcote and Mr Gibson may have said to the Ch. Secretary in depreciation of Sir John Hay's Motion before Easter, it seems now highly probable (judging at least from the *Standard* and *Morning Post*) that the temptation to help the Radicals to embarrass the Govt will be too strong for the Conservative party to resist.

But the cause which quite recently has brought matters to a crisis (Release or Not release of the Suspects) has been the most flimsy of all, namely, the quiet behaviour of the Parnellites on Wednesday afternoon, and the moderation of the Bill for the Amendment of the Land Act, which Mr Redmond and Mr Healy introduced and of which Mr Parnell is the author. From the moderation of this Bill and the very temporary civility of the Parnellites in introducing it, is concluded apparently that no further guarantees are needed for the maintenance of law and order in Ireland.

The new policy, according to this theory, is to be founded on fair promises and good feeling—about as safe a foundation to build on as an iceberg, both slippery and unstable. The existence of friendly relations between the Parnellites in the House of Commons and the Front bench will be of little comfort to an unpopular but perhaps innocent man in a disturbed part of Ireland, who may happen to be obnoxious to the Parnellite party out there, and who will see his danger increased by the withdrawal of the protection which the 'coercion policy' had given him.

What will be the effect on the law-abiding rent-paying part of the population in Ireland if they see the unconditional reconciliation between the Govt, which had undertaken to protect them from intimidation and outrage, and the leaders of the party who for their complicity in intimidation and outrage were imprisoned by this very Government?

Meantime hopeful deductions are drawn by the advocates of the good-feeling policy from Lord Spencer's appointment, and all sorts of speculations are afloat as to the probable fate of the Ch. Sec.—the *Spectator* amongst others condemning him to a peerage and the Colonies.

As for motives and probabilities, 'there is one thing', says Mother, 'which entirely baffles the newspapers, and that is when they have to do with a man who thinks only about what is best for the country and not about himself—they are as sharp as needles in detecting any selfish motives, but this rather puzzles them.'

A pouring wet morning. No walking to the Office. Mr Price and Ted to lunch. Drove with Mother in the afternoon; went to see the great painting now being exhibited by the Hungarian artist Munkasey, *Christ before Pilate*, a very fine painting, but not satisfying as a picture—single pictures more effective than the whole as a group.

Mr Cropper and Miss Sellar to tea. Father home at 6 o'clock to dress for the Academy dinner—a conference between him and Mother in the drawing room with closed doors.

A fearful gale sprang up this evening, thundering round the house, howling down the chimney, setting doors banging and windows creaking, and setting poor Mother's nerves still more on edge, her head already aching with the anxieties and trials of these trying days.

P.M.G. on 'Supersession of the Chief Secretary' [*Pall Mall Gazette*, 21 April 1882]

And why should this moment of all others be chosen for a renewal of the outcry? It is now known that the No Rent manifesto is proving practically a failure. It is no random assertion, invented for the argument of the day, but the actual truth that rents are now being paid in Ireland—perhaps better paid than they are in England. Surely this is a time, when the League seems to have been baffled, and when order is on the whole slowly beginning to revive (in spite of odious instances of crime in scattered places)—this is the very time when we should avoid these truculent appeals.

Who wonders that on such a system as this, so unintelligent, so maladroit, so perverse, Mr Forster does not find out the secret of managing the country?

Here we may drop a passing word of contempt on the effort that has been made to set down a piece of honest counsel as the fruit of we know not what mean design or personal intrigue.

But, we went on, though the country cannot change the Ministry, it is hard that affairs should therefore necessarily be left in the hands of an individual administrator who has not shown that he understands how to deal with them. You want a new policy—more intelligent, a better informed policy, and for this a new Irish Executive.[1]

[1] It was later to be alleged by Harcourt and others that this article had decided Forster to resign.

Father home late from the Academy and Club. He had found the dinner lively and pleasant, though fate had placed him between Sir William Harcourt and an empty place which should have been filled by Mr Chamberlain, who, however, was at Birmingham.

The Prince of Wales spoke to Father of the change in the Viceroyalty, adding: 'I understand now what was the reason I thought you were rather abrupt the other night'—a delicate lesson in manners from H.R.H.[1]

30 Apr., Sun.

As usual on a Sunday, Father was not left long undisturbed. Before we had finished breakfast, Mr O'Shea arrived, and Father was called off to interview him in the library.[2]

'An ambassador from Mr Parnell?' I ask when Father has left the room.

'Yes' says Mother, 'I can't say how much I hate him having any negotiations with them', and then no more is said even between ourselves, for I know these sort of transactions are most especially of the nature of a 'deadly'—and Mother has certainly no inclination to pursue the subject.

Oakel and I to church at St James the Less (Francie having already gone to the school), Mother at home with Father. Mr Jephson and Mr Clifford Lloyd to lunch. I cannot help having a strong feeling for Mr Clifford Lloyd; for I believe that his friendship and loyalty to the Chief Secretary are very sincere. . . .

He told me as he was leaving that he had just been saying goodbye to my Father, and that he had felt he was saying goodbye to him for good and all; and he said this and looked so much as if he really felt it, that I liked him better than ever before.

There will be a great deal that will be sad in saying goodbye to those who have stood by us, and whom we have come to know in these bad times in Ireland.

Mother and Francie went off immediately after lunch to St Paul's to hear Canon Liddon.

I with Father in a hansom to Lord Granville's I had intended to remain in the cab while he went in for his interview, but this he would not allow; fortunately for me, Lady Granville accepted my compulsory intrusion most amiably, and I spent a pleasant half-hour with her and her two fair-haired little girls, while Father was closeted with Lord G.

---

[1] This is followed, in the TS, by the extract from the *Pall Mall Gazette* printed above.

[2] This was the interview at which O'Shea gave Forster a copy of a letter from Parnell, dated 28 Apr., stating his terms for a settlement with the government, and (as recorded by Forster) declared on behalf of Parnell that 'the conspiracy which has been used to get up boycotting and outrages will now be used to put them down and that there will be a union with the liberal party', providing that Parnell's land programme could be carried out, and with the hope that further coercion would be shelved (Reid, *Forster*, ii, 436–9). See below, pp 472, 497–8.

After leaving Carlton Terrace we walked to the Reform Club, drove from there to the Irish Office, where the Cabinet box which we had been carrying about with us all this time was put in circulation, and then walked across the Park and called on Lady Reay in Stanhope Street.

During this afternoon with Father I had the advantage of hearing from his own self how things were. He told me again, as he had said on Thursday, that he should in all probability be out of Office on Tuesday night. Mr Parnell's offers—as made through Mr O'Shea—he thinks are worth nothing, but of course the document has been sent down to Mr Gladstone. 'I wonder what he will think of what I have sent him?' Father speculates as we walk home together.

The great stumbling block is the question of unconditional release; as far as Father himself is concerned, he has clearly made up his mind that he cannot under those circumstances be responsible for the administration of the Government in Ireland. But then how about Lord Spencer? His views on the subject are surely the same as Father's, and how can he any more than the Chief Secretary consent to become the instrument of a contrary policy— supposing that policy is decided upon by the Cabinet? 'Spencer has been a fool' is Father's emphatic opinion; he was advised to wait and see how things turned out, but he became impatient, and declared that matters must be settled one way or another, and now it will make everything more difficult. As for Mr Gladstone, his chief wish with regard to the crisis seems to be to minimize and postpone as far as he can.

There was no Cabinet yesterday—the one on Monday was to be at 2 instead of 12—and the Chief Secretary is not to make his statement till the evening sitting on Tuesday.

Lord Granville, as Father had expected, was highly displeased at the situation, having a great objection to anything being pushed so far as to break up a Cabinet. 'I suppose he understood your point of view?' 'Yes, but he doesn't agree with me.'

The afternoon was fine and breezy and very pleasant for walking. Certainly no one would have guessed that Father was in the thick of troubles and anxieties, and beset with difficulties and responsibilities as grave as ever a public man had to deal with—not to speak of injustice and disappointment which might well have made him depressed and gloomy; instead of this, I never knew him more kindly and more serene—willing to talk, and absolutely without resentment against anyone—such an idea in fact never seeming to enter his head.

In walking home from Stanhope Street we met Mr Goschen, who had been to No. 80 in the hope of seeing Father and now turned back with us and came in to tea.

'I shall be very glad indeed to hear what you have to say' Father said to him, 'but I'm afraid I can't talk to you'—meaning as to how things stood with the

Cabinet; however as it was, the conversation between them was most interesting; at the present juncture Mr Goschen is a friend both in the personal and the political sense, and Father could talk over the pros and cons of Irish and parliamentary policy with him with freedom and, in the main, agreement. They discussed the state of Ireland at the present time, Father describing briefly what the Coercion Act (under his administration of it) had effected, and setting before Mr Goschen the state of things now, with its bad and its good features.

Mr Goschen from his position as an independent member was well able to report the state of feeling in the House amongst members on our side, with reference to the present agitation. According to him there is a strong feeling that the release of the suspects is impending—in fact is inevitable—there is 'surrender in the air', and it is being freely said in the lobby that, after the way Gladstone fell on Healy's neck on Wednesday, it is impossible for him to keep the 'political suspects' (as it now the fashion to call them) any longer in prison. As for the motive of this sudden agitation, Mr Goschen thinks that it is very much due to a mere gust of opinion in the House of Commons, which is eminently gullible, and that this ardent desire for unlimited concession to the Parnellites is by no means so strong in the country even amongst Liberal constituencies.

'But how comes it' asked Father, 'that the feeling against the outrages which was so violent when I went over to Ireland—so violent in fact, that I thought people were going too far and had rather lost their heads—seems so completely to have disappeared?'

'Well, there have been fewer outrages reported in the papers during the last few days.'

'Do you mean to say that people go so completely by what they read in the papers from day to day as all that?' said Father, considering I suppose that at this rate it would be difficult for the government policy to be sufficiently vacillating (a favourite accusation) to please the people behind them, or rather below the Gangway.

Then came the question which is the gist of the whole matter; 'how far is it politic to purchase an immediate cessation of outrage and apparent pacification of Ireland by the unconditional release of the suspects—the virtual revocation of the Government policy'.

'One thing to be considered' says Father, 'is that such a course would be a tremendous step towards Home Rule. It would be equivalent to admitting that these men are what they claim to be—but are not—the leaders and representatives of the Irish people, and that the Govt releases them in order to effect what it cannot accomplish itself—the pacification of Ireland and the maintenance of law and order. It will be open to Mr Parnell to represent the transaction in this light before the Irish people: "I got you the Land Act—the Govt shut me up for what I had done—but now finding that they cannot quiet Ireland without my influence they have had to let me out, to help to amend the Land Act and pacify the country"'.

'What would be the ultimate effect on the relations between England and Ireland of a peace—or at least a cessation of outrage—bought on such terms as these?'

'It would be a heavy price to pay' says Mr Goschen. 'Yes, but on the other hand' says Father, putting the opposite side as usual with perfect fairness, 'it may be said in favour of this policy that a bird in the hand is worth two in the bush; it would be a great thing to have a quiet time in Ireland, during which the Land Act might have the chance to take root'.

It would seem that, with Mr Gladstone, all his ideas concerning agitation and lawlessness in Ireland are more or less connected with opposition to the Land Act; provided the Parnellites show a disposition to use the Land Act, all danger must needs be over, and the necessity for repressive legislation ceases.

'The truth is' says Father, 'that in a great proportion of cases the crime and defiance of the law have nothing whatever to do with opposition to the Land Act as such, and therefore acceptance of the Land Act by the Land League chiefs and the people does not necessarily imply the absence of intimidation and outrage for the furtherance of Land League principles.'

(It is none the less true that for the people to venture to use the Land Act freely, and still more for the Parnellite leaders to come forward and openly accept it (as they do by bringing forward such a bill as Mr Healy's) shows plainly to what extent the Government has triumphed in establishing the law of the land as opposed to the law of the Land League.

This has been done under the system and by the methods which it is now proposed to repudiate. *Because* the policy carried out by the Ch. Secretary has been so far successful that the Land League chiefs, instead of breathing out defiance and contempt against the Govt. and teaching the Irish people to despise the 'Parchment Lie' (as they were adjured in poetry) and to 'avoid the Land Courts' (as they were exhorted in prose), now come forward in the House to propose reasonable amendments of the Land Act, and to present themselves in the light of misunderstood politicians whose one aim is to assist the Govt in making their useful legislation for Ireland still more effective—because this is the result, the logical Radical sequence is to reverse the policy and turn out the Minister who carried it into effect.)

Mr Harris Gastrell and his sons to supper.

The day's work, as usual on Sunday, did not end till late. A call on Father from Mr Hooper, of the *Daily Telegraph*.

Mr Gladstone's answer returning the Parnell and O'Shea communication.

Certainly this does seem a most extraordinary negotiation. Father, in speaking in the afternoon of the proposal had said 'there was nothing in it'. 'Mr Parnell agrees' he told me this evening, when I was down in the library to help him as usual write his arrears of journal, 'that if we pass an Arrears bill he will undertake to do all he can to stop the outrages. O'Shea considers the affair as good as settled.'

'But is Mr Gladstone impressed with this?'

'Oh, Gladstone is delighted—he only thinks it's too good to be true.'

'He had better get Mr Parnell to take your place!' I suggest, as Father gathers together his papers and we prepare to go upstairs.

'Well that is rather the line of his ideas at present' says Father.

1 May, Mon.

The *Daily News* this morning in high spirits over the coming 'New departure' and full of lively speculation as to Ministerial changes—either Mr Shaw LeFevre or still better Mr Shaw to be Chief Secretary.

Mother closeted with Father in the library.

A short visit from Lord Monck to assure Father of the bad effect it would have in Ireland—an opinion shared even by some Irish Home Rulers—to go in for unconditional release of the Suspects.

According to Mr Blake, M.P. for Waterford, the effect would be disastrous— 'the Government would be thought to be throwing up the sponge'.

Walked with Oakel to the Irish Office that he might enquire of West (the Office keeper) whether he had any news of our dear Rob. Nothing is known as yet, but West, who is in connection with all the dog trainers (i.e. dog stealers) in London, does not despair of our recovering him.

Father to the Office and afterwards at 2 to the Cabinet—an eventful Cabinet for him.

Drove with Mother in the afternoon—calls—to the Hospital.

Father home at about 7 o'clock—a tête-à-tête with Mother in the drawing room—and then to dinner at Grillion's.

We heard from Mother that he had practically resigned, but things were not positively settled—there was to be another Cabinet tomorrow.

A quiet evening—Oakel at his debating Society. A talk with Mother in her room; these are very hard times for her. Father home late, having had a pleasant dinner at Grillion's, and been afterwards to the Club.

2 May, Tu.

The papers full of the crisis. The *Daily News* has given up the theory that Lord Spencer's appointment was made with the object of crowding out Mr Forster, and now explains that it was in fact made with the approval of Mr Forster himself (it does not say at his suggestion and request).

Two Cabinet boxes arrived before 11 o'clock. At half past 11 I drove with Father to Lord Spencer's (before his going on to the Cabinet) thereby having a few words with him.

'Has anything new happened?'

'Those who are of my way of thinking are doing all they can to keep me in—they don't wish to go out themselves—and I'm very glad of it, for I don't wish to break up the Government; they are trying to find some arrangement that I shall agree to—a middle course which would be neither one thing nor the other.

'If ever there was a fool it's Spencer; he was warned that he had better wait, but he wouldn't listen, in a really childish determination to get the thing settled somehow.' As to the probability of his speaking himself to-night he could not say, for he did not know what was the etiquette in these cases, and there was no one he could consult—except Mr Gladstone himself.

We were to come down to the House at the beginning of the Morning sitting, for he thought it possible he might have to make a statement then—if he was out, he did not know how it would be about his answering the questions.

At 2 o'clock Mother, Francie and I went down to the House, calling on the way at the Irish Office and finding that Father was not there.

Mother not wishing to confront many of her acquaintance, especially in the uncertainty as to what had actually happened at the last Cabinet, I ran up first to see if there were many people in Lady Brand's Gallery. No one—but a sealed letter for Mother which Father had entrusted to Wilson. I took it down to her in the carriage, and on hearing that the Gallery was empty she came up.

'He has resigned' she told us as we went upstairs. Lord Granville had gone down to Windsor, and no statement would be made till he returned.

A quiet-looking afternoon House, the Chief Secretary undergoing the usual catechism from the gang opposite, his red box beside him, from which was produced sheet after sheet of paper, from which he answered with his usual patient good temper the innumerable queries put to him in different tones of surliness and insult by the Parnellite members.

To us, who knew the strain on mind and feelings which he had been going through for some time past, and which had reached a climax that day, he looked tired, as well he might; one of the last answers he had to give was about [County] Inspector Smith[1]—a renewed condemnation of his circular, but a refusal to condemn the man himself, or to promise that he should be removed from his post for the gratification of Mr Healy.

As soon as the questions were over, the Chief Secretary took up his red box, and walked out of the House behind the Speaker's chair, no one but ourselves up in the Gallery and one or two of his colleagues below knowing that he was leaving his familiar seat by the side of Mr Gladstone on the Front Bench for the last time.

In a few minutes he came up to Lady Brand's Gallery and had a short interview with Mother in the back room, and shortly after she and Francie and I left the House, being told that no statement would be made till the evening sitting.

'Have any of his colleagues gone out with him?' we asked.

[1] See above, pp 454, 456.

'No—Lord Selborne was very near doing it, but Father persuaded him not to.'[1]

'Gladstone was very much moved at parting with him, and so was Father.'

At 7 o'clock, Uncle John arrived. 'Well, so he has resigned?' were his first words, much to our surprise since no statement was to have been publicly made till the evening. However it appears that, Lord Granville having made the announcement in the Lords, Mr Gladstone had determined to do the same in the Commons, without waiting till the evening sitting.

A little before 8, Father himself appeared and gave us a most cheery account of all that had taken place. He too had fully expected that nothing would be said that afternoon, and was surprised when Mr Bruce said to him; 'So I hear Gladstone is going to make his statement this afternoon'.

'Is he?' said Father with astonishment. 'Well, you ought to know' was the not unnatural answer.

Not wishing to be in the House when Mr Gladstone spoke, and yet [wishing] to hear what was said, Father took refuge in Lady Brand's Gallery where were only Mrs Gladstone and her daughter.

Having heard the statement, he betook himself to the Athenaeum, where he was greeted with acclamation at the Whist tables in the light of an old player restored to his friends.

Much cheerful talk at dinner, but a curious feeling of excitement, and as though the tears were not very far off one's eyes.

'Well' said Father, 'I think you might all drink the health of the right honourable gentleman the Member for Bradford, as Gladstone called me to-night'.

'I am very glad of one thing, and that is that I was able to get that done (extra pay) for the Constabulary before I went out of office.'[2]

People were coming to the house the whole evening, the first to call being Mr James Richardson, to express his sorrow at Father's departure from Ireland. Then followed newspaper people, whom Oakel was sent out to interview, telegrams, and cards, but fortunately no one else whom it was necessary to see.

We played a short game of whist, sent out for the latest edition of the papers to see Mr Gladstone's speech, and then Father was glad to go early to bed, being very tired.

Certainly such a day as this, with all that it has involved of political anxiety

---

[1] 'I agreed with Forster as to the necessity for such an act [additional powers], and I placed no more trust in Parnell than he did. I should have resigned as he did, if the cabinet of the first of May had not, by general consent, determined to bring in the necessary bill. . . . The question whether the release of suspects should precede or follow the passing of such a bill . . . did not seem to me, upon reflection, to be one on which I ought to part from my colleagues' (Selborne, *Memorials*, II, ii, 52). Selborne adds that he did not think Forster would have considered it a resigning matter if his relations with Gladstone had not been shaken.

[2] A special grant of £160,000 for this purpose had been added to the constabulary vote for 1882–3.

and personal sorrow, in parting company with old friends and colleagues, must seem to have the wear and tear of a whole year compressed into it.

As for Mother, no one can tell what she has been going through—but her face shows something of it.

3 May, Wed.

The newspapers full of Father's resignation, and the 'New departure'.

A letter to Father from the Queen following her telegram of the previous night. 'Have received your kind letter and will write, but give at once permission to give explanation desired.'

The letter was most gracious and gracefully expressed, and one that an English Minister might well be proud to receive from his Sovereign. The Queen's letter was only the prelude to scores of letters which Father has received from his fellow-citizens in all parts of the United Kingdom, deploring the loss of his services to the country, and expressing their regret and admiration for himself.

An exciting, distracting morning—only Father himself seeming perfectly serene, though rather sad. At 11 I walked with Oakel—Father being at work in the library.

To be with Oakel is always congenial to me, and this morning especially so, when both in our hearts and minds we were feeling so entirely alike.

As for poor old Oakel he had not closed his eyes till 5 in the morning, and was looking rather haggard—'he had not thought he should feel it all so much'.

I found that Father had just been telling him all the facts about the Parnell arrangement, so on this as on almost all other matters we could talk quite freely. Oakel had seen Mr Parnell's letter, and the notes taken down at the time by Father of his conversation with Mr O'Shea on Sunday morning.

The extraordinary nature of the undertaking is even more extraordinary than I had known. Mr Parnell, according to Mr O'Shea, would undertake not only in a vague way to discourage outrage, but to cause Mr Sheridan, the Land League organizer, to do the same. The organization of the League, which has hitherto been put in motion and directed by Mr Sheridan towards the commission of outrage and intimidation, is now, by Mr Parnell's influence, to be used in an opposite direction—conditionally of course on the Govt carrying such a Measure about arrears as should be satisfactory to the Parnellites in Parliament.

It seems that Mr Gladstone does not realize the bad effect it would have on the Government if the letter of Mr Parnell were to come out—still more if Mr O'Shea's offers on his behalf and with his sanction should become known. But as long as the matter is in Father's keeping the Government is quite safe.[1]

[1] O'Shea repeated the assurances he had given Forster in a later conversation with Gladstone, when it was arranged that O'Shea would send to Gladstone, for transmission to Spencer, the

Various members of the family came to the house in the course of the morning—Aunt Fan from Cobham to stay with us.

Father at home to lunch. I walked with him afterwards to the Irish Office—for the last time; how many hopes and fears and anxieties, Father and I have talked over during our many walks along this familiar road.

Of one thing I am sure, that whoever, for generations to come, may succeed our beloved Chief Secretary at the Irish Office, there will *never*—because there can never—be a man who will serve Ireland, and the cause of all that is good in Ireland, with more ungrudging, wholehearted devotion and courage. No one who has not lived close to him can know what he has had to contend against during these two years; or how much of all the good that has been done, and the evil that has been successfully resisted, has been owing to him, and to him personally.

'History' says the *Pall Mall Gazette* airily, 'will record that his (Mr Forster's) two years administration was a dreary failure', but, happily for the sake of truth, and of Father's fair fame, History will not be written solely by Mr Morley and the *Pall Mall Gazette*.

On our way down to the Office we met Mr Gibson, who took off his hat to Father and greeted him cheerfully—'Good luck and happiness to you my friend!'

Father has never seen much of Mr Gibson privately, but he has always had a liking for him, and maintained that he of all the late Conservative Ministers had behaved really well and patriotically towards the Govt in the Irish difficulty. Mr Gibson is an Irish Conservative who has never been tempted, by party hostility to the Government, to play into the hands of the agitators or to try and weaken the hands of Ministers, in dealing with disorder and crime, by indiscriminate abuse of the Executive.

At the Office—where Father wished me to come in for a moment—we found Mr Villiers Stuart—come to express his regret at Father's resignation. As for the step which had just been taken (the unconditional release of the three members), he thought it a mistake, and was the more sorry, since a Meeting of Irish Members of different shades was just now to have been held from which much good had been hoped. This would now probably fall through, as moderate Members who would have been willing to meet Mr McCarthy would refuse to meet Mr Parnell.

All manner of rumours are afloat as to Father's successor, the general impression being that Mr Chamberlain will become Chief Secretary. Amongst his friends his appointment is thought desirable on its merits and as the natural corollary of a 'good feeling' policy; whilst those who have resented his

names of suspects who could if released assist the work of pacification (Gladstone's memorandum, 5 May 1882, B.L., Add. MS 44766, ff 71–2). 'As nothing can be more clear', wrote Gladstone, 'than that he [Parnell] has used lawlessness for his ends, so O'Shea's statements tend to impress [?] the belief that he is now entirely in earnest about putting it down; but that he feels himself in some danger of being supplanted by more violent men.'

supposed connection with the 'intrigue' against Father are anxious to see him accept the post much in the spirit (as one newspaper says) in which they would like to watch him handle a red-hot poker.

Father and Mother dined in the evening at the Charles Roundells'.

Aunt Fan with Canon Bell to the Wordsworth Meeting at Lord Coleridge's—Oakel and I in the evening to Mrs Molton's—Francie with Father and Mother to Mrs Gladstone's and Lady Brand's.

A family conclave in Mother's room at 12 o'clock, to hear the experiences of the evening.

Poor dear Mother herself desperately tired and exhausted. She said that at Mrs Gladstone's it had been almost too trying an ordeal—like being at one's own funeral—every one coming up to speak to her with such deep feeling about Father—half condoling, half congratulating—and all full of sympathy and friendliness.

But in spite of all the kindness and friendliness—how much of what is said at a time like this, as Father and I were agreeing in the morning, is entirely wide of the mark.

One very interesting piece of news they brought back with them—not as yet a public fact—namely, the appointment of Lord Frederick Cavendish as Chief Secretary. Knowing them and liking them both as we do, it was a great pleasure to think of their being our successors at the C.S. Lodge.

4 May, Th.

The stream of letters still continuing—in fact the demonstration that has been made by all sorts of people and in all sorts of ways has been something worth remembering. By writing letters, sending telegrams, and leaving cards in sheafs, people of different kinds and stations give vent to their strong personal and public feelings towards the ex-Chief Secretary. Even the decorous calling-cards are in many cases made interesting by the vehement little messages scrawled upon them, and the usually terse form of a telegram is not allowed to interfere with the sender's wish to give full expression to his feelings. We could not help being amused at the following outburst having been submitted to the calm scrutiny of the post office officials at Bradford:

I Radical of Radicals congratulate you—hold the fort, stand by the guns. Gladstone said [at] Leeds no force no power of force, no power of force through ruin shall allow lawlessness to override the law, and the resources of civilization were not yet exhausted. Heart of Bradford will leap when you come. God save England.

But of all the letters those which most go to my heart are from our Irish friends; it is their deep regret at the Chief Secretary's departure which makes it seem hardest to leave Ireland—and yet is at the same time the best consolation in leaving.

Lunched with Mary Ward, going down afterwards to the House, where Lady Brand had kindly given us 4 places in her Gallery. I arrived before the others, in fact during prayers. I was alone in possession of the gallery. This I was glad of, for it was with strange feelings that I looked down on Father making his way to a seat on the third bench behind Ministers—obliged to come down thus early to the House in order to secure his place.

Never have I seen the House so crowded in every part—literally from floor to ceiling—Members standing in double rows in the galleries on either side of the House, the Peers' gallery filled to overflowing—even the standing room there occupied; in a short time Lady Brand's Gallery was also filled, amongst others present being Lady Spencer, Lady Harcourt, Lady Rosebery, the Duchess of Manchester, Mrs Gladstone etc. The Prince of Wales and the Crown Prince of Denmark were over the Clock.

Our Oakeley with Mr Jephson and Mr West were under the Gallery, amongst their near neighbours being Cardinal Manning, and a brother of Mr Dillon's.

There was everything to add to the dramatic interest of the occasion; the three Members from Kilmainham were an important part of the dramatis personae; Father putting up his glasses to scan them more closely as he discovered Mr Dillon's white face and black hair amongst the close packed ranks opposite.

The excitement and tension in the air were very evident during question time when various little scenes took place—lively demonstrations of opinion, cheers and counter cheers—significant questions—explanations, protests—an outburst of cheers and groans of derision when the name of the new Chief Secretary was disclosed by Lord Kensington coming forward to move for a new writ in consequence of the appointment of Lord Frederick Cavendish.

A still more curious and marked demonstration of ironical cheers greeted Mr Chamberlain when he came up to the table to answer some question about the adulteration of cotton, and was obliged to stand silent for a few moments until this very back-handed ovation had subsided.

At last question time was over, during which the Parnellites had been enchanted to hear of the intended release of Mr Davitt,[1] and Mr Gladstone had to stand the brunt of a succession of questions pointing to 'an arrangement between the Govt and Kilmainham'—an imputation which he repeatedly repudiated.

At 7 minutes past 5 the ex-Chief Secretary rose, and as he spoke in a low voice the opening words—'Mr Speaker I have received Her Majesty's gracious permission to make a statement'—the excited House, after a cordial outburst of cheers, subsided into perfect silence and attention.

All eyes were turned towards him as he stood erect in his unaccustomed

---

[1] The typescript reads 'Dillon' (who was already released) but the MS (see above, introduction, p. xxvii), shows this to be a misreading of 'Davitt'.

place, speaking low, but without hesitation or faltering—except once when he spoke of Mr Gladstone—with an air of quiet unaffected dignity which suited well with his words, and made him in appearance as well as in reality a most worthy central figure in this impressive scene.

A short time after Father had begun his speech, and as though to complete the dramatic effect of the situation, Mr Parnell entered the House, and made his way to his seat in full view of all beholders and amidst the cheers of his own followers.

At the close of Father's speech he was cheered from all parts of the House, everyone agreeing, one may believe, at any rate in the conviction which he told them had led him to resign—'that no public good is really advanced by an act of private dishonour'—and that, holding the belief he did about the danger of the New policy, he could not honourably consent to be responsible for it.

Father was followed[1] by Mr Gladstone—pale and speaking with suppressed feeling. He opened his speech by declaring that the statement of his right hon. friend 'had been such as he had expected from him, from the experience of a long and close association, which had given him abundant means of appreciating his personal qualities'. But in spite of his friendly personal allusion, it was painful to feel that from the circumstances of the case, Mr Gladstone's speech was of necessity a hostile answer to his late Chief Secretary; and one realized sadly what it must be to a man to have to take the step which Father has just taken—to separate himself from his old friends and colleagues, to find himself in public opposition to them, to be used as a weapon of offence against his own party and its leaders, and to have to suffer the ostentatious patronage of an Ashmead Bartlett and an Alderman Fowler.

No one who does not know how strong are Father's feelings of loyalty to his party and his political 'esprit de corps'—not to speak of devotion to Liberal principles—can imagine what a sacrifice it must have been to him to accept even for a time the position of an 'independent Member', using the word in the Parliamentary sense of the term.

The *Daily News* and *Pall Mall* talk angrily of the possibility of a 'cave', and take every opportunity to suggest that a defection from the Liberal ranks will be an intended result of Father's action.

'They know very little of Father', says Mother, scornfully, 'if they suppose he will ever make a "cave"!'

It must be owned that on this evening Mr Gladstone did not carry the House, or even his own side, with him; not ostensibly at least, for there is no doubt that in reality the loyalty of the majority to him is unswerving. But from a debating point of view, his speech was not the triumph which an oratorical effort usually is with him, and I never heard him so little cheered by his supporters.

[1] O'Kelly made a brief interposition, asking Forster to explain his imprisonment for treasonable practices.

Later on, an altercation which he was forced into with Mr Parnell was melancholy to witness; he looked pale and harassed and the ill behaviour and insolent cheers and interjections of some of the Conservatives, delighted at what they considered his embarrassment, made one thankful when this whole interlude was over.

The idea of an 'arrangement' in which Mr Gladstone, Mr Parnell, and Mr O'Shea were all mixed up, had got possession of the Conservatives, and once or twice in the course of the evening they came dangerously near the truth.

About 7 o'clock Father came up to us in the Ladies' Gallery, and at half past 7—the others having already gone back—I returned with him, feeling very proud and thankful as we left the heat and excitement of the House behind us for a few moments, and walked out through Palace Yard in the quiet freshness of the evening air.

After dinner Mother and I went back with Father to the House, Mother hardly fit to do so, but insisting upon it in her anxiety to hear Mr Goschen, who it was thought might speak. However in this we were disappointed, the principal speech being a vigorous attack on the 'New policy' by Mr Gibson. 'You are turning over a new leaf', said Mr Gibson, at which Members opposite cheered approvingly—'a new leaf in the chapter of accidents'[1]—on which conclusion the cheers came from the other side. The debate degenerating into Mr O'Donnell, Mother and I came away about 12 o'clock.

So ended another day—another crisis in which Father has played the prominent part, not certainly to his dishonour. Mr Parnell and his friends are again on the scene—having been released unconditionally and with flying colours—the obnoxious Chief Secretary is deposed, and the new policy of 'good feeling and conciliation' fairly started on the basis of an amicable understanding between the Front bench and the Parnellite Members.

5 May, Fri.

All the newspapers full of accounts of last night in the House, and articles on Father's explanation.

'There can be only one opinion with respect to the manner of Mr Forster's speech'—says *The Times*; 'it was dignified, manly, and impressive'.

This opinion seems to be that of all the papers except the *Daily News* and *Pall Mall Gazette*, which are naturally annoyed with Mr Forster for having troubled the public with any version but their own of his position with regard to Ireland and the New policy. 'It would have been better for Mr Forster's enduring reputation with the country', says the *Daily News* with a considerate regard for his prestige, 'if Mr Forster had followed the usual custom on such occasions, and merely stated in a few direct words his personal reasons for resigning office'; 'in any case his main argument was thin and poor'.

[1] A slightly different wording is in *Hansard 3*, cclxix, 179.

Times, May 5

There can be only one opinion with respect to the manner of Mr Forster's speech. It was dignified, manly and impressive. It was not graced by rhetorical adornments or even by an effective choice of language; but as a plain statement, inspired by strong convictions, it won sympathy and applause on both sides of the House.

Nobody can doubt that a Minister holding the opinions which Mr Forster holds, and which he has held all along as he yesterday reminded the House,[1] was under an obligation to resign when he found that his colleagues were determined to pursue a course involving, in his judgment, grave danger to the State. As the late Ch. Sec. has said himself, 'no public good is really advanced by an act of private dishonour'. It was necessary, however, that he should explain why he has been unable to follow the rest of the Cabinet upon their new line of policy, and he has done so frankly.

At the same time he has acknowledged that his opinion is only that of one man against that of 13, for he alone has left the Ministry.

It is possible that events may justify him in his view, but in the meantime he has been out-voted in the Cabinet, and his colleagues, however reluctantly, have made up their minds to deprive themselves of his services and to reject the warnings of his experience.

This is the general line—the exceptions of course being the *Daily News* and *Pall Mall Gazette*.

The *D. News*, however, thinks that Mr F's speech was an able and ingenious statement, 'but that its ability and ingenuity consisted mainly in the elaborate art with which Mr Forster seems to have set himself to damage his old colleagues'. That 'it would have been better for Mr Forster's enduring reputation with the country if he had followed the usual custom of such occasions, and merely stated in a few direct words his personal reasons for resigning office—in any case Mr Forster's main argument seemed to the *Daily News* 'to be thin and poor'.

As for the *Pall Mall Gazette*—'there is nothing (of the speech) that it would be beneficial to say—with the exception of certain passages it was unobjectionable'.

Shoals of cards and callers[2] again in the afternoon—amongst others the Archbishop of Canterbury.

Father and Mother to Windsor to dine and sleep.

I with Aunt Fan at half past [   ] to a Livery Stables in Regent St., in connection with Rob. Was taken into a stable and greeted by a beautiful colley, but not our own dear dog.

A quiet evening—read the Irish papers—all the accounts friendly towards Father—even the *Freeman* personally civil, and 'impressed with his dignity'.

[1] In the original, 'all along' follows 'the House'.
[2] As in MS; the TS reads: 'Shoals of letters and cards'.

6 May, Sat.

To Paddington in the morning to meet Father and Mother, on their return from Windsor. They had had a pleasant visit—the Queen very bright and gracious; but the Royalty they both lost their hearts to was the young Princess of Hesse,[1] who appears to have made herself charming.

Spent an hour in the library reading the 'rebel' papers; judging from their tone of triumph, and the sweeping nature of their 'demands' for the future, the Govt have little to hope from the moderation and practicability of the party they have undertaken to conciliate.

Read also a pile of letters received that morning which Father had left with me: a most remarkable collection—amongst the most interesting, two from friends of his old days—Mr Ludlow[2] and Thomas Cooper.

The former urged Father not to be too much cast down at having seemed to fail in solving what was under existing circumstances an insoluble problem— for the Irish question could never be settled until it was taken up in connection with the complete reorganization of the Empire. In this, Father emphatically agrees, and says that he has for long past held the same opinion.

As for Thomas Cooper, he speaks sadly of the present crisis being due to 'Gladstone's old fault—impatience', and Father feels that to some extent he speaks the truth.

(Nothing is more heart-breaking in this crisis, with all that it involves of risk and pain, than to feel that, with a little longer patience on Mr Gladstone's part, the good results of Father's laborious patient policy would have had time to show themselves; that what is being done now, with every appearance of a triumph for the Parnellites and the disloyal, might equally have been done a little later as the avowed result of the victory of law, won by the hard and persistent efforts of the Irish Executive during the past two years.

There is nothing more bitter in the present situation than to feel, as many of Father's correspondents point out, that he who has guided the ship all through the worst times is now forced to give up the helm when smoother waters seem within measurable distance.)

Having borne the whole brunt of the unpopularity attending the administration of the Government's Coercion policy, he is thrown over by his colleagues, and his opinion disregarded—when the time for 'conciliation' is thought approaching, the new policy having been only made possible by the successful administration of the old.

The man who 'launched' the Land Act in Ireland in the face of violent and

[1] Probably Victoria Alberta Elisabeth Mathilde Marie (1863–1950): granddaughter of the queen, daughter of Grand Duke Ludwig IV (1837–78) of Hess and by Rhine, and later mother of Earl Mountbatten.

[2] Probably John Malcolm Forbes Ludlow (1821–1911): founder-member of Christian Socialist movement and editor of the weekly *Christian Socialist*; helped to found and run the Working Men's College, Crowndale Road, London N.W.1, since 1854; chief registrar of friendly societies since 1875. For Cooper, see above, pp 137, 142.

organized hostility, who upheld the authority of the law and the right of individual liberty in the midst of what Mr Gladstone called a 'social revolution', has been compelled to leave the Government because the Cabinet, influenced by various minor considerations, would not defer to the opinion of the Irish Secretary as to the sequence of two measures both of which were held by all parties to be in themselves, and eventually, desirable.

'Take sufficient guarantees for the repression of crime and the complete establishment of lawful authority, and then come forward to open the prison doors and announce your purpose of conciliation and remedial legislation', said the Chief Secretary after two years' experience of the state of society in Ireland and intimate knowledge of the various forces at work there.

'Let us first do something to appease those who make our life a burden with their complaints of you and of "coercion", and then see if they will not out of gratitude for this "conciliation" help us to keep order without the immediate necessity for formal guarantees in the way of repressive legislation' said the Government, after one evening's experience of Moderation and good behaviour on the part of the Parnellite Members, and three weeks' vehement and unceasing[1] instigation from the *Pall Mall Gazette*.

The unconditional release of the three Members having been resolved on as a first instalment of conciliation, Father felt himself bound to leave a Govt in which it would have been his special business to vindicate and justify this step.

Father and Francie to Epping Forest—a great function on the occasion of the Queen's formally opening the Forest to the public.[2] It seemed strange that Father should have leisure to spend a day in this manner, but in many ways the first cessation of all office pressure, and the sudden removal of all official responsibility for what happens in Ireland, must seem very strange to one who has been for two years as it were the very centre and controlling power of government there. Even to us there is something curious in this side of our altered circumstances. It is like the feeling of going from a room full of eager talk and stir and excitement into an ante-room where there is space and silence, and whence[3] one can still see all that is going on, though without taking any share in it.

An afternoon at home—writing Menus etc.

Soon after six Lady Frederick Cavendish came to talk over matters concerning the Chief Secretary's Lodge. She responded with grateful readiness to Mother's friendly words of encouragement and pleasure in the thought of Lord Frederick's appointment, for she had evidently been pained, as was natural, at the chorus of indignant disapproval of it in the newspapers.

It is a week to-day since that evening, and I can see her bright sympathetic

---

[1] As in MS; the TS reads 'unnecessary'.

[2] The opening of the forest to the public was largely due to Sir Henry Selwin-Ibbetson (see above, p. 408).

[3] As in MS; the TS reads 'where'.

face now, as she sat on the sofa, talking pleasantly with Mother over various things and people connected with her future surroundings at the Chief Secretary's Lodge. As she was standing up to go and something was said about Lord Frederick being missed at his old department in London, she said with a pretty look of pride and happiness in the thought—'Oh yes, they are all in sackcloth and ashes over his leaving at the Treasury; it is very pleasant to think that he will be so much regretted by the people who have known him there'.

I went down with her into the hall, and she kissed me, as I said goodbye and told her how glad we were that it was she and Lord Frederick who were going to succeed us at the Chief Secretary's Lodge.

It must have been just at this time that it was all happening in the Phoenix Park!

A dinner party in the evening—the Dodsons, Monteagles, Rathbones, Richardsons, Fowlers, Colonel Colthurst and Mr F. Cullinan.

All the talk was of Ireland. Mr Cullinan told me that Lord Spencer had had a very good reception—cheering in the streets etc.; 'but all that doesn't really mean anything', he said gloomily, words which struck me at the time, and which I remembered afterwards.

There was much talk about the affray at Ballina, in which the police, it was feared, had fired without due justification, causing much injury and natural indignation. It was strange to see Father coming to Mr Cullinan for information about events passing in Ireland—'You will tell me anything you rightly can', he said to him quietly as he was leaving.

What follows I wrote down on the evening itself.

I went this evening after our own dinner party with Father to the Admiralty—an evening party to meet the Duke and Duchess of Edinbro'—the entrance hall and passages carpeted with red and filled with flowers.

After leaving my cloak, Father and I were preparing to enter the drawing room filled with people, and a buzz of talking and lights, but were met by Sir William Harcourt and Mr Howard Vincent.[1] Sir William took Father aside to speak to him—as I supposed about some question of parliamentary tactics—and I was left to talk to Mr Vincent. By the look of Father's face as he came towards me I could see that something was the matter, but I was frightened when he said to me 'Put your things on—we must go'. As soon as we were outside I entreated him to tell me what had happened, seeing that he had called a hansom and was I thought going to drive off and leave me to return home in this fearful suspense. But he said nothing—only signed me to get into the hansom, and left word with the servants that the carriage was to go home.

Then he said to me 'They've shot Burke, and dangerously wounded Lord Frederick'.

---

[1] Charles Edward Howard Vincent (1849–1908): founder and director of the criminal investigation department at Scotland Yard, 1878–84; conservative M.P. for Central Sheffield, 1885–1908; C.B., 1880; knighted, 1896.

'They've killed Burke', he added. After some minutes silence between us, he said 'It is awful!'

'I don't understand it', I said.

'They find the pressure taken off', he answered, adding after another silence 'I shall go tomorrow and ask if they'll take me back as Irish Secretary'. 'They'll find out now the sort of people they have to deal with.'

When we went upstairs, Mother called to us cheerfully out of her back room, where she and Francie were sitting, surprised that Father should be back so soon.

He said 'There is very bad news from Dublin'—and at once told her the whole truth, as far as we knew it then.

Poor darling Mother, who has had a great deal to bear lately, could not bear this; she cried out, and then put up her hands to her head and cried pitifully. Father stood over the fire, leaning his head on his hand, and speaking very quietly, but in short sentences as if he could not trust his voice.

Apart from the horror of this, he had a sincere friendship for Mr Burke. 'I feel it most about Burke', he said.

Sir W. Harcourt says the murder is by Fenians, but Father thinks he does not know for certain. As for us we know nothing. I can hardly think of anyone but Miss Burke—and then of Lady Frederick, Lord Spencer and Mr Gladstone.

7 May, Sun.

This has been a terrible day. The full tidings from Dublin were even worse than we had heard last night.

Francie (who had seen the *Observer*) came to tell me, before I went downstairs, that Lord Frederick and Mr Burke had both been stabbed to death in the Phoenix Park.

The ghastly details stared us in the face, set down in black and white in the newspapers. They had been walking home through the Park about half past 7 in the evening—still quite light, and many people about. A car with four men on it followed them, and when they had nearly reached the Phoenix column the murderers jumped off the car and attacked them. Lord Frederick, it is thought, must have been killed almost at once, but Mr Burke after a fierce struggle, for his hands were badly cut, and there were the signs of it on his face.

I can hardly bear to write of it—the look of his fine spirited face, with its flashing eyes, has been before my mind all day, and the thought of what I have just described keeps haunting me.

I had a few moments with Mother in her room, and then we all met together in the dining room, Oakel coming in pale and unable to speak having only just heard what had happened.

'I think we might have a few prayers', Mother said, and when she read with a faltering voice the prayer for 'those who are in any ways afflicted or distressed', one felt that, for once at least, the heart of everyone in the room was going fervently with the words.

While we were at our silent breakfast, a telegram was brought to Father from the Queen—a kind message saying that she knew what a shock this news must be to him and Mrs Forster, and asking how they both were.

Then came a man from the Press Association, whom Oakel was sent out to speak to and get rid of; a note from Lady Monck; a telegram from the Bishop of Exeter, asking if the terrible report was true; and both requiring answers.

At half past 10, Father went out to the Reform Club, and to see Mr Gladstone and Lord Hartington, Oakel going out with him.

Aunt Fan and Francie to church at St John's.

Dearest Mother wrote a few lines, such as only she could have written, to Miss Burke for whom we are feeling more than words can express, in the horror and desolation of her great loss. She lived for her brothers, and 'Tom' was above all the pride and centre of her life; all her movements and plans were arranged with a view to him, and I believe he was as deeply attached to her as she to him.

About 12 o'clock a message was brought up to Mother from Mr Brett (Lord Hartington's private Secretary) to say that Sir William Harcourt wished to see Father; and also to tell us that Lady Frederick was bearing up very courageously.

On considering this message Mother thought it possible that Lady Frederick might like to see her; she resolved at any rate to go and enquire for her, so we took a cab to Carlton House Terrace, and Mother was at once admitted to see Mrs Gladstone, who was in the house. She did not come out again for a quarter of an hour or twenty minutes, and then told me that she had been sitting with Lady Frederick herself.

Nothing could be more beautiful than her bearing, more touching in its sweet naturalness and unselfishness; she liked to talk to Mother about him, and could find comfort in Mother's suggestion that, even out of such darkness as this, there might come light—in the horror and revulsion that would be caused in Ireland against such crime as this, and all who were in any way connected with it.

Lady Frederick told Mother that she did not regret that her husband had gone to Ireland—and she had said this to Lord Hartington, not wishing to add to the bitterness of his grief the thought that she regretted Lord Frederick's having taken the appointment. She had told her husband that if he felt himself that he was equal to the task, she thought he ought to undertake it.

She was very sweet and affectionate to Mother, remembering from her call here yesterday that she must be sure and sit with her back to the light 'because of her poor eyes'.

'Amongst all the things we thought of yesterday we never thought of this', she said to her, and then added 'I suppose that among all your troubles, you never feared this?'—not knowing that Mother never passed a day at the C.S. Lodge last autumn without the fear of it before her mind.

Lady Frederick is not going over to Dublin, but 'she is to see him again', she told Mother, for the body is to be brought over to Chatsworth, and she will see him there—his face they say quite peaceful and unchanged.

Poor Mrs Gladstone had heard the news last night from Lord Northbrook. He came up to her and said: 'You must come away; there has been terrible news from Dublin'. 'Not Freddy?', she said—and then he told her of Lord Spencer's telegram to Sir William Harcourt. The first version to Lady Frederick, broken to her by Lady Louisa Egerton,[1] was the same that we had heard, 'Lord Frederick dangerously wounded', and it was only this morning that she knew the whole truth. But even now, of course, she has not seen the awful story in the newspaper, and believes also that the attack was really directed against Mr Burke, not against her husband who, as she says, 'was still quite innocent'.

We do not know as yet what was the special object of the murderers—but Father believes that it was 'to strike terror' according to the principles of the O'Donovan Rossa Fenians, and that Lord Frederick was probably the original object of attack as being Chief Secretary—Mr Burke not being sufficiently prominent to have been murdered for himself. Moreover he has been going about unprotected for months past; and what has been done now might have been done long before with equal impunity.

It may be that the police protection during the autumn and winter in Dublin has really been the means of saving Father's life, and that the Chief Secretary was only not murdered before by Irish-American assassins because he was well guarded.

On the first occasion that the Chief Secretary was known to be unprotected, he was murdered, notwithstanding that he was Lord Frederick Cavendish instead of Mr Forster.

According to Oakel's supposition, the plan for the murder had been laid, and lots drawn for the men to carry it out, some time back, and they have done it now at all hazards, and even under the altered circumstances, to escape being killed themselves for breach of agreement. It is known that several of the recent Fenian murders in Dublin have been for such a reason as this.

After leaving Carlton House Terrace Mother and I drove to the Irish office for her to leave her note to Miss Burke, and enquire if anything further had been heard from Dublin. Mr Cullinan gave us the copy of a telegram which he was just sending off to Father. It added little to what we already knew, except the extraordinary fact that a Captain Greatorex[2] had actually seen the death struggle going on, but thinking it was only a drunken brawl had not come to the rescue, only calling out to the men who drove past him after they had done the murder 'You have handled them rather roughly'. Captain Greatorex thinks

[1] Only sister of Lord Frederick Cavendish.
[2] Given in *Thom 1882* as Lt F. W. Greatrex of the 1st Royal Dragoons, stationed in Dublin.

he could identify one, and the gate keeper, two, of the men. Meantime no clue has been found to them or the car: orders have been given to stop all ships leaving the ports—fortunately Captain Talbot is back in Dublin.

Father and Oakeley came in at lunch time; Father had seen Mr Gladstone, but it was not yet decided whether the Cabinet would wish him to go over tonight to Dublin as he had offered to do.

Oakel told us that there had very nearly been a 'scene' at the Westminster Palace Hotel this morning, where most of the Parnellites lodge. Mr O'Kelly, Mr Davitt and Mr Dillon were sitting at a table together when a man came in, charged them to their faces with being a gang of assassins, and was on the point of attacking them with his stick when the waiter interfered.

Immediately after lunch Father went again to Mr Gladstone's, Mother driving on to St James's Square to see the Cowpers, whom she found just going off to Lady Spencer's.

Oakel having gone out, I was left to look through Father's drawerful of threatening letters for a certain one which he believed he had received lately, and which professed to be a warning against murder by stabbing instead of shooting. I was not able to find it, and he has since remembered that he sent it to the Authorities instead of putting it amongst his other letters. He had been reminded of it to-day by Count Munster, who had observed to him 'that almost all the effectual attempts at assassination in history had been by stabbing'.

To church with Mother at half past 3 at St Michael's—afterwards to Chesham Place[1] to ask Lady O'Hagan if she had heard any later news of Miss Burke. She had received a telegram from her asking her to come to her, but this, owing to her very delicate health, Lord O'Hagan would not allow. Lady O'Hagan had seen Colonel Burke that morning, and he had promised to try and bring his poor sister with him—in which case Lady O'Hagan would go and meet her at Holyhead.

Father came home between 6 and 7 o'clock; it is decided that he does not go to Dublin. His offer was referred by the Govt to Lord Spencer, who has telegraphed his thanks but declines the suggestion.

Mother says she does not see how the Govt under the circumstances could have agreed to his return to Dublin. Whatever the real reason, such a step would certainly have been interpreted as a return to the 'old policy' and would moreover have caused exasperation in Ireland. With a view to the future prospects of the New policy, more than to the immediate stress of the present time, they are wise, she thinks, to decline accepting his services.

On the other hand, Oakeley declares that Father's return to Dublin at this juncture was fully expected at the Clubs to-day; in fact, so much so that one or two people assured him that Mr Forster had actually gone.

---

[1] The London residence of Lord and Lady O'Hagan.

Meantime, Father has to hear the pain and anxiety of this terrible time, without the relief of being able to do anything, or to give a helping hand, when he of all people in England could give it the most effectively.[1]

It must be no small trial to feel himself shut out of the Cabinet, and shut out of the Castle at a crisis like this, not to speak of the deep personal sorrow which is weighing down his spirits; but in spite of everything he keeps his perfect temper, and patience, and consideration for others, and it is only by his flushed face, and the deep sighs he heaves as he sits with his head sunk between his hands, that we can tell the burden of care and perplexity that is upon him.

After 5 o'clock, various people came; Uncle Walter, who said he had never in his life seen such outward signs of excitement at the Club as this afternoon; Lord Monteagle, looking pale and distressed, and as if he had passed through a severe illness since we all met at dinner last evening; Mr Rathbone, who set himself deliberately to 'pump' Mother as to Mr Forster's opinion, Mr Forster himself being at the time closeted with Mr Becker in the library; Mr Tom Hughes, Mr Bevan Braithwaite, and Mr Cullinan—with a telegram from poor Mr Jephson who has been down at Bournemouth, and cannot reach London till 4 this morning.

At 8.15 Mother read aloud to Aunt Fan, Francie, and me one of Newman's sermons—almost[2] the only quiet quarter of an hour we have had during the day.

Supper at 9—letter writing to excuse from dinner parties on Monday and Tuesday—prayers—Father reading the 42nd of Isaiah—and then at last bedtime for Father—to be disturbed however after he was actually in bed by a note from *The Times* office requiring an immediate answer.

As for the newspaper people, cards and telegrams that have been coming to the house all day, I have not counted them.

Now at last the house is at any rate externally quiet: it has just struck 1, and I too am tired, for we have all, more or less, had a good deal to go through to-day. May there come light out of the darkness, both for our friends and for our country.

8 May, Mon.

A 'Manifesto' published in the papers this morning signed by Messrs Parnell, Davitt, and Dillon, expressing their abhorrence of the crime, conjuring their countrymen to testify the same by their conduct, and expressing their profound sympathy with the people of Ireland 'in the calamity that has befallen our cause'.

No one doubts that in this expression of their feelings the Land League leaders are perfectly sincere. Nothing can describe, no future historian can exaggerate, the all-penetrating thrill of horror and dismay and excitement felt

[1] As in MS; the TS reads 'effectually'.
[2] As in MS; the TS has 'about'.

in every corner of England this morning. The mere look of the newspapers—every column filled with facts and theories and comments about the one terrible and absorbing subject—from all parts of the world was a thing which impressed itself upon one's mind, and seemed a fit reflection of the universal feeling.

To us, even the smallest details came home with fearful distinctness, from our knowledge not only of the people but of the place—every inch of the ground being so familiar to us.

The bodies were taken first to Steevens Hospital,[1] and then to our Lodge. The post-mortem examination was made in the ball-room, and the bodies were afterwards laid in two of the bed-rooms (we heard from Mrs Adams that they were the two on the ground floor—Mr West's and Oakel's rooms).

All the accounts from Dublin and indeed from every part of Ireland describe the attitude of the people as being one of genuine distress and consternation at the crime which has disgraced their country—the first political assassination in our country since the Murder of the Duke of Buckingham.

There are many statements in the papers that Father is going at once to Dublin. In this crisis the public look to him with greater confidence than ever. What has happened is popularly held to be a direct justification of his recent conduct, and a proof that he was the one man in the Government who rightly understood the state of things in Ireland, and the sort of people with whom any English Government must reckon.

The 'rebel' papers which recorded with triumphant satisfaction last week that 'Mr Forster crept out of the House of Commons a ruined man' (*United Ireland*, May 6th) are now forced to acknowledge that 'Mr Forster in the eyes of the English public has been justified and vindicated' (*Irishman*, May 13th).

At the same time there is a fine absence throughout this country of blind hostility to the Irish people generally, and even in the first fervour of indignation and grief there has been a determination to persevere in justice to Ireland, and an anxious endeavour to discriminate in condemnation between the innocent and the guilty. This has been noticed, and commented on, to the honour of England in all parts of Europe. Writing from Pesth, Mr Pulzsky says

One symptom of the public feeling and opinion in England has struck me very much, and likely to prove a great example to us on the Continent. This is the calm unimpassioned spirit in which, even now, Irish matters are discussed and decided upon in spite of the outrage upon all feelings and hopes.

Walked with Oakel to the Club. The Tom Hugheses and Uncle Matt to lunch. Mr Hughes spoke of the extraordinary outward effect even, which this terrible shock has made in London society; every one carries the look of it in their faces, and people who, in ordinary times, would nod and pass by, now

[1] Near Kingsbridge (now Heuston) Station, across the river and about half a mile from the scene of the murders.

stop to speak to each other of this, for no one can think of anything else, and it is a relief to speak.

After lunch walked with Father to the Club; he said aloud to me, as we walked, the words he wished to say that afternoon in the House about Mr Burke, if he could find the opportunity.

Met Admiral Egerton,[1] who told us that 'Lucy was bearing up wonderfully'— she had had five hours sleep last night, and was now gone down to Chatsworth.

On returning to No. 80, I found Mr Ross of Bladensburg come in to see Mother for a few moments—he, like every one else, looking haggard and worn out. He had been sent over by Lord Spencer to the Cabinet, and was now just back from Windsor. He told us it was not true that Lord Spencer had actually seen the struggle from the Vice-Regal gardens—it was the man coming to call for help, after the murders, who first attracted the attention of Lord Spencer and Colonel Caulfield.[2]

At 4 o'clock I went down to the House. Mother did not feel that she could bear it, so I went, thinking that, if Father spoke, he would like one of us to be there. The Ladies' Gallery was overflowing, many going away, but thanks to Wilson's suggestion and Lady Brand's kindness I was allowed to have standing room in her Gallery as Mother's representative.

Even Lady Brand's Gallery was so crowded that I waited for a quarter of an hour in the anteroom—and thereby heard the cheers, which, I supposed at the time, and found afterwards to be the case, greeted Father when he came in through Westminster Hall.

Again the House was thronged in every part, but this time there was no excitement in the atmosphere, no side-acts, no breaking into cheers or outcry on any chance opportunity, such as often fills up the time when the House has met for some important occasion and is in lively and expectant humour.

Some of the ordinary 'private business' was transacted amidst a murmur of subdued talking, and then—soon after 4 o'clock—the Speaker put the Motion 'that this House do now adjourn'.

When Mr Gladstone rose and began to speak in low broken tones, it was in a silence so profound that I, standing far back where I could not catch a glimpse of the speaker, could yet hear plainly every word he said; there were sobs from amongst the ladies round me, and I could well understand Mrs Gladstone's feelings when she whispered at the end, 'I am so thankful it's over'.

Mr Gladstone was followed by Sir Stafford Northcote, speaking in grave and becoming words on behalf of the Opposition, and then Mr Parnell rose, dressed in mourning, and looking deadly pale. The few words he said were not distasteful to the House, and were quietly received in all parts.

[1] Husband of Lady Louisa Egerton, sister of Lord Frederick Cavendish; see above, p. 213.
[2] For Spencer's own account of the murders, given orally to Robert Spence Watson on 6 Nov. 1889, see A. B. Cooke and J. R. Vincent (ed.), 'Lord Spencer on the Phoenix Park murders' in *Irish Historical Studies*, xviii, no. 72 (Sept. 1973), pp 583–91.

Then Father spoke. First a few words of Lord Frederick, and then a tribute to Mr Burke, as full of true and discerning friendship and expressed in such simple and touching words that, even if it had been spoken by a man I did not know, and about a man I did not know, I should have thought it one of the most beautiful personal speeches that I had ever heard in the House.

Mr Lowther followed, speaking also of Mr Burke, and then the House adjourned till the next day.

The rumours of Father's departure for Ireland so persistent that at 6 o'clock Mr West came to enquire if it was really true that he was going over that evening. He had been told positively that since the Cabinet that afternoon it had been decided that Father should go to Dublin. However, Father himself appeared at 7 o'clock, and declared finally that he was *not* going, which settled the question.

Mr Jephson to dinner at 7.15, before crossing, very sad at returning under these circumstances to take up his old work at the Castle—'he should not know Dublin without Tom Burke'—he had worked under him for seven years.

9 May, Tu.

Mr Burke was buried to-day at Glasnevin.

The excitement over the tragedy of Saturday, and everything connected with it, as intense as ever. Demonstrations of public feeling from all parts of the kingdom—including Ireland.

The Parnell illuminations at Cork have been postponed. There can be no doubt that, on the lowest grounds of self-interest—not to speak of natural humanity—the Land League Members are profoundly distressed at the crime which has been committed by the most extreme section of the anti-English party.

Mr Parnell told his hearers at New Ross a year and a half ago that murder, 'where there was a suitable organization, was unnecessary', and no one questions that he and other Land League chiefs hold these murders in the Phoenix Park to be not only 'unnecessary' for the advancement of their cause but disastrous to it.

Their abhorrence of crime is in this instance perfectly sincere. At the same time, it is impossible for those who were in Ireland during the Land League agitation of 1880 to forget with what complete indifference (if not encouragement) these same men looked on the daily commission of private crime and outrage in the interests of a political cause which they thought at that period would be advanced and not hindered by such means.

Nor can one forget, when Mr Parnell is brought forward as the only legitimate and trustworthy representative of Irish opinion in Parliament, that he was the man who a few months back declared to an Irish audience that, if the working of the Land Act did not prove entirely to their taste, it would be advisable to carry on the agitation on the old lines and by the old methods. The favourite method of Mr Parnell is Boycotting; the favourite method of other members of the Land League, including especially the supporters of Mr Egan and the No Rent Manifesto, is mutilation and firing into houses; the favourite method of the Fenians is assassination.

A visit to Father from old Lord Fitzwilliam, come up from Yorkshire apparently for no other reason than to sit for a quarter of an hour in the library and express his sympathy with the late Chief Sec., returning the same day.

A visit to Mother from Lady Burdett Coutts—the same object. Calls also from Mr Ross of Bladensburg, and Mary de la Poer[1]—the latter returning home with her baby, very sad and in evident anxiety as to the state of things she should find at Gurteen. Mr de la Poer is in the midst of a conflict with his tenants, and they are moreover very poor, so much so that her husband was obliged to meet her at Waterford instead of Dublin in order to avoid the expense of the extra journey.

Mr Trevelyan has been appointed Chief Secretary. It is said that the post was offered to Sir C. Dilke but that he declined, in consequence of a seat in the Cabinet not being attached.

A Mr Hamilton[2] from the Admiralty Office has been appointed Under-Secretary—at any rate temporarily—and Colonel Brackenbury, said to be a very efficient and distinguished officer, succeeds Colonel Hillier as head of the Constabulary.[3]

Amongst the many drawbacks which Father has had to contend against during his two years' administration, Colonel Hillier at the Constabulary has been one.

In England, Mr Campbell-Bannerman[4] goes to Mr Trevelyan's place, Mr Courtney to the Treasury, and Mr Evelyn Ashley to the Colonies.

Walked with Father to the Club, pushing our way through the crowd in the Mall collected for the Drawing Room.

In Pall Mall met Mr Fison, who informed Father with much importance and glee that he was on his way to despatch a telegram announcing 'the Honourable

[1] Mary Monsell, Lord Emly's daughter: married, 1 June 1881, Edmond de la Poer (1841–1915), papal count, M.P. for Waterford County, 1866–73, and owner of 13,448 acres in Waterford and 76 in Tipperary, valued at a total of £4,982.

[2] Robert George Crookshank Hamilton (1836–95): assistant secretary to board of trade, 1872–8; accountant-general to navy, 1878–82; 8 May 1882, appointed secretary to admiralty. As under-secretary (1882–6), he was later noted for his sympathies with home rule.

[3] Henry Brackenbury (1837–1914): joined Royal Artillery, 1856; served in India, Ashanti, Zululand, and the Franco-German war; private secretary to viceroy of India, 1880; military attaché at Paris, 1881–2; organiser of Cyprus police; one of the foremost military administrators of the time. Brackenbury was in fact appointed to the newly-created post of assistant under-secretary for police and crime, intended as a stop-gap before the creation of a post of chief special commissioner, commanding both R.I.C. and D.M.P. The proposed reforms were never carried out.

[4] Henry Campbell-Bannerman (1836–1908): liberal M.P. for Stirling 1868–1908; financial secretary to the war office, 1871–4, 1880–82; secretary to the admiralty, 1882–4; chief secretary for Ireland, 1884–5; from 1899, liberal leader.

Alfred Gathorne-Hardy' as the Conservative candidate in the Northern Division of the West Riding [Yorkshire], where Mr Isaac Holden is standing for the Liberals.[1]

Mr Evelyn Ashley and Mr Edward Dicey to dinner.

It seemed strange to see anyone whose one and absorbing interest is not Ireland—but with Mr Dicey it is Egypt.

10 May, Wed.

A letter to Father from Mr Jephson giving a most gloomy account of the bad feeling amongst the lowest classes in Dublin.

In spite of all that is said about the universal abhorrence of the murders and the wish to assist the police in their search for the assassins, there seems no doubt that amongst a portion of the population the feeling is one of hardly-secret exultation. Those who have moved about in the crowds collected round the spot where the murders took place, and that lined the Quays when the bodies were being taken to their burial, report that it was muttered curses and savage satisfaction, that was heard, as well as lamentation and regret.

The horrid belief seems gaining ground that the assassins are not strangers who came from America to do their deed and have already fled from the country which they have disgraced, but that they are men familiar with Dublin and with some at least of its inhabitants, and that the slums of the city from which they emerged have now received them back, and are harbouring them in safety.

Morning sitting at the House, Father going afterwards with Mother to lunch at Mrs Jeune's[2] and meet Princess Christian—no one but themselves and Lady Tavistock.

Drove with Mother in the afternoon—called on the Miss Monks, and tried to see Mrs Trevelyan. They are in trouble from other causes than Ireland, Mr Trevelyan's sister, Mrs Dugdale, having just lost her husband, killed from the injuries he received in going down into one of his collieries at Atherstone to rescue men hurt in an explosion. It was only last August that I was at Merevale and saw so much of Mr and Mrs Dugdale and their two little boys.

Alone at dinner this evening. This day had been originally fixed for a dinner party, then after Father's resignation this was put off in favour of his proposed meeting at Bradford, and then came last Saturday—and this too was postponed.

Father in the evening to the Cos.

---

[1] The seat had been Lord Frederick Cavendish's. Alfred Erskine Gathorne-Hardy (1845–1918) was third son and later biographer of the first earl of Cranbrook; conservative M.P. for Canterbury, 1877–80. Isaac Holden (1807–97), self-made textile manufacturer, at Bradford since 1864; liberal M.P. for Knaresborough, 1865–8 (see below, p. 502).

[2] Formerly Mrs John Stanley.

11 May, Th.

Father left London at 9.40 for Chatsworth to be present at Lord Frederick's funeral. 300 Members going down by a special train.

Just after he had left, a packet was brought from Lady Ely containing the Queen's letter to Miss Burke which she wished Father to see before sending it off. I [was] sent off by Mother to Lady Ely's to explain that he had just gone. The Queen, Lady Ely told me, was terribly distressed by the news of Saturday, and very unhappy about Ireland—'you know, my dear, she has no confidence in Mr Gladstone'.

It does seem very hard and very incongruous that under all the circumstances there should be another Drawing Room to-day. Certainly no one can feel in the mood for it—least of all the Queen herself.

Mother received this morning a letter from Mrs Adams with a most sad and touching account of poor Miss Burke—during all Sunday she spoke to no one, and could not shed a tear, but sat looking on vacancy. On Monday she was brought over to the Chief Secretary's Lodge, and when she saw her brother, she threw herself upon the body and burst into a flood of tears, which, it is said, was a relief to her.

Lady O'Hagan had gone over to Dublin and hoped to bring Miss Burke back with her.

Father returned from Chatsworth a little before 8. He had been very much impressed by the order and the profound respectful sympathy of the immense crowd—30,000 people were present having come in by train from all the surrounding parts, and from Yorkshire. But above all he had been struck by the sight of Lady Frederick Cavendish; as she came out of the church leaning on the Duke's arm, she passed quite close to him—'I never saw anything so like an angel as her face—she was looking up with a sort of rapt expression', Father said. He had been touched too by the sight of Lord Hartington, and of the old Duke who has lost his favourite son. ('My Freddy', was all he said when he heard the terrible news, and he has not been able to talk or to mention his name since—Lady Taunton told Mother when she came to see her on Friday.) As for Lord Hartington, he looks ten years older, Father says.

Lady Ely dined with us. She and I went down to the House afterwards, Father coming up with us to Lady Brand's Gallery.

The scene again so different to when I was last here, three days ago.

Sir William Harcourt brought in the Bill for the Repression of crime in Ireland; in accordance with Mr Gladstone's announcement on Monday that what had happened had led the Govt 'to reconsider and in some degree to recast their arrangements'.[1] This Bill is to take precedence of arrears legislation and indeed of everything else. English public feeling may have been restrained and discriminating with reference to what happened on Saturday,

[1] *Hansard 3*, cclxix, 321.

but it is none the less strong, and all parties are agreed—even, professedly, the Parnellites—that the Govt had no choice but to bring forward at once some measure for the repression and if possible the punishment of crime. There had been a supposition that, so general was this feeling, even the Parnellites themselves would not greatly oppose the bill. False hopes as usual.

Sir W. Harcourt opened his speech with mournful suavity, elaborately polite to Irish members, full of metaphors implying that the crime it was proposed to deal with existed only amongst a small knot of assassins—was a 'plague spot'—'a cancer' etc.—only requiring to be cut out to leave the whole body perfectly sound; having finished this long and would-be soothing preliminary, he proceeded to unfold the new proposals of the Govt, the House listening with increasing attention and surprise, as clause after clause was laid before them.

Strong measures indeed! was the general impression—the Coercion Bill was mild to this. Suspension of Trial by Jury—a Commission of three Judges—renewal of the Aliens Act—power of domiciliary search not only for arms but for the 'apparatus of murder'—authority to the Lord Lieutenant to stop Meetings and seize newspapers—summary jurisdiction to be exercised by two Magistrates—power to charge the cost of extra police upon a limited district, and to levy a money compensation for injury to person as well as property—power to arrest strangers in a disturbed district, and persons found out of doors at night, etc.—In short the Bill seemed to include every suggestion in the way of 'strong measures' which one has so often heard suggested and longed for in Ireland during the past winter, but which then there appeared little probability of Parliament being induced to grant.

One can understand the bitterness with which Irish people observe that it takes the murder of an Englishman to open the eyes of English Liberals to the true state of things in Ireland, and to the necessity for something besides 'remedial legislation' for the prevention of daily crime, outrage and intimidation.

Sir William Harcourt was followed by Sir Stafford [Northcote]—approving but non-committal, then [by] Mr Chaplin who declared his belief that [this] was the strongest Coercion Bill ever brought forward in Parliament, and challenged Mr Bright and Mr Chamberlain to say if they still held to their theory that 'Force was no remedy', to which Mr Bright replied in a short and dignified speech.

Father made a powerful and effective speech, declaring his approval of the bill and his reasons for so approving, and also taking the opportunity to refute Mr Chaplin's assertion that in his administration of Ireland he had been 'thwarted' by his colleagues; differences of opinion there might have been, but when once a course of action had been decided upon he had been allowed full freedom in carrying it out. Whatever mistakes or faults had been committed, it was he who must be held responsible for them.

Mr Parnell, speaking apparently in a white heat of passion, denounced the Bill, and Mr Dillon in a very genuine and dramatic fury followed his example.

There is always something impressive in Mr Dillon's tragical face and manner, and the belief in his undoubted honesty and political unselfishness never fail to get him a respectful hearing from the House.

But tonight his gloomy fury and his outrageous threats were almost more than the House could tolerate even from Mr Dillon, and the excitement caused by the speech itself was heightened by the loud outburst of indignation which greeted some of his wild statements, and predictions conveyed in the form of threats. Mr Dillon with his white face and coal black hair, standing up with outstretched arm and ringing voice to prophesy all manner of evil, and to denounce with passionate intensity the proposed 'strong measures' and every one connected with them, seemed a curious ending to a debate which had begun so quietly and with such confident expression of confidence in the co-operation and good intentions of all parties in the House.

Mr O'Donnell getting up to speak soon afterwards, Lady Ely and I came away.

A talk with Mother in her room—she wondering over the way in which the Govt. have managed their business. 'The whole situation seems unchanged—repressive measures—Irish irritation etc., the same round of obstruction and bitter hostility in prospect—everything the same as before except that it is minus Father, and plus two murders and the three Land League Members'.

12 May, Fri.

Father went down this morning 1.45 to Bradford to speak at a Meeting at St George's Hall, on behalf of Mr Holden—Oakel going with him.

I, with Oakel, before they started, to the Irish Office where he had to search for & copy a passage from Mr Parnell's famous 'boycotting' speech at Ennis.

After lunch Francie and I in a hansom to a tobacconist's shop in Notting Hill, to enquire if an advertized 'found dog' was our Rob. Another disappointment.

Copied and sent off a letter from Oakel to the *Standard*, in answer to one published by them on Thursday from Mr Davitt.[1]

Aunt Fan left us this afternoon for Greenhithe and elsewhere—it has been an unspeakable comfort to Mother having her full and delightful sympathy in these bad times.

A quiet evening, Mother very anxious about the Meeting. How would it go off? Would the Irish element make a disturbance?

[1] Davitt had written on 10 May to the *Standard* in reply to its appeal for assistance in locating the assassins, pointing out that he had been imprisoned for the past fifteen months, that his denunciations of outrage had been thereby silenced, and that he had no information that would help to bring the Phoenix Park murderers to justice (*Standard*, 11 May).

13 May, Sat.

A splendid Meeting at St George's Hall and Father's reception more enthusiastic than he has ever received before—even in Bradford.

An excellent report of his speech in all the papers, especially the *Standard*, and allusions to the warm greeting he had received—the audience standing up, waving their hats, and cheering.

(Extract from *Bradford Observer*, May 13th)
Mr Forster's reception yesterday evening was as might have been anticipated, enthusiastic beyond measure—in this respect also the meeting of last night may be taken as representative of the feelings of the great majority of the English people.

The late Irish Secretary indeed has been placed by the event of last Saturday in a unique position. Though outside of the Government, he is at this moment probably the most popular man in the country.

The Government was wrong, and Mr Forster was right—such was the conviction which found expression in every cheer at last night's meeting and which, being undoubtedly shared by the majority of people all over the country, makes Mr Forster in his present unofficial position more powerful on the question of the day than any other man, official or unofficial.

The Government never stood in greater need of support. That is the first fact which we have to impress upon our minds. The second is that the Government has no more loyal supporter than Mr Forster.

The speech was worthy of the occasion—one of the most forcible—and indeed eloquent—that he has ever made; it almost seems as if with going out of office his gift of speech had been increased.

It would have been hard to find a more inspiriting electioneering speech, and no one could deny that, as Father put the case, it came with a good grace and with perfect consistency from the man who had first felt it his duty to resign his official position in the Liberal party, though without abandoning its principles.

So ungrudging and so invaluable at a time like this was Father's support of the Ministerial candidate, that the *Daily News* intermitted for one morning its attack upon the ex-Chief Secretary, in order to fill its leading article with extracts from his speech—of course without any acknowledgment that the generous surmises of itself and the *Pall Mall* as to the probability of Mr Forster forming a 'cave', had been mistaken.

The principal speeches after Father's were Mr Illingworth's, and Mr George Howard's.

Mr Illingworth has behaved most honourably to his much-abused colleague all through the last two years, and the Chief Secretary's Radical enemies have never had the least encouragement or assistance from the Radical Member for Bradford.

Mr Howard's speech was most cordial to Father personally—both kindly intentioned, and well and effectively expressed. In fact there was no sign of a 'split' or disintegration of the Liberal party, as represented at this great York-shire meeting.

Mother and Francie in the afternoon to Claydon, meeting Father at Bletch-ley. The cross journey from Yorkshire had been rather complicated, and, if it had not been for the zealous civility of all the railway officials in stopping trains to suit his convenience, Father would hardly have been able to manage it. Everywhere along the line both in going to and coming from Yorkshire, he was recognized and cheered by the people at the stations. At Burley on Friday night he was received with a band and torches, and had to make a little speech to the people at the station; in Leeds the next day he was also received with en-thusiasm wherever he was seen. If Father has bitter enemies, he certainly also has many friends throughout England, and especially at this time.

Went to see Mother and Francie off at Euston, the station from which I have so often started for Ireland—never without pleasure in doing so.

The illustrated papers which we bought here this time were full of pictures of the Phoenix Park, and of the Chief Secretary's Lodge—with the hearses standing at the front door.

Portraits too of Lord Frederick and of Mr Burke—of the latter very unsatis-factory, and doing no justice at all to the handsome keen-eyed face.

A quiet evening alone—read the Bradford papers, and wrote till 12 o'clock.

14 May, Sun.

To the Sunday school in the morning—afterwards to St James the Less. In the afternoon to St Peter's, and to tea at Grosvenor Crescent.

On my way back, I met Mr George Howard, and had the opportunity of speaking to him about his friendly speech at Bradford. He spoke very pleasantly of the satisfaction it had given him to be able to say what he had been thinking of Father and wishing to say publicly.

As for the Meeting he had been greatly impressed by our Bradford audience—as every one must be who comes to speak before them for the first time—and as for the splendid reception Father received, he said 'we ought to have been there to see it'.

He did not seem over sanguine as to Mr Holden's chances of a large majority. He had not been a good candidate personally, and there being some impression that he was too much the nominee of a 'Radical clique' . . .

A long visit to Mrs Perceval—glad to hear all I could tell her about Dublin and other things.

Oakel appeared to my great delight about 9 o'clock, having spent the day at Peterborough.

He told me more about the Meeting, and described the way in which Father three times tried to speak, and was each time met with such an uproar of cheers that he had to wait and begin again.

Oakel was glad he had been with him on this occasion—'he had been in so many queer holes with him lately'. The last time he heard him address an audience outside the House was from the hotel window at Tullamore.

There had been one cry of 'Buckshot' in the Gallery at St George's Hall on Friday, but the audience was not favourable to such demonstrations, and there were such angry shouts of 'Throw him over', 'Turn him out' etc. that the man, whoever he was, wisely refused to identify himself, and kept silence from hostile interruptions for the rest of the evening.

(Father, Mother and Francie spent this Sunday at Claydon—meeting Sir George and Lady Grey and the Fred. Verneys.)

15 May, Mon.

The Claydon party home about 1 o'clock.

Father wrote a letter to Mr Gladstone about the grant for Miss Burke— £300 was proposed, which he considered under all the circumstances much too small. The result of his letter was to get [a pension of] £400—he had wished for 5.[1]

The Arrears Bill brought in this afternoon by Mr Gladstone—'one year's arrears [of] rent to be paid by the tenant, one by the State, the rest to be blotted out'.

The principle of the measure to be 'gift and compulsion', not a loan and voluntary agreement, as was the case with the Arrears clause in the Land Act.

The Arrears Bill unfortunately was not the only subject which occupied the House this afternoon.

A question put from the Conservative side brought up the whole story of the 'Kilmainham Compact'—with results which made this week about the most disagreeable that Father has had to go through in all his Parliamentary experience.

The 'documentary evidence' which Mr Gladstone had once unfortunately alluded to, was enquired for—the letter in question being from Mr Parnell to Mr O'Shea.[2] Mr Gladstone made some demur about producing it, whereupon Mr Parnell volunteered to read it himself.

But what he read was not the whole letter—a passage was left out. Father rose to ask if the whole letter had been read. Mr O'Shea made some answer about having read from a copy,[3] whereupon Father produced and handed to

[1] The decision was announced by Granville in the house of lords next day (*Hansard 3*, cclxix, 825).

[2] Parnell to O'Shea, 28 Apr. 1882, in Joseph Chamberlain, *A political memoir, 1880–92*, ed. C. H. D. Howard (London, 1953), pp 49–50. This was the letter of which O'Shea gave Forster a copy at their meeting in Forster's London home on 30 Apr. (see above, p. 465), and which contained the substance of the 'Kilmainham treaty'.

[3] This telescopes the Hansard account, in which Parnell said he had read from a possibly incomplete copy, and O'Shea said he had not the document with him, whereupon Forster gave him a copy (*Hansard 3*, cclxix, 672–4).

him an ungarbled copy of the letter, which was then read by him to the House, after a pantomime of hesitation and refusal. The omitted passage contained a suggestion from Mr Parnell to the effect that if certain specified things (arrears and so forth) were done, he and his party should be able in future to co-operate with the Liberal party.

The interpretation of all this by the Conservatives was that a bargain had been struck between Mr Parnell and Mr Gladstone, and that, notwithstanding the Premier's emphatic assertion 'that nothing has been given, and nothing taken', there had most effectually been an arrangement, by virtue of which Mr Parnell and the other Members were released, on the understanding that they should not only assist in pacifying Ireland, but also give their support to the Liberal party in the House.

The mystery about the letter and the incomplete version of it just produced not unnaturally confirmed this impression, and Father was put in the very painful position of being supposed to have unmasked the intrigues of his late colleagues by his demand for the whole truth.

(Father had told me a week ago that, if any part of the letter was referred to, he should insist on the whole being produced—so what he did, disagreeable as it was, was not on an impulse of the moment to be regretted afterwards.)

But the worst was not over with the reading of the letter; later on in the evening the affair came up again, and this time—by way of showing plainly what there was in the Gladstone–Parnell understanding which had driven him to resign rather than be responsible for its consequences, Father felt bound to read to the House the Memorandum of his conversation with Mr O'Shea on that memorable Sunday morning. The effect of this incident was to renew tenfold all the disagreeables connected with the production of the letter; the true nature of the Government's new allies, and the unsatisfactory cause of their promised influence in stopping outrage were made known to the House and to the country, but it was at the cost of much pain and annoyance to Father, owing to the manner in which he himself had been made the instrument of disclosing the truth, of embarrassing his late colleagues, and affording unbounded delight to the Opposition.

The amicable readjustment of relations between himself and his Ministerial friends which seemed to have been coming about so naturally, over the North Riding election, and Father's generous speech at Bradford, appeared now to be checked if not absolutely destroyed.

Father dined at Grillion's.

16 May, Tu.

Astonishment and to some degree consternation in seeing from the papers this morning what had been happening in the House last night.

The *Daily News* of course furious, and abusive of Father; the *Standard* improving the occasion as against the Govt with great satisfaction—the last of the Kilmainham Treaty, etc., etc.

Walked with Father to Lady Ely's, he afterwards to the House—morning sitting.

Colonel Pearson to lunch. Even he full of last night's scene—evidently the talk of the clubs—'a tremendous blow to the Government'.

Mrs Trevelyan at half past 5 to talk things over with Mother: we felt much drawn towards her, she was very despondent and much moved, throwing her arms round Mother when she went away, and speaking with much feeling. She was expecting Mr Trevelyan back that evening. So was Lady Frederick expecting her husband back from Ireland when she came to see Mother last Saturday week.

A dinner party here in the evening—Tenterdens, Slaggs, Algernon Wests, Baron Solvyns, Mrs Buxton and May, Mr Nadal, Hibberts, and Mr Errington.

Everyone informing us separately that it had been a dreadful afternoon at the House. The Kilmainham affair again—Mr Balfour violent, talking of 'infamy'—Mr Gladstone excited almost to passion—Mr O'Shea personally insulting to Father—everyone agreeing that the afternoon had been supremely unpleasant and unprofitable. Father so tired that he could hardly keep up the semblance of talk at dinner.

Nothing can be more trying than the present situation for him; one feels that personally it is almost worse to bear than anything we have had yet. And yet it had to be done, under the circumstances which arose on Monday.

If nothing had been said, Father would have kept silence to the end of time, so far as his own personal justification alone was concerned; but for the sake of the effect in Ireland, if for nothing else, a false version—a false impression— could not be left unchallenged by the one man of all others who was able to let the truth be known before it was too late.

The attacks on him for his conduct on Monday are of course unusually bitter and offensive, the matter being regarded as a purely personal affair, in which the ex Chief Secretary, out of vindictiveness against his late colleagues and Mr Parnell, has condescended to make an unfair and disloyal use of Cabinet documents, with no other object than to damage the reputation and prospects of political opponents and quondam political friends.

This, needless to say, is the opinion of the *Pall Mall Gazette*, the *Nonconformist*, the *Sussex Daily News*, and other authorities quoted by the *P.M.G.*

But there are others who, from the first, have seen that the sole object of Mr Forster's action was a public one, and that, however disagreeable to himself in its immediate consequences, no other action would have been possible for him.

He would have belied the whole principle on which his recent course has been founded if he had not interfered, when he saw a false version being put before the country of the relations between the Land League and the Govt.; for it was no abstract question of historical truth ('history', says the *P.M.G.* truly, 'can afford to wait') that was involved, but the very foundation on which the policy of this country towards Ireland at the present juncture, and the relations between the Irish people and their would-be leaders, were to be based.

With a view to action in the immediate future it was well that two truths should at once be made known—one especially in Ireland, the other especially in England. The first that Mr Parnell, 'the uncrowned prince', the head of the 'National Land League', had not only thought it advisable to tender conditional support to the Liberal party, but also to keep that offer secret by suppressing the passage in his letter referring to it. Second, that the agents whose services had been proffered by Mr Parnell to the Govt for the suppression of outrage in Ireland were the identical men whose avowed mission it had been to promote and organize outrage when the cause of Mr Parnell and the League had required it.

Hence the disclosures made on Monday night, however inconvenient and even painful in their immediate consequences, served a more important public end in the long run—the chief moral being that neither from the Irish nor the English point of view is it wise to found a policy on private arrangement with men as to whose motives and methods there is very reasonable ground for suspicion.

With certain violent exceptions the general opinion as to Father's conduct on Monday is friendly, the belief being freely expressed, and the most so by those who understand Ireland as well as England, that under the circumstances he could not have done differently.

17 May, Wed.

Walked with Father to the Central Liberal Office in Parliament St. Talked over yesterday, and this miserable affair (which made me more unhappy at first than now when I have come to think it over).

'The party are furious with me', Father said.

A consultation with Mr Sellar as to whether a 'pair' could not be found for the election of Thursday; very doubtful—the tories were making an unwonted push to send down all their available men. Finally Father decided to go himself in any case, thinking it might have a good effect on the election, which gives cause for anxiety.

Mr Sellar thinks that recent events will have a damaging effect at a General Election, but at the same time quite agrees that Father, even in this last affair, was bound to act as he did.

'Some of the more violent spirits are angry', but he does not think there is hostility to Father in the country.

As for the *Pall Mall* in this matter, it represents, so Mr Sellar says, nothing beyond its own clique, certainly not the country.

'Would not what has happened be against Oakeley's chance of being accepted as the Liberal candidate at Devonport—at any rate for the time?' Mr Sellar thought decidedly not. So far as Liberal opinion in Devonport was divided at all, it would be in Father's favour.

Father to the House.

I, in the afternoon to Lady Monteagle's. She read several interesting but sad letters from Ireland—very gloomy, almost despairing about the country; the demonstrations and condolence about the Murders very hollow and artificial, the real feeling amongst the people is of indifference if not worse.

Every one agrees in this: there is no longer any natural horror at murder amongst the people, still less murder of an Englishman and an official.

One's hope that the air might in some measure have been purified by this last appalling shock, that some leverage point might have been found from which the priests and natural leaders of the people might have raised the degraded conscience of their countrymen, must now be given up. The gospel of hate has been preached too long and taken root too deeply for any sentiment of mere humanity to move the hearts of the Irish people.

The general feeling at present seems to be simply one of expectation—waiting to see what will be the next development, a desire to get some advantage out of whatever happens, whether it be a new Arrears Bill or a fresh murder.

Father, Mother and I dined at the Peases'. Father and I afterwards to the State Ball—many friends here to tell Father most cordially that he could not have acted differently. The Prince of Wales very pleasant and sensible. Fortunately H.R.H. has not got the Queen's antipathy to Mr Gladstone. Many of our Irish acquaintance present, Lord Cowper, Lord Powerscourt, Ch. Justice Morris, etc., the latter very cross about the proposed Commission of Judges—in fact this part of the bill is not well received, especially by the Judges.[1]

Father very tired. 'This sort of personal thing takes it out of you more than anything', he said as we drove home.

18 May, Th., Ascension Day

Mr Jephson to see Mother, having just returned from Dublin. There is still no clue to the murderers. The police theory now is that the assassinations were planned from Paris by Mr Egan, one reason being [that] the plot must have involved a great expenditure of money, and that the O'Donovan Rossa gang are known to be very poor. Mr Egan has control of the American Land League money, and he is said to have entirely broken with Mr Parnell, whose policy he would have no objection to defeat.

---

[1] The law officers at the end of April had been opposed to the idea of any such special tribunals; Law remarked: 'No Irish judge, as I believe, nor any Irish barrister *worth having*, would accept the position' (B.L., Add. MS 44628, ff 81–3). The clause was however passed as part of the crimes act, but never put into force.

The greatest precautions are now being enforced in Dublin for the protection of all the Castle officials: Mr Jephson (who has been appointed private Secretary to Mr Trevelyan) is always followed by a policeman, and Lord and Lady Spencer and Mr Trevelyan never go out without an escort of soldiers, police and armed detectives.

To church at St Peter's with Aunt Fanny Lucy; Mrs Tom Hughes, Gertrude Robinson, and Dr Perry to lunch. Drove with Mother—calls.

Alone at dinner.

Debate on Prevention of Crime Bill continued. Radicals pressing for amendments—press regulations objected to—also summary jurisdiction of Magistrates (about the most important feature in the bill).

Excellent speech by the new Chief Secretary—just the line Father would have taken; lament by one of the Parnellites 'that in one week the Chief Secretary should already have fallen under the influences of Dublin Castle', i.e. was not obliged to rely for information on newspaper reports, and statements by gentlemen of the Land League.

Father returned about 9 o'clock from Bradford—everywhere he had been most cordially cheered by our Yorkshire friends, and seemed inspirited by this friendly intercourse with Yorkshire Liberals after the abuse he has been receiving from certain London ones.

Father to the House.

19 May, Fri.

Letter in the paper from Mr O'Shea—ill-natured but not worth answering, being in fact no contradiction to Father's original statement.

News of the North Riding Election; very satisfactory, and under the circumstances most opportune—a majority of 2027, larger by a great deal than had been expected.[1]

Uncle Matt and Aunt Fanny Lucy to lunch. According to Uncle Matt, the general London opinion, even amongst strong Liberals, is that Father did quite right—on the other hand Lord Coleridge disapproves.

Drove with Mother in the afternoon. Tea at Mrs Magniac's.

Father home to dinner: talk over possibilities for Whitsuntide. Mother very anxious on all grounds that Father should prolong his time away at Whitsuntide and that we should go to Switzerland; due to his colleagues—the way in which he is used against them, involuntarily, must be irritating; a little absence might have a calming effect.

As for poor dear Mother herself she is nearly broken down with all that has happened lately, coming after the strain of the 2 years in Ireland.

Father back to the House (Opening Museums on Sunday).

[1] Isaac Holden was elected for the northern division of the West Riding on 18 May by 9,892 votes against Gathorne-Hardy's 7,865; see above, p. 491.

20 May, Sat.

Spectator goes against Father in the O'Shea affair—laments over his severance from the Liberal Party, regarding this apparently as an accomplished fact.

The Dean of Durham and Mrs Lake to lunch. Calls with Mother in the afternoon.

Father to the City—Turkish Bath—writing letters at the Club—whist. No Cabinet for him now-a-days on Saturday afternoon—not that he himself ever alludes to this.

To dinner with Mary and Humphry in Russell Sq. Sellars, Huxleys, etc. I had a very friendly and interesting talk with Mr Sellar. We spoke of the really hard part about the resignation—his having to give up at a time when his two years' work was beginning to tell, and the law to regain its ascendancy.

Mr Sellar had just had a letter from an Englishman in a bad part of Ireland giving the same impression.

We hear it also from other quarters.

21 May, Sun.

An article in the *Observer* which gave Father great satisfaction, so thoroughly understanding his personal position in the recent affair and seeing what the motives had been which had induced him to act as he did.

To church at St John's. Father at work over his speech on the Arrears Bill.

Father and Mother after lunch to Lady O'Hagan's to see Miss Burke. She thanked Father for what he had said in the House about her brother.

Calls here from Mr Vesey Fitzgerald, Cola Ball, etc. To G.F.S. Room. Church at St John's. A quiet Sunday. Helped Father in the evening with his arrears of journal, not written since the O'Shea Sunday.[1] We talked over the affair and Father agreed that the worst of it was over.

'I shan't write any more now', he said, as he shut up his diary,

I don't want to write about that horrid mess. I think if I had it over again, I should do differently. As for the letter I have no doubts about that, but I think it was a mistake to have read the Memorandum myself—I had better simply have got up and said 'that's not true'.

However he agreed that to have done even this would perhaps only have led to the same result in the end—as he would certainly have been forced by either one side or the other to produce the grounds for his contradiction.

Mr Gladstone wrote a friendly note to him last night asking if he would object to his showing his own letter to Father (written on the O'Shea Sunday) to Sir Drummond Wolff (who was pressing for more documentary evidence).

Father had none so far as he was concerned, but on the Government's

[1] 30 Apr. 1882; see above, p. 465.

account thought (privately) that Mr Gladstone would do better not to produce the letter—which he read me.

Certainly it would show amongst other things, that the ex Chief Secretary, however much he was cognisant of the negotiations, was very far from approving of them at any stage.

So far as Father is concerned this letter could only go to justifying him still further, both in what he has said and done.

22 May, Mon.

A violent and altogether discouraging speech of Mr Davitt's at Manchester reported in this morning's paper. Practically an invitation to further crime on the ground of the Land League having been suppressed—the Phoenix Park murders a natural climax. Repudiation of the Kilmainham compact, and general defiance of England, and English legislative reform in Ireland.[1]

Apparently a bid for the reversion of Mr Parnell's place *vice* the 'uncrowned prince' deposed.

Walked with Oakel to the Press Agency. He told me that police precautions are still being taken, and with very good reason, for Father's protection. 'They' (the murder gang) 'are very angry with him', and Oakel receives information, showing that precautions are not superfluous.

He himself does all he can to be with him at night so that he may not return from the House on foot alone.

Drove with Mother in the afternoon—to tea at Mrs Jacob Bright's; to the Hospital.

Father not back to dinner, dining at Grillion's. A note from him to Mother saying that he had got well through his arrears speech; that Gladstone was not going to answer Sir Drummond Wolff to night; and that Sir Erskine May had told him that he had just written to 'the Occidental' offering him a Clerkship in the House of Commons.

Arrears debate—Conservative obstruction—House sat till 3. Debate adjourned.

23 May, Tu.

Walked with Oakel—to Mr Baldwin Brown's Lecture on Greek Art.

Call on Father from Mr Francis Buxton and from Lady and Miss (Thomas) Gladstone.

Father at home to lunch. Lady Hobart to lunch.

---

[1] Florence is unduly hard on Davitt, whose speech (*F.J.*, 22 May 1882) was a characteristic, if slightly truculent, piece of rhetoric, rejecting the Kilmainham policy but also denouncing violence. Davitt was far from aspiring to replace Parnell as the national leader. See Moody, *Davitt*, pp 538–9.

Arrears Debate at the House continued.

Second Reading passed.

Drove with Mother—Calls—Mrs Harold Browne.

I went afterwards to see Miss Burke, who had said she would be willing to see me. I shall not soon forget the impression which I received of quiet, tearless, hopeless, sadness. She was very kind to me, and talked with perfect composure—but with silences, and with a look in her eyes that I had never seen before.

She will never go back to Ireland, but looks forward eventually to settling with her brother 'Gussy' in London.

At present she says she feels as if she were living in a sort of nightmare, and does not at all care what happens to her, or where she lives.

A dinner party here in the evening—Moncks, Aberdares, F. Verneys, Evelyn and Harry Anstruther, Croppers, Mr Dickson, Mr Bright, and Mr West.

The Members back to the House for the Repression of Crime—some excitement over the fact that a split had declared itself amongst the Parnellites, Mr Parnell walking out on a division with 6 or 7 others, including Mr O'Kelly and Mr O'Donnell, with Mr Dillon and 13 others insisting on voting against the Govt.

Oakel and I in the evening to the George Smiths'.

Some pleasant talk with Mrs Smalley—I fear there is much danger of Mr Lowell being recalled. President Arthur needs the Irish vote at the next election, and Mrs Smalley seemed to think that he might very likely be induced to sacrifice Mr Lowell to the exigencies of the Irish and their supporters and protegées.

The Irish vote is happily to some extent, but only partially, counteracted by the German, which is always cast on the right side (from our point of view and the U.S. Republican).

24 May, Wed.

With Father to the House at 12, in consequence of a charge made by Mr Lowther last night to the effect that Mr Forster's late colleagues had carried on secret negociations behind his back. Mr Gladstone had asked him to make an explanation. He did so in a few words of complete contradiction—the House cheered him—Mr Chaplin (on behalf of Mr Lowther, absent at the Derby) accepted the explanation, and Mr Gladstone entered a protest against his right honourable friend's having used the word 'negociation', which he did not think was applicable under the circumstances.

Mr Gladstone, no doubt by the prudent advice of his colleagues, has declined to show Sir Drummond the letter referred to.

Repression of Crime Bill continued. A cynically defiant and outrageous speech from Mr Dillon—'he never had denounced outrage, and he never should until the Govt denounced eviction'—defence of 'boycotting' on the ground that it was as necessary as Lynch law in California—demand that coercion should be dropped—threats—predictions of evil—unceasing opposition to the Bill, etc., etc.[1]

Mr Gladstone replied—one of his finest speeches—declaring that Mr Dillon's speech was 'heart-breaking', and showing with splendid eloquence what it was that he had really said, drawing occasional protests and attempts at palliation even from Mr Dillon himself.

As to demands for sweeping modifications and amendments of the Bill, he announced the intention of the Govt not to withdraw from their original position.

The effect of Mr Dillon's speech was very great even upon Radicals who had hitherto been inclined to join the Parnellites in their opposition. Mr Anderson, a Scotch member, declared that it made him think that we should have to come to Martial law instead of modifying the strength of Repressive Measures.

Mr Borlase announced that he should withdraw an Amendment in favour of mitigating some of the stronger clauses of the Bill.

Altogether the result of Mr Dillon's attack was to strengthen immeasurably the position of the Govt, and frighten off Radicals who had been inclined to aid the Parnellites in their opposition to the Bill.

Mrs Ball to lunch. Drove with Mother in the afternoon. Dined in the evening at the Beckett Denisons'—Father afterwards to the Cos.

25 May, Th.

Attempt in the *Daily News* (with which paper Mr Justin McCarthy is intimately connected) to minimize the disastrous effect of Mr Dillon's speech.

Father at home to lunch—very tired and depressed.

Mlle Sturmfels and Evelyn Anstruther, and Uncle Walter to 5 o'clock tea. Oakel and I to dinner with the Croppers. Mr Augustus Burke to dinner at home.

A remarkable speech by Mr Parnell this afternoon,[2] with the object of explaining away Mr Dillon's defence of outrage and boycotting.

If only Mr Parnell had spoken in this way in Ireland and at a time when his influence in directing the cruel land agitation of 1880 might have had much effect, things would probably have never come to the pass they have now. Unhappily the Land League system of occasional moderate speeches in the House of Commons, counteracted by violent and seditious speeches in Ireland, is too familiar for this move of Mr Parnell's to cause any hope of more reasonable political action on the part of the Land League being seriously intended.

[1] *Hansard 3*, cclxix, 1537.   [2] Ibid., 1618–30.

26 May, Fri.

Judging from slight indications during last evening's debate and question time, the Irish Magistrates—especially men who have the misfortune to be obnoxious to Mr Healy and his friends—will cease to have the same loyal and generous support from their chief which they never failed to receive from the ex Chief Secretary.

It will be hard if their task of maintaining the law in bad and hostile districts, and of defending innocent men from those cruel boycotting practices (which Mr Parnell himself confessed were often abused, and employed against the wrong people) is to be made more difficult by the consciousness that they are liable not only to be spitefully and persistently attacked in the House of Commons, but to be defended in such half-hearted fashion as to give the impression that the Minister is at bottom ashamed of his subordinates.

However as long as Lord Spencer is Lord Lieutenant there is no real danger of men like Mr Clifford Lloyd being thrown over—and of course, if it is thought that verbal conciliation of Mr Healy in the House can tend to pacify Ireland and help to make the 'new departure' a success, it would be foolish to let mere personal feelings of loyalty to a subordinate stand in the way.

Spent most of the morning in the library. Father at home to lunch, and afterwards to the House, where he made a short speech in Committee on the question of Land League huts—explaining that it had never been the practice to interfere with their erection for the purposes of charity, but only for intimidation. This is exactly the same distinction which the present Executive will make, and they will have to form their opinions and derive their information from the same sources.

However, with the Parnellites and some of their friends there is a great deal in a name, and Lord Spencer and Mr Trevelyan may hope to receive credit for good intentions where Mr Forster came in for nothing but suspicion and abuse.

Mr West to dinner with us before our departure for 'abroad' at 8 o'clock.

We shall all be very sorry to say good-bye to the 'Occidental', whom we have come to like very much during our two years intimate connection with him. And I like him not only for himself, but for his devotion to Father which I believe has been most genuine.

We left Victoria at 8 p.m. for Normandy, where Father and Mother had finally decided to spend a short Whitsuntide holiday. The party included Francie, Oakel and me, and also Williams.

I cannot say how sad it was to be coming abroad for the first time almost for six years without our beloved Rob, the most charming and happiest of travelling companions during so many pleasant journeys.

29 May, Mon.; Caen

I shall now take a rest from writing these notes which I have been working rather hard over for two years, and the last chapter of which, as it were, I finished on the night we left the Chief Secretary's Lodge in January to begin the Session of 1882.

So very much has happened since, and the times through which I have written have been so full of grave events and of strange and varied feelings, that I have sometimes felt inclined to give up trying to write altogether, when all that I could do seemed so poor and so inadequate and incomplete.

However, I had my reasons for going on—and at any rate I have done the best and the most truthful that I could.

June

While we were still abroad the House met again, and the Prevention of Crime Bill was gone on with, Sir William Harcourt taking it in charge and doing his work very well. Progress, however, was naturally slow.

6 June, Tu.

Father and I returned via St Malo and Southampton to London, Mother and Francie remaining in France—partly that Mother might have a longer time out of London, but still more that Father might have an ostensible reason for coming away again if he found it better for him to be away from the House during the debates on the Repression of Crime Bill.

He was anxious to return and see how things were—and desired also to put in an appearance, partly on Mr Goschen's account.

On the very first night that he was in the House, he was wantonly attacked by Mr Parnell, and when he rose (as he was compelled to in self defence) was insulted by Mr O'Kelly, who got up to ask if the right hon. gentleman was to be allowed to make any more of his infernal speeches.

This expression Mr O'Kelly was forced to withdraw and apologize for having used.

7 June, Wed.

Father told me at breakfast of the O'Kelly affair in the House last night. This had finally decided him to go abroad again—the more willingly that he saw the Govt were not going to give in to the Parnellites on the Bill.

As for himself, there seemed to be a general feeling in the House that his presence would have a bad effect in provoking extra opposition from the Parnellites. As Father says, a violent personal attack on him in the House is a safe and easy method of pleasing the Irish American press, and Mr Parnell and his friends are likely to resort to it often. Nothing could have been more gratuitous and unprovoked than Mr Parnell's attack on Father yesterday, and no doubt it was made on some such calculation.

As for Mr O'Kelly, he simply relapsed into his usual style of language—doubtless quite unintentionally.

8 June, Th.

Father was insulted in the House to-night by Mr Callan. 'It is like walking through mud', says Father.

We dined at the Childers'. Heard of the murder of Mr Walter Bourke in Galway.[1]

9 June, Fri.

Father left London to join Mother and Francie at Compiegne.

[16 June, Fri.]

On Friday 16th they returned home, both Father and Mother looking much the better for their time abroad. In fact if Mother had not gone away when she did, she must have broken down altogether.

Pall Mall Gazette, June 10th 1882

All these things, since the supersession and retirement of Mr Forster, the Government have done or diligently set about doing. It may seem little, but it is all that is possible: dragooning would do no better, as it did no better in the Tithe War.

As for the Bill before the House, we wholly fail to see how any of its clauses, if they were all in full operation, will help to prevent such crimes as those which afflict us to-day. Mr Trevelyan said that the ninth clause is directed against such outrages as these. But what is the ninth clause? It is to the effect that if a constable finds a stranger in a proclaimed district under suspicious circumstances he may arrest such stranger and bring him before a justice, and if the man cannot give a good account of himself, then he may be required to give sureties to keep the peace, on pain of imprisonment for a month. Then there is the clause giving certain powers in the case of men found out of doors between the sunrise and sunset [*sic*]. But all the outrages on Thursday took place between the hours of three and six in the afternoon.

Once more it is to the Irish Executive, and not to the British Legislature, that we must look, and in looking to the Irish Executive we shall do well to moderate our expectations

[1] Walter J. Bourke, who had had trouble with his tenants, was driving home from Gort at about 3.20 p.m. on 8 June when he and his escort, Cpl Robert Wallace of the 1st Royal Dragoons, were killed by a volley from behind a wall, and their weapons taken. Three men were arrested but discharged for want of evidence (S.P.O, I.C.R., Returns of outrages, 1882).

of prompt success, and, above all, to resist all crude rhetorical invitations from leading journals to believe that passion and precipitancy will win battles.

22 June, Th.

Father and Mother went down to Bradford for the opening of the new Technical College by the Prince and Princess of Wales.

In the procession through Bradford the next day Father was greeted everywhere with the utmost friendliness; cheered through miles of streets by the crowds.

'His enemies do not seem to have made much impression in Bradford', Mother says.

8 July, Sat.

I have given up writing my notes for the past month, and find it very difficult to go back to the habit again.

It is unpleasant enough doing so, and yet I feel that, if I do not try now, it will only become more and more impossible for me to pick up the thread of my dull chronicle. Not that events have been dull. What with Egypt and Ireland public events have been exciting enough, and certainly my interest in things has not decreased; but to write about them, even in my fragmentary style, is detestable.

The conduct of Arabi Pasha, leader of the Military and anti-European party in Egypt, had been causing anxiety and embarrassment to England and France for some time past. The Khedive Tewfik, a loyal coadjutor of the Western Powers in their attempts to re-organize Egyptian finance by means of 'the Control', was in danger of being overturned by his so-called War Minister, Arabi Pasha, who professes to represent the National party in Egypt in their legitimate objection to foreign interference.

Being at the head of the Army, and himself a fanatical and ignorant Mussulman, with power of appeal to the religious fanaticism of his countrymen, Arabi was a dangerous person, and becoming a powerful one.

The English and French Governments demanded his dismissal from the Ministry and departure from the country. But Arabi remained War Minister, and did not leave the country. Whereupon England sent iron-clads towards Alexandria, and France suggested a European Conference, a proposal which was not received with great favour by any of the Powers.

On Sunday, 11th June (or 18th?)[1] there was a sudden uprising of the native population in Alexandria, and a massacre of Europeans. The anxiety which had been steadily growing now became alarm and indignation. A general panic—departure of all the Europeans that could get away, gradually even the chief officials leaving their posts—all public works suspended—anarchy

[1] 11 June is correct.

complete. Arabi Pasha master of the situation, so much so that in certain quarters in England it was proposed to give up considering him an ignorant fanatical rebel raised into a dangerous position of authority by means of his influence with a discontented soldiery, and to regard him as the patriotic leader of the 'National Party', much more deserving of sympathy and support than the Europeanized Khedive.

Meantime a Conference being held at Constantinople to discuss the best means of ending the present confusion. The alternatives—English intervention, Anglo-French intervention, European intervention, Turkish intervention (1 as Suzerain—or 2 as 'Mandataire' of the Powers).

Dervish Pasha sent by the Sultan to Cairo, Arabi still dominant—panic and general insecurity continuing. Europeans insulted in the streets. Assurances of Arabi that he would be responsible for the preservation of order. Growing indisposition, on the part of England especially, to be contented with the prolongation of a 'status quo' based on such guarantees as Arabi's assurances. General feeling that his despotism was not working well even for the 'National party' and that his regime meant misery—not emancipation for the 'fellaheen'.

Impatience at the passive attitude of the Fleet in face of outrages upon British subjects relieved by the adoption of energetic war preparations by the Govt.

A clear understanding that if Arabi and his friends continued their defiance of the Khedive and the Powers, and insisted on going on with the erection of earthworks and pointing of guns against the Fleet, the English Admiral had instructions to use force—in fact to bombard Alexandria, quite independent of the proceedings of the Conference or the consent of France to join in the demonstration.

As regards France there seems a general impression that our present difficulties have been in great part owing to the anxiety of our Govt to 'keep step with France'—a policy which has involved us in the dangerous practice of making demands which neither we nor still less the French Govt were prepared to enforce by arms.

It is said that the Joint Note issued in the interests of the Bond holders, and at the strong instance of the French Govt, was the beginning of all our troubles, since it irritated the Egyptian people without producing any result [other] than that of giving Arabi a further advantage in his attempt to foster discontent with the Anglo-French Control, with all that it involved in the way of European administration of Egypt.

However I write with more than usual ignorance—the Egyptian question having only lately come to the front in such a manner as to make one think much of that, or of anything except Ireland.

As for Ireland, a great many things have happened which I can only mention without attempting, even if I could, to go into detail over.

I fear it can hardly be said that during the past month there has been much visible inprovement.

The murder of Mr Walter Bourke and his escort has been followed by the murder of Mr Blake, agent to Lord Clanricarde. Mr Blake was an elderly man, long resident in the country, and it was believed popular—as it appears he had every right to be. He was shot from behind a loop-holed wall as he was driving past on a car with his wife and a servant.

After Mr Blake had fallen off the car, a second volley was fired which killed the servant and wounded Mrs Blake. She is not expected to recover.[1]

There have been numerous other cruel outrages committed on tenants suspected of paying their rent, and other boycotted and unpopular persons.

We should have been having many black days if Father had been in office this month. Lord Spencer we hear is looking sad and harassed, as well he may; he is working like a tiger—9 or 11 hours a day, with a whole staff of efficient men working all day with him.

Mr Trevelyan's work seems limited pretty much to Parliament, which is in itself sufficient occupation.

Now that Father is out of it, and the parliamentary and administrative [work] is divided, one wonders how he can ever have continued for two years to combine them both as he was obliged to do; especially when one remembers that, over and above the legitimate parliamentary work, he had to labour day after day in the face of most illegitimate insult and obstruction.

This Mr Trevelyan is happily spared, the Parnellites preferring to employ their bad language chiefly against the Home Secretary, who conducts the Repression of Crime Bill with great ability, firmness and good temper.

Amongst the events of the past month have been the seizure of a Fenian Armoury at Clerkenwell;[2] the departure of Mr Davitt for America, and threatening split between him and Mr Parnell (the one holding to the Communistic, the other to the Land League Peasant Proprietor, theory);[3] and the culmination of Parnellite obstruction and misconduct in the House with an all-night sitting (June 30) and the suspension of all the Parnellite Members.[4]

On July 7th another curious Parliamentary incident took place. During the Committee on the Repression of Crime Bill, Mr Trevelyan as a concession to the Parnellites had accepted an amendment by which the police were forbidden to search houses at night for the purpose of finding arms, documents or 'the apparatus of murder'—i.e. masks and other disguises used by the 'Moonlighters'). On Friday afternoon it was proposed by Mr George Russell that the

---

[1] John Henry Blake, aged 75, and his servant Thady Ruane, aged 50, were killed outside Loughrea at about 11.30 a.m. on 29 June. Two men were arrested but discharged for lack of evidence. (S.P.O., I.C.R., Returns of outrages, 1882.)

[2] 400 Snider rifles, 25 cases of revolvers and large quantities of ammunition were found on 17 June at premises hired by Thomas Walsh, who was charged with feloniously receiving and dealing with firearms (*Annual Register, 1882*, p. 24).

[3] See Moody, *Davitt*, pp 534–40.

[4] The twenty-second night of the bill in committee opened at 3.15 p.m. on 30 June; the house adjourned at 8 p.m. on 1 July, after the suspension of 25 M.P.s (*Hansard 3*, cclxxi, 937–1211, especially 1140–41 and 1204–5).

amendment should be left out, and the original clause—giving complete right of search—restored. Mr Russell was supported by several Members on that side of the House, including Mr Goschen; Father, however, pleaded on behalf of the Govt that if, as was stated, Lord Spencer himself was desirous of being without the power, it would be wise not to force it on the Executive.

Mr Gladstone himself took a very high line about the matter, almost going to the length of making it a question of resignation—if the amendment were thrown out 'he would have to re-consider his personal position'. Mr Bright also very vehement, the House excited and restive. Finally a division in which the Govt were beaten by 19 in a House of 400.[1] The Parnellite Members on whose behalf Mr Gladstone was making this stand viewed the scene from the Gallery, declining the pressing invitations to them to come down and vote for their own amendment. Having declared and protested over and over again that this right of search at night was a wrong and an outrage on their country which they were bound to resist at all costs, the Parnellite Members now preferred to see their country outraged, rather than forego the momentary pleasure of spiting the Govt for having suspended them a day or two before.

Very natural no doubt, but not patriotic in the ordinary sense of the word.

(I find that the easiest way to keep up any sort of chronicle is in journal form. Though out of office, we are still enough in contact with public events to make our daily life take us through a great deal that is interesting.)

9 July, Sun.

Father and I went down after church to spend the day at Mr Pender's, of the Eastern Telegraph Company, at Gray's Foot, Sidcup, in Kent (Sergeant Ballantyne travelling in the same carriage.)

We arrived just in time for lunch. The party included the Tweedmouths (late Majoribanks), Hussey Vivians, Mr Evelyn Ashley, Sir George Elliot, Lord Lymington, and Mr Forster of the Ottoman Bank at Constantinople.

We could not have been at a better place for hearing Egyptian news, Mr Pender receiving telegrams from Alexandria twice in the course of the day. The fortifications being still continued by Arabi in spite of warnings from the British Admiral, formal notice had been given that the forts would be bombarded by the fleet in 12 hours from the time of warning. All British subjects believed to have left Alexandria.

General opinion amongst Egyptian authorities at Mr Pender's (including the host himself) that the sooner the bombardment begun and was over the better the chance for the restoration of order, and the averting of total ruin from those who had been forced by recent events to leave everything behind them and break off their business in Egypt.

[1] The division was 194:207.

10 July, Mon.

No news in the 1st edition of the papers of the bombardment having actually begun; but it was soon being cried in the streets. Two forts already silenced—great excitement—fresh items of news arriving at intervals during the day—the best reports being from the *Standard* correspondent on board the *Invincible*.

The sound of the bombardment had been heard at Malta, a thousand miles off. Great destruction apparently of the Egyptian fortifications, but impossible to tell what was happening in the town.

Much anxiety as to the safety of the Khedive who had declined the offer of safe quarters on board the fleet, preferring to remain with his people in spite of the obvious danger of his position.

11 July, Tu.

Father's birthday. This day last year, he was one of Her Majesty's Ministers, responsible to the country for the wise government of Ireland—working and fighting, and contriving from day to day, almost without an hour's intermission, with every faculty called into play, every nerve strained, with large powers in his hands, and the sole responsibility for their rightful exercise resting upon him. In short he was experiencing what it is to *govern*, to have to maintain law, order and justice amongst a demoralized and for the most part hostile people.

Now he is out of everything, with no more power or responsibility or knowledge of what is going on than any private member.

But while he is thus obliged to stand aside, he has at any rate the satisfaction of seeing the government of Ireland carried on on the lines which he followed and by the methods which he to a great extent initiated. His enemies have had to be content with vilifying and getting rid of him; they have not succeeded in enforcing their own theories with regard to the actual administration of affairs in Ireland.

Lord Spencer and the Special Magistrates in Ireland, and Mr Trevelyan at the Irish Office in London, continue the work of the late Chief Secretary, strengthened with the extra powers given them by the new Repression of Crime Bill.

Whether or not Father feels very keenly his enforced inaction and isolation it would be impossible for any one to guess from his outward bearing. He seems as serene, as much interested in everything (especially Irish affairs), as full of occupation as though he had never known any more exciting experience than presiding at Anti-Cruelty Meetings and attending Emigration Committees at the House.

But every now and then, when he is looking over and arranging the documents of his two years at the Irish Office, or when he is talking to some Irish friends, a single sentence or tone of voice will show to those who know him that his present position is not always as easy to bear as might be supposed from his imperturbable cheerfulness and generous readiness to take up any useful work that is still open to him.

The great centre of interest now is Alexandria. Every few hours telegrams arrive describing the progress of the bombardment.

A measure undertaken purely in self-defence, according to the Govt theory, but none the less exciting grave discontent below the Gangway.

A vigorous speech at the afternoon sitting from Mr Gladstone in reply to reproaches from Sir Wilfred Lawson and Mr Rylands (just returned from Egypt).

Father and Mother to Meeting for Working Girls Homes, at Lord Aberdare's.

Miss Mary Whately, Sir George Elliot, Mr Forster (of the Ottoman Bank) and Mr Broadhurst to dinner.

12 July, Wed.

The Repression of Crime Bill became law to-day.[1] Whether it will do good or not depends, it is said, entirely on the way it is worked by the local authorities in Ireland. Meantime the feeling of those who know the country and see at close quarters how things are going on is one of profound gloom and uneasiness.

Murder is on the increase. Within the last few days a poor herdsman (Doloughty) has been murdered in the County Clare, and a man named Kenny in the streets of Dublin.[2]

This last is a Fenian murder. The impression abroad amongst the people in the city is that he was one of the Phoenix Park murderers (or the car-man), and that he was killed by his confederates on the suspicion that he meant to 'split' on them.

In some of the Country districts the Murder Societies are as active as in Dublin.

Round Loughrea, and in fact throughout Galway, the danger of assassination by Members of a well-organized Secret Society (whether called Land League, Fenian or Whiteboy) is so serious that several families have been warned by the authorities not to return home at present, and those who remain are placed under protection.

One item to the good, of late, has been the unanimous prohibition of the Ladies Land League in the Bishops' Manifesto. Curates have at the same time

[1] Prevention of Crime (Ireland) Act, 1882 (45 & 46 Vict., c.25).
[2] John Doolaghty was shot in the face on his return from mass on 9 July and died the next day. Francis Hynes, whose family had formerly employed Doolaghty, was hanged for the murder on 11 Sept. John Kenny, a Dublin labourer, was shot and stabbed at about 1 a.m. on 4 July (S.P.O., I.C.R., Returns of outrages, 1882; *F.J.*, 4 July 1882).

been forbidden by the same authority to take part in Meetings without the express permission of their parish priests.[1]

This Manifesto has excited the displeasure and astonishment of *United Ireland*, and in so far may be considered to have been a move in the right direction. But not much good is to be hoped from this sort of intervention at the present stage of social demoralization in Ireland.

If only it had come a little sooner.

How earnestly we used to look for any such restraining influence from the Bishops and Clergy during the two years in which every bad and false passion was allowed free course, and how seldom any word of warning or remonstrance was ever heard.

Another feature in the situation which is new since our time, and which may have a good deal of effect—whether for good or ill—is the Land Corporation. This was started last winter, when a Meeting was held at the Mansion House, and subscriptions raised;[2] but for some time nothing more was heard of the proceedings of the Landlords Defence Association then formed, and it was only last month that the scheme which had been in course of quiet preparation for some time past was brought before the public, and explained in a long letter to *The Times* by Mr Kavanagh.[3]

The object of the Corporation is to enable landlords and others by combined effort on the principles of a Joint Stock Company, to buy, occupy and work, at their own expense, farms which individual landlords have been compelled by the Land League organization to leave 'derelict'.

Very large sums have already been invested in this scheme, but not more than will be required, since in many cases to work a farm in opposition to the Land League will involve the employment not only of a staff of imported labourers, but also of men to protect these labourers; and it is obvious that a farm which could be made to pay under these circumstances would have to be an unusually productive one.

However it will be a great thing if any legitimate combination can be found to check the illegitimate combination of the League, which depends also upon financial support but assisted by the power of intimidation and outrage.

Provided the Corporation is worked with prudence and not in a spirit of mere anti-tenant hostility, it may prove a benefit not only to defrauded landlords but to many labourers and small farmers who must have been suffering

[1] Archbishop Croke denied this, and generally played down the force of the pronouncements in a letter of 11 July to *F.J.* (12 July 1882). For the context of this letter see Emmet Larkin, *The Roman Catholic church and the creation of the modern Irish state, 1878–1886* (Philadelphia and Dublin, 1975), pp 169–74.

[2] Forster had then (7 Dec. 1881) suggested to Gladstone that it was worthy of support, as 'one of the few manifestations of that self-help which we are trying to stimulate'. Anticipating the question 'is it desirable for England to interfere in an Irish class struggle?', Forster replied 'If America helps one side, England may help the other' (B.L., Add. MS 44159, ff 126–9).

[3] *The Times*, 24 June 1882.

almost as much as the landlords from the embargo placed by the League on all independent action.

The new scheme has of course been received with great indignation by the League party, who naturally called loudly on the Government to interfere and prevent their being met in Ireland with [their] own weapons, i.e. money and combination.

News from Egypt that Arabi had hoisted a flag of truce, in consequence of which the bombardment was suspended.

A dinner party here in the evening—De Vescis,[1] Lady O'Hagan, Villiers Stuarts, Lawrence Smalleys, H. Wards, and Mr Townsend. This last distinguished himself by talking in such a random, exasperating manner about Ireland that Lady de Vesci and Lady O'H. could hardly contain themselves, and even Father was surprised and had to make the best excuse he could for him after he was gone.

One cannot help wishing that newspaper writers and editors and others 'put in authority over us', or at least over the opinion of the English public, were compelled by law to pass six months a year in Ireland by way of qualification for enlightening the world on the subject of that country.

To Mrs Childers' and Lady Herschell's in the evening.

13 July, Th.

Father suddenly home at lunch time with evening papers under his arm, and a look of bad news on his face. Bad news indeed from Egypt.

The flag of truce had been merely a pretext to gain time for Arabi to withdraw his troops in safety.

Under cover of it, he had left Alexandria, after first setting fire to the town and releasing the convicts from the prison in order that they might join his own soldiers in the work of plundering and massacreing all the remaining Christians and Europeans whom they could lay hands on.

While these horrors were being committed, the fleet was helpless; no troops were landed, because the force at Admiral Seymour's[2] disposal was not sufficiently large to cope with Arabi's army, and to land a small body of men would only have resulted in their own destruction, whilst they would have been powerless to prevent the work of murder and havoc which was now in full force.

A most painful state of things—all the more so from the consciousness that rightly or wrongly the responsibility for these horrors would to some degree be fastened upon England.

A garden party this afternoon at Marlborough House.

---

[1] As in MS; the typescript reads 'De Vesci'.
[2] Frederick Beauchamp Paget Seymour (1821–95): commander-in-chief, Mediterranean fleet, 1880–83.

Report spread by Masarus Pacha that the Khedive had been killed. This happily contradicted in the course of the evening in the House.

Mr P. J. Smyth to dinner.

14 July, Fri.

The newspapers very black reading this morning with the news from Alexandria. The town in flames—'two miles of fire' visible from the fleet—the place deserted—refugees from the Massacre taken on board the fleet. Arabi's movements quite unknown.

Resignation of Mr Bright.[1]

Oakel and I in the evening to the Gaiety to see a performance by Irish amateurs on behalf of those who had suffered from agrarian outrages in Ireland, the families of murdered herdsmen, small farmers, and others.

The streets swarming with newsboys advertizing fresh news from Egypt, more or less true, and recent. All sorts of items shouted by the rival newsboys—'Arrest of the Khedive by Admiral Seymour', etc.

15 July, Sat.

Oakel and I to Richmond, rowing up the river with the F. Verneys as far as Kingston.

A dinner party here, Selbornes, Arthur Russells, the O'C. Don and Madam O'Conor, the Bishop of Philadelphia and Mrs Stevens, Havelock Allens, Colonel Burke, etc.

16 July, Sun.

Father after lunch to Claremont to the Duke and Duchess of Albany's—meeting there Lord and Lady Clarendon and the Russian Ambassador.

The latter (Prince Lobanoff) had told the Duke of Albany that the truth about General Skobeloff's sudden and unexpected death was believed to be that he had poisoned himself, in alarm lest his complicity with the Nihilists should be discovered. It is also said that General Ignatieff is involved with them.

Reports and so-called 'new Editions' cried in the streets all the afternoon. No fresh crisis. A battle expected, but our force not yet sufficiently large, though troops being steadily despatched from England and Malta.

Arabi entrenched in the neighbourhood of Alexandria—order being gradually re-established. The conduct of Lord Charles Beresford and the naval officers assisting him excites general approval. The American fleet has landed men to help us in the task of restoring order, and doing justice on incendiaries and murderers.

[1] This was not generally known until the following day.

Meantime there is great anxiety for Cairo where massacres are apprehended, and to which we have been unable to send troops.

17 July, Mon.

Growing impatience at our Military inaction in Egypt. Chorus of laments from all the special correspondents—Arabi's power and influence increasing in proportion to our delay. Having struck once and so produced the terrible effects now visible at Alexandria, we are bound to strike again and bring the present state of misery and danger to a termination.

Why did we not land troops before the bombardment and so prevent the city falling into the power of Arabi and his ruffians?

The Govt from their relations to other Powers are obliged to be reserved in their communications. They are urged vehemently to take isolated action, if need be, to protect British interests in Egypt without waiting either for the co-operation of France or the assent of Europe—having acted on their own responsibility and alone in such an important step as the bombardment of Alexandria, why not go on alone, give up all embarrassing regard for the European Concert or the decisions of a Conference, and plunge boldly into an Egyptian war, unhampered by the checks and delays caused by diplomatic circumvention?

Probably the present delay, which must certainly have a bad effect from a military point of view, and so far as Arabi himself is concerned, is occasioned by the endeavours being made by the Govt to ensure the benevolent neutrality if not co-operation of our neighbours in the work we have before us in Egypt.

We are to strike, and to strike alone, but only after such a clear understanding of our position has been arrived at that we shall have only one enemy to deal with and not half a dozen, as might have been the case if England had proceeded suddenly from the bombardment (which Europe had allowed to be an act of self-defence) to the instant landing of troops and attack of Arabi Pasha, which Europe might have considered an invasion of Egypt, inconsistent with England's signature of the 'protocole de desintéressement' at Constantinople.

Whatever the causes, the result in the present state of Egypt is very unsatisfactory.

Arabi gaining in power—the English and other Europeans in isolated places, and even in the suburbs of Cairo, hunted out and cruelly murdered—the water supply of Alexandria threatened and already decreasing from Arabi's tampering with the canal—the most unhealthy time of year approaching, and fears entertained that by flooding the country Arabi can make a decisive campaign almost impossible.

Mr Bright made his statement concerning his resignation this evening.

18 July, Tu.

Walked with Father to the Athenaeum.

Mr Mahaffy to lunch. He gave us a curious account of things in Dublin. A complete change since we were there—everyone guarded up to the eyes—a cricket match at the Vice Regal Lodge the other day, with the ground lined with soldiers and police—cars that stopped on the grass outside to look on compelled to move off by the police. General conviction that the Phoenix Park Murderers are perfectly well known to very many in Dublin, and are probably in the city at this moment.

Lord and Lady Kilmaine to dinner (just going back to West Meath), also the Roundells, and a Mr Eugene Collins—a dull man imported by Father as an authority on Russia. His experiences chiefly confined apparently to the hotels, shops, and railway carriages.

19 July, Wed.

Oakel left in the morning for Devonport to be examined by the Liberal Committee, and if accepted to hold a public Meeting with his colleague, Mr Medley, on the following Friday.

A dinner party in the evening—Lord Fitzgerald, the Garnet Wolseleys, Uncle Matts, Websters, Mr Perry, Mr Mahaffy, Sir H. James, and Mr Chenery.

Afterwards to Lady Aberdeen's, and Lady Haytor's. Met Mr Blenner-hasset—very gloomy about Ireland; he himself just returned after an unpleasant experience there from his place in Kerry.

Lady Reay announced to Father the fact of Colonel Brackenbury's[1] resignation—which however he knew already. This is thought to be very wrong of Col. Brackenbury—and various reasons are given to explain his giving up such an important post at this critical juncture. It is said that he wanted to go with Sir Garnet Wolseley to Egypt, that Sir Garnet insisted on having him, that he had quarrelled with Lord Spencer, etc., etc.

Whatever the cause, the effect of his sudden departure is felt to be very hard on the Irish Executive.[2]

20 July, Th.

Saw in the papers that Oakel had been accepted by the Liberal Committee as their candidate at the next election. In a Committee of 150 the minority opposed to him (on Irish grounds) dwindled down to 3.

To tea in the afternoon with Mrs Trevelyan, who gave me a clove carnation out of the kitchen garden at the C.S. Lodge. She goes over there on the 10th

[1] See above, p. 490.   [2] See below, pp 526–7.

with her little boys; she told me her spirits about the prospect vary from time to time according as to what she hears. As a rule people from Dublin are not very encouraging—she is told even the children will have to be guarded.

Walked with Mother in the evening to Lady Galway's. The result of Mr Chenery's having dined with us and afterwards put a paragraph in *The Times* to the effect that 'Mr Forster and family were going to Russia and the East of Europe', has been that information and experience about Russia is volunteered us from all sides.

21 July, Fri.

Oakel's Meeting at Devonport.

A succession of people in the morning to see Father, Lords Gosport and Lurgan (to complain of Sub-Commissioners, especially of a Mr Meek who seems to be giving great offence), Lord Carlingford, a Miss Otway to talk about a Women's College for Belfast, etc.; it seemed quite like old times.

Sydney and Conny Buxton, Mr Isaac Wilson, and Mr Acland to dinner.

The Arrears Bill (including the improved Emigration Clauses) passed to-day.[1] No more Irish Legislation for the present. Great relief of English Members.

22 July, Sat.

Papers full of 'War Preparations'. Battle expected but nothing happened as yet.

Father in the afternoon to Greenhithe to give the prizes on board the *Shaftesbury*, the School Board Training ship.

Mother and I to Fox Warren. Father arriving in time for dinner.

23 July, Sun.

At Fox Warren—a fine day, but on the whole the weather is giving great cause for uneasiness, especially in Ireland where the consequences of a bad harvest would be very serious.

Quite lately there has been a lull in the outrages, and there is (except in Dublin) a slight sense of improvement; rent is being fairly well paid, and there are signs of the people becoming tired of agitation.

The very virulent 'Ladies Land League' in Wexford has come to a voluntary end; finding themselves with only 12/- in hand and having applied in vain to the Central L.L.L. for fresh funds, the Wexford ladies have closed their branch altogether.

The party staying in the house at Fox Warren included Mr Harcourt of

---

[1] It became law as Arrears of Rent (Ireland) Act, 1882 (45 & 46 Vict., c. 47) on 18 Aug.

Nuneham, Lord and Lady Egmont, Mr Herbert Gladstone, Mr Lane Fox (of the Electric Light) and the Sydney Buxtons.

To church at Hatchford in the morning.

A walk 'en masse' in the afternoon. Herbert Gladstone, May, and I to Pain's Hill Cottage, where Francie was staying.

24 July, Mon.

No fresh news from Egypt.

Our troops arriving. Arabi entrenching himself before Ramleh—a suburb of Alexandria, now occupied and held by our troops.

Arabi having proclaimed the Khedive a traitor, the Khedive has now proclaimed Arabi a Rebel.

It is hoped that this may have some effect though it is considered rather too late to do much good.

On our arrival in London we found the Devonshire papers with reports of Oakel's Meeting. His speech was really excellent and he seems to have already become a favourite in Devonport. Edward went all the way from Yorkshire to hear Oakel; it was not till he came on to the platform after the Meeting was over that Oakel knew who had been amongst his audience.

Oakel got back about 1—having spent Sunday in Salisbury. Walked with him to the Hospital (and House) in the afternoon, and heard more about Devonport. He seems to have made a good beginning of his political career.

24 July, Mon.

Egyptian debate in the House—Mr Gladstone's speech in asking for the Vote of Credit. No opposition to this from the Conservatives, though of course much criticism of Govt policy.

Certainly the effect is better when war preparations have to be made by a Liberal government than by a Conservative—the country is allowed to appear united in its action, which is not possible when a Liberal Opposition feels bound to protest against every penny spent in Military preparations, as was the case with the last Vote of Credit.

The Reserves have been called out, and Indian troops are to be brought to Egypt.

25 July, Tu.

Statement in the *Daily News* that Lord Kimberley was going to take the Chancellorship of the Duchy.

Uncle Matt to lunch—in some excitement, having heard from Lord Monck that this meant Father going to the Colonies, an arrangement they both thought excellent—a good way for Father to re-join the Cabinet, and a good thing also for the Colonies.

Lord Monck 'knew' that Mr Forster had been sounded on the subject—so much for people's knowledge in these sort of matters. In this case Father did not know it himself.

Both he and Mother feel strongly that Mr Gladstone cannot possibly ask Father to re-enter the Cabinet at present. If the present vacancies are filled up it will have to be in such a way as to please the Radical and *P.M. Gazette* section of the party, who would probably look upon the return of the late Chief Secretary to office under present circumstances as a personal insult.

Amongst the names favoured by the *Daily News* are those of Sir C. Dilke, Mr Fawcett, and Lord Rosebery; at present however no new appointments have been made, and Lord Kimberley does the light work of the Duchy in addition to his own at the Colonial Office.

With Oakel in the afternoon to a garden party at Mrs Medley's.

A dinner party here, de Bunsens, Lady Strangford, Mr Shaw LeFevre, Mr Knowles, the Miss Monks, and Mr A. Elliot and Mr Newdigate.

Egyptian debate continued—speech by Sir Charles Dilke.

26 July, Wed.

Father and I to Bradford. Prize giving and Speech by Father to the Bradford Grammar School at St George's Hall. A large, peaceful and friendly assemblage—all very pleased to see Father.

To Wharfeside in the evening. The dear place looking very pretty—buried in green, and the river brimful and shining under the quiet evening light. The garden full of flowers, the kitchen garden especially being gay with white lilies, phlox, poppies, and sweetwilliams.

Inside the house everything unchanged—except a new paper in Francie's and my room.

I have not been home since last April year,[1] and a great deal has happened since.

The dogs were enchanted to see me. It seemed quite like being back at the C.S. Lodge to sit alone at lunch and tea with a book in front of me, and my Puck on one side and dear old Yarrow on the other.

27 July, Th.

Father to Leeds to speak at the Education Council.

A long and pleasant day at Wharfeside. On the river in the morning with the dogs. A wet afternoon—a visit from Mrs Fison. Father back to tea. Dined with

[1] See above, p. 123.

Edward and Edith at Cathedine. Sat up till past 12 arranging a bundle of old newspapers (*General Evening News*) dating from 1787 to 1802, filed at the Weymouth Bank, and lately discovered by Mr Wharton in the attic.

The Irish news of those days, especially during the Rebellion, made one feel that things might have been worse during our two years' experience even than they were.

28 July, Fri.

Returned to London. Called at Cathedine to say goodbye to Edith, and to the dear little children, whom I could only see through the window—as they were supposed (wrongly as it turned out) to be sickening for measles.

Lunched in Leeds with Mr Jackson who has been very ill and was downstairs to-day for the first time. Nothing could have been more kind and affectionate than he was to me, and so loving about Father.

We travelled up to London with Mr Powell.

Evening papers full of 'Arabi sueing for peace'—a story that he had offered to make peace and retire to a Monastery in Syria etc., etc. Very satisfactory if true.

Mother and Francie met us at the station.

Father to the House, and afterwards home to dinner. No confirmation of Arabi's surrender.

29 July, Sat.

All untrue about Arabi. The situation unchanged. British troops arriving. Arabi encamped before Ramleh—uneasiness in Cairo. Conference still going on at Constantinople—efforts being made to induce the Sultan to intervene and put down Arabi himself.

France desperately afraid of being drawn into active interference in Egypt. The most ventured upon by M. de Freycinet a demand for a small note of credit towards the defence of the Canal in co-operation with England. Even this granted with much reluctance, and severe lectures to the Government from various quarters.

Meantime popular feeling in England rather relieved at being free of French co-operation; general impression that France has kept out of joint action with us long enough for all the odium of the recent strong measures to fall exclusively upon us, and had now better keep out of it altogether, and leave us to finish the work our own way.

Father, Mother and Francie to Warlies[1] for the Sunday—Oakel and I to Cobham.

---

[1] A Buxton house at Waltham Abbey.

30 July, Sun.

A beautiful day: in fact the weather has decidedly 'taken up' and the prospects for the hay and harvest are improving.

To church in the morning. Read Montalembert on Lacordaire lent me by Mr Jackson.

Lucy, Oakel, and I to Fox Warren in the afternoon—meeting there Mr J. G. Butcher and Herbert Gladstone; heard from the latter that Mr Clifford Lloyd is quieting Loughrea as he quieted Clare.

31 July, Mon.

Resignation of M. de Freycinet—this time definitely.

Father, Mother, and Francie returned from Warlies about 12. Oakel and I rather later. Heard from Mr West that Mr Clifford Lloyd had called, having come over from Ireland on a flying visit to the authorities.

The papers all reproduce the statement that he is to succeed Colonel Brackenbury.

Father to dinner at Grillion's.

1 Aug., Tu.

Dearest Mother's birthday.

Mr Clifford Lloyd to breakfast. He looked better in health than when we last saw him, in spite of the bad times he has been having in Loughrea, and seemed glad to see Father and all of us again. Certainly there is very little resemblance between the Clifford Lloyd of *United Ireland* and the *Pall Mall Gazette*, and the real man. It was very interesting to hear his account of things in the Loughrea district. He has hopes now, thanks to the Crimes Bill, [that] the Loughrea suspects, when they return from Kilmainham, as they soon will, will find themselves less able to do harm than before.

'Not that', as Mr Lloyd says, 'you can expect to make much permanent improvement by means of "brute force"', which is what a severe administration of the Crimes Act amounts to. The hope is that, as a result of the vigorous enforcement of the law, the side of order as against outrage may become the winning side, in which case the people will have a strong inducement to become well-disposed.

Already there have been signs, even in Loughrea, that there are people who have no sympathy with the outrage societies, if only they dared come forward; and very soon after his arrival Mr Lloyd received a curious anonymous letter to this effect.

Information too is beginning to be volunteered more freely, which is an improvement. At the same time there can be no relaxation in the fight on the part of the Magistrates.

The Secret organizations are known to be in full activity, and bent on murder. Several times quite recently the police have found the walls round Loughrea loop-holed for shooting purposes.

We heard from Mr Lloyd that there was no truth in the rumour of his being appointed to fill Col. Brackenbury's post. We are very glad of it.

With Father to the city—to Silver's for travelling bags, cushions, etc. for Russia—if we ever go there.

Mrs and Miss Cartwright, Lord Monteagle, and Mr O'Connor Power to dinner. I felt rather inclined to ask Mr O'Connor Power if he now felt at liberty to remember having come to the Chief Secretary's Lodge one afternoon in the autumn of 1880, a circumstance which he wrote to the Rebel papers to deny at the beginning of this year when some of the Parnellites charged him with it.

The House of Lords, having passed the 2nd Reading of the Arrears Bill in its original form, have since put into it an Amendment of Lord Salisbury's practically nullifying the whole object of the Government. Compulsion on the landlords to accept the provisions of the Bill has been changed into option. A second Amendment 'obliges' instead of 'permits' the Commissioners to take the Tenant's interest in his farm into account in their administration of the Act.

2 Aug., Wed.

Considerable commotion over the Lords' treatment of the Arrears Bill. Lord Salisbury's Amendment can never be accepted by the Govt, and then what will happen if the Lords on their side refuse to give way? Quite a 'constitutional crisis' like the one we had this time last year over the Land Act.

All our plans for going abroad thrown into confusion. There is talk of a prorogation to the 19th of this Month, then a second Session, the Bill to be sent up again to the Lords in its original shape—and then if they again reject it a Dissolution which would turn not so much on the Arrears Bill, as on the House of Lords.

Uncle Matt to lunch.

Father and Mother to dinner with the Fairbairns; Hamlet Philpot here.

3 Aug., Th.

Mr Jenkinson,[1] formerly a distinguished Indian official and now Private Secretary to Lord Spencer, has been appointed to succeed Col. Brackenbury.

The latter will receive no appointment in Egypt. Great interest has been made on his behalf, but both the Duke of Cambridge and Mr Childers are

[1] Edward George Jenkinson (1835–1919): served in Indian Civil Service, 1856–80, retiring with impaired health; cousin of Lord Northbrook.

resolved that he shall not this second time desert his post without taking the consequences. It appears that there was no disagreement between him and Lord Spencer, and no urgent summons to him from Sir Garnet; he simply asked for 24 hours leave and then telegraphed from London to say he should not return to Dublin.

I believe that, as a matter of fact, he was not making a success of the new Detective Department, finding the detective system in the country districts an impossibility, as those with experience of Ireland had foretold it would be.[1] The *P.M. Gazette* was never tired of recommending this sovereign remedy against outrage—'organize a detective police, the constabulary are nothing but a military body'.

This is what the plan has come to so far.

Military preparations and the departure of troops occupying public attention at present more than anything else.

Sir Garnet Wolseley has just left to take the chief command.

Much discontent in England at the prospect of Turkish troops co-operating (?) with us in Egypt—the unwelcome result of diplomacy at the Conference which is still going on.

Uncle Walter to dinner.

4 Aug., Fri.

Father and Mr West at work all the morning over arranging papers.

Colonel King Harman to dinner. Talk over the Land Corporation and its prospects. So far the effect has been good, and there can be no doubt that the mere preparations for it have alarmed the Land Leaguers. One very tangible result has been the prompt payment of Lord Digby's rents by tenants who were well able to pay, but had steadily refused to do so till they saw Lord Digby's name amongst the subscribers to the Land Corporation. Then the fear seized them that he might bring down Scotch and English farmers to take their places, and they preferred under these circumstances to avoid all chance of eviction by paying their rents.

Colonel King Harman also mentioned that the attacks on the Land Corporation, in a series of *Freeman* leading articles, had exactly and literally quadrupled the amount of the subscriptions to it. (He told us the figures but of course I have forgotten them.)

---

[1] The correspondence between Brackenbury and Spencer in the Spencer papers at Althorp does not support Florence's conjecture. Brackenbury's plans for detective work had concentrated on international Fenianism, not on secret societies in the country (a field later greatly developed by Jenkinson). He had strong feelings on the necessity for renewing the P.P.P. act, over which he apparently differed from Spencer; but this would not have caused him to resign—indeed, he seems to have been taken aback when Spencer insisted on treating his application to go to Egypt as a resignation. One of his arguments for wanting to go was that the reorganisation was now so complete that anyone could take over the direction of the police and crime department.

Mr Davitt's loudly advertised opposition will not, he thinks, prove very formidable. A circular has been issued by Mr Parnell, Mr Davitt and others representing the Corporation as an English Company, and calling for subscriptions to support the evicted families.

In view of this fresh necessity for National funds, it is announced that the movement for the payment of Members will be postponed for the present.

On the whole Colonel King Harman seemed to agree with Father that the Land League had to some extent lost its ascendancy in Ireland, and that the effect of this was visible both there and in the House.

Various things combine to give the Irish Executive a good chance at present. The Lord Lieutenant will not have to govern under the same disadvantages as the ex Ch. Secretary; what he would have given to have had such an instrument to work with as this new Act, which was every bit as much needed in 1881 as in 1882!

Again, the Magistrates are now being weeded out, and incompetent men got rid of, by allowing them liberal retiring pensions. In Father's time this process, quite as necessary last year as this, and felt by him to be so, could not be carried out because the Treasury could not see their way to guarantee the extra money.

Since that terrible 6th of May many things have been different, and yet in reality it is more English opinions than Irish facts which have altered.

Of some of our friends the latest reports are more cheerful than when we used to hear of them in the autumn and winter.

Mrs Power Lalor has entirely got the better of her enemies in Tipperary. The shopkeepers who 'boycotted' her so severely have lately sent her a humble request that she will forgive the past, and let byegones be byegones.

Captain and Mrs White in Leitrim have also I believe seen the worst of their troubles.

There is much uneasiness at present over the agitation spreading amongst the Constabulary.[1] Mr Trevelyan gave a reassuring and minimizing answer on the subject in the House on Thursday (or Friday),[2] but Father fears there is grave cause for anxiety.

With all his inefficiency Colonel Hillier, says Father, 'had the faculty of dealing well with the Constabulary, and so preventing their grumbling from becoming serious'.

The present movement seems to be a combined agitation spreading through the country for an increase in pay and pensions—to be called a strike or a

---

[1] At the beginning of Aug. there were demonstrations of discontent among the R.I.C. in Cork, Limerick, and other centres, arising from delay in distributing the special grant of £160,000, and giving rise to demands for consideration of general grievances. On 4 Aug. Clifford Lloyd, in a widely-publicised incident, reminded the Limerick force that insubordination in an armed force was a serious matter. On 7 Aug. the inspector general issued a circular stating that the government would not consider any claims while the agitation persisted. On 10 Aug. he was able to issue a second expressing Spencer's satisfaction at the ending of the agitation, and his intention to investigate grievances forthwith (*Hansard 3*, cclxxiii, 1626; 12 Aug. 1882).

[2] Fri., 4 Aug.; *Hansard 3*, cclxxiii, 754–6.

mutiny according as the Force is considered as a civil or a military body. Anyhow, coming at this time, discontent amongst the Irish Constabulary is very dangerous.

A violent and vulgar attack on Mr Jenkinson last night by Mr O'Donnell—ably defended by Mr Trevelyan. 'Mr Jenkinson will perhaps be the new Chief Secretary's Clifford Lloyd.'[1]

5 Aug., Sat.

No Cabinet has yet been formed in France. Father and Mr West at work all the morning over papers in the library.

Miss Tuttle an American School Mistress from Massachusetts to lunch.

Father and Mother to dinner at the Hubbards' to talk about Russia—our prospects, however, (thanks to Lord Salisbury) still quite uncertain.[2]

Florence Arnold-Forster

End of Journal

[1] O'Donnell's main theme had been Jenkinson's guilt, by association, for the horrors of the Indian mutiny of 1857 (*Hansard 3*, cclxxiii, 683–99).

[2] The TS ends with 'our prospects, however', being the final words on the last leaf of the MS. But several of the succeeding leaves of the MS 'Contemporary notes' have survived among the W. E. Forster papers in T.C.D. Library, and the remaining words of the entry for 5 Aug. have been supplied from this source.

The projected visit to Russia did take place. The lords, after delaying the arrears bill by a flood of amendments, finally gave way on 10 Aug., and the bill became law on 18 Aug., on which day both houses adjourned. In Sept. and Oct. 1882 Forster and his wife, with Oakeley and Florence, made a 'delightful journey' to Russia, during which they spent ten days at Moscow. (Private journal, 1879–85, p. 160.)

APPENDIX

Notes on certain persons and matters mentioned in the text

The criteria of inclusions of persons are (a) that they are Florence's relatives or members of the Forster circle during the period of Forster's chief secretaryship; (b) that they are mentioned at least nine times in the diary. The information given usually relates only to the period covered by the diary. The sources are enumerated in the bibliography at the end of the volume.

An asterisk means that relevant information is also to be found in this appendix under the word asterisked.

Titled persons who received their titles after August 1882 are entered under their family names, not under their titles.

ARNOLD AUNTS AND UNCLES. Children of Thomas Arnold, D.D. (1795–1842), headmaster of Rugby (1828–42), and his wife Mary Penrose (d. 1873)—see Arnold, Matthew, Thomas, Frances, Walter; Hiley, Mary; Cropper, Susannah Elizabeth Lydia

ARNOLD COUSINS. Children of Matthew Arnold, of Thomas Arnold, and of Susannah Cropper

ARNOLD, Frances (1833–1923). Youngest daughter of Dr Arnold; unmarried; lived at Fox How, near Ambleside, till her death, aged 90 ('Aunt Fan')

——, Frances Lucy. Wife of Matthew Arnold ('Aunt Fanny Lucy')

——, Matthew (1822–88). Eldest son of Dr Arnold; poet and man of letters; inspector of schools, 1851–83; married Frances Lucy Wightman, 1851, and had six children, of whom three, all boys, were dead by 1869; Richard Penrose (Dick), Lucy (married Frederick Whitridge, 1885), and Eleanor, survived; professor of poetry at Oxford, 1857–67; took house in Chester Square, London S.W., 1859; he lived at Pain's Hill, near Cobham, Surrey, from 1873; his publications include *On the study of Celtic literature* (1867); Edmund Burke, *Letters, speeches, and tracts on Irish affairs*, collected and arranged by Matthew Arnold (1881); and *Irish essays and others* (1882). ('Uncle Matt')

——, Thomas (1823–1900). 2nd son of Dr Arnold; inspector of schools, Tasmania, 1850–56; married Julia (d. 1888), daughter of William Sorell, of Hobart, 1850; received into Roman Catholic church, 1856, and left Hobart; taught English literature in Newman's Catholic University of Ireland, 1856–62; classical master at Birmingham Oratory School, 1862–5; left Roman Catholic church, 1866, but rejoined it in 1876; coached boys at Oxford; professor of English literature at University College, Dublin, and fellow of Royal University of Ireland, 1882; married Josephine Benison of Slieve Russell, Cavan, 1890; of his eight children the eldest, Mary Augusta*, married Humphry Ward, and the second daughter, Lucy (b. *c.* 1858), married Rev. E. C. Selwyn, headmaster of Uppingham

——, Walter (1835–93). Youngest son of Dr Arnold

ARNOLD-FORSTERS. The four children of William Delafield Arnold (1828–59) and his wife Frances Anne Hodgson (d. 24 Mar. 1858); adopted after the death of their father (9 Apr. 1859, at Gibraltar) by their Aunt Jane and her husband William Edward Forster, they formally assumed the name Arnold-Forster in 1878—see Arnold-Forster, Edward Penrose, Florence Mary, Hugh Oakeley, Frances Egerton

ARNOLD-FORSTER, Edward Penrose (b. Aug. 1851, India). Eldest child of William Delafield Arnold; managed his adopted father's Greenholme Mills at Burley-in-Wharfedale, living at Cathedine (now The Court), a house about a mile from the Forster home, Wharfeside; married Edith Mary Ford, 1875, and had four children: Delafield, Vernon, Iris Mary, William Howard

ARNOLD-FORSTER, Florence Mary (3 July 1854 (Bayswater, London)–8 July 1936). 2nd child of William Delafield Arnold; married Robert Vere O'Brien ('Robin'), of Old Church, Co. Limerick, 10 July 1883, and had four children: Aubrey, Hugh, Jane, Florence; died at her home, Ballyalla, Co. Clare, aged 82; author of a life of the Hungarian patriot-statesman, *Francis Deák* (London, 1881; Hungarian translation, BudaPest, 1881)

—, Frances Egerton (1857 (Dharmsala, India)–1921). 4th child of William Delafield Arnold; unmarried; author of *Heralds of the cross* (London, 1882) ('Francie')

—, Hugh Oakeley (19 Aug. 1855 (Dawlish, Devon)–12 Mar. 1909, London). 3rd child of William Delafield Arnold; called to the bar, 5 Nov. 1879; private secretary to W. E. Forster (1880–82) when chief secretary for Ireland; strongly hostile to the Land League (published *The truth about the Land League* in Apr. 1882); married, 1885, Mary Lucy, daughter of Mervyn Herbert Nevil Story-Maskelyne, and had four sons; a strenuous advocate of army and navy reform, and a prolific writer on political and social subjects; joined the liberal unionist party in 1886 on Gladstone's adoption of home rule; M.P. for West Belfast, 1892–1906; for Croydon, 1906–9; secretary of state for war, 1903–5, in Balfour's conservative administration

ASHLEY, Anthony Evelyn Melbourne (1836–1907). Son of 7th earl of Shaftesbury; liberal M.P. for Poole, 1874–80, and for Isle of Wight, 1880–85; parliamentary secretary to board of trade, 1880–82; owner of 12,426 acres in Co. Sligo, valued at £5,801

AUNT SARAH. Sarah Forster*, sister of W. E. Forster's father

BALL, John and his wife. Family friends of the Forsters; John Ball accompanied W. E. Forster on trips to Austria in 1865 and to Constantinople and Asia Minor in 1867

BESSBOROUGH COMMISSION. Royal commission under earl of Bessborough, appointed on 29 July 1880 to inquire into working of land act of 1870; reported, 4 Jan. 1881, in favour of the '3 Fs' (fair rent, fixity of tenure, and freedom for the tenant to sell his interest)

BIGGAR, Joseph Gillis (1828–90). A Belfast merchant and presbyterian who joined the home rule party and the Irish Republican Brotherhood, and was received into the catholic church; M.P., Co. Cavan, 1874–90; became notorious as a pioneer of uninhibited obstructionism in the house of commons; a principal colleague of Parnell; one of the treasurers of the Land League; a hunchback with a rasping voice and uncouth manner, of unbounded courage and indifference to hostile opinion; a fervent nationalist

BOYLE, 'Nelly'. Daughter of Emily Mary Buxton*

BRADLAUGH, Charles (1833–91). Freethinker and radical politician, notorious for atheism, republican views, and advocacy of birth control; elected M.P. for Northampton in Apr. 1880, he claimed the right to affirm instead of swearing the parliamentary oath, but his claim was rejected and he was unseated; he refused to accept defeat, and a struggle began in which the electors of Northampton repeatedly reelected him till in Jan. 1886 he was allowed to take his seat, which he held till his death

BRAND, Sir Henry Bouverie William (1814–92). Liberal M.P. for Lewes, 1852–64, and for Cambridgeshire, 1868–84; speaker of the house of commons, 1872–84; on 2 Feb. 1881 (see pp 62–3), at the height of Parnellite obstruction, when the machinery of the house was threatened with breakdown, he ended a 41-hour debate on his own authority, after consultation with the prime minister (Gladstone) and the leader of the conservative opposition (Northcote)—the first step in the control of members' right of unlimited obstruction; G.C.B., Aug. 1881; created Viscount Hampden, 1884; succeeded his elder brother as 23rd Viscount Dacre

—, Lady Eliza, daughter of General Robert Ellice; married Henry B. W. Brand, 1839; d. 1899

BRIGHT, John (1811–89). Son of Jacob Bright, a quaker miller of Rochdale; worked in his father's mill, and became partner in the business, 1839; leader with Cobden in anti-corn-law agitation; independent M.P. for Durham, 1843–7; for Manchester, 1847–57; for Birmingham, 1857–89; deeply concerned about the famine in Ireland, which he visited in 1849; enunciated a policy of identifying and removing the causes of Irish discontent; advocated legislation to facilitate sale of encumbered estates, creation of peasant proprietorship, and disestablishment of protestant episcopal church; visited Ireland again and was widely acclaimed, 1866; denounced Crimean war, 1853–6; as president of board of trade, 1868–71, he was part author of the disestablishment act of 1869 and secured the inclusion of land-purchase provisions (the 'Bright clauses') in the land act of 1870; withdrew from public life owing to illness, 1871–3; chancellor of duchy of Lancaster, 1873–4; again chancellor of duchy, 1880–82; condemned lords' rejection of Forster's compensation for disturbance bill, 16 Nov. 1880 ('Force is not a remedy'), but felt compelled to approve coercion bill, Feb. 1881; land act of 1881 went far to fulfil his agrarian aims; resigned over bombardment of Alexandria by Royal Navy (July 1882); parted from Gladstone over home rule bill of 1886

BRYCE, James (1838–1922). Eldest son of James Bryce, schoolmaster and geologist, of Belfast, and nephew of Reuben John Bryce, headmaster of Belfast Academy; fellow of Oriel College, Oxford, 1862–89; won, 1863, Arnold historical prize with essay on the Holy Roman Empire, which, as rewritten and published in 1864, brought him European acclaim; called to bar, 1867; joined northern circuit, and practised there till 1882; lectured in law at Queens College, Manchester, 1868–84; regius professor of civil law at Oxford, 1870–93; became an authority on the eastern question and champion of Armenian national claims; liberal M.P. for Tower Hamlets, 1880–85; for South Aberdeen, 1885–1906; in parliament deeply concerned with Irish problems and generally supported Gladstone's measures; as chancellor of duchy of Lancaster (1892–4) helped to prepare home rule bill of 1893; chief secretary, 1905–6; U.K. ambassador at Washington, 1907–13; created viscount, 1914; one of founders of *English Historical Review*, 1885; a prodigious traveller and climber; editor and contributor, *Handbook of home rule*, with preface by Earl Spencer (1887); author of *The American commonwealth* (1888), *Studies in history and jurisprudence* (1901), *Modern democracies* (1921), and other works

BURKE, Marianne Aline Alice. Only sister of Thomas Henry Burke, for whom she kept house in the Under-secretary's Lodge, Phoenix Park, Dublin; after her brother's murder she received a government pension of £400

—, Thomas Henry (1829–82). Second son of William Burke, a catholic landowner of Knocknagur, Co. Galway; clerk in Chief Secretary's Office, 1847; under-secretary for Ireland, 1869–82; unmarried, lived with his sister, Marianne, in the Under-secretary's Lodge in the Phoenix park; assassinated with Lord Frederick Cavendish in the Phoenix Park, 6 May 1882, by a party of 'Invincibles'

BURLEY-IN-WHARFEDALE. A village about ten miles north of Bradford, on the river Wharfe, in Yorkshire, where W. E. Forster and his partner, William Fison, established a worsted manufactory, driven by water power, called Greenholme Mills (1850); above the river, near the mill, Forster built a house, Wharfeside, which was his permanent home from 1852

BUXTON, Emily Mary. Eldest daughter of Sir Henry Holland (1788–1873) and widow of Charles Buxton (1823–71), who was grandson of Thomas Fowell Buxton and thus cousin of W. E. Forster; she lived near Byfleet, Surrey, in the house Fox Warren, designed and built by her husband; their children included Eleanor Margaret (Nelly) (who married Cecil William Boyle, Sept. 1877), Mary Emma (who married Albert Osliff Rutson, 1887), Bertram Henry (1852–1934), Richenda, and Sydney Charles (1853–1934), member of London school board, 1876–82; unsuccessful liberal candidate for Boston, 1880; published *Handbook to political questions of the day* (1880); liberal M.P. for Peterborough, 1883–5; married (3 Feb. 1882) Constance Mary, daughter of Sir John Lubbock; viscount, 1914; earl, 1920

BUXTON, Sir Thomas Fowell (1837–1915), 3rd baronet. Son of Sir Edward North Buxton (1812–58), 2nd baronet, and grandson of Sir Thomas Fowell Buxton (1786–1845); married Lady Victoria Noel, 1862, and had five sons and five daughters; liberal M.P. for King's Lynn, 1865–8; many philanthropic interests at home and abroad; governor of South Australia, 1895–8; G.C.M.G., 1899

CARLINGFORD, Chicester Samuel Parkinson Fortescue (1823–98), 1st Baron Carlingford. Youngest son of Lt-col. Chichester Fortescue, of Glyde Farm, Ardee, Co. Louth; liberal M.P. for Co. Louth, 1847–74; married, 1863, Frances Elizabeth Anne (1821–79), Countess Waldegrave; chief secretary for Ireland, 1865, 1868–71, in which capacity he was co-author with Gladstone of Irish disestablishment act, 1869, and land act, 1870; created Baron Carlingford, 1874; lord privy seal, May 1881; carried second Gladstone land act through house of lords, 1881; president of council, 1883–5; parted from Gladstone on home rule issue, 1886; owned 1,452 acres, valued at £1,719, in Co. Louth

CARPENTERS. Family employed in household staff of Chief Secretary's Lodge

CATHEDINE. Home of Edward and Edith Arnold-Forster, in Burley-in-Wharfedale, about a mile from the Forster home, Wharfeside; house now called The Court

CAVENDISH, Lord Frederick Charles (1836–82). 2nd son of 7th duke of Devonshire and younger brother of Lord Hartington*; private secretary to Granville*, 1859–64; married, 1864, Lucy Caroline, second daughter of Lord Lyttleton and niece of Mrs Gladstone; liberal M.P. for northern division of W. Riding of Yorks, 1865–82; private secretary to Gladstone, 1872–3; junior lord of treasury, 1873–4; financial secretary to treasury, Apr. 1880–May 1882, in which capacity he visited Forster in Dublin on several occasions; succeeded Forster as chief secretary; was assassinated in Phoenix Park, Dublin, 6 May 1882

CHAMBERLAIN, Joseph (1830–1914). Industrialist, social reformer, and politician; leader of radical element in liberal party; liberal M.P. for Birmingham, 1876–85; opposed to coercion policy in Ireland; involved in negotiations resulting in 'Kilmainham treaty' with Parnell, Apr. 1882; broke with Gladstone over home rule bill, 1886; secretary of state for colonies in Salisbury's third administration, 1895–1903

CHATTENOOGA. The Forster cat

CHURCHILL, Lord Randolph Henry Spencer (1849–94). Younger son of 6th duke of Marlborough, lord lieutenant of Ireland, 1876–80, with whom he spent lengthy visits at the Vice-Regal Lodge; conservative M.P. for Woodstock, 1874–85, for Paddington South, 1885–94; leader, in 1880s, of new 'fourth party'*; secretary of state for India, 1885–6; chancellor of the exchequer and leader of the house of commons, July–Dec. 1886

COWEN, Joseph (1831–1900). Liberal politician and journalist, of Newcastle upon Tyne; inherited a lucrative fire-brick business from his father; actively interested in revolutionary movements on the Continent; sympathised with chartists; liberal M.P. for Newcastle upon Tyne, 1873–86; supported home rule movement; proprietor and editor of *Newcastle Chronicle*

COWPER, Francis Thomas de Grey (1834–1905), 7th Earl Cowper. Succeeded his father, 1856; inherited large properties in Herts, Notts, Lancs, and Beds, and many titles; married Katrine Cecilia, daughter of marquis of Northampton, 1870; no issue; lord lieutenant of Ireland, May 1880–Apr. 1882; opposed Gladstone's home rule bill, 1886; chairman of royal commission on working of Irish land acts of 1881 and of 1885 (1887)

CROKE, Thomas William (1824–1902), archbishop of Cashel. Studied for priesthood at Paris, Menin, and Rome; D.D. 1847; curate of Charleville, 1849; professor of ecclesiastical history at the Catholic University of Ireland, 1854–8; president of St Colman's College, Fermoy, 1858–68; bishop of Auckland, N.Z., 1870–75; archbishop of Cashel, 1875–1902; home-ruler; strongest defender of Land League among the catholic bishops; patron of Gaelic Athletic Association, 1884

CROPPER, James (1823–1900). Eldest son of John Cropper (1797–1874), of Dingle Bank, Liverpool; of Ellergreen, Kendal; paper manufacturer, Kendal; J.P. and D.L. of Westmorland; high sheriff, 1874; chairman of Kendal board of guardians; chairman of Westmorland county council; liberal M.P. for Kendal, 1880–85; married (1845) Fanny Alison Wakefield (d. 1868), of Sedgwick, Westmorland; children, Frances Anne (who married J. W. E. Conybeare (1870)), Mary Wakefield, and Charles James (1852–1924), who married (1876) Hon. Edith Emily Holland (d. 1923), daughter of Sir Henry Thurstan Holland*

——, John Wakefield (1830–), 2nd son of John Cropper of Dingle Bank, Liverpool; married (23 Aug. 1853) Susannah Elizabeth Lydia (1830–1911), 3rd daughter of Dr Arnold

CULLINAN, Frederick J. Clerk in Irish Office, 18 Great Queen Street, Westminster, S.W.; another Cullinan, William F., was draftsman of parliamentary bills in the same office

DAVITT, Michael (1846–1906). Son of an evicted small tenant of Straide, Co. Mayo; spent childhood and youth in industrial town of Haslingden, Lancs, losing his right arm in a factory accident, 1857; joined Irish Republican Brotherhood (the Fenian organisation), 1865; sentenced at Old Bailey to 15 years penal servitude for Fenian arms-traffic, 1870; released from Dartmoor on ticket of leave, Dec. 1877; in America, with John Devoy, formulated a programme of cooperation between revolutionary and constitutional nationalists under Parnell, 1878; leader of agrarian agitation resulting in foundation of Irish National Land League (Oct. 1879), with Parnell as president and himself as principal inspiration and organiser; rearrested, Dublin, 3 Feb. 1881; in Portland prison till 6 May 1882; released as a result of 'Kilmainham treaty', which he denounced, aiming at revival of land agitation with national ownership of the land as its objective

DAWSON, Charles (b. 1842). High sheriff of Limerick, 1876–7; home rule M.P. for Carlow, 1880–85; lord mayor of Dublin, 1882–3

DE VERE, Aubrey Thomas (1814–1902). Son of Sir Aubrey de Vere, 2nd baronet, of Curragh Chase, Co. Limerick; younger brother of Sir Stephen Edward de Vere*; nephew of 1st Baron Monteagle; poet and man of letters; critic of English rule in Ireland but supporter of the union; friend of Wordsworth, Landor, Tennyson, Browning, Newman; joined catholic church, 1851; professor of political and social science in Catholic University of Ireland, 1854–8; unmarried; author of many volumes of poetry and some political writings

——, Sir Stephen Edward (1812–1904). 2nd son of Sir Aubrey de Vere; called to the bar, 1836; made journey to Canada on emigrant ship, 1847, to expose sufferings of famine emigrants; joined catholic church, 1848; liberal M.P. for Limerick County, 1854–9; succeeded his brother, Vere Edmond, as 4th baronet, 23 Sept. 1880; man of letters and translator; owner of 4,163 acres in Co. Limerick, valued at £2,108

DE VESCI, John Robert William Vesey (1844–1903), 4th Viscount de Vesci. Eldest son of

Thomas, 3rd Viscount de Vesci; J.P., Queen's County; lieut. col. 1st Coldstream Guards; married Hon. Evelyn Charteris, eldest daughter of Lord Elcho, 1872; succeeded his father, 1875; lord lieutenant of Queen's County, 1883; created Baron de Vesci of Abbeyleix (U.K.), 1884; founder of Irish Loyal and Patriotic Union, to resist home rule, 1885; owned 15,069 acres, valued at £9,410, in Queen's County

DILLON, John (1851–1927). Son of John Blake Dillon (1816–66), Young Ireland leader; elected to council of Home Rule League, 1877; vehement supporter of Parnell; early recruit to land agitation and member of original committee of Land League, 1879; with Parnell on his American mission, Jan.–Mar. 1880; M.P. for Tipperary County, 1880–83; on Land League executive, Apr. 1880; appointed Land League's head of organisation, Feb. 1881; imprisoned in Kilmainham jail, 1881, 1881–2; retired from politics, 1882–5; M.P. for Mayo East, 1885–1918; in party 'split' took anti-Parnell side, 1890–91; chairman of anti-Parnellite party, 1896–9; firmest ally of Davitt as agrarian radical, and close personal friend

ECCLESTON SQUARE, no. 80. The Forster residence in London, S.W., near Victoria station

EDITH. Wife of Edward Penrose Arnold-Forster, elder brother of Florence

EGAN, Patrick (1841–1919). Successful businessman, as employee, and finally managing director, of North Dublin City Milling Co.; co-proprietor, with James Rourke, of City Bakery; member of supreme council of I.R.B. and leading Fenian supporter of home rule movement; resigned from supreme council, Mar. 1877; treasurer of Land League, Oct. 1879–Oct. 1882, operating from Feb. 1881 in Paris; went to New York, Feb. 1883, to escape arrest, and had a second career in business and politics in the U.S.; president of National League of America, 1884–6; U.S. minister to Chile, 1889–93

ELY, Jane (d. 1890). Dowager marchioness of Ely; Member of Royal Order of Victoria and Albert (3rd class); lady of the bedchamber to Queen Victoria; married (1844) John Henry Loftus, who became 3rd marquis of Ely 1845 and d. 1857

EMLY, William Monsell (1812–94), Baron Emly. Only son of William Monsell of Tervoe, Co. Limerick; liberal M.P. for Limerick County, 1847–74; received into catholic church, 1850; privy councillor; under-secretary of state for the colonies, 1868–71; postmaster general, 1871–3; created Baron Emly, 1874; married as second wife Berthe, youngest daughter of Comte de Montigny, 1857, and had two children, Gaston William Thomas (married Frances Power, 5 Sept. 1881), and Mary Olivia Augusta (married Count Edward de la Poer, 1 June 1881); owner of 2,246 acres, valued at £1,987, in Co. Limerick

ERRINGTON, George (1839–1920). J.P. for Counties Tipperary and Longford; liberal M.P. for Longford County, 1874–85; unofficial contact at Rome between British government and papacy, 1880–85; baronet, 1885

FITZGERALD, John David (1816–89). Q.C., 1847; liberal M.P. for Ennis, 1852–60; solicitor general, 1855–6; attorney general, 1856–8, 1859; privy councillor, 1856; justice of queen's bench, 1860–82; lord of appeal with life peerage and English privy councillor, 1882; owner of 1,393 acres, valued at £622, in Co. Clare, of 1,324 acres at £702 in Co. Limerick

FORSTER, Jane Martha (1821–99). Eldest child of Dr Thomas Arnold; married (1850) William Edward Forster; no issue

——, Sarah. Sister of W. E. Forster's father, William (1784–1854); unmarried; lived at the family home of the Forsters at Tottenham, and died there, 14 Sept. 1880 ('Aunt Sarah')

——, William Edward (1818–86). Only child of William and Anna (née Buxton) Forster; married (1850) Jane Martha Arnold; no issue

'FOURTH PARTY'. A group of four freelance members of the conservative party in the parliament of 1880–85—Lord Randolph Churchill*, J. E. Gorst*, Sir Henry Drummond Wolff, Arthur James Balfour; exponents of an aggressive and unorthodox toryism, attacking the weakness of conservative opposition, supporting Bradlaugh*; favouring conciliation towards Ireland while denouncing home rule and the compensation for disturbance bill, and promoting conservatism among the working classes

FOX GHYLL. A house beside Fox How*, acquired by W. E. Forster in 1873 as a holiday home

FOX HOLM. A house about a mile east of Byfleet, Surrey, apparently owned by the Buxtons of Fox Warren, about a mile south. Francie spent some time 'every summer for the past five or six years' at Fox Holm, as guest of Rev. F. J. Holland* and his wife (Journal of Frances Arnold-Forster, iv (1879–83), p. 73 (28 June 1881))

FOX HOW. A house near Ambleside, Westmorland, at the foot of Loughrigg, in the valley of the Rothay, built in 1834 by Dr Arnold, and after his death (1842) maintained by his widow (d. 1873) and his youngest daughter, Frances, till her death in 1923, as a centre for the Arnolds and their connections; 'a place of hallowed memories' (Mary Arnold-Forster, *Hugh Oakeley Arnold-Forster* (London, 1910), p. 4)

FOX WARREN. A house about a mile south-east of Byfleet, Surrey, designed by its owner, Charles Buxton, whose widow, Emily Mary*, lived there

FRANCIE. Frances Egerton Arnold-Forster*, younger sister of Florence

GIBSON, Edward (1837–1913). Called to bar, 1860; conservative M.P. for Dublin University, 1875–85; attorney general for Ireland, 1877–80; created Baron Ashbourne, 1885; lord chancellor of Ireland, 1885, 1886–92, 1895–1905; carried land purchase act (Ashbourne act), 1885

GLADSTONE, Catherine. Eldest daughter of Sir Stephen Richard Glynne, of Hawarden castle, Flint; married W. E. Gladstone, 1839

—, Helen (1849–1925). Fourth daughter of W. E. Gladstone; vice-principal of Newnham College, Cambridge, 1882–96

—, Herbert John (1854–1930). Youngest son of W. E. Gladstone; liberal M.P., Leeds, 1880–85, West Leeds, 1885–1910; junior lord of the treasury, 1881–5, in which capacity he made frequent visits to Ireland; viscount, 1910

—, William Ewart (1809–98). Leader of the liberal party; prime minister, 1868–74, 1880–85, 1886, 1892–4

GORST, John Eldon (1835–1916). Fellow of St John's College, Cambridge, 1857–60; civil commissioner of Waikato, New Zealand, 1861–3; called to the English bar, 1865; conservative M.P. for Cambridge, 1866–8; reorganised machinery of conservative party, 1868–74; M.P. for Chatham, 1875–92, for Cambridge University, 1892–1906; member of 'fourth party'*, 1880–84; solicitor general, 1885–6; knighted, 1885; under-secretary of state for India, 1886; financial secretary to treasury, 1891–2

GOSCHEN, George Joachim (1831–1907), 1st Viscount Goschen. Son of W. H. Goschen, City of London banker; director of Bank of England, 1858; liberal M.P. for City of London, 1863–80; for Ripon, 1880–85; for Edinburgh East, 1885–6; president of poor law board, 1868–71; first lord of admiralty, 1871–4; opposed to radicalism of Chamberlain and Dilke and to home rule policy of Gladstone; joined Hartington in forming liberal unionist party, 1886; chancellor of the exchequer, 1886–92; liberal unionist M.P. for St George's, Hanover Square, 1887–1900; first lord of the admiralty, 1895–1900; created viscount, 1900

GRANT-DUFF, Sir Mountstuart Elphinstone (1829–1906). Liberal M.P., Elgin Burghs, 1857–81; under-secretary for India, 1868–74; under-secretary for the colonies, 1880–81; C.I.E., 1881; governor of Madras, June 1881–Dec. 1886; an authority on foreign affairs, a prolific writer, and widely travelled; wrote the preface to Florence's *Francis Deák* (1880); G.C.S.I., 1887

GRANVILLE, Lord. Granville George Leveson-Gower (1815–91), 2nd Earl Granville; Whig M.P. for Morpeth, 1836–8, and for Lichfield, 1841–6; succeeded his father, the 1st Earl Granville, 1846; secretary of state for foreign affairs, 1851–2, 1870–74, 1880–85; secretary of state for colonies, 1868–70, 1886; leader of house of lords when liberals were in office, 1855–86; supported Gladstone on home rule

GRAY, Edmund Dwyer (1845–88). Son of Sir John Gray, of the *Freeman's Journal*; succeeded his father as owner and editor of that paper, 1875; home rule M.P. for Tipperary county, 1877–80; for Carlow county, 1880–85; for Dublin (St Stephen's Green), 1885–8; lord mayor of Dublin, 1880; high sheriff, 1882

GREGORY, Sir William Henry (1817–92) of Coole Park, Gort, Co. Galway; conservative M.P. for Dublin, 1842–7; high sheriff of Galway, 1849; liberal-conservative M.P. for Galway county, 1857–71; joined liberal party, 1865; trustee of National Gallery, 1867–92; governor of Ceylon, 1871–7; K.C.M.G., 1876; married (1880) as second wife Isabella Augusta (1852–1932), daughter of Dudley Persse, of Roxborough, Co. Galway; owned 4,893 acres in Co. Galway, valued at £2,378

HARCOURT, Sir William George Granville Venables Vernon (1827–1904). Called to the bar, 1854; contributor to *Saturday Review*, 1855–9; liberal M.P. for Oxford City, 1868–80; independent critic of first Gladstone government; Whewell professor of international law at Cambridge, 1869–87; solicitor general for England, 1873–4; knighted, 1873; M.P. for Derby, 1880–95; home secretary, 1880–85; supported Gladstone on home rule; chancellor of the exchequer, 1886, 1892–5; leader of liberal party in house of commons, 1894–8; M.P. for Monmouth West, 1895–1904

HARTINGTON, Spencer Compton Cavendish (1833–1908), marquis of Hartington. Eldest son of 8th duke of Devonshire; elder brother of Lord Frederick Cavendish; cousin of Lord Granville; liberal M.P. for Lancashire North, 1857–68; marquis of Hartington, 1858; secretary of state for war, 1866–7; M.P. for Radnor Boroughs, 1869–80; chief secretary for Ireland, 1871–4; led liberal party during Gladstone's retirement, 1875–80; M.P. for Lancashire North-east, 1880–85; for Rossendale, 1885–91; secretary of state for India, 1880–82; for war, 1882–5; opposed to Gladstone's home rule policy and approved of coercion in Ireland; with Chamberlain founded liberal-unionist party; succeeded his father as 9th duke of Devonshire, 1891

HEALY, Timothy Michael (1855–1931). Born at Bantry, Co. Cork, elder son of Maurice Healy and nephew of A. M. Sullivan*; went to Dublin at 13 to make a living; largely self-taught; of acute mind, prodigious memory, and great intellectual vitality; quick-witted, sharp-tongued, and fluent; worked as shorthand writer at Newcastle upon Tyne for North-Eastern Railway, and became secretary of local home rule association; moved to London, 1878, to become contributor of a weekly parliamentary letter to the *Nation*; went in 1880 at Parnell's request to organise the latter's lecturing campaign in the U.S. and Canada; home rule M.P. for Wexford town (1880–83), Monaghan county (1883–5), Londonderry South (1885–6), Longford North (1887–92), Louth North (1892–1910), Cork North-east (1911–18); distinguished himself by his mastery of the complexities of the land bill of 1881, of which the 'Healy clause' (pt II, sect. VIII (9)), providing that a tenant's improvements should not be taken into account in assessing a fair rent, was his amendment; married (1882), Erina, daughter of T. D. Sullivan and niece of A. M. Sullivan; called to the bar, 1884; first governor general of Irish Free State, 1922–8

HILLIER, George Edward. Commissioned 5th Lancers; A.D.C. to governor general of India, 1840–47; retired with rank of lieutenant-colonel, 1864; inspector general of R.I.C., 1876–82; retired after Phoenix Park murders

HILEY, Mary. Second daughter of Dr Arnold, and wife (1858) of Rev. A. Hiley, of Wood-house, near Loughborough ('Aunt Mala')

HOLLAND, Francis James (1828–1907). 2nd son of Sir Henry Holland (1788–1873), and brother of Sir Henry Thurstan Holland* and of Emily Mary Buxton*; minister of Quebec Chapel, Bryanston Street, Marylebone W.1, 1861–83; married (1855) Mary Sibylla, daughter of Rev. Alfred Lyall, of Harbledown, Kent; children, Mary Agnes (d. 1928), married (1889) Rev. William Henry Bolton (d. 1902)

——, Sir Henry Thurstan (1825–1914), 2nd baronet. Son of Sir Henry Holland (1788–1873), physician, 1st baronet; assistant under-secretary for the colonies, 1870–74; conservative M.P. for Midhurst, 1874–85, and for Hampstead, 1885–8; privy councillor, 1885; vice-president of committee of council on education, 1885–6, 1886–8; created Baron Knutsford, 1888; secretary of state for the colonies, 1888–92; viscount, 1895; married (1) Elizabeth (d. 1855), youngest daughter of Nathanial Hibbert, (2) in 1858, Margaret Jean, eldest daughter of Sir Charles E. Trevelyan; children of first marriage, Sydney George (b. 1855), Arthur Henry Hibbert (b. 1855), Edith Emily; of second marriage, Cecil Trevelyan (b. 1862), Lionel Raleigh (b. 1865), Margaret Alice

IRISH OFFICE. The London base of the chief secretary's department, at 18 Great Queen St., Westminster, S.W.

MR JACKSON. Edward Jackson (d. 1892); LL.B. (Cantab.) 1829; curate of St James, Leeds, 1846; honorary canon of Ripon cathedral, 1875; chaplain of Leeds workhouse; precentor of Ripon diocese, 1880

JEPHSON, Henry. Clerk in chief secretary's office, 1865–72; private secretary to T. H. Burke as under-secretary, 1872–80; private secretary to W. E. Forster as chief secretary, 1880–82, and to his successor, Sir George Otto Trevelyan, 1882–4; author of *Notes on Irish questions* (1870) and other pamphlets on Irish subjects

JOHNSON, William Moore (1828–1918). Called to the bar, 1853; law adviser to Irish government, 1868–74; liberal M.P. for Mallow, 1880–83; solicitor general (24 May 1880–17 Nov. 1881); attorney general (17 Nov. 1881–3 Jan. 1883); justice of queen's bench, 1883–1909; knighted, 1909

'KILMAINHAM TREATY'. An informal understanding between Parnell, imprisoned in Kil-mainham jail, and the Gladstone government, negotiated by W. H. O'Shea*, Justin McCarthy*, and Joseph Chamberlain*, Apr. 1882; government to settle question of arrears of rent on an equitable basis, Parnell and his colleagues to have no-rent manifesto* withdrawn and to do their utmost to stop outrages and intimidation; cabinet agreed, and Parnell and the other imprisoned leaders were released (2 May 1882)

LAND LEAGUE. The Irish National Land League, founded by Davitt and Parnell in Dublin on 21 Oct. 1879 'to bring about a reduction of rack rents' and 'to facilitate the obtaining of the ownership of the soil by the occupiers'; leaders tried for conspiracy, Dec. 1880–Jan. 1881, but acquitted through disagreement of jury; issued 'no-rent manifesto', 18 Oct. 1881; suppressed by Irish government, 20 Oct. 1881; voluntarily wound up, 17 Oct. 1882

LAW, Hugh (1818–83). Called to the bar, 1840; Q.C., 1860; drafted Irish church act (1869) and land act (1870); solicitor general, 1872–4; attorney general, 1874; liberal M.P. for Londonderry county, 1874–81; attorney general, 10 May 1880–17 Nov. 1881; conducted prosecution of land-leaguers, Dec. 1880–Jan. 1881; active in committee stage of land bill, 1881; lord chancellor, 11 Nov. 1881–10 Sept. 1883

LITTON, Edward Falconer (1827–90). Called to the bar, 1849; J.P. for Counties Cork, Tyrone, and Wicklow; liberal M.P. for Co. Tyrone, 1880–81; member of land com-mission under land act of 1881

LLOYD, Charles Dalton Clifford (1844–91). Son of Col. Robert Lloyd of 68th Durham Light Infantry; grandson of Bartholomew Lloyd, provost of T.C.D., 1831–7, and nephew of Humphrey Lloyd, provost, 1867–81; educated at Sandhurst; began his public career in the Burma police and administration, 1862–72; read law at Lincoln's Inn, 1872–5; called to the bar, 1875; R.M. for Co. Down, 1874–81; for Longford, Jan.–May 1881, for Limerick, May–Dec. 1881; special R.M. for Limerick, Clare, and Galway, Dec. 1881–Sept. 1883; in service of Egyptian government, 1883–4; R.M. for Co. Londonderry, Mar.–Nov. 1885; governor of Mauritius, 1885–6; consult at Erzerum, 1889–91; author of *Ireland under the Land League* (Edinburgh and London, 1892)

LOWELL, James Russell (1819–91). Professor of modern languages, Harvard College, 1855–86; founder-editor of *Atlantic Monthly*, 1857–61; joint editor of *North American Review*, 1864–72; U.S. minister to Spain, 1877–80, and to Great Britain, 1880–85; author of many volumes of poems, essays, and commentaries on public questions, all marked by shrewd observation, independence of mind, wide-ranging sympathy, and good humour

LUBBOCK, Sir John (1834–1913). Banker, scientist, and public benefactor; liberal M.P. for Maidstone, 1870–80, and for London University, 1880–1900; vice-chancellor of London University, 1872–80; trustee of British Museum, 1878; created Baron Avebury, 1900; author of *The hundred best books* (1891) and many scientific, sociological, and ethical works; one of his daughters, Amy Harriet, married Andrew Mulholland, 1877; another, Constance Mary, married Sydney Charles Buxton, 1882

MCCABE, Edward (1816–85), archbishop of Dublin. Born in Dublin, the son of poor parents; educated at Maynooth; ordained curate of Clontarf, Dublin, 1839; parish priest of St Nicholas Without, Dublin, 1856; of Kingstown, 1865; assistant bishop to Paul Cullen, archbishop of Dublin, 1877; archbishop of Dublin, 1879–85; cardinal, 12 Mar. 1882; the most hostile of the catholic bishops to Land League; continually denounced agrarian outrage

MCCARTHY, Justin (1830–1912). Born near Cork and brought up in 'genteel poverty' (his own words); involved in Young Ireland movement, 1848; went to London, 1859, and joined staff of *Morning Star*, of which he was editor, 1864–8; in 1866 published *Paul Massey*, the first of many successful novels that included *Dear Lady Disdain* (1875) and *Miss Misanthrope* (1878); parliamentary leader-writer on *Daily News* from 1871; his reputation as a literary man was established by his *History of our own times* (4 vols, 1879–80); entered active politics at Parnell's instance as home rule M.P. for Longford county, 1879–85; elected vice-chairman of parliamentary party under Parnell's chairmanship, 27 Dec. 1880; M.P. Longford North (1885–6), Derry City (1886–92), Longford North (1892–1900)

MAHAFFY, John Pentland (1839–1919). Son of Rev. Nathaniel Mahaffy, a small landowner of County Donegal; B.A., Dublin University, 1859; ordained, 1864; elected fellow of Trinity College, Dublin, 1864; professor of ancient history, 1871–1900; provost, 1914–19; G.B.E., 1918; author of *Prolegomena to ancient history* (1871), *Kant's critical philosophy for English readers* (1871), *Greek social life from Homer to Menander* (1874), *A history of Greek classical literature* (1880), and many other works, mainly on Greek history and literature; famous alike as man of letters, academician, wit, and raconteur

MONCK, Charles Stanley (1819–94), 4th Viscount Monck of Charleville, Enniskerry, Co. Wicklow; called to the bar, 1841; succeeded his father as viscount, 1849; conservative M.P. for Portsmouth, 1852–7; lord of treasury, 1855–8; governor general of British North America, 1861–7; of dominion of Canada, 1867–8; created Baron Monck of U.K., 1866; G.C.M.G., 1869; member of Irish church temporalities commission, 1869–81; commissioner of national education, 1871–94; lord lieutenant of Co. Dublin, 1874–94; owned 3,434 acres, valued at £1,556, in Co. Wicklow, 5,663 at

£2,896 in Co. Wexford, 5,385 at £3,498 in Co. Kilkenny (total 14,482 acres valued at £7,950)

MONTEAGLE, Thomas Spring Rice (1849–1926), 2nd Baron Monteagle. Of Mount Trenchard, Foynes, Co. Limerick; elder son of Stephen Edmond Spring Rice; succeeded his grandfather, Thomas, 1st Baron Monteagle (1790–1866); married (1875) Elizabeth (1849–1908), eldest daughter of Samuel Butcher, bishop of Meath; owner of 2,310 acres in Kerry and 6,445 acres in Limerick, together valued at £6,137

—, Mary Anne, dowager Lady Monteagle. Eldest daugher of John Marshall of Hall-steads, Cumberland, and widow of 1st Baron Monteagle; d. 1889, aged 89

MORLEY, John (1838–1923). Wrote articles for *Saturday Review*, 1863–7; editor, 1867–82, of *Fortnightly Review*, which he made a leading organ of liberal opinion; published *Voltaire* (1872), *Rousseau* (1873), *Burke* (1879), *Life of Cobden* (1881), and many other works including *Life of Gladstone* (3 vols, 1903); collaborated in a programme of radical reform with Chamberlain and Dilke; editor of *Pall Mall Gazette*, 1880–83; fierce critic of Forster's regime in Ireland; liberal M.P., Newcastle upon Tyne, 1883–95; Montrose Burghs, 1896–1908; chief secretary for Ireland, 1886, 1892–5; secretary of state for India, 1905–10; created Viscount Morley of Blackburn, 1908; lord privy seal, 1910–14; resigned from cabinet over its decision to enter war in 1914

MRS BRAND'S GALLERY. The ladies' gallery in the house of commons under the control of Mrs Brand (from Aug. 1881 Lady Brand), as wife of the speaker of the house of commons, H. B. W. (from Aug. 1881 Sir Henry) Brand*

MULHOLLAND, Amy Harriet. Daughter of Sir John Lubbock*; married Andrew Mul-holland (1877) who died in the same year

NAISH, John (1841–90). Called to the bar, 1865; law adviser to Irish government, 1880–83; solicitor general, 1883–5; lord chancellor, 1885, 1886; lord justice of appeal, 1885, 1886–90; an eminent lawyer and the second catholic chancellor since 1690

NELLY. Eleanor Arnold, younger daughter of Matthew Arnold and cousin of Florence

NORTHCOTE, Sir Stafford Henry (1818–87). Called to the English bar, 1847; succeeded as 8th baronet, 1851; private secretary to Gladstone, 1842–51; author, with Sir Charles Trevelyan, of report (23 Nov. 1853) on the permanent civil service, later embodied in legislation; conservative M.P. for Dudley, 1855–7; for Stamford, 1858–66; for North Devon, 1866–85; secretary to treasury, 1859; president of board of trade, 1866–7; secretary of state for India, 1867–8; chancellor of the exchequer, 1874–80; and (from 1876) leader of house of commons; tried unsuccessfully to provide against Parnellite obstruction; as leader of the opposition (1880–85) was strongly criticised by 'fourth party'*; created earl of Iddesleigh and Viscount St Cyres, 1885; first lord of treasury, 1885–6; foreign secretary, 1886–7; an eminently mild, cautious, and disinterested politician, and an authority on public finance

NO-RENT MANIFESTO. Manifesto, following the arrest and imprisonment of Parnell and Land League colleagues (13–15 Oct. 1881), in which, as the executive of the league, they called on the tenant farmers to pay no rents to their landlords 'until the govern-ment relinquishes the existing system of terrorism and restores the constitutional rights of the people'; written by William O'Brien and signed by Parnell, Andrew Kettle, Thomas Brennan, John Dillon, and Thomas Sexton, and also bearing the names of Michael Davitt (in Portland prison) and Patrick Egan (in Paris); issued to the public by the central body of the Land League on 18 Oct. 1881; a gesture to extreme elements in the land movement, it was rejected by a large majority of the league's supporters and by the catholic clergy generally, including not only Arch-bishop McCabe* but also Archbishop Croke*; though it proved a failure, it encouraged, and was probably intended to encourage, lawlessness while the leaders of the league were interned; its withdrawal by them was an essential condition of the 'Kilmainham treaty'*

OAKEL. Hugh Oakeley Arnold-Forster*, younger brother of Florence

O'BRIEN, Charlotte Grace (1845–1909). Younger daughter of William Smith O'Brien (1803–64), Young Irelander; on her mother's death in 1861 looked after her father till his death; kept house for her brother, Edward William*, at Cahirmoyle, Co. Limerick, after his first wife died in 1868, and mothered his three young children till his second marriage, to Julia Marshall in 1880; her home for the rest of her life was at Foynes, on the Shannon; beginning in 1878 she published books, articles, and poems reflecting her fervent conviction on home rule for Ireland, the land question, and the Irish poor; fiercely attacked Forster's government in the *Pall Mall Gazette*; exposed the exploitation of girls emigrating through the port of Queenstown, set up in 1881 a large boarding-house for them in the town, and made several steerage passages to America to promote improved conditions of accommmodation for them on ship-board, and to provide for their reception at New York; joined the catholic church in 1887

——, Edward William (1837–1909). Eldest son of William Smith O'Brien (1803–64) of Cahirmoyle, Co. Limerick; cousin of 14th Baron Inchiquin and of Robert Vere O'Brien*; by a settlement with his father he took over the Cahirmoyle estate in 1863; married (1) Mary Spring Rice (1863) daughter of Stephen Edmond Spring Rice (d. 1868), and (2) Julia Mary Garth Marshall (31 Jan. 1880), daughter of James Garth Marshall (1802–73), of Monk Coniston, Ambleside, Westmorland; assistant commis-sioner for land act of 1881

——, Elinor. Widow of Hon. Robert O'Brien of Old Church, Co. Limerick; eldest daughter of Sir Aubrey de Vere, 2nd baronet, of Curragh Chase, Co. Limerick; sister of Aubrey* and Stephen* de Vere and mother of Robert Vere O'Brien*; d. 1889

——, Murrough John (1842–1914). Younger son of Rev. Henry O'Brien (1815–95); cousin of 14th Baron Inchiquin, of Edward William O'Brien*; and of Robert Vere O'Brien*; married (16 Sept. 1873) Eleanor Waller (d. 1916); one of three inspectors of estates under church temporalities commission; chief agent of land sales for land commission under land act of 1881; land commissioner, Nov. 1892; bought Mount Mapas, Kil-liney, Oct. 1879

——, Robert Vere (1842–1913) ('Robin'). Younger son of Hon. Robert O'Brien, of Old Church, Co. Limerick; cousin of 14th Baron Inchiquin and of Edward William O'Brien*; married Florence, 10 July 1883; children: Aubrey, Hugh, Jane, Florence

——, William (1852–1928). Born Mallow, second son of James O'Brien, solicitor's clerk; student at Queen's College, Cork; reporter on Cork *Daily Herald*, 1869; special corres-pondent for *Freeman's Journal*, 1875; *Christmas on the Galtees*, 1878; on *Freeman's Jour-nal* commission of inquiry into distress, 1879; editor of the Parnellite weekly, *United Ireland*, Aug. 1881; imprisoned in Kilmainham with Parnell and other leaders, 15 Oct.; writes 'no-rent manifesto'*, 18 Oct.; released, 2 May 1882; home rule M.P. for Mallow, 1883–5; for Tyrone South, 1885–6; for Cork North-east, 1887–92; for Cork City, 1892–5, 1900–09, 1910–18; co-author with John Dillon of 'plan of campaign', 1886; opposed to Parnell in 'split', 1890–91; founded United Irish League, 1898; leading figure in land conference (1902–3) which prepared the way for the decisive Wyndham land act of 1903; author of *Recollections* (1906), and many other works

O'CONNOR, Thomas Power (1848–1929). Eldest son of Thomas O'Connor, a shopkeeper of Athlone; student at Queen's College, Galway (B.A., 1866); began career in journal-ism in 1867 on staff of *Saunders' Newsletter*, Dublin conservative daily; moved to London in 1870, and obtained employment on *Daily Telegraph* and then on New York *Herald*; free-lancing in London, 1873–80; his *Life of Lord Beaconsfield* (1879), a hostile study of the prime minister, first gained him publicity; home rule M.P. for Galway City, 1880–85, distinguishing himself as one of the most strenuous talkers among the Parnellites; M.P. for the Scotland division of Liverpool, 1885–1929; he combined politics with journalism without ever becoming a leading member of his party or a distinctive influence on public opinion; first president of board of film censors, 1917; 'father' of the house of commons; author of *The Parnell movement* (1886), *Memoirs of an old parliamentarian* (1929), and other works

O'DONNELL, Frank Hugh (1848–1916). Son of Bernard O'Donnell, of Carndonagh, Co. Donegal, captain in Northumberland Fusiliers; b. Devonport; student at Queen's College, Galway (B.A., 1865, M.A., 1868); joined staff of *Morning Post* (London); initiated into I.R.B. in London by Mark Ryan; vice-president of Home Rule Confederation of Great Britain, Aug. 1876; home rule M.P. for Dungarvan, 1877–85; leading ally of Parnell in obstructionist policy, but parted with Parnellites over Land League; founded Farmers' Alliance, in London, as means of Irish intervention in British politics, July 1879; intellectually gifted, and a fluent speaker but politically ineffectual owing to extreme egotism and eccentricity; prolific author, works including *A history of the Irish parliamentary party* (1910)

O'HAGAN, John (1822–90). Second son of John Arthur O'Hagan, of Newry, Co. Down; called to bar, 1842; Young Irelander and contributor to the *Nation*; member of board of national education, 1861; married Frances, daughter of Thomas O'Hagan, 1865; county court judge, 1878–81; appointed judicial commissioner of land commission under land act of 1881

——, Thomas (1812–85). Only son of Edward O'Hagan, catholic merchant of Belfast; called to the bar, 1836; edited *Newry Examiner*, 1836–40; friend and supporter of O'Connell, but opposed to repeal of the Union; member of board of national education, 1858; solicitor general, 1860–61; attorney general, 1861–5; liberal M.P. for Tralee, 1863–5; judge of court of common pleas, 1865–8; lord chancellor (the first catholic to hold the office since 1690), 1868–74; created Baron O'Hagan of Tullahogue, 1870; member of intermediate education board, 1878; vice-chancellor of Royal University of Ireland, 1880; lord chancellor, May 1880–Nov. 1881

O'SHEA, William Henry (1840–1905). Son of Henry O'Shea, a Dublin catholic solicitor and clerk of the peace for Co. Limerick; in 18th Hussars, 1858–62; married (1867) Katharine, youngest daughter of Rev. Sir John Page Wood; home rule M.P. for Clare, Apr. 1880–Nov. 1885; voted for Parnell as leader of parliamentary party, 17 May 1880; by Oct. 1880 his wife and Parnell had become lovers, thus producing an obscure and complicated triangular relationship kept from public knowledge for nine years; in Apr. 1882 O'Shea was involved in negotiations between Parnell, imprisoned in Kilmainham jail, and leading members of the government that resulted in the 'Kilmainham treaty'; in 1884–5 he was again intermediary between Parnell and Chamberlain about a 'central board' scheme for Ireland; returned M.P. for Galway city, Feb. 1886, through Parnell's influence; did not vote on the second reading of the home rule bill, 7 June 1886, and resigned his seat next day; divorce decree against his wife, Nov. 1890, Parnell being cited as co-respondent, led to Parnell's deposition as leader by majority of party on 6 Dec. 1890

'THE OCCIDENTAL'. Horace West*

PARNELL, Charles Stewart (1846–91). Fourth son of John Henry Parnell (1811–59), of Avondale, Co. Wicklow; owner of 4,678 acres, valued at £1,245, in Co. Wicklow; high sheriff of his county, 1874; home rule M.P. for Meath, 1875–80, and a leading figure in obstructionist group in Irish parliamentary party; president of Land League, 1879–81; conducted fund-raising mission in U.S. and Canada, Jan.–Mar. 1880; M.P. Cork city, 1880–91; chairman of Irish parliamentary party, 17 May 1880–6 Dec. 1890;

prosecuted, with other land-leaguers, for conspiracy, Dec. 1880–Jan. 1881; imprisoned as 'suspect' in Kilmainham jail, 12 Oct. 1881, with other leading land-leaguers; released 2 May 1882, as a consequence of the 'Kilmainham treaty'*; attained a peak of political success with Gladstone's home rule bill (Apr.–June 1886) and the liberal alliance (1886–90); deposed from the leadership of the parliamentary party (6 Dec. 1890) as a consequence of the divorce suit brought by W. H. O'Shea* against his wife

PORTER, Andrew Marshall (1837-1919). Son of Rev. John Scott Porter, unitarian minister of first presbyterian church, Belfast; called to the bar, 1860; liberal M.P. for Londonderry county, 1881–4; solicitor general, 17 Nov. 1881–9 Jan. 1883; attorney general, 3 Jan.–19 Dec. 1883; master of the rolls, 1883–1906; baronet, 1902

POWER, John O'Connor (1846–1919). Born in Ballinasloe, Co. Galway, of obscure parentage, and spent part of his childhood in local workhouse; went to live, c.1861, with relations in Rochdale, and learnt trade of house-painter; joined I.R.B. and became one of its leading members; imprisoned in Kilmainham, Feb.–July 1868; at St Jarlath's College, Tuam, where he acquired a belated secondary education while actively engaged in arms-trafficking, Jan. 1871–July 1874; earned high reputation as orator; pioneered policy of Fenian cooperation with home rule movement; home rule M.P. for Co. Mayo, 1874–80; expelled from supreme council of I.R.B., Mar. 1877; prominent member of obstructionist group in Irish parliamentary party and advocate of advanced land-reform; aspired to leadership of party; hostile to Parnell; attended earliest land-meetings in west, 1879; reelected M.P. for Mayo, Apr. 1880; proposed compensation for disturbance bill, 28 May 1880, which precipitated the government's first initiative on land question; proposed withdrawal of Irish party from parliament, Feb. 1881, but voted for Gladstone's land bill and separated from Land League, eventually (1883) joining the liberal party; called to the English bar, 17 Nov. 1881; unsuccessful candidate for seat in parliament for Kennington as radical, in 1885, and for Mayo West as independent nationalist, in 1893; married widow of H. S. Weiss, F.R.C.S., 1893

POWERSCOURT, Mervyn Wingfield (1836–1904), 7th Viscount Powerscourt. Of Powerscourt Castle, Enniskerry, Co. Wicklow; lieut, 1st Life Guards; deputy-lieutenant for Wicklow, and J.P. for Wicklow, Dublin, and Tyrone; elected representative peer for Ireland, 1865; art collector; elected Member of Royal Irish Academy, 1885; owner of 50,454 acres, valued at £14,282 (38,725 acres (£9,829) in Wicklow, 11, 729 (£4,453) in Wexford)

PUCK. Florence's dog

REDINGTON, Christopher Thomas Talbot (1847–99). Eldest son of Sir Thomas Nicholas Redington (1815–62), under-secretary, 1846–52; deputy lieutenant and J.P. for Co. Galway; member of senate of Royal University of Ireland, 1880, and vice-chancellor, 1894; high sheriff of Co. Galway, 1893; close friend of Herbert Gladstone; catholic landlord, owning 9,626 acres, valued at £4,393, in Co. Galway, and 2,954 acres, valued at £1,487, in Co. Wexford

REDMOND, John Edward (1856–1918). Son of William Archer Redmond, home rule M.P. for Wexford, 1872–80; clerk in house of commons, 1880; home rule M.P. for New Ross, Jan. 1881–1885; for Wexford North, 1885–91; for Waterford, 1891–1918; Parnell's principal supporter in the 'split' (1890–91); leader of Parnellites in parliament, 1891–1900, and of reunited Irish party, 1900

RICHARDSON, James Nicholson (1846–1921). Son of John Grubb Richardson (1813–90) quaker founder of linen mills and model village at Bessbrook, Co. Armagh (1846–7); entered his father's business, 1863; married (1867) Sophia, daughter of William Malcolmson of Portlaw, and settled at Mount Caulfield, Bessbrook; liberal M.P. for Co. Armagh, 1880–85; strongly opposed Gladstone home rule policy

Rob. One of the Forster dogs; lost in Buckingham Palace Rd, 13 Apr. 1882, and never found; photograph in Mary Arnold-Forster, *Hugh Oakeley Arnold Forster* (London, 1910), facing p. 42

Ross-of-Bladensburg, John Foster (1848–1926), of Rostrevor, Co. Down. Asst private secretary to W. E. Forster, 1881–2; on staff of Spencer (1882–5) and of Carnarvon (1885–6) as lords lieutenant; chief commissioner, Dublin Metropolitan Police, 1901–14; K.C.B., 1903

Royal Hibernian Military School, Phoenix Park, Dublin. A boys' school, founded 1769 to prepare orphans of soldiers for apprenticeships or service in the regular army; Florence often attended Sunday service in the chapel (now R.C.) attached to this school, which was in the 'Fifteen Acres', not far from the Chief Secretary's Lodge; now St Mary's Hospital

Russell, Charles (1832–1900). Son of Arthur Russell of Newry (d. 1845); and nephew of Charles William Russell, professor of ecclesiastical history at Maynooth College, 1845–57, and president, 1857–80; educated at Belfast, Newry, Castleknock College, and T.C.D.; admitted solicitor, 1854, and practised in county courts of Down and Antrim; moved to London and entered Lincoln's Inn, 1856; called to English bar and joined northern circuit, 1859, acquiring very lucrative practice there; independent liberal M.P. for Dundalk, 1880–85; generally voted with Irish parliamentary party; adopted home rule, 1885; liberal M.P. for South Hackney, 1885–94; attorney general for England, 1886, 1892–4; leading counsel for Parnell before *Times*–Parnell commission, 1888–9; lord of appeal and life peer as Baron Russell of Killowen, 1894; lord chief justice, 1894–1900; author of *New views on Ireland; on Irish land: grievances, remedies* (1880) and other works

Rutson, Alfred Osliff (1836–90). Fellow of Magdalen College, Oxford, 1860–70; B.L., 1864; unsuccessful liberal candidate for Northallerton, Apr. 1880; married (27 Oct. 1887) Mary Emma Buxton, daughter of Emily Mary Buxton*

St James the Less. Church and school in Garden St., Vauxhall Bridge Rd, S.W.1, built (1859–61) by George Edmund Street (1821–81), R.A. and pioneer of arts and crafts movement, 'one of the most original and remarkable churches in London'

Salisbury, Robert Arthur Talbot Gascoyne-Cecil (1830–1903), 3rd marquis of Salisbury; Fellow of All Souls, Oxford, 1853; conservative M.P. for Stamford, 1853–68; secretary of state for India, 1866–7, 1874–8; succeeded his father as marquis, 1868; foreign secretary, 1878–80; leader of opposition in house of lords on Beaconsfield's death (Apr. 1881); prime minister, 1885–6, 1886–92, 1895–1902; contributed 33 articles to *Quarterly Review*, 1860–83; a formidable opponent of democracy and defender of unsentimental conservatism; uncle of Arthur James Balfour

Selborne, Roundell Palmer (1812–95), Baron Selborne. Fellow of Magdalen College, Oxford, 1835; conservative M.P. for Plymouth, 1847–52, 1853–7; liberal M.P. for Richmond (Yorks), 1861–72; solicitor general for England, 1861–3; knighted, 1861; attorney general, 1863–6; refused peerage and lord chancellorship, 1868, over Gladstone's Irish disestablishment bill; lord chancellor, 1872–4; Baron Selborne of Selborne, 1872; lord chancellor, 1880–85; earl, Dec. 1882; refused office, 1886, owing to his opposition to Gladstone's home rule bill

Sexton, Thomas (1848–1932). Born in Co. Waterford, son of constable of R.I.C.; leader writer on *Nation*, 1867; joined home rule party; as Parnellite candidate for Sligo County, Apr. 1880, he defeated the sitting member, E. R. King-Harman, a great landowner and conservative home-ruler; M.P. Sligo County, 1880–85; fluent speaker and valued member of obstructionist group in parliamentary party; member of Land League executive, 1880–81; imprisoned with Parnell and others in Kilmainham, 1881; M.P. Belfast West, 1886–92; Kerry North, 1892–6

SHAW, William (1823–95). Son of Rev. Samuel Shaw, of Passage West, Co. Cork, congregationalist minister; followed his father's calling, 1846–50, at Cork, but abandoned it for a business career in 1850, when he married Charlotte Clear, daughter of a wealthy Cork merchant; founded Munster Bank, 18 Oct. 1864; liberal M.P. for Bandon, 1868–74; home rule M.P. for Co. Cork, 1874–85; chairman of home rule party in parliament, June 1879–May 1880; member of Bessborough commission*, 1880–81; defeated by Parnell in vote for chairmanship of parliamentary party, 17 May 1880; seceded from party, Jan. 1881, over agrarian policy of Parnellites; declared bankrupt, 1886, following failure of Munster Bank

SHAW-LEFEVRE, George John (1831–1928). Son of Sir John George Shaw-Lefevre; founder-member and first chairman of Commons Preservation Society, 1866; liberal M.P. for Reading (1863–85), for Central Bradford (1886–95); secretary to board of trade, 1869–71; secretary to admiralty, 1871–4; first commissioner of works, 1880–83, 1892–4; president of local government board, 1894–5; active member of London County Council, 1897–1912; created Baron Eversley, 1906; an authority on land questions at home and abroad and an advocate of peasant proprietorship; author of *The working of the Bright clauses of the Irish land act, 1870* (1879), *Freedom of land* (1880), *English and Irish land questions* (1881), *Incidents of coercion: a journal of visits to Ireland in 1882 and 1888* (1888), *Agrarian tenures* (1893), *Commons, forests, and footpaths* (1894), *Gladstone and Ireland* (1912)

SHEEHY, Eugene (1841–1917). Educated at Mungret College and Irish College in Paris; ordained there, 1868; curate in Kilmallock parish, Co. Limerick, 1877–84; extreme land-agitator, and president of Kilmallock branch of Land League; imprisoned in Kilmainham jail, 20 May 1881, the first priest to be arrested during land war; released, 29 Sept.; on Land League delegation to Chicago convention of American Land League, 30 Nov.–2 Dec.; parish priest of Rockhill, Co. Limerick, 1886–1909

SMYTH, Patrick James (1826–85). Son of a prosperous tanner of Dublin; educated at Clongowes Wood College; joined Repeal Association, 1844; involved in Young Ireland rising of 1848; escaped to America and became prominent in Irish national movement there; conducted escape of John Mitchel and others from imprisonment in Tasmania, 1853; home rule M.P. for Westmeath, 1871–80, for Tipperary, 1880–82; critical of Parnell and hostile to Land League; resigned his seat, 1882; appointed secretary of Irish Loan Reproductive Fund, 1884, but died within a few weeks (on 12 Jan. 1885)

SPENCER, John Poyntz Spencer (1835–1910), 5th Earl Spencer. Liberal M.P. for South Northants, Apr. 1857; succeeded his father as earl, Dec. 1857; groom of the stole to Prince Albert, 1859–61; to Prince of Wales, 1862–7; K.G., 1865; lord lieutenant of Ireland without seat in cabinet, 1868–74; lord president of council, 1880–85; lord lieutenant of Ireland, retaining his seat in cabinet, 3 May 1882–June 1885; combined firmness with conciliation as lord lieutenant and supported Gladstone's home rule policy; first lord of admiralty, 1892–5

SPRING RICE, Alice and Frederica. Daughters of Stephen Edmond Spring Rice, and sisters of Lord Monteagle*, of Mount Trenchard, Co. Limerick

STANLEY, Mrs John (d. 1931). Mary Susan Elizabeth, elder daughter of Keith William Stewart-Mackenzie; married (1) 1871, Hon. Col. John Constantine Stanley (1837–78), 2nd son of 2nd Baron Stanley of Alderley; (2) 1881, Francis Henry Jeune (1843–1905), a successful barrister who became a high court judge in 1891 and was ennobled as Baron St Helier in 1905; a leading London hostess

STEELE, General Sir Thomas Montague (1820–90). Eldest son of Major-general Thomas Steele, and cousin of William Drogo Montagu, 7th duke of Manchester; commissioned in Coldstream Guards, 1838; served with distinction in Crimean war; major general, 1865; K.C.B., 1871; commanded Dublin military district, 1872–4; lieutenant general, 1874; commanded Aldershot Military Division, 1875–80; general, 1877; commander of the forces in Ireland, 1 Oct. 1880–85; G.C.B., 1887

SULLIVAN, Alexander Martin (1830–84). Born at Bantry, Co. Cork; second son of Daniel Sullivan and uncle of T. M. Healy*; assistant editor of the *Nation*, 1855; sole editor and proprietor, 1858; strongly opposed Fenian movement, but was imprisoned (1868) for an article on the three executed Fenians, Allen, Larkin, and O'Brien; founder member of Butt's home rule movement, 1870; home rule M.P. for Co. Louth, 1874–80; for Co. Meath, 1880–82; in 1876 advocated more 'active' policy for home rule party; called to bar, 1876, and transferred his property in the *Nation* to his elder brother, T. D. Sullivan; received special call to English bar, and moved his residence to London, 1877; defence counsel for Parnell and other land-leaguers in conspiracy trial, Dec. 1880–Jan. 1881; resigned his seat for Meath owing to ill health, 1882; author of *The story of Ireland* (1870), *New Ireland* (1877)

MR TAYLER. Edward Tayler (1828–1906), portrait painter and miniaturist; first exhibited at the Royal Academy, London, 1849

TED. Edward Penrose Arnold-Forster*, elder brother of Florence

TREVELYAN, George Otto (1838–1928). Son of Sir Charles E. Trevelyan; nephew of Lord Macaulay; liberal M.P. for Tynemouth, 1865–8; for Border (Hawick) Burghs, 1868–86; civil lord of the admiralty, 1868–70; resigned over Forster's education bill; parliamentary secretary to admiralty, 1881–2; chief secretary for Ireland, May 1882–Oct. 1884; secretary for Scotland, 1886, but resigned over Gladstone's home rule bill; succeeded his father as 2nd baronet, 1886; adopted home rule and elected M.P. for Bridgton division of Glasgow, 1887; secretary for Scotland, 1892–5; retired from public life, 1897; author of *Life and letters of Lord Macaulay* (1876), *The early history of Charles James Fox* (1880), *The American revolution* (1899–1914)

TUKE, James Hack (1819–96). Member of long established quaker family; employed in his father's wholesale tea and coffee business at York, 1835–52; partner in banking firm of Sharples & Co. of Hitchin, Herts, from 1852; engaged in famine-relief work in Ireland, with W. E. Forster, 1846–7; his pamphlet *A visit to Connaught in 1847* (1847) had wide public impact; distributed quaker relief in Paris after German evacuation, 1871; early in 1880 at instance of W. E. Forster, he spent two months in the west of Ireland administering relief funds privately subscribed by quakers; his pamphlet *Irish distress and its remedies: a visit to Donegal and Connaught in the spring of 1880* (1880), advocated the 3 Fs, the gradual creation of peasant proprietorship through state-aided land purchase, for the poorest tenants 'family emigration', the promotion of light railways, and of fishing and other local industries by government; his proposals received immediate and widespread recognition, and were nearly all put into effect before he died; 'for the last sixteen years of his life his advice on nearly all Irish questions was sought by the chief secretaries of both political parties' (*D.N.B.*); a personal friend of Forster, who both officially and privately collaborated with him in his philanthropic works for Ireland

UNCLE JOHN. John W. Cropper*, husband of Susannah Arnold

UNCLE MATT. Matthew Arnold*, eldest son of Dr Thomas Arnold

UNCLE TOM. Thomas Arnold, second son of Dr Thomas Arnold

UNCLE WALTER. Walter Arnold, youngest son of Dr Thomas Arnold

VERNON, John Edward (1816–87). Of Erne Hill, Belturbet, Co. Cavan, where he owned 1,766 acres, valued at £1,165; J.P. and D.L., Co. Cavan; high sheriff, 1864; land commissioner under land act of 1881; J.P. of Dublin, Wicklow, and Monaghan; agent to earl of Pembroke and Montgomery

WARD, Agnes. Sister of Humphry Ward and sister-in-law of Mary Augusta Ward*

WARD, Mary Augusta (1851–1920). Eldest daughter of Thomas Arnold; cousin of Florence; born in Tasmania; her father came back to England in 1856; Mary lived in Oxford from 1867, and married, 1872, Thomas Humphry Ward, fellow and tutor of Brasenose College; involved in movement for higher education of women; first secretary of Somerville College, 1879; contributed to *Dictionary of Christian biography*; moved with her husband to London, 1881; author of *Miss Brotherton* (1884), *Robert Elsmere* (1888), a best seller, and many other works, including *A writer's recollections* (1918)

WEST, Horace (b. 1859). Assistant private secretary to W. E. Forster, 1880–82; son of Sir Algernon West, private secretary to W. E. Gladstone (1868–72); private secretary to H. H. Asquith, 1892–5; 'the occidental'

WILLIAMS. Lady's maid to Mrs Forster

WOLSELEY, Sir Garnet Joseph (1833–1913). Eldest son of Major Garnet Joseph Wolseley (d. 1840) of Golden Bridge House, Co. Dublin; educated in Dublin; commissioned, 1852; served in Burma, the Crimea, India during the mutiny, China, Canada, 1852–70; as assistant adjutant-general at war office, 1871–4, strongly supported army reforms of Edward Cardwell, secretary of state for war; first administrator of Cyprus, 1878–9; completed defeat of Zulus and granted Transvaal status of crown colony, 1879; as quartermaster general at war office, 1880–82, began comprehensive programme of army reform against resistance of commander-in-chief, the duke of Cambridge; adjutant general, 1882–9; commander-in-chief in Ireland, 1890–95; commander-in-chief of British army, 1895–9; 'he recreated the British army, which had fallen into inanition and inefficiency after the Napoleonic wars' (*D.N.B.*); author of *The soldier's pocket book* (1869) and other works

WOODHOUSE. A house near Loughborough, Leics, the home of Mary Hiley ('Aunt Mala'), second daughter of Dr Thomas Arnold and wife of Rev. A. Hiley

YARROW. A collie, one of the Forster dogs

BIBLIOGRAPHY

For the purposes of this book, comprehensive listings of works on the land war or on contemporary British politics are neither practicable nor necessary; both are substantially to be found in the bibliography of T. W. Moody, *Davitt and Irish revolution, 1846–82* (Oxford, 1981). The sources listed below, therefore, are those specifically mentioned in footnotes to the text.

The sources most commonly consulted for the purposes of annotation have not been generally cited in footnotes. Biographical details have been compiled from such standard sources as the *Dictionary of national biography*; *Burke's peerage*; *Burke's landed gentry*; *Burke's landed gentry of Ireland*; *Who was who*, vols i–iv (London, 1920–52); Frederic Boase, *Modern English biography* (6 vols, Truro, 1892–1921); *Crockford's clerical directory*; and the *Army list*. Details of the extent and valuation of estates in Ireland are drawn from U. H. Hussey de Burgh, *The landowners of Ireland: an alphabetical list of owners of estates of 500 acres or £500 valuation and upwards, in Ireland* (Dublin, 1878). A wide range of valuable information is in *Thom's Irish Almanac and Official Directory of the United Kingdom of Great Britain and Ireland for the year 1880* [etc.; the title changed to *Thom's Official Directory...* in 1881] (Dublin, 1880 [etc.]). Statements in the text about speeches and voting in parliament have been checked against *Hansard*, and newspaper reports, where possible, against the files of those journals. Details of crimes and legal proceedings have been checked against the official returns in the series of bound volumes of 'Irish crimes records' in the State Paper Office, Dublin Castle; particularly the monthly returns of outrages for 1877–82, the annual returns for 1879–93, and the lists of arrests and persons in custody under the Protection of Person and Property Act, 1881.

Arnold, Matthew. The incompatibles. In *Nineteenth Century*, ix, no. 50 (Apr. 1881), pp 709–26; ix, no. 52 (June 1881), pp 1026–43.

— *Letters of Matthew Arnold, 1848–1888. Ed.* George W. E. Russell. 2nd ed. 3 vols. London, 1904.

— *Unpublished letters of Matthew Arnold. Ed.* Arnold Whitridge. New Haven, 1923.

Arnold-Forster, H. O. A civilian's reply to Sir Garnet Wolseley. In *Nineteenth Century*, ix, no. 52 (June 1881), pp 905–16.

— The Gladstone government and Ireland. In *North American Review*, cxxxiii, no. 301 (Dec. 1881), pp 560–77.

— *The truth about the Land League. . . . By 'One who knows'.* London, 1882.

Arnold-Forster, Mary. *The right honourable Hugh Oakeley Arnold-Forster: a memoir by his wife.* London, 1919.

Arnstein, Walter L. *The Bradlaugh case: a study in late Victorian opinion and politics.* Oxford, 1965.

— Parnell and the Bradlaugh case. In *I.H.S.*, xiii, no. 51 (Mar. 1963), pp 212–35.

Becker, Bernard H. *Disturbed Ireland: being the letters written during the winter of 1880–81.* London, 1881.

Chamberlain, Joseph. *A political memoir, 1880—92. Ed.* C. H. D. Howard. London, 1953.

Cooke, A. B., and Vincent, J. R. (ed.). Herbert Gladstone, Forster, and Ireland, 1881–2. [Journal kept by Herbert Gladstone in Ireland, 1881–2.] In *I.H.S.*, xvii, no. 68 (Sept. 1971), pp 521–48; xviii, no. 69 (Mar. 1971), pp 74–89.

Cooke, A. B., and Vincent, J. R. (ed.). Lord Spencer on the Phoenix Park murders. In *I.H.S.*, xviii, no. 72 (Sept. 1973), pp 583–91.

Davitt, Michael. *The fall of feudalism in Ireland*. London and New York, 1904.

Derby, earl of [E. H. Stanley]. Ireland and the land act. In *Nineteenth Century*, x, no. 56 (Oct. 1881), pp 473–93.

'Distinguished Irishwomen, their professions, pleasures, and pursuits'. In *The Lady of the House*, Christmas, 1895. Dublin, 1895.

Duffy, Charles Gavan. *Conversations with Carlyle*. London, 1890.

Edwards, Owen Dudley. American diplomats and Irish coercion, 1880–1883. In *Journal of American Studies*, i, no. 2 (Oct. 1967), pp 213–32.

Forster, William. *Memoirs of William Forster. Ed.* Benjamin Seebohm. 2 vols. London, 1865.

Garvin, J. L. *The life of Joseph Chamberlain*. 3 vols. London, 1932–4. Julian Amery completed the work in three further vols (1951–69).

Gore, John. *Sydney Holland, Lord Knutsford: a memoir*. London, 1936.

Grey, Earl [H. G. Grey]. Ireland. In *Nineteenth Century*, xi, no. 64 (June 1881), pp 977–1012.

Gwynn, S. L., and Tuckwell, G. M. *The life of the rt hon. Sir Charles W. Dilke, Bart., M.P.* 2 vols. London, 1917.

Hawkins, Richard. Gladstone, Forster, and the release of Parnell, 1882–8. In *I.H.S.*, xvi, no. 64 (Sept. 1969), pp 417–45.

—— An army on police work: Ross of Bladensburg's memorandum. In *Irish Sword*, xi, no. 43 (winter 1973), pp 75–117.

—— Liberals, land, and coercion in the summer of 1880: the influence of the Carraroe ejectments. In *Galway Arch. Soc. Jn.*, xxxiv (1974–5), pp 40–57.

Holland, Bernard. *Life of Spencer Compton Cavendish, marquis of Hartington and eighth duke of Devonshire*. 2 vols. London, 1911.

Jones, Enid Huws. *Mrs Humphry Ward*. London, 1973.

Larkin, Emmet. *The Roman Catholic church and the creation of the modern Irish state, 1878–1886*. Philadelphia and Dublin, 1975.

Lloyd, C. D. Clifford. *Ireland under the Land League: a narrative of personal experiences*. Edinburgh and London, 1892.

Lyons, F. S. L. *John Dillon: a biography*. London, 1968.

—— *Charles Stewart Parnell*. London, 1977.

McCarthy, Justin Huntly. *England under Gladstone, 1880–84*. London, 1884.

McGrath, Terence [H. A. Blake]. *Pictures from Ireland*. London, 1880; 2nd ed. 1881.

MacKnight, Thomas. *Ulster as it is: or, twenty-eight years' experience as an Irish editor*. 2 vols. London, 1896.

Mahaffy, J. P. The Irish landlords. In *Contemporary Review*, xli (Jan. 1882), pp 160–76.

Moody, T. W. *Davitt and Irish revolution, 1846–82*. Oxford, 1981; paperback ed., 1984.

O'Connor, T. P. *Gladstone's house of commons*. London, 1885.

—— *Memoirs of an old parliamentarian*. 2 vols. London, 1929.

O'Halpin, Eunan. The secret service vote and Ireland, 1868–1922. In *I.H.S.*, xxiii, no. 92 (Nov. 1983), pp 348–53.

Palmer, Norman Dunbar. *The Irish Land League crisis*. New Haven, 1940. (Yale Historical Publications Miscellany XXXVII.)

Pigott, Richard. The Irish question. In *Macmillan's Magazine*, xlv (1881–2), pp 165–76.

Reid, T. Wemyss. *Life of the right honourable William Edward Forster*. 2 vols. London, 1888.

Robinson, Sir Henry. *Memories: wise and otherwise*. London, 1923.

Ross of Bladensburg, John. With Mr Forster in Ireland in 1882. In *Murray's Magazine*, ii (Aug. 1887), pp 165–86.

—— See also Hawkins, Richard.

Russell, Charles. *New views on Ireland*. London, 1880.

Russell, G. W. E. *Lady Victoria Buxton: a memoir*. London, 1919.

Selborne, earl of [Roundell Palmer]. *Memorials*. 4 vols. London, 1896–8.

Shaw-Lefevre, G. J. *Incidents of coercion: a journal of visits to Ireland in 1882 and 1888*. London, 1888.

Short, K. R. M. *The dynamite war: Irish-American bombers in Victorian Britain*. Dublin and London, 1979.

Stanley, A. P. *The life and correspondence of Thomas Arnold, D.D.* 12th ed. 2 vols. London, 1881.

Transactions of the central relief committee of the Society of Friends during the famine in Ireland in 1846 and 1847. London, 1852.

Trevor, Meriol. *The Arnolds: Thomas Arnold and his family*. London, 1973.

Tuke, James Hack. *Irish distress and its remedies*. London and Dublin, 1880.

Vaughan, W. E. Richard Griffith and the tenement valuation. In G. L. Herries Davies and R. C. Mullan (ed.), *Richard Griffith, 1784–1878* (Dublin, 1980), pp 103–22.

de Vere, Aubrey. *Recollections of Aubrey de Vere*. London, 1897.

Victoria. *Letters of Queen Victoria*, series II, vol. iii. *Ed.* G. E. Buckle. London, 1928.

Ward, Mary Augusta ('Mrs Humphry Ward'). *A writer's recollections*. London, 1918.

Ward, Wilfred. *Aubrey de Vere: a memoir*. London, 1904.

West, Algernon. *Recollections, 1832–1886*. 2 vols. London, 1899.

Woods, C. J. Ireland and anglo-papal relations, 1880–85. In *I.H.S.*, xviii, no. 69 (Mar. 1972), pp 29–60.

Wordsworth, William and Dorothy. *The letters of William and Dorothy Wordsworth: the later years. Ed.* Ernest de Selincourt. 3 vols. Oxford, 1939.

Yarnall, Ellis. *Wordsworth and the Coleridges*. New York and London, 1899.

INDEX

There are a few names that appear throughout the text, for which the entries are correspondingly large. In the cases of Gladstone, Parnell, Frances and Oakeley Arnold-Forster, and Mrs Forster, a broadly chronological listing of references has been adopted. But with W. E. Forster and Florence herself, this could not be done without virtually reproducing the journal in abbreviated form. A selection of entries has therefore been made, which as a selection is necessarily incomplete.
The following special abbreviations have been used: Fl. (Florence); WEF (W. E. Forster).